Dracula in Visual Media

Dracula in Visual Media

Film, Television, Comic Book and Electronic Game Appearances, 1921–2010

by JOHN EDGAR BROWNING *and* CAROLINE JOAN (KAY) PICART

with a foreword by DACRE STOKER *and an afterword by* IAN HOLT

McFarland & Company, Inc., Publishers
Jefferson, North Carolina, and London

Frontispiece: Bram Stoker, ca. 1906

LIBRARY OF CONGRESS CATALOGUING-IN-PUBLICATION DATA

Dracula in visual media : film, television, comic book and electronic game appearances, 1921–2010 / by John Edgar Browning and Caroline Joan (Kay) Picart ; with a foreword by Dacre Stoker and an afterword by Ian Holt.
p. cm.
Includes filmographies.
Includes bibliographical references and index.

ISBN 978-0-7864-3365-0
softcover : 50# alkaline paper

1. Stoker, Bram, 1847–1912. Dracula.   2. Stoker, Bram, 1847–1912 — Film adaptations.   3. Dracula, Count (Fictitious character)   4. Dracula films — History and criticism.   5. Dracula films — Catalogs.   6. Animated films — Catalogs.   7. Vampires on television.   8. Comic books, strips, etc.— History and criticism.   I. Browning, John Edgar.   II. Picart, Caroline Joan, 1966–
PR6037.T617D7827   2011   791.43'651— dc22   2010037135

British Library cataloguing data are available

© 2011 John Edgar Browning and Caroline Joan Picart. All rights reserved

No part of this book may be reproduced or transmitted in any form or by any means, electronic or mechanical, including photocopying or recording, or by any information storage and retrieval system, without permission in writing from the publisher.

Front cover: Christopher Lee in *Dracula Has Risen from the Grave*, 1968 (Warner Bros./Photofest)

Manufactured in the United States of America

McFarland & Company, Inc., Publishers
Box 611, Jefferson, North Carolina 28640
www.mcfarlandpub.com

Kay devotes this book to her family,
who have been the only enduring constant
in a life of constant evolution.
Most especially, Kay thanks her husband,
Jerry Rivera, whose love, devotion and
loyalty are without peer.

John wishes to devote this book to all the women
and men of Dracula and of Dracula's brood
who inspired him as a young man:
Skal, Melton, Miller, Youngson, Wolf, McNally,
Florescu, Hart, Auerbach, Guiley, Glut, Leatherdale,
Pirie, Frayling, Riccardo, Barker, Dresser and Haining.

We are especially grateful for and dedicate this book to
Donald F. Glut and his work *The Dracula Book* (1975),
whose legacy we continue in these pages.

Table of Contents

Foreword
    Dacre Stoker   1

Preface and Acknowledgments   3

Part I. Dracula in Film, Television, Documentary, and Animation   9

Introduction — Dracula: Undead and Unseen
    David J. Skal   11

Filmography   18

Part II. Dracula in Adult Film   191

Introduction — I Want to Suck Your…: Dracula in Pornographic Film
    Laura Helen Marks   193

Filmography   200

Part III. Dracula in Video Games   213

Introduction — Vampire Bytes and Digital Draculas
    Dodd Alley   215

Video Gameography   219

Part IV. Dracula in Comic Books   237

Introduction — The Darker Cape: Dracula, Vampires, and Superheroes in Comics
    Mitch Frye   239

Comics Listing   244

Japanese Manga   261

Afterword
    Ian Holt   263

Appendix 1. Dracula *in Print: A Checklist*
    Robert Eighteen-Bisang *and* J. Gordon Melton   265

Appendix 2. Film, Television, and Video Game Chronology   273
Appendix 3. Notable Dramatizations Featuring Dracula   284
Bibliography   289
About the Authors and Contributors   291
Index   293

Foreword

Dacre Stoker

I am very proud of my Stoker family heritage, but, typical of most Canadians, humble at the same time. As a child, I would be asked, especially around Halloween, "Hey, are you related to that guy who wrote *Dracula*?" Even to this day people are usually surprised when I say, "Yes, I am his great-grandnephew." George Stoker, my great-grandfather, was the youngest of seven Stoker siblings, and is said to have had the closest relationship with Bram.

Over the last several years, I believe I have come to know my great-granduncle, but it was not easy. Many more books are written about *Dracula* and its most famous character than about the man who gave them to us. Four well-researched biographies have been written about my great-granduncle, and yet we actually know very little about him from his personal writings, largely because Bram wrote precious few words about himself. In addition to *Dracula*, Bram wrote seventeen other books, numerous short stories and articles, but nothing in the way of autobiographical. He is remembered as the manager of Sir Henry Irving and the Lyceum Theatre in London and as the author of *Dracula*, but not as the interesting man I have found him to be. Bram Stoker was a man who focused his considerable energy and attention toward those for whom he worked, without giving any thought to writing about the actual part he played in the lives of these people or his personal dealings with them.

Dacre Stoker, great-grandnephew of Bram Stoker and co-author of the Stoker family-sanctioned sequel, ***Dracula: The UnDead*** (photograph by Jan Cobb).

Bram Stoker was a modest man, not at all self-important. He was also a gentleman, and although *Dracula* was considered not for the faint of heart, any sexual overtones in the novel were merely subtle innuendo, stemming more, I believe, from over-analysis by readers than from any intention on Bram's part.

Bram would surely be surprised at the great number of works, books, movies, television shows, comics, etc., apparently inspired by, or in some way connected to, the vampire figure he created. But, more than the sheer volume, I believe he would be shocked at a great deal of the content and graphic sexual themes that have become prevalent in the many iterations of his greatest work. I am sure he would not have identified with much of it at all.

The early history of the novel is quite the tragic story. Bram Stoker died in 1912, before *Dracula* became popular. Ten years later, one of history's most famous cases of plagiarism involved F.W. Murnau's 1922 silent film, *Nosferatu*, based without permission on *Dracula*. Afterwards, Florence Stoker, Bram's widow, sued the studio, and following a three-year battle all prints of the film were ordered destroyed. However, one copy of the film survived.

As Florence Stoker negotiated a deal to sell the movie rights to Columbia Pictures in the early 1930s, attorneys soon realized that although Bram had applied for American copyrights for the novel, he had not complied with all the copyright requirements. So, the copyright was not valid, and thus the book fell into the public domain, where it has remained ever since in the United States. Because of this oversight, there has been no family control over what could be done with and to the original story and its characters during the last century. As a result, the Stoker family hasn't received U.S. royalties from any of the *Dracula* derivations or licensing for *Dracula*. Ironically, this copyright technicality can be credited with allowing the Dracula character to proliferate to all corners of the world. If producers and writers were required to gain family approval and pay a license fee, then possibly Dracula would not have sprung up with such frequency in movies, games, costumes, toys and cereal boxes, to name a few.

Ian Holt and I shared the same desire to bring Dracula back to the pages of a book that Bram Stoker could relate to, and hopefully be proud of. For me, our sequel to *Dracula*, entitled *Dracula: The Un-Dead*, represents a quest to reclaim *Dracula* for Stokers all over the world.

I have been asked how I came to embark on writing a sequel to this immortal classic. Part of the answer to this question is reflected in this book, by John Edgar Browning and Caroline Joan (Kay) Picart. Their work is a testimony to the incredible fascination cultures from all around the world have had and continue to have with vampires. Just as vampires are able to take on so many forms, so, too, do the titles and subject matter chronicled within this book. They are truly immortal shapeshifters, difficult to keep down!

I have enjoyed looking through these pages, which have helped me realize the impossible amount of catching up I have to fill in the gaps in my cinematic education.

It is staggering to imagine the entirety of *Dracula*'s indelible influence on pop culture. The economic balance sheet alone would have been enough to make a small country proud. If my great-granduncle were still here, this book would have made an awfully good place for him to start to get an idea of the legacy and achievement he would have scarcely believed during his lifetime.

Preface and Acknowledgments

> *The* Chronicle *pronounces that "the impossibilities of the subject [of vampires] are handled with such fertility and ingenuity that* Dracula *is not likely to leave room for imitators. Mr. Stoker's vampire will remain unique."*
> — *"Book Reviews Reviewed,"* The Academy *(31 July 1897)*

Given the breadth of the present book, we hope to convey the *Chronicle*'s gross miscalculation. In truth, what *Dracula*'s uniquity has left little room for, in the last 113 years since the novel's publication, is competition. For no other vampire — or no other character in horror, for that matter — has been emulated more times than the nefarious Count, whose legacy we attempt to chronicle in these pages. Count Dracula, the novel's most ubiquitous character, is indeed survived by a vast genealogy of "imitators." Thus, our goal ultimately is to expose this vastly familiar, yet largely underestimated body of work that spans nearly film's entire length as a historical period.

John Polidori's short story "The Vampyre" (1819), first published in *The New Monthly Magazine* under Lord Byron's name, gave us the first "modern" literary vampire. Polidori developed the plot from a shorter unfinished piece by Lord Byron, for whom Polidori had worked as a travelling physician during that fateful summer in Geneva that also gave readers *Frankenstein* (1818). Polidori's short story was an instant success throughout Europe, metamorphosing the peasantry's corpse-like revenant (or vampire) that had dominated folklore for centuries, into the suave, attractive aristocratic vampire, or "Fatal Man"[1] as David Pirie writes. However, the epitome of these fatal men would not emerge until during the *fin de siècle* with the publication of *Dracula* in 1897.

"[A]rguably, the last of the great Gothic horror novels," writes Veronica Hollinger[2] of Stoker's *Dracula*. It became the benchmark after which later vampire narratives were patterned. This development, however, was not immediately realized until the 1920s. While Stoker's novel successfully established such vampiric tropes as tombs or "coffins" (although Dracula journeyed to England with "crates" or boxes, not coffins), and firmly cemented the vampire's metamorphosis into a bat, the real impact (which we shall discuss at length momentarily) occurred, initially, with the Hamilton Deane (1924) and Hamilton Deane–John L. Balderston (1927) stage versions,[3] then, more prominently, with the Universal (1931) and Hammer (1958) film versions. In the early part of the twentieth century, film became the fastest growing entertainment medium in the world, and film-goers needed to be neither wealthy nor literate to enjoy the art form. Because *Dracula* (1931) was the first horror "talkie," it should come as little surprise then that its release would in turn play catalyst to Dracula's domination — be it directly or indirectly—in vampire literature and film. In the end, Béla Lugosi's unforgettable portrayal initiated into popular entertainment not only Stoker's indelible character but the horror genre as a whole.

Over 700 citations on domestic and international Dracula films, television programs, documentaries, adult features, animations, and video games comprise the bulk of this book; additionally, we have documented nearly a thousand domestic and international comic book titles and stage adaptations. While all of these titles may vary widely on matters of length, significance, quality, genre, moral character, country, and format, they do share one characteristic: they explore, with great variation, the Dracula cinema myth. Some of the titles make considerable effort to adapt Stoker's original narrative, while others diffuse beyond this traditional strain of films, often merely adopting the markers or tropes that became associated with Dracula during the initial theatrical and cinematic portrayals. However, in nearly all the titles we catalog, Dracula, or some semblance of him (i.e., a Dracula-type vampire), makes a literal appearance.

Stefan Dziemianowicz aptly remarks, "The success of *Dracula* can be measured by how faithfully the vampires of most stories written in its wake are modeled on Stoker's Transylvanian Count."[4] To provide a starting point for understanding the classificatory and organizational schemata we employ in qualifying specific titles for inclusion, it is necessary to outline the particular conventions lying at the center of "Dracula" narratives. Perhaps it was Béla Lugosi who said it best in 1935, when he wrote for *Film Weekly* that "there is a popular idea that portraying a monster of the Dracula type requires no acting ability. People are apt to think that anyone who likes to put on a grotesque make-up can be a fiend. That is wrong."[5] Dracula and Dracula-type vampires typically invoke a host of recognizable tropes that the London and Broadway theatrical adaptations of Stoker's novel helped to engender in the 1920s. In time, Béla Lugosi's and Christopher Lee's respective filmic portrayals in the 1930s and 1940s (Universal, Metro) and the 1950s to the 1970s (Hammer) would help to extend and solidify these markers. Briefly sketched, these markers include clothing (cape [with or without stand-up collar], crest ring, dark tuxedo or suit, black-red coloration, medallion), mannerisms (Eastern European accent, suave), physical features (tall, piercing stare, dark and/or slicked-back hair [with or without widow's peak]), and engagements (moving into town and buying up real estate, searching for lost or reincarnated loved ones). More recently, Gary Oldman's portrayal (Columbia, 1992), helped to institute what would become new staples: long, rather than slicked-back hair; princely, rather than county status; and a "Romanian" accent specifically. Further, in the wake of the Columbia picture, we have come to know Dracula on a first name basis (i.e., as "Vlad"), which is particularly relevant for the purposes of this book because the letter V has come to figure more and more prominently in the nomenclature of Dracula-type vampires (whereas before it was more commonly the letter D or the suffix -ula).[6]

In some of the films cataloged, Dracula plays the lead character, while in others he may make only a cameo or bit appearance. Some titles in which auxiliary characters from the novel appear (Mina or Van Helsing, for example), but do so without Dracula, are also cataloged, because in general these auxiliary characters still make significant references to Dracula, often by name. In cases dealing with titles featuring Dracula-type vampires, generally deciding whether these titles fit the description is often incredibly arbitrary. Moreover, just when we think we have excised a definitive definition for "Dracula-ness," we discover a title that proves utterly problematic to these efforts. Thus have we opted for inclusion in some cases rather than exclusion. However, of one thing can we be certain: Dracula is inextricably like the genre he parented, for he, too—like horror—can not be fully encapsulated by any sort of reduction, nor is he restricted to national or geographical borders.

Tommy ("Hypnotic Quaker") Baker plays Dracula for Universal Studios in Castle Theatre's popular production of *Castle Dracula*, which ran from Friday, June 13, 1980, to January 31, 1983 (photograph by Sandy Fields).

Since Dracula's inception, we have continuously censored his portrayals and encoded him with our politics. Dracula is an amalgam of social fears and desires, and just when we think we can predict his movement, his expansion and contraction, or his thematic demise, Dracula's flexibility and porosity enable him to metamorphose again and again, in new and unforeseeable directions. This volume is therefore not complete; missed titles are found

"HAMMER HOUSE" 113-117 WARDOUR STREET · LONDON · W.1
TELEPHONE: GERRARD 9707 (6 LINES) · TELEGRAMS: "HAMMER FILM · GERRARD 9707 · LONDON"
REGISTERED OFFICES: 113 WARDOUR STREET · LONDON · W.1
DIRECTORS: WILLIAM HAMMER · LT. COL. JAMES CARRERAS, M.B.E. · ANTHONY HINDS
MICHAEL CARRERAS · SECRETARY: JAMES DAWSON, F.C.C.S.
BANKERS: BARCLAYS BANK LTD, LONDON · BANK OF AMERICA · NATIONAL TRUST AND SAVINGS ASSOCN, LONDON

BY HAND

OUR REF AH/PA/52   YOUR REF   DATE 11th February, 1958

J. Nicholls, Esq.,
The British Board of Film Censors,
3 Soho Square,
LONDON, W.1.

Dear Mr. Nicholls,

"DRACULA"

I have just returned from America and heard of the objections raised by the Board in connection with this film. I have today been through the whole picture with my cutter, Mr. James Needs, and we have made the following alterations in accordance with your requirements:

REEL 2:   The shot of the Vampire Woman's sinking her teeth into Jonathan's neck has been removed entirely.

REEL 7:   All shots of the stake being driven into the girl's heart have been removed entirely.

REEL 9:   The disintegration of Dracula: (i) The shot of his hand tearing the flesh from his face has been removed entirely.

(ii) All further shots of disintegration have been trimmed to the minimum.

I trust that you will find this satisfactory when you see the film tomorrow.

Yours sincerely,
HAMMER FILM PRODUCTIONS LTD.

H. Anthony Hinds

A letter from Anthony Hinds of Hammer Films to John Nicholls of the British Board of Film Censors concerning the release of *Dracula* (1958; *Horror of Dracula* [U.S.]) (courtesy John Edgar Browning).

nearly each week, and new titles are produced in various countries each year.

Dracula has endured with considerably more ease than vampires of the more common variety. For while these ordinary vampires generally carry with them no more distinction than a pair of incisors and cold, pallid skin, Dracula has distinguished himself by appropriating, in addition to these common traits, the set of highly recognizable, highly marketable tropes that we outlined. As a result, Dracula has become standardized, therefore allowing him not only to outperform his competition, but also birth an entire genealogy of vampires imbued with his tropes. Scholars have frequently remarked on Stoker's modernization of the vampire myth and the Gothic literary tradition by situating much of the novel in contemporary England. "The plot is ingenious," *The British Review* (July 3, 1897) comments, "and the more interesting that it is laid chiefly in England at the present day." Yet, equally beneficial to Dracula's development, though frequently overlooked, is the way in which Stoker constructed much of the novel's plot around, rather than about, Dracula—a fact that becomes all too obvious by Chapter 4, after which Dracula seldom appears again in the text. As a result, we fail to gain access to Dracula's psychology in the same way we do with most of the other characters through the various letters and journal entries contained in the novel. Thus, Dracula remains, throughout the novel, much as he has remained throughout the last century: a very mysterious, ambivalent figure. And therein perhaps may lie the key to his morphology: that someone who, to the public, is so familiar and yet so "unknown" allows us, in moments of crisis and need, to reshape and reconfigure quite fluidly the character of Dracula whenever it suits us. This could not be more evident than in the present, as we bear witness to one of the most prominent waves of vampire fandom since the early 1990s, just prior to and following the release of *Bram Stoker's Dracula* (1992). It is also no coincidence that the recent vampire phenomenon has occurred with the economic recession. After all, the vampire's tendency to stand in for prevailing phobias of the day is matched only by its capacity for generating tremendous revenue.[7] Whatever the reason for our continued fascination with Dracula, or vampires, this volume is a testament to his universally recognized, indomitable iconography.

A book like this would not have been produced without the kind assistance of numerous individuals, institutions, and private collections. In particular, we would like to gratefully acknowledge the assistance of some very talented researchers: Toni Borel, David Callison, Allison Chancy, Wyatt Chandler, Nicholas Comeaux, Kelsey Copperberg, Matthew Deshotels, Gloria Dupre, Andrew Ficklin, Christian Gonzalez, Jordan Goynes, Douglas Harper, Blake Jones, Matthew Lousteau, Christopher Martin, William Moss, Leslie Schrof, Kyle Sibley, Justin Thibodeaux, Skylar White, and Jacob Williams.

Of particular note is Frank Henchy, whose invaluable knowledge, and willingness to help and contribute to this book, made possible the breadth of information on Dracula in video games contained in these pages. Similarly, Wayne Stein was especially helpful in tracking down several rare Asian titles. Both Frank and Wayne have our sincerest thanks.

We are also infinitely grateful to several graduate students and faculty, without whose generous help and time some of our more challenging film citations would have gone unresearched: Andrew Banecker, Anne M. Canavan, Conor Picken, Catherine Riley, and Dejan Ognjanovic. Considerable thanks are due also to Helana Brigman and Kristopher Mecholsky, who generously devoted their time and proofreading skills to help bring this book to completion after five years.

Special thanks also go to Carrie Swetonic at Dutton (part of Penguin Group [U.S.] Inc.); Joe Rubin, Hardcore Film archivist; Mike Raso, film archivist and founder of Alternative Cinema; and Hethalein Mares, publicist at Wicked Pictures.

Finally, we would like to express our sincerest gratitude to the contributors of this work — David J. Skal, Dacre Stoker, Ian Holt, Robert Eighteen-Bisang, J. Gordon Melton, Laura Helen Marks, Mitch Frye, and Timothy Dodd Alley — whose respective areas of expertise, dedication, and love for the genre have given this catalog its comprehensiveness. To J. Gordon Melton and CESNUR (Center for Studies on New Religions), Robert Eighteen-Bisang, Jeanne Youngson, David J. Skal, Justin Humphreys, Simon Santos, and Wayne L. Kinsey, we are especially grateful, for their willingness to share their invaluable research, knowledge, and photographs.

We hope readers enjoy reading and using this book. We would also like to elicit the generous help of our readership to submit film, video game, and comic book additions and corrections to: draculafilmsourcebook@live.com.

Notes

1. David Pirie, *The New Heritage of Horror* (I.B. Tarius, 2009), 3–7. We defer here also to the "Wandering Jew." For further discussion, see also: Orit Kamir, *Every Breath You Take: Stalking Narratives and the Law* (University of Michigan Press, 2004) and H. L. Malchow, *Gothic Images of Race in Nineteenth-Century Britain* (Stanford University Press, 1997).

2. Veronica Hollinger, "The Vampire and the Alien: Gothic Horror and Science Fiction," in *Bram Stoker's Dracula: Sucking Through the Century, 1897–1997*, ed. Carol Margaret Davison (Toronto: Dundurn, 1997), 213.

3. See David J. Skal, ed., *Dracula: The Ultimate, Illustrated Edition of the World-Famous Vampire Play* (New York: St. Martin's, 1993).

4. Stefan Dziemianowicz, "Introduction," in *Dracula: Prince of Darkness* (New York: DAW, 1992), ed. Martin H. Greenberg, 9.

5. Béla Lugosi, "I Like Playing Dracula," *Film Weekly*, July 1935.

6. Here, we have adapted and extended the list of Dracula-type markers initially compiled by Wayne Stein and John Edgar Browning in their essay "The Western Eastern: Decoding Hybridity and Zyber*Zen* Goth(ic) in *Vampire Hunter D* (1985)" in *Asian Gothic: Essays on Literature, Film and Anime* (McFarland, 2008), ed. Andrew Hock Soon Ng, 221; reprinted in revised form in *Draculas, Vampires, and Other Undead Forms: Essays on Gender, Race, and Culture* (Scarecrow, 2009), ed. John Edgar Browning and Caroline Joan (Kay) Picart, 290–291.

7. We draw from John Edgar Browning's discussion of "Gothic Economics" and the economic recession, which first appeared in "Interviews with the Vampires: The Real Story behind New Orleans's Vampire Subculture," *Deep South Magazine* 1 (Spring 2010).

PART I

Dracula in Film, Television, Documentary, and Animation

Introduction —
Dracula: Undead and Unseen

David J. Skal

You hold in your hands the most comprehensive compilation of Dracula film credits to date, and, like all such compilations, ample testimony to the vampire king's robust afterlife in the media, a feat so far unmatched by any other fictional character.

Since Dracula has clocked so much screen time, it may be useful to consider his many absences from the picture: already an offstage (but always anticipated) character for most of Bram Stoker's novel, his many failures to be conjured on screen, and elsewhere, amount to a chronicle in itself. The history of *Dracula* has largely been one of nonpresence, missed chances, grand plans, failures, invisibility and unaccountability. Stoker himself was only dimly aware of the emerging technology of the motion picture, but believed that his book should be theatrically performed. The famous refusal of his employer, the actor-manager Sir Henry Irving, to even consider playing the title role ("Whenever I talk about it, he just laughs at me," Stoker once said) was the first missed chance, and emblematic of a pattern that was to follow: *Dracula* was fated to be overestimated in its dramatic potential (as in Stoker's 1897 copyright reading, maddening in its scant documentation), or underestimated (as in Irving's purported exclamation, "Dreadful!")

Ambivalence has been at the core of this devilish game of approach/avoidance — one might say that dramatic adaptations of *Dracula* have been in a protracted state of "development hell" now lasting well over a century.

One early *Dracula* that went unseen, if not overlooked, by Bram Stoker's widow, Florence, was F.W. Murnau's 1922 expressionist classic *Nosferatu: A Symphony of Horror*. A blatant copyright infringement by any standard, *Nosferatu* was moved against aggressively by Mrs. Stoker, who succeeded after two years of litigation in having the film ordered destroyed by the German courts. There is no record she actually saw the film, or even felt the need to.

Early in her campaign against *Nosferatu*, Stoker's widow maintained that she had been involved in motion picture negotiations "for some time," which might have been bluster, but it is also possible that unspecified silent filmmakers besides [Murnau] had their own ideas brewing. Nothing is known about a purported 1917 unauthorized stage version, the existence of which surprised Florence Stoker, who disavowed any connection to it. One lost curiosity of the period is a Hungarian silent entitled *Drakula halála* (*The Death of Drakula*) and directed by Karoly Lathjay in 1921. Only fragmentary information and a handful of tantalizing photos survive, but Lathjay's now invisible effort was the first media appropriation of the name. The film's impact was not widely felt, and the cover artist for the 1926 Hungarian edition was clearly more inspired by Murnau than Lathjay.

Although *Nosferatu* cheated death at Florence Stoker's hands, and *Drakula* escaped her wrath, another visual incarnation of *Dracula* in the early 1920s was successfully condemned to widow-oblivion. Approached with a proposal for the celebrated Irish artist Harry Clarke (1889–1931) to illustrate an edition deluxe of *Dracula*, Stoker found the terms unacceptable and dismissed the project summarily. Clarke's tragically unrealized illustrations, evocative of Aubrey Beardsley's best, would have made an indelible public impression, much like those Clarke penned for Poe's *Tales of Mystery and Imagination*. As Neil Gaiman has written of Clarke's imagery, "It will inextricably color your reading of the story. It will remain in your head until you die." The influence of the Clarke illustrations was still in evidence in promotional graphics for Roger Corman's screen adaptations of Poe in the 1960s, and it can only be wondered what cinematic reach and influence a Clarke *Dracula* might have wrought.

When Carl Laemmle's Universal Pictures bought the screen rights in 1930 (after having considered the property as early as 1915), the studio developed a number of treatments and scripts, all attempting in their own ways to reconcile a problematic original novel with a proven stage adaptation. The results (including the finished film) were all clumsily handled, but a number of interesting moments went unproduced. The most elaborate treatment, by novelist Louis Bromfield, ran 50 pages and included more dialogue than is customary in a treatment. It made the most of key moments from the novel, especially Dracula crawling down the wall of his castle, and the graphic staking of Lucy Westenra, complete with a bloodcurdling "wild cry." Both would ultimately be jettisoned, the latter if only to avoid censorship. Bromfield also included opportunities for special makeup effects, likely because Universal thought it might woo the silent superstar and "Man of a Thousand Faces" Lon Chaney. Had he actually played the part (and it was never a realistic proposition, for many reasons other than the most serious one: Chaney had terminal cancer), it is a safe bet the actor would have incorporated Dracula's metamorphosing wall-crawl, much in the manner he scaled cathedral brick as Quasimodo in *The Hunchback of Notre Dame* (1923). As for his makeup, Bromfield included a typed sidebar to the treatment: "In his unnatural unearthly manifestations the Count De Ville [the overly cute alias was actually Stoker's idea] assumes the wolfish appearance of Dracula. His eyes grow dilated and his canine teeth appear to grow much longer."

Gruesome details such as these grew scarcer and scarcer, and in the final shooting script by Garrett Fort and Dudley Murphy, with an unbilled assist from director Tod Browning, the last remaining script reference to fangs (during Dracula's deadly sea voyage) was ignored, and Lucy's death was simply cut, continuity be damned. Among the unseen elements and artifacts from Browning's *Dracula* are more than ten minutes of studio cuts that were never preserved in negative or positive. The simultaneously produced Spanish language version of the film used the entire shooting script, and, while the production is usually praised as being technically superior to Browning's version, the English-language film is more effective in editing Dracula's stand-off with Van Helsing as a single scene, and not intercut with Mina's attempted seduction of Harker as specified in the script and realized in the Spanish version.

Universal's surviving negotiation and legal files on *Dracula* have never been made public; all that has been so far accessed is the studio's correspondence with the agent for Florence Stoker, John L. Balderston, and *Dracula*'s first dramatist, Hamilton Deane, and Balderston's marvelously chatty reports on the negotiations. Balderston found the finished film disappointing, and, when little of his material for *Return of Frankenstein* (released in 1935 as *Bride of Frankenstein*) was appreciated or used, happily provided rival producer David O. Selznick a treatment for *Dracula's Daughter*—a problematic concept brimming with sexual sadism. Whether Selznick really intended to produce the film or just profitably resell his rights to Stoker's short story "Dracula's Guest" to Universal is not known, but he made good on the latter gambit. Carl Laemmle, Jr., turned the project over to director James Whale, who hoped he would be finished with horror films after *Bride of Frankenstein* (1935). In collaboration with R.C. Sherriff, who scripted Whale's *The Old Dark House* and *The Invisible Man* (1933), he deliberately crafted a script so outrageous it would never interfere with projects he really cared about, most specifically the musical version of Edna Ferber's *Show Boat*.

In his autobiography, *No Leading Lady*, Sherriff doesn't even acknowledge his substantial work on the project, perhaps understanding the whole thing as a joke or delaying gambit for Whale, and not a serious script. Whale had entertained himself with an extended game of cat-and-mouse with the censors over *Bride of Frankenstein* and knew how to play them for time. The script has been the object of much speculation, but only recently has been published. Sherriff's narrative is obviously written with Lugosi in mind (and the studio used Lugosi's image prominently in trade announcements), but it is the actor's contemporaneous, torture-minded turn as Dr. Vollin in Universal's *The Raven* (1935) rather than *Dracula* that Sherriff seems to anticipate. Although Dracula is described as being clad completely in black, as per Stoker's description, Sherriff never mentions a cape. Think of Lugosi's Roxor in *Chandu the Magician* (1932), minus the turban. The reader can almost hear Lugosi's familiar, purring cadences as the proposed scenes unfold.

Béla Lugosi

"You have eaten my food, dear friends—you have drunk my wine and honoured a lonely man in his lonely Castle with your innocent gaiety and delicate jokes," Dracula tells his gluttonous guests, decadent aristocrats from all over Europe. "In return I've prepared for each of you a little dish gathered freshly from the fields this very morning." In reality, he has kidnapped young women from their beds. "I wouldn't like to see these delicate morsels damaged before they are eaten." The guests throw dice to pick their prizes. But the fiancé of one of the victims has smuggled himself into the castle, and is seized by Dracula's men.

"There's no need for my little girl to be afraid," Dracula assures the girl, who now commands special interest. "Your lover will come to you, and you will be together again.... He will come to you and place his strong arm around you; you will be together again, husband and wife—and I shall adopt you as a daughter. Doesn't it thrill that fluttering little heart? Dracula's daughter!"

She is taken to a room where a male figure in Arabian robes appears. He raises a hand, and she recognizes his ring. She runs to him — and pulls away a hacked off arm. Dracula throws off his disguise. "The girl, as if fighting a terrible nightmare, gazes round. Her lover's severed arm still hangs over her shoulder — it drops down between her back and the cushion of the couch when she moves — and the hand sticks up like a drowning soldier's from the sea." Dracula has kept his promise: "The strong arm of your lover has come to comfort you."

If the question immediately arises, how did they possibly think such a scene would ever be filmed, the answer is obvious: they didn't.

Dracula's crimes prompt the outraged townsfolk to retain the services of a wizard named Talifer — a role believed to have been written with Boris Karloff in mind — who confronts Dracula and his debauchers and curses them magically down the evolutionary ladder: "The CAMERA focuses on the terrified Baron — his bulbous eyes shrink up — his nose broadens — his fat arms shrink within their sleeves — and sitting at the table — ridiculous in the rich robes of the Baron Heydendorf — sits a great grunting hog that struggles and squeals in terror." Others become monkeys, snakes and spiders. But for Dracula Talifer saves a special kind of punishment — to be trapped forever between the human and animal realms as a bloodthirsty vampire.

Then, as if the already grotesque spectacle is not enough, comes a final flourish: "The CAMERA sweeps down the long table. A moment previously it has been lavishly set with dishes of food — fine decorations and magnificent ornaments — but as the CAMERA moves over it, everything crumbles to hideous decay. Great dust-hung cobwebs cling to the dishes — the fruit crumbles into black dirt — a boar's head falls to a whitened skull; through the cobwebs creeps the giant Spider, and upon a tattered napkin sits the great impassive toad.... The CAMERA moves swiftly as the Great Hall disintegrates: we see the magnificent tapestries crumble and the stately curtains that cover the windows drip into rags. The walls themselves crumble and the roof falls in with a sudden crash."

Dracula flies to the arm-traumatized girl and, as a vampire bat, seroconverts her into undeath. For the balance of the film, Sherriff cleverly inverts the original Stoker plot and characters: Dracula's blood-adopted daughter travels to London, where she invades the lives of two male friends, one of whom grows hysterical and weak under her predation, but ultimately turns against her and destroys her during a sea voyage back to Transylvania.

Dracula's back story amounted to a third of Sherriff's script. Unfortunately, it was also the most cinematic material, and its removal for the censors was effectively the death knell for the production. James Whale went on to his triumphant production of *Show Boat*, and a completely new version of *Dracula's Daughter* was concocted by screenwriter Garrett Fort and involved quasi-lesbian Countess Zaleska, her name likely inspired by Sherriff's Countess Szelinski) who burns the staked body of her father at the beginning of the film. Lambert Hillyer ultimately directed the production, and Béla Lugosi was paid for the use of his face (barely recognizable) in the cremation scene.

Throughout the 1940s and 1950s, Dracula appeared, usually as a supporting character, in a handful of films. A particularly intriguing, but abandoned, adaptation first proposed in 1957 would have featured Boris Karloff as the Count, who accepted the idea with the proviso, "Just so long as I don't have to imitate Béla!" However, the idea was swept away in the wake of Hammer Studios' *Horror of Dracula* (1958; *Dracula* [U.K.]) and the immensely successful franchise that would follow.

In 1972, Shane Briant, a rising British stage actor, was approached by Hammer with the offer of a term contract, which, tantalizingly, included the chance to play Bram Stoker in a proposed biographical feature called *Victim of His Imagination*. Two Hammer actors were well-suited to play the actor Henry Irving, now widely presumed to be the inspiration of Stoker's vampire. Christopher Lee and Peter Cushing, who had, respectively, played Dracula and Van Helsing in *Horror of Dracula* (and continued to reprise the roles) would have both been splendid in the part, and a graphic depiction of Lee's would appear in a Hammer trade announcement of the project. It is possible that Cushing was also initially considered for the role of Stoker before Briant, but the casting details remain maddeningly vague.

"How interesting!" Briant himself recently told this writer. "I didn't think anyone knew about this proposed film. I was asked to become a Hammer contract player for two years. My agent had talks with Michael Carreras at Hammer and the idea — the incentive/lure — was that I should play the lead in a bio of Bram Stoker. The second proposed film was to be a re-make of a non–Gothic classic film — I wish I could remember what it was. I was, you see, unsure at that time whether I wanted to commit to two years of horror films if they were to be run of the mill horrors. I had just been nominated by the London Theatre Critics for Best Newcomer of the Year for my portrayal of the young man in *Children of the Wolf* [1969] at the Apollo in London's West End. Ultimately the lure proved too tempting and I signed for two years. But instead of the films that were proposed, I ended up making *Demons of the Mind, Straight on Till Morning* [both 1972], *Frankenstein and the Monster from Hell* and *Captain Kronos, Vampire Hunter* [both 1974]. I never saw the Bram Stoker script, I'm afraid, and I was *very* disappointed to be doing *Demons* rather than Bram Stoker." Briant would, however, be given the chance to deliver an impressive Stoker-era performance in the title role of *The Picture of Dorian Gray* for television producer Dan Curtis in 1973.

The *Victim* script Briant never saw was a detailed, 29-page treatment by Don Houghton, who had just scripted *Dracula A.D. 1972* and would write and produce *The Satanic Rites of Dracula* (1973) and *Legend of the Seven Golden Vampires* (1974). At the time of the *Victim* project, Houghton had only one Stoker biography to consult: *A Biography of Dracula* (1962) by Harry Ludlam. He comes to dramatic and psychological conclusions not explicitly drawn by Ludlam but which are certainly suggested in the book. Stoker is presented as having suffered from terrifying visions and nightmares since an early age, turning to writing horror stories to exorcise his own demons. Stoker's well-documented adoration of Walt Whitman is elaborated by Houghton into the receipt of creative advice from the American poet, namely, "that BRAM should continue writing, should unload the dark shadows, into his stories and books, thereby cleansing himself of the unknown spectre that haunts him. WHITMAN is certain that BRAM's sanity is not in jeopardy, but it could become so if he allows the nightmare to take control of his mind." Stoker responds by using "every spare moment of his already crowded tour schedule to jot down notes and thoughts for proposed stories and novels."

The exercise only exhausts him; back in London, lovemaking with his wife is aborted when Florence Stoker's caressing fingers melt into hideous, writhing worms. Houghton: "a perpetually returning theme, BRAM's preoccupation with hands, tortured, tormented, constantly referred to in fact and in the fantasy of his stories, must have a deep significance ... in almost every story written by BRAM STOKER he finds it necessary to describe the hands of his characters in great detail. It may or may not be significant. For the purpose of this treatment I have made it so." The deathbed doctor who attends Stoker engages in some strained psychoanalytic sleight-of-hand to root out the writer's primal conflict, ultimately found in repressed childhood memories of the ghastly cholera scourge that swept Ireland in the 1850s, and to which Stoker's family was witness. The images of death, blood, and clutching hands culminate in Stoker's mother severing the arm of a frenzied cholera victim, in a scene that strikingly anticipates the house-under-siege set-piece of countless modern zombie narratives: "A MAN, his face yellow, drawn and ghastly ... his teeth bared in fury, appears at the window, forced forward by the mob behind him. In terrible detail the child sees the horror of what happens next. The MAN thrusts his arm through the glass to tear at the boards barring the window. The arm, white with disease, gropes into the room, like an ugly tentacle, wavering like a monstrous worm."

The story that Henry Irving's personality inspired or informed the character of Count Dracula has now achieved such mythic status that it is surprising that Houghton makes so little of it. It is equally strange that biographer Ludlam made no such connection whatsoever, especially considering his direct access to Stoker's son and Hamilton Deane. Houghton may be, in fact, the first biographical writer of any kind to have considered a direct Irving/Dracula connection, seemingly drawn from nowhere but his own instincts as a screenwriter. Irving's celebrated production of *Macbeth* is now featured prominently in most studies that explore Irving-as-Dracula, but Houghton scores a more original point as Irving's Othello, killing Desdemona in her bed, morphs into Dracula attacking a victim. Stoker's wife and mother watch on hungrily in the guise of vampire wives. Ellen Terry, Irving's acting partner — his Desdemona — warns Stoker that Irving "feeds off his good nature and calm competence." Houghton: "These words seem to stick in Bram's mind. To feed off him. To suck him dry." Later, when the real Irving lies dead on a hotel lobby floor, Dracula's death scene flashes in Stoker's brain. Houghton is ultimately less interested in Henry Irving than in cholera as an inspiration for *Dracula*, and includes horrific dramatized excerpts from Stoker's short stories "The Squaw"(1893), "The Burial of the Rats (circa. 1893)," and his final novel, *Lair of the White Worm* (1911). At the end, in a fevered delirium, Stoker wrestles with Irving's demon: "He feels guilt and terrible remorse. Did he, he asks, really *hate* Irving? Did he, like so many people suggested, resent the actor's hold over him?" It is at this point that he fully surrenders to the awful cholera visions. As Stoker's own death swiftly approaches, Irving is exonerated. "BRAM is quiet, contemplative. The lines of torment are slowly soothed away. Now his life has a pattern, an ordered reason for everything that has happened. He can take leave of it now in peace. The vision of Hell and Purgatory is vanished."

The real story behind *Dracula* has yet to be seen on screen, but in 2009, a promising musical-in-development, *Children of the Night* by Scott Martin, put the Stoker/Irving relationship at stage center, and recently enjoyed a not-for-profit run at the Beverly Hills Playhouse. Unlike *Victim of his Imagination*, this production benefited from several decades of Stoker scholarship and speculation that followed Ludlam, much of it psychosexually driven. Among the most notable unproduced screen adaptations of *Dracula* in this vein was the sex-propelled script written in 1978 by Ken Russell and presumably shelved in light of the film version then being prepared by Universal with Frank Langella and Laurence Olivier.

Russell's conception, envisioned as a star vehicle for Mick Fleetwood, opens with Jonathan Harker's familiar wild ride to Castle Dracula, in which the wolves, bats, flames, and frightened peasants are all part of an elaborate joke on the visitor. But lest the viewer think that this Dracula is a harmless prankster, things quickly turn truly weird. For instance, as Dracula's wives approach Harker for their midnight nip, Aubrey Beardsley's most erotic imagery looms over the proceedings: "The CAMERA pans over the wallpaper showing four men with giant erections dancing before an audience of beautiful women." ("Beardsley was surely one of your finest artists," Dracula laments. "It is to my everlasting regret that I never met him. So talented, and to die so young. A tragedy! I might have helped him." Jonathan: "Are you a doctor, sir?" Dracula (laughing): "I dabble a little in acupuncture, certainly; I'm also something of a patron of the arts." Later, when Dracula plays a recording of Shubert's 8th — the famously unfinished — Symphony, Jonathan quips, "Pity you weren't around to help him as well. He might have finished it." "Yes," says Dracula, this time seriously, "that is one of the great regrets of my life."

This Dracula, we learn, is a die-hard arts philanthropist, with a special appreciation for the vocal gifts of opera diva Lucy Weber — Stoker's transmogrified Lucy Westenra, this time not Mina Murray's friend, but her employer. Weber is dying of leukemia, but evidently strong enough to mount a farewell tour for her morbid, mournful public. When she finally meets the Count, he offers his trademark brand of dracupuncture, and she finally recognizes those eyes she had often seen just beyond the footlights at theatres all over Europe. Lucy's voice, in Dracula's estimation, "has more colour than Turner ever dreamed of, there is more music in your every movement than in a romance by Silbelius, more poetry in your smile than a verse by Baudelaire." And after Lucy's death, undeath, and final death, Dracula tells Mina that "some of our greatest artists are 'Nosferatu' ... have you never pondered on the resemblance between Beethoven and Sibelius? And does not Rembrandt look like Picasso, just a little bit?"

The script continues to follow Stoker's general plot, with more of Russell's clever embellishments. The madman Renfield is another leukemia victim, who ill-advisedly sought a miracle cure in Transylvania. When Dracula's coffin-filled ship lands in England, it also plows through a concert pier where Lucy and Mina are enjoying (what else?) Strauss' overture to *Die Fleidermaus*. Beyond the usual mesmeric ministrations, Dracula's seductions involve psychedelic lectures on hematology. And after Dracula's naked, Icarus-like demise, his two surviving wives lament, "He could not love; he could not love!"

Russell's *Dracula* achieved an offscreen afterlife; the unproduced screenplay partially inspired the choreography of a 1996 production by the Yorkshire-based Northern Ballet Theatre, then under the artistic direction of dancer/actor Christopher Gable, who had appeared in Russell's *Women in Love* (1969), *The Music Lovers* (1970), and, perhaps most pertinently, *Lair of the White Worm* (1988). Russell was given a prominent credit on the original posters, but the synopsis that accompanies the 1996 CD recording includes none of Russell's plot embellishments. In any event, the production is unlikely to ever be seen again — chalk up one more invisible vampire — having been replaced in the NBT repertoire by a new *Dracula* (2005) taking visual inspiration on a spectrum ranging from Tod Browning to Francis Ford Coppola.

The three examples of unrealized films examined barely hint at the degree to which *Dracula* has fired the imaginations of filmmakers and other performance artists. Even the misfires are fascinating, the failed attempts often as interesting as the ones that came to fruition. *Dracula* is surely unique in narrative history, with its origins in oral folklore, its longevity in print, and its apparently unstoppable afterlife in the realm of the moving image. Like Dracula himself, the story's ability to endlessly shapeshift seems to be an essential key to its immortality.

Sources

Briant, Shane. Correspondence with author, October 10, 2009.

Gable, Christopher. Liner notes for compact disc recording of Tim Feeney's ballet score for *Dracula*. Naxos/HNH International, 1996.

Houghton, Don. *Victim of His Imagination* (screenplay treatment, January 1972). Author's collection.

Ludlam, Harry. *A Biography of Dracula: The Life Story of Bram Stoker* (London: W. Foulsham, 1962). Reprinted as *A Biography of Bram Stoker: Creator of Dracula* (London: New English Library, 1977).

Riley, Philip J., ed. *James Whale's Dracula's Daughter* (Albany, GA: Bear Manor, 2009).

Russell, Ken. *Dracula* (second draft screenplay; August 18, 1978). Author's collection.

Sherriff, R.C. *No Leading Lady* (London: Victor Gollancz, 1968).

Filmography

The ABC Saturday Superstar Movie (TV Series [1972–1974]), episode "Daffy Duck and Porky Pig Meet the Groovie Goolies"; U.S., 16 December 1972; Horror, Comedy, Family/Television, Animation; 60 minutes/color/English/Mono; Filmation Associates, Warner Bros. Animation.

Producers: Norm Prescott, Lou Scheimer; *Writing Credits*: Len Janson, Chuck Menville; *Director*: Hal Sutherland; *Film Editing*: Doreen A. Dixon, Joseph Simon; *Original Music*: Ray Ellis (as Yvette Blais), Norm Prescott (as Jeff Michael); *Cast*: Mel Blanc (Daffy Duck/Porky Pig/Elmer Fudd/Yosemite Sam/Tweety Pie/Road Runner/Wile E. Coyote/Pepe LePew/Foghorn Leghorn/Sylvester/Charlie Dog), Larry Storch (Count Tom Dracula/The Phantom), Howard Morris (Franklin "Frankie" Frankenstein/Wolfgang "Wolfie" Wolfman/Orville Mummy), Jane Webb (Hagatha/Petunia Pig [as Joanne Louise]), Len Janson (uncredited), Chuck Menville (uncredited)

Daffy Duck (Mel Blanc) is a movie producer in Hollywood filming a movie about King Arthur and his Knights of the Round Table. The Looney Toons and the Groovie Goolies, including Count Tom Dracula, go to Hollywood to star in Daffy's movie.

The ABC Saturday Superstar Movie (TV Series [1972–1974]), episode "The Mad, Mad, Mad Monsters"; U.S., 23 September 1972; Horror, Comedy, Family/Television, Animation; 60 minutes/color/English; Rankin-Bass Productions, Mushi Studio, Videocraft International.

Producers: Jules Bass, Basil Cox, Arthur Rankin Jr.; *Writing Credits*: William J. Keenan, Lou Silverman; *Director*: Jules Bass, Arthur Rankin Jr.; *Film Editing*: Irwin Goldrese; *Original Music*: Maury Laws; *Cast*: Bradley Bolke (voice), Rhoda Mann (Additional Voices [voice]), Bob McFadden (Additional Voices [voice]), Allen Swift (Frankenstein/The Creature from the Black Lagoon/The Invisible Man/The Invisible Boy/Dracula/Dracula's Son/Ron Chanley/Dr. Jekyll/Mr. Hyde/Rosebud [voice]).

Baron Von Frankenstein and Igor plan to build a girl monster to partner with Frankenstein's Monster. Joining them too is Dracula.

ABC Weekend Specials (TV Series [1977–1997]), episode "Bunnicula, The Vampire Rabbit"; U.S., Season 5, Episode 3, 9 January 1982; Adventure, Comedy, Drama/Television, Animation; 23 minutes/color/English; Taft Entertainment Company/Ruby-Spears Productions.

Producers: Joe Ruby, Ken Spears; *Writing Credits*: Mark Evanier, Deborah Howe, James Howe; *Director*: Charles A. Nichols; *Film Editing*: Mary Nelson-Duerrstein, Chip Yaras; *Original Music*: Dean Elliot; *Cast*: Jack Carter (Harold, Roy), Howard Morris (Chester — Stockboy, Hank), Pat Petersen (Toby Monroe), Alan Young (Mr. Monroe — Storekeeper), Janet Waldo (Mrs. Monroe — Gertie, Alice), Alan Dinehart (Boss — Andy), Joshua Milrad (as Josh Milrad).

When workers at Mr. Monroe's factory begin finding the carrots and other vegetables sucked dry of their juices, Harold the Dog and Chester the cat, along with the other neighbors, suspect that the new rabbit in town might be a Dracula-type vampire.

The Addams Family (TV Series 1973–1975), episode "The Fastest Creepy Camper in the West"; U.S., Season 1, Episode 4, 29 September 1973; Comedy, Horror, Family/Television, Animation; 30 minutes/color/English; Hanna-Barbara Studios.

Producers: Iwao Takianoto, William Hanna, Joseph Barbera, Paul Sommer, Maurice Pooley; *Writing Credits*: Bill Raynor, Bud Atkinson, Jack Mendelsolm, Miles Wilder, Dick Conway, Gene Thompson; *Director*: Charles A. Nichols, John Halas, Joy Batchelor; *Original Music*: Hoyt Curtin; *Cast*: Leonard Welanib (Gomez), Janet Waldo (Morticia, Granny), Jackie Coogan (Uncle Fester), Ted Cassidy (Lurch), Jodie Foster (Pugsley), Cindy Henderson (Wednesday), Josh Albee, Howard Caine, John Carver, Pat Harrington, Jr., Bob Holt, Don Messick, John Stphenson, Herb Vigran.

The Addams Family engages in a race with Count Evil and The Race Ace. Aided by Uncle Fester's latest invention, "Festerine," they win one million dollars towards "Vulture Culture," their favorite class at The Ghoul School of Dracula University.

The Adventures of Elmo in Grouchland; U.S., 1999; Adventure, Family, Comedy, Fantasy/Animation; 73 minutes/color/English/Dolby Digital, SDDS; Children's Television Workshop (CTW), The Jim Henson Company, Jim Henson Pictures.

Producer: Stephanie Allain, Martin G. Baker, Timothy M. Bourne, Kevin Clash, Brian Henson, Marjorie Kalins, Alex Rockwell; *Writing Credits*: Mitchell Kriegman, Mitchell Kriegman, Joey Mazzarino (as Joseph Mazzarino); *Director*: Gary Halvorson; *Cinematography*: Alan Caso; *Film Editing*: Alan Baumgarten; *Original Music*: John Debney; *Art Direction*: William G. Davis; *Make-Up*: Cecilia Verardi; *Special Effects*: James Chai, Phil H. Fravel, David Hill, Larry Jameson, Walter Kiesling, Thomas Kittle, Tom Newby, William Purcell, Michael Schorr, Joseph Quinn Simpkins; *Cast*: Kevin Clash (Elmo/Pestie/Grouch Jailer/Grouch Cab Driver [voice]), Mandy Patinkin (Huxley), Vanessa Williams (Queen of Trash), Sonia Manzano (Maria), Roscoe Orman (Gordon), Fran Brill (Zoe/Pestie/Prairie Dawn [voice]), Stephanie D'Abruzzo (Grizzy/Pestie [voice]), Dave Goelz (Humongous Chicken [voice]), Joey Mazzarino (Bug [voice]) (as Joseph Mazzarino), Jerry Nelson (Count/Pestie/Grouch Mayor/Grouch Cop [voice]), Carmen Osbahr (Rosita [voice]), Martin P. Robinson (Telly/Pestie/Laundromad Guy [voice]), David Rudman (Baby Bear/Fat Blue/Caterpillar/Pestie/Collander Stenchman/Ice Cream Customer [voice]), Caroll Spinney (Big Bird/Oscar [voice]), Steve Whitmire (Ernie/Stuckweed/Football Stenchman/Ice Cream Vendor/Parrot [voice]), Alison Bartlett (Gina [as Alison Bartlett-O'Reilly]), Frank Oz (Bert/Grover/Cookie Monster [voice]), Ruth Buzzi (Ruthie), Emilio Delgado (Luis), Loretta Long (Susan), Bob McGrath (Bob), Drew Allison (Additional Muppet Performer [voice]), Bill Barretta (Additional Muppet Performer [voice]), John Boone (Additional Muppet Performer [voice]), R. Lee Bryan (Additional Muppet Performer [voice]), Leslie Carrara (Additional Muppet Performer [voice] [as Leslie Carrera]), Lisa Consolo (Additional Muppet Performer [voice]), Jodi Eichelberger (Additional Muppet Performer [voice]), Rowell Gormon (Additional Muppet Performer [voice]), Mary Harrison (Additional Muppet Performer [voice]), Rob Killen (Additional Muppet Performer [voice]), Bruce Lanoil (Additional Muppet Performer [voice]), Bob Lynch (Additional Muppet Performer [voice]), Ed May (Additional Muppet Performer [voice]), Tim Parati (Additional Muppet Performer [voice]), Annie Peterle (Additional Muppet Performer [voice]), Andy Stone (Additional Muppet Performer [voice]), Lisa Sturz (Additional Muppet Performer [voice]), Kirk R. Thatcher (Additional Muppet Performer [voice] [as Kirk Thatcher]), Matt Vogel (Big Bird/Ernie [assistant] [uncredited])/Additional Muppet Performer [voice]), Matt Yates (Additional Muppet Performer [voice]).

Elmo and his friend Zoe get into a tug-of-war match with Elmo's favorite fuzzy blue blanket, sending it to Grouchland, a faraway place inhabited by grouchy creatures, stinky garbage, and the villainous Huxley. Mustering all his courage and determination, Elmo sets out after his favorite blanket on an action-packed rescue mission. Characters from Sesame Street, including Count von Count, follow after Elmo to Grouchland to get him back.

The Adventures of Young Indiana Jones: Masks of Evil; U.S., 1999; Adventure, Horror; 95 minutes/color/English, Italian, Turkish, German, Icelandic; Amblin Television.

Producers: George Lucas, Rick McCallum, Doris Kirch; *Writing Credits*: Rosemary Anne Sisson, Jonathan Hensleigh, George Lucas; *Director*: Dick Maas (segment "Transylvania"); *Cinematography*: David Tattersall; *Film Editing*: Edgar Burcksen, Louise Rubacky; *Original Music*: Laurence Rosenthal, Curt Sobel; *Art Direction*: Ricky Eyres, Lucy Richardson, Karel Vacek; *Make-Up*: Katerina Erbanova, Pat Hay, Meinir Jones-Lewis, Eva Vytlelová; *Cast*: Sean Patrick Flanery (Indiana Jones [also archive footage]), Katherine Butler (Molly [archive footage]), Keith Szarabajka (Colonel Waters [archive footage]), Peter Firth (Stefan [archive footage]), Bob Peck (General Targo [archive footage]), Ahmet Levendoglu (Mustafa Kemal [archive footage]), Philippe Smolikowski (Etienne [archive footage]), Huseyin Katircioclu (Nico [archive footage]), Boris Isarov (Vasily [archive footage]), Tristram Jellinek (Victor [archive footage]), Mehmet Birkiye (Sadallah [archive footage]), Nüvit Özdogru (Sultan [archive footage] [as Nuvit Ozdogru]), Emrah Kolukisa (Mahmoud [archive footage]), Ali Taygun (Enver Pasha [archive footage]), Zuhal Olcay (Halide Edib [archive footage]), Hüseyin Köroglu (Young Turkish Officer [archive footage]), Nuri Ersan (Young Turkish Man [archive footage]), Suna Pekuysal (Fortune Teller [archive footage]), Kevork Malikyan (Armenian Agent [archive footage]), Sean McCabe (Monty [archive footage]), Sara Baydur (Turkish Girl #1 [archive footage]), Tumay Keles (Jale [archive footage]), Zeynep Cem (Turkish Girl #2 [archive footage]), Neslihan Yazici (Turkish Girl #3 [archive footage]),

Simone Bendix (Maria [archive footage]), Paul Kynman (Nicholas Hunyadi [archive footage]), Sam Kelly (Dr. Heinzer [archive footage]), Michael Mellinger (Paretti [archive footage]), William Roberts (Stanfill [archive footage]), William Armstrong (The Major [archive footage]), Steven Hartley (Agent Picard [archive footage]), Anne Tirard (Tarot Reader [archive footage]), Petr Svárovský (Venetian Policeman [archive footage]), David Gilliam (Agent Thompson [archive footage]), Petr Jákl (German General [archive footage]), Jiri Kraus (French General [archive footage]).

General Targo is discovered by Indiana Jones to be impaling prisoners he takes from the German P.O.W. camps. Targo lives in Transylvania and is acting just like Vlad Tepes from long ago.

Adventures of Young Van Helsing: The Quest for the Lost Scepter; U.S., 2004; Action-Adventure, Horror; 114 minutes/color/English; Scorpio Pictures, Totality Films LLC.

Producers: Jerome Pettaman, Kevin Summerfield; *Writing Credits*: Craig Clyde, Kevin Summerfield, Kevin Summerfield; *Director*: Kevin Summerfield; *Cinematography*: Brad Walker; *Film Editing*: Brendan Davis, Kevin Summerfield, Brendan Walsh; *Original Music*: Quentin Chiappetta; *Make-Up*: Robert H. Bennett, Jeannie Fry, Pete Gerner, Brian Spears; *Special Effects*: Robert H. Bennett, Pete Gerner, Steve Tolin; *Cast*: Ken Mitzkovitz (Abraham Van Helsing), Freddie Sabaugh (Aki), Ned Narang (Professor Arad), Rabiah Elaawar (Estabon), Tomm Bauer (Danny Morgan [as Thomas Bauer]), Amneek Sandhu (Aldonza [as Amneek Sandha]), Nahid Zoha (Fernando), Kara Edwards (Rita), Omar Porter (Campbell), Joe Zaso (Simon Magus), Kimberly Botbyl (Morgan LeFay), Keith Jordan (Michael Harris/Michael Van Helsing), Johnny Alonso (Karl Andrews), Ken Beal (Mr. Syler), Joy Griffin (Mary Ellen), Beauty Jackson (Beth), Thomas Haskell (Teacher Andrews), Lisa Willis (Aunt Molly Harris), T.J. Sicilia (Preston), Daniel J. Allen (Anthony), Melvyn Wallace (Mr. Morgan), Bo Mitchell (Little Danny Morgan), Jonathan Adock (Will Brown).

Michael Harris (Keith Jordan) is the descendant of Abraham Van Helsing. Abraham found the scepter of God, an artifact forged by an angel, and hid it. Demons are now attacking Michael in an attempt to get the scepter.

AFI's 100 Years ... 100 Heroes & Villains (*AFI's 100 Years, 100 Heroes & Villains: America's Greatest Screen Characters* [U.S., complete title]); U.S., 2003; Documentary; color/English; American Film Institute (AFI), The Gary Smith Company, SFM Entertainment.

Producers: Melinda Cote, Bob Gazzale, Dann Netter, Frederick S. Pierce, Jason Schoenagle, Gary Smith, Zack Smith, Robb Wagner, Jeffrey L. Wilcox (as Jeff Wilcox); *Writing Credits*: Bob Gazalle; *Director*: Gary Smith; *Film Editing*: Ali Grossman Debra Light Tim Preston; *Original Music*: Toby Foster (music mixer), Ian Fraser (music arranger), Ian Fraser (musical director), Bill Hughes (music contractor), Edward Karam (music arranger, as Eddie Karam), Diane Prentice (music clearance); *Make-Up*: Stacy L. Hodgson (makeup artist: Mr. Stallone); *Cast*: Kathy Bates (Herself), Anthony Hopkins (Dr. Hannibal Lecter, #1 Villain), Hayden Christensen (Himself), Glenn Close (Herself), Wes Craven (Himself), Geena Davis (Herself), Kirk Douglas (Himself), Robert Englund (Himself), Sally Field (Herself), Louise Fletcher (Herself), Harrison Ford (Himself), Milos Forman (Himself), Jodie Foster (Herself), William Friedkin (Himself), Antoine Fuqua (Himself), Celeste Holm (Herself), Dennis Hopper (Himself), Michael Keaton (Himself), Frank Langella (Himself), Angela Lansbury (Herself), Janet Leigh (Herself), George Lucas (Himself), Sidney Lumet (Himself), Malcolm McDowell (Himself), Roger Moore (Himself), Peter O'Toole (Himself), Arthur Penn (Himself), Christopher Reeve (Himself), Susan Sarandon (Herself), Ridley Scott (Himself), Sylvester Stallone (Himself), Oliver Stone (Himself), Robert Towne (Himself), Sigourney Weaver (Herself), Arnold Schwarzenegger (Himself, Host), Gordon Smith (Himself—U.S. senator, Oregon), Erin Brockovich-Ellis (Herself, as Erin Brockovich), Jean Firstenberg (Herself, as Jean Picker Firstenberg), Mary Badham (Herself), Randy Thomas (Announcer, voice), rest of cast listed alphabetically: Carl Bernstein (Himself), Elmore Leonard (Himself), Gregory Peck (Atticus Finch), Anthony Perkins (Norman Bates, #2 Villain).

The American Film Institute selected its 100 greatest heroes and villains, among which is Dracula, played by Frank Langella in the 1979 Universal film.

El Águila Descalza (*The Barefoot Eagle* [undefined]); Mexico, 1971; Comedy, Crime, Drama; 90 minutes/color/Spanish; Producciones Jaguar S.A. de C.V.

Producers: Juan Abusaid Rios, Lucas Haces Gil, Heriberto Mendez Pons; *Writing Credits*: Alfonso Arau, Emilio Carballido, Pancho Cordova, Hector Ortega; *Director*: Alfonso Arau; *Cinematography*: Alex Phillips Jr.; *Film Editing*: Eufemio Rivera; *Cast*: Alfonso Arau (Poncho/Jonathan Eaglepass/Mascalzzone), Ofelia Medina (Chona), Christa Linder (Sirene Martinez), José Gálvez (Don Carlos Martinez), Eva Muller (Bailarina China), Virma González (Adelita, paciente Manicomio), Roberto

Cobo (El Apostol, paciente Manicomio), Tamara Garina (Brigitte, paciente manicomio), Victor Eberg (Mafioso alto), Héctor Ortega (Trabajador factoria/Policia de transito), Alfonso Munguía (Engeniero factoria), MaríaLuisa Serrano (Tia Chofi), Eduardo López Rojas (Trabajador factoria), Ernesto Gómez Cruz (Trabajador factoria), Pancho Córdova (Encargado de Manicomio), Omar Jasso (Borracho), Nacho Contla (Juez), Margarita Narváez (Borracha), Celia Viveros (Borracha), Roberto Ramírez Garza (Policia), Willie Wilhelmy (Paciente Manicomio), Florencio Castelló (Don Alejo), Victorio Blanco (Anciano), José Dupeyrón (Chavita), Armando Acosta (Trabajador factoria), Marta Aura (Trabajador factoria), Ana Ofelia Murguía (Trabajador factoria), Salvador Zea (Trabajador factoria), Álvaro Carcaño (Trabajador factoria), Juan Gabriel Moreno (Trabajador factoria), Adan Guevara (Trabajador factoria), Juan Manuel Díaz (Trabajador factoria), Adrian Ramos (Trabajador factoria), Luis Torner (Trabajador factoria), Isabel Larios (Soprano), Jose Maria Cora (Comandante policia), Joe Carson (Mafioso), René Barrera (Mafioso telefono), Arturo Alegro (Leon, paciente Manicomio), Rodrigo Puebla (Moctezuma, paciente Manicomio), Abel Cureño (Vecina), Cecilia Leger (Trabajador vidrios), Clara Osollo (Dona Tencha), Gerardo Zepeda (Trabajador Manicomio), Nathanael León (Trabajador Manicomio), Guillermo Ayala (Trabajador Manicomio), Jorge Allende (Trabajador Manicomio), Tomas Fernandez (Trabajador Manicomio), Queta Carrasco (La Llorona, paciente Manicomio), Giovanni Korporaal (El Cosmaonauta, paciente Manicomio), Carlos Quintero (Dracula, paciente Manicomio), Carlos Castañon (Hippie, paciente Manicomio), Daniel Benítez (El Pajaro, paciente Manicomio), Susana Gamboa, Daniel Albertos (Hermano de Sirene), Gilberto Chacon.

A masked vigilante decides to take the law into his own hands and becomes a hero in a small town. Carlos "Che" Quintero plays a mental patient named "Drácula."

Akui ggot (*The Bad Flower* [undefined]); South Korea, 1961; Horror; black and white/Korean; Lee Yong-min Productions.

Producer: Yongmin Lee; *Writing Credits*: Taekwon Nam; *Director*: Yongmin Lee; *Cinematography*: Ho-jin Choi; *Film Editing*: Yongmin Lee; *Original Music*: Mun-pyeong Hwang; *Art Direction*: Yim Myung-sun; *Cast*: Ye-chun Lee, Geumbong Do, Seon-ae Ko.

A botanist, after dedicating years of research to plotting his revenge, succeeds in making a flower that, upon his order, drains its victims of their blood. He uses it to take revenge upon his enemies in this film that is adapted, in part, from Bram Stoker's *Dracula*.

Las Alegres Vampiras de Vögel (*Vampires of Vogel* [English title]); Spain, 1975; Horror, Comedy; 99 minutes/color/Spanish; Titanic Films.

Producers: Julio Pérez Tabernero; *Writing Credits*: Antonio Baylos, Julio Pérez Tabernero; *Director*: Julio Pérez Tabernero; *Cinematography*: Emilio Foriscot; *Film Editing*: Domingo García; *Original Music*: Alfonso G. Santisteban; *Cast*: Ágata Lys, María José Cantudo, Germán Cobos, Rafael Conesa, J. Alonso Vaz, Mary Cruz, Elke Jhonsen, Liza S. Leon, Sara Mora, Juan Antonio Patiño (as Marqués de Toro), Paula Pattier, María Pinar, Débora Rey, Juan Tabernero, José María Tasso, María Vidal.

The ruins of an old castle where the vampire Count tortures and drinks the blood of his prisoners looms over the Transylvanian town of Vögel. As luck would have it, two stranded young girls seek shelter in the remote European castle, and the Count is delighted to receive them.

Alfred Hitchcock Presents (TV Series [1985–1989]), episode "Night Creatures"; U.S., Season 4, Episode 17, 29 April 1989; Mystery, Thriller; 30 minutes/color/English/Mono; Michael Sloan Productions, Universal TV.

Producers: Robert De Laurentiis (as Robert DeLaurentis), Mary Kahn, Jon Slan, Michael Sloan; *Writing Credits*: Michael Sloan; *Director*: Richard J. Lewis; *Cinematography*: Maris H. Jansons; *Film Editing*: Tom Joerin; *Original Music*: Christopher Dedrick; *Art Direction*: Katherine Mathewson; *Make-Up*: Irma Parkkonen, Divyo Rae Putney; *Cast*: Jason Blicker (Freak), Brett Cullen (Cooper), Alfred Hitchcock (Himself—Host) (archive footage), Ray James (Max Cantilever), Michael Rhoades (Martin Lecross), Stevie Vallance (Holly [as Louise Vallance]).

A reporter becomes interested in a Dracula-type vampire turned rock star.

All My Children (TV Series [1970–present]), episode "Episode dated 31 October 2002"; U.S., 31 October 2002; Drama, Romance, Mystery, Soap Opera/Television; 60 minutes/color/English/Mono; American Broadcasting Company.

Producers: Casey Childs, Lisa Connor, Enza Dolce; *Writing Credits*: Craig Carlson, Lisa Connor, Christina Covino, Frederick Johnson, Mimi Leahey, Karen Lewis, Gordon Rayfield, Amanda Robb, Louise Shaffer, Rebecca Taylor, Addie Walsh; *Director*: Albert Alarr, James A. Baffico, Andrew Lee, Michael V. Pomarico, Andrew Giles Rich, Barbara M. Simmons; *Original Music*: Billy Barber, David Benoit; *Cast*: Kal Cauthen (Kal),

Greg Messina (Doctor), David Zappone (Dracula).

Alucard; U.S., 2003; Horror; 156 minutes/color/English; Brain Damage Film/Darkstone Entertainment.

Producer: John Johnson; *Writing Credits*: Spenser Tomson; *Director*: John Johnson; *Cinematography*: Sergio Lescari; *Original Music*: Lisa Hammer; *Cast*: Jay Barber (Dr. John Seward), Liam Smith (Jonathon Harker), Rebecca Taylor (Miss Mina Murray), David Harscheid (Dr. Abraham Van Helsing), Karthik Srinivasan (Arthur Holmwood), Mariah Smith (Lucy), John Van Patterson, Hal Handerson (Count Alucard), John Johnson (Quincey P. Morris).

Bram Stoker's classic novel gets a modern makeover in this low-budget adaptation from director John Johnson. An old Transylvanian count is planning to move to the more populated city of Nilbog, and Jonathan Harker, a young lawyer, has been employed to oversee the process. Harker ventures to the nobleman's countryside and discovers that the local superstitions are indeed true: Count Alucard ("Dracula" spelled backwards) is, in fact, a vampire. Harker therefore seeks the aid of Dr. Van Helsing.

Alucarda, la hija de las tinieblas (*Alucarda* [U.S.]; *Innocents from Hell* [U.S.]; *Mark of the Devil 3* [U.S.]; *Sisters of Satan* [U.S.]; *Pieklo* [Poland]); Mexico, 1978; Horror, Thriller; 85 minutes/color/English/Mono/35mm; Films 75, Yuma Film.

Producers: Max Guefen, Juan López Moctezuma, Eduardo Moreno; *Writing Credits*: Sheridan Le Fanu (novella "Carmilla"), Alexis Arroyo (story), Tita Arroyo (story), Juan López Moctezuma (story), Yolanda López Moctezuma (story), Alexis Arroyo (screenplay), Juan López Moctezuma (screenplay); *Director*: Juan López Moctezuma; *Cinematography*: Xavier Cruz; *Film Editing*: Maximino Sánchez Molina, *Original Music*: Anthony Guefen; *Art Direction*: Kleomenes Stamatiades; *Make-Up*: Ramírez del Río; *Special Effects*: Abel Contreras; *Cast*: Claudio Brook (Dr. Oszek/Hunchbacked Gypsy), David Silva (Father Lázaro), Tina Romero (Alucarda/Alucarda's Mother), Susana Kamini (Justine), Lili Garza (Daniela Oszek), Tina French (Sister Angélica), Birgitta Segerskog (Mother Superior), Adriana Roel (Sister Germana), Antonia Guerrero, Martin LaSalle (Brother Felipe), Manuel Dondé (Wagon Driver), Adriana Riveroll, Susan Inman, Alejandra Moya, Agustín Isunza (Monk), Paloma Woolrich, Marina Isolda, Sonia Rangel, Beatriz Martínez (Nun), Colombia Moya, Damián Dueñas, Tito Novaro (Monk), Victorio Blanco (Monk [uncredited]), Rosa Furman (uncredited), Edith González (Village Girl [uncredited]), Juan López Moctezuma (Monk [uncredited]), Kleomenes Stamatiades (uncredited).

After the death of her parents, a young girl moves into a convent because she has nowhere else to turn. Her arrival to the convent sets off a series of unexplainable events. There, an evil presence surrounds the girl and her new mysterious friend, as they take part in vampirism, Satanic worship, and demonic possession.

Amantul marii doamne Dracula (TV Series [2005]); Romanian; Drama/Television; color/Romanian.

Writing Credits: Fanus Neagu (novel); *Director*: Constantin Dicu; *Cast*: Agatha Nicolau (Elena Ceausescu), Cristian Motiu (Bob Orlando), George Motoi, Daniela Nane (Izabel Capitanita), Margareta Pogonat, Alexandru Repan, Valentin Uritescu.

The Amazing Adrenalini Brothers! (TV Series [2006–2007]), episode "Fangs of Horror" (*Y Brodyr Adrenalini* [U.K., Welsh title]); U.K./Canada, Season 1, Episode 3, 2006; Family, Comedy, Adventure/Television, Animation, Short; 22 minutes/color/English; Pesky Ltd., Studio B Productions.

Producers: David Hodgson, Tatitana Kober; *Writing Credits*: Nick Ostler; *Director*: Dan Chambers, Claire Underwood.

The Adrenalini Brothers crash in Transylvania and discover that they have landed right in front of Count Dracula's castle. Xan looks identical to the Count, and no one can tell who is who. When they get into trouble, Erk rides in on a giant vampire bat to save them.

Animaniacs (TV Series [1993–1998]), episode "Draculee, Draculaa/Phranken-Runt"; U.S., Season 1, Episode 29, 29 October 1993; Family, Comedy/Television, Animation; 10 minutes/color/English; Warner Brothers Television Animation.

Producers: Rich Arons, Rusty Miller, Peter Hastings, Sherri Stoner, Steven Spielberg, Tom Ruegger; *Writing Credits*: John P. McCann; *Director*: Michael Gerard, Byron Vaughns; *Film Editing*: Joe Gall, Al Breitenbach, Kelly Ann Foley, Theresa Gilroy-Nielson, Susan Odjakjian; *Original Music*: Richard Stone, Steven Bernstein, Julie Bernstein; *Art Direction*: Jeff DeGrandis (storyboard artist), Ken Harsha (storyboard artist), Byron Vaughns (storyboard artist); *Cast*: Jess Harnell (Wakko), Rob Paulsen (Yakko, Dr. Otto Scratchansniff), Tress MacNeille (Dot, Hello Nurse), Frank Welker (Ralph the Guard), Dan Castellaneta (Dracula).

While trying to get to Pennsylvania to meet their parents, the Warner siblings end up in Transylvania. They decide to stay in Dracula's castle. During the night, Dracula tries to bite Dot. The siblings then pull out Dracula's teeth and put them in Dot's hair to make her look like Sheena Easton.

Animaniacs (TV Series [1993–1998]), episode "Randy Beaman's Pal #6" *Steven Spielberg Presents Animaniacs* [U.S.]); U.S., 3 May 1994; Comedy, Family, Fantasy, Musical/Television, Animation; 30 minutes/color/English/Stereo; Akom Production Company.

Producers: Steven Spielberg, Rich Arons, Rusty Miller, Peter Hastings, Sherri Stoner; *Director*: Jon McClenahan; *Film Editing*: Joe Gall, Al Breitenbach, Kelly Ann Foley, Theresa Gilroy-Nielson, Susan Odjakjian; *Original Music*: Richard Stone, Steven Bernstein, Julie Bernstein; *Cast*: Colin Wells (Colin [voice]).

Randy Beaman imagines that he is Dracula, when in actuality he really is Dracula.

Animaniacs—Spooky Stuff; U.S., 1997; Comedy, Family; 60 minutes/color/English/Dolby/35mm; 20th Century–Fox Television.

Producer: Barbra J. Gerard; *Writing Credits*: Dave Finkel, Nick Dubois, Ralph Soll, Steven Spielberg, Wendell Morris; *Director*: Charles Visser, Peter Bonerz; *Cast*: Rob Paulsen, Jess Harnell, Tress MacNeille, Frank Welker, Maurice LaMarche.

This "spooky" compilation of Animaniacs episodes includes "Draculee Dracula," in which Yakko, Wakko, and Dot find another way to vanquish Count Dracula by annoying him to death! Elsewhere, Slappy the Squirrel trick or treats, and more. Other episodes include "Meatballs or Consequence," "Scare Happy Slappy," and "Runt's Heroics."

Aqua Teen Hunger Force (TV Series [2001–present]), episode "Bus of the Undead"; U.S., Season 1, Episode 3, 30 September 2001; Comedy/Television, Animation; 15 minutes/color/English; Radical Axis.

Producers: Keith Crofford, Jay Edwards, Michael Lazzo, Matt Maiellaro, Vishal Roney, Dave Willis; *Writing Credits*: Matt Maiellaro, Dave Willis; *Director*: Matt Maiellaro, Dave Willis; *Film Editing*: Jay Edwards; *Original Music*: Schooly-D; *Special Effects*: Scott Fry; *Cast*: Dana Snyder (Master Shake [voice]), Carey Means (Frylock [voice]), Dave Willis (Meatwad/Carl Brutananadilewski [voice]), C. Martin Croker (Dr. Weird/Steve [voice]), H. Jon Benjamin (Mothmonsterman [voice]), Don Kennedy (Assisted Living Dracula), Mary Kraft (Nurse to Assisted Living Dracula), Schooly-D (Narrator [voice] uncredited).

The episode starts out with Shake wearing a lid that has lots of bright spot-lights. The Mothmonsterman, attracted to all the lights, shows up to the Aqua Teen's house. Shake mistakes the moth creature, telling everyone it is Dracula. The next day, the Mothmonsterman shows up outside the house demanding the lights be turned back on. To prove that it is not Dracula, Frylock brings the group to Dracula's grave in Memphis.

Aqua Teen Hunger Force (TV Series [2001–present]), episode "Little Brittle"; U.S., Season 3, Episode 6, 5 September 2004; Comedy/Television, Animation; 15 minutes/color/English; Radical Axis.

Producers: Keith Crofford, Jay Edwards, Edward Hastings (as Ned Hastings), Matt Maiellaro, Vishal Roney, Dave Willis; *Writing Credits*: Matt Maiellaro, Dave Willis; *Director*: Matt Maiellaro, Dave Willis; *Film Editing*: John Brestan, Edward Hastings; *Original Music*: Schooly-D; *Cast*: Dana Snyder (Master Shake [voice]), Carey Means (Frylock [voice]), Dave Willis (Meatwad/Carl Brutananadilewski/Ignignokt [voice]), Andy Merrill (Oglethorpe [voice]), Mike Schatz (Emory [voice]), Chris Ward (Little Brittle [voice]), Matt Maiellaro (Err/Vampire [voice]).

MC Pee Pants returns to Earth as a crazy old rapper, Little Brittle, who is on his hospital death bed. Meatwad visits Little Brittle with a solution to how he can live longer. He tells Little Brittle to get bitten by and transformed into a vampire. When Little Brittle is finally turned into a vampire, he leaves the hospital during the day and is killed by the sunlight.

Ashes of Doom; Canada, 1970; Horror, Comedy/Short; 2 minutes/color; National Film Board of Canada (NFB).

Producers: Wolf Koenig, Robert Verrall; *Writing Credits*: Don Arioli; *Director*: Don Arioli, Grant Munro; *Cinematography*: Jacques Fogel; *Film Editing*: Grant Munro (as William G.P. Munro); *Original Music*: Karl du Plessis, Eldon Rathburn; *Art Direction*: Earl G. Preston (set designer); *Cast*: Grant Munro (Dracula), Nadia Salnick.

El Ataúd del Vampiro (*Der Sarg des Vampiro* [West Germany]; *El ataud del muerto* [Mexico, alternative spelling]; *El returno del vampiro* [Mexico, alternative spelling]; *La bara del vampiro* [Italy]; *The Vampire's Coffin* [undefined]); Mexico, 1958; Horror, Mystery, Thriller; 80 minutes/black and white/Spanish/Mono; Cinematográfica ABSA.

Producers: Abel Salazar; *Writing Credits*: Ramón Obón, Alfredo Salazar, Raúl Zenteno; *Director*: Fernando Méndez; *Cinematography*: Víctor Herrera; *Film Editing*: Alfredo Rosas Priego; *Make-Up*: Ana Guerrero; *Special Effects*: Juan Muñoz Ravelo; *Cast*: Abel Salazar (Dr. Enrique Saldívar), Ariadna Welter (Marta González), Germán Robles (Count Karol de Lavud), Yerye Beirute (Baraza [as Yeire Beirute]), Alicia Montoya (María Teresa), Guillermo Orea, Carlos Ancira (Dr. Marion), Antonio Raxel, Alicia Rodríguez (uncredited).

Graverobbers inadvertently stumble upon the

Poster for *El Ataúd del Vampiro* (Mexico, 1958).

tomb Count Karol de Lavud, a vampire, who turns them into the walking dead to do his bidding: to locate and hunt down beautiful women.

Attack of the Killer Tomatoes (TV Series [1990–1991]), episode "Spatula, Prinze of Dorkness"; U.S., 1990; Comedy, Science Fiction, Thriller/Television, Animation; 23 minutes/color/English/Stereo; Akom Production Company, American Film Technologies, Four Square Productions, Fox Children's Network Inc, Marvel Productions.

Producers: John De Bello, Boyd Kirkland, Stephen Peace, Joe Taritero; *Writing Credits*: Richard Mueller; *Film Editing*: Jay Bixsen; *Original Music*: Shuki Levy, Haim Saban; *Art Direction*: Bobby Haynes (color tagger), Tom O'Mary (post-production art director), Tom Tataranowicz (storyboard artist); *Special Effects*: Patrick Neary (digital artist), Brad Constantine (assistant director of animation/lead animator), David McGrath (animator), Mark Risley (assistant animator, 1990/animator, 1991), Steve Troop (animator); *Cast*: Maurice LaMarche (Zoltan/Tomato Guy [voice]), Kath Soucie (Tara Boumdeay [voice]), Christian Guzek (Chad Finletter [voice]), S. Scott Bullock (FT [voice]), John Astin (Dr. Putrid T Gangreen [voice]), Cam Clarke (Igor Smith [voice]), Thom Bray (Wilbur Finletter [voice]), Neil Ross (Whitley White [voice])

Zoltan gets turned into a vampire in an experiment performed by Dr. Gangreen and Igor Smith. He dubs himself "Spatula, Prinze of Dorkness" and goes around biting people on their necks. Tara Boumdeay and her disguised tomato FT have escaped from Dr. Gangreen and found a job working at Wilbur Finletter's pizza parlor. She meets his nephew, Chad, and they attempt to stop Dr. Gangreen and Spatula's evil intentions. The episode is narrated by Count Dracula.

Awake (*Bajo anesthesia* [Argentina/Peru]; *Acordado* [Portugal]; *Anestezi* [Turkey]; *Awake—A Vida Por Um Fio* [Brazil]; *Awake—Anestesia cosciente* [Italy]; *Conscient* [Canada]; *Consciente* [Mexico]; *Despierto* [Spain]; *Przebudzenie* [Poland]; *Siopilos efialtis* [Greece]); U.S., 2007; Crime, Thriller; 84 minutes/color/English, Japanese/Dolby Digital; GreeneStreet Films.

Producers: Kelly Carmichael, Donny Deutsch, Amy J. Kaufman, Jason Kliot, John Penotti, Fisher Stevens, Tory Tunnell, Joana Vicente, Bob Weinstein, Harvey Weinstein, Tim Williams; *Writing Credits*: Joby Harold; *Director*: Joby Harold; *Cinematography*: Russell Carpenter (director of photography); *Film Editing*: Craig McKay; *Original Music*: Samuel Sim; *Art Direction*: Ben Barraud; *Make-Up*: Chris Bingham (makeup department head), Michelle Johnson (hair stylist: J. Alba and L. Olin), Anna Krommydas (department head hair) Evelyne Noraz (makeup artist: J. Alba and L. Olin), Barney Burman (prosthetics makeup consultant [uncredited]); *Special Effects*: Russell Berg (special effects foreman), Peter Kunz (special effects), Dan Crawley (special effects technician [uncredited]), Anthony Grow (special effects technician [uncredited]), Hill Vinot (mold maker: Burman Studios [uncredited]); *Cast*: Hayden Christensen (Clay Beresford), Jessica Alba (Sam Lockwood), Terrence Howard (Dr. Jack Harper), Lena Olin (Lilith Beresford), Christopher McDonald (Dr. Larry Lupin), Sam Robards (Clayton Beresford Sr.), Arliss Howard (Dr. Jonathan Neyer), Fisher Stevens (Dr. Puttnam), Georgina Chapman (Penny Carver), David Harbour (Dracula), Steven Hinkle (Young Clay [as Stephen Hinkle]), Denis O'Hare (Financial News Analyst), Charlie Hewson (Brian the Orderly), Court Young (Officer Doherty), Joseph Costa (Dr. Elbogen), Poorna Jagannathan (Dr. Neyer's Nurse), Lee Wong (Mr. Waturi), Kae Shimizu (Asian Translator), Steven Rowe (Teacher), Jeffrey Fierson (Head Chef), John C. Havens (Policeman), Richard Thomsen (Minister), Joshua Rollins (Funeral Minister), Brenda Schad (Pregnant Woman), Sam Pitman (Zombie), Ross Klavan (Financial News Analyst #2).

The film focuses on a man who suffers from "anesthetic awareness," finding himself awake and aware, but paralyzed, during heart surgery. His mother must wrestle with her own demons as a drama unfolds around them. Dracula makes an appearance as well.

Il Bacio di Dracula (TV mini-series) (*Dracula* [U.S.]; *Dracula's Curse* [U.S., DVD Title]); Italy/Germany, 2002; Horror/Television; 173 minutes/Italian, English/color/Stereo/35mm; Lux Vide (as A Lux Video), Beta Film (in association with), RaiTrade, Rai Fiction, KirchMedia.

Producers: Roberta Cadringher, Paolo De Crescenzo, Ferdinand Dohna, Michele Greco, Paolo Lucidi; *Writing Credits*: Bram Stoker (novel), Roger Young (teleplay), Eric Lerner (teleplay); *Director*: Roger Young; *Cinematography*: Elemer Ragalyi (as Elmer Ragalyi); *Film Editing*: Alessandro Lucidi; *Original Music*: Harald Kloser, Thomas Wanker; *Make-Up*: Giancarlo Del Brocco (makeup supervisor), Anna Tesner (assistant makeup artist); *Special Effects*: Gabor Kiszelly (special effects technician), Fernc Ormos (special effects supervisor); *Cast*: Patrick Bergin (Vladislav Tepes/Dracula), Giancarlo Giannini (Dr. Enrico Valenzi), Hardy Krüger Jr. (Jonathan Harker [as Hardy Krüger Jr.]), Stefania Rocca (Mina), Muriel Baumeister (Lucy), Kai Wiesinger (Dr. Seward [as Kay Wiesinger]), Alessio Boni (Quincy), Conrad Hornby

(Arthur Holmwood), Brett Forest (Roenfield [as Brett Forrest]), Alessia Merz (Fair Woman), Piroska Kiss (Dark Woman), István Göz (Male Nurse [as Istvan Goz]), Barna Illyés (Border Guard [as Barna Illyes]), Csaba Pethes (Captain of the Tug), Balázs Tardy (Tug Crew Member 1 [as Balazs Tardy]), Levente Törköly (Tug Crew Member 2 [as Levente Torkoly]), Ilona Kassai (Woman at the Hotel), Imola Gáspár (Woman at the Manor [as Imola Gaspar]), Andrew Divoff (Doctor [uncredited]), Csilla Bakonyi (uncredited), Petra Hauman (uncredited), Tibor Kenderesi (uncredited).

Engaged to Mina Murray, Jonathan Harker, a real estate agent, is summoned to Romania to meet a new client. Upon arrival, he meets Vladislav Tepes, who is looking for a place for his uncle. As the story unfolds, it is revealed that Tepes is actual the famous Count Dracula, and is looking for new blood.

Bandh Darwaza (*The Closed Door* [India]); India, 1990; Horror; 145 minutes/color/Hindi/Mono; Ramsay Productions.

Producers: Shyam Ramsay, Tulsi Ramsay, Anjali Ramsay, Kanta Ramsay; *Writing Credits*: Dev Kishan (dialogue), Dev Kishan (story), Shyam Ramsay (screenplay); *Director*: Shyam Ramsay, Tulsi Ramsay; *Cinematography*: Gangu Ramsay; *Film Editing*: Keshav Hirani; *Original Music*: Anand Chitragupth, Milind Chitragupth; *Art Direction*: T.K. Desai; *Make-Up*: Srinivasa Roy, Salim (assistant); *Special Effects*: Baldev Malik (opticals), Krishan Malik (opticals), Harish Patel (main titles), Jogesh Patel (main titles); *Cast*: Hashmat Khan, Manjeet Kullar, Kunika, Vijayendra Ghatge (Thakur), Satish Kaul, Anita Sareen, Anirudh Agarwal (Nevla), Aruna Irani, Shamsher Khan, Raza Murad, Beena Banerjee (Mrs. Pratap Singh) (as Beena), Ashalata, Chetana Das (Bijli [as Chetna]), Sunil Dhawan, Jack Gaud, Bishnu Kharghoria (Thaaya [as Bishnu]), Johnny Lever, Karunakar Pathak, Rajnibala, Shyamalee, Ashalata Waghdegare.

The Indian version of *Dracula*, *Bandh Darwaza* tells the story of a childless woman who visits the lair of a magician in order to conceive a child. After the child is born, the evil magician demands that the woman hand over her baby girl. The woman refuses and has the magician killed. Many years later, the magician is revived as the undead and searches for the now-teenage girl to make her his slave.

Banpaia bantâ D (*Vampire Hunter D: Bloodlust* [U.S., DVD box title]; *D, o kynigos vampir: Dipsa gia aima* [Greece, DVD title]; *Vampire Hunter D* [U.S.]; *Vampire hunter D — Zadza krwi* [Poland, DVD title]); Japan/Hong Kong/U.S., 2000; Action, Horror, Science Fiction, Romance, Western/ Animation; 103/color/English/Dolby Digital; BMG Funhouse.

Producers: Meileen Choo, Masao Maruyama, Taka Nagasawa, Mataichiro Yamamoto; *Writing Credits*: Brian Irving (uncredited), Yoshiaki Kawajiri, Hideyuki Kikuchi (novel "D — yousatsukou"); *Director*: Yoshiaki Kawajiri, Jack Fletcher (English language version), Tai Kit Mak (co-direction [credited as Asian prints]); *Cinematography*: Hitoshi Yamaguchi; *Original Music*: Marco D'Ambrosio; *Art Direction*: Yuji Ikehata; *Cast*: Hideyuki Tanaka (D), Ichirô Nagai (Left Hand), Kôichi Yamadera (Meier Link), Megumi Hayashibara (Leila [voice]), Emi Shinohara (Charlotte Elbourne), Yûsaku Yara (Borgoff), Hôchû Ôtsuka (Kyle), Rintarou Nishi (Mashira), Keiji Fujiwara (Benge), Yôko Soumi (Caroline), Toshihiko Seki (Grove), Ryûzaburô Ôtomo (Nolt), Chikao Ôtsuka (Barbarois Elder), Takeshi Aono (Polk), Motomu Kiyokawa (John Elbourne), Kôji Tsujitani (Alan Elbourne), Chiharu Suzuka (D's Mother), Akiko Yajima (Young Leila), Rikiya Koyama (Public Official), Mika Kanai (Leila's Granddaughter), Unshô Ishizuka (Priest), Bibari Maeda (Carmila), Andrew Philpot (D [voice]), John Rafter Lee (Meier Link [voice]), Pamela Adlon (Leila [voice] [as Pamela Segall]), Wendee Lee (Charlotte [voice]), Michael McShane (Left Hand [voice]), Julia Fletcher (Carmila [voice]), Matt McKenzie (Borgoff [voice]), John Di Maggio (John Elbourne/Nolt/Mashira [voice]), Alex Fernandez (Kyle [voice]), Jack Fletcher (Grove [voice]), John Hostetter (Polk [voice]), Dwight Schultz (Benge/Old Man of Barbarois [voice]), Mary Elizabeth McGlynn (Caroline [voice]), Naomi Amamiya (Young Leila/Leila's Granddaughter [HK version] [voice]), Sonny Chang (Public Official [HK version] [voice]), Jordan Chan (D. the vampire hunter [HK version] [voice]), Lindsay Chan (Leila [HK version] [voice]), Kelly Chen (D's Mother [HK version] [voice]), Billy Chow (Barbarois Elder/Polk [HK version] [voice]), John DeMita (Alan Elbourne/Priest [voice]), Debi Derryberry (Girl [voice]), Martina Duncker (Caroline [German version] [voice]), Norbert Gastell (Barbarois Elder [German version] [voice]), Joachim Geisler (Left Hand [German version] [voice]), Julia Haacke (Charlotte Elbourne [German version] [voice]), Martin Halm (Grove [German version] [voice]), Hou Hsiao (John Elbourne [HK version] [voice]), Christoph Jablonka (Nolt [German version] [voice]), Crock Krumbiegel (Meier Link [German version] [voice]), Jan Lamb (Kyle [HK version] [voice]), Lichun Lee (Priest [HK version] [voice]), Tobias Lelle (Kyle [German version] [voice]), Katharina Lobinski (Camilla [German version] [voice]), Laura Lössl (Leila [German version] [voice]), Ta-yu Lo (D's Left Hand [HK version] [voice]), Elaine Lui (Camilla [HK version] [voice]), Ah Mei (Charlotte Elbourne [HK version] [voice]), Francis Ng (Meier Link [HK version] [voice]), Judy Ongg (Caroline [HK version] [voice]), Ole Pfennig (Machira [HK version] [voice]), Horst Raspe (Polk [German version] [voice]), Sabou (Mahira [HK version] [voice]), Holger Schwiers (Borgoff [German version] [voice]), Tommy So (Alan Elbourne [HK version] [voice]), Christine Stichler (Leila [German version] [voice]), Oliver Stritzel (D [German version] [voice]), Kai Taschner (Bengia [German version] [voice]), Manfred Trilling (Allan [German version] [voice]), Walter von Hauff (Sheriff [German version] [voice]), David Wu (Benge [HK version] [voice]), Shi-Kwan Yen (Nolt [HK version] [voice]).

Meier Link (Kôichi Yamadera) embodies the classic Dracula: tall, thin, pale, suave, and gentlemanly. He has kidnapped Charlotte Elbourne (Emi Shinohara) from her parents, setting off a race against time. Charlotte's parents enlist the help of vampire bounty hunters and a specialist known as D (Hideyuki Tanaka). D is a dhampir (part vampire and part human), making him the ultimate vampire killing machine. D and the other hunters must track down Meier Link before Charlotte's life is over.

Banquete das Taras; Brazil, 1982; Horror; 90 minutes/color/Portuguese; W.C. Filmes.

Producers: J.C. Penna, Zulfo Epifânio Pereira; *Writing Credits*: Carlos Alberto Almeida; *Director*: Carlos Alberto Almeida; *Cinematography*: Jorge da Silva; *Film Editing*: Severino Dadá; *Make-Up*: Elisabeth Fairbanks; *Cast*: Aladir Araújo, Cidéia Barbosa, Jotta Barroso (Gregor Nastase), Kelly Berg, Bianca Blonde, Sônia Bruna, Eva Canto, Newton Couto, Elisabeth Fairbanks, Francis, Ed Heath, Maurício Herdy, Cristina Keller, Sérgio Madureira (Vladmir Vladislav), Roberto Marconi, Cláudia Marly, Paulo Neves, Leda Prado, Jorge Queiroz, Ademir Ribeiro, Youssef Salim, Newton Souto, João Carlos Teixeira, Edmundo Telles.

Gregor Nastase pays a visit to Vladmir Vladislav, a young sculptor in Nova Friburgo, Brazil who is Count Dracula's direct descendant. Gregor demands that they find four young women to sacrifice to fulfill his uncle's wishes. Vlad ignores him at first but soon changes his mind when, as though by magic, Gregor materializes an oil painting of Count Dracula himself.

Bara no Konrei -Mayonaka ni Kawashita Yakusoku (*Bridal of Rose - The Promise Exchanged at Midnight* [U.S.]); Japan, 2001; Drama, Horror, Thriller, Musical; 85 minutes/color/Japanese and English inter-titles/Silent (orchestrated); Gaga Communications, Inc & KSS, Inc.

Director: Hiroyuki Muto; *Original Music*: Malice Mizer; *Cast*: Klaha (Klaha), Kozi (Kozi), Mana (female vampire nun), Yu-ki (Earl of Dracula), Terumi Nagoyosi (Cecil).

Before marrying Cecil in England, Klaha visits the Earl of Dracula in Transylvania while on a business trip. When Klaha returns, he finds Cecil is possessed by demons. More importantly, she is Dracula's bride to be. Dracula then visits England and takes her to Transylvania. Klaha follows after them to save her and destroy Dracula.

El Barón Brakola (*Santo vs. Baron Brakola* [U.S.] (video box title); Mexico, 1967; Action, Adventure, Fantasy, Horror, Mystery, Thriller; 77 minutes/black and white/Spanish, English/Mono; Filmica Vergara S.A, Cinecomisiones.

Producers: Luis Enrique Vergara (as Luis Enrique Vergara C.); *Writing Credits*: Jose Diaz Morales, Rafael Garcia Travesi, Fernando Oses; *Director*: Jose Diaz Morales; *Cinematography*: Eduardo Valdes; *Film Editing*: Juan Jose Munguia; *Cast*: Santo (Santo), Fernando Oses (Baron Brakola), Mercedes Carreno (Silvia), Antonio de Hud (Eduardo), Andrea Palma (Rebeca's Mother), Ada Carrasco (Aurora), Susana Robles (Rebeca), Miguel Macia (Don Fernando), Manuel Arvide (Don Luis), Rosa Vinay, Jorge Fegan (Servant), Cesar Gay, Enrique Ramirez, Jorge Mateos, Roberto Porter, Quasimodo, Beny Galan (Wrestler), Juan Garza (Wrestler), Margarita Luni (Spectator), Antonio Padilla "Picoro" (Ring Announcer [as Picoro]).

The Baskervilles; Canada, 2002; Comedy, Family/Television; 30 minutes/color/English; CINAR Entertainment, Alphanim.

Producer: Cassandra Schafhausen; *Writing Credits*: Tony Barnes, Alastair Swinnerton; *Director*: Nick Martinelli; *Cast*: Suzy Aitchison (April Baskerville and others), Rob Brydon (Brian Baskerville, Old Nick and others), Gary Martin (The Boss, Colin and others), Rachel Preece (Janet Baskerville and others).

The Baskervilles move to a theme park owned by The Boss (Gary Martin), where good and bad are reversed and new neighbors that include the Dracula family, the Frankenstein's, and other well-known monsters.

Batman Dracula (*Dracula* [U.S., short title]); U.S., 1964; Fantasy, Horror; black and white/English/Mono.

Producer: Andy Warhol; *Director*: Andy Warhol; *Cast*: Gregory Battcock, David Bourdon, Tally Brown, Rufus Collins, Dorothy Dean, Beverly Grant, Sam Green, Bob Heide, Jane Holzer (as Baby Jane Holzer), Mark Lancaster, Naomi Levine, Ron Link, Gerard Malanga, Mario Montez, Billy

Name, Ivy Nicholson, Ondine, Jack Smith (Batman/Dracula), Sam Wagstaff.

Produced and directed by Andy Warhol, and screened only at his art exhibits, this film features the Batman character without DC Comics's consent. Warhol, a fan of the Batman serials, pays "homage" to the series with this rarely seen film.

Batman Fights Dracula (*Baty and Roby Against Crime* [Philippines: English title]); Philippines, 1967; Action, Fantasy, Horror, Comedy; color; Fidelis Productions.

Writing Credits: Bert R. Mendoza, Bob Kane, Bram Stoker; *Director*: Leody M. Diaz; *Original Music*: Tony Maiquez; *Cast*: Jing Abalos (Batman/Bruce Wayne), Dante Rivero (Dracula), Vivian Lorrain (Marita Banzon), Rolan Robles (Ruben), Ramon D'Salva (Dr. Zerba), Nort Nepomuceno (Turko), Angel Confiado, Ruben Ramos, Greg Lansang, Tiva Lava, Lope Policarpio, Isaias Betsayda (as Sai Betsayda), Jeanette Gonzalez, Rudy Dominguez, Marcelo Bernardo, Eddie Castro, Buddy De Jesus, Johannes Christof von Heinsburg (Mevik [uncredited]).

The superhero Batman (Jing Abalos) fights Dracula (Dante Rivero), the villain. Both Batman and Dracula battle it out with their bat-like characteristics.

Batman vs Dracula: The Animated Movie (*The Batman vs Dracula: The Animated Movie* [Hungary]; *Batman vs Drácula—La película animada* [Venezuela]); U.S., 2005; Action, Thriller/Animation; 83 minutes/color/English; Warner Bros. Animation.

Producers: Duane Capizzi, Michael Goguen, Kimberly Smith; *Writing Credits*: Duane Capizzi (written by), Bob Kane (Batman characters), Bram Stoker (Dracula character); *Director*: Michael Goguen; *Art Direction*: Wendy Guin (animation coordinator), Thomas Perkins (character designer), Justin Schultz (animation checker); *Cast*: Jeff Bennett (Arkham Asylum Inmat, Additional Voices [voice]), Alastair Duncan (Alfred Pennyworth [voice]), Richard Green (Additional Voices [voice]), Tom Kenny (Oswald Cobblepot, The Penguin [voice]), Kevin Michael Richardson (The Joker [voice]), Rino Romano (Bruce Wayne/The Batman [voice]), Neil Ross (Additional Voices [voice]), James Sie (Additional Voices [voice]), Peter Stormare (Dracula [voice]), Tara Strong (Vicky Vale [voice]).

Batman must defend Gotham City from the terror of Count Dracula.

Batuta ni Drakula (*Batuta ni Dracula* [Canada]); Philippines, 1971; Horror; color/Filipino; FGO Film Productions.

Producers: Jon Miedzik, R.G. Pitica; *Writing Credits*: Carlos Empaynado (story and screenplay); *Director*: Luis San Juan; *Cinematography*: Tommy Marcelino; *Original Music*: Pablo Vergara; *Cast*: Eddie Garcia (Drakula), Marilou Ver, Vina Morena, Vicky Sandoval, Panchito, Pugak, Jerry Pons, Matimtiman Cruz, Pabo (as Pabo Zapata), Angge, Mauricio, Louie St. John, Nick Ocampo, Nelson Esparga, Jess Santos.

The Beatles (TV Series [1965–1969]), episode "Misery"; U.K., Season 1, Episode 5, 23 October 1965; Musical, Comedy/Television, Animation; 15 minutes/English/color; King Features Production, Artransa/Graphik, CanaWest Studios, TVC-London.

Producers: Al Brodax, Jack Gettles, Mary Ellen Stewart; *Writing Credits*: Al Brodax (creator), Dennis Marks; *Director*: John W. Dunn (as John Dunn); *Cast*: The Beatles (The Beatles [singing voices]).

The Beatles go to a wax museum to see themselves as wax figures. While there, the Count Dracula figure comes to life and begins chasing them. The band ends up having to burn their wax figures to save themselves.

Behind the Fame: The Munsters/Addams Family; U.S., 2002; Documentary, Television; 60 minutes/color/English; Starcast.

Producers: Geoffrey Mark Fidelman, James Romanovich, Sarah L. Sterling; *Writing Credits*: Robert Corsini, Geoffrey Mark Fidelman; *Director*: Robert Corsini, Geoffrey Mark Fidelman; *Original Music*: John Ross; *Cast*: James Romanovich (Narrator).

This documentary explores the indelible characters from two of America's most fiendishly popular families. Included among them is Grandpa "Vladimir Dracula" Munster.

Béla Lugosi Scrapbook; U.S., 197?; Documentary, Television; 60 minutes.

Cast: Béla Lugosi (himself [archive footage]).

This documentary is comprised of Lugosi appearances, outtakes, flubs, and trailers. This documentary of the horror film actor includes his classic screen roles as well as flubbed outtakes and other novelty footage.

Beloved Count; U.S., 2007; Documentary, Short; 27 minutes/color, black and white/English; Funhouse Pictures.

Producers: Malik B. Ali, Carl Daft, Greg Newman; *Director*: David Gregory; *Cinematography*: Emilio Schargorodsky; *Film Editing*: John Cregan, David Gregory (as Tod Corman); *Cast*: Jesus Franco (Himself), Harry Alan Towers (Himself), Peter Cushing (Prof. Van Helsing [archive footage,

Ad for *Batuta ni Drakula* (Philippines, 1971).

uncredited]), Francisco Franco (Himself [archive footage, uncredited]), Klaus Kinski (Renfield [archive footage, uncredited]), Christopher Lee (Count Dracula [archive footage, uncredited]), Herbert Lom (Prof. Van Helsing [archive footage, uncredited]), Béla Lugosi (Count Dracula [archive footage, uncredited]), Soledad Miranda (Lucy Westenra [archive footage, uncredited]), Paul Muller (Dr. Seward [archive footage, uncredited]), Vincent Price (Himself [archive footage, uncredited]), Maria Rohm (Mina Murray [archive footage, uncredited]), Fred Williams (Jonathan Harker [archive footage, uncredited])

Director Jesus Franco tells about making his film adaptation of Bram Stoker's classic novel, which starred Christopher Lee.

Benyamin kontra Drakula (*Drakula Mantu* [Indonesia]); Indonesia, 1974; 95 minutes/Indonesian; P.T. Ratna Indah Kartika Film.

Director: Nya Abbas Akup; *Cinematography*: Asmawi; *Original Music*: Mus Muali; *Cast*: Benyamin S, Tan Tjeng Bok, Pong HardJatmo, Netty Herawati, Rice Marghareta Gerung, Wahab Abdi, Syamsudin Syafei, Intan Nurcahya, Benny Gaok, Judi As, Asfal Fuad Salim.

Billy & Mandy's Big Boogey Adventure; U.S., 2007; Comedy, Family, Fantasy, Adventure/Television, Animation; 80 minutes/color/English/Dolby Digital 5.1; Cartoon Network Studios.

Producers: Maxwell Atoms, Shaun Cashman, Louis J. Cuck, Brian A. Miller, Jennifer Pelphrey; *Writing Credits*: Maxwell Atoms (story), Nina G. Bargiel (as Nina Bargiel), Jeremy J. Bargiel (as Jeremy Bargiel), Maxwell Atoms (creator: Billy & Mandy); *Director*: Robert Alvarez, Russell Calabrese, Shaun Cashman, Phil Cummings, Matt Engstrom, Eddy Houchins, Gordon Kent, Christine Kolosov, Michel Lyman (as Mike Lyman), Sue Perrotto, Kris Sherwood; *Original Music*: Gregory Hinde, Drew Neumann; *Film Editing*: Illya Owens; Visual Effects: Azariah Owens; *Cast*: Grey DeLisle (Mandy/Mandroid/Older Mandy/Milkshakes/Some

Kid [voice]), Greg Eagles (Grim/Sperg/Pirate #6 [voice]), Richard Steven Horvitz (Billy/Billybot/Harold/Pale Ghoulish Juror/Chippy the Squirrel [voice, as Richard Horvitz]), Vanessa Marshall (Irwin/Pirate #5/Unicorn [voice]), Maxwell Atoms (I'll Cut You Guy/Pirate #2/Horrorbot/Burnt Skeleton Guard [voice]), George Ball (Peequay [voice]), Jane Carr (Bride of Frankenstein [voice]), Greg Ellis (Creeper/Horror's Hand/Pirate #3/Paperboy [voice]), Bart Flynn (Giant Cyclops/Ugly Pirate [voice]), C.H. Greenblatt (Fred Fredburger/Pirate #4 [voice]), Jennifer Hale (Billy's Mom [voice]), Dorian Harewood (Older Irwin [voice]), Phil LaMarr (Space Villain/Glacier of Evil/Dracula/Judge Roy Spleen/Underworld Cop [voice]), Rachael MacFarlane (2 Headed Parrot [voice]), George Segal (Horror [voice]), Armin Shimerman (General Skarr/Pirate #7 [voice]), James Silverman (Executioner/Pirate #1 [voice]), Lauren Tom (Numbuh Three [voice]), Billy West (Pirate #8/Miniature Cyclops/Spider Clown Mailman/Beast Master [voice]), Fred Willard (The Boogey Man [voice]).

After having his powers taken from him, Boogey tries to get the "Hand of Horror" so he can take over the world, and finally be scary. As the hand can unlock peoples' worst nightmares, all the creatures of the night, including Dracula, are in the race to get it.

Billy the Kid Versus Dracula; U.S., 1966; Western, Horror; 73 minutes/color/English/Mono/35mm; Circle Productions Inc.

Producer: Carroll Case; *Writing Credits*: Carl K. Hittleman, Jack Lewis (uncredited); *Director*: William Beaudine; *Cinematography*: Lothrop B. Worth; *Film Editing*: Roy V. Livingston; *Original Music*: Raoul Kraushaar; *Cast*: John Carradine (Vampire), Chuck Courtney (Billy the Kid), Melinda Plowman (Elizabeth Bentley), Virginia Christine (Eva Oster), Walter Janovitz (Frank Oster), Bing Russell (Dan "Red" Thorpe), Olive Carey (Dr. Henrietta Hull), Roy Barcroft (Sheriff Griffin), Hannie Landman (Lisa Oster), Richard Reeves (Pete), Marjorie Bennett (Mary Ann Bentley), William Forrest (James Underhill), George Cisar (Joe Flake), Harry Carey Jr. (Ben Dooley), Leonard P. Geer (Yancy), William Challee (Tim), Charlita (Indian Maiden), Max Kleven, Jack Williams.

David Carradine plays Dracula in *Billy the Kid Versus Dracula* (U.S., 1966).

When Franz (Walter Janovitz) and Eva (Virginia Christine) Oster's daughter Lisa (Hannie Landman) is killed by Dracula, the Osters swear to fight this menace. Dracula shows up again in the guise of Uncle James Underhill (John Carradine), newly arrived in town to help out at the Double Bar B Ranch. Betty begins to awaken with bites on her neck. When Underhill comes to take Betty back to the ranch, the doctor holds up a mirror and sees no reflection. Sure now that Underhill is a vampire, the doctor springs Billy from jail and the three of them (Billy, doctor, and Sheriff Griffin [Roy Barcroft]) pursue the vampire and Betty out to the abandoned mine where Dracula has his coffin stored.

Biography (TV Series [1987–present]), episode "Bram Stoker"; U.S., 11 December, 2004; Documentary, Television; 50 minutes/color; A&E Home Video.

Cast: Neil Ross (Narrator).

This film documents author Bram Stoker and the events in his life that led him to write his most famous novel, *Dracula*, which has fueled the imaginations of people for more than a century.

Birth of the Vampire; U.S., 2003; Drama, Fantasy, Action, Horror/Short; 28 minutes/color/English/Stereo; Northstar Films.

Producers: Matt Kaplan, Monella Kaplan. Heather Mara Rem, Rodney Wilson; *Writing Credits*: Monella Kaplan; *Director*: Monella Kaplan; *Cinematography*: Jon Aaseng (as John Aaron Aaseng); *Film Editing*: Monella Kaplan; *Original Music*: Enis Rotthoff; *Make-Up*: Sheila Frasier; *Cast*: Lance C. Williams (Prince Dracula), Emanuel Gironi (The Devil), Bjorn Johnson (Count Kiraly [as Bjoern Johnson]), Chris Jolliff (Gravedigger), Monella Kaplan (Anna), James Hiser (Manole), Wayne Beach (Mason), Donald Cox (Mason), Nathan Rose (Mason), Arlos Chodwell (Mason), Soumaya Akaboun (Witch), Earnie Spetter (Mason), Ariane Nicole Navarra (Witch), Ginger Welker (Witch), Christian Pichler (Mason).

Prince Dracula, having been in jail for 12 years, makes a pact with the Devil to retake his throne. The pact states that Prince Dracula must bring the Devil a certain woman. This troubles Dracula because the particular woman he must bring to the Devil is the same with which he is in love.

B.J. and the Bear (TV Series [1979–1981]), episode "A Coffin with a View" (*B.J. und der Bär* [West Germany]; *El camionero y su mono* [Spain]; *Truck Driver* [Italy]); U.S., Season 1, Episode 3; 10 March 1979; Comedy; 60 minutes/color/English/Mono; Universal TV.

Producers: Lester Wm. Berke, Joe Boston, Glen A. Larson, Richard Lindheim; *Writing Credits*: Michael Sloan; *Director*: Ray Austin; *Cinematography*: Frank Beascoechea; *Film Editing*: Buford F. Hayes; *Original Music*: William Broughton; *Cast*: Greg Evigan (B.J. McKay), Foster Brooks (Terry Morgan), John Carradine (Transylvanian Caretaker), Christopher Carroll (Detective Tony Grimes), Christina Cummings (Nancy Duvall), Jack Ging, Pamela Hensley (Holly Tremaine), Robert F. Hoy (Officer Kling), William Kux (Detective Stinson), George Lazenby (Paul Desmond), Robert Lussier (Bo Bender), Danny Glover (Matt Thomas, TV Reporter [uncredited]).

B.J. is contracted to arrive at a boat dock at night and haul two Transylvanian coffins that will be in a vampire movie, but little does he know that Dracula may be hiding in one of them.

Black Inferno; U.S., 1956; Horror/Short; 8 minutes/black and white; Adventure Films Productions.

Producer: Tony Brzezinski; *Director*: Tony Brzezinski.

This film includes a scene in which Dracula lures a female into a cemetery.

Blacula; U.S., 1972; Horror; 93 minutes/color/English/Mono; American International Pictures.

Producers: Samuel Z. Arkoff, Norman T. Herman, Joseph T. Naar; *Writing Credits*: Raymond Koenig, Joan Torres; *Director*: William Craine; *Cinematography*: John M. Stephens; *Film Editing*: Allan Jacobs; *Original Music*: Gene Page; *Make-Up*: Fred B. Phillips; *Special Effects*: Roger George; *Cast*: William Marshall (Mamuwalde/Blacula), Vonetta McGee (Luva/Tina), Denise Nicholas (Michelle), Thalmus Rasulala (Dr. Gordon Thomas), Gordon Pinsent (Lt. Jack Peters), Charles Macaulay (Dracula), Emily Yancy (Nancy, Photographer), Lance Taylor Sr. (Swenson, Undertaker), Ted Harris (Bobby McCoy), Rick Metzler (Billy Schaffer), Ji-Tu Cumbuka (Skillet), Logan Field (Sgt. Barnes), Ketty Lester (Juanita Jones, Cabbie), Elisha Cook Jr. (Sam [as Elisha Cook]), Eric Brotherson (Real Estate Agent), The Hues Corporation (Group performing in club), Flemming Williams (Himself [as The Hues Corporation]).

In 1972, two gay antique dealers attend an estate sale at a castle in Romanina and procure, among other things, a coffin, in which the body of an African prince (who had been bitten by Dracula centuries before) lies dormant. They ship it to Los Angeles, where Blacula (William Marshall), the coffin's inhabitant, is unleashed upon the city.

Blade: Trinity (*Blade: Trinity* [Argentina/Brazil/Chile/Finland/Germany/Greece/Spain]; *Blade 3* [Japan]; *Blade III — La trinité* [Canada]; *Blade: Kolmik* [Estonia]); U.S., 2004; Action, Horror, Thriller; 113 minuets/color/English/Dolby Digital; New Line Cinema, Shawn Danielle Productions Ltd, Amen Ra Films, Marvel Enterprises, Imaginary Forces.

Producers: Avi Arad, Cale Boyter, Toby Emmerich, Kevin Feige, Peter Frankfurt, David S. Goyer, Lynn Harris, Stan Lee, Art Schaeffer, Wes-

Poster for *Blacula* (U.S., 1972).

ley Snipes; *Writing Credits*: David S. Goyer (written by), Marv Wolfman (character), Gene Colan (character); *Director*: David S. Goyer; *Cinematography*: Gabriel Beristain (director of photography); *Film Editing*: Conrad Smart, Howard E. Smith; *Original Music*: Ramin Djawadi; *Art Direction*: Patrick Banister, Eric Fraser; *Make-Up*: Jill Bailey, Ken Banks, Joel Echallier, Mike Elizalde, Gerald Gibbons, Rebecca Lee, Lisa Love, Harlow MacFarlane, Shauna Magrath, Hayley Miller, Rob Miller, Beverly Moncrief, Ryan Nicholson, Cyndi Reece-Thorne, Yoichi Art Sakamoto, Sydney Silvert, Christ Stanley, Bill Terezakis, Monique Venier; *Special Effects*: Cara E. Anderson, Cara E. Anderson, Brent Baker, Roland Blancaflor, Michael Bolan, Darin Bouyssou, Norman Cabrera, Rhaban Canas, Rory Cutler, Jon Dawe, Joel Dobzewitz, André Dominguez, Mary Elizalde, Thomas Floutz, Steve Fox, Frederick Fraleigh, Derek Heselton, Graham S. Hollins, Carlos Huante, Timothy Huizing, Bill Jacob, Carol Jones, Hiroshi Katagiri, Charles Kuzela, Don Lanning, Russell Lukich, Kyle Martin, Cass McClure, W. David McGuire, Kevin McTurk, Scott Millenbaugh, Jeff Miller, Jaimie Nakae, Mark Obedinski, David Perteet, Rob Phillips, Scotty Pringle, John Reynolds, Christopher Schreiber, Mark Setrakian, Kevin Stadnyk, Siegfried Stock, Wayne Szybunka, Adam Tayler, Kazuhiro Tsuji, Dale Vrba, Brian Walsh, Steve Wang, Lisa Welton, Lawrence Wray; *Cast*: Wesley Snipes (Blade), Kris Kristofferson (Whistler), Dominic Purcell (Drake), Jessica Biel (Abigail Whistler), Ryan Reynolds (Hannibal King), Parker Posey (Danica Talos), Mark Berry (Chief Martin Vreede), John Michael Higgins (Dr. Edgar Vance), Callum Keith Rennie (Asher Talos), Paul Levesque (Jarko Grimwood), Paul Anthony (Wolfe), Françoise Yip (Virago), Michael Rawlins (Wilson Hale), James Remar (Ray Cumberland), Natasha Lyonne (Sommerfield), Haili Page (Zoe), Patton Oswalt (Hedges), Ron Selmour (Dex), Christopher Heyerdahl (Caulder), Eric Bogosian (Bentley Tittle), Scott Heindl (Gedge), John Ashker (Campbell), Clay Cullen (Stone), Steven McMichael (Denlinger), Paul Wu (Ellingson), Kimani Ray Smith (Doh), Darren McGuire (Emond), Shannon Powell (Woman Bystander), Jill Krop (Reporter), Jordan Hoffart (Squid), Kett Turton (Dingo), Cascy Beddow (Flick), Simon Pidgeon (Proof), Michael St. John Smith (FBI Agent), Stephen Spender (Agent), Kwesi Ameyaw (Agent), Alejandro Rae (Goth Guy Wannabe), Erica Cerra (Goth Vixen Wannabe), Garvin Cross (Hoop), Raymond Sammel (Security Guard), John Ulmer (Security Guard), Justin Sain (Security Guard), Darryl Scheelar (Doctor), Camille Martinez (Hysterical Mother), Michelle Stoll (Vance's Assistant), Dawn Mander (Biomedica Technician), Gabriel Beristain (One-Eyed Newspaper Vendor [uncredited]), Michel Cook (SWAT Member [uncredited]), Chris Gorak (Doctor [uncredited]), Johanna Olson (Shanghai Dancer [uncredited]), Brian Steele (Drake Creature [uncredited])

The vampire nation awakens Dracula, the ruler of the vampires. In order to defeat him, Blade (Wesley Snipes) joins up with a group of vampire hunters called the Nightstalkers. The vampires want to use Dracula's blood to become daywalkers, while at the same time Blade is working on a virus to wipe out all vampires.

Blood; U.S., 1974; Horror; 74 minutes/color/English/Mono; Bryanston Distributing.

Producer: Walter Kent; *Writing Credits*: Andy Milligan; *Director*: Andy Milligan; *Film Editing*: Andy Milligan (as Gerald Jackson); *Make-Up*: Ted Donovant (special makeup designer); *Cast*: Allan Berendt (Dr. Lawrence Talbot [alias Orlovsky]), Hope Stansbury (Regina Dracula Talbot [alias Orlovsky]), Patricia Gaul (Carrie), Michael Fischetti (Orlando), Pichulina Hempi (Carlotta), Pamela Adams (Prudence Towers), John Wallowitch (Carl Root), Martin Reymert (Mr. Markham [realtor]), David Bevans (Johnny [Carrie's brother]), Eve Crosby (Petra [the hag]), Joe Downing (The New Realtor), Lawrence Seelars (Baron von Frankenstein), Sophia Andoniadis (Mme. von Frankenstein), Hazel Wolffs (Woman Next Door).

Dr. Orlovsky, the son of a werewolf, decides to marry the daughter of Count Dracula. They maintain a garden with man-eating plants in order to extract the fluid that gives them life to use as a substitute for blood. Eventually Dracula's daughter decides it's not enough. Bats also fly around the city, and when bitten, people are turned into flesh eating cannibals.

Blood for Dracula (*Dracula cerca sangue di vergine ... e morì di sete!!!* [Italy]; *Andy Warhol's Dracula* [U.S./West Germany]; *Sangre para Drácula* [Argentina/Venezuela]; *Aima gia ton Drakoula* [Greece [reissue title]]; *Andy Warhol's Young Dracula* [undefined]; *Dracula* [undefined]; *Dracula vuole vivere: cerca sangue di vergine!* [Italy]; *Drakoulas dipsaei gia aima parthenas ... kai pethainei dipsasmenos!, O* [Greece]; *Drakoulas me to tsekouri, O* [Greece [reissue title]]; *Du sang pour Dracula* [France]; *Sangue Virgem para Drácula* [Portugal]; *Young Dracula* [undefined]); Italy, 1974; Horror; 103 minutes/color/English/Mono/35mm; Compagnia Cinematografica Champion.

Producers: Andrew Braunsberg, Andy Warhol, Jean Yanne; *Writing Credits*: Pat Hackett (uncredited), Paul Morrissey, Bram Stoker (character [uncredited]); *Director*: Paul Morrissey; *Cinematogra-*

phy: Luigi Kuveiller; *Film Editing*: Jed Johnson (credited in U.S. print), Franca Silvi; *Original Music*: Claudio Gizzi; *Art Direction*: Gianni Giovagnoni; *Make-Up*: Mario Di Salvio, Paolo Franceschi; *Special Effects*: Carlo Rambaldi (special effects); *Cast*: Joe Dallesandro (Mario Balato, the Servant), Udo Kier (Count Dracula), Vittorio De Sica (Il Marchese Di Fiore), Maxime McKendry (La Marchesa Di Fiore), Arno Juerging (Anton, the Count's Servant), Milena Vukotic (Esmeralda), Dominique Darel (Saphiria), Stefania Casini (Rubinia), Silvia Dionisio (Perla), Inna Alexeievna, Gil Cagne (Townsman [as Gil Cagnie]), Emi Califri, Eleonora Zani, Giorgio Dolfin (uncredited), Stefano Oppedisano (uncredited), Roman Polanski (Man in Tavern [uncredited]).

A dying Count Dracula is in need of virgin (pronounced "wirgin") blood, so he travels to a Catholic country supposedly known for its virgins, Italy. There he befriends the landowner Marchese di Fiori and attempts to feed off of Fiori's four reputedly "virgin" daughters.

The Blood Is the Life: The Making of Bram Stoker's Dracula; U.S., 2007; Documentary, Short; 27 minutes/color/English/Dolby Digital; ZAP Zoetrope Aubry Productions.

Producers: Kim Aubry, Anne Mason; *Director*: Kim Aubry; *Cinematography*: Eli Adler, Daniel Yarussi; *Film Editing*: Ken Schneider; *Original Music*: Wojciech Kilar; *Art Direction*: Jeffrey Roth (graphic designer); *Cast*: Gary Oldman (Himself), Francis Ford Coppola (Himself), Winona Ryder (Herself), Anthony Hopkins (Himself), Keanu Reeves (Himself), Richard E. Grant (Himself), Bill Campbell (Himself), Cary Elwes (Himself), Sadie Frost (Herself), James V. Hart (Himself), Stephen Salvati (Van Helsing).

Through interviews and off-screen footage, this documentary offers both an in-depth look at the making of the Hollywood blockbuster *Bram Stoker's Dracula*, and a detailed look at the classic Universal *Dracula*.

Blood Lines: Dracula — The Man, the Myth, the Movies; U.S., 1992; Documentary, Short; 29 minutes/color/English; Columbia Pictures Corporation.

Producers: Kenneth Fuchts, Kincaid Jones, Bonny LeFebre, Robert Solomon, Jeff Werner; *Writing Credits*: Kincaid Jones; *Director*: Jeff Werner; *Cinematography*: Daniel Yarussi (as Dan Yarussi); *Film Editing*: Oreet Rees; *Make-Up*: Ann Masterson; *Cast*: Francis Ford Coppola, Gary Oldman, Dr. Donald A. Reed, James V. Hart, Anthony Hopkins, Keanu Reeves, Norine Dresser, Winona Ryder, Michael Ballhaus, Sadie Frost.

Blood of Dracula (*Blood Is My Heritage* [U.K.]; *Blood of the Demon* [Canada]); U.S., November 1957; Horror/Romance; 68 minutes/black and white/English/Mono; American International Pictures (AIP), Carmel Productions.

Producers: Herman Cohen, Austen Jewell; *Writing Credits*: Aben Kandel (as Ralph Thornton); *Director*: Herbert L. Strock, Austen Jewell (Assistant director); *Cinematography*: Monroe P. Askins; *Film Editing*: Robert Moore; *Original Music*: Paul Dunlap; *Make-Up*: Phillip Scheer; *Cast*: Sandra Harrison (Nancy Perkins), Louise Lewis (Miss Branding), Gail Ganley (Myra), Jerry Blaine (Tab), Heather Ames (Nola), Malcolm Atterbury (Lt. Dunlap), Mary Adams (Mrs. Thornedyke), Thomas Browne Henry (Mr. Paul Perkins [as Thomas B. Henry]), Don Devlin (Eddie), Jean Dean (Mrs. Doris Perkins [as Jeanne Dean]), Richard Devon (Det. Sgt. Stewart), Paul Maxwell (Mike, the young doctor), Shirley Delancey (Terry [as Shirley De Lancey]), Michael Hall (Glenn), Craig Duncan, Edna Holland (Miss Rivers), Carlyle Mitchell (Stanley Mayther), Voltaire Perkins (Dr. Lawson), Barbara Wilson (Ann), Jimmy Hayes (Joe), Lynn Alden (Linda).

Nancy Perkins (Sandra Harrison) becomes victim of her teacher Miss Branding's (Louise Lewis) science experiment. Miss Branding, using an amulet, puts Nancy under hypnosis to ease the pain after Nancy gets hurt in a laboratory accident. While Nancy is under hypnosis, Miss Branding also takes away Nancy's will using the same amulet, which she bought from an immigrant woman from the Carpathian Mountains. Unknowingly to Nancy, this amulet turns her into a vampire.

Blood of Dracula's Castle (*Aima sto spiti tou Dracoula* [Greece]; *Dracula und seine Opfer* [West Germany]; *Verilinna* [Finland]); U.S., 1969; Horror; 84 minutes/color/English/Mono; Paragon International Pictures.

Producers: Al Adamson, Ewing Miles Brown, Rex Carlton, Martin B. Cohen, Samuel M. Sherman, Jerome Wexler; *Writing Credits*: Rex Carlton; *Director*: Al Adamson, Jean Hewitt; *Cinematography*: László Kovács (as Leslie Kovacs); *Film Editing*: Peter Perry Jr.; *Original Music*: Don Hulette; *Make-Up*: Jean Hewitt, Ken Osborne (special effects makeup); *Cast*: Alexander D'Arcy (Count Dracula, alias Count Charles Townsend), Paula Raymond (Countess Townsend), Gene Otis Shayne (Glen Cannon), Jennifer Bishop (Liz Arden) Robert Dix (Johnny), John Carradine (George, the butler) Ray Young (Mango), Vicki Volante (Ann, motorist-victim), John "Bud" Cardos (as John Cardos).

Living in a dungeon, the Count and his wife capture young beautiful girls and feed on them till

Poster art for *Blood of Dracula* (U.S., 1957).

their death to satisfy their own insatiable need for blood.

Blood Scarab; U.S., 2008; Horror; 81 minutes/color/English/Surround Sound; Frontline Entertainment.

Producers: Jackeline Olivier, Rock Riddle; *Director*: Donald F. Glut; *Cinematography*: Roberto Correa; *Original Music*: Terry Huud; *Art Direction*: Bruce Barlow, Oliver Rayon; *Make-Up*: Ayla Dew, Melissa Chmielowski, Turner Walker; *Cast*: Bruce Barlow (Mummy), Lamik Blake (Nubian Guard), Susan Brock (Ingrid), Ernest Carter (Nubian Guard), Tony Clay (Dracula), Sagreb De La Torre (Delphine), Natasha Diakova (Mina), Buddy Friedman (Embalmer), Michael Gavino (Video Store Customer), Donald F. Glut (Mr. Sarno), Doug Goodreau (Embalmer), Lee Hexum (Mummy Scavenger), Del Howison (Renfield), Crystal Isherhoff (Maria), Jessie Lilley (Museum Personnel), Nicolette Lupian (Flashback Handmaiden), Ange Maya (Hathor's Handmaiden), R.A. Mihailoff (Dungeon Master), Angelica Monro (Hathor), Christina Morris (Samantha), James M. Myers (Mr. Ostfeld), David Norberg (Video Store Customer), Jackeline Olivier (Elana), Monique Parent (Countess Elizabeth Bathory), Sasha Peralto (Princess Hat-Em-Akhet), Edward L. Plumb (Mummy Scavenger), Cindy Pucci (Tanya), Oliver Rayon (Video Store Customer), Rock Riddle (Rude Wrestler), Alisa Robinson (Serving Wench), Sam Silver (Edgar), Brinke Stevens (Professor Foran), Joleen Thornton (Flashback Handmaiden), Kent Vaughan (Museum Personnel), Veronica (Hathor's Handmaiden), Mary Votava (Lucia), Delpano Wills (Nubian Guard), Mia Zottoli (Hor Sep Sut [as Ava Niche]), Ted Newsom (Security Guard [uncredited]).

The vampire Countess Elizabeth Bathory (Monique Parent) comes to Los Angeles from Transylvania to take over the castle of her husband, Dracula (Tony Clay). Dracula is killed by the rising sun, and Elizabeth nearly suffers the same fate. In order to live during the day without being destroyed by the sun, she tasks her servant Renfield (Del Howison) with finding a mummy that will give her this ability.

Blood Son (*Drink My Red Blood* [U.S.]); U.S., 2006; Horror/Short; 15 minutes/color/English; Buffalonickel Films.

Producers: Tom Macdonald, Michael McGruther, Michele Santos; *Writing Credits*: Richard Matheson (short story), Michael McGruther (screenplay); *Director*: Michael McGruther; *Cine-*

matography: Timothy Nuttall; *Film Editing*: Michael McGruther, Timothy Nuttall; *Original Music*: Matt Heider; *Make-Up*: Ingrid Okola; *Cast*: Robert Hancock (Antique Shopkeeper), Julie Finch (Teacher), Paul Coughlan (Dracula), Joseph M. Somma (Jim Christianson), Mandi Bedbury (Mother), Aldous Davidson (Manny), Arthur Lupetti (The Doctor), Joseph Somma (Father), Alan Tavarez (Rico), Cash Tilton (Principal), Lucas Wotkowski (Jules).

Adapted from Richard Matheson's "Drink My Blood," this film reveals the story of a teenaged boy who is obsessed with vampirism. He gains knowledge about them through literature. He matures throughout the story to find his true identity.

Blood Suckers (*Boogeyman Vampire Club 4* [International English title] *I Want to Be a Vampire* [U.S. working title] *Nothing Generation* [U.S. working title]); U.S., 1997; Horror; 85 minutes/color/English; Black Cat Enterprises.

Producer: Ulli Lommel; *Director*: Ulli Lommel; *Cinematography*: Duane Osterlind Jürg V. Walther; *Cast*: Michelle Bonfils (Darling Dead), Peter Sean (Dr. Ghoul), Ulli Lommel (Angelo/Santano), Christopher Rogers (Nuggy), Samantha Scully (Schnibble), Stephanie Feury (Virginia), George "Buck" Flower (Grampa), Catherine Campion (Vampire student), Matthias Hues (Reporter), Christopher Kriesa (Sheriff [as Chris Kriesa]), Ron Robbins (Nuggy's Father), Adrian Staton (Vampire), Rayder Woods (Vlad Dracula).

A teenage girl wants to become a vampire and sets out to do so. In her quest, she finds good and bad vampires who test her determination to become undead.

Bloodlines: The Dracula Family Tree; U.S., 2003; Documentary, Television; 50 minutes/color, black and white/English; A&E Television Networks.

Film Editing: Roger Dacier; *Cast*: Radu Florescu (Himself), Raymond McNally (Himself [archive footage]), Bram Stoker (Himself [archive footage]).

In this documentary, Radu Florescu, Boston professor whose research with Raymond McNally in the 1970s exposed the truth about the historic Dracula, Vlad Tepes ("The Impaler"), shares some of the incredible untold stories from his and McNally's journey, like how the hunt for Dracula eventually resulted in death, strange diseases, and illness; the repeated disappearance of key documents; and the peculiarities surrounding Dracula's decapitated body.

Bloodspit; Australia/U.S., 2006; Horror, Comedy; 80 minutes/color/English/Dolby Digital Stereo; Troma Team Video.

Producers: Leon Fish, Duke Hendrix; *Writing Credits*: Leon Fish, Duke Hendrix; *Director*: Duke Hendrix; *Cinematography*: Okan Gumus, Duke Hendrix, Jed Hendrix; *Film Editing*: Duke Hendrix; *Original Music*: Tracy Lundgren; *Cast*: Angus (Tom Simmons), Spanky Doll (Lilly), Leon Fish (Dr. Ludvic), Duke Hendrix (Count Blaughspich), Zenda Markhova (Countess Blaughspich).

Dr. Ludvic (Leon Fish), who had battled the vampire Count Blaughspich (Duke Hendrix), must prevent the Count and his Minions from rejuvenating themselves in the mirror world.

Bloodsucking Cinema (*Blod på vita duken* [Sweden]); U.S., 2007; Documentary, Television; 56 minutes/color; Insight Film Studios & Vamp Productions

Producers: Christopher Black, Brad McAfee, Wendy McKernan, Michael Ruggiero, Kirk Shaw, Laura Amelse Watson; *Writing Credits*: Barry Gray; *Director*: Barry Gray; *Original Music*: Don MacDonald; *Cinematography*: Todd Craddock; *Film Editing*: Andrew Notman; *Cast*: Uwe Boll (Himself), Everett Burrell (Himself), John Carpenter (Himself), David S. Goyer (Himself), Corey Haim (Himself), Harry Jay Knowles (Himself), John Landis (Himself), Kristanna Loken (Herself), Leonard Maltin (Himself), Cheech Marin (Himself), Gregory Nicotero (Himself), Joel Schumacher (Himself), Stephen Sommers (Himself), Stuart Townsend (Himself), Stan Winston (Himself), Len Wiseman (Himself), Marv Wolfman (Himself)

This documentary examines why vampire films are so popular in cinema, and how the legend of Dracula, both fictionally and historically, has influenced films from the silent era to more recent vampire films like *Underworld* and *Van Helsing*. John Carpenter, John Landis, Joel Schumaker, Uwe Boil, and others discuss their own films as well as the ones that inspired them. Considerable time is also spent focusing on the Mexican *Dracula* films that have been made over the past few decades.

Bonnie & Clyde vs. Dracula; U.S., 2008; Action, Crime, Horror; color/English; Big Atom Productions.

Producers: Joseph Allen, Jennifer Friend, Emily Iorg, Tiffany Shepis, Robert Shultz, Janet Sourk, Deny Staggs, Jeff Chitty; *Writing Credits*: Timothy Friend; *Director*: Timothy Friend; *Cinematography*: Todd Norris; *Film Editing*: Timothy Friend; *Original Music*: Joseph Allen; *Art Direction*: Nita Norris; *Make-Up*: Amy Hubbard, Staci Broski, Bennie Hamilton, Tony Redmond, Karen Redmond; *Special Effects*: Ryan Oliphant, Jeff Sisson; *Cast*: Jordan Baranowski (Moonshiner), Katie Barker (Dead Prostitute), Ari Bavel (Older Moonshiner), Chris Carter (Vampire #7), Jessica Cooper (Vampire #16), Anita Cordell (Liza), Haley Cordell (Fruitstand Girl), Bryan Davis (Vampire #1), Donna M. Davis

(Vampire #2), Scott Decker (Vampire #18), Emily Foster (Vampire #15), Edward Franklin (Vampire #11), Austin Fraser (Vampire #13), Michael Friedlander (Cop #2), Alex "Fish" Friend (Moonshine Kid), Jennifer Friend (Annabel), Russell Friend (Dracula), F. Martin Glynn (Henry), T. Max Graham (Jake), Garland Greiner (Dinner Guest #4), Trent Haaga (Clyde), Thomas Hadden (Corpse), Harley (The Dog), Siouxxsie Harper (Prostitute), Penny Harzi (Vampire #3), Sam Hendrix (Vampire #5), JoAnn Imre (Vampire #19), Allen Lowman (Dr. Loveless/Chick), Seymour Noone (Farmer), Anthony Paxton (Vampire #10), Kari Paxton (Vampire #9), Brook Edward Penca (Cop #1), Robert Potter (Vampire #4), Rebecca Ray (Dinner Guest #5), Jared Reck (Horace), Sadie Rehnke (Hallway Body), Lance Schellhorn (Vampire #17), Tiffany Shepis (Bonnie), Robert Shultz (Dinner Guest #3), Jeff Sisson (Hillbilly Rapist #2), Janet Sourk (Dinner Guest #2), Toby Tolbert (Lead Hillbilly), Amber Underwood (Vampire #8), Kim Varner (Vampire #12), Carl Wallace (Ed), Gretchen L. Webster (Vampire #14), Ron L. Wilborn Jr. (Vampire #20), Mary Wilkens (Dinner Guest #1), Anne Willow (Rosie/Farmer's Wife), Audrey Wilson (Vampire #6).

Bonnie (Tiffany Shepis) and Clyde (Trent Haaga) seek refuge in a mansion after a botched robbery attempt. Inside the mansion Dracula (Russell Friend) has recently been revived, and Bonnie and Clyde must face him and the many horrors that await them within the mansion.

Boo; U.S., 1932; Comedy, Horror/Short; 10 minutes/black and white/English/Mono; Universal Pictures.

Producer: Albert DeMond; *Writing Credits*: Albert DeMond; *Director*: Albert DeMond; *Film Editing*: Lynn Harrison; *Original Music*: James Dietrich (composer: stock music [uncredited]), Heinz Roemheld (composer: stock music [uncredited]); *Cast*: Morton Lowry (Man reading "Dracula"), Mae Clarke (Elizabeth [edited from "Frankenstein"] [archive footage] [uncredited]), Lawrence Grant (Crosby [edited from "The Cat Creeps"] [archive footage] [uncredited]), Raymond Hackett (Paul [edited from "The Cat Creeps"] [archive footage] [uncredited]), Boris Karloff (Frankenstein's Monster [edited from "Frankenstein"] [archive footage] [uncredited]), Elizabeth Patterson (Susan [edited from "The Cat Creeps"] [archive footage] [uncredited]), Max Schreck (Dracula-Nosferatu [edited from "Nosferatu"] [archive footage] [uncredited]), Helen Twelvetrees (Annabelle West [edited from "The Cat Creeps"] [archive footage] [uncredited]), Edward Van Sloan (Dr. Waldman [edited from "Frankenstein"] [archive footage] [uncredited]), Gustav von Wangenheim (Hutter [edited from "Nosferatu"] [archive footage])

A narrator, Morton Lowry, mocks footage containing Frankenstein's monster and Dracula.

Boris Karloff and Béla Lugosi; France, 2002; Television, Documentary, Short; 26 minutes/color/English; Striana Productions.

Writing Credits: Laurent Preyale; *Director*: Laurent Preyale; *Cast*: Boris Karloff (himself [archive footage]), Béla Lugosi (himself [archive footage].

Brácula Condemor II; Spain, 1997; Comedy; 88 minutes/color/Spanish; Producciones A.S.H. Films S.A.

Producer: Julio Parra; *Writing Credits*: Andrés Sáenz de Heredia, Álvaro Sáenz de Heredia; *Director*: Álvaro Sáenz de Heredia; *Cinematography*: Tomás Mas; *Film Editing*: Andrés Sáenz de Heredia; *Original Music*: Andrés Sáenz de Heredia; *Special Effects*: José Ramón Molina Jr. (special effects technician); *Cast*: Chiquito de la Calzada (Condemor/Brácula), Bigote Arrocet (Lucas), Héctor Cantolla (Conde Drácula), Rubén Gálvez (Arnaldo Daviñón), Carla Hidalgo (Lucía), Javivi (Barón), Nadiuska (Baronesa), Aramis Ney (Señoría Ilustrísima/Mago Negro).

Condemor and Lucas take a ship to Europe, and it sinks. In an attempt to save their lives, they climb on to a coffin and float to shore. When they get to shore, a group of scary characters mistake Condemor for Dracula whom they have been expecting for quite some time.

Bram Stoker's Dracula (*Bram Stokers Dracula* [Finland/Germany/Sweden]; *Dracula* [Czech Republic/Italy/Poland]; *Drácula de Bram Stoker* [Brazil/Portugal]; *Drácula, de Bram Stoker* [Argentina/Spain]; *Bram Stokeri Dracula* [Estonia]; *Bram Stokerin Dracula* [Finland]; *Dracula d'après Bram Stoker* [France]; *Dracula d'après l'oeuvre de Bram Stoker* [Canada]; *Dracula de Bram Stoker* [Brazil]; *Drakoulas* [Greece]; *Drakula* [Slovenia]); U.S., 1992; Horror, Romance; 128 minutes/color/English/Dolby Digital; American Zoetrope, Columbia Pictures Corporation, Osiris Films.

Producers: Michael Apted, Francis Ford Coppola, Susan Landau Finch, Fred Fuchs, James V. Hart, Charles Mulvehill, Robert O'Connor, John Veitch; *Writing Credits*: Bram Stoker (novel "Dracula") James V. Hart (screenplay); *Director*: Francis Ford Coppola; *Cinematography*: Michael Balhaus; *Film Editing*: Anne Goursaud, Glen Scantlebury, Nicholas C. Smith; *Original Music*: Wojciech Kilar; *Art Direction*: Andrew Precht; *Make-Up*: David P. Barton, Linda Benevente-Notaro (as Linda Notaro), John Blake, Roland Blancaflor, Michele Burke, Greg Cannom, Mitch Devane (as Mitch DeVane), Matt Falls (as Mat Falls), Glen Hanz,

J.C. Logan, Mike Measimer, Gilbert A. Mosko, Matthew W. Mungle, Larry Odien, Steve Prouty, Carol Schwartz, Rick Stratton, Todd Tucker, Robert E. Watson (as Rob Watson), Joel Harlow, Keith VanderLaan; *Special Effects*: Yarek Alfer (as Jarosian G. Alfer), David Blistein, Michael Lantieri, Darrell Pritchett (as Darrell D. Pritchett), Paul Barnes, Randy Cabral, Jeanna Crawford, Kim Derry, Thomas R. Hornsher, Michael Hubert, Matt McDonnell, Tom Pahk, Brian Tipton, Harold Weed; *Cast*: Gary Oldman (Dracula), Winona Ryder (Mina Murray/Elisabeta), Anthony Hopkins (Professor Abraham Van Helsing), Keanu Reeves (Jonathan Harker), Richard E. Grant (Dr. Jack Seward), Cary Elwes (Lord Arthur Holmwood), Bill Campbell (Quincey P. Morris), Sadie Frost (Lucy Westenra), Tom Waits (R.M. Renfield), Monica Bellucci (Dracula's Bride), Michaela Bercu (Dracula's Bride), Florina Kendrick (Dracula's Bride), Jay Robinson (Mr. Hawking), I.M. Hobson (Hobbs), Laurie Franks (Lucy's Maid), Maud Winchester (Downstairs Maid), Octavian Cadia (Deacon), Robert Getz (Priest), Dagmar Stanec (Sister Agatha), Eniko Öss (Sister Sylvia [as Eniko Oss]), Nancy Lineharn Charles (Older Woman), Tatiana von Furstenberg (Younger Woman), Jules Sylvester (Zookeeper), Hubert Wells (Zookeeper), Daniel Newman (News Hawker), Honey Lauren (Peep Show Girl), Judi Diamond (Peep Show Girl), Robert Buckingham (Husband), Cully Fredrickson (Van Helsing's Assistant), Ele Bardha (Grave Digger [uncredited]), Christina Fulton (Vampire Girl [uncredited]), Moreen Littrell (Impaled Dancer [uncredited]), Joe Murkijanian (Monk [uncredited]), Adamo Palladino (Dock Loader [uncredited]), Philip Pucci (Lorryman [uncredited]), Heidi Schooler (Courtesan [uncredited]).

Jonathan Harker (Keanu Reeves) travels to Transylvania to meet with Count Dracula (Gary Oldman) to close a real estate contract with him for property the Count is buying up in London. Mina (Winona Ryder), Jonathan's fiancée, falls in love with Dracula upon his arrival to England. Jonathan, along with Professor Abraham Van Helsing (Anthony Hopkins) and others, pursue Dracula and follow him all the way from England to his home land in order to put an end to his reign of terror.

Bram Stoker's Vampire Diaries: Renfield (*Vampire Diaries: Renfield* [short title]); U.S., 2010; Horror; color/English; Champion Entertainment, Poison Apple Entertainment.

Producers: Yankie Grant, Vance Johnson, Melissa Nichols, Melissa Nichols, Phil Nichols, J. Eddie Peck Bob Willems; *Director*: Jaroslav Vodehnal; *Cinematography*: David Tattersall; *Film Editing*: Joseph Profit; *Original Music*: Julye Newlin; *Art Direction*: Melissa Nichols; *Make-Up*: Leslie Chambers (first assistant special makeup effects), Melissa Nichols (special makeup effects artist), Phil Nichols (makeup supervisor), Heather Warnock (wig maker); *Cast*: Tiffany Shepis Paula Craig [ru-

Gary Oldman plays Prince Vlad Dracula in *Bram Stoker's Dracula* (U.S., 1992).

mored]), J. Eddie Peck (Cranston), Phil Nichols (Renfield), Yankie Grant (D. A. Branch), Roxy Cook (Mina), Calvin Lafiton (Landon [rumored]), Eduardo Enriquez Jr. (Count Dracula [rumored]) or Kane Hodder (Count Dracula [rumored]), Melissa Nichols (The Oracle), Vance Johnson (Dr. Seward), Glen Lambert (Willard Caine [rumored]), Austin Colt (Quincy).

Dracula's old slave R. N. Renfield is now on his own. Now a vampire himself, he has gone insane and terrorizes the metropolis of Bayou City.

Bram Stoker's Way of the Vampire (*Cesta upírů— Van Helsing vs. Dracula* [Czech Republic (DVD title)]; *Van Helsing vs. Drácula* [Venezuela]; *Van Helsing's Way of the Vampire* [U.S.]); U.S., 2005; Horror, Thriller; 90 minutes/color/English/Dolby Digital 5.1; The Asylum.

Producers: David Michael Latt, David Rimawi, Sherri Strain, Rick Walker, Kevin Carraway; *Writing Credits*: Karrie Melendrez, Sherri Strain, Michael Stewart; *Director*: Sarah Nean Bruce, Eduardo Durao; *Cinematography*: Zack Richard; *Film Editing*: David Michael Latt, Dustin Voigt; *Original Music*: Ralph Rieckermann; *Art Direction*: Dominic Ceci; *Make-Up*: Keith Beck, Rocky Faulkner, Elizabeth Fox; *Special Effects*: Keith Beck, Richard Miranda; Visual Effects: David Michael Latt; *Cast*: Rhett Giles (Dr. Abraham Van Helsing), Paul Logan (Dracula), Andreas Beckett (Sebastien), Denise Boutte (Arianna), Brent Falco (Emily), Alix Henning (Yvonne), Anthony Turk (Father Cefalu), James Ashby (Dominic), Drew Berenc (Norris), Ulf Björlin Jr. (Walsh), Butterfly (Solana), Lisa Clark (Essence), Jared Cohn (Roman), Matt Dallas (Todd), Edward DeRuiter (Jake), Whitney Deutch (Martika), Ed Flanagan (Ivanovich), Bogdan Ioana (Lorenzo), Claudia Katz (Leona), Shannon Kemp (Det. Donn), Sean Lust (Colin), Nadra Macuish (Paula), Renée Mignosa (Diana), Brian Nichols (Det. Shirani), Kristina Proulx (Josie), Rey Reyes (Julio), Trina Robinson (Elena), Lawrence Sara (Wilson), Amanda Ward (Natalia), Mark Romero Wilson (Joseph).

Van Helsing is granted immortality by the Church after defeating Dracula in order to vanquish all future vampires. His hunt leads him through time and across continents to a bloody stand-off between his fellow hunters and an army of the undead. The army is led by Sebastian, Van Helsing's arch-enemy who took away the only woman he has ever loved.

Breakfast with Dracula (*Breakfast with Dracula: A Vampire in Miami* [U.S.]; *Vampire in Miami, A* [U.S.]; *Vampiro a Miami, Un* [Italy]); Italy/U.S., 1993; Horror; 90 minutes/color; Victoria Film.

Producer: Tod Barrell; *Writing Credits*: Tod Barrell; *Director*: Tod Barrell; *Original Music*: Donald Brent; *Cast*: David Warbeck (Sheriff), Anthony Foster, Christine Garrison, Deborah Murphy.

A man has nightmares about a girl running through a graveyard while being attacked by the living dead. Eventually, he discovers that he himself has become a vampire.

The Breed; U.S./Hungary, 2001; Action, Adventure, Horror, Science Fiction; 91 minutes/color/English, German/Dolby Digital/35 mm; Motion Picture Corporation of America.

Producers: Jim Burke, Kelli Konop, Brad Krevoy, Adam Richman, Joyce Schweickert, Annette Vait; *Writing Credits*: Christos N. Cage (written by), Ruth Fletcher (written by [as Ruth C. Fletcher]); *Director*: Michael Oblowitz; *Cinematography*: Chris Squires; *Film Editing*: Matthew Booth, Emma K. Hickox; *Original Music*: Roy Hay; *Art Direction*: Tibor Lazar; *Make-Up*: Sean Anderson (special makeup effects artist), Katalin Jakots (makeup department head), Gabi Nemeth, Balazs Novak (assistant makeup artist), Ivan Poharnok (special makeup effects artist); *Special Effects*: Janos Berki (special effects [as Janos Berki]), Gabor Kiszelly (special effects technician), Ferenc Ormos (special effects supervisor); *Cast*: Adrian Paul (Aaron Gray), Bokeem Woodbine (Steve Grant), Ling Bai (Lucy Westenra), Péter Halász (Cross), James Booth (Fleming), Lo Ming (Seward [as Ming Lo]), Paul Collins (Calmet), Debbie Javor (Section Chief), Reed Diamond (Phil), John Durbin (Boudreaux), Zen Gesner (West), István Göz (Dr. Orlock), William Hootkins (Fusco), Brandy Miller (Goth Poser #1), John Rado (Detective [as Janos Rado]), Barna Illyés (Man), Erzsebet Bodor (Woman), Antal Leisen (Bystander), Norbert Növényi (Nazi Soldier #1), Soma Zámbori (Nazi Soldier #2), Lajos Szücs (Vampire Cop #1), Zsolt Sáfár Kovács (Vampire Cop #2 as Zsolt Safar-Kovacs]), Dianna Camacho (Dr. Bathory), Szonja Oroszlán (Newscaster), Imre Csuja (Polish Bartender), Jake Eberle (Lowlife).

In the far future exists a society where human and vampire peacefully coexist. When a flurry of murders begins to draw interest from the law, the suspect is a Dracula-type vampire, who is accompanied by other characters deriving from Stoker's novel and various other vampire literature.

The Brides of Dracula (*Maîtresses de Dracula, Les* [France]; *Dracula— blodtörstig vampyr* [Sweden]; *Dracula und seine Bräute* [Germany]; *Spose di Dracula, Le* [Italy]); U.K., 1960; Horror; 85 minutes/color/English/Mono; Hammer Film Productions, Hotspur Film Productions Ltd.

Producers: Michael Carreras; Anthony Hinds;

Anthony Nelson Keys; *Writing Credits*: Peter Bryan (screenplay), Anthony Hinds (uncredited), Edward Percy (screenplay), Jimmy Sangster (screenplay); *Director*: Terence Fisher; *Cinematography*: Jack Asher; *Film Editing*: Alfred Cox; *Original Music*: Malcolm Williamson; *Art Direction*: Thomas Goswell (uncredited); *Make-Up*: Roy Ashton, Freda Steiger; *Special Effects*: Sydney Pearson (special effects); *Cast*: Peter Cushing (Dr. J. Van Helsing); Martita Hunt (Baroness Meinster); Yvonne Monlaur (Marianne Danielle); Freda Jackson (Greta); David Peel (Baron Meinster); Miles Malleson (Dr. Tobler); Henry Oscar (Herr Otto Lang); Mona Washbourne (Frau Helga Lang); Andree Melly (Gina); Victor Brooks (Hans, a Villager); Fred Johnson (The Cure, Father Stepnik); Michael Ripper (Coachman); Norman Pierce (Johann, Landlord); Vera Cook (Landlord's Wife); Marie Devereux (Village Girl (as Marie Deveruex); Susan Castle (Elsa, School Maid [uncredited]); Michael Mulcaster (Latour, The Man in Black [uncredited]); Harry Pringle (Karl [uncredited]); Harold Scott (Severin [uncredited]); Stephanie Watts (Foxy Girl [uncredited]).

Marianne Danielle (Yvonne Monlaur), a student teacher on her way to the Bachstadt Lady's Academy, is forced to take up lodging at Baroness von Meinster's (Martita Hunt) castle. As she attempts to sleep, she comes to discover the Baroness's son, Baron von Meinster (David Peel), chained to his room. She then searches for the key and gives it to the Baron so that he may escape. While on her way to the Academy the following morning, Marianne, accompanied by Dr. van Helsing (Peter Cushing) a vampire hunter, discovers a young girl with bite wounds on her neck, which van Helsing recognizes as a vampire bite. A string of supernatural events soon unfolds.

Buck Rogers in the 25th Century (TV Series [1979–1981]), episode "Space Vampire"; U.S., Season 1, Episode 14, 3 January 1980; Adventure, Science Fiction/Television; 60 minutes/color/English/Mono; John Mantley Productions, Glen A. Larson Productions, Universal TV.

Producers: Jock Gaynor, Medora Heilbron, Bruce Lansbury, Glen A. Larson, David J. O'Connell, David G. Phinney; *Original Music*: Robert Prince; *Cinematography*: Ben Colman; *Film Editing*: George Potter; *Art Direction*: Hub Braden, Fred Luff III; *Special Effects*: David M. Garber, William Guest, Wayne Smith; *Cast*: Gil Gerard (Capt. William "Buck" Rogers), Erin Gray (Col. Wilma Deering), Tim O'Connor (Dr. Elias Huer), Christopher Stone (Space Station Commander Royko), Nicholas Hormann (Vorvon), Lincoln Kilpatrick (Dr. Ecbar), Patty Maloney (Twiki), Mel Blanc (Twiki (voice), David Moses (Technician), Phil Hoover (Helson) Jeannie Fitzsimmons (Captain), William Conrad (Narrator (voice) (uncredited), Eric Server (Dr. Theopolis [voice] [uncredited]).

Buck Rogers (Gil Gerard) and Wilma are on their way to vacation on the planet Genesia but stop first at Theta Station to drop off Twiki, who is in need repair. While there, a craft appears and crashes into the space station. Searching the vessel only to discover the entire crew dead (before the ship crashed), Space Station Commander Royko (Christopher Stone) places the station under quarantine, fearing the virus EL-7. However, the real culprit is in fact the Vorvon, a large-fanged, Dracula-type vampire (a la *Nosferatu*) from deep space who drains soul, rather than blood, from the living.

Bud Abbott and Lou Costello Meet Frankenstein (*Meet Frankenstein* [original title]; *Abbott and Costello Meet Frankenstein* [U.S., short title]; *Abbott and Costello Meet the Ghosts* [U.K.]; *The Brain of Frankenstein* [U.S.; original script title]); U.S., 1948; Comedy, Horror, Romance, Science Fiction; 83 minutes/black and white/English/Mono; Universal International Pictures (UI).

Producer: Robert Arthur; *Writing Credits*: Mary Shelley, Bram Stoker, Robert Lees, Frederic I. Rinaldo, John Grant; *Director*: Charles Barton; *Cinematography*: Charles Van Enger; *Film Editing*: Frank Gross; *Original Music*: Frank Skinner; *Art Direction*: Hilyard M. Brown, Bernard Herzbrun; *Make-Up*: Carmen Dirigo, Bud Westmore, Jack Kevan, (uncredited), Emile LaVigne (uncredited); *Special Effects*: Jerome Ash, David S. Horsley, Fred Knoth (uncredited); *Cast*: Bud Abbott (Chick Young), Lou Costello (Wilbur Grey), Lon Chaney Jr. (Larry Talbot/The Wolf Man [as Lon Chaney]), Béla Lugosi (Count Dracula), Glenn Strange (The Frankenstein Monster), Lenore Aubert (Dr. Sandra Mornay), Jane Randolph (Joan Raymond), Frank Ferguson (Mr. McDougal), Charles Bradstreet (Dr. Stevens), Bobby Barber (Waiter [uncredited]), George Barton (Man [uncredited]), Harry Brown (Photographer [uncredited]), Joe Kirk (Man at costume party in fez [uncredited]), Howard Negley (Harris [insurance man] [uncredited]), Vincent Price (The Invisible Man [voice] [uncredited]), Carl Sklover (Man at costume party [uncredited]), Helen Spring (Woman at baggage counter [uncredited]), Paul Stader (Sergeant [uncredited]), Clarence Straight (Man in armor [uncredited]), Joe Walls (Man [uncredited]).

Opposite: **Spanish poster for *The Brides of Dracula* (U.K., 1960).**

Béla Lugosi, left, plays Dracula opposite Glen Strange as Frankenstein's Monster in *Bud Abbott and Lou Costello Meet Frankenstein* (U.S., 1948) (courtesy Justin Humphreys).

While the remains of Frankenstein and Dracula were being shipped to Europe to be displayed in a house of horror, Dracula suddenly awakened. He planned to bring Frankenstein back to life with a new brain. With a little help Dracula kidnaps Wilbur. Chick and Talbot want to save Wilbur, but it is too late.

Bud Abbott and Lou Costello Meet the Monsters!; U.S., 2000; black and white, color/English; Universal Studios Home Video.

Producer: David J. Skal; *Writing Credits*: David J. Skal; *Director*: David J. Skal; *Film Editing*: Keith Clark; *Original Music*: Kathleen Mayne; *Cast*: Bob Burns (Himself), Chris Costello (Herself), Béla Lugosi Jr. (Himself), Bob Madison (Himself), Ron Palumbo (Himself), David J. Skal (Host).

Buenas Noches, Señor Monstruo; Spain, 1982; Comedy, Musical; 80 minutes/color/Spanish/Stereo; José Frade Producciones Cinematográficas S.A.

Producer: José Frade; *Writing Credits*: Antonio Merceo, José Ángel Rodero; *Director*: Antonio Mercero, Josetxo San Mateo; *Cinematography*: Manuel Rojas; *Film Editing*: Javier Morán; *Original Music*: Manuel Cubedo, Félix Lapardi; *Art Direction*: Julio Esteban, Humberto Cornejo; *Make-Up*: Fernando Florido, Dolores Gracía Rey; *Special Effects*: Fernando Pérez, Tomás Urbán; *Cast*: Jaime Benet (Jaime [as Regaliz]), Astrid Fenollar (Astrid [as Regaliz]), Eva Mariol (Eva [as Regaliz]), Eduard Navarrete (Eduardo [as Regaliz]), Fernando Bilbao (El monstruo), Luis Escobar (Conde Dracula), Andres Mejuto (Doctor Frankenstein), Guilermo Montesinos (Quasimodo), Astrid Fenollar (Astrid [as Regaliz]), Eva Mariol (Eva [as Regaliz]), Eduard Navarrete (Eduardo [as Regaliz]), Fernando Bilbao (el monstruo), Luis Escobar (Conde Dracula), Andres Mejuto (Doctor Frankenstein), Guillermo Montesinos (Quasimodo), Paul Naschy (El Hombre Lobo), Miguel Angel Valero (El Hijo de Dracula [as Miguel Angel Valero]), Lorenzo Ramirez (Guia del museo), Rosa Redondo (Senorita Sara), Nina Ferrer (Senorita), Amelie Jara (Jaime [voice, uncredited]), Julio Nunez (El hombre lobo [voice, uncredited]).

Buffy the Vampire Slayer; U.S., 1992; Horror, Action, Comedy; 86 minutes/color/English/Dolby/

35mm; Twentieth Century–Fox Film Corporation, Kuzui Enterprises, Sandollar.

Producers: Carol Baum, Alex Butler, Sandy Gallin, Fran Rubel Kuzui, Kaz Kuzui, Dennis Stuart Murphy, Howard Rosenman; *Writing Credits*: Joss Whedon; *Director*: Fran Rubel Kuzui; *Cinematography*: James Hayman; *Film Editing*: Jill Savitt, Camilla Toniolo; *Original Music*: Carter Burwell; *Art Direction*: James R. Barrows, Randy Moore; *Make-Up*: Ann Brodie, Michelle Bühler, Bill Forsche, Mark Maitre, Angela Moos, Thomas E. Surprenant, Tyger Tate, Dean Gates (uncredited); *Cast*: Kristy Swanson (Buffy), Donald Sutherland (Merrick), Paul Reubens (Amilyn), Rutger Hauer (Lothos), Luke Perry (Pike), Michele Abrams (Jennifer), Hilary Swank (Kimberly), Paris Vaughan (Nicole), David Arquette (Benny), Randall Batinkoff (Jeffrey), Andrew Lowery (Andy), Sasha Jenson (Grueller), Stephen Root (Gary Murray), Natasha Gregson Wagner (Cassandra), Mark DeCarlo (Coach), Thomas Jane (Zeph), Candy Clark (Buffy's Mom), James Paradise (Buffy's Dad), David Sherrill (Knight), Liz Smith (Reporter), Paul M. Lane (Robert Berman), Toby Holguin (Vampire Fan), Eurlyne Epper (Graveyard Woman), Andre Warren (Newscaster), Bob "Swanie" Swanson (Referee), Erika Dittner (Cheerleader), J.T. Cole (Biker), Michael Kopelow (Student), Ricky Dean Logan (Bloody Student), Bobby Aldridge (Vampire), Amanda Anka (Vampire), Chino Binamo (Vampire), Al Goto (Vampire), Terry Jackson (Vampire), Mike Johnson (Vampire), Sarah Lee Jones (Vampire), Kim Robert Koscki (Vampire), Clint Lilley (Vampire), Chi Muoi Lo (Vampire), Jimmy N. Roberts (Vampire), David Rowden (Vampire), Kenny Sacha (Vampire), Ben Scott (Vampire), Kurtis Epper (Vampire), Sharon Schaffer (Vampire), Lincoln Simonds (Vampire), Diamond Yukai, Ben Affleck (Basketball Player #10 [uncredited]), Bryan Goeres (Basketball Player [uncredited]), Ricki Lake (Charlotte [uncredited]), Paul Pesco (Vampire [uncredited]).

Buffy Summers leads a typical teenage life with cheerleading, shopping, and dating the captain of the basketball team, that is, until her life gets turned upside down when a mysterious stranger, Merrick, tells her that her true calling is to be "the Slayer," a woman called to defend the world from vampires. Her greatest challenge is Lothos, a master (Dracula-type) vampire.

Buffy the Vampire Slayer (TV Series [1991–2003]), episode "Buffy vs. Dracula" (*BtVS* [U.S.: promotional abbreviation]; *Buffy* [U.S.: short title]; *Buffy, the Vampire Slayer: The Series* [U.S.: long title]; U.S., Season 5, Episode 1, 26 November 2000; Drama, Action, Fantasy/Television; 42 minutes/color/Dolby Digital; 20th Century–Fox Television.

Producers: Marc D. Alpert (as Marc David Alpert), Gail Berman, Gareth Davies, Jane Espenson, David Fury, Sandy Gallin, David Greenwalt, Fran Rubel Kuzui, Kaz Kuzui, Marti Noxon, John F. Perry, Douglas Petrie, David Solomon, Joss Whedon; *Writing Credits*: Joss Whedon, Marti Noxon; *Director*: David Solomon; *Original Music*: Thomas Wanker; *Make-Up*: Robin Beauchesne, Gloria Pasqua Casny, Steve Fink, Todd McIntosh, Brigette A. Myre (as Brigette Myre-Ellis), Lisa Marie Rosenberg, John Vulich; *Cast*: Sarah Michelle Gellar (Buffy Summers), Nicholas Brendon (Xander Harris), Alyson Hannigan (Willow Rosenberg), Marc Blucas (Riley Finn) Emma Caulfield (Anya), James Marsters (Spike), Anthony Head (Rupert Giles [as Anthony Stewart Head]), Rudolf Martin (Dracula), Michelle Trachtenberg (Dawn Summers), Amber Benson (Tara Maclay), Kristine Sutherland (Joyce Summers), Edward James Gage (Mover #1 [as E.J. Gage]), Scott Berman (Mover #2), Marita Schaub (Vampire Girl #1), Lesli Jean Matta (Vampire Girl #2 [as Leslee Jean Matta]), Jennifer Slimko (Vampire Girl #3).

Buffy runs into Dracula while chasing another vampire. She is flattered that he came all the way to her town to meet her. Giles plans to go back to London because Buffy doesn't need him as a watcher anymore. Dracula makes Xander a vampire and he bites Buffy. Buffy hides the bite, but she is enticed by Dracula who told her he would give her full power.

Call Him Jess (*Llámale Jess* [Spain: Original title]); Spain, 2000; Documentary; color/Spanish/Dolby Digital; Media park S.A., Mamen Boué, Mariona Tella.

Writing Credits: Joan Ferré, Manel Mayol,, Carles Prats; *Director*: Manel Mayol, Carles Prats; *Cinematography*: Pere Ballesteros; *Film Editing*: Eugenio Campos; *Original Music*: Christian Rey Salvador Rey; *Cast*: Jesus Franco (Himself), Lina Romay (Herself).

In this documentary, Jesus Franco talks about many of his films, one of which is his filming of *Dracula*, starring Christopher Lee.

Canucula! (*Dracula in Canada*); Canada, 2008; Horror; 49 minutes/black and white/English; Anthony D.P. Mann presents...

Producer: Anthony D.P. Mann; *Writing Credits*: Anthony D.P. Mann; *Director*: Anthony D.P. Mann; *Film Editing*: Anthony D.P. Mann; *Original Music*: Anthony D.P. Mann; *Cast*: Anthony D.P. Mann (Dracula), Pamela Tomsett (Ruby Dires), Michael Pontbriand (Michel Richard), Terry Snider (Smythe Von Sloan), Joanna Szczepanski (Desdemona),

Steve Heron (Wally Gorkin), Mark Snider (Rob), Richard M. Piperni (The Vagrant), Melissa Shook (The Junkie).

This film takes place around one hundred years following the events in the original *Dracula* novel. Dracula finds himself in Canada and discovers a distant relative of his former love. The protagonist, a hockey player, must save the young lady from Dracula's intentions.

Captain Berlin Versus Hitler; Germany, 2009; Horror, Comedy, Sci-fi, Action; 75 minutes/color/German; Vonblitzenfilm.

Producers: Jörg Buttgereit, Thilo Gosejohann, Julia Naunin; *Writing Credits*: Jörg Buttgereit; *Director*: Jörg Buttgereit; *Cinematography*: Thilo Gosejohann; *Film Editing*: Thilo Gosejohann; *Original Music*: Mark Reeder Peter Synthetic; *Art Direction*: Melissa Nichols; *Make-Up*: Leslie Chambers (first assistant special makeup effects), Melissa Nichols (special makeup effects artist), Phil Nichols (makeup supervisor), Heather Warnock (wig maker); *Special Effects*: Hannes Heiner; *Cast*: Adolfo Assor (Dracula), Jürg Plüss (Captain Berlin), Sandra Steffl (Maria), Claudia Steiger (Ilse von Blitzen).

Ilse von Blitzen has hired Dracula to bring Hitler's brain back to life in an actual body. She plans to pay Dracula with the beautiful daughter of Captain Berlin. Captain Berlin must save his daughter by defeating von Blitzen, Dracula, and the brain of Hitler himself.

Captain N: The Game Master (TV Series [1989–1991]), episode "Return to Castlevania"; U.S., Season 3, Episode 3, 28 September 1991; Family, Science Fiction/Television, Animation; 30 minutes/color/English; DiC Entertainment.

Producers: Jaimie Edlin (live action main title), Robby London, John O'Sullivan Francis Jr.; *Writing Credits*: Matt Uitz; *Director*: Kit Hudson; *Original Music*: Shuki Levy, Haim Saban; *Cast*: Matt Hill (Kevin "Captain N" Keene/Narrator [voice]), Long John Baldry (Poltergeist King [voice]), Alessandro Juliani (Kid Icarus [voice]), Andrew Kavadas (Simon Belmont [voice]), Venus Terzo (Princess Lana [voice]), Shane Meier (Additional Voices), Anthony Holland (Additional Voices), Al Jorden (Additional Voices), Dorian Barag (Kevin Keene [Live Action Sequences]), Lee Jeffrey (Additional Voices), Tomm Wright (Duke the Dog), Donald Brown (Additional Voices), Marcy Goldberg (Additional Voices).

At the Simon Belmont Awards, Kevin and Simon have a scuffle with one of Dracula's agents who is impersonating the King Poltergeist. To rescue the real King, Kevin and Simon have to get past Dracula's obstacles.

Capulina Contra los Vampiros; Mexico, 1971; Comedy, Fantasy, Mystery; 85 minutes/color/Spanish; Producciones Zacarías S.A.

Producers: Miguel Zacarías, Gaspar Henaine (uncredited); *Writing Credits*: René Cardona (screenplay), Mario Vaena (story); *Director*: René Cardona; *Cinematography*: Raúl Martínez Solares; *Film Editing*: Gloria Schoemann; *Original Music*: Sergio Guerrero; *Make-Up*: Ana Guerrero, Agripina Lozada; *Cast*: Gaspar Henaine (as Gaspar Henaine Capulina), Rossy Mendoza, Aurelio Pérez, Carlos Agostí, Juan Gallardo, Armando Acosta, Guillermo Hernández Jr., Francisco Meneses, Violeta Corral (Vampira), Sara Benítez (Vampira), María Teresa León (Vampira), Stephanie Lover (Vampira), María Claudia Esquivel (Vampira), Leonor Madera (Vampira), Ivonne Govea (uncredited).

Beloved Mexican comedian Capulina (Gaspar Henaine) stars in a wacky horror-comedy hybrid, which finds the hapless funnyman accidentally reviving a vampire. Capulino is pursued by a few thousand bats emerging at night to search for blood.

Carry on Christmas; U.K., 1969; Comedy, Family; 50 minutes/color/English; Thames Television.

Producer: Peter Eton; *Writing Credits*: Talbot Rothwell; *Director*: Ronnie Baxster; *Cast*: Sid James (Ebenezer Scrooge), Terry Scott (Dr. Frank N. Stein, Convent Girl, Mr. Barrett, Baggie the Ugly Sister), Charles Hawtrey (Spirit of Christmas Past, Angel, Convent Girl, Buttons), Hattie Jacques (Elizabeth Barrett, Nun, Bemused Passer-By), Barbara Windsor (Cinderella, Fanny, Spirit of Christmas Present), Bernard Bresslaw (Bob Cratchit, Frank N. Stein's Monster, Spirit of Christmas Future, Convent Girl, Town Crier, Policeman), Peter Butterworth (Dracula, Street Beggar, Convent Girl, Haggie the Other Ugly Sister), Frankie Howerd (Robert Browning, Fairy Godmother).

Ebenezer Scrooge is mean and grumpy, withholding money from people as well as not participating in spreading joyous Christmas cheer. He is visited by three ghosts who show him how his attitude has been affecting those around him. Along the way he meets characters such as Cinderella, the Fairy Godmother, and Dracula.

Il Castello dei morti vivi (*Castillo de los muertos vivientes, El* [Venezuela]; *Castle of the Living Dead* [U.S.]; *Château des morts vivants, Le* [France]; *Crypt of Horror*); Italy, 1964; Horror, Science Fiction, Thriller/Film; 91 minutes/black and white/Italian/35mm; Filmsonor.

Producer: Paul Maslansky; *Writing Credits*: Michael Reeves, Lorenzo Sabatini (as Warren Kiefer); *Director*: Luciano Ricci (as Herbert Wise),

Lorenzo Sabatini (as Warren Kiefer), Michael Reeves (uncredited); *Cinematography*: Aldo Tonti; *Film Editing*: Mario Serandrei; *Original Music*: Angelo Francesco Lavagnino; *Art Direction*: Carlo Gentili; *Make-Up*: Guglielmo Bonotti; *Cast*: Christopher Lee (Count Drago), Gaia Germani (Laura), Philippe Leroy (Eric), Mirko Valentin (Hans), Donald Sutherland (Sgt. Paul/The witch/The old man), Antonio De Martino (Nick [as Anthony Martin]), Luigi Bonos (Marc [as Lewis Bonos]), Jacques Stany (Bruno [as Jack Stany]), Luciano Pigozzi (Dart [as Luke Pigozzi]), Ennio Antonelli (Gianni), Renato Terra (Policeman [uncredited]).

Count Drago invites a group of entertainers to his castle. Count Drago secretly poisons them one by one with a drug that embalms its victims immediately after killing them.

Castlevania; U.S., 2011; Action, Horror; color/English; Crystal Sky Pictures, Grosvenor Park Productions, Impact Pictures, Konami Corporation, Rogue Pictures.

Producers: Paul W.S. Anderson, Jeremy Bolt, Benedict Carver, Steven Paul; *Writing Credits*: Paul W.S. Anderson, Andrew Hyatt, Ian Jeffers; *Director*: Sylvain White; *Art Direction*: Dominic Lavery, Howard Swindell; *Special Effects*: Cheryl Bainum, Deak Ferrand.

The year is 1691, Transylvania has been at peace for 100 years, and the time when vampires and chaos ruled the local peasantry has nearly passed out of memory. There are those, however, who still remember that Count Dracula returns every 100 years. Indeed, the count returns to Castlevania, his ancestral home, to call upon his minions to strike at the hearts of humans. And so it was that Simon Belmont, of the ancient Belmont line, takes up "Vampire Killer," the family's legendary whip, and sets forth on a legendary quest to vanquish Dracula and his army of creatures.

Casualty (TV Series [1986–present]), episode "Trials and Tribulations"; U.K., Season 9, Episode 18, 11 February 1995; Drama/Television; 50 minutes/color/English/Stereo/35mm; British Broadcasting Corporation (BBC).

Producers: Corinne Hollingworth; *Writing Credits*: Lilie Ferrari; *Director*: Lilie Ferrari; *Cast*: Thea Bennett (TV Presenter), Ian Bleasdale (Josh Griffiths), Steven Brand (Adam Cooke), Roger Burfield (Court Usher), Robert Cavanah (James Barnes), Lisa Coleman (Jude Korcanik), Thomas Craig (Graham Evans), Sorcha Cusack (Kate Wilson), Sue Devaney (Liz Harker), Alice Douglas (Izzy), Sean Gilder (D.S. Hennessy), Richard Goodfield (Security Guard), Vivienne Goodfield (Jury Foreman), Jane Gurnett (Rachel Longworth), Martin Hill-Jones (Pastor), Mark Lewis Jones (Alison), Nikki Kyle (Receptionist), Clive Mantle (Mike Barratt), Barry McCarthy (Opie), Glenn McCrory (Vlad the Impaler), Jason Merrells (Matt Hawley), Ben Miller (Daniel Murdoch), Joan Oliver (Eddie Gordon), Tessa Peake-Jones (Jenny Hodges), Christine Pollon (Dr. Jacobs), Peter Reeves (Judge), Patrick Robinson (Martin "Ash" Ashford), Anna Rose (Sally Porter), Daniel Ryan (Mark Hitchens), Derek Thompson (Charlie Fairhead), Andrew Woodall (Tom Hodges), Hugh Young (Clerk of Court).

Ash's case comes to trial while Matt has an important decision to make. Jude's personal and professional lives collide when a young man with AIDS is rushed into the ER.

Il Cav. Costante Nicosia demoniaco, ovvero: Dracula in Brianza (*Dracula in the Provinces* [undefined]; *Drakoulas dagonei ponira, O* [Greece] [reissue title]; *Drakoulas dagonei ... sta malaka, O* [Greece] [reissue title]; *Erotiaris vrykolakas* [Greece]; *The Demonic Womanizer Costante Nicosia, or: Dracula in Brianza* [undefined] [informal literal English title]; *Young Dracula* [undefined]); Italy, 1975; Comedy; 100 minutes/color/Italian/Mono; Coralta Cinematografica.

Producers: Mario Mariani, Alfonso Donati; *Writing Credits*: Mario Amendola, Pupi Avati, Bruno Corbucci, Enzo Jannacci, Giuseppe Viola; *Director*: Lucio Fulci; *Cinematography*: Sergio Salvati; *Film Editing*: Ornella Micheli; *Original Music*: Vince Tempera, Fabio Frizzi, Franco Bixio; *Art Direction*: Pier Luigi Basile; *Cast*: Lando Buzzanca (Costante Nicosia), Rossano Brazzi (Dr. Paluzzi), Sylva Koscina (Mariù—wife of Costante), Moira Orfei (Bestia Assatanata), Christa Linder (Liù Pederzoli), John Steiner (Count Dragulescu), Francesca Romana Coluzzi (Wanda Torsello), Grazia Di Marzà (Prostitute), Antonio Allocca (Peppino), Grazia Spadaro (Aunt Maria), Franco Nebbia (Meniconi), Michele Cimarosa (Salvatore Cannata), Giampaolo Rossi (Brother-in-Law), Ciccio Ingrassia (Salvatore, the Wizard of Noto), Valentina Cortese (Olghina Franchetti), Franca Martelli (Gia), Mauro Vestri (TV Journalist), Ugo Fangareggi (Battai, Count's servant), Carlo Bagno (Head Worker), Renato Malavasi (Arnaldo), John Bartha (Concierge), Barbara Musci (Georgia), Gianfranco Bocca (Colombo), Belsana Arfenone (Nicosia's assistant), Dori Dorika (Night club singer) (uncredited), Ilona Staller (Gianka) (uncredited).

Costante Nicosia (Lando Buzzanca) is a snobbish and conceited businessman who treats others rudely with a lack of concern for their emotions. After encountering the vampire Count Dragulescu (John Steiner) on a business trip to Romania, Costante returns home only to find that he has a craving for blood and exhibits homosexual tendencies.

Ceremonia Sangrienta (*Forca do Diablo, A* [Brazil]; *Blood Castle* [undefined]; *Bloody Ceremony* [undefined]; *Comtesse des Grauens* [West Germany]; *Countess Dracula* [undefined]; *De dödas slot* [Sweden]; *Kauhujen linna* [Finland]; *Kuolleitten linna* [Finland]; *The Bloody Countess* [undefined]; *The Female Butcher* [undefined]; *The Legend of Blood Castle* [undefined]; *Vergini cavalcano la morte, Le* [Italy]); Spain/Italy, 1973; Horror; 102 minutes/color/Spanish, English/Mono; Luis Film.

Producers: José María González Sinde; *Writing Credits*: Sandro Continenza, Jorge Grau (screenplay), Jorge Grau (story), Peter Sasdy (novel), Juan Tebar; *Director*: Jorge Grau; *Cinematography*: Fernando Arribas, Oberdan Troiani; *Film Editing*: Pedro del Rey; *Original Music*: Carlo Savina; *Make-Up*: Carlos Peradela; *Cast*: Lucia Bosé (Erzsebet Bathory), Espartaco Santoni (Karl Ziemmer), Ewa Aulin (Marina), Ana Farra (Housekeeper), Silvano Tranquilli (Doctor), Lola Gaos (Carmilla), Enrique Vivó (Mayor), María Vico (Maria Plojovitz), Ángel Menéndez (Magistrate), Adolfo Thous (Judge), Ismael García Romen (Captain), Raquel Ortuño (Irina), María Dolores Tovar (Sandra [as Dolores Tovar]), Franca Grey (Nadja), Ghika (Inge), Miguel Buñuel (Secretary), Fabián Conde (Constable), Estanis González (Innkeeper), Antonio Puga (Claus), Francisco Agostín (Postman), Antonio De Mossul (Falconer), Rafael Vaquero (Painter [as Rafael Vakero]), Roberto Daniel (Plojovitz), Ángel Rodal (Young Mario), Juan José Otegui (Servant), Mari Paz Ballesteros (Maid), Sergio Alberti (Sergeant), Sofía Nogueiras (Laura), Kino Pueyo (Boy at inn [as Joaquín Pueyo]), Fernando De Bran (Rector), Rafael Frías (Boy on horse).

To regain her health and beauty, the Countess must take the blood of her maid.

Cetrdeset Dana see under **Forty**

Chair; U.S., 2001; Comedy, Horror/Short, Documentary; color, black and white/English.

Director: Gary Don Rhodes, Bob Stovall; *Cast*: Actor (role played): Gary Don Rhodes, James F. Cain (The Sound Man), Béla Lugosi (Himself [archive footage]), John Springer.

This mockumentary deals with Rhodes' procurement of Béla Lugosi's chair and the consequences.

Challenge of the SuperFriends (TV Series [1978]), episode "Attack of the Vampire"; U.S., Season 2, Episode 6, 14 October 1978; Action, Family/Television, Animation; 30 minutes/color/English; Hanna-Barbera Productions.

Producers: Joseph Barbera, William Hanna, Don Jurwich, Iwao Takamoto; *Writing Credits*: Carmine Infantino (characters [uncredited]), Bob Kane (characters: Batman, Robin, Scarecrow, Riddler [uncredited]); *Director*: Ray Patterson, Carl Urbano; *Film Editing*: Nancy Massie (color key); *Original Music*: John Beal (composer: additional music), John Beal (orchestrator); *Art Direction*: Iraj Paran (graphics), Tom Wogatzke (graphics); *Cast*: Lewis Bailey (voice), Melanie Chartoff (voice), Henry Corden (voice), Al Fann (voice), Bob Hastings (voice), Bob Holt (voice), Renny Roker (voice), Louise Williams (voice).

The SuperFriends try to stop Dracula after he returns from the grave and tries to turn innocent civilians into vampires.

Chappaqua; U.S./France, 1966; Drama; 82 minutes/color, black and white/English/Mono/35mm; Minotaur.

Producers: Francis Bouche, Louis-Emile Galey, Conrad Rooks; *Writing Credits*: Conrad Rooks; *Director*: Conrad Rooks; *Cinematography*: Étienne Becker, Robert Frank, Eugen Schüfftan; *Film Editing*: Kenout Peltier; *Original Music*: Ravi Shankar; *Make-Up*: Jacqueline Pipard, Jean Pipard; *Cast*: Jean-Louis Barrault (Dr. Benoit), Conrad Rooks (Russel Harwick), William S. Burroughs (Opium Jones), Allen Ginsberg (Messiah), Ravi Shankar (Sun God), Paula Pritchett (Water Woman), Ornette Coleman (Peyote Eater), Swami Satchidananda (The Guru), Moondog (The Prophet), Jill Lator (Sacrificed One), John Esam (The Connection), Ed Sanders (The Fugs), Rita Renoir, Penny Brown, Jacques Seiler, Moustique, Sophie Stelboun, Elder Wilder, Peter Orlovsky, Pascal Aubier, France Crémieux, Rene Serisier, The Fugs (Themselves), Hervé Villechaize (Little Person [uncredited]).

This is a semi-autobiographical film about Conrad Rooks's struggle with alcoholism and drug addiction. His struggle is depicted through different psychedelic images and scenes. One of these sequences involves a Dracula-type vampire.

Les Charlots contre Dracula; France, 1980; Comedy; 85 minutes/color/French/Mono; Belstar Productions, Stephan Films, Films de la Tour.

Producers: Véra Belmont, Jacques Dorfmann; *Writing Credits*: Jean-Pierre Desagnat, Gérard Filipelli (writer [as Les Charlots]), Stéphan Holmes (idea), Olivier Mergault, Fernand Pluot, Gérard Rinaldi (writer [as Les Charlots]), Jean Sarrus (writer [as Les Charlots]); *Director*: Jean-Pierre Desagnat, Jean-Pierre Vergne (uncredited); *Cinematography*: Ramón F. Suárez; *Film Editing*: Michel Lewin; *Cast*: Gérard Filipelli (Phil), Gérard Rinaldi (Gérard), Jean Sarrus (Jean), Amélie Prévost (Ariane), Andréas Voutsinas (Count Dracula),

Gérard Jugnot (Gaston Lepope), Vincent Martin (Igor), Dora Doll (Commisaire Gluck), Jacqueline Alexandre (Femme Etranglee), Eugène Berthier (Homme qui se rase), Michel Duplaix (Commisaire [as Michel Dupleix]), Jean-Pierre Elga (Elic), Tomas Hnevsa (Costaud), Marc Henry (Voyageur Clandestin), Alain Mercier (Sosie Lepope), Maria Verdi (Bertha), François Maisongrosse (Taxi) Jacques Ramade, Romain Soler (Dracounet), Jacques Nolot (uncredited).

A group of misfits tries to stop Dracula's reign of terror.

Chi o suu bara (*Bloodsucking Rose* [undefined]; *Evil of Dracula* [U.S.]; *The Bloodthirsty Roses* [undefined]); Japan, 1974; Drama, Horror; 87 minutes/color/Japanese/Mono/35mm; Toho Company, Toho Eizo Co.

Producers: Henry G. Saperstein (1980 U.S. TV release), Fumio Tanaka; *Writing Credits*: Ei Ogawa, Bram Stoker (character), Masaru Takesue; *Director*: Michio Yamamoto; *Cinematography*: Kazutami Hara; *Film Editing*: Michiko Ikeda; *Special Effects*: Teruyoshi Nakano; *Cast*: Toshio Kurosawa (Professor Shiraki), Kunie Tanaka (Doc Shimimura), Katsuhiko Sasaki (Professor Yoshi), Shin Kishida (The Principal), Mariko Mochizuki (Kumi), Mio Ohta (uncredited), Mika Katsuragi (uncredited), Keiko Aramaki (uncredited), Yûnosuke Itô (uncredited).

Dracula ends up in Japan in the 1600s after getting shipwrecked there. At that time, Christianity was illegal. So, he was forced to turn his back on the cross and roam the desert alone. After cutting himself, he began to drink his own blood until he acquired a taste for it, even attacking a local citizen. The story then flashes forward to the present day, where a teacher moves to a new school and is then asked by the principal to take over. The principal's wife died in a car wreck, so he begins keeping her in the cellar to see if she will come back to life. The teacher investigates and gets caught up in the world of vampires.

Chickula: Teenage Vampire; U.S., 1995; Comedy/Short; 4 minutes/color/English.

Producer: Kristina Malder; *Writing Credits*: Angela Robinson; *Director*: Angela Robinson.

A parody of 1950s horror trailers, this short features a lesbian vampire who terrorizes a suburban high school.

Children of Dracula; U.S., 1994; Documentary; 60 minutes/color/English; Remington York Inc.

Producers: Bret McCormick, David Stephens, Schnele Wilson; *Writing Credits*: Bret McCormick; *Director*: Bret McCormick, Christopher Romero (reenactment segment); *Cinematography*: T. G. Weems; *Film Editing*: Keith Kjornes; *Special Effects*: T. G. Weems (computer graphics); *Cast*: Tony Brownrigg, Joe Estevez (Narrator [voice]), John Fiklin, Mika James, Jason Lockburn, Robert Maciejewski, John McCarty (Himself), Gregory S. O'Rourke (Himself), Jennisen Svendsen, Cassandra Timmins, Schnele Wilson.

This documentary features a number of interviews with persons who claim to be real vampires.

Cinderelmo; U.S., 1999; Family, Comedy, Fantasy/Television, Animation; 65 minutes/color/English/Dolby Digital 2.0 Stereo.

Producer: Jill Lopez Danton; *Writing Credits*: Tony Geiss; *Director*: Bruce Leddy; *Cinematography*: James Jansen; *Make-Up* Linda Grimes; *Cast*: Keri Russell (Princess), Kathy Najimy (Stepmother), Caroll Spinney (Big Bird [voice]), French Stewart (Prince), Oliver Platt (Frank/Fairy Godperson), Mizuho Akiba (Cast), Chad Azadan (Cast), Fran Brill (Zoe [voice]), Kevin Clash (Elmo), Kristina Copeland (Cast), Paul Cruz, Michelle Elkin (Cast), Tim Fournier (Cast), Scott Hislop (Cast), Laurie Kanyok (Cast), Vicky Lambert (Dancer), Joey Mazzarino (King Fred [voice]), James McKnight (Suitor), Jerry Nelson (Count von Count/Mr. Johnson [voice]), Frank Oz (Bert/Grover/Cookie Monster [voice]), Martin P. Robinson (Telly Monster/Aloysius "Snuffy" Snuffleupagus [voice]), David Rudman (Baby Bear [voice]), James Tortora (Suitor), Barry Wernick (Suitor), Steve Whitmire (Ernie/Kermit the Frog/Prince the Dog [voice]).

Elmo stars in this remake of the Cinderella story that uses human actors and Sesame Street characters, including Count von Count.

Cineastes contra magnats (*Filmari proti magnátum* [Czech Republic]; *Filmmakers vs. Tycoons* [International]); Spain, 2005; Documentary; 97 minutes/color/Spanish/Dolby Digital; Kilimanjaro Productions.

Writing Credits: Ferrán Alberich, Carlos Benpar; *Director*: Carlos Benpar; *Cinematography*: Xavier Camí, Tomàs Pladevall; *Film Editing*: Manu de la Reina; *Original Music*: Xavier Oro, Pep Solórzano; *Cast*: Marta Belmonte (Marta), Woody Allen (Himself), Marco Bellocchio (Himself), Jack Cardiff (Himself), Henning Carlsen (Himself), Manuel De Sica (Himself), Jesús Ángel Domínguez (Bufó), Stanley Donen (Himself), Federico Fellini (Himself [archive footage]), Richard Fleischer (Himself), Milos Forman (Himself), Luis García Berlanga (Himself), Adoor Gopalakrishnan (Himself), John Huston (Himself [archive footage]), Víctor Jerez (Caballer), Burt Lancaster (Himself [archive footage]), Santiago Lapeira (Projeccionista), Daniel Medrán (Navarrete), Robert Ellis

Miller (Himself), Giuliano Montaldo (Himself), Maurizio Nichetti (Himself), José María Nunes (Himself), Arthur Penn (Himself), Sydney Pollack (Himself), Antonio Regueiro (Felipe II [as Toni Regueiro]), Elliot Silverstein (Himself), Vilgot Sjöman (Himself), Enric Suñol (Acomodador), Liv Ullmann (Herself), Tunet Vila (Fraile), Fred Zinnemann (Himself [archive footage]), Roscoe "Fatty" Arbuckle (archive footage, uncredited), John Barrymore (Svengali [in "Svengali," archive footage] uncredited), Humphrey Bogart (Sam Spade [in "The Maltese Falcon," archive footage] uncredited), Marlon Brando (archive footage [uncredited]), Yul Brynner (Himself [archive footage] uncredited), Gary Cooper (Link Jones [in "Man of the West," uncredited, archive footage]), Joseph Cotten (Holly Martins [in "The Third Man," archive footage, uncredited]), Tony Curtis (Albert DeSalvo [in "The Boston Strangler," archive footage, uncredited]), James Dean (Jim Stark [in "Rebel Without a Cause," archive footage, uncredited]), Vittorio De Sica (Himself [archive footage, uncredited]), Kirk Douglas (Einar [in "The Vikings," archive footage, uncredited]), Cary Grant (Peter Joshua [in "Charade," archive footage, uncredited]), Sterling Hayden (Johnny "Guitar" Logan [in "Johnny Guitar," archive footage, uncredited]), Audrey Hepburn (Regina "Reggie" Lampert [in "Charade," archive footage, uncredited]), Rock Hudson (Burke Devlin [in "The Tarnished Angels," archive footage, uncredited]), José Isbert (Don Pablo, el alcalde [in "Bienvenido Mr. Marshall," archive footage, uncredited]), Buster Keaton (archive footage [uncredited]), Caterina Sylos Labini (Maria Piermattei [in "Ladri di saponette" [archive footage] [uncredited]), Christopher Lee (Dracula [archive footage], [uncredited]), Janet Leigh (Morgana [in "The Vikings" [archive footage] [uncredited]), Julie London (Billie Ellis [in "Man of the West" [archive footage] [uncredited]), Béla Lugosi (Dracula [archive footage] [uncredited]), Dorothy Malone (LaVerne Schumann [in "The Tarnished Angels" [archive footage] [uncredited]), Marian Marsh (Trilby O'Farrell [in "Svengali" [archive footage] [uncredited]), Groucho Marx (archive footage [uncredited]), Toshirô Mifune (archive footage [uncredited]), Peter O'Toole (T.E. Lawrence [in "Lawrence of Arabia" [archive footage] [uncredited]), Gregory Peck (Harry Street [in "The Snows of Kilimanjaro" [archive footage] [uncredited]), Anthony Perkins (Josef K. [in "Le Procès" [archive footage] [uncredited]), Francisco Rabal (archive footage [uncredited]), Paul Richter (Siegfried [in "Die Nibelungen: Siegfried" [archive footage] [uncredited]), Edward G. Robinson (archive footage [uncredited]), Romy Schneider (Leni [in "Le Procès" [archive footage] [uncredited]), Max Schreck (Graf Orlok [in "Nosferatu" [archive footage] [uncredited]), Omar Sharif (Sherif Ali [in "Lawrence of Arabia" [archive footage] [uncredited]), Robert Stack (Roger Schumann [in "The Tarnished Angels" [archive footage] [uncredited]), Enzo Staiola (Bruno [in "Il Ladri di biciclette" [archive footage] [uncredited]), James Stewart (archive footage [uncredited]), King Vidor (Himself [archive footage] [uncredited]), Erich von Stroheim (archive footage [uncredited]), Raoul Walsh (Himself [archive footage] [uncredited]), Orson Welles (Himself [archive footage] [uncredited]), Darryl F. Zanuck (Himself [archive footage] [uncredited]).

Cities of the Underworld (TV Series 2007–Current), episode "Dracula's Underground"; U.S., Season 1, Episode 10, 9 July 2007; Documentary, Television; 50 minutes/color/English; Authentic Entertainment, Thirty Four Productions (in association with), Scorekeepers Music.

Producers: Lauren Lexton, Tom Rogan; *Writing Credits*: Sean Dash; *Cinematography*: Anne Etheridge; *Film Editing*: Emre Sahin, Cary Lin; *Original Music*: Adam Small; *Cast*: Don Wildman (Host [as himself]), Eric Geller.

The History Channel explores underground worlds in some of the most popular and historic cities, and in this particular episode, the alleged home of Vlad the Impaler.

Close-Up (TV Series [1994–2007]), episode "Béla Lugosi: Dracula's Dubbelganger"; Netherlands/Germany/Belgium, 16 December 2007; Documentary; 57 minutes/color/Dutch/Stereo; AVRO Television, Belgische Radio en Televisie (BRT), Zweites Deutsches Fernsehen (ZDF).

Producers: Joke Beemer, Rachèl van Gelder; *Director*: Florin Leapin; *Cinematography*: Rafael Vasilcin; *Film Editing*: Wolfgang Cehmann; *Cast*: Peter Muller (Himself), Dorothy West (Herself [archive footage]), Gary Don Rhodes (Himself [as Gary D. Rhoades]), István Szabó (Himself), Elisabeth Alder (Herself [archive footage]), Otilia Hedesan (Herself), Helen Richman (Herself), Béla Lugosi Jr. (Himself), Bud Abbott (Himself [archive footage]), Lon Chaney (Himself [archive footage]), Cary Grant (Himself [archive footage]), Adolf Hitler (Himself [archive footage]), J. Edgar Hoover (Himself [archive footage]), Eric Johnston (Himself [archive footage]), Boris Karloff (Himself/The Monster/Various [archive footage]), Béla Lugosi (Himself/Dracula/Ygor/Various [archive footage]), Ervin Nyiregyhazi (Himself [archive footage]), Ronald Reagan (Himself [archive footage]), J. Parnell Thomas (Himself [archive footage]), Edward D. Wood Jr. (Himself/Glen/Glenda [segment "Glen or Glenda"] [archive footage]).

Codename: Kids Next Door (TV Series [2002–2008]), episode "Operation S.P.A.N.K."; U.S., Season 2, Episode 2, 10 October 2003; Action, Adventure, Family/Television, Animation; 30 minutes/color/English/Stereo; Curious Pictures.

Producers: Tom Warburton, Richard Winkler, Bruce Knapp; *Writing Credits*: Tom Warburton, Mo Willems; *Director*: Tom Warburton; *Original Music*: Thomas Chase, Steve Rucker; *Cast*: Dee Bradley Baker (Numbuh 4/Mr. Fibb/Delightful Children From Down the Lane [voice]), Grey DeLisle (Lizzie Devine [voice]), Ben Diskin (Numbuh 1/Numbuh 2/Carlos/Delightful Children From Down the Lane [voice]), Tom Kenny (Mr. Wink/Carlos' Dad [voice]), Daran Norris (Count Spankulot/Judge [voice]), Cree Summer (Numbuh 5/Delightful Children from Down the Lane/Carlos' Mom [voice]), Lauren (Tom Numbuh 3/Judge's Wife [voice]).

Count Spankulot was in jail for spanking the wrong child, but now that he is out, he wants to help kids. He wants to join up with the Kids Next Door, but not all of them want him there.

The Comic Strip (TV Series), segment, "The Mini-Monsters"; U.S., 1987; Family, Comedy/Television, Animation; Rankin/Bass Productions.

Producers: Jules Bass, Lee Dannacher, Arthur Rankin Jr.; *Writing Credits*: J. Larry Carroll, Julian P. Gardner, Peter Lawrence, Matthew Malach, Romeo Muller, Chris Trengrove; *Original Music*: Bernard Hoffer; *Cast*: Donald Acree (voice), Josh Blake (voice), Camille Bonora (voice), Gary V. Brown (voice), Jim Brownnold (voice), Carmen De Lavallade (voice), Danielle DuClos (voice), Seth Green (voice), Earl Hammond (voice), Larry Kenney (voice), Bob McFadden (voice), Jim Meskimen (voice), Peter Newman (voice), Gordy Owens (voice), Gerrian Raphael (voice), Ron Taylor (voice), Maggie Wheeler (voice as Maggie Jakobson), Tanya Willoughby (voice), Daniel Wooten (voice).

This two-hour series ran as a marathon with four first-run cartoons in a single episodic adventure each week. The four shows included: "The Karate Kat," "The Mini-Monsters," "The Street Frogs" and "The Tigersharks."

El Conde Drácula (*Count Dracula* [U.K./U.S.]; *Nachts, wenn Dracula erwacht* [West Germany]; *Bram Stoker's Count Dracula* [undefined]; *Conde Drácula* [Brazil]; *Conte Dracula, Il* [Italy]; *Demone nero, Il* [Italy]; *Dracula 71* [undefined]; *Komis Drakoulas xanahtypa, O* [Greece, reissue title]; *Komis Drakoulas, O* [Greece]; *Nuits de Dracula, Les* [France]; *Nights of Dracula, The* [undefined]; *Verenhimoinen Dracula* [Finland]); Spain/West Germany/Italy/Liechtenstein, 1970; Drama, Horror; 98 minutes/color/English/mono/35mm; Corona Filmproduktion, Filmar Compagnia Cinematogra-

Poster art for *El Conde Drácula* (Spain/West Germany/Italy/Liechtenstein, 1970).

fica, Fénix Cooperativa Cinematográfica, Towers of London, Etablissement Sargon, Korona Film, Towers Productions.

Producers: Arturo Marcos, Harry Alan Towers; *Writing Credits*: Bram Stoker, Dietmar Behnke, Milo G. Cuccia, Carlo Fadda, Augusto Finocchi, Jesus Franco (as Jesús Franco), Erich Kröhnke, Harry Alan Towers (as Peter Welbeck); *Director*: Jesus Franco (as Jesús Franco); *Cinematography*: Manuel Merino, Luciano Trasatti; *Film Editing*: Bruno Mattei, Derek Parsons; *Original Music*: Bruno Nicolai; *Make-Up*: Gerry Fletcher, José Luis Vázquez, Ricardo Vázquez; *Special Effects*: Sergio Pagoni; *Cast*: Christopher Lee (Count Dracula), Herbert Lom (Prof. Abraham Van Helsing), Klaus Kinski (R.M. Renfield), Soledad Miranda (Lucy Westenra), Maria Rohm (Mina Murray), Fred Williams (Jonathan Harker), Paul Muller (Dr. John Seward [as Paul Müller]), Jack Taylor (Quincey Morris), Jesús Puente (Minister of Interior), José Martínez Blanco (Traveller/Dr. Seward [voice: Spanish version] [as J. Martinez Blanco]), Emma Cohen (Vampire woman [uncredited]), Jesus Franco (Van Helsing's servant [uncredited]), Colette Giacobine (Greta, housekeeper [uncredited]), Teresa Gimpera (Crying mother [uncredited]), Jeannine Mestre (Vampire woman [uncredited]), Moisés Augusto Rocha (Servant behind Prof. Van Helsing in Wheelchair [uncredited]).

In this Jess Franco retelling of Bram Stoker's classic novel, Count Dracula is an old man who dines on the blood of young maidens to grow younger.

The Conde Mácula (*Mortadelo y Filemón, agencia de información: El conde Mácula* [Spain] [series title]); Spain, 1971; Comedy/Short, Animation; 17 minutes/Spanish/color/Mono; Estudios Vara.

Director: Rafael Vara.

Mortadelo and Filemón know a scientist with a machine that can alert them to Conde Macula's activity. When it shows Conde Macula emerging from his coffin, they then use the same machine to teleport themselves to Conde Macula's castle to investigate.

Count Dracula (*Great Performances: Count Dracula* [U.S.]; *Conde Dracula, El* [Venezuela]; U.K., 1977; Horror/Television; 150 minutes/color/English/Mono; British Broadcasting Corporation (BBC).

Producer: Morris Barry; *Writing Credits*: Gerald Savory (adaptation), Bram Stoker (novel); *Director*: Philip Saville; *Cinematography*: Peter Hall; *Film Editing*: Richard Bedford; *Original Music*: Kenyon Emrys-Roberts; *Make-Up*: Suzan Broad; *Cast*: Louis Jourdan (Count Dracula), Frank Finlay (Abraham van Helsing), Susan Penhaligon (Lucy Westenra), Judi Bowker (Wilhelmina "Mina"

Louis Jourdan plays Dracula opposite Susan Penhaligon as Lucy in the BBC's *Count Dracula* (U.K., 1977) (courtesy John Edgar Browning).

Westenra), Jack Shepherd (Renfield), Mark Burns (Dr. John Seward), Bosco Hogan (Jonathan Harker), Richard Barnes (Quincey P. Holmwood), Ann Queensberry (Mrs. Westenra), George Raistrick (Bowles), George Malpas (Swales), Michael Macowan (Mr. Hawkins), Susie Hickford (Dracula's Bride), Belinda Meuldijk (Dracula's Bride), Sue Vanner (Dracula's Bride), Bruce Wightman (Coach Passenger), Izabella Telezynska (Coach Passenger), O.T. (Coach Passenger).

This television adaptation follows closely the plotline of Bram Stoker's classic novel. In preparation to move to England, Jonathan Harker visits the Count in Transylvania. The Count becomes enchanted by a photo of Harker's fiancée and sister. The Count imprisons Harker, and moves to London to sets his sights on these two beautiful young. Dr. Van Helsing is the only person that can try to save these women from Dracula's horrible curse of immortality.

Count Dracula, The True Story; Canada, 1979; Documentary.

Director: Yurek Filjalkoski.

Filmed in Romania, this documentary examines Vlad Tepes ("the Impaler"). To date, no copies have been sold.

Count Duckula (TV Series) (*Comte Mordicus* [France]; *Conte Dacula* [Italy]; *Count Duckula* [Greece]; *El conde Pátula* [Argentina]; *Graaf Duckula* [Netherlands]; *Graf Duckula* [West Germany]; *Kreivi Duckula* [Finland]); U.K., 1988–1993; Comedy, Family, Horror/Television, Animation; 22 minutes/color/English; Cosgrove Hall Films (as Cosgrove Hall Productions), Nickelodeon Network, Thames Television.

Producers: Brian Cosgrove (15 episodes, 1988–1989), Mark Hall (15 episodes, 1988–1989), John Hambley (15 episodes, 1988–1989), Chris Randall (15 episodes, 1988–1989); *Writing Credits*: Jimmy Hibbert (36 episodes, 1988–1993), Peter Richard Reeves (15 episodes, 1988–1990), Brian Trueman (11 episodes, 1988–1993), Chris Randall (4 episodes, 1988), Jan Needle (2 episodes, 1989–1993); *Director*: Chris Randall; *Film Editing*: Zyggy Markiewicz (9 episodes, 1988–1989), Patrick Haggerty (5 episodes, 1988), Eilis Ward (2 episodes, 1988–1989); *Original Music*: Mike Harding; *Art Direction*: Vincent James (designer/storyboard artist [16 episodes, 1988–1993]), Chris Randall (designer/storyboard artist [16 episodes, 1988–1993]), Margaret Riley (designer [16 episodes, 1988–1993]), Paul Salmon (designer/storyboard artist [16 episodes, 1988–1993]), Dan Whitworth (designer [16 episodes, 1988–1993]), Edmund Williams (designer [16 episodes, 1988–1993]), John Stevenson (storyboard artist [13 episodes, 1988–1991]), Andy Roper (designer/storyboard artist [3 episodes, 1988–1993]), Ben Turner (storyboard artist [2 episodes, 1988]); *Special Effects*: Carlos Alfonso (special effects [13 episodes, 1988]), Garry Owen (special effects [2 episodes, 1988–1989]), Murti Schofield (special effects [2 episodes, 1988–1989]); *Cast*: Jack May (Igor [35 episodes, 1988–1993]), Brian Trueman (Nanny [35 episodes, 1988–1993]), Jimmy Hibbert (Sviatoslav [35 episodes, 1988–1993]), David Jason (Count Duckula [34 episodes, 1988–1993]), Barry Clayton (Narrator [34 episodes, 1988–1993])

Count Duckula is a vegetarian vampire duck who lives in a castle that can go anywhere the Count pleases. He lives with Nanny, and Igor, his butler. A vampire hunter follows Duckula around with a gun loaded with wooden stakes.

The Count of Calle Ocho (*The Count of Little Havana* [working title]; *The Count* [U.S., new title]); U.S., 2010; Horror, Comedy, Family, Romance; color/English.

Producer: Charles Cotayo; *Writing Credits*: Charles Cotayo; *Director*: Charles Cotayo

This film is a satire on the vampire mythology. Two Cuban-American sisters rent a spare bedroom in their broken down old house to "the Count." Things become complicated upon the arrival of their run-away-nun sister, who has been homeless, and the antagonist, an evil wizard accompanied by an apprentice.

Count Yorga, Vampire (*Junges Blut für Dracula* [Austria/West Germany]; *Comte Iorga, el vampir* [Spain: Catalan title]; *Conde Yorga, Vampiro* [Brazil]; *Conde Yorga, vampiro* [Spain]; *Teufelsausrottung* [West Germany]; *The Loves of Count Iorga, Vampire* [U.S.]; *Vampyrernas blodiga borg* [Sweden]; *Vampyyrikreivin haaremi* [Finland: TV title]; *Vrykolakas, o satanas tou Skotous* [Greece]; *Wampir — hrabia Yorga* [Poland]; *Yorga il vampiro* [Italy]; *Yorga, o vrykolakas* [Greece: reissue title]); U.S., 1970; Drama, Horror, Romance; 90 minutes/color/English/Mono; Erica Productions Inc.

Producers: Bob Kelljan, Michael Macready; *Writing Credits*: Bob Kelljan; *Director*: Bob Kelljan; *Cinematography*: Arch Archambault; *Film Editing*: Tony de Zarraga (as Tony de Zárraga); *Original Music*: Bill Marx (as William Marx); *Make-Up*: Master Dentalsmith, Mark Rogers; *Special Effects*: James M. Tanenbaum (special effects [as James Tanenbaum]); *Cast*: Robert Quarry (Count Yorga/Dracula), Roger Perry (Dr. James "Jim" Hayes), Michael Murphy (Paul), Michael Macready (Michael "Mike" Thompson), D.J. Anderson (Donna) (as Donna Anders), Judy Lang (Erica Landers) (as Judith Lang), Edward Walsh (Brudah), Julie Conners (Cleo), Paul Hansen (Peter), Sybil

Scotford (Judy), Marsha Jordan (Donna's mother), Deborah Darnell (Vampire woman), Erica Macready (Babette, the nurse), George Macready (Narrator) (voice), Stella Thomas (Vampire woman) (uncredited).

After losing his girlfriend, Count Yorga (Robert Quarry) holds a séance to speak with her. After the séance, one of the couples who was present, Paul (Michael Murphy) and Erica (Judy Lang), get attacked and Erica is found to have lost a lot of blood. Erica becomes a vampiress and stalks the streets of Los Angeles with Yorga.

Countess Dracula (*Comtesse Dracula* [France]); U.K., 1971; Drama, Horror; 93 minutes/color/English/Mono/35 mm; Hammer Film Productions, The Rank Organization.

Producer: Alexander Paal; *Writing Credits*: Jeremy Paul, Alexander Paal, Peter Sasdy, Gabriel Ronap, Valentine Penrose (uncredited); *Director*: Peter Sasdy (director), Ariel Levy (assistant director); *Cinematography*: Kenneth Talbot; *Film Editing*: Henry Richardson; *Original Music*: Harry Robertson; *Make-Up*: Tom Smith; *Special Effects*: Bert Luxford; *Cast*: Ingrid Pitt (Countess Elisabeth Nodosheen), Nigel Green (Captain Dobi the Castle Steward), Sandor Elès (Lt. Imre Toth), Maurice Denham (Master Fabio, [Castle Historian]), Patience Collier (Julie Sentash, the Nurse), Peter Jeffrey (Captain Balogh — Chief Bailiff), Lesley-Anne Down (Ilona Nodosheen, Elisabeth's Daughter), Leon Lissek (Sergeant of Bailiffs), Jessie Evans (Rosa, Teri's Mother), Andrea Lawrence (Ziza, Shepherd's Inn Whore), Susan Brodrick (Teri the Countess Chambermaid), Ian Trigger (Clown at the Sheperd's Inn), Nike Arrighi (Fortune Telling Gypsy Girl), Peter May (Janco the Mute Gamekeeper), John Moore (Priest), Joan Haythorne (Second Cook), Marianne Stone (Kitchen Maid), Charles Farrell (The Seller), Sally Adcock (Bertha the Goat Girl), Anne Stallybrass (Pregnant Woman), Paddy Ryan (Man), Michael Cadman (Young Man), Hülya Babus (Belly Dancer at the Shepherd's Inn), Lesley Anderson (Gypsy Dancer with Circus), Biddy Hearne (Gypsy Dancer with Circus), Diana Sawday (Gypsy Dancer with Cir-

Poster for *Countess Dracula* (UK, 1971).

cus), Andrew Burleigh (1st Boy finding the Fortune Teller's Body), Gary Rich (2nd Boy finding the Fortune Teller's Body), Albert Wilkinson (Circus Midget), Ismed Hassan (Circus Midget).

After Count Nodosheen dies, the aging Countess Elisabeth (Ingrid Pitt) harshly rules in medieval Europe with the help of her lover Captain Dobi (Nigel Green). She somehow finds out that bathing in the blood of young virgin girls makes her become young again. She orders Dobi to begin abducting likely candidates. After becoming younger, the Countess, pretending to be her own daughter, starts dallying with Lt. Imre Toth (Sandor Elès), a younger man, much to Dobi's annoyance.

The Creeps; U.S., 1997; Comedy, Science Fiction, Horror; 80 minutes/color/English/Mono/35mm; Full Moon Pictures.
Producers: Charles Band, Kirk Edward Hansen; *Writing Credits*: Benjamin Carr; *Director*: Charles Band; *Cinematography*: Adolfo Bartoli; *Film Editing*: Steven Nielson; *Original Music*: Carl Dante; *Art Direction*: Joel Weber; *Make-Up*: Gabriel Bartalos; *Cast*: Rhonda Griffin (Anna Quarrels), Justin Lauer (David Raleigh), Bill Moynihan (Winston Berber), Kristin Norton (Miss Christina), Jon Simanton (Wolfman), Joe Smith (Mummy), Thomas Wellington (Frankenstein's Monster), Phil Fondacaro (Dracula), J.W. Perra (Video Store Customer), Andrea Harper (Stella, Video Store Clerk [as Andrea Squibb]).

A horror-obsessed scientist tries to recreate his favorite characters, including Dracula, Frankenstein, and The Mummy, but the problem is that he has created them too small. The creatures are all about three feet, and are out to regain their size.

Cuadecuc, vampir (*Vampir* [undefined]); Spain, 1970; Horror/Documentary; 67 minutes/black and white/English/mono; Films 59, Pere Portabella.
Writing Credits: Joan Brossa (idea), Pere Portabella (idea); *Director*: Pere Portabella; *Cinematography*: Manuel Esteban; *Film Editing*: Miguel Bonastre; *Original Music*: Carles Santos; *Cast*: Christopher Lee (Himself), Herbert Lom (Himself), Soledad Miranda (Herself), Jack Taylor (Himself); Emma Cohen (Herself [uncredited]), Jesus Franco (Himself [uncredited]), Paul Muller (Himself [uncredited]), Maria Rohm (Herself [uncredited]), Fred Williams (Himself [uncredited]).

Essentially an abridged version of *Count Dracula*, this documentary uses behind-the-scenes footage to show how the original movie was made. It shows all the characters from *Count Dracula* as themselves, getting their make-up put on, and shooting their scenes.

The Curse of Dracula (TV Series) (*Cliffhangers: The Curse of Dracula* [U.S., alternative title]; *Dracula '79* [U.S., alternative title]; *The Loves of Dracula* [U.S., recut version]; *The World of Dracula* [U.S., alternative title]); U.S., 1979; Horror, Thriller/Television; 20 minutes/color/English/Mono; Universal TV.
Producers: Kenneth Johnson, Richard Milton, Laura R. Rokowitz, Paul Samuelson, B.W. Sandefur, Dean Zanetos; *Writing Credits*: Myla Lichtman (episode "Demons of the Dark") (episode "Pleas of the Damned") (episode "Sealed in Blood") (episode "Sepulcher of the Undead"); *Director*: Jeffrey Hayden, Richard Milton, Sutton Roley, Kenneth Johnson; *Cinematography*: Mario DeLio, Robert F. Liu; *Film Editing*: Gene Palmer, Lawrence J. Vallario, Edward W. Williams; *Original Music*: Les Baxter, C.R. Cassey, Joseph Harnell; *Art Direction*: Gary A. Lee; *Make-Up*: Jim Gillespe (makeup artist and designer); *Special Effects*: Wayne Rose; *Cast*: Michael Nouri (Count Dracula), Stephen Johnson (Kurt Von Helsing), Carol Baxter (Mary Gibbons), Antoinette Stella (Antoinette), Mark Montgomery (Darryl), Bever-Leigh Banfield (Christine), Louise Sorel (Amanda Gibbons), Joanne Strauss (Sister Theresa), Brad Crandall (uncredited)

Count Dracula is teaching night classes at South Bay College in southern California. He uses his position as professor to lure young, attractive college girls to him so he can bite them. All the while, the von Helsing family is hot on his trail.

Cyberchase (TV Series [2002–Present]), episode "Castleblanca"; Canada, U.S., Season 1, Episode 2, 23 January 2002; Comedy, Family, Mystery, Science Fiction/Television, Animation; 30 minutes/color/English; Nelvana.
Producer: Arash Hoda; *Writing Credits*: George Arthur Bloom, Dan Elish; *Director*: Larry Jacobs; *Original Music*: David W. Shaw; *Cast*: Christopher Lloyd (The Hacker), Gilbert Gottfried (Digit), Jacqueline Pillon (Matt), Bianca Marie DeGroat (Bianca), Novie Edwards (Jackie), Erin Fitch (Wendy), Annick Obonsawin (Inez).

Three kids travel to the creepy country of Castleblanca in a quest to rescue the important cyberscientist Dr. Marbles. Before "The Hacker" can transfer his brain into a diabolical robot and take over Cyberspace, the three kids must use data collection and data graphing to figure out which creepy castle in which Dr. Marbles is being held captive.

Danny Phantom (TV Series [2004–2007]), episode "Material Instinct"; U.S., Season 1, Episode 17, 18 February 2005; Action, Adventure, Family, Science Fiction/Television, Animation; 30 minutes/color/English/Stereo; Billionfold.

Producers: Deirdre Brenner, Butch Hartman, Steve Marmel, Bob Boyle, George Goodchild; *Writing Credits*: Butch Hartmon; *Director*: Butch Hartman, Wincat Alcala, Kevin Petrilak, Gary Conrad; *Film Editing*: Mark Banker; *Original Music*: Guy Moon; *Art Direction*: Stephen Silver, Shannon Tindle; *Cast*: David Kaufman (Danny Fenton/Danny Phantom), Martin Mull (Vlad Masters/Vlad Plasmius).

Danny goes to a science conference in Florida, but this conference is organized by Vlad Masters (a Dracula-type character), who just so happens to be Danny's enemy. Vlad is trying to launch a ghost attack on Fenton Works.

Darakula; Philippines, 1982; Comedy, Horror; color/Filipino, Tagalog; Centercinema Entertainment.

Writing Credits: Angel Labra; *Director*: Angel Labra; *Cast*: Redford White (Darakula), Rodolfo "Boy" Garcia (Erpat), Alita San Diego, Juana Morena, Lito Anzures (Bully), Pugak (Wyatt Erap), Popoy (Hotel Waiter), Ruel Vernal (Porpirio), Juana Morena (Schwangere Patientin), Lynn Gomez (Mariachi Singer), Rita Rios (Herself), Gelyne del Rio (Outta Sight Singer #2), Claudia Zobel.

Dark Prince: The True Story of Dracula (*Dracula: The Dark Prince* [U.S., video title]; *Fürst der Finsternis—Die wahre Geschichte von Dracula* [Germany, video title]; *Dark Prince: Legend of Dracula* [U.K., video title]; *Passions of Dracula: A True Story* [U.S., working title]; *Drakoulas: I alithini istoria tou prigipa ton Karpathion* [Greece, DVD title]; *Pimeyden ruhtinas: Tositarina Draculasta* [Finland]; *Príncipe de las tinieblas—La verdadera historia de Drácula, El* [Venezuela]; *Printul noptii* [Romania]; *Vlad the Impaler* [U.S., working title]; U.S., 2000; Horror, Thriller/Television; 92 minutes/color/English/Dolby; The Kushner-Locke Company, Pueblo Productions.

Producers: Matt Earl Beesley, Teresa Garber, Avram "Butch" Kaplan, Donald Kushner, Peter Locke, Vlad Paunescu; *Writing Credits*: Thomas Baum; *Director*: Joe Chappelle; *Cinematography*: Dermott Downs; *Film Editing*: Joe Rabig; *Original Music*: Frankie Blue; *Art Direction*: Cristian Baluta; *Make-Up*: Vivian Baker (makeup department head), Daniela Busoiu, Letitia Ghenea (assistant makeup artist), Rachel Kick (key makeup artist); *Special Effects*: Lucian Iordache (special effects supervisor), Ionel Popa (special effects artist); *Cast*: Rudolf Martin (Vlad Dracula the Impaler), Jane March (Lidia), Christopher Brand (Bruno), Peter Weller (Father Stefan), Roger Daltrey (King Janos), Michael Sutton (Radu), Razvan Vasilescu (Aron), Radu Amzulescu (Inquisitor), Maia Morgenstern (Woman at Fountain), Claudiu Bleont (Sultan Mohamed), Claudiu Trandafir (Prince Karl), Dan Bordeianu (Vlad III — Age 18), Victor Ungureanu (Vlad III — Age 8), Dan Badarau (Vlad Dracula's Father), Sebastian Lupea (Teen Vlad Dracula), Niels Brinks (Teen Radu), Eugen Cristea (Andrei), Orodel Olanu (Orodel), Mircea Stoian (Bald Noble), Serban Celea (Turkish Emissary), George Grigore (Orthodox Priest), Laura Cret (Lady in Waiting), Roxana Marian (Maria), Marius Capota (Prince Karl's Soldier), Constantin Barbulescu (Sentry [uncredited]).

This film is based on the life of Vlad Dracula, an historical nobleman famous for his gruesome and merciless treatment of his enemies. The story, told as flashbacks during a hearing by Greek orthodox priests, is used to illustrate Dracula's colorful past while the priests decide whether or not to excommunicate him from the ruling church.

Dark Shadows (TV Series [1966–1971]) (*Shadows on the Wall* [U.S., working title]; *Sombras da Noite* [Brazil]; *The House on Storm Cliff* [U.S., working title]; *Yön vampyyrit* [Finland]); U.S., Season 2–5, 1967–1971; Horror, Drama/Television; 30 minutes/color, black and white/English/Mono, Stereo; Dan Curtis Productions.

Producer: Dan Curtis, Robert Costello, Peter Miner, Lela Swift, Sy Tomashoff, George DiCenzo; *Writing Credits*: Dan Curtis, Art Wallace, Gordon Russell, Sam Hall, Ron Sproat, Malcolm Marmorstein, Violet Welles, Joseph Caldwell, Francis Swann, Ralph Ellis; *Director*: Lela Swift, Henry Kaplan, John Sedwick, Sean Dhu Sullivan, Dan Curtis, Jack Sullivan, John Weaver, Pennberry Jones, Dennis Kane; *Original Music*: Bob Cobert; *Make-Up*: Vincent Loscalzo, Dennis Eger, Dick Smith; *Cast*: Jonathan Frid (Barnabas Collins), Grayson Hall (Dr. Julia Hoffman), Nancy Barrett (Carolyn Stoddard), Joan Bennett (Elizabeth Collins Stoddard), Alexandra Isles (Victoria Winters), Louis Edmonds (Roger Collins), Kathryn Leigh Scott (Maggie Evans), David Selby (Quentin Collins), David Henesy (David Collins), Lara Parker (Angelique), Thayer David (Professor Timothy Stokes), John Karlen (Willie Loomis), Joel Crothers (Joe Haskell), Roger Davis (Jeff Clark), Christopher Pennock (Cyrus Longworth), David Ford (Sam Evans), Jerry Lacy (Gregory Trask), Mitch Ryan (Burke Devlin), Humbert Allen Astredo (Nicholas

Blair), Don Briscoe (Chris Jennings), Clarice Blackburn (Mrs. Sarah Johnson), Jim Storm (Gerard Styles), Robert Rodan (Adam), Denise Nickerson (Amy Jennings), Kate Jackson (Daphne Harridge), Dennis Patrick (Jason McGuire), Diana Millay (Laura Collins), Terrayne Crawford (Beth Chavez), Marie Wallace (Megan Todd), Michael Stroka (Aristede), Bob O'Connell (Bartender Bob Rooney), Kathleen Cody (Hallie Stokes), Anthony George (Burke Devlin), Keith Prentice (Morgan Collins), Addison Powell (Dr. Eric Lang), Sharon Smyth (Ghost of Sarah), Dana Elcar (Sheriff George Patterson), Donna Wandrey (Roxanne Drew), Robert Gerringer (Dr. Dave Woodard), Virginia Vestoff (Samantha Drew Collins), Timothy Gordon (Ghost of Jeremiah), Lisa Blake Richards (Sabrina Stuart), John Lasell (Dr. Peter Guthrie), Donna McKechnie (Amanda Harris), Alex Stevens (The Werewolf), Christopher Bernau (Philip Todd), Conard Fowkes (Frank Garner), Craig Slocum (Harry Johnson), John Harkins (Horace Gladstone), Peter Murphy (Caretaker), Elizabeth Eis (Buffie Harrington), Frank Schofield (Bill Malloy), James Shannon (Thomas Findley), Geoffrey Scott (Sky Rumson), Tom Gorman (3rd Judge), Peter Turgeon (Dr. Dave Woodard), Michael McGuire (Judah Zachary), Betsy Durkin (Victoria Winters), Vince O'Brien (Sheriff George Patterson), Duane Morris (Monster), Lee Beery (Joanna Mills), Paul Kirk Giles (Judge), Daniel Keyes (Eagle Hill Cemetary Caretaker), Michael Maitland (Michael Hackett Todd), John Beal (Judge Vail), Ed Riley (Sheriff Davenport), Mark Allen (Sam Evans), Natalie Norwick (Edith in the coffin), Paula Laurence (Hannah Stokes), Hugh Franklin (Richard Garner), Dorrie Kavanaugh (Body in coffin in Maggie's dream), David Jay (Alexander Todd), Colin Hamilton (Inspector Hamilton), Jered Holmes (Ghost of Damion Edwards), Paul Michael (King Johnny Romano), James Hall (Willie Loomis), Leslie Barrett (Judge Hanley), Jane Draper (Suki Forbes), Isabella Hoopes (Edith Collins), Michael Currie (Sheriff Jonas Carter), Florence Stanley (Sobbing Josette), Norman Parker (Headless man), Tom Markus (Judge), Gene Lindsey (Randall Drew), Ken McEwen (Larry Chase), Mary Cooper (Josette DuPres Collins), Michael Hadge (Buzz Hackett), Conrad Bain (Mr. Wells, the clerk at the Collinsport Inn), Dan Morgan (Riggs), Alice Drummond (Nurse Jackson), Rosemary McNamara (Ghost of Josette), Marin Riley (Widow), Carol Crist (Susie), George McCoy (Blue Whale customer), Joy Nicholson (Widow), Charles Rush (Figure attacking Julia), Peter Lombard (Oberon), Henry Judd Baker (Istvan), Diana Davila (Julianka), Kay Frye (Pansy Faye), Gaye Edmond (Stella Young), Tom Happer (Jeremy Grimes), Cliff Cudney (John Hart), Liliane Sandor (Cloaked figure), Brian Sturdivant (Claude North), John Connell (Lt. Dan Riley), Cavada Humphrey (Janet Findley), Vala Clifton (Maude Browning), Anita Sharp-Bolster (Bathia Mapes), Abe Vigoda (Ezra Braithwaite), Dennis Johnson (Deputy Fred), John Baragrey (James Blair), Carolyn Groves (Victoria Winters), George Mitchell (Matthew Morgan), Colleen Kelly (Susie), Anthony

Jonathan Frid plays Barnabas Collins, a Dracula-type vampire, in the television series *Dark Shadows* (U.S., 1966–1971).

Goodstone (Bailiff), Bridget O'Donnell (Widow), Howard Honig (Gaoler), Hansford Rowe (Judge), Alexander Cort (Tate's creation), Deborah Loomis (Tessie Kincaid), Camila Ashland (Minnie DuVal), Emory Bass (Mr. Best), Don Crabtree (Sheriff), Chuck Morgan (Emory Pace), Martin Brent (the Rev. Johnson), David Hurst (Justin Collins), Elizabeth Wilson (Mrs. Hopewell), Joseph Julian (Wilber Strake), Angus Cairns (Sheriff George Patterson), Richard Woods (Dr. Dave Woodard), Erica Fitz (Leona Eltridge), Audrey Larkins (Crystal Cabot), Gail Strickland (Dorcas Trilling), Rebecca Shaw (Barmaid at the Eagle), Edward Marshall (Ezra Braithwaite), Ed Crowley (Policeman), Ted Beniades (Policeman), Fred Stewart (Dr. Reeves), Margo Head (Phylliss Wicke), Frances Helm (Nurse), Alfred Hinckley (Dr. Ian Reade), Betty Beaird (Ghost), Jacqueline Bertrand (Ghost), Harvey Keitel (Blue Whale customer), Fran Anthony (Julia in David's dream), House Jameson (Judge Crathorne), Katherine Quint (Blue Whale customer), David Groh (Ghost of One-Armed Man), Paul Craffey (Spectator), Scott Upright (Spectator), Ronald Dawson (Ed the Records Clerk), Kenneth McMillan (Bartender at the Eagle), Jim Hale (Executioner), Robin Lane (Haza), Jenny Egan (Hortense Smiley), Paul Geier (Amos Ross), Roger Hamilton (Constable Jim Ward), Marilyn Joseph (Lorna Bell), Joseph Mosca (Hanging man), Carl Nicholas (Judge), George Strus (Steve), Barbara Tracey (Figure holding a knife), Steve Calder (Executioner), Jordan Keen (Guard).

This intensely popular Gothic soap opera centers on the Collins family of Collinsport, Maine. The family's lavish estate, Collinwood, falls victim to enumerable supernatural circumstances, including an extended-stay visit from the family's "cousin from England," Barnabas Collins, a 175 year old Dracula-type vampire.

Dark Shadows (TV Series) (*Dark Shadows Revival* [U.S., video box title]; *La malédiction de Collinwood* [France]); U.S., 1991; Drama, Romance, Thriller, Horror/Television; 60 minutes/color/English/Stereo; Dan Curtis Productions, MGM Television.

Producers: Steve Feke, Bill Blunden, Jon Boorstin, Dan Curtis, William Gray, Armand Mastroianni; *Writing Credits*: Dan Curtis, Steve Feke, Hall Powell, Bill Taub, Jon Boorstin, Matthew Hall, Sam Hall; *Director*: Armand Mastroianni, Dan Curtis, Matthew Hall, Mark Sobel; *Cinematography*: Dietrich Lohmann, Chuy Elizondo; *Film Editing*: Bill Blunden, Stephen Butler, Terry Williams; *Original Music*: Bob Cobert; *Make-Up*: David Dittma, Jene Fielder, John Goodwin, Jack Petty; *Special Effects*: Greg Curtis, Michael Meinardus; *Cast*: Ben Cross (Barnabas Collins), Joanna Going (Victoria Winters), Joseph Gordon-Levitt (David Collins), Jim Fyfe (Willie Loomis), Roy Thinnes (Roger Collins), Barbara Steele (Dr. Julia Hoffman), Barbara Blackburn (Carolyn Stoddard), Jean Simmons (Elizabeth Collins Stoddard), Veronica Lauren (Sarah Collins), Julianna McCarthy (Mrs. Johnson), Michael T. Weiss (Joe Haskell), Stefan Gierasch (Joshua Collins), Michael Cavanaugh (Sheriff George Patterson), Ely Pouget (Maggie Evans), Lysette Anthony (Angelíque), Eddie Jones (Bailiff Henry Evans), Ellen Wheeler (Phyllis Wicke), Steve Fletcher (Deputy Jonathan Harker), Rebecca Staab (Daphne Collins), Adrian Paul (Jeremiah Collins), Wayne Tippit (Dr. Hiram Fisher), Apollo Dukakis (the Reverend Amos), Brendan Dillon (Judge Isiah Braithwaite).

A revival of the popular soap opera, this television series begins with Victoria Winters, who arrives at Collinsport, Maine, an isolated costal town where, in the great Collinwood mansion, she will work as a governess for the Collins family. Soon, however, she finds herself involved in a string of unnatural occurrences filled with vampires, ghosts, and a centuries-old curse that still haunts the Collins family. Most of all, she will meet Barnabas Collins, a Dracula-type vampire who has survived the last two centuries.

Dark Shadows: Behind the Scenes (*Dark Shadows Revival [U.S.]*); U.S., 1991; Horror/Documentary; 60 minutes/English/color; Dan Curtis Productions.

Producers: Jim Pierson; *Writing Credits*: Sam Hall, Gordon Russell; *Director*: Dan Curtis; *Original Music*: Bob Cobert; *Make-Up*: Don Semmens; *Cast*: Jonathan Frid (Himself/Barnabas Collins), Nancy Barrett (Herself/Carolyn), Joan Bennett (Herself), Clarice Blackburn (Herself/Mrs. Johnson), Don Briscoe (Chris Jennings [archive footage]), Terrayne Crawford (Herself), Joel Crothers (Joe Haskell [archive footage]), Thayer David (Professor Stokes [archive footage]), Roger Davis (Himself), Louis Edmonds (Himself/Roger Collins), Grayson Hall (Herself/Julia Hoffman [archive footage]), David Henesy (David Collins [archive footage]), Alexandra Isles (Herself/Victoria Winters), Kate Jackson (Herself/Daphney), John Karlen (Himself/Willie Loomis), Jerry Lacy (Himself/the Reverend Trask), Donna McKechnie (Herself), Diana Millay (Herself), Denise Nickerson (Amy Jennings [archive footage]), Lara Parker (Herself/Angelique), Dennis Patrick (Himself), Christopher Pennock (Himself), Lisa Blake Richards (Herself), Robert Rodan (Himself/Adam), Jane Rose (Mrs. Mitchell [archive footage]), Mitch Ryan (Himself), Kathryn Leigh Scott (Herself/Maggie), David Selby

(Himself/Quentin Collins), Sharon Smyth (Herself/Sarah Collins), Jim Storm (Himself), Michael Stroka (Himself), Lela Swift (Herself), Marie Wallace (Herself/Eve), Donna Wandrey (Herself).

Focused on the *Dark Shadows* soap opera's short-lived 1991 revival, which featured vampires as well as other supernatural entities, this collection includes behind-the-scenes footage from the revival series.

Dark Shadows: Bloopers; U.S., 1993; Documentary; 45 minutes/English/color, black and white; MPI Home Video.; *Cast*: Jonathan Frid (Barnabas Collins [archive footage]), Joan Bennett (Elizabeth [archive footage]), Grayson Hall (Julia Hoffman [archive footage]), Nancy Barrett (Carolyn Stoddard [archive footage]), David Henesy (David Collins [archive footage]), Alexandra Isles (Victoria Winters [archive footage]), Lara Parker (Angelique [archive footage]), David Selby (Quentin Collins [archive footage]).

Focused on the *Dark Shadows* soap opera, which featured vampire Barnabus Collins, this collection is a series of outtakes, missed lines, and other bloopers from the original series.

Dark Shadows 1840 Flashback; U.S., 1967; Horror/Television; 52 minutes/English/color; Dan Curtis Productions.

Producers: Jim Pierson; *Writing Credits*: Sam Hall, Gordon Russell; *Director*: Dan Curtis *Original Music*: Bob Cobert *Make-Up*: Don Semmens; *Cast*: Jonathan Frid (Barnabas Collins), Lara Parker (Angelique), Grayson Hall (Julia Hoffman), Nancy Barrett (Carolyn), Louis Edmonds (Roger Collins), Christopher Pennock (Cyrus Longworth), Michael Stroka (Aristide), Michael McGuire (Judah Zachary).

A condensed compilation of some of the 1840s episodes from the *Dark Shadows* soap opera, this film features vampire Barnabus Collins, who travels back to the middle of the 19th century to stop an evil plot.

Dark Shadows: Music Videos; U.S., 1991; Documentary; 40 minutes/English/color, black and white/HiFi Sound; MPI Home Video.

Directors: Paul Lynch, Rob Bowman, Dan Curtis, Matthew Hall, Mark Sobel; *Original Music*: Bob Cobert; *Cast*: Jonathan Frid (Barnabas Collins [archive footage]), David Selby (Quentin Collins [archive footage]).

Focused on the *Dark Shadows* soap opera, which featured vampire Barnabus Collins, this collection highlights the original music composed for the show, and is interspersed with scenes from the original series.

Dark Shadows Resurrected: The Video; U.S., 1997; Documentary; minutes/English/color; MPI Home Video.

Cast: Dan Curtis (Himself).

Following in the wake of the series revival of the *Dark Shadows* soap opera, which featured vampires as well as other supernatural entities, this documentary includes interviews with the cast as well as creator Dan Curtis, behind-the-scenes footage, original promotional films, outtakes, and bloopers.

Dark Shadows' Scariest Moments; U.S., 1991; Documentary; 41 minutes/English/color, black and white.

Producers: Dan Curtis; *Writing Credits*: Dan Curtis; *Cast*: Jonathan Frid (Barnabas Collins), Lara Parker (Angelique DuPres), Nancy Barrett (Carolyn Stoddard), Joan Bennett (Elizabeth Collins Stoddard), Grayson Hall (Julia Hoffman), Alexandra Isles (Victoria Winters).

This documentary is a compilation of the most frightening moments from the original *Dark Shadows* soap opera, which featured vampire Barnabas Collins.

Dark Shadows: 30th Anniversary Tribute; U.S., 1996; Documentary; 60 minutes/color, black and white/English; MPI Home Video.

Producers: David Del Valle, Barbara Steele; *Original Music*: Bob Cobert; *Cast*: Jonathan Frid (Himself [Barnabas Collins]), David Selby (Himself [Quentin Collins]), Lara Parker (Herself [Angelique DuPr'es]), Louis Edmonds (Himself [Roger Collins]), Kathryn Leigh Scott (Herself [Maggie Evans/Josette DuPres]), John Karlen (Himself [Willie Loomis]), Kate Jackson (Herself), Dennis Patrick (Himself [Jason MacGuire]), Marie Wallace (Herself), Michael Stroka (Himself [Aristide]), Diana Millay (Herself [The Phoenix]), Mitch Ryan (Himself), Chris Pennock (Himself [Leviathan]), Donna Wandrey (Herself), Robert Rodan (Himself [Adam]), Denise Nickerson (Herself), Conrad Bain (Himself), Joan Bennett (Herself/Elizabeth Collins Stoddard [archive footage]), Grayson Hall (Herself/Dr. Julia Hoffman [archive footage]), Craig Hamrick (Himself), Alexandra Isles, Victoria Winters (archive footage).

Focused on the *Dark Shadows* soap opera, which featured vampire Barnabus Collins, this collection offers cast reunion footage, promotional appearances by the actors, episode highlights and bloopers, comments from the fans, and interviews with the cast.

Dark Shadows: 25th Anniversary Tribute; U.S., 1991; Documentary; 60 minutes/English/color, black and white/HiFi Sound; MPI Home Video.

Producers: Dan Curtis; *Writing Credits*: Dan

Curtis; *Original Music*: Robert Cobert; *Cast*: Jonathan Frid (Barnabas Collins), Lara Parker (Angelique DuPres), Louis Edmonds (Roger Collins), Nancy Barrett (Carolyn Stoddard), Kathryn Leigh Scott (Maggie Evans/Josette DuPres), John Karlen (Willie Loomis), Dennis Patrick (Jason MacGuire), Marie Wallace (Megan Todd), Michael Stroka (Aristide), Diana Millay (The Phoenix), Christopher Pennock (Leviathan), Donna Wandrey (Roxanne Drew), Robert Rodan (Adam), Joan Bennett (Elizabeth Collins Stoddard), Grayson Hall (Julia Hoffman), Alexandra Isles (Victoria Winters), Terry Crawford, Alexandra Moltke.

Focused on the *Dark Shadows* soap opera, which featured vampire Barnabus Collins, this film features footage from the 1991 *Dark Shadows* Festival in Los Angeles.

Dark Shadows: Vampires and Ghosts; U.S., 1995; Documentary; 60 minutes/English/color, black and white.

Producers: Dan Curtis; *Writing Credits*: Dan Curtis; *Cast*: Jonathan Frid (Barnabas Collins), Lara Parker (Angelique DuPres), Nancy Barrett (Carolyn Stoddard), Joan Bennett (Elizabeth Collins Stoddard), Grayson Hall (Julia Hoffman), Alexandra Isles (Victoria Winters).

This documentary is a compilation of the supernatural characters from the original *Dark Shadows* soap opera, which featured vampire Barnabus Collins.

Dark Shadows: Video Scrapbook; U.S., 1999; Documentary; 128 minutes/English/color, black and white; MPI Home Video.

Cast: Dan Curtis (Himself), Nancy Barrett (Carolyn Stoddard).

A collection of featurettes focusing on the original *Dark Shadows* series; *Dark Shadows on Location* with Nancy Barrett (Carolyn Stoddard); *Inside the Shadows* with program creator Dan Curtis; and *Dark Shadows Nightmares & Dreams*.

Dead to the Last Drop; U.S., 2007; Horror; 60 minutes/color; Savage Film Group.

Producers: Rock Savage (executive producer); *Writing Credits*: Rock Savage (screenplay); *Director*: Rock Savage; *Original Music*: Marvin Kennedy Jr.; *Cinematography*: Rock Savage; *Film Editing*: Marvin Kennedy Jr.; *Cast*: Eric Koger (Rex Jones), Mod Mutilator (Himself), Rock Savage (Harry Gross).

This film features three tales of vampires in Retro City. In the "Omega Wrestler," a group of vampires surrounds the home of the Mod Mutilator as he's trying to enjoy a quiet evening. Next, in "The Vampire Pierre," Investigator Harry Gross fights to recover a ring of Dracula's from a sexy vampire with plans to take over America. In the third short, "Bloodsucking Sheiks," a secret agent named Rex Jones battles a Nazi/Arab/Vampire with a terrorist plot.

Deafula (*Young Deafula* [U.S.]); U.S., 1975; Horror; 95 minutes/black and white/English, American Sign Language/Mono/16mm; Signscope.

Producers: Gary R. Holstrom; *Writing Credits*: Peter Wolf (writer [as Peter Wechsburg]); *Director*: Peter Wolf (as Peter Wechsburg); *Cinematography*: J. Wilder Mincey; *Make-Up*: Katherine Wilson; *Cast*: Peter Wechsberg (Deafula/Steve Adams), James D. Randall (minister [Steve's father]), Lee Darrel (detective), Dudley Hemstreet (assistant detective), Katherine Wilson (mother of Steve), Cindy Whitney (young Amy), Norma Tuccinardi (old Amy), Dick Tuccinardi (Zork [Amy's servant]), Gary R. Holstrom (Count Dracula), voice of Count Dracula (Dan Becker), Bob L. Fowler (Dr. Moon), Raymond Reichle (Dr. Reichle), Errol Wechsberg (baby Deafula), Von Wechsberg (young Deafula), Toni Below (tall woman in bedroom), Sheila Pope (young woman in living room), William M. Glenn (black man in alley), Ray D.

Gary Holstrom as Dracula in *Deafula* (U.S., 1975) (courtesy John Edgar Browning).

Lunceford (motorcyclist), Gail Platt (motorcyclist's girl friend), Mike Averett (lover), Catherine Adams (lover), Tom Leitner (man in unknown room), Barry Taylor (policeman), Christine McCoy (hanging girl), Henry Stack (newscaster), Michael Fetts, Mark Hoshi (boys in alley), James M. McGrann, Bill Darcy (policemen in alley), Garry Hood (waiter), Elizabeth Behrens (elevator operator), Russ Fast (voice of Steve Adams), Dan Becker (voice of minister [Steve's father]), Rob Lawson (voice of detective), B. Joe Medley (voice of assistant detective), Jackie Fowler (voice of mother of Steve), Chrisse Roccaro (voice of young Amy), Lyn Terrell (voice of old Amy), Dan Becker (voice of Dracula), Monte Merrick (voice of Dr. Moon), Rodney Graham (voice of newscaster).

A theology student turns into a vampire and begins to hunt other students. Peter Wechsberg plays the role of Deafula and Gary R. Holstrom plays the role of Count Dracula. Steve Adams is the deaf son of a preacher and wishes to follow in his father's footsteps. Standing in Steve's way of joining the cloth is a mysterious blood disorder that requires him not only to receive monthly transfusions from his father, but to stalk victims for fresh blood in his alternate vampiric form (Deafula). To Steve's horror, he discovers his true father to be none other than Count Dracula himself, one of Satan's messenger's who made a pact with Steve's mother who died during labor.

Defenders of the Earth (TV Series [1986–1987]), episode "Dracula's Potion"; U.S., Episode 42, 4 November 1986; Family, Action/Television, Animation; 30 minutes/color/English/Mono; Marvel Productions, LTD.

Writing Credits: Allan Cole, Chris Bunch; *Director*: Will Meugniot; *Film Editing*: Nicholas James; *Original Music*: Robert J. Walsh; *Art Direction*: Gary Hoffman; *Cast*: Adam Carl (Kshin), Ron Feinberg (Ming the Merciless), Buster Jones (Lothar), Loren Lester (Rick Gordon), Sarah Partridge (Jedda Walker), Diane Pershing (Dynak X), Peter Renaday (Mandrake the Magician), Lou Richards (Flash Gordon), Peter Mark Richman (The Phantom), Dion Williams (L.J.), William Callaway (Ming the Merciless).

When a young archeologist disappears in Transylvania, The Defenders head to the region to investigate. In Transylvania, they are invited to the castle of a man named Vlad who spikes their drinks, which turns them into animals. After receiving the antidote, the defenders shine lights onto Vlad, turning him back into the young archeologist who was possessed by an ancient vampire.

Demons (TV-Series [2009]) (*The Last Van Helsing* [U.K.] [working title]); U.K., 2009; Drama, Family, Fantasy, Thriller/Television; 60 minutes/color/Stereo/English; Shine.

Producers: Johnny Capps (producer [5 episodes, 2009]), Julian Murphy (producer [5 episodes, 2009]), Dean Hargrove (executive producer, Sony Pictures Television International [3 episodes, 2009]); *Writing Credits*: Johnny Capps (3 episodes, 2009), Julian Murphy (3 episodes, 2009), Peter Tabern (3 episodes, 2009); *Director*: Tom Harper (3 episodes, 2009); *Cinematography*: Geoffrey Wharton (4 episodes, 2009); *Film Editing*: Mark Eckersley (2 episodes, 2009); *Original Music*: Jack C. Arnold (5 episodes, 2009); *Art Direction*: Maudie Andrews (assistant art director [5 episodes, 2009]), Dominic Roberts (supervising art director [3 episodes, 2009]); *Make-Up*: Shaune Harrison (prosthetics designer/prosthetics supervisor [6 episodes, 2009]), Emma Scott (hair & makeup designer/makeup designer [6 episodes, 2009]); *Cast*: Holly Grainger (Ruby [6 episodes, 2009]), Philip Glenister (Rupert Galvin [6 episodes, 2009]), Zoe Tapper (Mina Harker [6 episodes, 2009]), Christian Cooke (Luke Van Helsing [6 episodes, 2009]), Saskia Wickham (Jenny Rutherford [4 episodes, 2009]), Andy Wareham (Noisy Boy 1 [2 episodes, 2009]), Terry Kvasnik (Noisy Boy 2 [2 episodes, 2009]), Terry Lamb (Noisy Boy 3 [2 episodes, 2009]), Mackenzie Crook (Gladiolus Thrip [2 episodes, 2009]), Richard Wilson (Father Simeon [2 episodes, 2009]), Peter G. Reed (Zippy [2 episodes, 2009]), Thomas Arnold (Jay Van Helsing [2 episodes, 2009])

This television series follows Luke, the last descendant of Abraham Van Helsing, who must pick up from where his ancestor left off by hunting demons, creatures, and vampires. Luke is also aided by Mina Harker, a medium who helps him locate the demons. In Mina's blood flows that of Dracula.

Destruction Kings; U.S., 2006; Horror, Comedy; 71 minutes/color/English/Digital; Low Budget Pictures, Splatter Rampage.

Producers: Chris Seaver; *Writing Credits*: Debbie Rochon (idea), Lauren Seavage, Chris Seaver; *Director*: Chris Seaver; *Cinematography*: Jock Queaf De; *Film Editing*: Henrique Couto; *Original Music*: The Planet Smashers; *Special Effects*: George Troester; *Cast*: Chris Seaver (Mr. Bonejack), TeenApe (Himself [as Casey Bowker]), Ariauna Albright (Brandy Kaufman), Brad Austin (Dracula), Jason McCall (Funkenstein), Travis Indovina (Eddie/Wolfman), Shawn Green (Steffon), A.J. Stabone (Mowgli), Noel Williams (Katie), Henrique Couto (Agent Budnick), Matt Meister (Thunderball), Jesse Ames (Luscious), Brett Kelly (Milo), Katie Lesnick (Marsha), Emilie La Diablesse, Fawn

LaRoche, Nichole LaRoche (Crystal Chandelier and Vampire), Heather Maxon, Andrew Mitchell, Sherry Purcell.

Dracula, the Wolfman, and Funkenstein team up to take over the world with an army of sexy female vampires. Mr. Bonejack and TeenApe, along with the PIA (Paranormal Investigation Agency), attempt to put a stop to their plan for world domination.

La Dinastía de Dracula (*Dynastie Dracula* [Germany]); Mexico, 1981; Horror, Mystery, Thriller; 85 minutes/color/Spanish; Conacite Dos.

Writing Credits: Jorge Patino; *Director*: Alfredo B. Crevenna; *Original Music*: Rogelio Zuñiga; *Cast*: Fabián Aranza (Dracula) (as Fabian), Silvia Manríquez, Magda Guzmán, Rubén Rojo, Roberto Nelson, Erika Carlsson, Víctor Alcocer, José Nájera, Kleomenes Stamatiades, Arturo Fernández, Alvaro Tarcisio, Roberto Espriu (as Roberto Spriu), Roy De La Serna, Martha de *Cast*ro, Armando Madrigal, José Manuel Moreno, Baltazar Ramos.

During the inquisition, an evil noble is killed by order of the Holy Church and is buried in a cursed grotto. Three hundred years later, vampire Baron Von Helsing, the son of the noble, prowls the countryside killing young girls, while the local doctor and priest discover a prophecy predicting that the noble will rise again from the dead. Doctor Fuentes and Father Juan set out to destroy the father and son.

Doctor Dracula (*Doktor Dracula* [Sweden]; *Docteur Dracula* [France video title]; *Lucifer's Women* [U.S. working title]; *Svengali* [U.S.]); U.S., 1978; Horror; 88 minutes/color/English/Mono; Rafael Film Associates.

Producers: Edward H. Margolin, Lisa Rich, Lou Sorkin; *Writing Credits*: Paul Aratow, Cecil Brown, Gary Reathman, Samuel M. Sherman; *Director*: Paul Aratow, Al Adamson; *Cinematography*: Gary Graver, Robbie Greenberg; *Film Editing*: Michael Bockman, Michael Bourne, David Webb Peoples; *Make-Up*: Kathleen Rochester, Mark Rodriguez; *Cast*: John Carradine (Radcliff), Don "Red" Barry (Elliot [as Donald Barry]), Larry Hankin (Wainwright), Geoffrey Land (Gregorio), Susan McIver (Stephanie), Regina Carrol (Valerie), Jane Brunel-Cohen (Trilby), Norman Pierce (Sir Steven), Paul Thomas (Roland [as Philip Toubus]), Tweed Morris (Barbara), Clair Dia (Mary [as Emily Smith]), Vic Kirk (Bobo), Robert W. Carr (Jeremy [as Robert Carr]), Michael Renner (Jean), Noel Welch (Dancer), Susan Catherine (Party Girl), Kathy Spencer (Party Girl), Laurie Gross (Magician's Assistant), Nike Zachmanoglou (Victim).

John Wainwright is the living reincarnation of an ancient hypnotist. When he is asked to help a girl named Stephanie by contacting her dead mother, she begins acting possessed. A psychiatrist — who happens to be Dracula — is called in to find the cause of the mother's death. When he offers to bestow vampirism upon the daughter as he did the mother, Stephanie refuses and kills both herself and Dracula in a car explosion.

Dr. Terror's Gallery of Horrors (*Alien Massacre* [1966]; *Blood Suckers* [1967]; *Gallery of Horror* [1981]; *Gallery of Horrors* [1966]; *The Witch's Clock* [1966]); U.S. 1967; Horror, Science Fiction; 83 minutes/color/English/Mono; American General Pictures/Borealis Enterprises Inc., Dorad Corporation.

Producers: Ray Dorn, David Hewitt, Gary Heacock; *Writing Credits*: Russ Jones; *Director*: David L. Hewitt; *Cinematography*: Austin McKinney; *Film Editing*: Tim Hinkle; *Art Direction*: Ray Dorn; *Make-Up*: Jean Hewitt; *Cast*: Lon Chaney Jr. (Dr. Mendell [as Lon Chaney]), John Carradine (Narrator/Tristram Halbin), Rochelle Hudson (Helen Spalding), Roger Gentry (Bob Farrell/Mob Leader/Dr. Sevard/Harker), Ron Doyle (Brenner/Dr. Spalding/Dr. Cushing), Karen Joy (Julie Farrell/Vampire [Medina]), Vic McGee (Dr. Finchley/Desmond/Amos Duncan/The Burgermeister), Ron Brogan (Marsh), Margaret Moore (Mrs. O'Shea), Gray Daniels (The Coachman), Mitch Evans (The Count [Alucard]), Joey Benson (Dr. Sedgewick)

Several people in London find themselves victim to a "King of the Vampires." But when the Chief Homicide Investigator, Marsh, follows the trail of the vampire, he is surprised to find that the vampire is a woman: his secretary, Miss Clark, also known as Vampiress Medina. Things get more complicated when Mr. Harker brings a new count in town, Count Alucard.

Doctor Who (TV Series [1963–1989]), serial ***The Chase***, episode "The Executioners" (*Doctor Who* [Argentina/Spain/West Germany]; *Dr. Who* [Greece/U.K., alternative spelling]; *Docteur Who* [France]); U.K., Season 2, Episode 30, 22 May 1965; Adventure, Drama, Science Fiction/Television; 25 minutes/black and white/English/Mono/16mm; British Broadcasting Corporation (BBC).

Producers: Verity Lambert; *Writing Credits*: Terry Nation; *Director*: Richard Martin; *Original Music*: Dudley Simpson; *Make-Up*: Sonia Markham; *Cast*: William Hartnell (Dr. Who), William Russell (Ian Chesterton), Jacqueline Hill (Barbara Wright), Maureen O'Brien (Vicki), Robert Marsden (Abraham Lincoln), Roger Hammond (Francis Bacon),

Vivienne Bennett (Queen Elizabeth I), Hugh Walters (William Shakespeare), Richard Coe (Television Announcer), Peter Hawkins (Daleks [voice]), David Graham (Daleks [voice]), Robert Jewell (Dalek), Kevin Manser (Dalek), John Scott Martin (Dalek), Gerald Taylor (Dalek), Jack Pitt (Mire Beast), John Maxim (Frankenstein's Monster), Malcolm Rogers (Count Dracula), George Harrison (Himself [archive footage, uncredited]), John Lennon (Himself [archive footage, uncredited]), Paul McCartney (Himself [archive footage, uncredited]), Ringo Starr (Himself [archive footage, uncredited]).

The Doctor races through time and space to avoid Daleks who want to assassinate him. They all find themselves in the Mary Celeste, the Empire State Building, and a haunted house.

Doctor Who, serial, ***The Chase***, episode "Journey into Terror" (*Doctor Who* [Argentina/Spain/West Germany]; *Dr. Who* [Greece/U.K., alternative spelling]; *Docteur Who* [France]) (TV Series [1963–1989]); U.K., Season 2, Episode 33, 12 June 1965; Adventure, Drama, Science Fiction/Television; 23 minutes/black and white/English/Mono/16mm.

Producers: Verity Lambert; *Writing Credits*: Terry Nation; *Director*: Richard Martin; *Original Music*: Dudley Simpson; *Make-Up*: Sonia Markham; *Cast*: William Hartnell (Dr. Who), William Russell (Ian Chesterton), Jacqueline Hill (Barbara Wright), Maureen O'Brien (Vicki), John Maxim (Frankenstein), Malcolm Rogers (Count Dracula), Roslyn DeWinter (Grey Lady), Peter Hawkins (Daleks [voice]), David Graham (Daleks [voice]), Robert Jewell (Dalek), Kevin Manser (Dalek), John Scott Martin (Dalek), Gerald Taylor (Dalek), Edmond Warwick (Robot Doctor [uncredited]).

The Daleks are after the Doctor and his friends with a time machine of their own. The groups travel to a few different places then end up on the same planet, planet Mechanus, where the Daleks use a robot body double of the Doctor to try to kill his companions. Everyone is taken prisoner by the mechanoids, the native robots. The Daleks go to battle with the mechanoids and they both eventually destroy each other, and the Doctor and his friends escape in the Daleks time machine.

Don Dracula (TV Series); Japan, 1982; Comedy, Fantasy/Animation; 30 minutes/color/Japanese; Jin Productions.

Producers: Kimio Ikeda, Toshiki Toriumi, Masatoshi Yui; *Writing Credits*: Osamu Tezuka; *Director*: Masamune Ochiai; *Cast*: Kenji Utsumi (Earl Don Dracula [voice]), Saeko Shimazu (Chocola [voice]), Takao Ôyama (Igor [voice]), Tomie Katayama (Blonda [voice]), Kaneta Kimotsuki (Bat Yasube [voice]) Junpei Takiguchi (Professor Helsing [voice]) Masaru Ikeda (Inspector Murai [voice]).

Earl Don Dracula, who feeds on the blood of virgin women, moves to Japan from Transylvania. His adversary, Professor Helsing, follows him to Japan in hopes of killing him, but develops hemorrhoids instead and has to give up his hunt.

Doom of Dracula; U.S., 1966; Horror/Short; 8 minutes/black and white/English/Mono/16mm and 8mm; Universal Pictures.

Producers: Paul Malvern; *Writing Credits*: Curt Siodmak; *Director*: Erle C. Kenton; *Cast*: John Carradine (Count Dracula), Boris Karloff (The Madman), J. Carrol Naish (The Hunchback), Anne Gwynne (Rita, the girl), Peter Coe (Rita's Husband), George Zucco (Prof. Lampini), Lionel Atwill (Arntz, police official), Sig Ruman (The Burgomaster), Gino Corrado (face in the crowd [extra, uncredited]).

This short is an excerpt from the 1944 film *House of Frankenstein*.

Dororon Emma-Kun (TV Series); Japan, 1973–1974; Family, Action, Adventure/Television, Animation; 25 minutes/color/Japanese; Toei Animation Company.

Writing Credits: Masaki Tsuji, Tadaaki Yamazaki, Shunichi Yukimuro, Masami Uehara; *Director*: Kimio Yabuki, Keisuke Morishita, Takeshi Shirato, Fusahito Nagaki, Tomoharu Katsumata, Satoshi Dezaki; *Art Direction*: Yoshinori Kanada (animator); *Cast*: Masako Nozawa (Emma-kun [voice]).

The King of Hell finds out that his creatures sent to cause mayhem on Earth are secretly plotting to overthrow him. He proceeds to send his nephew to fix the problem. Count Dracula is their guide and helps them find the ones who have disobeyed the King.

Dracul cu scripca; Romania, 1969; Documentary; Romanian/MoNo.

Director: Ion Bostan.

Dracula (*Ksiaze Dracula* [Poland]); U.S., 1931; Horror; 75 minutes/black and white/English/Mono; Universal Pictures.

Producers: Tod Browning, Carl Laemmle Jr., E.M. Asher; *Writing Credits*: Bram Stoker, Hamilton Deane, John L. Balderston, Garrett Fort, Louis Bromfield (uncredited), Max Cohen (uncredited), Dudley Murphy (uncredited), Louis Stevens (uncredited); *Director*: Tod Browning; *Cinematography*: Karl Freund; *Film Editing*: Milton Carruth, Maurice Pivar; *Original Music*: Philip Glass; *Art Direction*: Charles D. Hall; *Make-Up*: Jack P. Pierce (uncredited); *Cast*: Béla Lugosi (Count Dracula), Helen Chandler (Mina Harker), David Manners

Poster for *Dracula* (U.S., 1931)

(John Harker), Dwight Frye (Renfield), Edward Van Sloan (Prof. Abraham Van Helsing), Herbert Bunston (Dr. Jack Seward), Frances Dade (Lucy Weston), Joan Standing (Briggs [a nurse]), Charles K. Gerrard (Martin [Charles Gerrard]), Anna Bakacs (Innkeeper's daughter [uncredited]), Nicholas Bela (Coach passenger [uncredited]), Daisy Belmore (Coach passenger [uncredited]), Barbara Bozoky (Innkeepers wife [uncredited]), Tod Browning (Voice of Harbormaster [uncredited]), Moon Carroll (Maid [uncredited]), Geraldine Dvorak (Dracula's wife [uncredited]), John George (Small Scientist [uncredited]), Anita Harder (Flower Girl [uncredited]), Carla Laemmle (Coach passenger [uncredited]), Donald Murphy (Coach passenger [uncredited]), Wyndham Standing (Surgeon [uncredited]), Cornelia Thaw (Dracula's wife [uncredited]), Dorothy Tree (Dracula's wife [uncredited]), Josephine Velez (Grace [English nurse] [uncredited]), Michael Visaroff (Innkeeper [uncredited]).

Renfield enters castle Dracula to meet with Count Dracula and discovers that he is a vampire. Dracula sucks the blood of Lucy Weston and turns her into a vampire, then discovers her friend, Mina Seward, the daughter of Dr. Seward. Van Helsing is called in as a specialist to diagnose Mina's poor health. Van Helsing realizes Dracula is a vampire and tries to warn Mina's fiancé, John Harker, and Dr. Steward of what is going to happen and how they are to prevent Mina from becoming one of the undead.

Drácula (*Spanish Dracula* [U.S.]); U.S., 1931; Drama, Fantasy, Horror; 104 minutes, black and white, Spanish; Hungarian, Mono; Universal Pictures.
Producers: Carl Laemmle Jr., Paul Kohner; *Writing Credits*: Baltasar Fernández Cué (Spanish adaptation); *Director*: George Melford; *Cinematography*: George Robinson; *Film Editing*: Arthur Tavares; *Original Music*: Heinz Roemheld (conductor [uncredited]), Heinz Roemheld (music supervisor [uncredited]); *Art Direction*: Charles D. Hall; *Cast*: Carlos Villarías (Conde Drácula [as Carlos Villar]), Lupita Tovar (Eva), Barry Norton (Juan Harker),

Carlos Villarías, left, plays Conde Drácula opposite Eduardo Arozamena as Van Helsing in *Drácula* (U.S., 1931).

Pablo Álvarez Rubio (Renfield), Eduardo Arozamena (Van Helsing), José Soriano Viosca (Doctor Seward), Carmen Guerrero (Lucía), Amelia Senisterra (Marta), Manuel Arbó (Martín), Geraldine Dvorak (Bride of Dracula [in catacombs] [uncredited]), Cornelia Thaw (Bride of Dracula [in catacombs] [uncredited]), Dorothy Tree (Bride of Dracula [in catacombs] [uncredited]).

Renfield and Drácula have traveled to England by ship, arriving in the harbor during a storm. Renfield is raving mad and is taken to Dr. Seward's sanitarium near London, while Drácula takes up residence in Carfax Abbey, which adjoins the sanitarium. Soon after, more victims turn up and Professor Van Helsing (Eduardo Arozamena) makes his way to England to find out why Renfield is a vampire. Matters complicate when a Eva and Harker, a young couple, are drawn into the tragic events.

Dracula (*Horror of Dracula* [U.S.]; *Drácula* [Argentina/Spain]; *Cauchemar de Dracula, Le* [Belgium] (dubbed version) (French title); *Dracula* [West Germany]; *Dracula 1958* [U.S.]; *Dracula il vampiro* [Italy]; *Drakoulas, o vrykolakas ton Karpathion* [Greece]; *Horror Draculi* [Poland]; *Horror de Drácula, O* [Portugal]; *Horror of Dracula* [U.S.]; *I Draculas klor* [Sweden]; *Nachtmerrie van Dracula, De* [Netherlands]; *Pimeyden prinssi* [Finland]; *Vampiro da Noite, O* [Brazil]); U.K., 1958; Horror, Thriller; 82 minutes/color/English/Mono; Hammer Film Productions.

Producers: Michael Carreras, Anthony Hinds, Anthony Nelson Keys; *Writing Credits*: Jimmy Sangster; *Director*: Terence Fisher; *Cinematography*: Jack Asher; *Film Editing*: Bill Lenny, James Needs; *Original Music*: James Bernard; *Art Direction*: Bernard Robinson; *Make-Up*: Philip Leakey, Henry Montsash, Roy Ashton (uncredited); *Special Effects*:

Poster for *Dracula* (U.K., 1958; *Horror of Dracula* [U.S.]).

Sydney Pearson, Les Bowie; *Cast*: Peter Cushing (Doctor Van Helsing), Christopher Lee (Count Dracula), Michael Gough (Arthur Holmwood), Melissa Stribling (Mina Holmwood), Carol Marsh (Lucy Holmwood), Olga Dickie (Gerda), John Van Eyssen (Jonathan Harker), Valerie Gaunt (Vampire Woman), Janina Faye (Tania) (as Janine Faye), Barbara Archer (Inga), Charles Lloyd Pack (Dr. Seward), George Merritt (Policeman), George Woodbridge (Landlord), George Benson (Frontier Official), Miles Malleson (Undertaker), Geoffrey Bayldon (Porter), Paul Cole (Lad).

Jonathan Harker attacks Count Dracula at his castle disguised as an employed librarian for the castle. Upon the failure and death of Harker, the Count moves to Harker's city and terrorizes the family of Harker's fiancée. Their only hope of evading Dracula is Dr. Van Helsing, Harker's dear friend and colleague, who sets out to kill Dracula.

Dracula; U.S., 1966; Horror/Short; 8 minutes/black and white/English/Mono; Universal Pictures.

Writing Credits: Garrett Fort; *Director*: Tod Browning; *Cast*: Béla Lugosi (Count Dracula), Helen Chandler (Mina), David Manners (John), Edward Van Sloan (Professor), Herbert Bunston (Mina's Father).

This short is a condensed version of Tod Browning's 1931 classic *Dracula*.

Dracula (*Bram Stoker's Dracula* [U.S.]; *Dan Curtis' Dracula* [undefined]; *Drácula, el último romántico* [Argentina]; *Il demone nero* [Italy]; *Kreivi Dracula* [Finland]; *O Drakoulas zei akoma sto Londino* [Greece, theatrical title]); U.K., 1973; Horror, Romance/Television; 100 minutes/color/English/Mono; Latglen Ltd.

Producers: Dan Curtis, Robert Singer; *Writing Credits*: Bram Stoker, Richard Matheson; *Director*: Dan Curtis; *Cinematography*: Oswald Morris; *Film Editing*: Richard A. Harris; *Original Music*: Bob Cobert (as Robert Cobert); *Make-Up*: Paul Rabiger; *Cast*: Jack Palance (Dracula), Simon Ward (Arthur), Nigel Davenport (Van Helsing), Pamela Brown (Mrs. Westenra), Fiona Lewis (Lucy), Penelope Horner (Mina), Murray Brown (Jonathan Harker), Virginia Wetherell (Dracula's Wife [as Virginia Wetherall]), Barbara Lindley (Dracula's Wife), Sarah Douglas (Dracula's Wife), George Pravda (Innkeeper), Hana Maria Pravda (Innkeeper's Wife [as Hanna-Maria Pravda]), Reg Lye

Jack Palance as Dracula in *Dracula* (U.S., 1973), produced and directed by Dan Curtis (courtesy Justin Humphreys).

(Zookeeper), Fred Stone (Priest), Roy Spencer (Whitby Inn Clerk), John Challis (Stockton-on-Tees Clerk), Nigel Gregory (Midvale Shipping Clerk), John Pennington (Richmond Shipping Clerk), Martin Read (Coastguard), Gita Denise (Madam Kristoff), Sandra Caron (Whitby Inn maid [uncredited]).

It is 1897 as an English real estate agent named Jonathan Harker arrives at a castle near the town of Bistritz to officiate the sell of English properties to a nobleman named Count Dracula. Harker soon discovers that the Count hides a terrible secret: He is a centuries-old vampire. Leaving Jonathan imprisoned in his castle to be terrorized by vampiric women, Dracula travels to England to seek out a lovely woman named Lucy, whom he believes is the reincarnation of his beloved from centuries past.

Dracula; Canada, 1973; Horror/Television; Canadian Broadcasting Company.

Writing Credits: Rod Coneybeare; *Director*: Jack Nixon-Browne; *Cast*: Norman Welsh (Dracula), Blair Brown (uncredited), Charlotte Hunt (uncredited), Nehemiah Persoff (Dr. Van Helsing).

Count Dracula is played by Norman Welsh, and his costume reveals the traditional white hair, large fangs, and cape that are commonly associated with the character. The show is popular because of the scene in which Van Helsing pierces Dracula's heart with a stake.

Dracula (*Dracula '79* [Germany]; *Dracula-Eine Love Story* [Austria]); U.S./U.K., 1979; Horror, Romance; 109 minutes/color/English, Dutch, Romanian/Dolby; Universal Pictures.

Producers: Marvin Mirisch, Walter Mirisch, Tom Pevsner; *Writing Credits*: Hamilton Deane (play), John L. Balderston (play), W.D. Richter (screenplay); *Director*: John Badham; *Cinematography*: Gilbert Taylor; *Film Editing*: John Bloom; *Original Music*: John Williams; *Art Direction*: Brian Ackland-Snow; *Make-Up*: Eric Allwright, Susie Hill, Colin Jamison, Peter Robb-King, Jane Royle; *Cast*: Frank Langella (Count Dracula), Laurence Olivier (Prof. Abraham Van Helsing), Donald Pleasence (Dr. Jack Seward), Kate Nelligan (Lucy Seward), Trevor Eve (Jonathan Harker), Jan Francis (Mina Van Helsing), Janine Duvitski (Annie), Tony Haygarth (Milo Renfield), Teddy Turner (Swales), Sylvester McCoy (Walter [as Sylveste McCoy]), Kristine Howarth (Mrs. Galloway), Joe Belcher (Tony Hindley), Ted Carroll (Scarborough Sailor), Frank Birch (Harbormaster), Gabor Vernon (Captain of Demeter), Frank Henson (Demeter Sailor), Peter Wallis (Priest).

Dracula is the lone survivor of a shipwreck and

Frank Langella as Dracula in Universal Studios' *Dracula* (U.S., 1979).

is rescued by the sickly Mina Van Helsing. After dining with Mina's caretakers, the Sewards, Dracula visits Mina's room and kills her. Mina's father, Abraham Van Helsing, tracks down his now vampire daughter and destroys her. He then begins chasing Dracula who now has Lucy Seward captive, on the road to becoming a vampire herself. On Dracula's escape vessel, Dracula stakes Van Helsing, but Van Helsing hoists Dracula into the sunlight before he dies.

Dracula; India, 1999; Horror; 92 minutes/color/ Hindi/35mm; Bhooshan Films.

Producers: Bhooshan Lal; *Writing Credits*: Rajesh Kundan; *Director*: Bhooshan Lal, Teerat Singh; *Cinematography*: R.M. Shah; *Original Music*: Sawan Kumar Sawan; *Cast*: Sadashiv Amrapurkar (uncredited), Ashna (uncredited), Mohan Joshi (uncredited), Kiran Kumar (Abdullah), Anil Nagrath (uncredited), Raj Premi (uncredited), Rami Reddy (uncredited), Jyoti Rana (uncredited), Priya Rao (uncredited), Sapna (uncredited), Deepak Shirke (uncredited), Vinod Tripathi (uncredited).

Drácula (TV Mini-Series); Argentina, 1999; Horror, Mystery, Romance, Thriller/Television; 60 minutes/color/Spanish/Stereo.

Director: Diego Kaplan; *Original Music*: Federico Jusid; *Cinematography*: Hernán Bouza; *Cast*: Carlos Calvo, Magalí Moro, Coraje Abalos, Alejandro Awada, Adriana Castro, Ulises Dumont, Baby Etchecopar, Carolina Fal, Iván González, Enrique Liporace, Juan Ignacio Machado, Julieta Ortega, Lorenzo Quinteros, Julio Riccardi.

Dracula; U.K., 2006; Horror; 90 minutes/color/ English, German; Granada Television, British Broadcasting Corporation (BBC [as BBC Wales]), WGBH.

Producers: Michele Buck, Rebecca Eaton, Julie Gardner, Damien Timmer, Trevor Hopkins; *Writing Credits*: Stewart Harcourt; *Director*: Bill Eagles; *Cinematography*: Cinders Forshaw; *Film Editing*: Adam Recht; *Original Music*: Dominik Scherrer; *Art Direction*: Paul Ghirardani; *Make-Up*: Nicola Frost; *Cast*: David Suchet (Abraham Van Helsing), Marc Warren (Count Dracula), Dan Stevens (Lord Holmwood), Sophia Myles (Lucy Westenra), Benedick Blythe (Lord Godalming), James Greene (Dr. Blore), Tom Burke (Dr. John Seward), Donald Sumpter (Alfred Singleton), Stephanie Leonidas (Mina Murray), Rafe Spall (Jonathan Harker), Ian Redford (Hawkins), Tanveer Ghani (Cotford), Rupert Holliday-Evans (DI Burton) (as Rupert Holliday Evans), David Glover (Stephens), Ian Gain (Sgt Kirk), Richard Syms (Priest), Diana Payne-Myers (Wraith [uncredited]).

London-based Arthur Holmwood, who suffers from syphilis, summons the help of Count Dracula. Lucy, Arthur's wife-to-be, is unaware of her fiancé's health condition, a disease that would hinder the consummation of their marriage. Arthur relies on Dracula's mystical powers for a cure; however, Dracula's intention is not to cure but to feed on those in London and produce others like himself. Arthur fights back, aided by Professor Abraham Van Helsing.

Dracula 2000 (*Dracula 2001* [U.K., Colombia, Spain, Finland, France]; *Wes Craven präsentiert Dracula* [Germany]; *Wes Craven—Dracula 2000* [Germany]; *Dracula 2002* [Belgium, English title video title]; *Wes Craven Presents Dracula* 2000 [U.S., complete title]); U.S., 2000; Action, Horror; 99 minutes/color/English/DTS; Carfax Productions Ltd., Dimension Films, Neo Art & Logic, Wes Craven Films.

Producers: Wes Craven, Marianne Maddalena, Andrew Rona, Bob Weinstein, Harvey Weinstein, Daniel K. Arredondo, W.K. Border, Ron Schmidt, Joel Soisson, Tony Steinberg; *Writing Credits*: Joel Soisson (story/screenplay), Patrick Lussier (story); *Director*: Patrick Lussier; *Cinematography*: Peter Pau; *Film Editing*: Peter Devaney Flanagan, Patrick Lussier; *Original Music*: Marco Beltrami; *Art Direction*: Elinor Rose Galbraith, Monroe Kelly; *Make-Up*: Wendi Lynn Allison, Carla Brenholtz, Rose-Mary Gubala; *Special Effects*: Dan Gibson, Walter Klassen; *Cast*: Gerard Butler (Dracula), Christopher Plummer (Abraham/Matthew Van Helsing), Jonny Lee Miller (Simon Sheppard), Justine Waddell (Mary Heller), Colleen Fitzpatrick (Lucy Westerman) (as Colleen Anne Fitzpatrick), Jennifer Esposito (Solina), Omar Epps (Marcus), Sean Patrick Thomas (Trick), Danny Masterson (Nightshade), Lochlyn Munro (Eddie), Tig Fong (Dax), Tony Munch (Charlie), Jeri Ryan (Valerie Sharpe), Shane West (J.T.), Nathan Fillion (Father David), Tom Kane (Anchor Man), Jonathan Whittaker (Detective Gautreaux), Robert Verlaque (Dr. Seward), Randy Butcher (Stakeman #1), Bill Davidson (Stakeman #2), Peter Cox (Stakeman #3), Chris Lamon (Stakeman #4), Herb Reischl Jr., Stakeman #5 (as Herb Reischl), Duncan McLeod (Stakeman #6), Wayne Downer (Desk Guard), Robert Racki (Door Guard), William Prae (Parade Cop), Kaaron Briscoe (Teen Co-Worker), Scarlett Huntley (Blood Doll), Harold Short (Black Angel of Death), David J. Francis (Jesus), Shimmy Silverman (Barker), Ed Mundell (Himself), David Wyndorf (Himself band member), Carlo Daquin (Featured guy [uncredited]), Peter Devaney Flanagan (Dead Londoner [uncredited]), Jeremy Galeaz (uncredited), Jeff Hanneman (Talking Guy [uncredited]), Eric Santana Illarmo (Young Reveler [uncredited]), Manou Lubowski (uncredited), Devin C. Lussier (Boy going to angel [uncredited]), Kelsey Matheson (Stripper [uncredited]), Gary J. Tunnicliffe (Dead Londoner [uncredited]).

A modernized version of the classic *Dracula*, *Dracula 2000* tells the story of a group of thieves that steals the sealed coffin of Dracula (Gerard Butler), inevitably setting the vampire free to feast on and terrorize the city of New Orleans. Learning of Dracula's escape, Abraham Van Helsing (Christopher Plummer) and his assistant Simon (Jonny Lee Miller) travel to the U.S. in order to recapture Dracula and protect Van Helsing's estranged daughter, Mary (Justine Waddell).

Dracula 3000 (*Dracula 3000: Infinite Darkness* [South Africa, English working title]); Germany/South Africa, 2004; Horror, Science Fiction; 86 minutes/color/English; Film Afrika Worldwide, ApolloProMedia GmbH & Co. 1. Filmproduktion KG (I), Fiction Film & Television Limited.

Producers: James Atherton, Jan Fantl, Frank Hübner, Brad Krevoy, David Lancaster, Julia Verdin, Jörg Westerkamp, David Wicht; *Writing Credits*: Ivan Milborrow, Darrell Roodt; *Director*: Darrell Roodt; *Cinematography*: Giulio Biccari; *Film Editing*: Avril Beukes, Ronelle Loots; *Original Music*: Michael Hoenig; *Art Direction*: Tiaan van Tonder; *Make-Up*: Isabella Acerbi, Sabine Palfi, Marnette Rossouw; *Special Effects*: Dennis Beechey, Rob Carlisle, Kevin Carter, Roly Jansen, Tyrell Kemlo, Wally Langer Cordell McQueen, Clinton Smith; *Cast*: Casper Van Dien (Capt. Abraham Van Helsing), Erika Eleniak (Aurora Ash), Coolio (187), Alexandra Kamp-Groeneveld (Mina Murry [as Alexandra Kamp]), Grant Swanby (Arthur "The Professor" Holmwood), Langley Kirkwood (Orlock), Tommy "Tiny" Lister (Humvee [as Tiny Lister]), Udo Kier (Capt. Varna).

A spacecraft piloted by Capt. Abraham Van Hellsing (Casper Van Dien) finds the lost ship Demeter adrift in deep space. The captain and his crew decide to investigate the found ship. Onboard they find a series of coffins, one of which contains the body of Count Orlock (Langley Kirkwood), a Dracula-type character who begins to feed upon the crew. It becomes a race for survival as the crew tries to reach the sun, hoping it will destroy Orlock.

Dracula II: Ascension (*Drácula II—Resurrección* [Spain]; *Drakoulas II: I epistrofi* [Greece]); U.S., 2003; Horror; 85 minutes/color/English/35 mm; Castel Film Romania.

Producers: W.K. Border, Nick Phillips, Ron Schmidt, Joel Soisson; *Writing Credits*: Joel Soisson, Patrick Lussier; *Director*: Patrick Lussier; *Cinematography*: Douglas Milsome; *Film Editing*: Diana Negoitescu; *Original Music*: Marco Beltrami, Kevin Kliesch; *Art Direction*: Gabi Bálint, Adriana Bucataru, Mihai Buciumeanu, Crina Cartos, Stefan Curelaru, Costin Dragan, Viorel Ghenea, Adriana Iurascu, Iasar Memedali, Petre Nicolescu, Ciprian Opreo, Mihaela Poenaru, Florin Samoila, Christian Simion, George Stanciu, Mihai Stanciu; *Make-Up*: Daniela Busoiu, Cristina Catanescu, Christopher K. Grap, Snowy Highfield, Marina Ionescu, Steven Lawrence, Viorel Militaru, Mirela Nitu, Gary J. Tunnicliffe; *Special Effects*: Kevin Carter, Lucian Iordache, Ionel Popa; *Cast*: Jennifer Kroll (Twins of Evil), Jason Scott Lee (Father Uffizi), Craig Sheffer (Lowell), Diane Neal (Elizabeth Blaine), Khary Payton (Kenny), Brande Roderick (Tanya), Jason London (Luke), Chris Hunter (Corello), Tom Kane (Doctor), John Light (Eric), Stephen Billington (Dracula II), Nick Phillips (Officer Smith), John Sharian (Officer Hodge), Dragos Balauca (Altar Boy), David Gant (Old Priest), Roy Scheider (Cardinal Siqueros), Daniela Nane (Cat-Woman), David J. Francis (Jesus), Vasile Albinet (Horseman), Silviu Olteanu (Young Priest).

This is the sequel to *Dracula 2000*. Scientists use Dracula's blood to cure a disease.

Dracula III: Legacy (*Dracula 3* [U.S.]; *Dracula: Resurrected* [U.S.]); U.S., 2005; Horror; 86 minutes/color/English/Dolby Digital/35 mm; Castel Film Romania, Buena Vista Pictures, Miramax Films, Neo Art & Logic.

Producers: Bob Weinstein, Harvey Weinstein, W.K. Border, Nick Phillips, Andrew Rona, Ron Schmidt; *Writing Credits*: Joel Soisson, Patrick Lussier; *Director*: Patrick Lussier; *Cinematography*: Douglas Milsome; *Film Editing*: Lisa Romaniw; *Original Music*: Kevin Kliesch, Ceiri Torjussen; *Make-Up*: Daniela Busoiu, Cristina Catanescu, Christopher K. Grap, Marina Ionescu, Mirela Nitu, Gary J. Tunnicliffe; *Special Effects*: Kevin Carter, Lucian Iordache, Ionel Popa; *Cast*: Jason Scott Lee (Father Uffizi), Stephen Billington (Dracula II), Diane Neal (Elizabeth Blaine), Jason London (Luke), Rutger Hauer (Dracula III), Ilinca Goia (Marta), George Grigore (Bruno), Roy Scheider (Cardinal Siqueros), Tom Kane (EBC Anchorman), Alexandra Wescourt (Julia Hughes), Serban Celea (Gabriel), Gavril Patru (Canadian Lieutenant), Giuliano Doman (French Sergeant), Valentin Popescu (French Captain), Nicodim Ungureanu (Pavel), Claudiu Bleont (Bogdan), Georgeta Marin (Red Shirt Girl) Domnita Constantiniu (Old Woman [as Domnita Costantin]), Constantin Codrescu (Old Man [as Consantin Codrescu]), Mircea Iulian Anca (Bishop Boy), Gary J. Tunnicliffe (Tommy), Carmen Stimeriu (Vampire Mom), Cosmin Chiriac (Vallon), Florin Porumb (Stiltman),

Ioan Ionescu (Ragman [as Ioan Andrei Ionescu]), Anne-Marie Caragea (Red Acrobat [as Ana-Maria Caragea]), Nicole Dutu (Rebel Woman), Ioana Ginghina (Dracula's Bride).

In this third installment (preceded by *Dracula 2000* and *Dracula II: Ascension*), Dracula (Rutger Hauer) has returned to Romania and captures Liz Blaine (Diane Neal). Her father Uffizi (Jason Scott Lee), a priest, is determined to seek out Dracula and rescue his daughter Liz. The church withdraws its support, saying that the priest has been tainted from his last encounter with Dracula and wishes for him to return to the church. Father Uffizi refuses the church, turns in his collar, and goes to rescue his daughter along with Luke (Jason London), her lover.

Dracula: A Chamber Musical; Canada, 2000; Drama, Musical/Television; 110 minutes/color/English; Ontario Educational Communications Authority (OECA).

Producers: Richard Ouzounian; *Writing Credits*: Richard Ouzounian; *Director*: Richard Ouzounian; *Film Editing*: Julian Lannaman; *Original Music*: Marek Norman; *Cast*: Juan Chioran (Count Dracula), Roger Honeywell (Jonathan Harker), June Crowley (Mina Harker), Benedict Campbell (Renfield), Michael Fletcher (Abraham Van Helsing), Amy Walsh (Lucy Westenra), Sadie Hoy (Demon Bride), Esther Maloney (Demon Bride).

Dracula: A Chamber Musical is a film based on Stoker's novel that uses music to explore the character's emotions without the use of gore and other traditional characteristics typical of Dracula adaptations.

Dracula: A Cinematic Scrapbook; U.S., 1991; Documentary; 60 minutes/color, black and white/English.

Writing Credits: Ted Newsom; *Director*: Ted Newsom.

This documentary follows the history of *Dracula* in film and print, using movie clips, and movie trailers.

Dracula A.D. 1972 (*Dracula '73'* [France]; *Dracula '72'* [U.K.] (working title), *Dracula Chelsea '72'* [U.K.] (working title), *1972: Dracula colpisce ancora!* [Italy]; *Dracula Today, Dracula jagt Mini-Mädchen* [Germany]; *Dracula Chases the Mini Girls* [U.K.] (working title), *Draculan kosto* [Finland]; *Drakoulas* [Greece]; U.K., 1972; Horror; 96 minutes/color/English/Mono; Hammer Film Productions.

Producers: Michael Carreras, Josephine Douglas; *Writing Credits*: Don Houghton (writer); *Director*: Alan Gibson; *Cinematography*: Dick Bush; *Film Editing*: James Needs; *Original Music*: Michael Vickers; *Make-Up*: George Blackler, Jill Carpenter, Barbara Ritchie; *Special Effects*: Les Bowie; *Cast*: Christopher Lee (Count Dracula), Peter Cushing (Professor Van Helsing), Stephanie Beacham (Jessica Van Helsing), Christopher Neame (Johnny Alucard), Michael Coles (Inspector), Marsha A. Hunt (Gaynor, as Marsha Hunt), Caroline Munro (Laura Bellows), Janet Key (Anna), William Ellis (Joe Mitcham), Philip Miller (Bob), Michael Kitchen (Greg), David Andrews (Detective Sergeant), Lally Bowers (Matron Party Hostess), Constance Luttrell (Mrs. Donnelly), Michael Daly (Charles), Artro Morris (Police Surgeon), Jo Richardson (Crying Matron), Penny Brahms (Hippy Girl), Brian John Smith (Hippy Boy), Tim Barnes (Rockgroup Member, as Stoneground), Sal Valentino (Rockgroup Singer/Guitarist, as Stoneground).

Dracula is unknowingly resurrected by Johnny (the great-grandson of the servant who buried the vampire's remains) and Jessica (the granddaughter of Abraham Van Helsing), whom Dracula plans to kill.

Dracula aema; South Korea, 1994; 85 minutes/color/Korean; Bando Young Sang.

Producers: Kyeong-hie Jeong; *Writing Credits*: Do-won Seok; *Director*: Do-wan Seok; *Cinematography*: Myeong-hun Kwak; *Film Editing*: Ki-hyeong Jo; *Original Music*: Jeong-rim Lee; *Cast*: Na-a Oh, Hyeong-jun Ko, Seok Won, Ae-jin Jeong.

A man meets a vampire bent on revenge after finding a strange computer disk.

Dracula Bites the Big Apple; U.S., 1979; Horror, Musical/Short; 22 minutes/English/color.

Producers: Richard Wenk; *Writing Credits*: Fred Olsen; *Director*: Richard Wenk; *Make-Up*: Laurie Aiello; *Cast*: Barry Gomolka (Renfield), Peter Loewy (Dracula), Steve Rubell (Himself), Karen Tull (The Girl), Whitey Wenk (Customs Official).

This 22-minute short follows Dracula throughout his trip to New York City.

The Dracula Business (*Tuesday's Documentary: The Dracula Business* [complete title]); U.K., 1974; Horror/Documentary; English; BBC Television.

Producers: Anthony de Lotbinière; *Cinematography*: Eugene Carr; *Film Editing*: Hugh Newsam; *Cast*: Daniel Farson (Himself).

Daniel Farson investigates our obsession with Dracula, the iconic figure Farson's great-uncle Bram Stoker created in 1897. Farson visits Romania to investigate the background of the novel and the myth. While in England, Farson talks to a number of people who have encountered vampire hunters or priests claiming to have performed exorcisms.

Drácula contra Frankenstein (*Die Nacht der offenen Särge* [West Germany]; *Dracula contro Frank-*

enstein [Italy]; *Dracula prisonnier de Frankenstein* [France]; *Dracula prisonnier du docteur Frankenstein* [France]; *Drácula contra el Dr. Frankenstein* [undefined]; *Dracula Against Frankenstein* [undefined]; *Dracula Prisoner of Frankenstein* [undefined]; *Dracula vs. Dr. Frankenstein* [undefined]; *Screaming Dead* [undefined]); Spain, 1972; 85 minutes/Eastmancolor/Spanish/Mono; Prodif Ets., Comptoir Français du Film Production (CFFP), Fénix Cooperativa Cinematográfica.

Producers: Arturo Marcos; *Writing Credits*: Paul D'Ales, Jesus Franco (foreword [as David H. Klunne], screenplay, story); *Director*: Jesus Franco; *Cinematography*: José Climent; *Film Editing*: María Luisa Soriano; *Original Music*: Bruno Nicolai, Daniel White; *Art Direction*: Antonio de Cabo; *Make-Up*: Monique Adélaïde, Elisenda Villanueva; *Special Effects*: Manuel Baquero; *Cast*: Dennis Price (Doctor Frankenstein), Howard Vernon (Drácula), Paca Gabaldón (María) (as Mary Francis), Alberto Dalbés (Doctor Jonathan Seward) (as Alberto Dalbes), Britt Nichols (Chica vampira), Geneviève Robert (Amira — la gitana) (as Genevieve Deloir), Anne Libert (Primera víctima de Drácula), Luis Barboo (Morpho) (as Luis Bar Boo), Brandy (El Hombre Lobo), Fernando Bilbao (El Monstruo), Josyane Gibert (Estela — la cantante de cabaret) (as Josiane Gibert), Antonio de Cabo (uncredited), Eduarda Pimenta (Wife, last victim besides her husband [uncredited]), Daniel White (Danny, the innkeeper [uncredited]).

After Doctor Jonathan Seward (Alberto Dalbés) discovers two puncture marks on his patient, he travels to Castle Drácula to confront the vampire. Meanwhile, Doctor Frankenstein (Dennis Price) and his assistant, Morpho (Luis Barboo), travel to the same town to awaken Drácula in an attempt to create an army to take over the world.

Poster art for *Drácula contra Frankenstein* (Spain, 1972)

Dracula: Fact or Fiction; U.S., 1992; Documentary; 40 minutes/color/English; Steve Michelson Productions, Worldvision Home Video.

Producers: Robert W. Sigman, Gary Delfiner, Arthur Kassel, Steve Michelson, Rebecca Locke, Marie Meacham; *Director*: Steve Michelson; *Cast*: Warren Weageant (narrator), Raymond T. McNally (Himself), Jeanne Keyes Youngson (Herself), Donald Reed (Himself).

The world's fascination with vampires provides the focus of this documentary, which looks at the bloody life of the 15th-century Romanian prince who is said to have been the model for Bram Stoker's classic novel. This documentary also examines vampire films over the years as well as modern-day real vampires.

Dracula: Forbidden Fruit — a Play Benefiting the Clemente Program; U.S., 2009; Documentary/Short; 18 minutes/color/English.

Producers: Angelique Gibson, Randy Grimes; *Director*: Angelique Gibson, Randy Grimes; *Cinematography*: Angelique Gibson, Felicia Allyn, Larry Brown, Randy Grimes, Lauren Hagen, Tim Renaud, Andrew Schiffbauer, Kiesha Simpson, Michael Weeks; *Film Editing*: Angelique Gibson; *Special Effects*: Angelique Gibson; *Cast*: Shaun Kraisman.

A school without a theater department puts on a high production play to support the local Clemente Program.

Dracula/Garden of Eden; 1928; Horror, Romance; 52 minutes/black and white/silent.

Cast: Louise Dresser, Alexander Granach, Corinne Griffith, Charles Ray, Max Schreck (Dracula).

This silent film combines the vampire film *Nosferatu* with *The Garden of Eden*. Tini Le Brun meets her new love interest while vacationing with her friend, a baroness.

Dracula Has Risen from the Grave (*Amanti di Dracula, Le* [Italy]; *Dracula nousee haudasta* [Finland]; *Dracula et les femmes* [France]); U.K., 1968; Romance, Horror; 92 minutes/color/English/Mono/35mm; Hammer Film Productions.

Producers: Aida Young; *Writing Credits*: Anthony Hinds (as John Elder); *Director*: Freddie Francis; *Cinematography*: Arthur Grant; *Film Editing*: Spencer Reeve; *Original Music*: James Bernard; *Make-Up*: Wanda Kelley, Heather Nurse, Rosemarie McDonald Peattie; *Special Effects*: Frank George, Bert Luxford (uncredited), Jimmy Snow (uncredited); *Cast*: Christopher Lee (Dracula), Rupert Davies (Monsignor Ernest Mueller), Veronica Carlson (Maria Mueller), Barbara Ewing (Zena), Barry Andrews (Paul), Ewan Hooper (Priest), Marion Mathie (Anna Mueller), Michael Ripper (Max), John D. Collins (Student), George A. Cooper (Landlord), Christopher Cunningham (Farmer [as Chris Cunningham]), Norman Bacon (Mute Boy), Carrie Baker (1st Victim [uncredited]).

Dracula has been "destroyed" and he now rests in the frozen river that flows alongside his castle. The monsignor arrives at Dracula's castle a year later to check up on things. He finds that the townsfolk refuse to attend Sunday Mass at the church because the shadow from Dracula's castle touches the church in the later part of the day. The monsignor exorcises Dracula's castle to show the townsfolk that there's nothing to be afraid of. But Dracula is soon resurrected, and he's out for revenge, and a new bride. What better bride than the monsignor's niece, Maria?

Dracula in the Movies; U.S., 1992; Documentary; 60 minutes/color, black and white/English; A Film Shows, Inc., GoodTimes Home Video Co.

Producers: Ken Cayre, Stan Cayre, Joe Cayre; *Writing Credits*: Sandy Oliveri (compiled by).

This documentary is a compilation of *Dracula* and vampire movie trailers and teasers.

Dracula in Vegas; U.S., 1999; Horror; 63 minutes/color/English; I.R.M.I. Films Corporation.

Producers: Frances Millard; *Writing Credits*: Nick Millard; *Director*: Nick Millard; *Cast*: Glen Eberspecher, Sam Gartner, Maximillian Grabinger (Max, a vampire), Miriam Krasny, April Leigh (Christine, a co-ed), Frances Millard (as Flora Myers).

Dracula Live from Transylvania; U.S., 1989; Documentary, Television; 92 minutes/English.

Producers: Gerry Arbeid, Pieter Kroonenburg, Michel Shane; *Director*: Roger Cardinal; *Cinematography*: Karol Ike; *Film Editing*: Jean Beaudoin; *Original Music*: Osvaldo Montes; *Cast*: George Hamilton, Leo Ilial, Françoise Robertson.

Vampire experts, people claiming to be vampires, and others are guests as George Hamilton hosts a show on vampire stories, live from Transylvania.

Dracula Mon Amour; France, 1993; Horror/Short; 8 minutes/color/French; Skopia Films.

Producers: Eric Bitoun; *Writing Credits*: Serge Abi-Yaghi; *Director*: Serge Abi-Yaghi; *Cinematography*: Nicolas Eprendre; *Cast*: Bruno Todeschini (Dracula), Natacha Amal, Benoît Vergne, Matthieu Rozé.

A woman is in love with Dracula.

Dracula: Pages from a Virgin's Diary; Canada, 2002; Horror, Musical/Ballet; 73 minutes/color, black and white/Silent (with English intertitles)/35mm; Vonnie Von Helmont Film, Canadian Broadcasting Corporation (CBC) (in association with), Dracula Productions Inc., Royal Winnipeg Ballet.

Producers: Danishka Esterhazy, Lesley Oswald, Robert Sherrin (CBC Television Arts Programming), Vonnie von Helmolt; *Writing Credits*: Mark Godden; *Director*: Guy Maddin; *Cinematography*: Paul Suderman (director of photography); *Film Editing*: Deco Dawson; *Original Music*: Bob Stewart (music editor); *Art Direction*: Deanne Rhode; *Make-Up*: Lori Caputi, Amanda Kuryk (key makeup artist) Doug Morrow (key special makeup effects) Jennifer Machnee (first assistant prosthetic makeup artist, uncredited); *Special Effects*: Ken Hart Swain; *Cast*: Wei-Qiang Zhang (Dracula, as Zhang Wei-Qiang), Tara Birtwhistle (Lucy Westernra), David Moroni (Dr. Van Helsing), Cindy-Marie Small (Mina), Johnny A. Wright (Jonathon Harker, as Johnny Wright), Stephane Leonard (Arthur Holmwood), Matthew Johnson (Jack Seward), Keir Knight (Quincy Morris), Brent Neale (Renfield), Stephanie Ballard (Mrs. Westernra), Sarah Murphy-Dyson (Maid/Nun/Vampiress), Carrie Broda (Maid/Nun), Gail Stefanek (Maid/Vampiress), Janet Sartore (Maid/Nun), Jennifer Welsman (Gargoyle/Nun), Emily Grizzell (Gargoyle/Nun), Chalnessa Eames (Gargoyle/Nun), Vanessa Lawson (Gargoyle/Nun), Michelle Lack (Nun), Kerrie Souster (Vampiress).

A menacing immigrant attacks innocent English women in this ballet rendition of Bram Stoker's

Zhang Wei-Qiang plays Dracula and Tara Birtwhistle stars as Lucy in *Dracula: Pages from a Virgin's Diary* (Canada, 2002).

Dracula. Subtitles, dance, and pantomime tell this tale in a style similar to the early twentieth century.

Dracula père et fils (*Die Herren Dracula* [West Germany]; *Dracula and Son* [U.S.]; *Dracula na emigracji* [Poland]; *Dracula padre e figlio* [Italy]; *Drakoulas tou mesonyhtiou, O* [Greece] (reissue title); *Drakoulas ... patir kai yios* [Greece]; *Pure, vampyyri, pure!* [Finland]); France, 1976; Comedy, Horror; 96 minutes/color/French/Mono; Productions 2000.

Producers: Alain Poire; *Writing Credits*: Claude Klotz (novel), Alain Godard, Edouard Molinaro, Jean-Marie Poiré; *Director*: Edouard Molinaro; *Cinematography*: Alain Levent; *Film Editing*: Monique Isnardon, Robert Isnardon; *Original Music*: Vladimir Cosma; *Art Direction*: Jacques Bufnoir, Gérard Viard; *Make-Up*: Jim Gillespie, Alex Archambault, Monique Archambault; *Cast*: Christopher Lee (Dracula père/Le prince des Ténèbres/Prince of Darkness), Bernard Menez (Ferdinand Poitevin, fils d'Herminie et du prince des Ténèbres/Son) Marie-Hélène Breillat (Nicole Clement), Catherine Breillat (Herminie Poitevin), Mustapha Dali (Khaleb), Xavier Depraz (Le majordome), Claude Génia (Marguerite), Jean-Claude Dauphin (Cristéa/Christian Polanski), Anna Gaël (Miss Gaylor), Gérard Jugnot (Le responsable de l'usine), Raymond Bussières (L'homme âgé à l'ANPE), Bernard Alane, Anna Prucnal, Jean Lescot, Albert Simono (Le vendeur de cercueils), Arlette Balkis, Geoffrey Carey, Lyne Chardonnet (L'infirmière), Robert Dalban (Le réceptionniste de l'hôtel), Carlo Nell, Guy Piérauld, Jean-Marie Arnoux, Jacques Boudet, Branko, Véronique Dancier, Jean-François Dérec (Le gardien de l'hôpital), Louise Dhour, Jean-François Duhamel, Cédric Dumond, Tudor Eliad, Patrick Feigelson (A Soldier), Jean-Paul Franky, Jacques Galland, Gill Gam, Jean-Pierre Garrigues, Maitena Galli, Jean-Yves Gautier, Raoul Guylad, Jacqueline Hopstein, Peter J. Kavanagh, Daniel Léger, Lucienne Legrand, Robert Lestourneaud, Sylvain Lévignac, Colin Mann, Moz-Djer, Patrice Pascal, Olivier Pierre, Henry Pillsbury (Henri Pillsbury), Daniel Popescu, Paul Rieger, Pierre-Olivier Scotto, Jean-Louis Tristan, Dominique Zardi (Un agent).

Dracula's son (Bernard Menez) is skeptical about carrying out the family tradition of being a vampire. After his family is banished from Romania, they all end up traveling to different places. Dracula's son ends up in France, while Dracula finds a career in British horror films. Once united, Dracula and his son end up falling for the same woman.

Dracula: Prince of Darkness (*Blut für Dracula* [West Germany]; *Disciple of Dracula*; *Drácula, príncipe de las tinieblas* [Spain]; *Dracula* [Sweden]; *Dracula — pimeyden ruhtinas* [Finland]; *Dracula 3*; *Dracula principe delle tenebre* [Italy]; *Dracula, prince des ténèbres* [France]; *Drakoulas, o arhon tou Skotous* [Greece]; *Revenge of Dracula*; *Bloody Scream of Dracula*); U.K., 1966; Horror; 90 minutes/color/English/Mono/35mm; Hammer Film Productions, Bray Studios.

Producers: Anthony Nelson Key; *Writing Credits*: Jimmy Sangster (as John Sansom), Anthony Hinds (as John Elder); *Director*: Terence Fisher; *Cinematography*: Michael Reed; *Film Editing*: Chris Barnes; *Original Music*: James Bernard; *Art Direction*: Don Mingaye; *Make-Up*: Roy Ashton, Frieda Steiger; *Special Effects*: Les Bowie; *Cast*: Christopher Lee (Count Dracula), Barbara Shelley (Helen Kent), Andrew Keir (Father Sandor), Francis Matthews (Charles Kent), Suzan Farmer (Diana Kent), Charles "Bud" Tingwell (Alan Kent) Thorley Walters (Ludwig), Philip Latham (Klove), Walter Brown (Brother Mark), George Woodbridge (Landlord), Jack Lambert (Brother Peter), Philip Ray (Priest), Joyce Hemson (Frau Koenig), John Maxim (Coach Driver), Peter Cushing (Doctor Van Helsing)

Ten years have passed since the demise of Dracula when a party of travelers finds itself stranded along a path near Dracula's castle. Seeking shelter for the night, the party ventures to the castle, where, by the next morning, two members of the party have gone missing. What they do not realize is that their friends have fallen prey to Dracula and his minion. A battle ensues shortly after.

Dracula: Prince of Marketing; U.S., 2008; Horror, Comedy/Short; 10 minutes/color/English/Stereo; AVClubProductions.

Writing Credits: Tim Hall; *Director*: Tim Hall; *Cinematography*: Chris Elliott; *Film Editing*: Tim Hall; *Original Music*: UniqueTracks; *Cast*: Adam Laupus (Alan du Trucco/Count Dracula), Tim Hall (Van Helsing), Alison Klapthor (bride), Lillie Mear (bride), Pamela Notarantonio (bride), Brian McKay (security guard), Phil Falco (Bob Enfield), Reka Simonsen (Elizabeth Van Helsing [photo]), Ronya Fattouh (Mina Carandini [photo]).

This short adaptation of Dracula is set in modern-day New York City, where Van Helsing works as a Victorian-clad desk clerk who attempts to kill the newly hired executive of marketing, Alan du Tracco, which is an anagram for "Count Dracula."

Dracula: Revamped; U.S., 2007; Comedy/Short; 14 minutes/color/English/Dolby; Noc-Off Productions.

Producers: Andrew Burks, Michael Cheeseman, Patrick Nicely; *Writing Credits*: Michael Cheeseman, Patrick Nicely; *Director*: Patrick Nicely; *Cinematography*: Andrew Burks; *Cast*: Karl Andrew (Count Dracula), Landen Celano (Billy "Porkchop" McGee), Brandon Flock (Gay Cowboy), Riley William Wood (Matthew "Turkey" McDaniels).

The legendary Count Dracula decides to give up a life of evil and move to California in order to start over. He enrolls in a local university and becomes best friends with his new roommates, Matt and Billy. Dracula's new life seems perfect — until he contracts AIDS.

Dracula Rising (*Dracula: il risveglio* [Italy]; *Corman's Dracula* [Germany, Hungary]); U.S., 1993; Horror, Romance; 85 minutes/color/English/Stereo/35 mm; New Horizon Picture Group.

Producers: Roger Corman, Mary Ann Fisher, Steven Rabiner; *Writing Credits*: Rodman Flender, Daniella Purcell; *Director*: Fred Gallo; *Cinematography*: Ivan Verimezov; *Film Editing*: Glenn Garland; *Original Music*: Ed Tomney; *Art Direction*: Mira Chang; *Cast*: Christopher Atkins (Vlad), Stacey Travis (Theresa), Doug Wert (Alec), Vessela Karlukovska (Michelle) Nikolai Sotirov (Timothy), Zahari Vatahov (Vlad the Impaler), Desi Stoyanova (Anna), Stancho Stanchev (Cab Driver), Nelli Vladova (Maid), Tara McCann (uncredited).

Theresa (Stacey Travis) meets Vlad (Christopher Atkins) at a gallery party where they dance all night. He disappears soon after and she starts to have dreams about him. Theresa is asked to restore a painting of Vlad the Impaler (Dracula) in Eastern Europe, and there she again runs into Vlad. Her employer wants her killed, but Vlad tries to save her.

Dracula, the Great Undead (*Drácula, el rey de los muertos vivos* [Venezuelan]; *Vincent Price's Dracula* [U.S.]); U.S., 1985; Horror/Documentary; 60 minutes/color/English/Mono; M&M Film Productions.

Producers: Vincent Price; *Director*: John Muller; *Cast*: Vincent Price (Host/narrator)

Vincent Price hosts this in-depth look at Hollywood's obsession and portrayal of the bloodsucking creature of the night, including several of Béla Lugosi's films. Archive footage includes: *Mark of the Vampire* (1935), *Nosferatu: Eine Symphonie des Grauens* (1922), *The Return of Dracula* (1958), *The Return of the Vampire* (1944), *Vampyr — Der Traum des Allan Grey* (1932).

Dracula the Impaler (*Vlad Tepes, the Impaler* [Romania] [working title]); Romania, 2002; Action, Docudrama, Horror; 90 minutes/color/English/35mm; Artis Film.

Producers: Cornelia Palos, Adrian Popovici; *Writing Credits*: Ioan Carmazan, Nicu Covaci, Ted Nicolaou, Radu Petrescu-Aneste; *Director*: Adrian Popovici; *Cinematography*: Marian Stanciu; *Film Editing*: Nita Chivulescu, Alfredo Mihaicut, Adrian Popovici; *Original Music*: Vlady Cnejevici; *Cast*: Marius Bodochi (Vlad), Adrian Pintea (Vambery), Gabi Andronache (Hagen), Marcel Iures (Vlad [voice]), Lamia Beligan, Vlad Radescu.

Vlad Dracula chooses to fight for humankind and begins a quest to destroy all other vampires. His journeys take him to a Gothic church where he meets Vambery, the vampire who cursed Dracula and who Dracula thought he had killed hundreds of years earlier.

Dracula: The Series (TV Series); U.S., 1990–1991; Drama, Horror/Television; 30 minutes/English; Cinexus/Famous Players.

Producers: Glenn Davis, Wendy Grean, William Laurin; *Writing Credits*: Phil Bedard, Larry Lalonde, Peter Meech; *Director*: Allan Eastman (7 episodes, 1990), Rene Bonniere (4 episodes, 1990–1991), Allan King (3 episodes, 1990–1991), Randy Bradshaw (2 episodes, 1990–1991), Allan Kroeker (2 episodes, 1991), Jeff Woolnough (2 episodes, 1991), Joe Dea (unknown episodes); *Cinematography*: C.W. Fallin (unknown episodes); *Film Editing*: Brian Q. Kelley (2 episodes, 1990); *Original Music*: Christopher Dedrick (unknown episodes); *Special Effects*: John Gajdecki (visual effects supervisor [unknown episodes]), Gudrun Heinze (animation co-ordinator/effects animator [unknown episodes]); *Cast*: Bernard Behrens (Gustav Helsing [21 episodes, 1990–1991]), Geordie Johnson (Alexander Lucard [21 episodes, 1990–1991]), Mia Kirshner (Sophie Metternich [21 episodes, 1990–1991]), Joe Roncetti (Christopher Townsend [21 episodes, 1990–1991]), Jacob Tierney (Max Townsend [21 episodes, 1990–1991]), Geraint Wyn Davies (Klaus Helsing [5 episodes, 1990–1991]), Phil Bedard ("Hot & Steamy" Schnitzel Delivery Boy [2 episodes, 1990–1991]), Patrick Monckton (Magnus St. John-Smythe [2 episodes, 1990]), Tamara Gorski (Alexa Singleton [2 episodes, 1991]).

Max and Chris Town are sent to Europe to live with their Uncle Gustav Helsing due to their mother's constant business affairs. After arriving at their uncle's place, they realize he's actually a vampire hunter, and his main target is business tycoon Alexander Lucard, who, unbeknownst to everyone else, is Dracula.

Dracula: The True Story; U.S., 1997; Documentary; English.

Director: Matthias Kessler.

This documentary examines the myth of Dracula. The director investigates Bram Stoker's inspiration for the book and the movies.

Drácula, Uma História de Amor (TV Series); Brazil, 1980; Horror, Romance/Television; Portuguese; TV Tupi.

Writing Credits: Rubens Ewald Filho; *Director*: Atílio Riccó; *Cast*: Rubens de Falco (Conde Vladimir Drácula), Carlos Alberto Riccelli (Rafael), Bruna Lombardi (Mariana), Cleyde Yáconis (Dona Marta), Isabel Ribeiro (Hannah), Paulo Goulart (Jonathan), Flávio Galvão, (Tonico), Paulo Castelli (Fernando), Cláudia Alencar (Alcina), Annamaria Dias, Marcos Plonka (seu Honorato), Maria Helena (Steiner), Matheus Carrieri (Edu).

Dracula Vs. Frankenstein (*Blodsmässa* [Sweden]; *Blood Freaks* [U.S., working title]; *Blood of Frankenstein* [undefined]; *Dracula à la recherche de Frankenstein* [France]; *Dracula contre Frankenstein* [France]; *Draculas Bluthochzeit mit Frankenstein* [West Germany]; *Drakula kontra Frankenstein* [Poland]; *Satan's Bloody Freaks* [undefined]; *Teenage Dracula* [undefined]; *The Blood Seekers* [undefined]; *The Revenge of Dracula* [undefined]; *Verimessu* [Finland]); U.S., 1971; Horror, Science Fiction; 90 minutes/color/English/Mono; Independent International Pictures (I–I).

Producers: Al Adamson, Mardi Rustam, Mohammed Rustam, Samuel M. Sherman, John Van Horne (as John Van Horn); *Writing Credits*: William Pugsley, Samuel M. Sherman (as Sam Sherman); *Director*: Al Adamson; *Cinematography*: Paul Glickman, Gary Graver; *Film Editing*: Irwin Cadden *Original Music*: William Lava; *Art Direction*: Ray Markham; *Make-Up*: Gary Kent, Sheldon Lee, Tony Tierney (special makeup), George Barr (uncredited); *Special Effects*: Ken Strickfaden; *Cast*: J. Carrol Naish (Dr. Frankenstein, aka Dr. Duryea), Lon Chaney Jr. (Groton, as Lon Chaney), Anthony Eisley (Mike Howard), Regina Carrol (Judith Fontaine), Greydon Clark (Strange), Zandor Vorkov (Count Dracula), Angelo Rossitto (Grazbo), Anne Morrell (Samantha), William Bonner (Biker), Russ Tamblyn (Rico), Jim Davis (Police Sgt. Martin), John Bloom (Frankenstein's Monster), Shelly Weiss (The Creature), Forrest J. Ackerman (Dr. Beaumont, as Forest J. Ackerman), Maria Lease (Jodie), Bruce Kimball (Biker), Albert Cole (Cop Killed by Creature), Gary Kent (Bob, Beach Boy), Irv Saunders (Policeman), Lu Dorn, Sean Graver, Barney Gelfan, Al Adamson (Man in Audience, uncredited), Gary Graver (Man on Beach, uncredited), Connie Nelson (Laura, Beach Girl, uncredited)

Doctor Duryea (J. Carroll Naish), a sideshow owner and mad scientist working on a blood serum, must collect the blood of women energized with fear. To do this, he uses his zombie, Groton (Lon Chaney Jr.), to behead them. Dracula (Zander Vorkov) visits Duryea, offering the remains of Frankestein's monster in exchange for the blood serum. But when Dracula falls for a woman, Judith Fontaine (Regina Carrol), looking for her sister, Frankenstein's monster appears to protect her.

Dracula Year Zero; U.S., 2011; Horror, Thriller, Drama, Romance, Docudrama; English; Universal Pictures, Michael de Luca Productions

Producers: Michael de Luca, Alissa Phillips, Jeff Kirschenbaum, Donna Langley; *Writing Credits*:

Zandor Vorkov, left, plays Dracula with Forrest J Ackerman as Dr. Beaumont in *Dracula Vs. Frankenstein* (U.S., 1971).

Matt Sazama Burk Sharpless; *Director*: Alex Proyas.

During the Turkish Invasion of Romania, Vlad the Impaler is willing to risk everything to save his country, even if it means he is forever cast to be a creature of the night.

Dracula's Baby; U.S., 1970; Musical.
Producer: Andy Warhol; *Director*: Andy Warhol.
This is a vampire musical.

Dracula's Bram Stoker; Ireland, 2003; Documentary, Television; 52 minutes [Norway]/color/English/Stereo; Ferndale Films.
Producers: Anne Marie Naughton, Noel Pearson; *Writing Credits*: Sinead O'Brien, Stephen Salvati; *Director*: Sinead O'Brien; *Original Music*: Richie Buckley; *Art Direction*: Sinead Kavanagh; *Cast*: John Hurt (Narrator), Owen Killian (Young Bram Stoker), Christopher Lee (Himself), Caitríona Ní Mhurchú (voice), Patrick Sutton (Bram Stoker).

This documentary examines the life of Bram Stoker, following closely the events that may have inspired him to write *Dracula*.

Dracula's Curse (*Bram Stocker's I katara tou Drakoula* [Greece (DVD title)]; *Bram Stoker's Dracula's Curse* [Australia (DVD title)]); U.S., 2006; Horror; 107 minutes/color/English; Timeless Media Group, Eagle Entertainment.
Producers: David Michael Latt, David Rimawi, Sherri Strain, Rick Walker; *Writing Credits*: Leigh Scott; *Director*: Leigh Scott; *Cinematography*: Steven Parker; *Film Editing*: Leigh Scott; *Original Music*: Eliza Swenson; *Art Direction*: Clint Zoccoli; *Make-Up*: Jennifer Greenberg, Eva Lohse, Kelley Mitchell, Erik Porn; *Special Effects*:

Thomas Downey; *Cast*: Thomas Downey (Rufus King), Eliza Swenson (Gracie Johannsen), Rhett Giles (Jacob Van Helsing), Christina Rosenberg (Countess Bathorly), Jeff Denton (Rafe), Amanda Barton (Darvulia), Tom Nagel (Rick Tattinger), Rebekah Kochan (Trixie McFly), Sarah Hall (Sadie Macpherson), Chriss Anglin (Rich "Nebraska"

Zulkowski), Justin Jones (Maximillian), Sarah Lieving (Alex Deveraux), Leigh Scott (The Old One), Marie Westbrook (Anastasia Ravenwood), Jennifer Lee Wiggins (Dorthea), Vanessa Rooke (Katarina), Marat Glazer (Ivan Iwazkiewicz), Vaz Andreas (Tsorak), David Shick (Lord Treykahn), Noel Thurman (Denise), Michael Tower (Crypt Watcher), Elissa Dowling (Pure Blood) (as Elissa Bree), Griff Furst (Konstantinos), Monique La Barr (Erzsi), Ruffy Landayan (Lau), Mia Moretti (Juditha), Crystal Napoles (Selene), Kat Ochsner (Vixen), Derek Osedach (Jimmy D'Amico), Rajah (Curtis), Erica Roby (Christina Lockheart), Nick Wall (Bouncer).

The Nine ia a group of vampire hunters who organize a treaty between several vampire clans. When the agreement is broken by an evil countess, Elizabeth Bathorly (Christina Rosenberg), the Nine is forced back together in a showdown with Bathorly.

Dracula's Curse: Behind the Scenes; U.S., 2006; Short, Documentary; 8 minutes/color/English; The Global Asylum.

Producers: David Michael Latt, Derek Osedach, David Rimawi, Sherri Strain; *Director*: Derek Osedach; *Film Editing*: Derek Osedach; *Cast*: Thomas Downey (Himself), Rhett Giles (Himself), Tom Nagel (Himself), Derek Osedach (Himself), Leigh Scott (Himself), Eliza Swenson (Herself).

This short documentary features the actors from the film *Dracula's Curse*, who provide commentary on their respective roles.

Dracula's Daughter (*Hija de Drácula, La* [Argentina/Spain]; *Córka Drakuli* [Poland]; *Draculas dotter* [Sweden]; *Figlia di Dracula, La* [Italy]; *Fille de Dracula, La* [France]; *Kori tou Drakoula, I* [Greece]); U.S., 1936; Drama, Horror; 71 minutes/black and white/English/Mono; Universal Studios.

Producers: Harry Zehner, E.M. Asher; *Writing Credits*: David O. Selznick (as Oliver Jeffries) Garrett Fort, John L. Balderston, Kurt Neumann, Charles Belden, Finley Peter Dunne, R.C. Sherriff; *Director*: Lambert Hillyer; *Cinematography*: George Robinson; *Film Editing*: Milton Carruth; *Original Music*: Heinz Roemheld (uncredited); *Art Direction*: Albert S. D'Agostino; *Make-Up*: Otto Lederer

Gloria Holden, right, plays Countess Marya Zaleska opposite Nan Grey as Lili in *Dracula's Daughter* (U.S., 1936).

(uncredited), Jack P. Pierce (uncredited); *Cast*: Otto Kruger (Dr. Jeffrey Garth), Gloria Holden (Countess Marya Zaleska), Marguerite Churchill (Janet Blake), Edward Van Sloan (Prof. Von Helsing), Gilbert Emery (Sir Basil Humphrey), Irving Pichel (Sandor), Halliwell Hobbes (Const. Sgt. Hawkins [as Halliwell Hobbs]), Billy Bevan (Const. Albert), Nan Grey (Lili), Hedda Hopper (Lady Esme Hammond), Claud Allister (Sir Aubrey Vail) (as Claude Allister), Edgar Norton (Hobbs) (Sir Basil's butler), E.E. Clive (Sgt. Wilkes), Agnes Anderson (Elena) (bride in Transylvania [uncredited]), John Blood (Bobby [uncredited]), David Dunbar (Motor bobby [uncredited]), Douglas Gordon (Attendant [uncredited]), Owen Gorin (Groom's friend [uncredited]), Gordon Hart (Mr. Graham) (host [uncredited]), Elsa Janssen (Wedding guest [uncredited]), Guy Kingsford (Radio announcer [uncredited]), George Kirby (Bookstore proprietor [uncredited]), Edna Lyall (Nurse [uncredited]), Eily Malyon (Miss Peabody) (nurse [uncredited]), Paul Mitchell (Messenger [uncredited]), Clive Morgan (Desk sergeant [uncredited]), Vesey O'Davoren (Butler [uncredited]), John Power (Police official [uncredited]), Hedwiga Reicher (Innkeeper's wife [uncredited]), Christian Rub (Coachman [uncredited]), William Schramm (Groom in Transylvania [uncredited]), George Sorel (Police officer [uncredited]), Pietro Sosso (Priest [uncredited]), Bert Sprotte (Wedding guest [uncredited]), Vernon Steele (Squires [uncredited]), Joseph R. Tozer (Dr. Graham) (attending Lili [uncredited]), Silvia Vaughan (Nurse [uncredited]), Wilhelm von Brincken (Policeman [uncredited]), Fred Walton (Dr. Beemish) (Chief of Staff [uncredited]), Paul Weigel (Transylvania innkeeper [uncredited]), Eric Wilton (Butler [uncredited]), Douglas Wood (Dr. Townsend) (attending Lili [uncredited]).

Before Professor Von Helsing (Edward Von Sloan) can be prosecuted for the murder of Dracula, a hypnotic woman steals the Count's body and cremates it. The beautiful woman is Hungarian Countess Marya Zaleska (Gloria Holden) who, after settling in London, soon displays her father's (Count Dracula) predatory affinity for blood, as drained corpses begin appearing in London again. Zaleska seeks the help of psychiatrist Jeffrey Garth (Otto Kruger) in trying to rid herself of her father's evil influence. The film is based on Bram Stoker's short work that was posthumously published by Florence Stoker as *Dracula's Guest* (1914).

Dracula's Dog (*Dracula contro Zombi* [Italy]; *Lykoskylo tou Drakoula,* [Greece (reissue title)]; *Perro de Satán, El* [Spain]; *Skylia tou Drakoula, Ta* [Greece]; *Zoltan — O Cão Vampiro de Drácula* [Brazil]; *Zoltan il cane di Dracula* [Italy]; *Zoltan,* *Draculas Bluthund* [West Germany]; *Zoltan, Hound of Dracula* [U.K.]; *Zoltan, le chien sanglant de Dracula* [France]); U.S., 1978; Horror; 90 minutes/color/English/Mono/35mm; EMI Television, VIC Productions.

Producers: Albert Band, Philip Collins, Frank Ray Perilli; *Writing Credits*: Frank Ray Perilli; *Director*: Albert Band; *Cinematography*: Bruce Logan; *Film Editing*: Harry Keramidas; *Original Music*: Andrew Belling; *Make-Up*: Zoltan Elek, Stan Winston; *Special Effects*: Stan Winston; *Cast*: Michael Pataki (Michael Drake/Count Dracula), Jan Shutan (Marla Drake), Libby Chase (Linda Drake), John Levin (Steve Drake), Reggie Nalder (Veidt Smith), Cleo Harrington (Pat Parks), Tom Gerrard (Maslov, the guard), Bob Miller (Lieutenant), Gordon McGill (Second Officer), Al Ferrara (Al, the deputy), Roger Pancake (Sheriff), Sally Marr (Camper), Merryl Jay (Camper), Jackie Drake (Camper), John Kirby (Traveler), Darlene Craviotto (Traveller), Lou Schumacher (Customs Inspector), Carl Morrison (Customs Inspector), Dimitri Logothetis (Corporal), Chris George (Soldier), Dwight Krizman (Soldier), Roger Schumacher (Hiker), Dominic Ferlan (Villager), Katherine Fitzpatrick (Dracula's Victim), Joan Leone (Car Rental Agent), Arlene Martel (Maj. Hessel), Simmy Bow (Fisherman), JoJo D'Amore (Fisherman), José Ferrer (Inspector Branco).

While digging in a field in Romania, Russian soldiers unearth Dracula's entire family tomb. When an earthquake knocks open one of the unnamed, one solider mistakenly removes the stake from the covered body. With the stake removed, a big black dog, Zolton, leaps from the coffin and kills the solider. Zolton, along with Dracula's renfield, Veidt Smith, travel to the United States to find the last remaining descendent of Dracula, Michael Drake, to make him their new vampire master.

Dracula's Family Visit; Netherlands, 2006; Comedy; 87 minutes/color/Dutch.

Writing Credits: Monique Breet; *Director*: Monique Breet; *Film Editing*: Mathijs Altena; *Cast*: Harrie Juijs (Dracula), Sander Kocken (Satan), Galyna Kyyashko (Sophie), Claudia Neeft (Angelica, the cook), Roel Peeters (Frank van Helsing, detective), Luca Schoonheijt (Lotti), Robin Schoonheijt (Luna), Alix Schoonhevt (Hoofddoekie), Carlo Smeets (Edwin, the driver), Veerle Snijders (Doris), Gwendolyn Snowdon (Alexi), Maria Stuut (Florentina), Roy van Breeman (Assi, dental assistant), Andre van Leeuwen (Styx), Marjolein van Ziel (Agaath), Jaro Wolff (Roderick, the butler).

Damion Dracula lives in a big house with his Siamese-twin daughters and his staff. His half-sister, Agaath, and her daughter Florentina come over to stay for a few days, followed soon after by two young female tourists. Dracula throws a big party, but it's not long before terrible things start to happen.

Dracula's Guest (*Bram Stoker's Dracula's Guest* [Australia]; *Bram Stokers Draculas Gast* [Germany, DVD title]); U.S., 2008; Adventure, Horror; 87 minutes/color/English; North American Entertainment.

Producers: Barry Barnholtz, Melvin Butters, Michael Feifer, Diane Healey; *Writing Credits*: Michael Feifer; *Director*: Michael Feifer; *Cinematography*: Charles Haine; *Film Editing*: Leaf Baimbridge; *Original Music*: Andres Boulton; *Art Direction*: Carlo Garduno; *Make-Up*: Melissa Anchondo; *Cast*: Amy Lyndon (Mrs. Witham), Wes Ramsey (Bram Stoker), Andrew Bryniarski (Count Dracula), Kelsey McCann (Elizabeth), Dan Speaker (Admiral Murray), Ryan Christiansen (Malcolm), Caia Coley (Mrs. Murray), Thomas Garner (Mr. Quartermane), Robert Smith (Johann [as Robert Ragis]), Maya Waterman (Shanty Woman), Stan Bly (Pierre), Robert William Madrigal (Dracula's Carriage Driver), Nino Simon (Herr Delbruch), Andy Parks (Conductor), Daniel Bonjour (German Captain), Daniel Tostenson (German Soldier #1), Jennifer House (Diana), Michael Feifer (Admiral's Carriage Driver), Dustin Clyde (Real Estate Office Client), Jennifer Bailey (Diana), Peter Bisson (Rat Person), Monica Braunger (Rat Person), Liana Bryer (Zombie), Jeffrey English (Rat Person/Soldier), David Flores (Soldier), David Flores (Soldier), Mark Irvingsen (Soldier), Mike Korich (Rat Person), Sarah Long (Dracula's Concubine), Jason Medbury (Rat Person/Soldier), Tom Oman (Dudley Stephens), Ragan O'Reilly (Dracula's Concubine [as Ragen O'Reilly]), Melissa Redmond (Dracula's Concubine), Christina Rivers (Dracula's Concubine), Sarah Scherger (Dracula's Concubine), John Searles (Rat Person/Soldier).

Bram Stoker and Elizabeth are young lovers whose union is forbidden by Elizabeth's father. Elizabeth, in an attempt to escape her father, runs away to London where she is kidnapped by Count Dracula. Dracula keeps Elizabeth prisoner at his castle in an effort to draw Bram there, where he will settle an old family dispute between the Stokers and the Draculas.

Dracula's Stoker; Ireland, 2009; Drama, Horror, Mystery/Documentary; 112 minutes/color/English/Dolby Digital; Eurofox Pictures.

Producers: Stephen Salvati; *Writing Credits*: Stephen Salvati; *Director*: Stephan Salvati; *Cinematography*: Stephen Salvati; *Film Editing*: Stephen Salvati; *Original Music*: Jerome Moore, Jeremy Soule, Julian Soule; *Art Direction*: Sergey Gusev, Stephen Salvati; *Make-Up*: Tihana Petrovic; *Special Effects*: John Lawless, Albert Monaghan, Stephen Salvati; *Cast*: Stephen Salvati (Van Helsing/Dracula), Sergey Gusev (Ancient Spirit), Audrey McCoy (Florence Balcombe), John Canning (Oscar Wilde), Sharon McCoy (Dracula's bride), Joe McCoy (Bram Stoker), Katerina Lavrenova (Dracula's bride), Lara Doree (Dracula's bride), Monica Salvati O'Neill (Dracula's Bride), Andrei Coliban (Johnathan Harker), Angelica Antonova (Vampiress).

This documentary examines Bram Stoker, the author of *Dracula*. It researches the influential places, people, and events of his life that may have led to the creation of his character Dracula.

Dracula's Wedding Day; U.S., 1967; Horror/Short; 4:45 minutes/black and white/Silent/16mm; The Film-Makers' Cooperative.

Producer: Mike Jacobson; *Director*: Mike Jacobson.

This underground silent, purple-tinted film features Dracula, who leads a girl he has just hypnotized into a cave at sunset.

Dracula's Widow; U.S., 1988; Horror; 86 minutes/color/English/Stereo; De Laurentiis Entertainment Group (DEG).

Producers: Stephen Traxler; *Writing Credits*: Christopher Coppola, Kathryn Ann Thomas; *Director*: Christopher Coppola; *Cinematography*: Giuseppe Maccari; *Film Editing*: Tom Siiter; *Make-Up*: Dean Gates, Melissa Walden, June Westmore; *Special Effects*: Greg Browning, William G. Davis, Todd Masters, Joe Quinlivan; *Cast*: Sylvia Kristel (Vanessa), Josef Sommer (Lannon), Lenny von Dohlen (Raymond), Marc Coppola (Brad), Stefan Schnabel (Helsing), Rachel Jones (Jenny), Duke Ernsberger (Bart), G.F. Rowe (Lou), Richard K. Olsen (The Drunk [as Richard Olsen]), Lucius Houghton (Willie), J. Michael Hunter (Dave), Traber Burns (Citrano), Dick Langdon (Nightwatchman), Adrienne Stout (Babs), Tracy Tanen (Juliet), Paul J.Q. Lee (Suit Officer), John Woodson (Uniform Officer), Kelly Cole (Scarface), Candice Sims (The Victim), Elizabeth Hayes (Reporter #1), Bill Brown (Reporter #2), George Stover (Coroner), Patricia Guinan (Rose), Rick Warner (Caulfield), Laurens Moore (Forensics Investigator), Laurie Quinlivan (Reporter #3), Tom McGovern (Questioner #1), Elliot Moffit (Questioner #2), Oseland (Jail Clerk), Bev Appleton (Guard), Jack Cannon (Orderly).

Raymond Everett (Lenny von Dohlen), owner of Hollywood House of Wax, waits for a shipment of artifacts from Romania to arrive for his Dracula display. Inside one of the crates is Dracula's wife, Vanessa (Sylvia Kristel), now a widow and discovering for the first time that Van Helsing killed her husband over a century ago. She tries to transform Raymond to help her get back to Romania. But when dead bodies start appearing in town, Lieutenant Lannon (Josef Sommer), aided by Helsing's grandson, Victor (Stefan Schnabel), set out to stop and kill Vanessa and rescue Raymond.

Draculina Video Magazine; U.S., 1996; Comedy, Horror/Documentary; 67 minutes/color/English.
Director: Hugh Gallagher; *Cast*: Debbie Rochon (Herself).

Draculito, mon Saigneur (*Draculie — Der gruftstarke Vampir* [Germany 1999]); Germany, 1992; Family, Fantasy/Animation; 23 minutes/color/French.
Writing Credits: Bruno-René Huchez (idea), Hélène Joubaud (scenario and adaptation); *Director*: Bruno-René Huchez, Bahram Rohani.

Dragstrip Dracula; U.S., 1962; Horror; black and white/English/16mm.
Producers: Don Glut; *Writing Credits*: Don Glut; *Director*: Don Glut; *Cinematography*: Don Glut; *Film Editing*: Don Glut; *Original Music*: Don Glut; *Make-Up*: Don Glut; *Special Effects*: Don Glut; *Cast*: Don Glut (Dracula).
An unsuspecting teenager finds the staked skeletal remains of a teenage Dracula (Don Glut). After reviving Dracula, the unsuspecting teenager becomes his next victim. *Dragstrip Dracula* is one of many amateur teenage monster films made by Don Glut.

The Drak Pack (TV Series); U.S., 1980; Adventure, Comedy/Television, Animation; 30 minutes/color/English/Mono; CBS-TV.
Producers: Art Scott, Joseph Barbera, William Hanna; *Writing Credits*: Doug Booth, Larz Bourne, Glenn Leopold, Cliff Roberts; *Director*: Chris Cuddington; *Film Editing*: Gil Iverson; *Original Music*: Hoyt Curtin; *Cast*: Alan Oppenheimer (Dracula), Jerry Dexter (Drak Jr.), Bill Callaway (Howler/Frankie), Chuck McCann (Mummy Man), Julie McWhirter (Vampira), Hans Conried (Dr. Dred), Don Messick (Toad, Fly).
Three teenagers — Franky, Howler, and Drak — discover that when they combine forces, they take on the characteristics of their Hollywood ancestors: Frankenstein, Wolfman, and Dracula. To make up for their ancestors' dark pasts, together they fight off the evil power of The Organization for Generally Rotten Enterprises (a.k.a. OGRE) and its leader, Dr. Dred.

Drakoulas & Sia (*Dracula and Me* [U.K.]); Greece, 1959; Comedy, Horror, Mystery; 78 minutes, black and white, Greek; Hrisma Films.
Writing Credits: Giorgos Giannakopoulos; *Director*: Errikos Iatrou; *Cinematography*: Gerasimos Kalogeratos; *Cast*: Costas Hajihristos (Thanasis Karatribouras); Ketty Diridaoua (Margie Bobots); Kostas Doukas (Apostolos); Linda Alma (Dancer); Nitza Avantagelou; Nikos Fermas; Giannis Flery (Dancer); Nana Gatsi (Theano); Katerina Gogou (as Kaiti Gogou); Despoina Gounaropoulou; Takis Hristoforidis (Giorgakis Polyzois); Dimitris Katsoulis; Sylvios Lahanas; Anna Matzourani; N. Palagarinos; Valentini Rouli; P. Sotiriou; Mimis Thiopoulos; D. Vasileiadis; Stratos Zamidis.

O Drakoulas ton Exarheion (*Dracula of Exarcheia* [International English title]); Greece, 1983; Comedy, Horror, Musical; 87 minutes/color/Greek/Mono; Allagi Films, Vimar, Movie Makers.
Producers: Vasilis Alatas, Nikos Zervos; *Writing Credits*: Vangelis Kotronis, Lili Panousi, Tzimis Panousis, Nikos Zervos; *Director*: Nikos Zervos; *Cinematography*: Spiros Nounesis; *Film Editing*: Atonis Tempos; *Original Music*: Tzimis Panousis, Mousikes Taxiarhies; *Art Direction*: Tzimis Panousis; *Make-Up*: Achilles Haritos, Loukia Stergiou; *Special Effects*: Yannis Samiotis; *Cast*: Konstantinos Tzouma (Victor Papadopoulos), Tzimis Panousis (uncredited), Vangelis Kotronis (Kotronis), Issavella Mavraki (Ioulieta), Maria Tsakalidou (uncredited), Nikolas Asimos (uncredited), Antonis Kafetzopoulos (uncredited), Dimitris Poulikakos (Police Officer), Johnny Vavouras (Aphrodite), Thekla Tselepi (uncredited), Fei Damianaki (uncredited), Sakis Boulas (uncredited), Hristina Aulianou (uncredited), Giannis Kouriotis (uncredited), Giannis Mihalakos (uncredited), Panayotis Kaldis (uncredited), Alekos Arpalias (uncredited), Mary Garitsi (Maria Garitsi), Lili Panousi (uncredited), Mousikes Taxiarhies (The Band), Kostas Bournazos (Body Builder), Spyros Bournazos (Body Builder), Angela Bournia (uncredited), Babis Dimoliatis (uncredited), Eleni Giokari (uncredited), Alexandros Havellas (uncredited), Ioanna Hristopoulou (uncredited), Kostas Koukios (uncredited), Giannis Koukos (Body Builder), Maria Kyriaki (uncredited), Katerina Lygiou (uncredited), Dimitris Mantzos (uncredited), Giorgos Margaritis (uncredited), Hristos Margaritis (uncredited), Vangelis Mikrelis (uncredited), Maria Mouhtaridou (uncredited), Martha Moutsaki (uncredited), Dimitra Neonaki (uncredited), Ioanna Panteli (uncredited), Valentina Ross (uncredited), Kalliopi Saivanidou (uncredited), Smaragda Skourta (uncredited), Anna Sotrini (uncredited), Sotiris Stefanopoulos (uncredited), Fay Tsanetopoulou (uncredited), Lili Tsi-

garida (uncredited), Vaso Tsigarida (uncredited), Hrysi Tsiouri (uncredited), Antonis Xydis (uncredited), Nikos Zervos (uncredited).

Dracula leaves for Athens from his Transylvanian homeland. While in Greece, Dracula and his servants fashion a Frankensteinian Monster out of body parts from legendary musicians (like Jimi Hendrix), in the hopes of turning their creation into a rock music superstar.

Drakula Goes to R.P.; Philippines, 1973; Comedy, Horror; Filipino, Tagalog/color; RVQ Productions.

Producers: Dolphy (as Rodolfo V. Quizon); *Writing Credits*: Bram Stoker, Ading Fernando; *Director*: Tony Cayado; *Cinematography*: Manuel Bolotano (as Manuel Bulotano); *Original Music*: Ernani Cuenco; *Cast*: Dolphy, Rod Navarro, Pugo, Maritess Revilla, Panchito, Marissa Delgado, Babalu, Virginia Montes, Teroy de Guzman, Georgie Quizon, Andres Centenera, Manny Tibayan, Bayani Casimiro.

Drakula halála (*The Death of Drakula*; *Drakula's Death*); Hungary/Austria, 1921; Horror, Thriller; black and white/Hungarian/silent.

Writing Credits: Károly Lajthay, Michael Curtiz (uncredited); *Director*: Károly Lajthay; *Cinematography*: Eduard Hoesch; *Cast*: Paul Askonas (Drakula), Carl Goetz (Funnyman), Károly Hatvani, Anna Marie Hegener, Aladár Ihász (assistant), Paula Kende, Dezsö Kertész (George), Margit Lux, Lene Myl (Mary Land), Oszkár Perczel, Lajos Réthey (The fake-doctor), Magda Sonja, Lajos Szalkai, Elemér Thury (doctor), Béla Tímár.

Ad for ***Drakula Goes to R.P.*** (Philippines, 1973) (courtesy Simon Santos).

A girl experiences frightening dreams after visiting a sanitarium where one of the patients, the girl's former music professor, has gone mad and claims to be the evil Drakula, an immortal who has lived for a thousand years.

Drakula Istanbul'da (*Dracula in Istanbul* [International (English title)]); Turkey, 1953; Horror; black and white/Turkish; And Film.

Producers: Turgut Demirag; *Writing Credits*: Umit Deniz (writer), Ali Riza Seyfi (novel adaptation); *Director*: Mehmet Mutar; *Cinematography*: Ozen Sermet; *Cast*: Atif Kaptan (Drakula), Annie Ball (Güzin), Bülent Oran (Azmi), Ayfer Feray (Sadan), Cahit Irgat (Turan), Münir Ceyhan, Kemal Emin Bara, Osman Alyanak, Eser Tezcan, Kadri Ögelman, Ahmet Danyal Topatan (Watchman of the cemetery [uncredited]).

This is a Turkish film based on the novel by **Bram Stoker**. Dracula (Atif Kaptan) recruits people into his undead legion. Guzin (Annie Ball) is a cabaret dancer that he threatens to recruit to take the place of Mina Seward, a demure innocent young woman.

Drakulita; Philippines, 1969; Horror; Filipino, Tagalog; Barangay Productions, RJF Bros. Pictures.

Paul Askonas plays Drakula in the Hungarian film *Drakula halála* (1921), now regarded as the first cinematic portrayal featuring Dracula.

Writing Credits: Rico Bello Omagap (story), Consuelo Osorio (screenplay); *Director*: Consuelo Osorio; *Original Music*: Demetrio Velasquez (as Demet Velasquez); *Cast*: Lito Legaspi, Rebecca, Gina Laforteza, Joseph Gallego, Rebecca Rocha, German Moreno, Ike Lozada, Nora Aunor, Tirso Cruz III, Edgar Mortiz, Ricardo "Bebong" Osario (as Bebong Osorio, Martin Marfil, Matimtiman Cruz, Ernie White, Efren Reyes Jr., Jessette, Tony Salgado, Angela Montes, Yola Nieva, Edgar Garcia, Lito Calzado, Rosanna Ortiz.

Poster art for *Drakula Istanbul'da* (Turkey, 1953; *Dracula in Istanbul* [International English title]) (courtesy David J. Skal).

Drum bun — Jo utat! (*Drum Bun — Gute Reise* [Germany]; Hungary/Germany/Switzerland, 2004; Comedy; 75 minutes/color/English, Hungarian, German, Romanian; Gute filme, Duna Televizio.
Producers: Gyorgy Durst, Robert Ralston; *Writing Credits*: Robert Ralston, Felix Theissen; *Director*: Robert Ralston; *Cinematography*: Gyorgy Boros; *Film Editing*: Christof Schilling; *Original Music*: Ben Abarbanel-Wolff, Kanizsa Csillagai; *Cast*: Bocskor Salló Lóránt (as Bocskor Lóránt), Krisztina Bíró (as Bíró Kriszta), Tibor Pálffy, Juliane Kindler, Ferenc Szélyes, Andrea Szélyes, Emő Szabadi, Alfréd Nagy, Attila Zsigmond, Tibor Csergő, László Gorové, Iuliu Fagarasan, Ioan Teran, Felix Theissen.

The story follows Martin, who has to go back to Transylvania (Romania) rather unexpectedly to obtain the remains of his father, Dracula. Once he arrives, he is overwhelmed with having to deal with a belligerent couple, and the trip turns into a drawn-out ordeal all over the eastern half of Romania.

Duck Dodgers (TV Series [2003–2005], episode "I'm Going to Get You, Fat Sucka" (*Duck Dodgers in the 24½th Century* [U.S., long title]; *Duck*

Ad for *Drakulita* (Philippines, 1969) (courtesy Simon Santos).

Dodgers [Greece]); U.S., Season 1, Episode 5, 20 September 2003; Adventure, Comedy, Family/Television, Animation; 30 minutes/English/color; Warner Bros. Television Animation, Cartoon Network Studios.

Producers: Paul Dini, Tom Minton, Bobbie Page, Linda Steiner; *Writing Credits*: Spike Brandt, Tony Cervone, Paul Dini, Tom Minton; *Director*: Spike Brandt, Tony Cervone; *Film Editing*: Rob Desales; *Original Music*: Robert J. Kral; *Art Direction*: Mark Whiting; *Special Effects*: Michael Viner; *Cast*: Joe Alaskey (Daffy Duck as Duck Dodgers/Drake Darkstar [voice]), Bob Bergen (Porky Pig as The Eager Young Space Cadet [voice]), Edward Asner (Guard Captain [voice]), Dee Bradley Baker (Rookie Guard [voice]), Jeff Bennett (Count Muerte [voice]), Grey DeLisle (Vampire Bride #1/Vampire Bride #3 [voice]), Michael Dorn (Krag the Klunkin [voice]), Kevin Michael Richardson (Cat Head Murphy/Slygoe [voice]), Tasia Valenza (Vampire #2 [voice]).

Daffy Duck and company are terrorized by a blood-sucking space vampire, the Dracula-type Count Muerte.

Dugo ng Vampira; Philippines, 1969; Horror; color/Filipino; VP Pictures.

Writing Credits: Emmanuel H. Borlaza (screenplay), Rico Bello Omagap (story); *Director*: Emmanuel H. Borlaza; *Cast*: Gina Pareño, Edgar Salcedo, Myrna Delgado, Tito Galla, Charlie Davao, Bella Flores, Aring Bautista, Glenn Bernardo, Venchito Galvez, Nenita Jana, Linda Martin, Ven Medina.

La Duodécima hora; Spain, 2007; Mystery/Short; 20 minutes/color/Spanish/Dolby SR/35 mm; Lolita Films.

Producers: Damián París, Juanma Ruiz; *Writing Credits*: Rodrigo Plaza, Juanma Ruiz; *Director*: Rodrigo Plaza, Juanma Ruiz; *Cinematography*: Juanma Ruiz; *Film Editing*: Juanma Ruiz; *Cast*: Paul Naschy (Expert), Luciano Berriatúa (Expert), Juan Luis Alvarez (Narrator), Ismael Serrano (Henry Jones Sr. [voice]), Ernesto Filardi (Icarus Sherrinford [voice]), Juanma Ruiz (Icarus Sherrinford).

Friedrich Wilhelm Murnau's diary is discovered by a film restorer, which leads him to discover a secret attempt to gain immortality.

The Electric Company (TV Series) (*The Reading Program* [U.S. working title]); U.S., 1971–1977; Family, Comedy/Television; 28 minutes/color/English/Mono; Children's Television Workshop (CTW).

Producers: Naomi Foner, David D. Connell, Joan Ganz Cooney, Andrew B. Ferguson Jr., Samuel Y. Gibbon Jr., Walt Rauffer, Wibby Ritchey, Edith Zornow; *Writing Credits*: Christopher Cerf Jeremy Stevens, John Boni, Amy Ephron, Paul Dooley, Thad Mumford, Sara Compton, Tom Dunsmuir, Elaine Laron, Jim Thurman, Tom Whedon; *Director*: Henry Behar, Bob Schwarz, John Tracy; *Film Editing*: Diana Wenman; *Original Music*: Clark Gesner, Joe Raposo, Gary William Friedman, Dave Conner, Tom Lehrer; *Special Effects*: Lee Harrison III, Len Rosolio; *Cast*: Jim Boyd (Andy), Morgan Freeman (Count Dracula), Judy Graubart (Jennifer of the Jungle), Skip Hinnant (Clam), Rita Moreno (Carmela), June Angela (Julie—Member of the Short Circus), Mel Brooks (Blond-Haired Cartoon Man), Luis Avalos (Dr. Doolats), Joan Rivers (Narrator of "The Adventures of Letterman"), Gene Wilder (Letterman), Zero Mostel (Spell Binder), Hattie Winston (Sylvia), Melanie Henderson (Kathy—Member of the Short Circus), Steve Gustafson (Buddy—Member of the Short Circus), Danny Seagren (Spider-Man), Lee Chamberlin (Brenda), Bill Cosby (Hank), Gregg Burge (Dwayne—Member of the Short Circus), Todd Graff (Jesse—Member of the Short Circus), Douglas Grant (Zack—Member of the Short Circus), Bayn Johnson (Kelly—Member of the Short Circus), Rodney Lewis (Charlie—Member of the Short Circus), Réjane Magloire (Samantha—Member of the Short Circus), Janina Mathews (Gail—Member of the Short Circus), Irene Cara (Iris—Member of the Short Circus), Denise Nickerson (Allison—Member of the Short Circus), Ken Roberts (Announcer), Carol Burnett (Herself), Walt Frazier (Himself), Lorne Greene (Himself), Willie Tyler (Himself), Caroll Spinney (Big Bird), Michael Landon (Himself), Gary Owens (Himself), Dick Martin (Himself), Dan Rowan (Himself), Lily Tomlin (Herself).

Dracula (played by Morgan Freeman), or Vincent the Vegetable Vampire, was one of several recurring characters in this children's television series for PBS. Dracula was frequently pitted alongside Frankenstein's monster (Skip Hinnant) and the Wolfman (Jim Boyd).

Elmo Saves Christmas; U.S., 1996; Family, Comedy, Fantasy, Musical/Animation; 60 minutes/color/English/Dolby Digital 2.0 Stereo; Children's Television Workshop (CTW), The Jim Henson Company.

Producer: Carol Colmenares, Nancy Kanter, Karin Young Shiel; *Writing Credits*: Christine Ferraro, Tony Geiss; *Director*: Emily Squires; *Film Editing*: Scott P. Doniger; *Make-Up*: Cidele Curo; *Art Direction*: Bob Phillips; *Cast*: Charles Durning (Santa Claus), Harvey Fierstein (Easter Bunny), Caroll Spinney (Big Bird/Oscar [voice]), Carlo Alban (Carlo), Maya Angelou (Narrator), Alison Bartlett (Gina Jefferson), Fran Brill (Zoe [voice]), Kevin Clash (Elmo [voice]), Emilio Delgado (Luis), Sonia Manzano (Maria), Joey Mazzarino (Lightning [voice]), Bob McGrath (Bob), Jerry Nelson (Count von Count/Mr. Johnson/News Flash Announcer [voice]), Roscoe Orman (Gordon), Carmen Osbahr (Rosita [voice]), Frank Oz (Cookie Monster/Grover [voice]), Martin P. Robinson (Snuffleupagus/Telly Monster [voice]), David Rudman (Baby Bear/Humphrey [voice]), David Langston Smyrl (Mr. Handford), Steve Whitmire (Kermit the Frog [voice]).

Elmo is determined to stay up all night on Christmas Eve so he can meet Santa Claus but is surprised to discover that Santa has become stuck in the chimney. Elmo frees Santa from the chimney and is offered, in return, a magic snow-globe that can grant him three wishes. Elmo proceeds to wish that Christmas could be every day. As a result of Elmo's wish, things go completely amuck. For example, businesses permanently close for the holiday, the elves fail to keep up with the new pace, carolers lose their voices, and Count von Count grows weary of counting all the Christmases. Elmo uses his last wish to set things straight.

Elmo Says Boo; U.S., 1996; Family, Comedy, Fantasy/Animation; 60 minutes/color/English, Spanish.

Producer: Nancy Kanter, Karin Young Shiel; *Writing Credits*: Annie Evans, Emily Perl Kingsley; *Director*: Emily Squires, Jim Henson, Jim Martin, Randall Balsmeyer, Victor DiNapoli, Ken Diego; *Cast*: Kevin Clash (Elmo), Jerry Nelson, Frank Oz, Jerry Nelson (Count von Count), Julia Roberts (Herself), Martin P. Robinson, David Rudman (Baby bear).

Elmo pays a visit to fellow Sesame Street muppet Count von Count at his castle, where Elmo becomes momentarily scared, that is, until more friends from the Sesame Street television program show up.

Elmo Visits the Doctor; U.S., 2005; Family, Comedy, Musical/Animation; 53 minutes/color/English; Sesame Workshop.

Producer: Tim Carter, April Chadderdon, Kevin Clash, Melissa Dino, Matt Goldman, Frank Hall Green, Deborah Mayer, Dionne Lynn Nosek, Carol-Lynn Parente, Joseph Pipher, Eva Saks,

Jennifer Smith; *Writing Credits*: Annie Evans, Christine Ferraro, Judy Freudberg, Eva Saks, Luis Santeiro; *Director*: Kevin Clash, Ken Diego, Jim Martin, Edward May; *Cinematography*: Mai Iskander, Ruben O'Malley, Lyle Vincent; *Film Editing*: Erin McKnight, Savvas Paritsis, José Peláez; *Original Music*: Mike Cole, Kendall Simpson; *Cast*: Alison Bartlett (Gina), Fran Brill, Kevin Clash (Elmo), Aiden Connell, Stephanie D'Abruzzo, Alice Dinnean, Kylie Goldstein (The Impatient Patient), Bill Irwin (Mr. Noodle), Eric Jacobson, John Kennedy, Nicole Kolman, Peter Linz, Michael Lisa, Loretta Long (Susan), Vincent Lumapan, Rick Lyon, Lara MacLean, Noel MacNeal, Jim Martin, Joey Mazzarino, Jerry Nelson (The Count), Oliver Oguma, Carmen Osbahr, Frank Oz, Chris Rafinski, David Rudman, Caroll Spinney (Big Bird), Matt Vogel, Steve Whitmire (Ernie [voice]), Hatsumi Yoshida.

Elmo visits the doctor's office for the first time and learns, along with his Sesame Street friends (including Count von Count), how doctor's visits can help earaches, fevers, and stuffy noses to feel better.

Elmopalooza; U.S., 1998; Family, Comedy, Fantasy, Musical/Television, Animation; 50 minutes/color/English/Dolby Digital 5.1.

Producer: Ginger Brown; *Writing Credits*: Annie Evans, Emily Perl Kingsley; *Director*: Emily Squires, Jim Henson, Jim Martin, Randall Balsmeyer, Victor DiNapoli, Ken Diego; *Cast*: Jon Stewart (Himself/Host), David Alan Grier (Himself), Rosie O'Donnell (Herself), Gloria Estefan (Herself), Cindy Herron (Herself [as En Vogue]), Kenny Loggins (Himself), Shawn Colvin (Herself), Jimmy Buffett (Himself), Dicky Barrett (The Mighty Mighty Bosstones), Richard Belzer (Himself), Chris Rock (Himself), Cindy Crawford (Herself), Tyra Banks (Herself), Kevin Clash (Elmo [voice]), Caroll Spinney (Big Bird/Oscar [voice]), Jerry Nelson (Announcer/The Count/Two-Headed Moster [I]/Biff/Cookie Monster [assistant]/Additional Muppets [voice]), Steve Whitmire (Ernie/Kermit the Frog [voice]), Martin P. Robinson (Telly/Snuffy/Slimey/Frazzle/Yip-Yip Martian [voice]), Fran Brill (Prairie Dawn/Zoe/Penguin [voice]), David Rudman (Baby Bear/Two-Headed Monster (II)/Sparky/Yip-Yip Marsian/Forgetfull Jones [voice]), Johnny "Vegas" Burton (The Mighty Mighy Bosstones), Terry Ellis (Herself [as En Vogue]), Maxine Jones (Herself [as En Vogue]), Bob McGrath (Himself), Jenn Pinto (Kid), Dawn Robinson (Herself [as En Vogue]), Joe Selph (Additional Muppets [voice]), Ivy Austin (Oinker Sister [voice] [uncredited]), Tony Bennett (Himself [archive footage] [uncredited]), Heidi Berg (Oinker Sister [voice] [uncredited]), Bill Corsair (Hank, the Handyman [uncredited]), Cheryl Hardwick (Oinker Sister [voice] [uncredited]), Madonna (Herself [archive footage] [uncredited]), Conan O'Brien (Himself [uncredited]), Judy Prianti (Make-up Lady [uncredited]), Will Smith (Himself [archive footage] [uncredited]).

Things get a little out of hand when Elmo and other Sesame Street friends, including Count von Count, take the lead in their own all-star tribute after the host becomes locked in his dressing room.

Elmo's Christmas Countdown; U.S., 2007; Family, Comedy, Musical/Television, Animation; 60 minutes/color/English; Gotham Group, Sesame Workshop.

Director: Gary Halvorson; *Art Direction*: Bradley Schmidt; *Cast*: Pam Arciero (Various Muppets), Tyler Bunch (Various Muppets), Leslie Carrara (Abby Cadabby), Kevin Clash (Elmo), Sheryl Crow (Herself), Stephanie D'Abruzzo (Various Muppets), Ryan Dillon (Various Muppets), Artie Esposito (Various Muppets), Jamie Foxx (Himself), James Godwin (Various Muppets), BJ Guyer (Various Muppets), Anne Hathaway (Herself), Andy Hayward (Various Muppets), Patrick Holmes (Various Muppets), Jennifer Hudson (Herself), Eric Jacobson (Grover), Kevin James (Santa Claus), John Kennedy (Various Muppets), Alicia Keys (Herself), Peter Linz (Various Muppets), Michael Lisa (Various Muppets), Noel MacNeal (Various Muppets), Amanda Maddock (Various Muppets), Ed May (Various Muppets), Joey Mazzarino (Stan the Snowball), Paul McGinnis (Various Muppets), Tracie Mick-Shoemaker (Various Muppets), Jerry Nelson (The Count [voice]), Carmen Osbahr (Various Muppets), Brad Paisley (Himself), Ty Pennington (Himself), Marc Petrosino (Various Muppets), Martin P. Robinson (Mr. Snuffleupagus), David Rudman (Cookie Monster), Steve Schirripa (Himself [voice]), Tony Sirico (Himself [voice]), Caroll Spinney (Big Bird/Oscar the Grouch), Ben Stiller (Stiller the Elf [voice]), Andy Stone (Various Muppets), Ian Sweetman (Various Muppets), Gabriel Velez (Various Muppets), Matt Vogel (Stiller the Elf), Steve Whitmire (Ernie [voice]), Bryant Young (Mr. Snuffleupagus [back half]).

Characters from Sesame Street, particularly Count von Count, assist Elmo in counting down the days left until Christmas.

Emotion: densetsu no gogo=itsukamita Dracula; Japan, 1966; Fantasy/Short; 40 minutes/color/Japanese/Mono.

Writing Credits: Nobuhiku Obayashi; *Director*: Nobuhiku Obayashi.

This is a short film in which a young girl's (possible) fantasy takes her to a city where she falls in love with a vampire.

Ernest Le Vampire; France, 1991; Family, Adventure/Television, Animation; 60 minutes/color/French/Dolby Digital 2.0; Studio SEK, Quartier Latin, Col. Ima. Son, France 3, W.D.R.

Producers: Ghyslaine Fizet, Bruno Desraissses, Michel Noll; *Writing Credits*: Francois Bruel; *Director*: Jean-Jacques Lonni, Jose Xavier (animation director); *Original Music*: Gabriel Yared; *Art Direction*: Rene Laloux

Ernest is an awkward, but creative vampire. All kinds of mishaps befall to him in his castle. He lives with a dragon, a bat, mice, and other visitors.

Escala en Hi-Fi; Spain, 1963; Comedy, Musical; 98 minutes/color/Spanish/4-track Stereo; Documento Films, Ízaro Films.

Writing Credits: Juan Cobos, Isidoro M. Ferry, Gustavo Quintana (story); *Director*: Isidoro M. Ferry; *Cinematography*: Francisco Sempere; *Film Editing*: José Antonio Rojo; *Original Music*: Waldo de los Ríos; *Cast*: Xan das Bolas, Nina Braccio, Francisco Camoiras, Cassen, Perla Cristal, Germaine Damar, Ángel del Pozo, Ignacio de Paúl, Arturo Fernández, María Isbert, Karina, Dan Milland, José Orjas, Dorothy Peterson (unconfirmed), Aida Power, José Rubio, Laly Soldevila, Manuel Zarzo.

This film contains a scene with a dream sequence in Castle Dracula.

Every Home Should Have One (*Eroticón, El* [Spain]; *Haferbrei macht sexy* [West Germany]; *Het på gröten* [Sweden]; *Jokaisella pitäisi olla se* [Finland]; *Kathe andras ehei apo ... mia* [Greece] (reissue title); *Kathe spiti prepei nahi apo mia...* [Greece]; *Marty Feldman — Ich kann alles* [West Germany]; *Ogni uomo dovrebbe averne due* [Italy]; *Papa en a deux* [France]; *Think Dirty*); U.K., 1970; Comedy/Television; 94 minutes/color/English/Mono; British Lion Film Corporation.

Producers: Terry Glinwood, Ned Sherrin; *Writing Credits*: Marty Feldman (writer), Herbert Kretzmer (story), Denis Norden (writer), Milton Shulman (story), Barry Took (writer); *Director*: Jim Clark; *Cinematography*: Ken Hodges; *Film Editing*: Ralph Sheldon; *Original Music*: John Cameron; *Art Direction*: Roy Stannard; *Make-Up*: Jeanette Freeman, Richard Mills; *Cast*: Marty Feldman (Teddy Brown), Judy Cornwell (Liz Brown), Patrick Cargill (Wallace Trufitt), Jack Watson (McLaughlin), Patience Collier (Mrs. Monty Levin), Penelope Keith (Lotte von Gelbstein), Dinsdale Landen (Vicar Geoffrey Mellish), Annabel Leventon (Chandler's secretary), John McKelvey (Colonel Belper), Moray Watson (Chandler), Sarah Badel (Joanna Snow), Michael Bates (Magistrate), Erika Bergmann, Shelley Berman (Nat Kaplan), Veronica Clifford (Hot Dog Girl), Roland Curram (Arthur/Mario), Ellis Dale (Leonard Crape), Dave Dee (Wednesday Play Star), Mischa De La Motte (Trufitt's Manservant), Frances de la Tour (Maud Crape), Julie Ege (Inga Giltenburg), Mark Elwes (Rokes), Robert Farrant (Porridge Eater #2), Ray Fell (Goldilocks Presenter), John Hamill (Porridge Eater #1), Hy Hazell (Mrs. Kaplan), Rose Hill (Shopping Woman #1), Vicki Hodge (Pippa), Winnie Holman (Shopping Woman #2), David Hutcheson (Stockbroker), Judy Huxtable (Dracula's Victim), Harold Innocent (Jimpson), Maggie Jones (Hetty Soames), Charles Lewsen (Arthur Soames), Garry Miller (Richard Brown), Diana Quiseekay (Elvira), Kenny Rodway (Porridge Eater #3), Bernard Sharpe (Shopping Man), John Wells (Tolworth), Alan Bennett (Defence Solicitor [uncredited]), Fiona Curzon (uncredited), Geraldine Gardner (Girl [uncredited]), Sheila Gish (Mother in TV commercial [uncredited]), Christopher Godwin (Magistrates' Clerk [uncredited]), David Lee (Ern [uncredited]), James Payne (Taxi driver with the dwarfs [uncredited]), Marianne Stone (TV Production Assistant #1 [uncredited]).

Terry (Marty Feldman) is trying to sell frozen porridge for the advertising company he works for. He gets the idea of adding some sex appeal to the product. This gets him in trouble with his wife, who is a member of the "Keep Television Clean" movement. During the scandal, Terry dreams about Dracula and becomes sexually intimate with a Swedish pair.

Everybody Loves Raymond (TV Series [1996–2005]), episode "Halloween Candy"; U.S., Season 3, Episode 6, 26 October 1998; Comedy/Television; 30 minutes/color/English; Warner Bros. Studios, Columbia Broadcasting System (CBS).

Producers: Tucker Cawley, Cindy Chupack (co-executive producer), Holli Gailen (co-producer), Lisa Helfrich, David Letterman, Ken Ornstein (coordinating producer), Ray Romano, Rory Rosengarten, Philip Rosenthal, Ellen Sandler (co-executive producer), Lew Schneider (supervising producer), Steve Skrovan, Stu Smiley, Jeremy Stevens (supervising producer), Kathy Ann Stumpe (co-executive producer); *Writing Credits*: Philip Rosenthal (creator), Steve Skrovan (writer); *Director*: Steve Zuckerman; *Cinematography*: Mike Berlin; *Original Music*: Rick Marotta, Terry Trotter; *Cast*: Ray Romano (Raymond "Ray" Barone), Patricia Heaton (Debra Barone), Brad Garrett (Robert Barone), Madylin Sweeten (Ally Barone), Sawyer Sweeten (Geoffrey Barone), Sullivan Sweeten (Michael Barone), Doris Roberts (Marie Barone), Peter Boyle (Frank Barone), Tina Arning (Angelina), Vinnie Buffolino (Dracula), Elizabeth Herring (Carrie Parker), Andy Kindler (Andy),

Joseph V. Perry (Nemo), Zachary Robinson (Trick-or-Treater), Ben Rosenthal (Trick-or-Treater), Nicholas Rossitto (Trick-or-Treater), Sam Skrovan (Trick-or-Treater), Susan Varon (Suzy)

Ray plans an evening of sex on Halloween, but his father (Frank) mistakenly hands out Ray's condoms to trick-or-treaters. Hilarity ensues.

Evil of Dracula; U.S., 1998; Animation, Short; 2 minutes/color/English.

Producers: Martha Colburn; *Writing Credits*: Martha Colburn; *Director*: Martha Colborn.

This short film features various old advertisements in which fangs have been drawn in to produce evil grins, thereby illustrating the money-grubbing, blood-thirsty nature of advertisement.

Fade to Black; U.S., 1980; Comedy, Drama, Horror, Romance, Thriller; 102 minutes/color/English/Mono/35mm; Leisure Investments, Movie Ventures.

Producers: George G. Braunstein, Ron Hamady, Sylvio Tabet, Joseph Wolf, Irwin Yablans; *Writing Credits*: Vernon Zimmerman; *Director*: Vernon Zimmerman; *Cinematography*: Alex Phillips Jr.; *Film Editing*: James Mitchell, Barbara Pokras; *Original Music*: Craig Safan; *Make-up*: Colin Booker; *Cast*: Dennis Christopher (Eric Binford), Tim Thomerson (Jerry Moriarty), Gwynne Gilford (Officer Anne Oshenbull), Norman Burton (Marty Berger), Linda Kerridge (Marilyn O'Connor), Morgan Paull (Gary Bially), James Luisi (Capt. M.L. Gallagher), Eve Brent (Aunt Binford), John Steadman (Sam), Marcie Barkin (Stacy), Mickey Rourke (Richie), Peter Horton (Joey), Hennen Chambers (Bart), Melinda O. Fee (Talk Show Hostess), Anita Converse (Dee Dee), Bob Drew (the Reverend Shick), Teddi Siddall (Jill), Sharon Schlarth (Mail Girl), David Daniels (Waiter at Food Stand), Marilyn Staley (Starlet), Al Tafoya (Newscaster), Clyde Primm (Bookstore Owner), Gilbert Lawrence Kaan (Counterman), Sharon McCreedy (Frightened Spectator), Bill Stack (SWAT Leader), Gregory Sage (Peter), J.K. Wiley (Gofer), Peggy Kaye (Midway Operator).

Eric Binford is a film geek whose sanity slips as he begins acting out his favorite scenes from the movies, including *Dracula*. In doing so, he manages to involve his enemies, and the scenes usually result in death.

El Fang-Dango; U.S., 1971; Short; 14 minutes.

Writing Credits: Tony De Nonno; *Director*: Tony De Nonno; *Cast*: Tony Travis (Dracula).

Fangland; U.S., 2011; Thriller, Horror, Suspense; English; DAS Films, Blumhouse Productions.

Producers: Tracy Underwood, Jason Blum, Sriram Das, Hilary Swank, Steven Schneider; *Writing Credits*: Mark Wheaton (based on John Mark's novel); *Cast*: Hilary Swank (Evangeline Harker).

Evangeline Harker (Hilary Swank) is a producer for the news show *The Hour*. She travels to Transylvania to interview Ion Torgu, an infamous Eastern European crime boss. Torgu ends up being a modern-day Dracula.

Fangs! A History of Vampires in the Movies; U.S., 1989; Documentary; 57 minutes/color, black and white/English; Pagan Video, E.I. Independent Cinema.

Producers: Carl Dietz; *Writing Credits*: Bruce G. Hallenbeck; *Director*: Bruce G. Hallenbeck; *Cinematography*: Antonio Panetta; *Film Editing*: Carl Dietz, Antonio Panetta; *Cast*: Veronica Carlson (Host/Narrator).

Narrated by Veronica Carlson, this documentary explores the evolution of vampires in film using a compilation of film clips and trailers.

El Fantasma de la opereta (*The Phantom of the Operetta* [International English]); Argentina, 1954; Horror; 70 minutes/black and white/Spanish/Mono/35 mm; Cinematográfica General Belgrano.

Writing Credits: René Marcial, Manuel Rey, Alfredo Ruanova; *Director*: Enrique Carreras; *Cinematography*: Alfredo Traverso; *Film Editing*: José Gallego; *Original Music*: Víctor Slister; *Art Direction*: Óscar Lagomarsino; *Make-Up*: Miguel Angel Casals; *Cast*: Amelia Vargas, Alfredo Barbieri, Tono Andreu, Gogó Andreu, Inés Fernández, Alfonso Pisano, Mario Baroffio

Not to be confused with Leroux's *Phantom of the Opera*, this movie is the story of a bloody serial killer named the Phantom who slashes and kills girls in a chorus.

The Fearless Vampire Killers*; or, *Pardon Me, but Your Teeth Are in My Neck (*Dance of the Vampires* [U.K.]; The *Fearless Vampire Killers* [U.S.]; *The Vampire Killers* [U.S., working title]; *Vampire Ball* [Europe, working title]; *Bal des vampires, Le* [Canada, France]; *A Dança dos Vampiros* [Brazil]; *Baile de los vampiros, El* [Spain]; *Der Tanz der Vampire* [Switzerland]; *Nieustraszeni pogromcy wampirów* [Poland]; *Nyhta ton vrykolakon, I* [Greece]; *Per favore, non mordermi sul collo* [Italy]; *Por Favor Não Me Morda o Pescoço* [Portugal]; *Tanz der Vampire* [West Germany]; *Vámpírok bálja* [Hungary]; *Vampyrernas natt* [Sweden]; *Vampyrdrådarna—Ursäkta, ja har era tänder i nacken* [Finland, Swedish title]; *Vampyrernes nat* [Denmark]; *Vampyyrintappajat* [Finland]); U.S./U.K., 1967; Comedy, Horror; 108 minutes/color/English/Mono; Cadre Films, Filmways Pictures.

Producers: Gene Gutowski, Martin Ransohoff; *Writing Credits*: Gérard Brach (story and screenplay), Roman Polanski (story and screenplay); *Director*: Roman Polanski; *Cinematography*: Douglas Slocombe; *Film Editing*: Alastair McIntyre; *Original Music*: Krzysztof Komeda; *Art Direction*: Fred Carter; *Make-Up*: Tom Smith; *Cast*: Jack MacGowran (Professor Abronsius), Roman Polanski (Alfred [Abronsius' Assistant]), Alfie Bass (Shagal, the Inn-Keeper), Jessie Robins (Rebecca Shagal), Sharon Tate (Sarah Shagal), Ferdy Mayne (Count von Krolock), Iain Quarrier (Herbert von Krolock), Terry Downes (Koukol) (the Servant), Fiona Lewis (Magda) (the Maid), Ronald Lacey (Village Idiot), Sydney Bromley (Sleigh Driver), Andreas Malandrinos (Woodcutter), Otto Diamant (Woodcutter), Matthew Walters (Woodcutter), Roy Evans (Vampire at ball [uncredited]).

Professor Abronsius (Jack MacGowran) and his assistant Alfred (Roman Polanski) travel to Transylvania in search of vampires. Alfred falls in love with the inn-keeper's daughter, Sarah (Sharon Tate), who is kidnapped by Count von Krolock (Ferdy Mayne), a Dracula-type vampire. The Professor and Alfred attempt to rescue Sarah from von Krolock's castle.

Fem døgn i august (*Fem dygn med Viveca* [Sweden]; *Five Days in August* [U.S.])

Norway, 1973; Drama; 95 minutes/color/Norwegian/Stereo; Comacico, A/S Elan-Film.

Writing Credits: Svend Wam; *Director*: Svend Wam; *Cinematography*: Fred Sassebo; *Cast*: Margarete Robsahm (Viveca), Kjersti Døvigen (Aud), Eli Anne Linnestad (Vivecas venninne), Stellan Skarsgård (Christer), Thomas Robsahm (Thomas), Harald Heide-Steen Jr. (Alfred), Einar Olsen (El Jucan), Kari Svendsen (Stina), Morten Andresen (Læregutten), Bente Børsum (Barnehagelærerinne), Maurice Budini (Plateknusers ass), Bela Csepcsanyi (Dracula), Sverre Gran (Naboen), Bredo Greve (Filmkunstneren), David Horsefield (David), William Jensen (Konferansier), Jorunn Kjellsby (I bankens kantine), Finn Lewin (Plateknuser), Gunnar Olram (I kantina), Marco Pannaggi (Jens), Liv Thorsen (Dame på trikken), Svend Wam (Fotografen).

31-year-old Viveca and her 6-year-old son have had enough of the hectic life they lead. She and her friend Aud start to move around with bohemians and artists, staying on the move. The movie follows the trio over the course of 5 days as they encounter many strange places and people, including Dracula.

La Fiancée de Dracula (*Draculas Braut* [Germany, DVD title]; *Retour de Dracula, Le* [undefined]); France, 2002; Horror; 91 minutes/color/French; Avia Films.

Producers: Andrea Angioli; *Writing Credits*: Jean Rollin; *Director*: Jean Rollin; *Cinematography*: Norbert Marfaing-Sintes; *Film Editing*: Janette Kronegger; *Original Music*: Philippe D'Aram; *Make-Up*: Christelle Laromanière, Bernard Tramier; *Cast*: Cyrille Iste (Isabelle), Jacques Orth (Le professeur [as Jacques Régis]), Thomas Smith (Thibault), Sandrine Thoquet (La vampire), Magalie Madison (L'ogresse/La folle [as Magalie Aguado]), Céline Mauge (Soeur Toutière), Marie-Laurence (Mère supérieure Paris), Danièle Servais-Orth (Mère supérieure îles Chausey), Denis Tallaron (Eric), Sabine Lenoël (Soeur Marthe), Céline Clémentel (Soeur Simplicité), Mira Petri (Soeur Cigare), Marianna Palmieri (Soeur Bouffarde), Bernard Musson (Le sorcier), Nathalie Perrey (La sorcière [as Natalie Perrey]), Catherine Castel (Soeur à la corde à sauter [as Cathy Castel]), Dominique Treillou (L'homme du cimetière [as Dominique Treilloux]), Frédéric Legrand (Le marin au pompon rouge), Brigitte Lahaie (La louve), Thomas Desfossé (Dracula).

A professor and his assistant are searching for Dracula and trying to destroy him. Their search reveals a "parallel world" where Dracula, strange people, and creatures exist. The two men find Dracula's fiancée in a bizarre convent and use her to get to Dracula.

La Fille de Dracula (*A Filha de Dracula* [Portugal]; *Daughter of Dracula* [undefined]; *Hija de Dracula, La* [Spain]; *Vloek van Dracula, De* [Netherlands]); France/Portugal, 1972; Horror, Mystery, Romance; 87 minutes/color/French/Mono/35mm; Comptoir Français du Film Production (C.F.F.P.)/Interfilm.

Producers: Victor de Costa; *Writing Credits*: Jesus Franco (as Jess Franco); *Director*: Jesus Franco (as Jess Franco); *Original Music*: Daniel White; *Cast*: Britt Nichols (Luisa Karlstein), Anne Libert (Karine), Alberto Dalbés (Inspector Ptuschko), Howard Vernon (Count Karlstein [Dracula]), Daniel White (Count Max Karlstein), Jesus Franco (Cyril Jefferson), Fernando Bilbao (Charlie the Reporter), Carmen Carbonell (Baroness Karlstein), Conchita Núñez (Margot the Waitress), Yelena Samarina (Ana Kramer), Eduarda Pimenta (First victim [uncredited]), Lina Romay (uncredited), Luis Barboo (uncredited).

Based on *Dracula's Daughter*, a young woman travels to visit her dying grandmother at their family's large estate. Once she arrives there and speaks with her grandmother, her grandmother tells her the dreaded family curse: they're all vampires. The young woman decides to take up residence at the estate with her uncle, cousin, and caretaker. What she soon finds out is that the curse is real.

Flesh and Blood: The Hammer Heritage of Horror; U.S./U.K., 1994; Horror/Documentary; 100 minutes/color, black and white/English/Mono;

Bosustow Media Group, Hammer Film Productions, Heidelberg Films.

Producers: Tee Bosustow, Joe Dante, Bill Kelley, Richard Nathan, Ted Newsom, Roy Skeggs; *Writing Credits*: Ted Newsom; *Director*: Ted Newsom; *Film Editing*: Tee Bosustow, Alexander Gittinger (as Alex Gittinger), Noriko Miyakawa, Sean Okin; *Original Music*: James Bernard; *Cast*: Christopher Lee (Himself/Narrator), Peter Cushing (Narrator/Himself [voice]), Roy Ward Baker (Himself), James Bernard (Himself), Martine Beswick (Herself [as Martine Beswicke]), Veronica Carlson (Herself), Michael Carreras (Himself), Hazel Court (Herself), Joe Dante (Himself), Freddie Francis (Himself), Val Guest (Himself), Ray Harryhausen (Himself), Anthony Hinds (Himself), Andrew Keir (Himself), Francis Matthews (Himself), Ferdy Mayne (Himself), Caroline Munro (Herself), Christopher Neame (Himself), Ingrid Pitt (Herself), Jimmy Sangster (Himself), Yutte Stensgaard (Herself [archive footage]), Raquel Welch (Herself).

Fonz and the Happy Days Gang (TV Series [1980–1981]), episode "The Vampire Strikes Back"; U.S., Season 1, Episode 7, 20 December 1980; Comedy/Television, Animation; 30 minutes/color/English; Hanna-Barbera Productions.

Producers: William Hanna, Joseph Barbera, Doug Paterson, Art Scott, Duane Poole, Tom Swale; *Writing Credits*: Ray Parker, Duane Poole (story), Tom Swale (story); *Director*: George Gordon, Carl Urbano, Rudy Zamora; *Film Editing*: Gil Iverson; *Original Music*: Hoyt Curtin, Paul DeKorte (Music Supervision); *Cast*: Henry Winkler (Fonzie), Ron Howard (Richie Cunningham), Donny Most (Ralph Malph), Frank Welker (Mr. Cool), Didi Conn (Cupcake), Marlene Aragon, Rene Auberjonois, Michael Bell, Mary Ann Chin, Henry Corden, Brad Crandall, Tandy Cronyn, Peter Cullen, Keene Curtis, Rick Dees, Dick Erdman, Kathy Garver, Joanie Gerber, Bob Holt, Buster Jones, Jackie Joseph, Zale Kessler, Allan Lurie, Ken Mars, Amanda McBroom, Mitzi McCall, Joe Medalis, Ron Palillo, Pat Parris, Clare Peck, Patrick Pinney, Henry Polic, Lou Richards, Bob Ridgely, John Stephenson, Alexandra Stoddart, Russi Taylor, Fred Travalena, B.J. Ward.

"The Fonz and the Happy Days Gang" is the story of Fonzie (Henry Winkler), Ralphie (Donny Most), Richie (Ron Howard), and Fonzie's dog, Mr. Cool (Frank Welker), as they travel through time with their new friend, Cupcake (Didi Conn). The gang travels through history as they help Cupcake repair her time machine. In the episode "The Vampire Strikes Back," the gang encounters Dracula during its adventures.

Fort Dracula; U.S., 2004; Comedy, Drama/Short; 34 minutes/black and white/English/Stereo.

Producers: Jeff Holt; *Writing Credits*: Jeff Holt; *Director*: Jeff Holt; *Cinematography*: Jeff Holt; *Film Editing*: Jeff Holt; *Cast*: Gerard Nazarian (The Count), Richard Brundage (Renfield).

The Count is living in a Brooklyn park because he has been expelled from his ancestral home, which is going to be demolished by the city. He sends his servant, Renfield, to look for a new place to live. After settling into his new place, he sends Renfield to find a woman for him.

40 [Cetrdeset] Dana; Serbia, 2009; Documentary; 22 minutes/color/Serbian/Stereo; Prodigy Advertising.

Producers: Bojan Đoković; *Writing Credits*: Bojan Đoković; *Director*: Boris Đurić; *Cinematography*: Milan Ilić; *Film Editing*: Boris Đurić; *Original Music*: Boris Kovač; *Cast*: Bojan Đoković, Marija Ilić, Negoslava Matić, Marija Trišanović, Paun Rucić

Based on Ana Radin's book *Motiv vampira u mitu i književnosti* (*The Motif of Vampire in Myth and Literature*), this documentary explores Serbian beliefs about afterlife, centering on the one which states that the soul of the deceased lingers in this world for 40 days after death. Experts from the Balcan Institute and Ethnological Museum talk about the ghosts, vampires and the undead, and their dicussion is accentuated by accounts from peasants who claim to have met the undead, and by inserts from vampire films, including *Nosferatu The Vampyre* (1979).

40 [Quaranta] gradi all'ombra del lenzuolo (*Sex with a Smile* [Philippines, English title]; *40 gradi sotto il lenzuolo* [Italy]; *Cuarenta grados a la sombra de la sabana blanca* [Spain]; *Destination livvakt* [Sweden]; *Müssen Männer schön sein?* [West Germany]; *Seksiä hymyillen* [Finland]; *Sex med ett leende* [Finland, Swedish title]); Italy, 1976; Comedy; 100 minutes/color/Italian/Mono/35mm; Medusa Produzione.

Producers: Luciano Martino; *Writing Credits*: Tonino Guerra, Tonino Guerra, Sergio Martino, Giorgio Salvioni, Giorgio Salvioni; *Director*: Sergio Martino; *Cinematography*: Giancarlo Ferrando; *Film Editing*: Eugenio Alabiso; *Original Music*: Guido De Angelis, Maurizio De Angelis; *Art Direction*: Marco Ortolani; *Make-Up*: Franco Di Girolamo, Mirella Ginnoto, Alessandro Jacoponi, Pierantonio Mecacci; *Cast*: Barbara Bouchet (The Woman [segment "I soldi in banca"]), Edwige Fenech (Emilia Chiapponi [segment "La cavallona"]), Dayle Haddon (Marina [segment "La guardia del corpo"]), Alberto Lionello (Filippo, the "Catch It While It's Hot" male [segment "L'attimo fuggente"]), Aldo Maccione (Adriano Serpetti, the "Dog's Day" male [segment "Un posto tranquillo"]), Tomas Milian (Cavaliere Marelli, the

"Dream Girl" male [segment "La cavallona"]), Enrico Montesano (Salvatore, the "One for the Money" male [segment "I soldi in banca"]), Giovanna Ralli (Esmeralda [segment "L'attimo fuggente"]), Sydne Rome (Marcella Fosne [segment "Un posto tranquillo"]), Marty Feldman (Alex, the "Bodyguard" male [segment "La guardia del corpo"]), Christian Aligny (Dracula [segment "La cavallona"]) (as Christian Alegny), Salvatore Baccaro (Client at the bar [segment "La cavallona"]), Fiammetta Baralla (Woman in the Bathroom [segment "I soldi in banca"]), Mimmo Craig (François [segment "La guardia del corpo"]) (as Mimmo Crao), Franco Diogene (Ignazio, her husband [segment "I soldi in banca"]), Nello Pazzafini (L'affita-auto [segment "L'attimo fuggente"]) (as Giovanni Pazzafini), Angelo Pellegrino (The Priest [segment "Un posto tranquillo"]), Renzo Rinaldi (as Enzo Rinaldi), Giuseppe Terranova.

This film is made up of a series of five short comic sketches, all unrelated to each other except for their Italian sexual humor. Dracula (Christian Aligny) appears in the segment titled, "La cavallona."

Fracchia Contro Dracula; Italy, 1985; Comedy, Horror; 94 minutes/color/Italian; Faso Films S rl, Bruno Altissimi, Claudio Saraceni.

Writing Credits: Franco Marotta, Laura Toscano, Neri Parenti (story), Paolo Villaggio (story), Carlo Mazzacurati (comic); *Director*: Neri Parenti; *Cinematography*: Luciano Tovoli; *Film Editing*: Sergio Montanari; *Original Music*: Bruno Zambrini; *Make-Up*: Laura Borselli, Paolo Franceschi, Tiziano Trani; *Special Effects*: Massimo Cristofanelli; *Cast*: Paolo Villaggio (Giandomenico Fracchia), Edmund Purdom (Count Dracula), Gigi Reder (Rag. Filini), Ania Pieroni (Contessina Oniria), Federica Brion (Stefania), Giuseppe Cederna (Boris), Susanna Martinková (Catarina), Andrea Gnecco, Filippo De Gara (Maggiordomo [as Filippo Degaras]), Paul Muller (Fracchia's boss), Romano Puppo (Frankenstein), Isabella Ferrari (Luna).

Mr. Filini comes to Fracchia, a down-on-his-luck realtor, with a nearly impossible house to find. Fracchia finds it for him — in Transylvania. The two travel to Transylvania to see it and meet its owner, Count Vlad. While visiting, the Count's daughter falls in love with Fracchia and a vampire hunter's sister seeks revenge for her brother's death at the hands of the Count.

Fraiser (TV Series [1993–2004]), episode "Halloween"; U.S., Season 5, Episode 3, 28 October 1997; Comedy/Television; 30 minutes/English/color/Dolby; Grub Street Productions, Paramount Network Television.

Producers: Mary Fukuto, Kelsey Grammer; *Writing Credits*: David Angell (creator), Peter Casey (creator), David Lee; *Director*: Pamela Fryman; *Original Music*: Andrew M. Chukerman (composer: additional music); *Make-Up*: Nanci Cascio, Adruitha Lee, Michele Payne; *Cast*: Kelsey Grammer (Dr. Frasier Crane), Jane Leeves (Daphne Moon), David Hyde Pierce (Dr. Niles Crane), Peri Gilpin (Roz Doyle), John Mahoney (Martin Crane), Dan Butler (Bob "Bulldog" Briscoe), Cindy Crawford (Dorothy [voice]), Jonathan Fraser (Man at Party), Camille Grammer (Eve [as Camille Donatacci Grammer]), Edward Hibbert (Gil Chesterton), Mark Munoz (Dr. Krovitz), Joey Zimmerman (Dracula), Moose (Eddie [uncredited]).

It's Halloween and Fraiser, after Roz tells him she thinks she's pregnant, goes to a costume party, which Dracula attends. He lets the news slip, and drunken misunderstandings take place.

Frankenstein and Me (*Ea si Frankenstein* [Romania]; *Frankenstein et moi* [Canada]; *Meu Amigo Frankenstein, O* [Portugal]; *Mi amigo Frankenstein* [Venezuela]); Canada, 1996; Family, Fantasy; 91 minutes/color/English/Dolby SR; France Film, Téléfilm Canada.

Producers: Richard Goudreau, René Malo, Jeffrey Tinnell; *Writing Credits*: Richard Goudreau, David Sherman, Robert Tinnell (story); *Director*: Robert Tinnell; *Cinematography*: Roxanne di Santo; *Film Editing*: Roxanne di Santo; *Original Music*: Normand Corbeil; *Art Direction*: René Gratton; *Make-Up*: Antoine Bergeron, Brian McManus; *Special Effects*: Karl Nettmann (uncredited); *Cast*: Jamieson Boulanger (Earl Williams), Ricky Mabe (Larry Williams), Polly Shannon (Elizabeth), Louise Fletcher (Mrs. Perdue), Myriam Cyr (Judy Williams), Burt Reynolds (Les Williams), Ryan Gosling (Kenny), Rebecca Henderson (Karen), Jason Cavalier (Billy), Mélany Goudreau (Suzie), Roc LaFortune (Sheriff Gonzalez), Lynne Adams (Aileen), Jean Guérin (Doctor), Charles Edwin Powell (Loved kid) (as Charles Powell), Joe De Paul (Ticker Soldier), Jeff Osterhage (Carl), Sam Stone (Carnival Owner), David Deveau (Stan), Conner Vandeer (Dracula), Véronique Cloutier (Vampire), Martine Marois (Vampire), Amanda Strawn (Nurse Himen), Anik Matern (Nurse Tilko), Émile Genest (Judge Ewing).

Young dreamer Earl Williams is obsessed with monsters, and his fantasies take him to a world of the classic monsters of Universal Studios. When the carnival comes to town, Earl encounters a host of creatures, including Frankenstein's monster, the Mummy, the Wolfman, and even Dracula himself.

Friday the 13th: The Series (TV Series [1987–1990]), episode "The Baron's Bride" (*The 13th Hour* [U.S.]; *Friday's curse* [U.K.]); U.S., Season 1, Episode

13, 15 February 1988; Horror, Thriller/Television; 60 minutes/color/English/Mono; Lexicon Productions, Triumph, Paramount Television.

Producers: Frank Mancuso Jr.; *Writing Credits*: Larry Gaynor; *Director*: Bradford May; *Cinematography*: Rodney Charters; *Film Editing*: Gary L Smith; *Original Music*: Fred Mollin; *Make-Up*: Ava Stone; *Special Effects*: Nicolette Beasley, Randy Daudlin, John Gajdecki, Bruce Turner; *Cast*: John D. LeMay (Ryan Dallion [as John D. Le May]), Louise Robey (Micki Foster [as Robey]), Chris Wiggins (Jack Marshak), Tom McCamus (Frank Edwards), Kevin Bundy (Abraham), Susannah Hoffman (Caitlin), Diana Barrington (Marie Simmons), John Shepherd (Constable), Emma Richler (Tart), Ron Tough (Man #1), Antun Percic (Newspaper Vendor).

While Micki and Ryan are fighting a vampire named Frank, they are all transported to 1875 London. There Ryan and Micki team up with a writer named Abraham to hunt down Frank who is terrorizing London.

Fright Night; U.S., 1985; Horror, Thriller; 106 minutes/color/English/Dolby; Columbia Pictures Corporation, Delphi IV Productions, Vistar Films.

Producers: Jerry A. Baerwitz, Herb Jaffe; *Writing Credits*: Tom Holland; *Director*: Tom Holland; *Cinematography*: Jan Kiesser; *Film Editing*: Kent Beyda; *Original Music*: Brad Fiedel; *Make-Up*: Ken Diaz, Rick Stratton, Dale Brady, Bill Sturgeon; *Special Effects*: Morton Greenspoon (as Dr. Morton K. Greenspoon), Albert Lannutti, Michael Lantieri, Dean W. Miller, Thaine Morris, Clay Pinney (as Clayton Pinney), Darrell Pritchett, Larry Odien; *Cast*: Chris Sarandon (Jerry Dandrige), William Ragsdale (Charley Brewster), Amanda Bearse (Amy Peterson), Roddy McDowall (Peter Vincent), Stephen Geoffreys ("Evil" Ed Thompson), Jonathan Stark (Billy Cole), Dorothy Fielding (Judy Brewster), Art Evans (Detective Lennox [as Art J. Evans]), Stewart Stern (Cook), Nick Savage (Bouncer #1), Ernie Holmes (Bouncer #2), Heidi Sorenson (Hooker), Irina Irvine (Teenage Girl), Bob Corff (Jonathan [as Robert Corff]), Pamela Brown (Miss Nina), Chris Hendrie (Newscaster), Prince Hughes (Bouncer #3 [as Prince A. Hughes]), Lene Hefner, Joy Michelle Moore (High School Student [uncredited]).

Charlie Brewster (William Ragsdale) has come to believe that his next door neighbor Jerry Dandridge (Chris Sarandon) is a vampire and is responsible for a string local prostitute murders. Dandridge therefore takes action, confronting Charlie in his own bedroom one night in an attempt to silence Charlie, or kill him. No one believes Charlie's story, so he enlists the help of Peter Vincent, a horror television host and film star.

Fright Night: Part 2; U.S., 1989; Horror, Thriller; 104 minutes/color/English/Ultra Stereo/35mm; TriStar Pictures.

Producers: Mort Engelberg, Herb Jaffe, Miguel Tejada-Flores; *Writing Credits*: Tom Holland, Tim Metcalfe, Miguel Tejada-Flores, Tommy Lee Wallace; *Director*: Tommy Lee Wallace; *Cinematography*: Mark Irwin; *Film Editing*: Jay Cassidy; *Original Music*: Brad Fiedel; *Special Effects*: Rick Josephsen, Ken Nosack, Scot Silver; *Cast*: Roddy McDowall (Peter Vincent), William Ragsdale (Charley Brewster), Traci Lind (Alex), Julie Carmen (Regine Dandridge), Jon Gries (Louie), Russell Clark (Belle), Brian Thompson (Bozworth), Merritt Butrick (Richie), Ernie Sabella (Dr. Harrison), Matt Landers (Mel), Josh Richman (Fritzy), Karen Anders (Mrs. Stern), Rochelle Ashana (Art Major), Blair Tefkin (Bernice), Alexander Folk (Sergeant), Scanlon Gail (Watch Captain), Grant Owens (Jailor), John Lafayette (Bartender), Gary Allen (Mr. Newberry), Brad Kepnick (Hip Young Guy), Neith Hunter (Young Admirer), Ed Quinlan (Newscaster), Jennifer Joan Taylor (Secretary), Jill Augustine (Ced), Gar Camppbell (Director), Ed Corbett (Stagehand), Robert Jenkins (2nd Stagehand), David Efron (Orderly), Bob Bergen (Additional Voices [Uncredited]).

Three years after killing the vampire in the original, Charlie has started to believe it was all his imagination and starts to forget that vampires truly exist — until four strangers, lead by Regina (a noted performance artist), arrive at Peter Vincent's house and start to have an unhealthy interest in Charlie, his friend Peter, and Charlie's new girlfriend, Alex. It becomes clear that Regina is Jerry's (the vampire in the original film) sister, who is determined to revenge his death and turn Charlie into a vampire so he can face his punishment for all eternity.

Galgali familywa Dracula (*The Galgali Family and Dracula* (International: English title); South Korea, 2003; Comedy, Family; 85 minutes/color/Korean.

Producers: Seung-dae Park; *Writing Credits*: Dong-yong Kim; *Director*: Ki-nam Nam; *Cast*: Jun-hyeong Park (Galgali), Jong-cheol Jeong (Ok Dong-ja), Seung-hwan Lee (Greasy Man), Hyeok-pil Lim (Dracula).

When Dracula comes to a strange town, three brothers try to stop him.

Gandy Goose in Ghost Town; U.S., 1944; Comedy/Animation; color/English; 20th Century–Fox.

Producers: Paul Terry; *Writing Credits*: John Foster (story); *Director*: Mannie Davis; *Original Music*: Philip A. Scheib; *Cast*: Arthur Kay (Gandy Goose, Sourpuss).

Gandy Goose and companion Sourpuss become

trapped in a ghost town in the desert. While in the town, the two come across a variety of ghosts and ghouls including Dracula and Frankenstein's monster.

Gandy Goose in G-Man Jitters; U.S., 1939; Animation; 7 minutes/black and white/English/Mono; Terrytoons, 20th Century–Fox.
Producers: Paul Terry; *Writing Credits*: John Foster (story); *Director*: Eddie Donnelly, Connie Rasinski; *Original Music*: Philip A. Scheib; *Cast*: Arthur Kay (Gandy Goose, Sourpuss).

Garfield and Friends (TV Series [1988–1995]), episode "Count Lasagna"; U.S., 20 October 1990; Family, Comedy/Television, Animation; 60 minutes/color/English/Stereo, Mono; Lee Mendelson Films, Paws, Inc., Film Roman Productions.
Producers: Bob Curtis, Bob Nesler; *Writing Credits*: Mark Evanier, Sharman Divono; *Director*: Jeff Hall; *Film Editing*: Timothy Borquez, Julie Gustafson, Sam Horta, Tim Terusa; *Original Music*: Ed Bogas, Desirée Goyette; *Cast*: Lorenzo Music (Garfield), Thom Huge (Jon, Binky), Gregg Berger (Odie, Floyd Mouse, The Mailman, Madman Murray), Desirée Goyette (Nermal), Julie Payne (Liz), Victoria Jackson (Penelope).

Jon submits a cartoon idea to Count Lasagna, a popular cartoon producer. The cartoon centers on Jon (as Count Dracula) and Garfield (as Count Lasagna), who steals Italian food from delivery people. Using pizza to lure Count Lasagna into a trap, the angry townspeople attempt to capture Garfield.

Gebissen wird nur nachts (*Happening der Vampire* [undefined]; *Mezzo litro di rosso per il conte Dracula* [Italy]; *Orgia tou Drakoula, Ta* [Germany]; *The Vampire Happening* [undefined]); West Germany, 1971; Comedy Horror; 102 minutes/color/German/Mono/35mm; Aquila Film Enterprises.
Producers: Pier A. Caminnecci; *Writing Credits*: Karl-Heinz Hummel, August Rieger; *Director*: Freddie Francis; *Cinematography*: Gérard Vandenberg; *Film Editing*: Alfred Srp; *Original Music*: Jerry van Rooyen; *Art Direction*: Hans Zehetner; *Make-Up*: Helmut Kraft, Jupp Paschke, Stefan Szenoner; *Cast*: Pia Degermark (Betty Williams/Clarimonde), Thomas Hunter (Jens Larsen), Yvor Murillo (Josef), Ingrid van Bergen (Miss Niessen), Joachim Kemmer (Martin), Oskar Wegrostek (Abt), Ferdy Mayne (Count Dracula), Lyvia Bauer (Gabrielle), Daria Damar (Kirsten), Kay Williams, Michael Janisch, Toni Wagner, Raoul Retzer, Bruno Frenzel (uncredited), Bernd Koschmidder (uncredited), Willfried Kovárnik (Transvestite, uncredited), Bernd Noske (uncredited), Reinhold Sobotta (uncredited).

An American actress inherits a castle in Transylvania. What she doesn't know is that her ancestor, the Baroness Catali, was a vampire countess. Catali emerges from her tomb to ravage the nearby village.

Get Smart (TV Series [1965–1970]), episode "The Wax Max"; U.S., 1965; Comedy, Crime, Mystery; 30 minutes/English
Producers: Burt Nodella, Harry R. Sherman, Leonard Stern; *Writing Credits*: James Komack, Mel Brooks (creator), Buck Henry (creator); *Director*: James Komack; *Cinematography*: Meredith M. Nicholson; *Film Editing*: William Cairncross; *Original Music*: Irving Szathmary; *Art Direction*: Archie J. Bacon; *Make-Up*: Bette Iverson, Ray Sebastian; *Special Effects*: Justus Gibbs; *Cast*: Don Adams (Maxwell Smart), Barbara Feldon (Agent 99), Edward Platt (Chief), Richard Devon (Waxman), Robert Ridgely (Dracula), Robert Lussier (Attendant), Simmy Bow (KAOS Agent), J.S. Johnson (Ticket Taker).

A visit to the park turns lethal when Max and Agent 99 are mistaken for KAOS agents. Dracula captures them and takes them to a KAOS agent, Waxman.

Geung see yee saang (*Doctor Vampire* [English]); Hong Kong, 1990; Comedy, Horror, Action, Romance; 98 minutes/color/Cantonese; Paragon Films.
Producers: Chua Lam, Stanley Lau; *Writing Credits*: Jamie Luk Kim-Ming; *Director*: Jamie Luk Kim-Ming; *Cinematography*: Yeung Jim; *Film Editing*: Peter Cheung Yiu-Chung; *Original Music*: Chui Yat-Kan; *Make-Up*: Chow Man-Guen, Lisa Boni; *Cast*: Bowie Lam Bo-Yi (Dr. Chiang Ta-Tsung), Ellen Chan (Alice), Seila Chan (May Chen), Peter Kjaer (Count, Vampire Master), David Wu (Doctor), Ni Kang (Taoist priest), Crystal Kwonk Gam-Yan (Joy Li), Lawrence Lau Sek-Yin (Dr. Chin).

While on a business trip in Scotland, Dr. Chiang is unknowingly bitten on his penis by a Chinese vampire-prostitute named Alice. Because Dr. Chiang's blood is potent from the ginseng he consumes, Alice and a Dracula-type Scottish Count follow Dr. Chiang when he returns to Hong Kong. Dr Chang's fiancée, May, doesn't like the ensuing vampire adventures, especially when Dr. Chiang starts to become Dracula-type in appearance.

Ghost Busters (TV Series [1986–1987]), episode "Shades of Dracula" (Filmation's Ghostbusters [U.S.]); U.S., Season 1, Episode 36, 16 May 1987; Action, Family/Television, Animation; Filmation Associates, Tribune Broadcasting Company.
Producers: Lou Scheimer; *Writing Credits*: Robby London, Barry O'Brien, Marc Richards (creator); *Director*: Bill Reed, Gwen Wetzler; *Film Editing*:

Joe Gall, Lida Saskova; *Art Direction*: John Grusd; *Special Effects*: Ashley Lupin, Brett Hisey, Randy Fullmer, Dardo Valez, Allan Stovall, Dan Chaika, Richard Coleman, Mark Myer, Peggy Cullen; *Cast*: Susan Blu (Belfrey the Bat/Futura/Jessica [voice]), Erika Scheimer (Additional Voices [voice]), Pat Fraley (Jake), Peter Cullen (Eddie), Alan Oppenheimer (Prime Evil), Linda Gary (Mysteria), Susan Blu, Erik Gunden.

Dracula retuns from the grave and attempts to reclaim his homeland of Transylvania. The Ghostbusters are called in to stop him, but they discover that much of their arsenal does not work on vampires.

Ghost Fever; U.S., 1987; Comedy, Horror; 86 minutes/color/English/Mono; Infinite Productions.

Producers: Edward Coe, Kenneth Johnston, Poemandres Rich, Ron Rich; *Writing Credits*: Oscar Brodney; *Director*: Lee Madden, Alan Smith; *Film Editing*: James Ruxin, Earl Watson; *Original Music*: James Hart; *Make-Up*: Martha Diosdado, Angelina Mendez, Tony Ramirez; *Special Effects*: Miguel Vazquez; *Cast*: Sherman Hemsley (Buford/Jethro), Luis Avalos (Benny), Jennifer Rhodes (Madame St. Esprit), Deborah Benson (Linda), Diana Brookes (Lisa), Myron Healey (Andrew Lee), Joe Frazier (Terrible Tucker), Pepper Martin (Sheriff Clay), Kenneth Johnston (Terrible Tucker's Manager), Roger Cudney (TV Announcer), Patrick Welch (Ring Announcer), Steve Stone (Reporter), Ramón Berumen (Referee), George Palmiero (Terrible Tucker's Trainer).

When two police detectives are sent on an assignment to serve an eviction notice, they become caught up in some ghostly happenings at a haunted mansion, where a Dracula-type vampire resides.

Ghost in the Water (TV Mini-Series); U.K., 31 December 1982; Drama, Family, Fantasy/Television; 440 minutes (total)/English/color; British Broadcasting Corporation (BBC).

Producers: Paul Stone; *Writing Credits*: Geoffrey Case, Edward Chitham (story); *Director*: Renny Rye; *Cast*: Judith Allchurch (Tess), Ian Stevens (David), Jane Freeman (Mrs. Willets), Dave Mitty (Mr. Willets), Joanne James (Jean Willets, Abigail Parkes)Hilary Mason (Nan), Paul Marks (Steve), Lynda Higginson (Tracy), Paul Copley (Mr. Reed), Peter Brooks (Mr. Milner), Neville Barber (Henry Parkes), Ysanne Churchman (Mrs. Parkes), Angus Kennedy (David Caddick), Samantha Gamble (Susanna Caddick), Ralph Lawton (Coroner), Simon Orme (Wayne), Val Hastings (Miss Jones), Daniel D'Arcy (Count Dracula), Mark Danesi (Boy in class), Johnny Thomas (Labourer).

Adapted from a story by Edward Chitham and Geoffrey Case, the story follows a young girl and her attempts to find information on a catastrophic event that occurred in the late 19th century. Different turns and twists plague the story, as the young woman attempts to find more information. Daniel D'Arcy plays Count Dracula.

Ghoul Mates; U.S., 2006; Horror, Comedy/Short; 5 minutes/black and white/English; Low Plains Production.

Producers: Rick Baldwin, Kelly Tippett; *Writing Credits*: Vicky L. Neal; *Director*: Kelly Tippett; *Film Editing*: Kelly Tippett; *Make-Up*: Rick Baldwin, Mollie Carnathan; *Special Effects*: Rick Baldwin; *Cast*: Rick Baldwin IV (Trick the Treat/Count Dracula), Elijah Hinshaw (Wolfie), Dallas Sullivan (Daria the Vamp), Kelly Tippett (Mummy Man).

On Halloween, four monsters living together are paid a visit by a trick-or-treater, and he just might have a trick that will get him all the candy.

Gilligan's Island (TV Series [1964–1967]), episode "Up at Bat" (*La isla de Gilligan* [Argentina/Venezuela]; *A Ilha dos Birutas* [Brazil]; *Gilligan's Travels* [U.S., working title]; *Gilligans Insel* [West Germany]; *L'île aux naufragés* [France, dubbed version]; *L'isola di Gilligan* [Italy]; *La isla de Gílligan* [Spain]); U.S., Season 3, Episode 1, 12 September 1966; Comedy/Television; 30 minutes/color/English/Mono; Columbia Broadcasting System (CBS), Gladysya Productions, United Artists Television.

Producer: Robert L. Rosen, Sherwood Schwartz; *Writing Credits*: Ron Friedman; *Director*: Jerry Hopper; *Cinematography*: Richard L. Rawlings; *Film Editing*: Larry Heath; *Original Music*: Gerald Fried; *Art Direction*: William Craig Smith; *Cast*: Bob Denver (Gilligan), Alan Hale Jr. (Jonas "The Skipper" Grumby), Jim Backus (Thurston Howell III), Natalie Schafer (Mrs. Lovey Howell), Tina Louise (Ginger Grant), Russell Johnson (Professor Roy Hinkley), Dawn Wells (Mary Ann Summers).

Gilligan fears he will turn into a vampire after he is bitten in the neck by a bat. Gilligan then falls asleep and is haunted by a dream in which he has, in fact, become a Dracula-type vampire living in some European castle in 1895.

Go for a Take (*Double Take* [U.S.]; *Crazy Movie*: *Das grobe Lachen* [West Germany TV Title]); U.K., 1972; Comedy; color/English/Mono; The Rank Organisation.

Producers: Roy Simpson; *Writing Credits*: Harry Booth, Alan Hackney; *Director*: Harry Booth; *Cinematography*: Mark McDonald; *Film Editing*: Archie Ludski; *Original Music*: Glen Mason; *Art Direction*: Lionel Couch; *Make-Up*: Patricia McDermott, Michael Morris; *Cast*: Johnny Briggs (Assistant Director), John Clive (Hotel Waiter), Julie

Ege (April), Bill Fraser (TV Studio Doorman), Jack Haig (Security Man), Melvyn Hayes (Ambulance Man), Anouska Hempel (Suzi Eckmann), John Levene (Assistant Director), Sue Lloyd (Angel Montgomery), David Lodge (Graham), Penny Meredith (Harem Girl), Aubrey Morris (Director), Patrick Newell (Generous Jim), Dennis Price (Dracula, actor), David Prowse (Actor), Norman Rossington (Jack Foster), Debbie Russ (Tiger), Peter Stephens (Director), Bob Todd (Security Man), Reg Varney (Wilfred Stone).

A 1970s comedy featuring many prominent British actors, the story goes that three friends are on the run from a man, Generous Jim, when they come across a movie studio and decide to seek refuge there. Little did they know that Generous Jim has business to tend to at the same studio.

Der Goldene Nazivampir von Absam: 2—Das Geheimnis von Schloß Kottlitz (*The Golden Nazi Vampire of Absam: Part II—The Secret of Kottlitz Castle* [International (English title)]); Germany, 2008; Comedy, Horror; 45 minutes/color/German/Dolby; Creative Gap Filmproduktion, Hochschule für Fernsehen und Film München (HFF), Münchner Filmwerkstatt.

Producers: Martin Blankemeyer, Christl Catanzaro, Mike Dehghan, Damien Donnelly, Daniel Fröhlich, Christoph Menardi, Cornel Schäfer, Robin Schäfer; *Writing Credits*: Lasse Nolte (screenplay), Christoph Menardi (story), Alexander Kometer (story), Wolfgang Menardi (story), Monty Arnold (text for RWU instruction film); *Director*: Lasse Nolte; *Cinematography*: David Emmenlauer; *Film Editing*: Lasse Nolte; *Original Music*: Tuomas Kantelinen; *Art Direction*: Cara Hutterer; *Make-Up*: Katharina Schultz, Nicole Weinfurtner; *Special Effects*: Sascha Kolmikow, Rainer Metz, Pit Rotter; *Cast*: Daniel Krauss (William "B.J." Blazkowicz), Götz Burger (Otto von Grimm), Hendrik Martz (Smokey Savallas), Walter Stapper (General Donovan), Kim Bärmann (Brick Bradford), Oliver Kalkofe (Adjudant von General Donovan), Guido Meyer (SS-Hauptsturmführer), Ferdinand Dörfler (SS-Scharführer), Christian Heiner Wolf (Corporal), Andreas Bendig (SS-Wache), Philippe Reinhardt (SS-Wache), Michael Schiller (SS-Wissenschaftler), Peter Heinrich (SS-Wissenschaftler), Alexander Kometer (Sanitätscorporal), Kerem Dagistan (Sanitätscorporal), Alexander Nadler (SS-Eskorte), Sebastian Badenberg (SS-Eskorte), Peter Thannisch (Dr. Szell), Joachim Hofmann (SS-Vampir bei Dr. Szell), Sven Blumenrath (SS-Funkervampir), Andreas Jaschke (SS-Torwache), Robert Krawczyk (Arischer Schönling), Peter Carpentier (Franzose), Monty Arnold (Erzähler im RWU-Lehrfilm, voice), Santiago Ziesmer (Spongebob [voice]), Kai Hauptmann (Vampir-Wache [uncredited]), Philipp Schall (Vampir-Wache [uncredited]), Torben Struck (Vampir-Wache [uncredited]).

The sudden appearance of "miracle weapons," murders, Dracula's bones, and secret laboratories and scientists in the Austrian Alps raises suspicion. To find answers, William Blazkowicz travels undercover, only to find that the events at Kottlitz Castle are among the most unimaginable.

Gorp; U.S., 1980; Comedy; 90 minutes/color/English, German/Mono; American International Pictures (AIP).

Producers: Lou Arkoff (producer [as Louis S. Arkoff]), Jeffrey Konvitz; *Writing Credits*: Jeffrey Konvitz, Jeffrey Konvitz (story), A. Martin Zweiback (story); *Director*: Joseph Ruben; *Cinematography*: Michel Hugo; *Film Editing*: Bill Butler; *Original Music*: Paul Dunlap; *Art Direction*: Joseph M. LeBaron; *Cast*: Michael Lembeck (Kavell), Dennis Quaid (Mad Grossman), Philip Casnoff (Bergman), Fran Drescher (Evie), David Huddleston (Walrus Wallman), Robert Trebor (Rabbi Blowitz), Lou Wagner (Federman), Richard Beauchamp (Ramirez), Julius Harris (Fred the Chef), Lisa Shure (Vicki), Deborah Richter (Barbara [as Debi Richter]), Rosanna Arquette (Judy), Dale Robinette (Irvington), Mark R. Deming (Lobster Newburg), Curt Ayers (Duffo Weiss), Steve Bonino (Batshit), Vincent Bufano (De Neckio), Rudy Diaz (Indian Joe), Douglas Dirkson (Bible Looie), Judith Drake (Big Bertha), Robert Elston (Mr. Kramer), Jim Greenleaf (Fat Solowitz [as James Greenleaf]), Shirley Gunther (Mrs. Walrus), Fred Hinds (The Seven Year Old Kid), Peter Marc Jacobson (Steinberg), DeWayne Jessie (Sweet Moe), John Reilly (Don Sharpe), Pete Robinson (Man in Bar), Janet Sarno (Mrs. Kramer), Four Scott (Kramer's Son), Marla Silverman (Zits Maguire), Glenn Super (Dracula Kesselman).

College students Kavell (Michael Lembeck) and Bergman (Philip Casnoff) spend their summers working as senior waiters at the summer camp Camp Oskemo. They court two attractive counselors at the camp, Evie and Vicki, while facing many conflicts with the junior waiters and camp owner, Wallman (David Huddleston). The two senior waiters bring havoc to the camp with many pranks, including showing a pornographic movie during Parent's Weekend.

Graf Dracula beißt jetzt in Oberbayern (*Dracula Blows His Cool* [undefined]; *Muérdeme abajo, Drácula* [Spain]; *Succhione, Il* [Italy]); West Germany, 1979; Comedy, Horror; 93 minutes, color, German, Mono, 35 mm; Bathonia Film.

Producers: Martin Friedman, Karl Spiehs; *Writing*

Credits: Carl Schenkel (as Carlos Ombra); *Director*: Carl Schenkel; *Cinematography*: Heinz Hölscher; *Film Editing*: Jutta Hering; *Original Music*: Gerhard Heinz; *Cast*: Gianni Garko (Stan/Count Stanislaus), Betty Vergès (Countess Olivia), Bea Fiedler (Mausi), Giacomo Rizzo (Mario), Ralf Wolter (Boris), Linda Grondier (Linda), Alexander Grill (Bürgermeister), Herta Worell (Gräfin), Ellen Umlauf (Lehrerin), Tobias Meister (Leopold), Georgina Steer, Herbert Stiny, Laurence Kaesermann, Dan van Husen (Franz), Rosl Mayr (Johanna), Werner Röglin (Beuler), Dolly Dollar (Hotel Guest [uncredited]), Margit Geissler (Hotel Guest [uncredited]).

Stanley has returned to Castle van Skrew, hoping to restore it. Joined by his girlfriend Linda, his younger brother Chubby, and a staff of models, Stan opens a nightclub and soft-core porn studio inside the castle. But he is unaware that Count Stanislaus Dracula and Countess Olivia sleep beneath them. They soon waken and begin feeding on the group, until they compromise and instead turn the castle into Hotel Dracula, with Disco Dracula.

Grampa's Monster Movies; U.S., 1990; Horror, Humor, Clip-show; 60 minutes/color/English; Passport International.

Cast: Al Lewis (Grampa Munster/Host)

An hour-long collection of trailers for classic Universal horror movies, hosted by *Munsters* star "Grampa" (Vladimir Dracula).

El Gran amor del conde Drácula (*Cemetery Girls* [U.S., reissue title]; *Cemetery Tramps* [undefined]; *Count Dracula's Great Love* [U.S.]; *Count Dracula's Greatest Love* [undefined]; *Diabolici amori di nosferatu, I* [Italy]; *Dracula's Great Love* [U.S., promotional title]; *Dracula's Virgin Lovers* [undefined]; *Draculan suuri rakkaus* [Finland]; *Grand amour du comte Dracula, Le* [France]; *The Great Love of Count Dracula* [undefined]; *Vampire Playgirls* [undefined]); Spain, 1972; Horror; 85 minutes/color/Spanish/Mono; Janus Films.

Writing Credits: Javier Aguirre, Alberto S. Insua, Paul Naschy (as Janito Molina); *Director*: Javier

Poster for *El Gran amor del conde Drácula* (Spain, 1972; *Dracula's Great Love* [U.S., promotional title]).

Aguirre; *Cinematography*: Raul Perez Cubero; *Film Editing*: Petra de Nieva; *Original Music*: Carmelo A. Bernaola; *Art Direction*: Jose Luis Galicia (as Galicia), Jaime Perez Cubero (as Cubero); *Make-Up*: Mercedes Guillot, Emilio Puyol; *Special Effects*: Pablo Perez; *Cast*: Paul Naschy (Count Dracula/Dr. Wendell Marlow), Haydée Politoff (Karen), Rosanna Yanni (Senta), Ingrid Garbo (Marlene), Mirta Miller (Elke), Víctor Alcázar (Imre Polvi, as Vic Winner).

An evil doctor captures four innocent woman who mistakenly spent the night in an old mountain sanitarium. He then forces them to perform vampiric acts on each other and on nearby virgins in a small town.

Gravedale High (TV Series) (*Rick Moranis in Gravedale High* [U.S. complete title]; *La escuela de los monstrous* [Spain]); U.S., 1990–1991; Horror,

Adventure, Family/Television, Animation; 30 minutes/color/English; Hanna-Barbera Studios.

Producers: Robert Dranko; *Writing Credits*: Ernie Contreras; *Director*: Robert Alverez, Oscar Dufao, Don Lusk, Paul Sommer, Carl Urbano; *Original Music*: Tyrell Music Group; *Cast*: Rick Moranis (Max Schneider), Shari Belafonte (Blanche), Roger Rose (Vinnie Stoker), Eileen Brennan (Miss Dirge), Georgia Brown (Headmistress Crone), Tim Curry (Mr. Tutner), Barry Gordon (Reggie Moonshroud), Sandra Gould (Miss Webner), Jackie Earl Haley (Gill Waterman), Ricki Lake (Cleopatra), Maurice Lamarche (Sid the Invisible Kid), Brock Peters (Boneyard), Kimmy Robertson (Medusa), Frank Welker (Frankentyke, J.P. Ghastly III), Jonathan Winters (Coach Cadaver).

Gravedale High is unlike any other high school. With the help of Max Schneider (Rick Moranis), the only living human faculty member at the school, this school serves a student body of scary, classic monsters, including mummies, werewolves, and even vampires, one of which (named Vinnie "Stoker") is distinctly Dracula-type.

Greasepaint and Gore: The Hammer Monsters of Phil Leakey; U.K., 2004; Documentary; 80 minutes/color/English; Tomahawk Films.

Producers: Bruce Sachs; *Writing Credits*: Bruce Sachs, Russell Wall; *Director*: Russell Wall; *Cinematography*: Paul Inott, Jonathan Young; *Cast*: Christopher Lee (Himself), Hazel Court (Herself), Philip Leakey (Himself [archive footage]), Val Guest (Himself), Jimmy Sangster (Himself).

This documentary's subject is Phil Leakey, a man who pioneered makeup effects for gory and gothic horror films. Experimenting with different materials, Leakey strived for more realistic effects in such movies such as *The Curse of Frankenstein*, and *Dracula*. Using interviews and makeup demonstrations, the film provides an interesting insight into the achievement of what is now called "Hammer Horror."

Greasepaint and Gore, Part 2: The Hammer Monsters of Roy Ashton; U.K., 2004; Documentary, Short; color/English; Tomahawk Films.

Producers: Bruce Sachs, Russell Wall; *Writing Credits*: Bruce Sachs, Russell Wall; *Director*: Russell Wall; *Cinematography*: Paul Inott, Russell Wall, Jonathan Young; *Film Editing*: David Smith; *Original Music*: Simon Hinkler; *Cast*: Roy Ashton (Himself), Elizabeth Ashton (Herself [Narrator]), Philip Leakey (Himself), Christopher Lee (Himself), Jimmy Sangster (Himself), Val Guest (Himself), Hazel Court (Herself), Barbara Shelley (Herself), Freddie Francis (Himself), Janette Scott (Herself), Eddie Powell (Himself), Bruce Sachs (Narrator [voice]), Russell Wall (Narrator [voice])

The Great Bear Scare (U.S., 1983; Family/Television, Animation; 30 minutes/color/English; DimenMark International.

Producers: Thomas A. Mayfield, Mary Roscoe; *Writing Credits*: John Barrett; *Director*: Hal Mason; *Film Editing*: Franklin Cofod; *Original Music*: William Loose, Edward Yelin; *Cast*: Tom Smothers (Ted E. Bear [voice]), Louis Nye (Dracula [voice]), Hans Conried (Professor Werner von Bear [voice]), Sue Raney (Patti Bear [voice]), Hal Smith (Mayor C. Emory Bear [voice]), Lucille Bliss (Miss Witch [voice]).

The bears from Bearbank have to confront their greatest fears when their neighbors come to visit. Nearby Monster Mountain is home to all the monsters of the world, including Dracula. When the monsters invade Bearbank, the bears pretend they're not there, and the monsters leave.

Great Books (TV Series [1993–2002]), episode "Dracula" ("Dracula: A Vampire for the Ages); U.S., 2001; Documentary, Television; 52 minutes/color, black and white/English/Mono; Cronkite Ward Company.

Producers: Trish Mitchell, Dale Minor, Ann Conanan, Richard Wells, Alexandra Middendorf, Jonathan Ward; *Writing Credits*: Trish Mitchell; *Cinematography*: Chip Nusbaum; *Film Editing*: Martin Nelson; *Original Music*: Cottrell-Mangum Music; *Art Direction*: Kin Remington; *Cast*: Donald Sutherland (Narrator), David J. Skal, Nina Auerbach, Elizabeth Miller, Leonard Wolf, Barbara Belford, Vlad, Sky, Val, James V. Hart, Ellie Nicoll, Chris Mangum, Terence Aselford, Bill Toscano, John Paglio, Niculai Siritanu, Margaret Norwood, Stas Wronka, Chris Davenport, James Gregorio, Scott Degraw, Virginia Itta Marcu, Dan Sanulescu.

This documentary explores both Bram Stoker's classic narrative and its impact on the vampire mythos, as well as the historical Dracula and the lives of "real life" vampires.

Grim & Evil (TV Series [2001–2007]), episode "Billy Idiot/Home of the Ancients"; U.S., Season 4, Episode 33, 30 June 2005; Family, Comedy, Fantasy/Television, Animation; 30 minutes/color/English/Stereo; Castle Creek Production, Cartoon Network.

Producers: Maxwell Atoms (83 episodes, 2001–2007), Louis J. Cuck (producer/line producer) (82 episodes, 2001–2007), Brian A. Miller (executive producer: Cartoon Network Studios/supervising producer: Cartoon Network Studios) (17 episodes, 2003–2007), Jennifer Pelphrey (supervising producer: Cartoon Network Studios) (16 episodes, 2004–2007), Shaun Cashman (supervising producer) (13 episodes, 2006–2007); *Writing Credits*: Maxwell Atoms; *Director*: Robert Alvarez, Sue

Perrotto; *Original Music*: Guy Moon; *Cast*: Grey DeLisle (Mandy/Owl/Student [voice]), Greg Eagles (Grim/Sperg/Slug) (voice), Richard Steven Horvitz (Billy/Billy's Dad/Myron/Grandpa) (voice) (as Richard Horvitz), Vanessa Marshall (Irwin) (voice), Jane Carr (Pud'n/Bride of Frankenstein) (voice), Chris Cox (Officer/Guy Guyerson) (voice), Jennifer Darling (Pollywinkle) (voice), Jennifer Hale (Marilyn) (voice), Phil LaMarr (Dracula/Narrator/Judge/Hector Con Carne/Mailman) (voice), Renee Raudman I (Kid/Nurse) (voice), Jason Spisak (Wolfman/Goblin) (voice), James Arnold Taylor (Front Desk Clerk/Director/Announcer) (voice).

The main characters, Grim (Greg Eagles), Billy (Richard Steven Horvitz), and Mandy (Grey DeLisle), meet many odd characters, like Wolfman (Jason Spisak) and Dracula (Phil LaMarr), in a retirement home.

Grim & Evil (TV Series [2001–2007]), episode "Fear and Loathing in Endsville" (*The Grim Adventures of Billy & Mandy* [U.S., new title]; *As Terríveis Aventuras de Billy E Mandy* [Brazil]; *Billy, Mandy & symmoria tis geitonias* [Greece]; *Demonio con carne y compañia* [Spain]; *Las macabras aventuras de Billy & Mandy* [Spain]; *Malices et menaces* [Canada, French title]; *Stygg og slem* [Norway, dubbed version]); U.S., Season 6, Episode 9, 12 May 2006; Family, Comedy, Fantasy/Television, Animation; 11 minutes/color/English/Stereo; Castle Creek Productions, Cartoon Network.

Producers: Maxwell Atoms, Louis J. Cuck; *Writing Credits*: Alex Almaguer, Maxwell Atoms, C. H. Greenblatt; *Director(s)*: Shaun Cashman, Juli Hashiguchi, Eddy Houchins, Sue Perrotto; *Film Editing*: Illya Cano; *Original Music*: Guy Moon; *Art Direction*: Rae McCarson; *Cast*: Grey DeLisle (Mandy/Small Girl/Gina), Greg Eagles (Grim), Richard Steven Horvitz (Billy/Billy's Dad), Vanessa Marshall (Irwin), Louie Anderson (Burt), Diedrich Bader (Hoss Delgado/Floss), Jane Carr (Pud'n), Brian Cummings (Orc/TV Host), Jim Cummings (Singer), Keith Ferguson (Sweetie), Phil LaMarr (Dracula), Armin Shimerman (Skarr), April Stewart (Waitress/Scorpion Mom), Dave Wittenberg (Harvey/TV Contestant).

Guess What Happened to Count Dracula (*Draculas lüsterne Vampire* [West Germany]; *Orgia del vampiro, L'* [Italy]; *Master of the Dungeon, The* [U.S., working title]); U.S., 1970; Comedy, Horror; 80 minutes/color/English/Mono/35mm; Merrick International Films.

Producers: Laurence Merrick, Leo Rivers; *Writing Credits*: Laurence Merrick; *Director*: Mario d'Alcala, Laurence Merrick; *Cinematography*: Jack Beckett, Robert Caramico; *Film Editing*: George Watters; *Art Direction*: Michael Minor; *Make-Up*: Tom Jones, Ric Sagliani; *Cast*: Des Roberts (Count Adrian), Claudia Barron (Angelica), John Landon (Guy), Robert Branche (Dr. Harris), Frank Donato (Imp), Yvonne Gaudry (Gypsy), Damu King (Hunch), Jim Settler (Runt), Sharon Bernardi (Vamp), Jeff Cady (Larry), Angela Carnon (Nurse), Beverly Gardner (uncredited), Harry Hampton (Drunk), John King III (Gil), Denny Lester (Igor), Leslie McRae (as Les MacRae), Nancy Simpson (uncredited), Sandra Steiner (uncredited), Gene Stowell (Miklos), Clancy Sylvan (uncredited), Andy Wilder (uncredited), James Young-El (Macumba Initiate).

Count Adrian runs a Hollywood nightspot, Dracula's Dungeon, where he sets his sights on Angelica, as the woman he wants to keep for eternity.

Hakaba Kitarô (TV Series) (*Graveyard Kitaro* [U.S.]), episode "Yasha tai dorakyura yon sei" ("Yasha vs. Dracula IV" [U.S.]); Japan, Season 1, Episode 2, 17 January 2008; Horror, Fantasy, Adventure/Television, Animation; Toei Animation, Fuji TV, Tokai TV; 23 minutes/color/Japanese.

Director: Kimitosi Chioka; *Original Music*: Kaoru Wada; *Cast*: Masako Nozawa (Kitaro); Hideyuki Hori (Yasha), Ryuzaburo Otomo (Dracula the 4th).

In this episode, Kitaro, a yokai (monster/boy) who lives in a cemetery, is harassed by two monsters as Yasha, a Japanese Demon, encounters Dracula IV, a Western demon.

Halloween with the New Addams Family; U.S., 1977; Horror, Comedy, Family/Television; 74 minutes/color/English/Mono; Los Angeles, California/Charles Fries Productions.

Producers: Charles M. Fries, Charles W. Fries, David Levy, Paul Pieratt; *Writing Credits*: Charles Addams; *Director*: David Steinmetz; *Cinematography*: Jacques R. Marquette; *Film Editing*: Ken Baker; *Original Music*: Vic Mizzy; *Art Direction*: Bill Ross; *Make-Up*: Carol L. Dary; *Special Effects*: Robbie Knott; *Cast*: John Astin (Gomez Addams), Alice Fries (Witch kid in Party Scene), Carolyn Jones (Moricia Addams), Jackie Coogan (Uncle Fester), Ted Cassidy (Lurch), Jane Rose (Grandmama Addams), Lisa Loring (Wednesday Friday Addams [senior]), Jenifer Suprenant (Wednesday Friday Addams [junior]), Ken Weatherwax (Pugsley Addams [senior]), Ken Marquis (Pugsley Addams [junior]), Felix Silla (Cousin Itt), Henry Darrow (Pancho Addams), Vito Scotti (Mikey), Parley Bear (Boss Crook), Patrick Campbell (Little Bo Peep), Dean Sothern (Fake Gomez), David B. Johns (Hercules), Terry Miller (Fake Morticia), Clinton Beyerle (Atlas), George Ranito Jordan (First Cop), Suzanne Krarna (Countess Dracula), Elvia Allman (Mother Frump).

The Addams's Halloween plans are put on hold as a band of thieves try to trick the family fortune out of Pancho, Gomez's brother, who has come to guard the family while Gomez is out of town. The criminals kidnap Gomez and Morticia and replace them with doubles.

The Halloween That Almost Wasn't (*The Night Dracula Saved the World* [U.S.]); U.S., 1979; Comedy, Family, Horror/Television; 30 minutes/English/color/Mono.

Producers: Richard Barclay, Gaby Monet; *Director*: Bruce Bilson; *Cinematography*: Peter Sova; *Film Editing*: Arthur Ginsberg; *Make-Up*: Bob O'Bradovich, Dossie Donaldson [uncredited]; *Cast*: Judd Hirsch (Count Dracula), Mariette Hartley (Winnie the Witch), Henry Gibson (Igor), Jack Riley (Wolf Man/Warren the Werewolf), Josip Elic (Zabaar the Zombie), Charles Fields (Boy dressed as Scarecrow [as Charlie Fields]), Robert Fitch (Mummy), Jamie Ross (Father), Maggie Peters Ross (Mother), John Schuck (Frankenstein's Monster), Kristin Williams (Girl dressed as witch).

In fear of losing Halloween, Count Dracula threatens to expel the classic horror monsters from his castle unless they regain and revamp their images to become more frightening and scary.

Hallow's End; U.S., 2003; Horror; 90 minutes/color/English/Dolby; Hallow's End Production, Highland Myst Entertainment.

Producers: Brandon Baker, Michael Baker, Richard T. Carey, Ned Foster, Jenna Hovland, Jon Keeyes, Randy Manis, Faras Rabadi, Robert H. Straight, Michele Taverna; *Writing Credits*: Chris Burdick (as Christopher J. Burdick); *Director*: Jon Keeyes; *Cinematography*: Brad Walker; *Film Editing*: Robert J. Castaldo; *Original Music*: David Rosenblad; *Art Direction*: Eric Whitney; *Make-Up*: Jason Cook, Amy Everett, Damaris Foster, Adrienne Hoverson, Stuart Kincaid; *Special Effects*: Marvin Day; *Cast*: Stephen Cloud (Tom Sharp), Brandy Little (Jill Tremaine), Amy Jo Hearron (Kira Clemens), Amy Morris (Heidi Campbell), Matt Moore (Dan Miller), Scott Barrett (Steve Johnston), Camille Chen (Lily Moore), John F. Beach (Gary Yeats [as John Beach]), Jim Dunn (Pumpkin Jack), Velinda Godfrey (Faith), Terry Gamble (Bob), Bill Sebastian (Frat Boy), Mark E. Howell (Tour Group Dad), Victoria Sokol (Red), Vironika Kirksey (80's Hair Girl), Damaris Foster (Southern Belle), Travis Helton (Morgue Attendant), David Carter (Headless Horseman), Dean Jarnig (Bone Daddy), Rick Greenwood (2nd Tour Guide), John Cronin (Evil Clown), Todd Jenkins (Bob Stand-in), Rick Herod (Brotherhood of Nine Leader), Scott Meissner (Brotherhood of Nine), Brandon Baker (Brotherhood of Nine), Mike Wallace (Brotherhood of Nine), Ned Foster (Brotherhood of Nine), Shelly Shivers (Brotherhood of Nine), Tommy Raley (Brotherhood of Nine), Joseph Brentlinger (College Kid), Deidre Roy (College Kid), Lauren Goode (College Kid), Jaime Johnson (College Kid), Carina Baker (College Kid), Suzanne Osmer (College Kid), J.T. Swierczek (College Kid), Lizzie Lander (College Kid), Valeria Perreault (College Kid), Chris Garcia (College Kid), Rebecca Stacey (College Kid), Kandice Wallace (College Kid [as Kandice Burke-Wallace]), Jason Lacker (College Kid), Spenser Turnage (College Kid), Nickie Ludwig (Costumed Patron), Andrew Magnus (Clown), Brandie McMinn (Mom), Sarah McMinn (Statue Of Liberty), William McMinn (Uncle Sam), Kevin Milligan (Pregnant Girl), Brandi Cacy Mumaw (Costumed patron), Dade Mumaw (Costumed patron), Drake Mumaw (Costumed patron), Michael Magnus (Haunted house attendant [uncredited]).

Eight college students find themselves trapped in a haunted house on Halloween. An ancient curse causes the eight kids to turn into their Halloween costumes, one of which is Dracula.

Haram alek (*Ismail Yassin Meets Frankenstein* [U.K.]; *Ismail and Abdel Meet Frankenstein* [U.S.] [informal title]; *Shame on You* [International English title]); Egypt, 1954; Comedy/Horror; black and white/Arabic; Studio Elgiza.

Writing Credits: Gamal Hamdi; *Director*: Essa Karama; *Cast*: Abdel Fatah Al Kasri, Ismail Yasseen

In this comedy based on the movie *Abbott and Costello Meet Frankenstein*, two men (Abdel Fatah Al Kasri and Ismail Yasseen) who work in an antique shop meet Dracula, Frankenstein, and a werewolf. In the film, Frankenstein is actually a mummy, and the werewolf is a man with whom Dracula's niece has fallen in love.

Harker; U.S., 2005; Horror/Short; 14 minutes/black and white/English; In the Dark Entertainment.

Producers: Anthony Steven Giordano, Heather Henson, Jason Murphy; *Writing Credits*: Anthony Steven Giordano, Jason Murphy, Scott Shoemaker; *Director*: Anthony Steven Giordano; *Cinematography*: Jason Murphy; *Film Editing*: Anthony Steven Giordano, Jason Murphy; *Original Music*: Tom Hoehn; *Cast*: Scott Silson (Harker), Tracie Mick-Shoemaker (Renfield), James Donmoyer (Nosferatu), Billy Horne (Additional Puppeteer), Scott Shoemaker (Additional Puppeteer), Jayme LaRosa (Additional Puppeteer).

This is a puppet version of a silent horror film, in the German Expressionist style.

Hay que matar a Drácula; Argentina, 1968; Horror; 90 minutes/black and white/Spanish/Mono; Proartel S.A.

Producers: Luis A. Catalano; *Writing Credits*: Maximo Soto; *Director*: Alberto Rinaldi; *Make-Up*: Narciso Ibáñez Menta; *Cast*: Narciso Ibáñez Menta (uncredited), Patricio Contreras (Arthur); Graciela Dufau (uncredited); María Ibarreta (Lucy); Ariel Keller (uncredited); Elizabeth Killian (Condesa); Luisa Kuliok (Nora); Gianni Lunadei (Conde Drácula); Pepe Novoa (Jonathan Harker).

Hello Dracula; Hong Kong, 1985; Comedy, Horror.

Director: Huey Lueng

Her Morbid Desires; U.S., 2008; Thriller, Comedy; color/English; Irena Belle Productions.

Producers: Shawna Baca, Edward L. Plumb, Kim Waltrip; *Writing Credits*: Edward L. Plumb, Brad Linaweaver (story); *Director*: Edward L. Plum; *Cinematography*: Stephen Rocha; *Film Editing*: Jim Knell; *Original Music*: Jack Lancaster, David Manning; *Make-Up*: Misa Aikawa, Mark Fenlason, Tammy Griggs, Lorraine Martin, Janet Walker, Tracy Wilcox; *Special Effects*: Timothy Michael Cairns, Tony Copolillo; *Cast*: Erica P. Hanson (Freddi/Tessa), Ronn Moss (Count Dracula), Molly Murphy (Queen of the Vampires), Tippi Hedren (Aunt Gloria), Robert Loggia (Bob, the Director), Kevin McCarthy (The Monk), William Smith (Bill, the Director), Seth Marten (Gerry Shah), Amanda Jordan (Girl With Blue Hair), Symone Humphris (Cyndi Meadows), Shawna Baca (Rebecca Dalia), Jessica Borden (The Virgin), Kandis Erickson (Jennifer), Del Howison (Glenn, The First AD), Nicole Panucci (Dark Haired Vampire), Diana Catania (Female Vampire Slayer), Princess Nali (Young Screaming Actress), Denae Cavadias (Theresa), Heather Montanez (Nurse Vampire), Leanna Chamish (Leather Vampire), Brinke Stevens (Brinke), Tara Norris (Ouija Board Vampire), Madison Warner (Fighting Vampire at Fountain), Danielle James (Elizabeth), Rebecca Rogers (Dead Body That Comes Alive), Kelli Blissard (Dead Body at Fountain), Hanna Harper (Trophy Wife), Danielle Arnold (Brunette Vampire at Fountain [as Danielle Renee]), Rod McKuen (Himself), Ray Harryhausen (Himself), Cassandra Peterson (Elvira), George Clayton Johnson (Opium Smoking Vampire), Peter Atkins (Guitarist), Marlene Mc'-Cohen (Vanessa's Assistant), Ginny Jones (Starlet at party), Jack Lancaster (Sax player), Robert Long II (Dead body), Erica Tucker (Secretary), Kelly Rosado (Queen's Pet), Leigh Foad (Dancer), John Pepe (Vampire Slayer), Kara Brackney (Girl at party), Chuck Hammill (Bartender), Michael Milner (Guitarist), Nell Rutledge (Courtyard Vampire), Vanessa Koman (Girl at party), Andrea Alexandra (Violinist), Chris Rogers (Uke player), Matt Sells (Drummer), Erica Michaelenko (Girl with Tambourine), Mayra Gomez (Vampire at wall), Brad Linaweaver (Harryhausen Interviewer), Diane King (Vampire against wall), Summer McClure (Lady at Party), Lorenzo Loco (Postman), Victor Koman (Man at Bar), Kiki Harbster (Body model vampire), Edward L. Plumb (Western director), Steven Iyama (Extra), Mark Montanez (Camera man), Barbara Steele (Vanessa Peabody).

Hercules: The Legendary Journeys (TV Series [1995–1999]), episode "Darkness Visible"; U.S., Season 6, Episode 4, 16 January 1995; Action, Adventure, Drama, Fantasy/Television; 50 minutes/ color/English/Dolby.

Producers: Sam Raimi; *Director*: Philip Sgriccia; *Writing Credits*: Phyllis Strong; *Original Music*: Joseph LoDuca; *Film Editing*: David E. Blewitt (as David Blewitt); *Cast*: Kevin Sorbo (Hercules), Michael Hurst (Iolaus), Rafe Battiste (Darius), Jon Brazier (Mateus), Tiffany de *Cast*ro (Nadia), Norman Fairley (Headmaster), Marcel Kalma (Bald Figure), Stephen Lovatt (Galen the Vampire Hunter), Irene Malone (Vendor), Jeffrey Meek (Vlad the Impaler).

Hercules receives help against vampires (including Vlad the Impaler) attacking his people, but he is hiding a secret.

Here Come the Munsters (*Eine unheimliche Familie zum Schreien* [Germany]; *Les monsters* [France]); U.S., 1995; Comedy, Horror, Science Fiction/Television; 96 minutes/color/English/Stereo/35mm; Bodega Bay Productions, MCA Television Entertainment (MTE), St. Clare Entertainment.

Producers: Leslie Belzberg, James A. Dennett, John Landis, Michael S. Murphey; *Writing Credits*: Bill Prady, Jim Fisher, Jim Staahl; *Director*: Robert Ginty; *Cinematography*: Paul Maibaum; *Film Editing*: Dale Beldin, Marshall Harvey; *Original Music*: Michael Skloff; *Make-Up*: Tom Cummins; *Special Effects*: Michael Roundy (special effects coordinator); *Cast*: Edward Herrmann (Herman Munster), Veronica Hamel (Lily Munster), Robert Morse (Grandpa), Christine Taylor (Marilyn Hyde [Munster]), Mathew Botuchis (Eddie Munster), Troy Evans (Detective Warshowski), Joel Brooks (Larry Walker), Sean O'Bryan (Detective Cartwell), Mary Woronov (Mrs. Dimwitty), Jeff Trachta (Brent Jeckyll), Max Grodénchik (Norman Hyde), Judy Gold (Elsa Munster Hyde), Amanda Bearse (Mrs. Pearl), Irwin Keyes (One-eyed man), Jim Fisher (Villager), Scotch Ellis Loring (Flight Attendant), Brian George (Immigration Official), Robertson Dean (Angry Dog Owner), Jim Staahl (Quarenteen Official), Keone Young (Ralph, the limo driver) Kellen Hathaway (Trick-or-Treator), Bill Prady (Paramedic), T.J. McInturff (Stanley), Francesca Smith (Monique), Jane Carr (Cassie

O'Leary), James Keane (Maitre d'), James Basile (Waiter) (as James Basil), Lynne Marie Stewart (Mrs. Waffer), Judy Kain (Mrs. Hersby), Tommy Bertelsen (Ted Walker), Ralph P. Martin (Sergeant), Jim Jackman (Front Desk Officer), Christina Venuti (Woman at Fundraiser), Aaron Paris (Transformed Band Leader), Yvonne De Carlo (Cameo appearance), Al Lewis (Cameo appearance), Butch Patrick (Cameo appearance), Pat Priest (Cameo appearance).

The Munsters have come home! Returning to America to search for Herman's brother-in-law, Norman Hyde, the Munsters discover that he has turned himself into Brent Jekyll, a suave politician who is running for congress. Grandpa immediately begins work on a formula to change Norman back.

Heroes of Horror; U.S., 2001; Documentary; color, black and white/English/Dolby Digital; A&E Television Networks.

Cast: Lon Chaney Jr. (Himself/Lawrence "Larry" Talbot/The Wolf Man/The Mummy/Frankenstein's Monster/Dracula/Bruno The Chauffeur/Akhoba [archive footage]), Boris Karloff (Himself/Frankenstein's Monster/Narrator & The Grinch/Prof. Morlant/Byron Orlok/Gorca [archive footage]), Peter Lorre (Himself/Hans Beckert/Joel Cairo/Ugarte/Doctor Gogol/Dr. Adolphus Bedlo/Hilary Cummins/Montresor Herringbone [archive footage]), Béla Lugosi (Himself/Count Dracula/Legendre/Dr. Vitus Werdegast/Joseph [archive footage]), Vincent Price (Himself/Prof. Henry Jerrod/Francios Delambre/Dr. Warren Chapin/Dr. Anton Phibes/Edward Lionheart/Propero [archive footage]).

A&E sets out to document the five most infamous horror movie stars, including Béla Lugosi as Dracula.

Herushingu (TV Series) (*Hellsing* [Greece/U.S.]); Japan, 2001–2002; Action, Fantasy, Horror/Television, Animation; color/Japanese.

Producers: Satoshi Fujii (producer [13 episodes, 2001–2002]); *Writing Credits*: Kohta Hirano (13 episodes, 2001–2002), Chiaki Konaka (11 episodes, 2001–2002), Yuji Hosono (2 episodes, 2001); *Director*: Umanosuke Iida, Yasunori Urata; *Original Music*: Yasushi Ishii; *Art Direction*: Shinji Katahira; *Special Effects*: Shin Inoie (10 episodes, 2001–2002), Naoyuki Fukuda (2 episodes, 2001); *Cast*: Jôji Nakata (Alucard [13 episodes, 2001–2002]), Yoshiko Sakakibara (Integra [13 episodes, 2001–2002]), Fumiko Orikasa (Seras [13 episodes, 2001–2002]), Crispin Freeman (Alucard [13 episodes, 2001–2002]), K.T. Gray (Seras Victoria [13 episodes, 2001–2002]), Victoria Harwood (Sir Integra Wingates Hellsing [13 episodes, 2001–2002]), Michael Parker (Captain Steadler [3 episodes, 2001–2002]), JB Blanc (Priest, Enrico Maxwell [2 episodes, 2001]), Craig Robert Young (Paul Wilson [unknown episodes]), Steven Brand (Paladin Alexender Andersong, Dr. Trevellian, Sir Richard Hellsing [unknown episodes]), Ananda Banc (Woman Ghoul, Jessica, Attendent [unknown episodes]), Tricia Dickson (Young Integra Wingates Hellsing, Servant [unknown episodes]), Siobhan Flynn (Hellsing Intelligence Operative, Laura [unknown episodes]), Minako Ichiki (Woman Ghoul [unknown episodes]), Taliesin Jaffe (Jack, Leif, Assistant, Hellsing Member A, Radio Voice, Army Helicopter Pilot, Army Soldier [unknown episodes]), Jason Miller (Hellsing Member, Servant, Army Soldier [unknown episodes]), Hiromi Otsuda (Woman Ghoul [unknown episodes]), Chikao Ôtsuka (Lionel Hellsing [unknown episodes]), Chris Pooley (Vampire [unknown episodes]), Li Xing Qin (Chinese Man [unknown episodes]), Paul D. Roberts (Host Vampire [unknown episodes]), Stephanie Sheh (Waitress, Female Vampire [unknown episodes]).

The Helsing foundation protects innocent people in modern-day London against vampires who terrorize the city. The development of a new drug that instills in humans a taste for blood really has made Van Helsing in dire need of help. With the aid of the ancient vampire Alucard ("Dracula" spelled backwards), Van Helsing is ready to do battle.

Heubhyeol hyeongsa na do-yeol (*Vampire Cop Ricky* [U.S.]); Korea, 2006; Action, Comedy, Crime, Fantasy, Romance; 110 minutes/color/Korean; Chungeorahm Films.

Producers: Choi Yong-bae, Lee Si-myeong; *Writing Credits*: Jeon Soon-wook, Kang Seong-ryong, Kim Hyeong-gi, Kim Se-Gyeom, Kim Soo-yeong, Lee Soo-jeong, and Nam Koong-gyoon; *Director*: Lee Si-myeong; *Film Editing*: Kyeong Min-ho; *Original Music*: Dong-jun Lee; *Cast*: Kim Su-ro (Ricky or Yeol Na Do), Jeon Ho-jin (Inspector Kang), Jo Yeo-Jeong (Yoeng-hee), Oh Kwang-rok (Vampire Hunter).

A mosquito bites Count Dracula in Transylvania and ends up on a plane that lands in South Korea, biting and infecting Ricky, a policeman. But he is a different type of vampire because he turns into a vampire only when he has an erection. At one point, his girlfriend is kidnapped and the local church sends a vampire hunter to kill him.

The Hilarious House of Frightenstein (TV Series); Canada, 1971; Comedy, Family/Television; 60 minutess/color/English/Mono; CHCH-TV.

Producers: Mitch Markowitz, Riff Markowitz; *Writing Credits*: Riff Markowitz; *Director*: Riff Markowitz; *Make-Up*: Hilda Healey, Robert Laden;

Cast: Billy Van (Bwanna Clyde Batty), Guy Big (Midget Count), Mitch Markowitz (Mosquito), Julius Sumner Miller (The Professor), Vincent Price (The Narrator), Fishka Rais (Igor), Joe Torbay (Harvey C. Wallbanger).

This series follows the scary and silly happenings at a mad scientist vampire's home/lab.

Historical Dracula, Facts Behind the Fiction; U.S./Romania, 1976; Documentary.

Director: Ian Boston.

This documentary examines the music and traditions of Transylvania, as well as the myths behind Vlad the Impaler and his vampiric counterpart in Bram Stoker's novel.

Hollywood on Parade No. A-8; U.S., 1933; Documentary, Short; 10 minutes/black and white/English/Mono; Louis Lewyn Productions.

Producers: Louis Lewyn; *Director*: Louis Lewyn; *Cast*: Eddie Borden (Host), Rex Bell (Himself), Dorothy Burgess (Herself), Béla Lugosi (Dracula), Charles Murray (Himself [as Charlie Murray]), Marie Prevost (Herself), Mae Questel (Betty Boop), George Sidney (Himself), Gayne Whitman (Himself).

In a Hollywood wax museum, Eddie Bordon comes to life and introduces the audience to various movie stars.

Hollywood's Greatest Villains; U.S., 2005; Documentary; 100 minutes/English/color. Lou Reda Productions.

Producers: Mark Etkind, Lou Reda; *Director*: Michael Emerson; *Writing Credits*: Dennis Kleinman; *Film Editing*: Tracey Jackson; *Cast*: (All as themselves) John Carpenter, Glenn Close, Scott Glenn, James Earl Jones, Jonathon Klutz, Martin Landau, George Lucas, Sharon Stone.

Home to Roost (TV Series [1985–1990]), episode "Open House"; U.K., Season 2, Episode 2, 12 September 1986; Comedy/Television; 30 minutes/color/English; Yorkshire Television (YTV).

Producers: Vernon Lawrence, David Reynolds; *Writing Credits*: Eric Chappell; *Director*: David Reynolds; *Original Music*: Peter Knight; *Make-Up*: Linda Crozier; *Cast*: John Thaw (Henry Willows), Reece Dinsdale (Matthew Willows), Elizabeth Bennett (Enid Thompson), John Rowe (Sally's Dad), Julia Gilbert (Dracula), Jean Rimmer (Tom's Mum).

Henry (John Thaw) comes home to find his son Mathew throwing a wild party. The episode features an appearance from a character referred to as Dracula (Julia Gilbert).

The Horror of Hammer; U.S., 2001; Documentary; 115 minutes/color, black and white/English/Mono; Image Entertainment.

Cast: Christopher Lee (himself [archive footage]), Peter Cushing (himself [archive footage]), Ingrid Pitt (herself [archive footage]).

This is a compilation of trailers from movies by Hammer Studios featuring Christopher Lee as Dracula.

Hotel Transylvania; U.S., 2011; Comedy/Animation; color/English; Sony.

Producers: Michelle Murdocca; *Writing Credits*: Don Rhymer; *Director*: Jill Culton, Anthony Stacchi, David Feiss

The Van Helsing family is a famous family of monster hunters who hunt vampires mostly. The youngest in the Van Helsing line, Simon, falls madly in love with Mavis, the daughter of Count Dracula himself. The two lovers try to bring their families together.

House of Dark Shadows (*Dark Shadows* [U.S., pre-release title]; *Das Schloß der Vampire* [West Germany]; *La casa dei vampiri* [Italy]; *La fiancée du vampire* [France]; *Nas Sombras da Noite* [Brazil]; *Sombras en la obscuridad* [Mexico]; *Sombras tenebrosas* [Chile]; *To spiti me tis mavres skies* [Greece]; *Vampyrens hus* [Sweden]; *Vampyyrien häät* [Finland]); U.S., 1970; Horror, Drama; 97 minutes/color/English/Mono; Metro-Goldwyn-Mayer (MGM).

Producer: Dan Curtis, Trevor Williams; *Writing Credits*: Gordon Russell, Sam Hall; *Director*: Dan Curtis; *Cinematography*: Arthur J. Ornitz (as Arthur Ornitz); *Film Editing*: Arline Garson; *Make-Up*: Robert Layden, Dick Smith; *Cast*: Jonathan Frid (Barnabas Collins), Grayson Hall (Dr. Julia Hoffman), Kathryn Leigh Scott (Maggie Evans), Roger Davis (Jeff Clark), Nancy Barrett (Carolyn Stoddard), John Karlen (Willie Loomis), Thayer David (Professor T. Eliot Stokes), Louis Edmonds (Roger Collins), Don Briscoe (Todd Blake), David Henesy (David Collins), Dennis Patrick (Sheriff George Patterson), Lisa Blake Richards (Daphne Budd, Elizabeth's Secretary [as Lisa Richards]), Jerry Lacy (Minister), Barbara Cason (Mrs. Johnson), Paul Michael (Old Man), Humbert Allen Astredo (Dr. Forbes [as Humbert Astredo]), Terrayne Crawford (Todd's Nurse [as Terry Crawford]), Michael Stroka (Pallbearer), Joan Bennett (Elizabeth Collins Stoddard), Camila Ashland (Collinwood Party Guest [uncredited]), Chip Coffey (Collinwood party guest [uncredited]), George DiCenzo (Deputy [uncredited]), Philip Larson (Deputy [uncredited]).

Willie Loomis searches the Collins's family crypt in search of the family's lost jewels and in the process unleashes the sleeping (Dracula-type) vampire Barnabas Collins. Soon, the family welcomes its long lost "cousin from England," Barnabas, as female members of the family, starting around the same time, begin to suffer attacks that drain them of blood. Dr. Julia Hoffman, a blood specialist, learns the truth of Barnabas's supernatural affliction and offers him the chance of a possible cure. All appears to be going well until Barnabas acquaints himself with Maggie Evans, the Collinwood governess, believing her to be his lost love Josette du Prés.

House of Dracula; U.S., 1945; Horror; 67 minutes/black and white/English/Mono; Universal Studios.

Producers: Joseph Gershenson, Paul Malvern; *Writing Credits*: Edward T. Lowe Jr., Dwight V. Babcock (story [uncredited]); *Director*: Erle C. Kenton; *Cinematography*: George Robinson; *Film Editing*: Russell F. Schoengarth; *Original Music*: William Lava; *Art Direction*: John B. Goodman, Martin Obzina; *Make-Up*: Carmen Dirigo, Jack P. Pierce; *Special Effects*: John P. Fulton; *Cast*: Lon Chaney Jr. (Lawrence Stewart Talbot/The Wolf Man [as Lon Chaney]), John Carradine (Count Dracula), Martha O'Driscoll (Miliza Morrelle), Lionel Atwill (Police Inspector Holtz), Onslow Stevens (Dr. Franz Edlemann), Jane Adams (Nina), Ludwig Stössel (Siegfried [as Ludwig Stossel]), Glenn Strange (The Frankenstein Monster), Skelton Knaggs (Steinmuhl), Joseph E. Bernard (Brahms — Coroner [uncredited]), Fred Cordova (Gendarme [uncredited]), Dick Dickinson (Villager [uncredited]), Beatrice Gray (Mother [uncredited]), Casey Harrison (Gendarme [uncredited]), Boris Karloff (Frankenstein Monster in Dream Sequence [archive footage (uncredited)]), Harry Lamont (Villager [uncredited]), Gregory Marshall (Johannes [uncredited]).

Dracula comes to Dr. Edleman about getting a cure for his vapirism but gets sidetracked by the doctor's beautiful female assistant. Meanwhile, Talbot, the Wolf Man, comes to Dr. Edleman to try and cure his lycanthropy. The first attempt at the

John Carradine, left, plays Dracula opposite Onslow Stevens as Dr. Franz Edlemann in *House of Dracula* (U.S., 1945) (courtesy John Edgar Browning).

cure fails, so Talbot jumps off a cliff in an attempt to end his life. This too fails, and Talbot survives the fall but discovers a series of caves, one containing a sleeping Frankenstein's monster. The two monsters battle it out to prove once and for all who is the strongest.

House of Frankenstein (*Chamber of Horrors* [U.S., working title]; *Doom of Dracula* [U.S., working title]; *The Devil's Brood* [U.S., working title]); U.S., 1944; Fantasy, Horror, Science Fiction; 71 minutes/black and white/English/Mono; Universal Studios.

Producers: Paul Malvern; *Writing Credits*: Edward T. Lowe Jr. (as Edward T. Lowe), Curt Siodmak; *Director*: Erle C. Kenton; *Cinematography*: George Robinson; *Film Editing*: Philip Cahn; *Original Music*: Hans J. Salter (as H.J. Salter); *Art Direction*: John B. Goodman, Martin Obzina; *Make-Up*: Jack P. Pierce (uncredited); *Special Effects*: John P. Fulton; *Cast*: Boris Karloff (Doctor Gustav Niemann), Lon Chaney Jr. (Lawrence Talbot), John Carradine (Dracula/Baron Latos), Anne Gwynne (Rita Hussman), Peter Coe (Karl Hussman), Lionel Atwill (Inspector Anz), George Zucco (Professor Bruno Lampini), Elena Verdugo (Ilonka), Sig Ruman (Burgomeister Hussman), William Edmunds (Fejos), Charles F. Miller (Tobermann [as Charles Miller]), Philip Van Zandt (Muller), Julius Tannen (Hertz), Hans Herbert (Meier), Dick Dickinson (Born), George Lynn (Gerlach), Michael Mark (Frederick Strauss), Frank Reicher (Ullman), Brandon Hurst (Dr. Geissler), Glenn Strange (Frankenstein Monster), Olaf Hytten (Hoffman), J. Carrol Naish (Daniel), Edmund Cobb (Coachman [uncredited]), Gino Corrado (Man in Audience at Dracula Exhibit [uncredited]), Joe Kirk (Schwartz [uncredited]), Belle Mitchell (Urla, Gypsy Woman [uncredited]), Charles Wagenheim (Jailer (uncredited).

Dr. Niemann shares his tales of scientific experimentation with brain switching with his hunchbacked cellmate, Daniel. He mentions to Daniel that he could possibly put his brain in a more suitable body. The prison is destroyed in a thunderstorm, and the men escape and run away with a traveling carnival. The men discover that the carnival owner has the skeleton of Count Dracula and knows how to revive him. The hunchback kills the carnival owner, and Dr. Niemann has Dracula kill those who sent them to prison. Daniel falls in love with a gypsy girl who later devastates him by falling in love with Talbot, the tormented human form of the Wolf Man locked inside of Frankenstein's castle.

The House That Dripped Blood; U.K., 1971; Horror, Mystery; 102 minutes/color/English/Mono; Amicus Productions.

Producers: Paul Ellisworth, Max Rosenberg (producer [as Max J. Rosenberg]), Milton Subotsky, Gordon Wescourt; *Writing Credits*: Robert Bloch; *Director*: Peter Duffell. *Cinematography*: Ray Parslow; *Film Editing*: Peter Tanner; *Original Music*: Michael Dress; *Art Direction*: Tony Curtis; *Make-Up*: Harry Frampton, Joyce James; *Cast*: John Bennett (Det. Insp. Holloway), John Bryans (A.J. Stoker), John Malcolm (Sgt. Martin), Jon Pertwee (Paul Henderson [segment "The Cloak"]), Ingrid Pitt (Carla Lynde [segment "The Cloak"]), Geoffrey Bayldon (Theo von Hartmann [segment "The Cloak"]), Richard Coe (Film *Director* [segment "The Cloak"] [uncredited]), Roy Evans (Hunchback [segment "The Cloak"] [uncredited]), Bernard Hopkins (Film Crewmember [segment "The Cloak"] [uncredited]), Joanna Lumley (Film Crew Girl [uncredited]), Jonathan Lynn (Set Designer [segment "The Cloak"] [uncredited]), Winifred Sabine (Tea Trolley Woman [segment "The Cloak"] [uncredited])

In the segment titled, "The Cloak," Paul Henderson buys a cloak from a costume store for his upcoming part in a movie as a vampire. However, the cloak belonged to a real vampire and was imbued with special powers. The cloak magically transforms Paul into a real-life Dracula-type vampire.

How My Dad Killed Dracula; U.S., 2008; Comedy, Family, Horror/Short; 14 minutes/color/English/Dolby Digital; Telltale Productions, The Marlowe-Pugnetti Company.

Producers: Nicholas Beard, Karin Chess (co-producer), Rae Kieffer Cohen, David Colley, Mark Dalton, John Huegel, Karen Huegel, John Manier, Brian Maris, James Marlowe, Geralyn Orcutt, John Orcutt, Steve Pierce, Brian Pugnetti, Juan Ramirez, Mathew Ramos, Ryan Ramos, Richard Sinatra, Sky Soleil, Sky Soleil, Timothy Stoefen, Elyssia Stratton, Paul Viets, Sharon Viets, Dulani Wallace, Jill Wright, Steven Wright; *Writing Credits*: Sky Soleil (story and screenplay); *Director*: Sky Soleil; *Cinematography*: Skye Borgman; *Film Editing*: Richard Sinatra; *Original Music*: Nathan Lanier; *Art Direction*: C.J. Henderson (carpenter), C.J. Henderson (prop designer), Brinson M. Thieme (storyboards); *Make-Up*: Megan Areford (makeup artist [segments]), Caroline Ramos (assistant makeup artist), Michelle Tabor (key hair stylist), Michelle Tabor (key makeup artist); *Special Effects*: Blake Bolger (special effects), Mark Richardson (smoke effects); *Cast*: Daniel Roebuck (Uncle Ronny), Neil Hopkins (Dracula), Victor Bonavida (Jason), Cooper Green (Steven), Maxim Knight (Todd), Cameron Palatas (Mark), Linh Chan (Shop Owner), Gerard Huegel (Man on Street).

A father tries to prove to some teens that he killed Dracula, who is played by Neil Hopkins.

Hrabe Drakula; Czechoslovakia, 1971; Horror; 76 minutes/black and white/Czech/Mono; Ceskoslovenská Televize.

Writing Credits: Oldrich Zelezný; *Director*: Anna Procházková; *Cinematography*: Vladimír Opletal; *Film Editing*: Milton Carruth; *Cast*: Ilja Racek (Count Drakula), Jan Schánilec (Jonathan Harker), Václav Mares, Klára Jerneková, Jirí Zahajský, Ota Sklencka, Hana Maciuchová.

This film is based on Bram Stoker's short work that was later published by Florence Stoker as *Dracula's Guest* (1914).

Hungarian Dracula; Hungary, 1983; Drama/Television; 68 minutes/color/Hungarian; Magyar Televízió Müvelödési Föszerkesztöség.

Writing Credits: Péter Müller; *Director*: Géza Böszörményi; *Cinematography*: Gyula Bornyi; *Film Editing*: Olga Polgáriné Herskovits; *Make-Up*: András Tolnai; *Cast*: Djoko Rosic (Csungi), Ildikó Bánsági (Rózsika), Gábor Reviczky (Rózner), András Bálint (ÁVH-s tiszt), Attila Andics, János Bucsi, Ferenc Deimanik, Gábor Dézsi Szabó, Károly Donnert, György Dörner, Mariann Dörnyei, László Dózsa, András Fekete, Károly F. Nagy, Gabriella Hegedûs, László Helyey (Bignicev), József Incze, Kálmán Nemes, Ildikó Pécsi (ÁVH-s), Edit Soós, Eta Szilágyi.

Hyakumannen chikyû no tabi: Bandâ bukku (*One Million-Year Trip: Bandar Book* [U.S.]); Japan, 1978; Action, Family/Television, Animation; 94 minutes/color/Japanese; Tezuka Production Company.

Writing Credits: Osamu Tezuka; *Director*: Hisashi Sakaguchi; *Film Editing*: Ei Itô; *Original Music*: Yuji Ono; *Art Direction*: Katsumi Handô (artboards); *Cast*: Masatô Ibu (Black Jack), Iemasa Kayumi (Dokudami), Kaneta Kimotsuki (Dr. Sharaku), Kiyoshi Kobayashi (Dr. Kudo), Mami Koyama (Mimuru), Yû Mizushima (Bandar), Reiko Mutô (Queen Tasuka), Yukiko Nikaido (Mrs. Kudo), Tôru Ôhira (King Zobi), Kousei Tomita (King Bolbox).

Young Bandar, a teenage Earthling, lives on a far-away planet with human-like shape-shifters who survive on a diet of vegetables and animal tails. An invasion by outsiders, including several classic horror icons, sparks violence.

Hysterical; U.S., 1983; Comedy, Horror; 87 minutes/color/English/Mono/35mm; H&W Filmworks, Cinema Group Venture.

Producers: William J. Immerman, Gene Levy; *Writing Credits*: Chris Bearde, Bill Hudson, Brett Hudson, Mark Hudson, Trace Johnston; *Director*: Chris Bearde; *Cinematography*: Thomas del Ruth; *Film Editing*: Stanley Frazen; *Original Music*: Bob Alcivar, Robert O. Ragland *Cast*: Bill Hudson (Frederic Lansing/Casper), Mark Hudson (Dr. Paul Batton), Brett Hudson (Fritz), Cindy Pickett (Kate), Richard Kiel (Captain Howdy), Julie Newmar (Venetia), Robert Donner (Ralph), Murray Hamilton (Mayor), Clint Walker (Sheriff), Franklyn Ajaye (Leroy), Charlie Callas (Dracula), Amanda H. Bearde (Teenage Girl), Pamela Bowman (New York Model #2), Robert Alan Browne (New York Press Man), Sue Casey (Bookstore Society Lady #2), Gene Castle (Lead Zombie Dancer), Kathy Cherry (Sexy Girl), Dick Chudnow (Looney), Pat Colbert (Hooker #1), Natalie Core (Bookstore Society Lady #1), Bud Cort (Dr. John), John Diehl (Taxi Driver), Mary Ellen Flaherty (Bookstore Society Lady #4), John Larroquette (Bob X. Cursion), Helena Mäkelä (Nurse), Gary Owens (TV Announcer), Indy Shriner (Hooker #2), Maurice Sneed (Looney), JoAnn Willette (Bookstore Society Lady #3), Keenan Wynn (Fisherman), Anne Gaybis (Waitress).

A writer goes to a town called Hellview to write a novel. The lighthouse he is renting is haunted because someone was killed there over 100 years ago. The woman who was killed was married to Dracula. He is resurrected and two adventure seekers are brought in to solve the case.

Ibulong mo sa hangin (*Blood of the Vampires* [U.S.]; *Creatures of Evil* [undefined]; *Curse of the Vampires* [International English title]; *Terrore ha la pelle di donna, Il* [Italy]; *Whisper to the Wind* [U.S.]); Philippines, 1966; Horror, Drama; 90 minutes/Eastmancolor/Tagalog, English, Philipino/Mono/35mm; AM Productions.

Producers: Amalia Fuentes (as Amalia Muhlach); *Writing Credits*: Ben Feleo (story and screenplay), Pierre L. Salas; *Director*: Gerardo de Leon; *Cinematography*: Mike Accion; *Film Editing*: Ben Barcelon; *Original Music*: Tito Arevalo; *Make-Up*: Ben Otico; *Cast*: Amalia Fuentes (Leonore Escodero), Romeo Vasquez (Daniel Castillo), Eddie Garcia (Eduardo Escodero), Johnny Monteiro, Mary Walter (Doña Consuelo Escodero de Victoria), Rosario del Pilar, Francisco Cruz, Quiel Mendoza, Luz Angeles, Andres Benitez, Tessie Hernandez, Linda Rivera, Paquito Salcedo.

Eduardo Escodero (Eddie Garcia) has been turned into a vampire by his vampire mother who has escaped from her dungeon prison in the basement of their castle-like estate. Eduardo, now a Dracula-type vampire, turns his girlfriend into a vampire, which incites her brother Daniel (Romeo Vasquez) to vow revenge. Daniel and other villagers must find a way to stop the vampire curse from spreading.

The Impaler: A Biographical/Historical Look at the Life of Vlad the Impaler, Widely Known

Ad for *Ibulong mo sa hangin* (Philippines, 1966; *Curse of the Vampires* [International English title]) (courtesy Simon Santos).

as Dracula; Canada, 2002; Documentary, Television; 48 minutes/color/English.

Director: George Angelescu.

This film documents the life of the historical Dracula, Vlad the Impaler, who lived during the 15th century.

El Imperio de Drácula (1967) (*The Empire of Dracula* [U.S.]); Mexico, 1967; Horror, Mystery, Thriller; 85 minutes/color/Spanish/Mono; Filmica Vergara Comisiones.

Producers: Luis Enrique Vergara; *Writing Credits*: Ramón Obón (screenplay), Bram Stoker (novel); *Director*: Federico Curiel, Ángel Rodríguez Vázquez (assistant director); *Cinematography*: Alfredo Uribe; *Film Editing*: Luis Sobreyra; *Original Music*: Gustavo César Carrión, Salvador Topete (music recordist), Gonzalo Gavira (sound effects), Jaime Rodríguez (boom operator), Jesus Sanchez (dialogue recordist); *Art Direction*: Arcadi Artis Gener; *Make-Up*: Armando Islas (makeup supervisor), Aida Sánchez (hair stylist); *Special Effects*: Ricardo Sáinz; *Cast*: Lucha Villa (Patricia), César del Campo (Luis Brener), Eric del Castillo (Baron Draculstein [as Erick del Castillo]), Ethel Carrillo (Diana), Guillermo Zetina (Dr. Wilson), Robin Joyce (Lily), Fernando Osés (Igor), Víctor Alcocer (Sr. Brener), Mário Orea (Inspector), Rebeca Iturbide (Sra. Brener), Altia Michel (as Atilia Michel), Gigi Moret (as Gigi Monet), Carlos Ortigoza (as Carlos David Ortigoza Jr.), José Dupeyrón (Chofer), Erick del Castillo Jr., Ortega (uncredited).

Luis Brener (Cesar del Campo) is sent by his dying mother to Castle Draculstein to avenge his father killed by Baron Draculstein (Eric del Castillo). There, several beautiful vampires try to lure him to their estate to feed on his blood.

In Camera: The Naïve Visual Effects of Bram Stoker's Dracula; U.S., 2007; Documentary, Short; 19 minutes/color/English; ZAP Zoetrope Aubry Productions.

Producers: Kim Aubry; *Director*: Kim Aubry; Cinematography: Stephen Salvati; *Film Editing*: Ken Schneider; *Cast*: Francis Ford Coppola (Himself), Roman Coppola (Himself), Gary Oldman (Himself [archive footage]), Keanu Reeves (Himself [archive footage]), Stephen Salvati (Van Helsing), Christopher Warren (Himself), Gene Warren Jr. (Himself).

Director Kim Aubry takes us behind the scenes with her second documentary about Francis Ford Coppola's 1992 remake of *Dracula*.

In Living Color (TV Series [1990–1994]), episode "Bram Stoker's Wanda"; U.S., Season 4, Episode 11, 11 December 1992; Horror, Comedy, Romance/Television; 4 minutes and 59 seconds/color, black and white/English/Stereo; Twentieth Century–Fox Television.

Producers: Keenan Ivory Wayans; *Writing Credits*: Robert Schimmel; *Original Music*: Nancy Severinson; *Cast*: Jamie Foxx (Wanda), Jim Carrey (Vampire).

Jim Carrey, who plays the Vampire, enters the room of Wanda, played by Jamie Foxx, while she is sleeping so that he can drink her blood. After the lights turn on, the Vampire no longer wants Wanda anymore, and tries to think of ways to leave. Wanda, on the other hand, tries to get him to stay by offering blood she has under her bed, breaking her mirrors, and pulling out a coffin. The Vampire finally kills himself by tricking Wanda into thinking he liked sunlight. By opening the curtains, he puts himself out of the misery of being with her.

In Search of Dracula with Jonathan Ross; U.K., 1996; Documentary, Television; 51 minutes/color/English; London Weekend Television (LWT).

Producers: Mark Tinkler; *Director*: Luke Jeans; *Cast*: Stephanie Beacham (Herself), Francis Ford Coppola (Himself), Sadie Frost (Herself), Richard E. Grant (Himself), Grace Jones (Herself), Christopher Lee (Himself), Gary Oldman (Himself), Jack Palance (Himself), Jonathan Ross (Himself/Host), Ken Russell (Himself).

This documentary examines the history of Dracula in film.

In Search of History: The Real Dracula; U.S., 2000; Documentary, Television; 47 minutes/English/color; A&E Television Networks.

Producers: Charlie Ryan; *Writing Credits*: Charlie Ryan; *Cast*: Radu Florescu (Himself), Raymond McNally (Himself).

This documentary examines the real Dracula, Vlad the Impaler, as well as the structures and towns he built in the fifteenth century that still stand in Romania. McNally and Florescu published the first work to treat the historical Dracula and film.

Inside Television's Greatest: Addams Family & The Munsters; U.S., 2001; Documentary; 60 minutes/color, black and white/English/NTSC Goldhil Entertainment.

Cast: James Reeves (narrator).

This documentary offers a behind-the-scenes look at the creation of two of television's most famously monstrous families and their lasting influence. Included among them is Vladimir "Grandpa" Munster.

The Inspector (TV Series [1965–1969]), episode "Transylvania Mania"; U.S., 1968; Comedy, Horror/Television, Animation, Short; 7 minutes/color/English/Mono; Mirisch-Geoffrey-DePatie-Freleng Productions.

Producers: David H. DePatie, Friz Freleng; *Writing Credits*: John W. Dunn (story); *Director*: Jerry Chiniquy; *Film Editing*: Lee Gunther; *Original Music*: Walter Greene; *Art Direction*: Warren Batchelder (animator), Manny Gould (animator), Tom O'Loughlin (background artist), Manuel Perez (animator [as Manny Perez]), Tom Ray (animator), Dick Ung (layout artist), Don Williams (animator); *Cast*: Pat Harrington Jr. (Inspector [voice]), Marvin Miller (Urg [voice]), Hal Smith (Vampire Scientist [voice]).

The Inspector arrives at the Vampire Scientist's castle in Transylvania to ask for directions. The Vampire Scientist decides to put the Inspector's brain in a robot. The Vampire Scientist and his assistant chase the Inspector after he runs away.

Inspector Gadget (TV Series [1983–1986]), episode "Haunted Castle"; U.S., Season 1, Episode 8, 29 October 1983; Family, Adventure/Television, Animation; 30 minutes/color/English; DIC Entertainment.

Producers: Jean Chalopin, Jean Chalopin, Andy Heyward, Tetsuo Katayama, Patrick Loubert; *Writing Credits*: Andy Heyward (creator), Jean Chalopin (creator), Bruno Bianchi (creator), Jean Chalopin (developer), Peter Sauder (head writer); *Director*: Dave Cox, Edouard David, Raymond Jafelice (as Ray Jafelice), Ken Stephenson; Cinematography: Katsuji Misawa, Tyi Nishimura (as T. Nishimura), Masahide Ueda; *Film Editing*: Peter Aries, Philippe Kotlarski (as Phillipe Kotlarski), Masatoshi Tsurubuchi; *Original Music*: Suki Levy, Haim Saban; *Art Direction*: Dave Cox, Scott Caple; *Cast*: Don Adams (Gadget [voice]), Cree Summer (Penny [as Cree Summer Francks]), Frank Welker ([voice]), Greg Duffell ([voice]), Jeri Craden ([voice] [as Jeri Cradden]), Melleny Brown ([voice]), Bernard Carez (Chef Gonthier [voice]), Patricia Darnot (Sophie [voice]), Victor Désy (Docteur Gang [voice]), Luc Durand (Gadget [French version] [voice]), Don Francks (Big M.A.D Agent), Dan Hennessey (M.A.D Agent), Hadley Kay (Additional Voices [voice]), Chris Wiggins (Chief Quimby [uncredited]).

Gadget, Penny and Brian travel to a scary castle in Transylvania, where the borderguard looks mysteriously like Count Dracula.

Is It Real? (TV Series [2005–Current]), episode "Vampires"; U.S., 2006; Documentary; color/English; National Geographic Channel, National Geographic.

Producers: Kathleen Cromley, Eleanor Grant, French Horwitz (senior producer), Vicky Matthews, Vicky Matthews (series producer), Natalia Mironova; *Writing Credits*: Vicky Matthews; *Cinematography*: Rich Confalone, Steve Conklin, Dominic DeSantis; *Film Editing*: Penny Lee; *Art Direction*: Ricardo Andrade, Nick Jernigan, Steve Yasin; *Special Effects*: Ricardo Andrade (visual effects); *Cast*: Ian Gregory (Narrator), Kevyn Settle (Dracula), Rebecca Taylor (Sarah).

National Geographic follows the story of the vampire: from folkloric accounts and fictional narratives, to historical figures (like Dracula) and present day practitioners (like Don Henrie).

The Jail Break; U.S., 1946; Animation; 5:58 minutes/color/English/Mono; 20th Century–Fox, TerryToon Cartoons.

Producers: Paul Terry; *Writing Credits*: John Foster; *Director*: Eddie Donnelly; *Original Music*: Philip A. Scheib; *Cast*: Tom Morrison (Mighty Mouse).

When Bad Bill Bunion escapes Alcatrez prison it is up to Mighty Mouse to capture him. Bad Bill Bunion commits a number of crimes before Mighty Mouse stops him and puts him back where he belongs.

Les Jeux de la Comtesse Dolingen de Gratz (*The Games of Countess Dolingen* [U.S.]); France, 1980; Drama; 114 minutes/color/French/Mono; Les Films du Nautile, Prospectacle.

Producers: Annick Colomes, Jacques Zajdermann; *Writing Credits*: Catherine Binet, Bram Stoker (short story "Dracula's Guest"), Jules Verne (novel), Unica Zürn; *Director*: Catherine Binet; *Cinematography*: William Lubtchansky; *Film Editing*: Catherine Renault, Boris Viard; *Original Music*: Carlos D'Alessio; *Make-Up*: Muriel Baurens; *Cast*: Michael Lonsdale (Bertrand Haines-Pearson), Carol Kane (Louise Haines-Pearson), Katia Wastchenko (La petite fille), Marina Vlady (La mère de la petite fille), Emmanuelle Riva (Une invitee), Roberto Plate (Le voyageur, Le voleur, L'étranger), Marilu Marini (La comtesse Dolingen de Gratz, La bonne), Robert Stephens (Le professeur), Marucha Bo (Nena), Antoine Binet (Le frère), Raoul Escari (Argentin 1), Tobie Schumer (Argentin 2), Carine Toly (La belle dame), Nathalie Goldnadel (La fille pubère), François Mouren-Provensal (L'homme sur la plage), Julien Etchevery (L'épicier), Tina Anzini (La patronne de l'hôtel), Isa Mercure (Une convive), France Valéry (Une convive), Yves Barsacq (Un convive), Jean Champion (Un convive), Gilles Guyot (Un convive), Alain Cuny Bram Stoker's "Dracula's Guest" (1914).

The film starts with a girl traveling by train back home. Upon her arrival, her father informs her that a countess has just passed away. While she is away doing other things, her husband is at home guarding his collection of wooden angels. One night a thief went down the chimney and stole several things. To make sure this doesn't happen again, he builds a caged trap for the creature. He leaves for a trip only to return with the creature trapped and dead in the cage.

Joe Nosferatu: Homeless Vampire; U.S., 2004; Comedy, Horror/Short; 42 minutes/color/English; Slayzoid Studios.

Producers: Timothy Herron, Bob Hinton; *Writing Credits*: Bob Hinton; *Director*: Timothy Herron, Bob Hinton; *Cinematography*: Bob Hinton; *Film Editing*: Bob Hinton; *Original Music*: Billy Darnell *Cast*: The Bone Jangler (Himself), Leanna Chamish (Vamp Girl), Henrique Couto (Dr. Freak), Dr. Creep (Himself), Shane Dallman (Remo D.), Ms. Demure (Herself), Richard Dyszel (Himself), Brian Easterling (Butch R. Cleaver), Jeanne Easterling (Patches), Timothy Herron (Joe Nosferatu), Bob Hinton (Honey Diptwat), Ken Kish (Himself), Jeff McClellan (J.R. Kiltsport), Nocturna (Herself), C.W. Prather (The Voice), Miss Scarlett (Herself), Suspira (Herself), Louu the Xxxmas Devil (Himself).

This is a "Dracumentary" about a vampire, Joe Nosferatu, who is looking for food, women, and respect.

Jonathan (*Vampire sterben nicht* [West Germany]) West Germany, 1970; Horror; 97 minutes/color/German/Mono; Atelier München-Unterföhring/Iduna Film Produktiongesellschaft.

Producers: Hellmut Haffner; *Writing Credits*: Hans W. Guissendorfer; *Director*: Hans W. Guissendorfer; *Cinematography*: Robby Müller (as Robert Müller); *Film Editing*: Wolfgang Hedinger; *Original Music*: Roland Kovac (as Roland Kovác); *Art Direction*: Hans Gailling; *Make-Up*: Ida Driessler (key makeup artist), Peter Kraus; *Cast*: Jürgen Jung (Jonathan), Hans-Dieter Jendreyko (Joseph (as Hans Dieter Jendreyko)Paul Albert Krumm (Count/Graf), Hertha von Walther (Thomas' Mutter), Oskar von Schab (Professor), Ilona Grübel (Eleonore), Sofie Strehlow (Alte Frau [as Sophie Strehlow]), Gaby Herbst, Henry Liposca (Gnom), Christine Ratej (Elisabeth), Arthur Brauss (Adolf), Hans-Dieter Kerky (Eberhard), Wilfried Klaus (Pfarrer [as Winfried Klaus]), Monica Teuber (as Monika Teuber), Walter Feuchtenberg (Lenas Vater), Kathi Telheim, Ilse Kunkele, (Lenas Mutter), Michael Hoffman, Michael Grimm, Bernd Schwamm, Thomas Astan (Thomas), Elenore Schminke (Lena), Angelika Werner, Peter Bauer (Junger Mann [uncredited]), Otmar Engel (Begleiter des Grafen), Walter Frank (uncredited), Gudrun Gundalach (uncredited), Heidi Hedinger (uncredited), Peter Heeg (Verfolger), Alexander May (Portier), Willy Schultes (uncredited).

This film takes places in the 16th century, a time when vampires, immune to sunlight, have taken over civilization. The oppressed humans rebel, and a battle for life and control of civilization ensues.

El Jovencito Drácula; Spain, 1977; Horror, Comedy; 86 minutes/color/Spanish/Mono; Los Films del Mediterraneo.

Producers: Victor Oller; *Writing Credits*: Jose Antonio Domenich, Patricio Raoran; *Director*: Carlos Benpar; *Cinematography*: Tomas Pladevall; *Film Editing*: Emilio Ortiz; *Original Music*: Juan Pineda; *Art Direction*: Ramón Ferré; *Make-Up*: Anna

Tarrasson; *Cast*: Carlos Benpar, Susana Estrada, Victor Israel, Veronica Miriel, Marina Ferri, Mir Ferry.

A descendant of Count Dracula inherits the castle of his ancestor. Van Helsing sets out to try and find and kill Dracula. Dracula's old servant, Renfield, escapes from prison and tries to rejoin his master. This is a comedy filled with quick and sexual humor.

Kaibutsu-Kun (TV Series) (*Carletto, il Principe dei Mostri* [Italian]); Japan, 1968; Family/Television, Animation; 25 minutes/black and white/Japanese; Tokyo Movie Shinsha.

Writing Credits: Haruya Yamazaki, Tsunehisa Ito, Takashi Hayakawa, Takashi Yamada, Hirokazu Mizude, Yoshio Urasawa.; *Director*: Masaaki Osumi, Tiji Okabe, Shinichi Suzuki, Hiroshi Fukutomi, Shinji Okuda, Makoto Nakahara; *Original Music*: Michio Okamoto, Yasei Kobayashi; *Art Direction*: Norio Kubii (Animation), Sadao Tominaga (Animation); *Cast*: Fuyumi Shiraishi (Kaibutsu-kun), Chiyoko Kawashima (Oneesan), Eiko Masuyama (Kaiko Chan), Hiroshi Ohtake (Dracula), Keiko Han (Ako-chan), Mariko Mukai (Ichimaru Kako), Masao Imanishi (Franken), Minori Matsushima (Ichimaru Hiroshi), Nagaharu Yodogawa (Narrator), Shingo Kanemoto (Werewolf), Takuzou Kamiyama (Werewolf), Ichirô Nagai, (uncredited), Jouji Yanami (uncredited), Kaneta Kimotsuki (uncredited), Katsue Miwa (uncredited), Kinto Tamura (uncredited), Kinya Aikawa (uncredited), Tadashi Nakamura (uncredited), Toku Nishio (uncredited), Yasuo Yamada (uncredited), Yoshiko Ohta (uncredited), Yutaka Ohyama (uncredited).

Based on the 1965 manga by Hiroshio Fujimoto, this TV Series follows the prince of Kaibutsu Land, Kaibutsu-kun, when he decides to go to the human world as part of his training to become the King.

Kaibutsu-kun (TV Series); Japan, 1980; Family/Television, Animation; 25 minutes/color/Japanese; Shinei Doga (Shin'ei Dôga) Co. Ltd.

Writing Credits: F. Fujio Fujiko (comics); *Director*: Eiji Okabe, Hiroshi Jinsenji, Masaaki Osumi, Shinichi Suzuki; *Original Music*: Michio Okamoto; *Cast*: Masako Nozawa (Kaibutsu-kun [voice]), Kaneta Kimotsuki (Dracula [voice]), Katsue Miwa (Hiroshi [voice]), Taro Sagami (Franken [voice]), Shingo Kanemoto (Franken [voice]), Takuzô Kamiyama (Ookami-otoko [voice]).

Kaibutsu-kun, prince of Kaibutsu, travels to the human world to train for being the next King.

Kamitsukitai/Dorakiyura yori ai-0 (*From Dracula with Love* [Japan (English title)]; *I Want to Bite You/From Dracula with Love* [unidentified]; *My Soul Is Slashed* [U.S.]); Japan, 1991; Comedy, Horror; color/Japanese; Toho Company.

Writing Credits: Takeshi Kawanmura; *Director*: Shusuke Kaneko; *Original Music*: Mylène Farmer (vocalist: theme song); *Cast*: Ken Ogata (Shutaro Ishikawa), Eisei Amamoto (Servant), Nina Blake, Tony Cetera, Sansho Fukami (TV; Director), Harumi Harada (Takeda), Sumiyo Hasegawa (Enokida), Natsumi Hayakawa, Shigeri Higuchi, Hirotaro Honda (Policeman), Gen Inayama, Hikari Ishida (Saeko), Shigesato Itoi (Inohara), Saburo Kadowaki, Miyuki Katô (Secretary), Shigeo Kato, Atsumi Kurasawa (Miwako), Kasumi Kushida (Junpei), Ken Mitsuishi (TV; Director), Takeo Morimoto (Kitahara), Kôji Naka (Kuroda), Miyuki Nakano (Ryoko), Noboru Nakaya (Keisuke Takashima), Junpei Natsuki, Itoku Nobuzane (Doctor), Nanako Shindo (TV reporter), Sanshô Shinsui (as Sanshô Shinsui), Hiroshi Tahara (TV; Director), Yoshiaki Taki, Kôichi Ueda (Takemura), Sachiko Wakayama (Yasuyo), Narumi Yasuda (Yuzuko), Hideko Yoshida (Kimi), Naoko Yoshimi (Umeda).

A devoted company worker is killed by the same company to which he is loyal. The hospital's attempt to save his life goes terribly wrong when he is accidentally given the blood of Count Dracula. After a year, he returns from the dead and tries to set things right, all the while resisting his transformation into a full vampire.

Kara boga (*The Black Bull* [International English title]); Turkey, 1974; Horror; color/Turkish; Örnek Film.

Producers: Yilmaz Kuzgun; *Writing Credits*: Bülent Oran; *Director*: Yavuz Figenli; *Cinematography*: Salih Dikisci; *Cast*: Behçet Nacar, Yonca Yücel, Altan Günbay, Baykal Kent.

Karmina Canada, 1996; Comedy, Horror, Romance; 110 minutes/color/English, French/Dolby; SR Lux Films.

Producers: Nicole Robert; *Writing Credits*: Ann Burke, Yves Pelletier, Andree Pelletier, Gabriel Pelletier, Yves Pelletier, Ann Burke (original story); *Director*: Gabriel Pelletier; *Cinematography*: Eric Cayla (as Eric Cayla); *Film Editing*: Gaetan Huot; *Original Music*: Patrick Bourgoise (composer/theme music); *Art Direction*: Etienne Lapointe Proulx (property master); *Make-Up*: Pierre Saindon; *Special Effects*: Francis Choquette (special effects technician), Louis Craig (special effects technician), Mario Dumont (special effects floor supervisor); *Cast*: Isabelle Cyr (Karmina), Robert Brouillette (Phillipe), Yves Pelletier (Vlad), France Castel (Esmeralda), Gildor Roy (Ghislain Chabot/Patrick), Raymond Cloutier (Baron), Sylvie Potvin (Baronne), Diane Lavallée (Linda), Mario Saint-Amand

(Pierre Boutin), Pierre Chagnon (David), Alexis Martin (Monsieur Martel), Mireille Thibault (Germaine), Jean-Guy Bouchard (Policier #1), Guy-Daniel Tremblay (Policier #2), André Gauthier (Voisin de Chabot), Gordon Masten (Curé), Monique Martel (Dame Église), Gaston Caron (Agent Douanier), Khanh Hua (Mister Wong), Sylvie Boucher (Colette), Denis Houle (Dromad), Adèle Reinhardt (Candidate névrosée), Sonia Vachon (Candidate à Mario), Armand Laroche (Amateur de mannequin), Michel D'Amico (Amateur de baseball), Frédéric Desager (Denis au Bar Western), Frank Déguisne (Rene Aquilin), Rosie Yale (Cliente du Lovecraft), Nicolas Van Lenan (Vampire bien en chair), Alain Gendreau (Valet de Vlad), Roger Michael (Serviteur au chateau), Giovanni Antonacci (Serveur Italien), Jasmin Roy (Skin Head).

Karmina, a vampire from Transylvania, is forced by her oppressive parents to marry the terrible Vlad. She escapes to Quebec where she falls in love with a young church organist.

Karmina 2 (*K2* [Canada, promotional abbreviation]; *Karmina 2: L'enfer de Chabot* [undefined]) Canada, 2001; Horror, Comedy, Romance; 97 minutes/color/French/Dolby Digital; Go Films.
Producers: Nicole Robert; *Writing Credits*: Gabriel Pelletier, Yves Pelletier; Director: Gabriel Pelletier; *Cinematography*: Daniel Villeneuve; *Film Editing*: Gaétan Huot; *Original Music*: Gaétan Essiambre; *Special Effects*: Louis Craig; *Cast*: Gildor Roy (Ghislain Chabot), Yves Pelletier (Vlad), Diane Lavallée (Linda), Robert Brouillette (Philippe), Sylvie Léonard (Julie Cazavant), Isabelle Cyr (Karmina), Julien Poulin (Vincent Proulx), Michel Courtemanche (Ti-Pit), France Castel (Esmeralda), Sylvie Potvin (La Baronne), Pierre Collin (Le Baron), Macha Limonchik (Petronia), Annie Dufresne (Sandra), Michel Laperrière (Inspecteur), Louis Champagne (Norm), Rychard Thériault (Psychiatre), Gary Boudreault (Voisin), Marie-Chantal Perron (Nancy), Christine Foley (Poupoune blonde), Isabelle Maréchal (Lectrice nouvelles), Myriam Bédard (Skieuse), Richard Lalancette (Petit homme chauve), Richard Fréchette (Restaurateur gastronomique), Francis Durocher (Client mécontent), Evelyne Bonvin (Échangiste), Francine Pilote (Échangiste), Nadia David (Échangiste), Pamela Koren (Échangiste), Linda Plamondon (Échangiste), Anie Pascale (Échangiste), Jojo Marangola (Échangiste), William A. Hasley (Échangiste), Frank D'Amico (Échangiste), David Di Carlo (Échangiste), Hubert Le Messurier (Échangiste), Pierre Perpall (Échangiste), Elliott Lefrançois (Piétrou), Michel Carrière (Livreur de pizza), Michèle Cadieux (Barmaid), Valérie Wiseman (Femme géante), Manon Harvey (Poupoune brune), Debbie-Anne Champagne (Belle fille), Édèse Lamy (Belle fille), Mélissa Lajoie (Belle fille), Normand Roy (Police tactique), Éric Legault (Police tactique), Richard Champagne (Police tactique), Mario Lalande (Police tactique), Sylvain Cyr (Policier #1), Stéphane Scrive (Policier #2), Daniel Zanell (Ambulancier #1), Ron Torchia (Ambulancier #2), Emmanuel Auger (Barman #1), Stanislav Kholnogorov (Guide Roumain), Sylvain Hubert (Policier #3), Yanick Rock (Policier #4), Yoland Roy (Médecin légiste #1), Gregoire Dunlevy (Médecin légiste #2).

The sequel to *Karmina*, *Karmina 2* is the story about some vampires who take a special potion in order to assimilate into society as humans. The potion maker's wife, Karmina (Isabelle Cyr), wishes to become a vampire, but her husband, Ghyslain Chatbot (Gildor Roy), refuses to allow her to become one. Karmina then throws Chatbot out of the house without any potion, and with the help of Vlad (Yves Pelletier), a fellow vampire, Chatbot attempts to recover the potion.

Khooni Dracula (*Deadly Dracula* [India, English title]); India, 1992; Horror; color/Hindi.
Director: Hainam Singh; *Cast*: Amrit Pal (Dracula), Kiran Pal (Dracula), Kaushal Singh, Usha Singh, Sonia Thakur.

The plot of the story follows much of the original *Dracula*. Khooni Dracula is reincarnated after blood leaking from a maid's dead body somehow reaches his mouth. Khooni is now enslaved by the man who murdered the maid. The master then gives Khooni instructions to rape and kill more people, and he sets Khooni loose on the city.

Kibris: La ley del equilibrio; Spain, 2005; Action, Adventure; color/Spanish; Blue Dragon Productions S.L.
Producers: Susana Chan; *Writing Credits*: Fina Fernandez, Jaume Gil i Llopart, German Monzo; *Original Music*: Oriol Sana; *Cinematography*: Marc Cuixart; *Cast*: Javier Aller, Lorena Bernal (Betty), David Fernandez, Eduardo Gomez, Isamu Hirano, German Monzo (Kuroi), Monica Perez, Jose Sancho (Dracula), Maria Santos, Edu Soto, Paula Vazquez (Lisa).

Killer Barbys Vs. Dracula (*Killer Barbys contra Dracula* [Spain]; *Killer Barbys vs. Dracula* [Germany]); Spain, 2002; Horror, Comedy; 90 minutes/color/English/Dolby Digital; Impacto Films, Quiet Village Filmkunst.
Producers: Michael Cholewa, Carsten Frank, Tim Luna (as Heiner Thimm), Jacinto Santos; *Writing Credits*: Jesus Franco (as Jess Franco), Lina Fomay (as Rosa M. Almirall), Jacinto Santos (story), José Roberto Vila; *Director*: Jesus Franco

(as Jess Franco); *Cinematography*: Emilio Schargorodsky; *Original Music*: Jesus Franco (as Jess Franco), Daniel White; *Art Direction*: Exequiel Caldas (as Ezequiel Cohen); *Make-Up*: Javier Díez, Javier Díez, Bea Millas, Bea Millas; *Cast*: Silvia Superstar (Silvia), Enrique Sarasola (Count Dracula) (as Kike Sarasola), Dan van Husen (Dr. Seward), Aldo Sambrell (Pepe Morgan) (as Aldo Sanbrell), Bela B. Felsenheimer (Béla Blasko Lugosi), Billy King (Billy), Lina Romay (Irina von Karstein), Katja Bienert (Katja van Barenboim), Pietro Martellanza (Dracula) (as Peter Martell), Carsten Frank (Albinus), Sandra Ibarra (Selena), Fata Morgana (Puri), Carmen Montes (Carmen), Paul Lapidus (Martin Fierro), Viktor Seastrom (Ivan Ivanovich), Javier Díez (Viscontino), José Roberto Vila (Inspector), Exequiel Caldas (Man with Guitar) (as Ezequiel Cohen), Rubén Sánchez (Assistant), Bea Millas (Policeman [uncredited]), Emilio Schargorodsky (Policeman [uncredited]).

Dracula (Enrique Sarasola) is awakened by the sound of the Killer Barbys. He becomes infatuated with Silvia (Silvia Superstar), one of the band members. Dracula runs around the concert attacking different people. He is taken down by Dr. Seward (Dan van Husen) with a stake through the heart. But this does not kill Dracula.

Kulay Dugo ang Gabi (*Blood is the color of Night* [U.S.]; *color of Night* [U.S.]; *Blood Drinkers, The* [U.S.]; *The Vampire People* [U.S., reissue title, TV title]); Philippines/U.S., 1964; Horror; 88 minutes/color/Tagalog, English, Filipino/Mono; People's Pictures, Hemisphere Pictures, Inc.

Producers: Cirio H. Santiago, Danilo Santiago; *Writing Credits*: Cesar Amigo, Rico Bello Omagap; *Director*: Gerardo de Leon; *Cinematography*: Felipe Sacdalan (director of photography, as Felipe J. Sacdalan); *Film Editing*: Atilano Salvador; *Art Direction*: Ben Otico; *Make-Up*: Tony Artieda (makeup artist), Rey Salamat (makeup artist); *Special Effects*: Hilario Brothers (special effects); *Cast*: Ronald Remy (Dr. Marco), Amalia Fuentes (Charito/Katrina), Eddie Fernandez (Victor de la Cruz), Eva Montes (Tanya, the vampire bride), Celia Rodriguez, Renato Robles Mary Walter (Charito's mother), Paquito Salcedo (Elias, the guardian), Felisa Salcedo, Andres Benitez, Fred Param, Eddie Arce, Conchita Cruz, Vicky Velasquez, Cesar Aguilar, Frank Saavedra, Evelyn Shreve, Renato Murado Jr., Rudy Bugarin, Ricardo Rivera, Luis Benedicto, Felix Dionisio, Ri Paulino, Ernesto David, Eriberto Amazan Jr, Jess Romam, Frankie Lastimoso, Philip Antivo, Felipe Dionisio, Mona del Cielo, Tiva Lava, Jess Buenaflor, Vic Diaz (Voice of priest and narrator, uncredited).

In order to resurrect his wife, Katrina, Dr. Marco (a Dracula-type vampire) aims to transplant her heart with that of her twin sister Cherito's. In the end, only through prayer can both be saved.

Kwansukui Dracula (*Dracula Rises from the Coffin* [International English title]; *Dracula Rises* [International English title]); South Korea, 1982; Horror; 92 minutes/color/Korean Taechang Productions.

Producers: Won-shik Lim; *Writing Credits*: Hiewoo Lee; *Director*: Hyeong-pyo Lee; *Cinematography*: Seong-seob Lee; *Original Music*: Cheolhyeok Lee *Cast*: Ji-hun Park (Jang Jung-han), Yong-seok Kang (Park Cheol-hwan), Yeong-rae Park (Kim, Seong-hye), In-hwan Jang.

Kyuketsuki Gokemidoro (*Body Snatcher from Hell* [U.S.]; *Distruggete DC 59, da base spaziale a Hong Kong* [Italy]; *Goke—Vampir aus dem Weltall* [West Germany]; *Goke the Vampire* [undefined]; *Goke, Body Snatcher from Hell* [undefined]); Japan, 1968; Horror, Science Fiction; 84 minutes/color/English, Japanese/Mono/35mm; Shochiku Kinema Kenkyû-jo.

Producers: Takashi Inomata; *Writing Credits*: Kyuzo Kobayashi, Susumu Takaku; *Director*: Hajime Sato; *Cinematography*: Shizuo Hirase; *Film Editing*: Akimitsu Terada; *Art Direction*: Shinei Bijutsu Kogei; *Special Effects*: P Productions; *Cast*: Teruo Yoshida (Sugisaka, the co-pilot); Tomomi Sato (Kuzumi, the stewardess); Eizo Kitamura (Mano, the senator); Hideo Ko (The Hijacker); Kathy Horan (Mrs. Neal); Yûko Kusunoki (Noriko Tokiyasu); Kazuo Kato (Dr. Momotake, the psychiatrist); Hiroyuki Nishimoto (The Pilot); Andrew Hughes (Assassinated Ambassador); Masaya Takahashi (Sagai, the scientist).

A plane is flying out of Tokyo, and there is a hijacker on board. The passengers think they see a UFO, and it makes them crash on an island. They struggle for food and water and to protect themselves from the weird things that seem to be going on.

Kyûketsuki hantâ D (*Vampire Hunter D* [U.S.]); Japan, 1985; Horror, Science Fiction, Action, Western, Romance/Animation; 80 minutes/color/Japanese/Stereo; CBS Sony Group Inc., Epic/Sony, Movic.

Producers: Hiroshi Kato, Mitsuhissa Koeda, Carl Maced (English version), Shigeo Maruyama, Yugo Nagasaki, Yutaka Takahashi (Executive Producer); *Writing Credits*: Yasushi Hirano, Hideyuki Kikuchi (novel author), Tom Wyner (English version); *Director*: Toyoo Ashida, Carl Macek; *Cinematography*: Yukio Sugiyama Kazushi Torigoshi; *Original Music*: Tetsuya Kamuro; *Art Direction*: Toyoo Ashida; *Cast*: Kaneto Shiozawa (D), Michael McCnnohie

(D voice: English version), Steve Bulen (additional voices), Lara Cody (Lamika), Barbara Goodson (Doris Rumm) Seizo Kato (Count Magnus Lee) Satoko Kifuji (Lamika), Motomu Kiyokawa (Dr. Feringo), Steve Kramer (additional voices), Joyce Kurtz (additional voices), Kerrigan Mahan (Reiganse), Edie Mirman (additional voices), Yasuo Muramatsu (Roman), Ichiro Nagai (D's left hand), Shinya Otaki (as Susumu Kotaki), Yoshiko Sakakibara (snake sister), Kazuyuki Sogabe (Rei Ginsei), Kazumi Tanaka, Kirk Thorton (additional voices), Keiko Toda (Dan Rumm), Kan Tokumaru (Danton), Michie Tomizawa (Doris Rumm), Jeff Winkless (additional voices), Tom Wyner (additional voices), Kazuko Yanaga (snake sister), Yusaku Yara (Greco).

Humans have faltered as the dominant species on the planet, which is now ruled by vampires. When Count Lee, a vampire descended form Count Dracula himself, falls in love with a human, his family becomes alarmed that he will pollute the family bloodline and tries to stop the union.

Lady Dracula; West Germany, 1978; Horror; 79 minutes/color/German/Mono; IFV Produktion.

Writing Credits: Brad Harris (story), Redis Read; *Director*: Franz Josef Gottlieb; *Cinematography*: Fritz Baader, Ernst W. Kalinke; *Cast*: Evelyne Kraft (Comtesse Barbara von Weidenborn/Lady Dracula), Brad Harris (Kommissar), Theo Lingen (Theo Marmorstein), Eddi Arent (Eddi), Christine Buchegger (Irene Ruhesanft), Walter Giller (Herr Oskar), Klaus Höhne (Herr Hubert), Roberto Blanco (Baggerführer Karli), Stephen Boyd (Graf Dracula), Ulrich Beiger, Marion Kracht (Comtesse Barbara als Mädchen), Georg Lehn, Edith Leyrer, Zdenka Procházková, Walter Feuchtenberg (Notar [uncredited]), Herbert Fux ([uncredited]), Willy Harlander (Taxifahrer [uncredited]), Wolfgang Hess (Inspector [voice] [uncredited]), Heinz Reincke (Betrunkener [uncredited]), Christine Schuberth ([uncredited]), Johann Sklenka (Augenzeuge [uncredited]), Rinaldo Talamonti (Bauarbeiter [uncredited])

A blonde woman who was bitten by Dracula and killed 100 years ago is dug up and released. She begins a killing spree that mainly targets other young, attractive women.

The Lair (TV Series); U.S., 2007–2009; Horror, Drama/Television; 60 minutes/color/English; Here! TV.

Producers: Kimberly A. Ray, Stephen P. Jarchow, Paul Colichman, Jeff Schenck, Fred Olen Ray; *Writing Credits*: Fred Olen Ray; *Director*: Fred Olen Ray; *Film Editing*: Randy Carter; *Original Music*: Chuck Cirino; *Make-Up*: Judi Lewin; *Cast*: David Moretti (Thom Etherton [28 episodes, 2007–2009]), Dylan Vox (Colin [28 episodes, 2007–2009]), Colton Ford (Sheriff Trout [28 episodes, 2007–2009]), Brian Nolan (Frankie [27 episodes, 2007–2009]), Peter Stickles (Damian [26 episodes, 2007–2009]), Johnny Hazzard (Tim [15 episodes, 2008–2009]), Bobby Rice (Richie [15 episodes, 2008–2009]), Grant Landry (Gary [13 episodes, 2008–2009]), Beverly Lynne (Laura [12 episodes, 2007–2008]), Alex Parisien (Dr. Kent [10 episodes, 2009]), Matty Ferraro (Ian [9 episodes, 2007–2008]), Matthew King (Jake [8 episodes, 2008]]), Ethan Reynolds (Jonathan [7 episodes, 2008]), Jesse Cutlip (Johnathan [6 episodes, 2007]), Sybil Danning (Von Hess [6 episodes, 2009]), Michael Von Steele (Eric [5 episodes, 2007]), Arthur Roberts (Dr. Belmont [5 episodes, 2007]), Bryan Pisano (Deputy Miller [5 episodes, 2008]), Thor Knai (Dennis [5 episodes, 2009]), Evan Stone (Jimmy [4 episodes, 2007]), Tigger Walker Jr. (Deputy Rogers [3 episodes, 2007]), Pony R. Horton (Mr. Spivey [3 episodes, 2008]), Ted Monte (Matt [3 episodes, 2008]), Brandon Ruckdashel (Riley [3 episodes, 2008]), Gerald Webb (EMT #1 [3 episodes, 2008]), Jeff Castle (Campbell [3 episodes, 2009]), Ted Newsom (Dr. Cooper [2 episodes, 2007]), Steve Goldenberg (Medic [2 episodes, 2007]), Dorit Avganim (Lawyer [2 episodes, 2008]).

The Lair, a private gay club, is run by vampires who use the club to lure attractive young men from which to feed. Local journalist Thom begins investigating a string of murders involving bodies drained of blood. The life of Thom's boyfriend is threatened when Thom's snooping around comes to the attention Damian, a Dracula-type master vampire who sees Thom as the reincarnation of his own dead lover.

Laser Fart; U.S., 2004; Comedy/Short; 47 minutes/color/English.

Producers: Dan Harmon, David Harman; *Writing Credits*: Dan Harmon; *Director*: Dan Harmon, David Hartman; *Original Music*: Craig Sharmat; *Cast*: Jeff Bryan Davis (Jeff), Jack Black (The Elegant Hunter), Matt Gourley (Robot Dick), Rob Schrab (Dracula/Gorilla), Dawn Cody (Dawn/Donna), Dan Harmon (Dan/Laser Fart), Justin Roiland (Person on the news), Derek C. Wallace (Angry Bartender).

After Dan has an unfortunate incident with a faulty microwave, he becomes endowed with the power of shooting lasers out of his anus. Throughout this 10-part series, Dan encounters many villains, including Dracula, an "elegant hunter" with a computerized member.

Last Rites (*Dracula's Last Rites*); U.S., 1980; Horror; 86 minutes/color/English/Mono/35mm; New Empire Features.

Producers: Kelly Van Horn; *Writing Credits*: Ben Donnelly, Domonic Paris; *Director*: Domonic Paris; *Cinematography*: Domonic Paris; *Film Editing*: Elizabeth Lombardo; *Original Music*: Paul Jost, George Small; *Art Direction*: Robert Johnson; *Make-Up*: Thomas Serra, Carla White; *Special Effects*: Cord Keller (special effects), Ron Kurash (special effects); *Cast*: Patricia Hammond (Marie [as Patricia Lee Hammond]), Gerald Fielding (Lucard), Mimi Weddell (Mrs. Bradley), Victor Jorge (Dr. Cummins), Michael Lally (Ted), Alfred Steinel (Sheriff Ordell), Eric Trules (Potter), Gordito (Gasher), John Juback (Hearse driver), Joe Perce (Bobby), Rain Worthington (Suzy), Dan Freedman (Aide), Suzy Brabeau (Young girl), Michael Valentine (Young man), Mark Bennett (Drowning victim), Leah Vitale (Girl), Steven Vitale (Boy), Brian Nonnenmacher (Boy).

A vampire doctor sends still-living victims and false death certificates to Dr. A Lucard, Dracula hiding as a town's mortician, to have their blood sucked out. An uncontrolled vampire accidently gets loosed when a family takes the body back before Dr. Lucard can properly stake the newly turned victim.

The Last Sect; Canada, 2006; Horror, Thriller; 90 minutes/English/color; Peace Arch Entertainment Group.

Producers: Kate Harrison, Lewin Webb; *Director*: Jonathan Dueck; *Writing Credits*: David Robbeson; *Cinematography*: Curtis Petersen, Brendan Steacy; *Film Editing*: Michele Francis; *Production Design*: Chris Irvine; *Art Direction*: Andrew Berry; *Cast*: David Carradine (Van Helsing), Natalie Brown (Sydney St. James), Deborah Odell (Anna), Julian Richings (Karpov), Sebastien Roberts (Sam), Jordan Dyck (Tone as Jordan Van Dyck), Christine Tizzard (Receptionist), Megan Fahlenbock (Jess), Erin Berry (Security Guard), Richard Blackburn (Luke), Joe MacLeod (Bike Courier), Rosalba Martinni (Fortune Teller), Nicole Sherman (Vampette #1), Kasia Vassos (Vampette #2), Claire Oleson (Vampette #3), Kimberly Plaxton (Vampette #4 as Ochen), Elle Boutilier (Vampirette #5), Yuan Yuan Yin (Vampirette #6), Christopher Cordell (Ghoul #2 as Chris Cordell), Ted Ludzik (Ghoul #1), Geoff Scovell (Ghoul #3), Stewart Easun (Ghoul #4), Ron Fountain (Janitor).

Journalist Sydney St. James is working on her new project, the online dating agency Artemis. She interviews the owner, Anna, who is actually ancient vampire Anastasia. Dr. Abraham Van Helsing, a vampire hunter, knows that the vampire sect needs to regenerate by using a woman host. Van Helsing and his partner go to Artemis and fight against the ancient vampire and her sect.

The League of Extraordinary Gentlemen (*Die Liga der außergewöhnlichen Gentlemen* [Austria/Germany]; *La ligue des gentlemen extraordinaires* [France/Canada, French video title]; *The League* [Sweden/U.S., promotional title]; *A Liga Extraordinária* [Brazil]; *A szövetség* [Hungary]; *Det hemmelighedsfulde selskab* [Denmark]; *Herrasmiesliiga* [Finland]; *I symmahia* [Greece]; *LXG* [U.S., promotional abbreviation]; *LXG: The League of Extraordinary Gentlemen* [U.S., trailer title]; *La leggenda degli uomini straordinari* [Italy]; *La liga de los hombres extraordinarios* [Spain]; *La liga extraordinaria* [Argentina]; *League of Legend* [Japan, English title]; *Liga izuzetnih dzentlmena* [Serbia]; *Liga niezwyklych dzentelmenów* [Poland]; *Liga výjimecných* [Czech Republic]; *Liga výnimocných* [Slovakia]; *Muhtesem kahramanlar* [Turkey]; *The league: Det hemmelighedsfulde selskab* [Denmark, DVD box title]); U.S./Germany/Czech Republic/U.K., 2003; Horror, Action, Adventure; 110 minutes/color, black and white/English, German, Italian/DTS, Dolby Digital; Angry Films, International Production Company, JD Productions, Mediastream Dritte Film GmbH & Co. Beteiligungs KG, Twentieth Century–Fox Film Corporation.

Producer: Trevor Albert, Rick Benattar, Sean Connery, Bruce Devan, Mark Gordon, Don Murphy, Michael Nelson; *Writing Credits*: Alan Moore, Kevin O'Neill, James Robinson; *Director*: Stephen Norrington; *Cinematography*: Dan Laustsen; *Film Editing*: Paul Rubell; *Original Music*: Trevor Jones; *Make-Up*: Jason Barnett, Brian Best, Stuart Bray, Tricia Cameron, Mark Coulier, Neill Gorton, Pauline Heys, Rob Hinderstein, Neil Morrill, Ian Morse, Gabriela Polakova, Paula Price, Yoichi Art Sakamoto, Jemma Scott-Knox-Gore, Lesley Smith, Michelle Taylor, Shaune Harrison, Glenn Hetrick, Duncan Jarman, Dave Snyder; *Special Effects*: Thomas D. Bacho Jr., Brent Baker, Nick Bauman, Christian Beckman, Mark Boley, David Borg, Darin Bouyssou, Patrick G. Brady, Dennis Briest, Milos Brosinger, Stephanie Caillabet, Tamara Carlson, Gary Cohen, Eric Coon, Andrew Cridland, Neil Davis, Rob Derry, Dawn Dininger, Kevin Draycott, Bernard Eichholz, Fernando Favila, Peter Fern, Ulrich Fickel, Eric Fiedler, Steve Fink, John Fontana, Nathan Franson, Dan Frye, George Gibbs, Terry Glass, Joe Gomez, Antonio Gomez-Rubio, Angelo Grech, Ernst Gschwind, Ted Haines, Karin Hanson, Glen Hanz, Moto Hata, Alan Hawes, Jeremy Hays, Jeff Himmel, James Hirahara, Ron Hone, Matthew Horton, Ondar Hrncir, Timothy Huizing, Mike Hyrman, Hiroshi "Kan" Ikeuchi, Dominik Janda, Hiroshi Katagiri, Mark Killingsworth, Dave Knowles, Peter Konig, Leon Laderach, Samy Langs, Terence Lathwell,

Timothy Leach, Cass McClure, Miroslav Miclik, Zuzana Milfort, Scott Millenbaugh, David Monzingo, Craig Narramore, Trevor Neighbour, Ken Niederbaumer, Peter Norcliffe, James Patterson, Drago Poldrugac, Margaret Prentice, Martin Pryca, Grant Rogan, Sarah Rubano, Don Rutherford, Johnnie Saiko, Steve Scotton, W.A. Andrew Sculthorp, Constantine Sekeris, Steve Shines, Jan Singh, David E. Smith, Karel Solc, Clay Sparks, Dana H. Suddath, Matt Ullman, Patricia Urias, Brian Van Dorn, Jirí Vater, Michael S. Vincent, Mark Viniello, Chris Walker, John Weldy, Amy Whetsel, Mark White, Trevor Williams, Ian Wingrove, Kristina Frisch, Laurence Harvey, Steve Newburn, Thomas Ovenshire, A.J. Venuto; *Cast*: Sean Connery (Allan Quatermain), Naseeruddin Shah (Captain Nemo), Peta Wilson (Mina Harker), Tony Curran (Rodney Skinner [The Invisible Man]), Stuart Townsend (Dorian Gray), Shane West (Tom Sawyer), Jason Flemyng (Dr. Henry Jekyll/Edward Hyde), Richard Roxburgh (M), Max Ryan (Dante), Tom Goodman-Hill (Sanderson Reed), David Hemmings (Nigel), Terry O'Neill (Ishmael), Rudolf Pellar (Draper), Robert Willox (Constable Dunning), Robert Orr (Running Officer), Michael McGuffie (Copper #1), Joel Kirby (Copper #2), Marek Vasut (Soldier), Ewart James Walters (Toby), Michal Grün (Assassin #3), Robert Vahey (Elderly Hunter), Sylvester Morand (Old Treveler), Mariano Titanti (Edgar Shreave), Huggy Leaver (Hanson Cab Driver), Pavel Bezdek (Marksman #1), Stanislav Adamickij (Marksman #2), James Babson (Marksman #3), San Shella (Terrified Crewman), Ellen Savaria (Recordist), Riz Meedin (Venice Conning Tower Crewman), Sartaj Garewal (Rocket Room Crewman), Neran Persaud (Crewman Patel), Andrew Rajan (Headphones Crewman), Daniel Brown (Stunned Guard), Aftab Sachak (Breathless Crewman), Guy Singh (Signal Crewman [as Guy Singh Digpal]), Harmage Singh Kalirai (Chrewman Chandra), Brian Caspe (Guard #1), Robert Goodman (Valet), Rene Hajek (Flame Thrower), Semere-Ab Etmet Yohannes (Witch Doctor), Winter Ave Zoli (Eva [uncredited]).

Legendary adventurer Allan Quatermain leads a team of extraordinary people with extraordinary powers. Included among these extraordinary people is Mina Harker, whose run-in with Count Dracula has left her with extraordinary abilities.

The Legend of the 7 Golden Vampires (*7 Brothers Versus Dracula* [undefined]; *7 Brothers and a Sister Meet Dracula* [undefined]; *7 Brothers of Dracula* [U.K.]; *7 Golden Vampires* [U.K.]; *7 hrysoi vrykolakes, Oi* [Greece]; *7 vampires d'or, Les* [France]; *Die 7 Goldenen Vampire* [Netherlands]; *Die Sieben goldenen Vampire* [West Germany]; *Dracula and the Seven Golden Vampires* [undefined]; *Kung Fu contra los siete vampiros de oro* [Spain]; *Kung Fu-mysteriet* [Denmark]; *Légende des 7 vampires d'or, La* [France]; *Legenden om 7 gyclone vampyrer* [Denmark, video title], *Leggenda dei 7 vampiri d'oro, La* [Italy]; *Seit-*

Poster for *The Legend of the 7 Golden Vampires* (Hong Kong/U.K., 1974).

semän vampyyrin legenda [Finland, TV title]; *Seven Golden Vampires: The Last Warning* [U.K.]; *The Last Warning* [U.K.]; *The Legend of the Seven Golden Vampires* [U.K. [alternative spelling]; *The Seven Brothers Meet Dracula* [U.S.]); Hong Kong/U.K, 1974; Horror, Action; 83 minutes/color/English, Manchu/Mono/35mm; Hammer Film Productions, Shaw Brothers.

Producers: Don Houghton, Vee King Shaw, Runme Shaw (executive producer [uncredited]), Run Run Shaw (executive producer [uncredited]); *Writing Credits*: Don Houghton (screenplay); *Director*: Roy Ward Baker, Cheh Chang (uncredited); *Cinematography*: Roy Ford, John Wilcox; *Film Editing*: Chris Barnes; *Original Music*: James Bernard; *Art Direction*: Johnson Tsao (as Johnson Tsau); *Make-Up*: Yen-Lien Peng (hair stylist [as Peng Yen-Lien]), Hsu-Ching Wu (makeup artist [as Wu Hsu Ching]); *Special Effects*: Les Bowie (special effects); *Cast*: Peter Cushing (Prof. Van Helsing), David Chiang (Hsi Ching), Julie Ege (Vanessa Buren), Robin Stewart (Leyland Van Helsing), Szu Shih (Mai Kwei [as Shih Szu]), John Forbes-Robertson (Count Dracula), Robert Hanna (British Consul), Shen Chan (Kah [as Chan Shen]), James Ma (Hsi Ta), Chia Yung Liu (Hsi Kwei [as Liu Chia Yung]), Fong Lah Ann (Hsiu Sung [swordsman] [as Feng Ko An]), Chen Tien Loong (Hsi San), Wong Han Chan (Leung Hon), David de Keyser (Dracula [voice] [uncredited]).

Professor Van Helsing is at Chung King University to lecture about ancient Chinese legends. After a lecture, a student tells Van Helsing that the legend of a village plagued by vampires is true and convinces the professor to travel with his kung-fu trained siblings and destroy the vampires. Waiting at the village are 6 vampires lead by Count Dracula.

Lexx (TV Series [1997–2002]) (*Lexx: The Series* [undefined]; *Tales from a Parallel Universe* [U.S.: first season title]), episode "Walpurgis Night"; Canada, 1997; Science Fiction, Fantasy/Television; 60 minutes/color/English/Stereo; Silverlight Ltd.

Producers: Chris Roland; *Writing Credits*: Paul Donovan (co-writer), Tom de Ville; *Director*: Colin Bucksey; *Cinematography*: Les Krizsan; *Film Editing*: Paul Green; *Art Direction*: Shelley Nieder; *Make-Up*: Helga Schikowski; *Special Effects*: Björn Friese *Cast*: Brian Downey (Stanley H. Tweedle), Michael McManus (Kai), Xenia Seeberg (Xev Bellringer), Minna Aaltonen (Vlad) Keith-Lee Castle (Renfield), Andrea Green (Davinia), Peter Guinness (Joseph Van Helsing), Angie Hill (Muffy), Lionel Jeffries (Father Borscht), Arthur Spray (Gypsy Servant), John Standing (Count Dracul), Anna Cameron (Older Vlad (uncredited).

This is a sci-fi series about a crew of misfits traveling through universes aboard the space craft *Lexx*. In "Wapurgis Night," the crew heads to Transylvania on an impulse, only to find Count Dracul, Van Helsing and superstitious villagers.

Li san jiao wei zhen di yu men (*Deadly Hands of Kung Fu* [International]; *Lee saam geuk wai jan dei yuk moon* [Hong Kong]; *Résurrection du dragon, La* [France]; *The Dragon Lives Again* [International]); Hong Kong, 1977; Action, Comedy; color/Cantonese/Mono; Cineworld Pictures, Citadel Films.

Producers: Alex Gouw; *Writing Credits*: Shek Ke, Wai Leung; *Director*: Kei Law (as Lo Ke); *Original Music*: Frankie Chan; *Cast*: Siu-Lung Leung (Bruce Lee [as Bruce Leong]), Lik Cheung, Alexander Grand (James Bond), Kwok Choi Hon, Jenny (Emmanuelle), Yat Fan Lau, Sarina Sai, Yat Lung San, Ie Lung Shen (Shin Il Lung), Ching Tan, Ching Tang, Eric Tsang (Popeye), Kah Wah, Fong Yie, Siu Tien Yuen, Lau Wai Yu.

After Bruce Lee dies, he finds himself in hell. Once there, he realizes that the most evil people in hell are conspiring to take over, and he sets out to stop the rebellion. Among the evil plotters are James Bond, Clint Eastwood, and Dracula.

Lil Creepers; U.S., 2004; Family/Animation, Short; 22 minutes/color/English; H2 Studios.

Producers: Donald Hacker, Toby Martin; *Writing Credits*: Brian Byers, Donald Hacker, Richard Hays, Kevin Hull, Toby Martin; *Director*: Brian Byers, Donald Hacker; *Original Music*: Glen Longacre *Cast*: Dylan Crowley (Sam [voice]), Michael Curran (Béla [voice]), Breana Jarvis (Melly [voice]), Katherine Lord (Elsa [voice]), Ryan Rhodes (Vinnie [voice]), Jeremy Tant (Boris [voice]).

After Sam and Melly move to a monster-filled town against their will, they are accepted into a group of tiny friends who call themselves the "lil Creepers." Throughout the series, they encounter many evil monsters that they must escape. Sam and Melly are surrounded by many fascinating little figures, such as Boris, who plays a Frankenstein-type character, and Béla, who is a tiny teething vampire who resembles Dracula.

Little Dracula (TV Series); U.S., 1991, 1999; Family/Animation; 30 minutes/color/English/Stereo; Hahn Productions, Island Animation.

Producers: Pawn Evans, Michael Hack (supervising producer), Steven Hahn, Mike Young, Marlene Sharp (coordinating producer); *Director*: Joe Pearson; *Original Music*: Stephen C. Marston; *Art Direction*: Craig Clark (storyboard artist), Alejandro Gutierrez (assistant animator); *Cast*: S. Scott Bullock (Igor), Joey Camen (Werebunny [voice]), Brian Cummings (Garlic Man [voice]), Joe Flaherty (Big Dracula [voice]), Edan Gross (Little

Dracula [voice]), Melvyn Hayes (Deadwood [voice]), Danny Mann (No Eyes/Twin-Beaks [voice]), Neil Ross (Maggot [voice]), Fran Ryan (Hannah the Barbarian [voice]), Kath Soucie (Mrs. Dracula/Millicent [voice]), Jonathan Winters (Igor/Granny [voice]).

Dracula's son, green-skinned Little Dracula, plans to fill his father's big shoes someday. In the meantime, Little Dracula would rather party, surf, and listen to rock-and-roll.

Lost Worlds (TV Series 2005–2007), episode "The Real Dracula"; U.K., Season 1, Episode 10, 4 September 2006; Documentary, Television; 50 minutes/color/English; Atlantic Productions.

Producers: Martin Kemp; *Director*: Martin Kemp; *Special Effects*: James Jordon (visual effects supervisor); *Cast*: Corey Lawson (Narrator).

Before Bram Stoker gave life to Count Dracula in fiction, there was the *real* Dracula, a Romanian prince who conquered most of his Eastern European domain. He built splendid castles and many villages, which The History Channel explores using computer science to recreate Dracula's world.

Love at First Bite (*Amor à Primeira Mordida* [Brazil]; *Amor al primer mordisco* [Spain]; *Amore al primo morso* [Italy]; *Drakoulas sti Nea Yorki, O* [Greece]; *Kärlek vid första bettet* [Sweden]; *Liebe auf den ersten Biss* [West Germany]; *Milosc od pierwszego ukaszenia* [Poland]; *Rakkautta ensi puraisulla* [Finland]; *Vampire de ces dames, Le* [Canada]); U.S., 1979; Comedy, Horror, Romance; 94 minutes/color/English/Mono/35mm; Melvin Simon Productions.

Producers: Joel Freeman, George Hamilton, Robert Kaufman, Harold Vanarnum; *Writing Credits*: Robert Kaufman (screenplay, story) Bram Stoker (character Dracula, uncredited); *Director*: Stan Dragoti; *Cinematography*: Edward Rosson; *Film Editing*: Mort Fallick, Allan Jacobs; *Original Music*: Charles Bernstein; *Art Direction*: Serge Krizman; *Make-Up*: Dorothy J. Pearl, William Tuttle; *Special Effects*: Allen Hall, Robert G. Willard; *Cast*: George Hamilton (Count Vladimir Dracula), Susan Saint James (Cindy Sondheim), Richard Benjamin (Dr. Jeffery Rosenberg/Van Helsing), Dick Shawn (Lieutenant Ferguson NYPD), Arte Johnson (Mr. Renfield), Sherman Hemsley (the

George Hamilton plays Dracula and Susan Saint James plays Cindy Sondheim in *Love at First Bite* (U.S., 1979) (courtesy Justin Humphreys).

Reverend Mike), Isabel Sanford (Judge R. Thomas), Barry Gordon (Flashlight Vendor), Ronnie Schell (Guy in Elevator), Bob Basso (T.V. Repairman in Elevator), Bryan O'Byrne (Priest in Elevator), Michael Pataki (Mobster in Elevator), Hazel Shermet (Mrs. Knockwurst [Lady in Elevator]), Stanley Brock (Erwin Newman [Cab Driver]), Danny Dayton (Billy, first bellboy), Robert Ellenstein (VW Man at JFK), David Ketchum (Customs Inspector), Lidia Kristen (Commissare Woman), Eric Laneuville (Russell, Young Punk), Susan Tolsky (Cindy's Modeling Agent), Robin Dee Adler (Woman in Nightgown), Jack Baker (N.Y. Thug [as John Anthony Bailey]), Paul Barselou (Bloodbank Guard), Laurie Beach (Little Girl), Jacque Lynn Colton (Lady on plane with Cat), Charlie Dell (Busboy), John Dennis (Motorcycle Cop), Kay Dingle (TWA Agent) (as Ding Dingle), Shelly Garrett (N.Y. Thug), Alan Haufrect (Photographer), Michael Heit (Bellboy #2 with fire extinguisher), David Landsberg (Morty), Ralph Manza (Limo Driver at JFK), Tiger Joe Marsh (Citizen Outside Castle), Ed Marshall (Edward Calvin, News Reporter), Joseph G. Medalis (Intern) (as Joe Medalis), Rose Michtom (Elderly Lady), Debbie Javor (Nurse at Bloodbank) (as Deborah Kim Moore), Robert Nadder (Bellevue Doctor), Dino Natali (Man Outside Castle), Jerold Pearson (Hippie in Customs), Judy Penrod (Stewardess), Hal Ralston (Police Sergeant), Lavelle Roby (Mourner), Merrie Lynn Ross (Lady in Apartment), Whitney Rydbeck (Male Commissare), Rolfe Sedan (Maitre d'), Cicely Walper (Grandmother), Basil Hoffman (Hotel Manager [uncredited]), Jody Jaress (Dancer [uncredited]), Jimmy Williams (Dancer in nightclub [uncredited]).

In this vampire spoof, Count Dracula is forced out of his Transylvanian castle and moves to New York, where he begins to look for his Bride. He finds that New York life isn't any easier on vampires than it is on people. He begins pursuing Cindy Soundheim, but her boyfriend, Dr. Jeff Rosenberg, realizes she has fallen under Dracula's spell and convinces Lt. Ferguson to help him stop Dracula and save his girlfriend.

Lucy en Miroir; France, 2003; Drama/Short; 47 minutes/black and white/French; Les Films Singuliere.

Producers: Raphael Bassan, Michel Poirier; *Writing Credits*: Raphael Bassan, Bram Stoker; *Director*: Raphael Bassan; *Cinematography*: Othello Vilgard; *Film Editing*: Frédérique Devaux; *Original Music*: Jeremy Chinor, Cyril Descans, Anthony Lerat; *Art Direction*: Pip Chordorov; *Cast*: Raphael Bassan (the narrator), Anne-Sophie Brabant (Lucy S.), Gerard Courant (Jonathan), Steffani D. Loppinot (the second girl who looks at the film), Elodie Imbeau (Lucy E.), Dominic Lange (the Filmmaker), Garance Leblanc (the Drawer), Joelle Le (the first girl who looks at the film), Marcel Maze (the photographer).

Lugosi: Hollywood's Dracula (*Béla Lugosi: Hollywood's Dracula* [U.S.]); U.S., 1997; Horror/Documentary; 55 minutes/color, black and white/English/16mm; Spinning on Wheels Productions.

Producers: Donald Rhodes, Richard Sheffield (co-producer), Alexander Webb; *Writing Credits*: Gary Don Rhodes; *Director*: Gary Don Rhodes; *Cinematography*: James F. Cain; *Film Editing*: Bob Stovall; *Original Music*: Art Greenhaw; *Art Direction*: James F. Cain; *Cast*: Robert Clarke (Himself [Narrator/Interviewee]), Louise Currie (Herself), Frank J. Dello Stritto (Himself), Dwight David Frye (Himself), Richard Gordon (Himself), Loretta King (Herself), Howard W. Koch (Himself), Joseph H. Lewis (Himself), Béla Lugosi (archive footage), Hope Lugosi (Herself), Béla Lugosi Jr. (Himself), Lucille Lund (Herself), Rue McClanahan (Herself), Sammy Petrillo (Himself), Helen Richman (Herself), Richard Sheffield (Himself), John Springer (Himself), Harry Thomas (Himself), Audrey Totter (Herself), George E. Turner (Himself), Robert Wise (Himself).

Lugosi: Hollywood's Dracula reveals the truths and legends behind Hollywood's most recognizable Dracula, Béla Lugosi. Narrated by Lugosi's costar Robert Clarke and Lugosi fan Rue McClanahan, the film incorporates rare film footage from 1918–1956, home movies, and previously unseen photographs.

Lugosi: The Forgotten King; U.S., 1985; Horror/Documentary, Television; 60 minutes/color, black and white/English; Operator 13 Productions.

Producers: Mark S. Gilman Jr. (co-producer), Dave Stuckey (co-producer); *Writing Credits*: Mark S. Gilman Jr., Dave Stuckey; *Director*: Mark S. Gilman Jr., Dave Stuckey; *Cinematography*: Leslie Anne Smith (director of photography); *Film Editing*: Dave Stuckey; *Cast*: Forrest J Ackerman (Himself/Host/Narrator), Ralph Bellamy (Himself), Carroll Borland (Herself), John Carradine (Himself), Alex Gordon (Himself).

Hosted by Forrest Ackerman, this one hour documentary celebrates the life and career of Hollywood's most infamous vampire, Béla Lugosi. The film includes interviews with John Carradine, Ralph Bellamy, Carroll Borland and movie producer Alex Gordon.

Macabre Pair of Shorts; U.S., 1996; Comedy/Horror; 76 minutes/color, black and white/English/Stereo; Magick Films.

Producers: Scott Mabbutt, Sean Manton, Aaron McNally, Albee Patnesky, Brian Patrick; *Writing Credits*: Scott Mabbutt, Sean Manton (segment "The Eggs"); *Director*: Scott Mabbutt; *Cinematography*: Mark J. Coyne Derek Dale (segment "Vamps"), Tor Rolf Seeman (segment "Overtime"); *Film Editing*: Scott Mabbutt, Arthur Springer (segment "Vamps"); *Original Music*: John W. Morgan; *Make-Up*: Noah Korda; *Cast*: Rick Benattar (Jack Diamond [special edition]), David Boreanaz (Vampire's victim), Patrick Bradley (The Mime/Vincent/Assistant), Chelsea Dodson (Daughter [special edition]), Erik Emmons (Walt Farberman), Tony Ferriter (Patrick [segment "Overtime"]), Kara Flynn (Katherine), Robert Harvey (Dr. Serling), Ashley Hill (Christine Hackell/Waitress/Computer), Noah Korda (Make up Guy [special edition]), Scott Mabbutt (Tracy Langan/Himself [special edition]), Shannon K. MacDonald (Elizabeth [special edition]), Sean Manton (Tim/The Headless Rider), Kathryn McAlister (Kathryn [special edition]), Aaron McNally (Night Guard [segment "Overtime"]), Michael Overton (Seymour Hackell), Albee Patnesky (The Old Gravedigger/Blues Player), Stephanie Pinola (Kate [special edition]), Alan Sanborn (Skyles Horton/Dracula), Vance Weaver (The Pyrate), King Wilder (Tony [special edition]).

This is a collection of skits, one of which parodies Dracula himself.

Macaroni tout garni; Canada, 1998; Family, Fantasy; French Productions Jeunesses Bouchard Morin Inc.

Producers: Marjolaine Bourgeois, Jean-Pierre Morin *Original Music*: Sebastien Robitaille; *Cast*: Luc Bourgeois (Remi Lamy), Anne Casabonne (Cleo), Chantal Collin (Chantal), Nathalie D'Anjou (Macaroni), Genevieve Desilets (Dyna), Louis-Martin Despa (Louis-Martin), Pierre Gendron (Comte Dracula), Jean Harvey (Crocus), Julie LeBreton (Snoro), Olivier Loubry (Zetto), Emile Mailhiot (Lancelot), Karina Michaud-Daigneault (Fannie), Kim Olivier (Nico), Samuel Robichaud (Moustique).

Mad Monster Party? (*Frankensteins Monster-Party* [West Germany]; *Mad Monster Party* [U.S., alternative spelling]; *Mad Monsters Party?* [undefined] *Monsterpartyt* [Sweden]); U.S., 1967; Comedy, Family, Fantasy, Horror, Musical/Animation; 94 minutes/color/English/Mono; Embassy Pictures Corporation, Rankin/Bass, Productions Videocraft International.

Producers: Joseph E. Levine, Arthur Rankin Jr. Larry Roemer; *Writing Credits*: Forrest J Ackerman (uncredited), Len Korobkin, Harvey Kurtzman, Arthur Rankin Jr.; *Director*: Jules Bass; *Cinematography*: Tadahito Mochinaga; *Original Music*: Maury Laws *Cast*: Boris Karloff (Baron Boris von Frankenstein [voice]), Allen Swift (Felix Flankin/Yetch/Dracula/Invisible Man/Dr. Jekyll/Mr. Hyde/Additional Voices [voice]), Gale Garnett (Francesca [voice]), Phyllis Diller (The Monster's Mate [voice]), Ethel Ennis (Title Song Singer [voice]).

Dr. Frankenstein is having a party to celebrate his retirement. All the classic monsters, including Dracula, are invited, and Frankenstein must choose his successor.

The Magic Christian; U.K., 1969; Comedy; 92 minutes/color/English/Mono; Commonwealth United Entertainment/Grand Films Limited.

Producers: Denis O'Dell, Anthony B. Unger; *Writing Credits*: Terry Southern (novel), Joseph McGrath, Graham Chapman, John Cleese, Peter Sellers; *Director*: Joseph McGrath; *Cinematography*: Geoffrey Unsworth; *Film Editing*: Kevin Connor; *Original Music*: Ken Thorne, Paul McCartney; *Art Direction*: George Djurkovic; *Make-Up*: Harry Frampton, Joynce James; *Special Effects*: Trading Post, Wally Veevers, Brian Gamby, Garth Inns, Curly Nelhams, Jimmy Ward; *Cast*: Peter Sellers (Sir Guy Grand KG, KC, CBE), Ringo Starr (Youngman Grand, Esq.), Isabel Jeans (Dame Agnes Grand), Caroline Blakiston (Hon. Esther Grand), Wilfrid Hyde-White (Capt. Reginald K. Klaus), Richard Attenborough (Oxford coach), Leonard Frey (Laurence Faggot), Laurence Harvey (Hamlet), Christopher Lee (Ship's vampire), Spike Milligan (Traffic warden #27), Roman Polanski (Solitary drinker), Raquel Welch (Priestess of the Whip), Tom Boyle (My Man Jeff), Victor Maddern (hotdog vendor), Terence Alexander (Mad Major), Peter Bayliss (Pompous Toff), Joan Benham (Socialite in Sotheby's), Patrick Cargill (Auctioneer at Sotheby's), John Cleese (Mr. Dougdale [director in Sotheby's]), Clive Dunn (Sommelier), Fred Emney (Fitzgibbon), Kenneth Fortescue (Snob in Sotheby's), Patrick Holt (Duke in Sotheby's), David Hutcheson (Lord Barry), Hattie Jacques (Ginger Horton), Jeremy Lloyd (Lord Hampton), David Lodge (Ship's guide), Ferdy Mayne (Eduoard [of Chez Edouard restaurant]), Dennis Price (Winthrop), Robert Raglan (Maltravers), Graham Stark (Waiter at Chez Edouard Restaurant), Michael Aspel (TV commentator [uncredited]), Michael Barratt (TV commentator [uncredited]), Sean Barry-Weske (John Lennon lookalike [uncredited]), Yul Brynner (Transvestite cabaret singer [uncredited]), Harry Carpenter (TV commentator [uncredited]), Graham Chapman (Oxford crew [uncredited]), Kimberley Chung (Yoko Ono lookalike [uncredited]), Jimmy Clitheroe (Passenger on Ship [uncredited]), George Cooper (Losng Boxer's

Second [uncredited]), Roland Culver (Sir Herbert [uncredited]), W. Barrington Dalby (TV commentator [uncredited]), Freddie Earlle (Sol [uncredited]), Maria Frost (Slave Girl [uncredited]), Gail Gilmore (Girl in bar [uncredited]), Peter Graves (Lord at ship's bar [uncredited]), John Le Mesurier (Sir John [uncredited]), Guy Middleton (Duke at Mantisbriar [uncredited]), Peter Myers (Lord Kilgallon [uncredited]), Nosher Powell (Ike Jones [uncredited]), Birthe Sector (Slave girl [uncredited]), Edward Sinclair (Park attendant [uncredited]), John Snagge (TV commentator [uncredited]), Leon Thau (Engine Room Toff [uncredited]), Frank Thornton (Police Inspector [uncredited]), Michael Trubshawe (Sir Lionel [uncredited]), Edward Underdown (Prince Henry [uncredited]), Rita Webb (Woman in Park [uncredited]), Alan Whicker (TV commentator [uncredited]), Polly Williams [uncredited].

Sir Guy Grand adopts homeless bum Youngman to be heir to his obscene wealth, and immediately begins bringing him into the intricacies of the family business, which is to prey upon people's greed by use of the vast holdings of the Grand Empire. They leave no stone unturned as sporting events, restaurants, art galleries, and traditional pheasant hunts turn into lurid displays of bad manners and profiteering. Things climax at the social event of the season, the inaugural voyage of the new pleasure cruiser The Magic Christian.

Magnificent Obsessions (TV Series); Canada, 2002–2003; Documentary; 22 minutes/color/English; Summit Films Ltd.

Producers: Lorne MacPherson, Erika MacPherson; *Director*: Shereen Jerrett, Erika MacPherson, Noah Erenberg; *Film Editing*: Bruce Little.

This is a documentary investigating the lives of six extremely passionate people with unique hobbies, including sandcastle building and studying Dracula.

Makai Senki Disgaea (TV Series) (*Netherworld Battle Chronicle Disgaea* [U.S.]); Japan, 2006; Comedy, Fantasy/Television, Animation; 25 minutes/color/Japanese and English; Ankoku Gikai, Oriental Light and Magic.

Producers: Kazuya Furuse (producer, d-rights), Rika Sasaki (producer, Geneon), Jun Nishimura (producer, Geneon), Sohei Niikawa (producer, Nippon Ichi), Katsuhiko Tsurumoto, Nobuko Kudo (assistant producer); *Director*: Kiyotaka Isako; *Cinematography*: Tomoyoshi Ishizuka; *Original Music*: Tenpei Sato; *Art Direction*: Junko Shimizu; *Cast*: Kaori Mizuhashi (Laharl, voice, Japanese), Yuko Sasamoto (Flonne, voice, Japanese), Tomoe Hanba (Etna, voice, Japanese), Chihiro Suzuki (Mid boss, voice, Japanese), Nobuo Tobita (Gordon, voice, Japanese), Chiwa Saito (Jennifer, voice, Japanese), Yurika Ochiai (Thursday, voice, Japanese), Hironori Miyata (Burgano, voice, Japanese), Junji Majima (Prinny A, voice, Japanese), Chikara Osaka (Prinny B, voice, Japanese), Sandy Fox (Flonne), Barbara Goodson (Laharl), Michelle Ruff (Etna).

Two years after Demon Overlord King Krichevskoy died, his son Laharl is awakened by his disrespectful vassal Etna. Prince Laharl, Etna, and the angel Flonne set off to claim Laharl's title of Overlord from the other upstart demons, and their first target is the castle of Count Vyers. Vyers, who calls himself the "Dark Adonis," speaks with an Eastern European accent, and wears a red-and-black outfit with a wing-shaped cloak. This Count's fangs, long dark hair, and other similarities reveal his Dracula-inspired heritage.

Making Béla; U.S., 2004; Documentary, Short; 8 minutes/color, black and white/English.

Producers: Dana Kinonen, Jennifer Peterson; *Film Editing*: Chris McKim *Cast*: Martin Landau (Himself/Béla Lugosi), Rick Baker (Himself), Béla Lugosi (Himself/Count Dracula [archive footage]), Johnny Depp (Himself/Edward D. Wood Jr. [archive footage]).

This very short documentary explores how actor Martin Landou learned how to become his character of Béla Lugosi, who once played Dracula.

Making 'Bram Stoker's Dracula'; U.S., 1992; Documentary, Television; color/English; EMI Films, Columbia.

Producer: Francis Ford Coppola; *Director*: Francis Ford Coppola; *Original Music*: John Beal.

This documentary, directed by Francis Ford Coppola, takes viewers behind-the-scenes of the making of *Bram Stoker's Dracula*.

Malenka (*Bloody Girl* (undefined); *Ekdikisi ton zontanon nekron, I* [Greece, reissue title]; *Fangs of the Living Dead* [U.S.]; *Malenka la risposta del vampiro* [Italy]; *Malenka the Vampire* (undefined); *Malenka, i komissa Drakoulas* [Greece]; *Malenka, la nipote del vampiro* [Italy]; *Malenka: la sobrina del vampiro* [Spain]; *Nipote del vampiro, La* [Italy]; *The Niece of the Vampire* [undefined]; *The Vampire's Niece* [undefined]); Spain/Italy 1969; Horror; 98 minutes (Italy), 90 minutes (Spain)/Spanish/color/Mono; Cobra films.

Producers: Aubrey Ambert, Rosanna Yanni; *Writing Credits*: Amando de Ossorio (screenplay, story); *Director*: Amando de Ossorio; *Cinematography*: Fulvio Testi; *Film Editing*: Antonio Gimeno; *Original Music*: Carlo Savino; *Art Direction*: Augusto Lega, Felix Michelena; *Make-Up*: Antonio Nieto, Manolita Ponte, Marisa Tilly, Anna Maria Zini;

Cast: Anita Ekberg (Malenka/Sylvia Morel), Gianni Medici (Dr. Pietro Lufuani [as John Hamilton]), Diana Lorys (Bertha Zemis), Rosanna Yanni (Freya Zemis), César Benet (Max [as Guy Roberts]), Carlos Casaravilla (Dr. Horbringer), Fernando Bilbao (Vladis the Coachman), Paul Muller (Innkeeper), Adriana Santucci (The Count's Maid), Aurelia Treviño (Village Woman), Juanita Ramírez (Brugard the Barmaid), Adriana Ambesi (Blinka [as Audrey Ambert]), Julián Ugarte (Uncle/Count Walbrooke), Keith Kendal (Man).

Sylvia is a young woman who is about to be married when she hears that she has inherited a castle following the death of her mother. She is greeted there by her Uncle, Count Waldrick, who never comes out during the day. As time goes by, it becomes apparent that her uncle is not a benevolent man, but an evil Dracula-type vampire.

Mama Dracula; Belgium, 1980; Comedy, Horror; 90 minutes/color/English, French/Mono/35mm; Radio Télévision Belge Francophone (RTBF).

Producers: Boris Szulzinger; *Writing Credits*: Tony Hendra (dialogue), Pierre Sterckx, Boris Szulzinger, Marc-Henri Wajnberg; *Director*: Boris Szulzinger; *Cinematography*: Rufus Bohez, Willy Kurant; *Film Editing*: Claude Cohen; *Original Music*: Roy Budd; *Make-Up*: Pascale Kellen, Nicole Mora (assistant makeup artist), Nora Puttemans; *Special Effects*: Jacques Campens (special effects), Jacqueline Swennen (special effects); *Cast*: Louise Fletcher (Mama Dracula), Maria Schneider (Nancy Hawaii), Marc-Henri Wajnberg (Vladimir), Alexander Wajnberg (Ladislas [as Alexandre Wajnberg]), Jimmy Shuman (Professor Van Bloed), Jess Hahn (Le commissaire), Michel Israel (Rosa), Suzy Falk (The nanny [Gram Stoker]), Vincent Grass (Fiancé), Marie-Françoise Manuel (Virginie), José Gral (The inkeeper), William Del Visco (The psychiatrist), Martine Willequet (The choryphée), Sandrard (Fat Fiancee), Oriane Gilmon (Customer), Laurence Erhat (The little girl), Nicola Donato (Head Waiter), Charles Besterman (Cemetery Man), Muriel D'Odemont (Cemetery Woman), Michel Waxman (Head Countryman), Antoine Carette (Ticket Collector), Andre Heudens (Musician), Radomir Jovanovic (Musician), Petar Stojkovic (Musician), Patricia Bonnet (Fiancee), Claire Dessicy (Fiancee), Noëlle Fontaine (Fiancee), Carine François (Fiancee), Ariane Lorent (Fiancee), Victor Verek (Fiance [as Victor Werek]), Pierre Sterckx (Inspector), Marcy Szwartzburg (Inspector), Roland Lethem (A priest), Hal Brav (Narrator), Georges Aminel (Récitant/Narrator [French version] [voice]), Dominique Ronse (Fiancee), Bonnie Sikowitz (uncredited).

Countess Dracula has to bathe in the blood of virgins to live, but virgins are starting to become rare in modern days. She invites a blood doctor to Transylvania to create a substitute while Mama Dracula's two sons abduct the virgins needed for the research from their clothing store.

Mga Manugang ni Drakula; Philippines, 1963; Horror; black and white/Tagalog, Filipino; Ambassador Productions.

Writing Credits: Bert R. Mendoza; *Director*: Artemio Marquez; *Cast*: Zaldy Zshornack, Dolphy, Panchito, Al Quinn, Berting Labra, Jose Vergara, Teresa Mendez, Caridad Sanchez, Marilou Muñoz,

Ad for *Mga Manugang ni Drakula* (Philippines, 1963) (courtesy Simon Santos).

Lucita Soriano, Elena Mercado, Tony Gosalvez (Drakula), Silvio Ramiro.

This vampire film plays off the Dracula milieu.

La Marca del Hombre-lobo (*Frankenstein's Bloody Terror* [U.S.]; *Hell's Creatures* [U.K./U.S.]; *Die Vampire des Dr. Dracula* [West Germany]; *Horos ton vrykolakon, O* [Greece]; *Notti di Satana, Le* [Italy]; *The Mark of the Wolfman* [International]; *The Vampire of Dr. Dracula* [undefined]; *The Werewolf's Mark* [undefined]; *The Wolfman of Count Dracula* [U.S. promotional title]; *Vampires du Dr. Dracula, Les* [France]; *Varulvens blodiga natt* [Sweden]); Spain, 1968; Horror; 88 minutes/color/Spanish/Mono (English version) and 4-Track Stereo in 70mm prints/70mm; Maxper Producciones Cinematograficas (Maximiliano Perez Florez).

Producers: Maximiliano Perez-Flores; *Writing Credits*: Paul Naschy (as Jacinto Molina); *Director*: Enrique Lopez Eguiluz; *Cinematography*: Emilio Foriscot; *Film Editing*: Francisco Jaumandreu; *Original Music*: Angel Arteaga; *Art Direction*: Julio Arribas (property master), Gray Morrow (art designer [U.S. Version]); *Make-Up*: Ines Gonzalez, Jose Luis Morales, Jose Luis Ruiz; *Cast*: Paul Naschy (Count Waldemar Daninsky), Dyanik Zurakowska (Countess Janice von Aarenberg), Manuel Manzaneque (Rudolph Weissmann), Aurora de Alba (Wandessa Mikhelov), Julian Ugarte (Dr. Janos Mikhelov), Jose Nieto (Count von Alen), Carlos Casaravilla (Gypsy Judge), Antonio Jimenez Escribano (Antonio G. Escribano), Beatriz Savon (Frau Hildegard, Antique shop owner), Maria Teresa Torralba (M. Teresa Torralba), Rosanna Yanni (Nascha), Gualberto Galban (Gyogyo), Victoriano Lopez (uncredited), Milagros Ceballos (uncredited), Pilar Vela (uncredited), Angela Rhu (uncredited), Antonio Orengo (uncredited), Juan Medina (uncredited), Rafael Alcantara (uncredited), Angel Menendez (uncredited).

A gypsy couple, stranded one night with car trouble, accepts an invitation to stay the night at a nearby castle owned by Count Waldemar Daninsky. Inside they stumble upon a crypt and decide to steal valuables from the coffins, but they hadn't counted on an entombed werewolf. They remove the silver dagger from his heart and the werewolf is resurrected. *(Illustration page 120)*

The Mark of Dracula; U.S., 1997; Horror; 88 minutes/color/English; Wildcat Entertainment.

Producers: Albert Gordon, Mark J. Gordon; *Writing Credits*: Ron Ford; *Director*: Ron Ford; *Film Editing*: Lewis Schoenbrun; *Original Music*: Ian Zapczynski *Cast*: Mark Vasconcellos (Dracula), Valerie Belardinelli, Roxanne Coyne, Wes Deitrick (Phil), John R. Ellis, Ron Ford (Sheriff Cobb), Randal Malone (Mortomer Poe), Max Schreck (Orlof [archive footage]), Tim Sullivan.

An ancient, angry, and vengeful Dracula returns from the dead to terrorize the innocent living in a small town.

Mark of the Vampire (*Das Zeichen des Vampirs* [Austria/Germany]; *Das Zeichen des Vampyrs* [Austria] (alternative spelling); *Marca del vampiro, La* [Spain]; *Marque du vampire, La* [France]; *Vampires of Prague* [undefined]; *Vampiri di Praga, I* [Italy]; *Vampyrens mærke* [Denmark]; *Znak wampira* [Poland]); U.S., 1935; Horror, Mystery; 60 minutes/black and white/English, Czech/Mono; Metro-Goldwyn-Mayer (MGM).

Producers: Tod Browning, E.J. Mannix (uncredited); *Writing Credits*: Guy Endore, Bernard Schubert, H.S. Kraft (uncredited), Samuel Ornitz (uncredited), John L. Balderston (uncredited), Tod Browning (story "The Hypnotist," uncredited); *Director*: Tod Browning; *Cinematography*: James Wong Howe; *Film Editing*: Ben Lewis; *Original Music*: Jack Virgil (uncredited); *Art Direction*: Cedric Gibbons; *Make-Up*: Jack Dawn (uncredited), William Tuttle (uncredited); *Special Effects*: Tom Tutwiler (uncredited); *Cast*: Lionel Barrymore (Professor Zelen), Elizabeth Allan (Irena Borotyn), Béla Lugosi (Count Mora), Lionel Atwill (Inspector Neumann), Jean Hersholt (Baron Otto Von Zinden), Henry Wadsworth (Count Fedor Vencenti), Donald Meek (Dr. Doskil), Jessie Ralph (Midwife [scenes deleted]), Ivan F. Simpson (Jan [as Ivan Simpson]), Franklyn Ardell (Chauffeur), Leila Bennett (Maria), June Gittelson (Annie), Carroll Borland (Luna Mora [as Carol Borland]), Holmes Herbert (Sir Karell Borotyn), Michael Visaroff (Innkeeper), Lionel Belmore (scenes deleted), Robert Greig (Fat Man [scenes deleted]), Baron Hesse (Bus Driver [scenes deleted]), Doris Lloyd (scenes deleted), Eily Malyon (Sick Woman [scenes deleted]), Torben Meyer (Card Player [scenes deleted]), Henry Stephenson (scenes deleted), Zeffie Tilbury (Grandmother [scenes deleted]), Guy Bellis (Ronnie, Englishman at inn [uncredited]), James Bradbury Jr. (Actor [uncredited]), Egon Brecher (Coroner [uncredited]), Louise Emmons (Gypsy Hag [uncredited]), John George (Gypsy [uncredited]), Rosemary Glosz (Innkeeper's Wife [uncredited]), Mrs. Lesovosky (Old Woman at Inn [uncredited]), Christian Rub (Deaf Man at Inquest [uncredited]), Clare Verdera (Englishwoman at inn [uncredited]).

Sir Karell Borotyn (Holmes Herbert) is murdered two weeks before his daughter Irena's (Elizabeth Allan) wedding. He is found drained of blood with two marks on his neck, and the town suspects Count Mora (Béla Lugosi) and his daughter

of being vampires. No evidence is found to support this, and the wedding plans continue. A short while later more suspicious things start to happen, and the police inspector and Professor Zelen (Lionel Barrymore) decide to put an end to things.

Mas vampiros en La Habana; Cuba, Spain, 2003; Animation; 80 minutes/color/Spanish; Iskra S.L.

Producers: Aramis Acosta, Norma Martinez, Juan Jose Mendy, Paco Prats, Camilo Vives; *Writing Credits*: Juan Padron, Senel Paz; *Director*: Juan Padron; *Cinematography*: Armando Alba; *Original Music*: Robert Egues; *Special Effects*: Ivan Alain Perez, Rayner Valdes; *Cast*: Irela Bravo (voice), Raul Espinosa (voice), Rigoberto Ferrera (voice), Luis Alberto Garcia, Carlos Gonzalez (voice), Frank Gonzalez, Mirella Giullot (voice), Juan Padron, Jorge Perugorria, Teresita Rua (voice)

This animation is a sequel to *Vampiros en La Habana.*

Matantei Loki Ragnarok (TV Series [2003]) (*Detective Loki* [U.S.]; *Loki El Detective Loki* [Spanish]; *Mythical Sleuth Loki* [Portuguese]), episode "Dorakyura Jyou no Wana" ("Twelfth Night — The Trap of Dracula's Castle" [U.S.]); Japan, Episode 12, 21 June 2003; Action, Adventure, Comedy, Mystery, Horror/Television, Animation; 30 minutes/color/Japanese; Studio DEEN, TV Tokyo.

Producers: Naoki Nakamura and Yoshihiro Hosaka; *Writing Credits*: Kenichi Kanamaki; *Director*: Hiroshi Watanabe; *Original Music*: Kei Kanemaki Japanese Voice *Cast*: Takahiro Sakurai as Loki (old), Yuriko Fuchizaki (young), Yui Horie (Daidouji Mayura), Hiroaki Ishikawa (Dracula) Spanish Voice *Cast*: Ariadna Himenez (old and young Loki), Rosa Moyano (Mayura Daidoushi) Catalan Voice *Cast*: Vicy Martines (young Loki), Roser Aldabo (Mayura Daidoushi) Latin American Voice *Cast*: Gonzalo Fumero (old and young Loki), Anabella Silva (Mayura) Italian Voice *Cast*: Benedetta Ponticelli (old and young Loki), Debora Magnaghi (Mayura) U.S. Voice *Cast*: Jose Dias (old Loki), Shannon Emerick as (young Loki), Kira Vincent-Davis (Mayura Daidoji) Tagalog Voice *Cast*: Antony Malejana (old Loki and young Loki), Grace Cornel (Mayura Daidouji) Portuguese Voice *Cast*: Diogo Marques (young Loki), Wendel Bezerra as (old Loki), Samira Fernandes (Mayura).

While trying to play the video game Dracula's Castle, Mayura becomes ensnared within its virtual walls. Detective Loki enters the game to save Mayura.

Matinee Theatre (TV Series [1955–1958]), episode "Dracula"; U.S., Season 1, Episode 49, 6 January 1956; Drama, Horror, Mystery, Romance/Television; 60 minutes/color/English/Mono; National Broadcasting Company (NBC).

Producers: George Lowther, Albert McCleery (episode producer); *Writing Credits*: Robert Esson (adaptation) Bram Stoker (story); *Director*: Lamont Johnson; *Cast*: John Carradine (Dracula), Lisa Daniels (Lucy Weston).

McCloud (TV Series [1970–1977]), episode "McCloud Meets Dracula"; U.S., Season 7, Episode 6, 17 April 1977; Crime, Drama/Television; 75 minutes/English/color/Mono; Glen A. Larson Productions.

Producers: Gilbert Bettman Jr., Glen A. Larson, Ron Satlof (producer [as Ronald Satlof]), Michael Sloan; *Writing Credits*: Glen A. Larson (written by), Herman Miller (creator); *Director*: Bruce Kessler; *Cast*: Dennis Weaver (Sam McCloud), J.D. Cannon (Peter B. Clifford), Terry Carter (Sergeant Joe Broadhurst), John Carradine (Loren Belasco), Diana Muldaur (Chris Coughlin), Michael Sacks (Dr. Harvey Pollick), Ken Lynch (Police Sergeant Grover), Ken Scott (Police Detective Polk), John Finnegan (1st Officer [as J.P. Finnigan]), Carole Mallory (2nd Girl), Gino Ardito (Cop), Booth Colman (Coroner), Victor Fisher (Stokes), Vince Howard (Reporter), Toni Lawrence (1st Girl), Dennis Levine (2nd Officer), Bobbie Mitchell (Angie), Reggie Nalder (Morris), Michael Pataki (Reporter), Tom Snyder (Himself).

McCloud is on a mission to track down a sniper and encounters multiple murder scenes where the victims had no blood left in their bodies and two puncture wounds on their necks. His investigations lead him to an old, retired Dracula actor who is trying to live the life of Dracula in the real world.

Meitantei Conan (TV Series [1996–present]), episode "Dracula Murder Case: Part 1"; Japan, Season 3, Episode 36, 26 January 1998; Action, Adventure, Comedy, Crime, Drama, Fantasy, Horror, Mystery, Romance, Science Fiction, Thriller/Television, Animation; 25 minutes/color/Japanese/Dolby Digital/Stereo/35mm; FUNimation Entertainment.

Producers: Gen Fukunaga; *Writing Credits*: Gosho Aoyama (creater), Andrew Rye (English adaptation); *Director*: Mike McFarland; *Original Music*: Katsuo Ono; *Cast*: Brice Armstrong (Foster Drake), Bob Carter (Stefan Van Croven), Chad Cline (Jonathan Tradonio), Colleen Clinkenbeard (Rachel Moore), R. Bruce Elliott (Richard Moore), Jerry Jewell (Jimmy Kudo), Akira Kamiya (Kogoro Mori), Kristin McCollum (Daiselle Van Croven), Jay Moses (Shamus O'Halliwell), Minami Takayama

Opposite: German poster for *La Marca del Hombre-lobo* (Spain, 1968).

(Conan Edogawa), Alison Viktorin (Conan Edogawa), Wakana Yamazaki (Ran Mori).

Shinichi Kudo, a seventeen-year-old master detective, is shrunken down to the size of a fourth grader when an experimental poison is tried on him. He goes to the goofball inventor that lives next door to him for help, and the inventor agrees to give him a hand. The inventor and Shinichi pass him off as a child named Conan Edogawa (in reference to Sir Arthur Conan Doyle). In each episode, Conan solves a different case in the style of all good detective shows, giving hints to help the viewer try to guess who the villain is, while trying to keep his true identity a secret.

Men of Action Meet Women of Drakula; Philippines, 1969; Villanueva.

Director: Artemio Marquez; *Cast*: Dante Varona, Eddie Torrente, Ruben Obligacion, Norman Henson, Ernesto Beren, Angelito Marquez, Martin Marfil, Liza Melmonte, Marco Antonio Arzate, Nemia Velasco, Silvio Ramiro, Miniong Alvarez.

Dracula and his vampire women fight with acrobats.

Merrie Melodies (Theatrical/TV Series 1931–1969), episode "Transylvania 6-5000"; U.S., 30 November 1963; Comedy, Family/Television, Animation, Short; 7 minutes/color/English/Mono; Warner Bros. Pictures, Inc., Vitaphone Releases.

Producers: David H. DePatie (producer, uncredited); *Writing Credits*: John W. Dunn (as John Dunn); *Director*: Chuck Jones; *Film Editing*: Treg Brown; *Original Music*: William Lava (as Bill Lava); *Cast*: Julie Bennett (Agatha and Emily — The Two-headed Vulture [voice]), Mel Blanc (Bugs Bunny [voice]), Ben Frommer (Count Bloodcount [voice]).

Bugs Bunny takes a wrong turn on his way to his vacation and winds up in Count Bloodcount's Transylvanian castle. He stays the night, and with some good luck and magic escapes to see the next day.

Method and Madness: Visualizing 'Dracula'; U.S., 2007; Short, Documentary; 12 minutes/color/English; ZAP Zoetrope Aubry Productions.

Producers: Kim Aubry; *Director*: Kim Aubry; *Film Editing*: Ken Schneider; *Art Direction*: Diana Landau, Anne Mason, Kenn Rabin; *Cast*: Francis Ford Coppola (Himself), Roman Coppola (Himself), Steven Anthony Jones (Himself [archive footage]), Peter A. Ramsey (Himself [as Peter Ramsey]).

Mickey's Gala Premier (*Mickey's Gala Premiere* [U.S.]); U.S., 1933; Comedy, Musical/Animation, Short; 7 min/black and white/English/Mono; Walt Disney Productions.

Producer: Walt Disney; *Director*: Burt Gillett; *Original Music*: Frank Churchill (uncredited); *Cast*: Walt Disney (Mickey Mouse [voice]), Marcellite Garner (Minnie Mouse [voice]).

Mickey Mouse is premiering a film at the Chinese Theatre, and many famous stars of Hollywood at the time show up to see Mickey's movie. Among the guests in the audience is a Dracula-type character enjoying Mickey's film.

Mighty Mouse: Mighty Mouse Meets Bad Bill Bunion; U.S., 1945; Animation; 6:02 minutes/color/English; 20th Century–Fox, TerryToon cartoons.

Producers: Paul Terry; *Writing Credits*: John Foster; *Director*: Mannie Davis; *Original Music*: Philip A. Scheib *Cast*: Tom Morrison (Mighty Mouse)

One day Mighty Mouse was going along with his everyday business when he was called for help. A gorgeous saloon singer is being kidnapped by an escaped prisoner, Bad Bill Bunion. Mighty Mouse comes to the rescue and takes down Bad Bill Bunion while saving the girl.

Mina and the Count (TV Series); 1995–2003, U.S.; Comedy, Family, Science Fiction, Adventure/Television, Animation, Short; 6:30–7:30 minutes/color/English; Hanna-Barbera Studios.

Producers: Buzz Potamkin, Larry Huber, Sylvia Edwards, Rob Renzetti; *Writing Credits*: Rob Renzetti; *Director*: Rob Renzetti; *Film Editing*: Paul Douglas; *Original Music*: Gary Lionelli; *Art Direction*: C. Miles Thompson; *Cast*: Michael Bell (Dad), Mark Hamill (Count/Janitor/Principal), Jeff Bennett (Igor/Frank/Reporter), Tara Clarenjoff (Mina).

In the first episode, "Interlude with a vampire," Mina, a little girl, begins to fall asleep one night when the Count, a Dracula-type vampire, awakens and heads off into the night. Arriving at Mina's house, the Count attempts to hypnotize Mina, but when he discovers that she is actually just a kid (and not the teenager for whom the Count's servant, Igor, had mistaken her), the Count becomes angered. Mina then wakes up and sees the Count not as a vampire but as her new playmate. The remaining episodes (six in all) concern the friendly adventures of Mina and the Count.

The Mini-Monsters: Adventures at Camp Mini-Mon; U.S., 1987; Comedy, Family/Animation, Short; 33 minutes/color/English.

Cast: Donald Acree (Voices).

The offspring of famous monsters such as Frankenstein, Dracula, Wolfman, the Mummy, the Wicked Witch of the West, and others are sent on a summer camp adventure where they cause mischief.

Mira corpora; France, 2004; Drama, Horror/Short; 45 minutes/color/French.

Producer: Stéphane Marti; *Writing Credits*: Stéphane Marti; *Director*: Stéphane Marti; *Cinematography*: Stéphane Marti; *Film Editing*: Stéphane Marti; *Original Music*: Berndt Deprez *Cast*: Amine Adjina (uncredited), Johan Amselem (uncredited), Christian Canciani d'Este (uncredited), Sarah Darmon (uncredited), Louis Dupont (uncredited), Samuel Ganes (uncredited), Élodie Imbeau (Élodie Jane), Marcel Mazé (uncredited), Orlan Roy (uncredited), Anders Ulrich (uncredited).

This is an experimental film that pays homage to Murnau's classic film.

Mr. and Mrs. Dracula (TV Series); U.S., 1980–1981; Comedy/Television; 30 minutes/color/English/Mono; ABC Circle Films.

Producers: Robert Klane, Stanley Korey; *Writing Credits*: Robert Klane; *Director*: Doug Rogers; *Cinematography*: Daniel Flannery; *Original Music*: Jack Elliott, Ken Lauber; *Cast*: Dick Shawn (Dracula), Carol Lawrence (Sonia Dracula [1980]), Paula Prentiss (Sonia Dracula [1981]), Gail Mayron (Minna Dracula), Anthony Battaglia (Sonny Dracula), Johnny Haymer (Gregor, the Bat), Barry Gordon (Cousin Anton), Rick Aviles (Mario).

After 618 years of marriage, Vladimir and Sonia Dracula are driven out of Transylvania by angry villagers. Vladimir and Sonia then resettle in the Bronx, New York with their son. Only two pilots of this show were ever shot.

Mistress of Seduction (*Dracula's Dirty Daughter* [U.S.]); U.S., 2000; Horror; color/English; Ventura Distribution.

Producers: Chet Bennett, Michael Raso; *Writing Credits*: Michele Pacitto; *Director*: Michele Pacitto; *Cinematography*: Pete Schuermann; *Film Editing*: Pete Schuermann; *Original Music*: Motor Dolls, DJ Gratcher; *Art Direction*: Jon Eberhardt; *Special Effects*: Milko Davis; *Cast*: Alysabeth Clements (Vampirina), Gentle Fritz (Corina), Thomas Martwick (John), Justiz Donaldson (Matt), Josh Dirmish (Pat), Michelle Tebow (Tanya), Kellie Brown (Kristal), Diane Skiba (Mercedes), Jim Prange (Professor Steele), Jack Leeper (Doorman), Jeff Haxton (Jimmy), Duane Clements (Bartender), Colin Smith (Mr. Buckner), Robert Samuelson (Himself), Jack Ray (Student), Stacy Storer (Student), Heather Trippleton (Student), Matt Jersey (Hot Tarts Patron), Bari Brenner (uncredited), Flame (uncredited), Lori Masters (uncredited).

Vampirina, a vampire and lesbian daughter of Dracula, seduces young college girls. Only their virginity can satisfy her cravings. Eventually, she discovers the girl who killed her father, but they become lovers.

Modern Vampires (*Revenant* [U.K., video title]; *Revenant— Sie kommen in der Nacht* [Germany]; *Revenant: Vampiros modernos* [Spain]; *Sie kommen bei Nacht* [Germany, cable TV title]; *The Revenant* [U.S., working title]; *Vampiros Modernos* [Brazil, cable TV title]; *Vamps* [Philippines, theatrical title]); U.S., 1998; Thriller, Horror; 91 minutes/color/English/Dolby; MU.S.E/Wyman, Storm Entertainment.

Producers: Lawrence Abramson (co-executive producer [as Larry Abramson]), Richard Elfman (co-producer), Jordan Gertner (co-executive producer), Chris Hanley (producer), H. Michael Heuser (executive producer), Casper Van Dien (co-executive producer), Brad Wyman (producer); *Writing Credits*: Matthew Bright; *Director*: Richard Elfman; *Cinematography*: Robin Brown; *Film Editing*: Larry Bock; *Art Direction*: Peter Kanter, Stacie B. London; *Make-Up*: Brad Boles (key makeup artist), Roy Knyrim (makeup effects supervisor, special makeup effects artist), Jerry Macaluso (makeup effects supervisor, special makeup effects artist), Roger Nall (special makeup effects artist); *Special Effects*: Sota F/X, Rick Baker (special effects consultant), G. Bruno Stempel (special effects coordinator [as Bruno Stemple]), Dan Winthrop (photographic effects); *Cast*: Casper Van Dien (Dallas), Natasha Gregson Wagner (Nico), Rod Steiger (Dr. Frederick Van Helsing), Kim Cattrall (Ulrike), Natasha Lyonne (Rachel), Craig Ferguson (Richard), Udo Kier (Vincent), Gabriel Casseus (Time Bomb), Robert Pastorelli (The Count), Natalya Andrejchenko (Panthia [as Natasha Andreichenko]), Boris Lee Krutonog (Concierge [as Boris Krutonog]), Marco Hofschneider (Hans [as Marco Hosschneider]), Stephen Porter (Harald), Ellia Thompson (The Count's Girlfriend), Peter Lucas (The Count's Henchman), Jason Ross-Azikiwe (Pimp [as Jason Asikiwe]), Roberta Hanley (Saleslady), Victor Togunde (Soda Pop), Cedrik Terrell (Li'l Monster [as Cedrick Terrell]), Flex Alexander (Trigger [as Flex]), Robert Peters (Cop #1), Rick Cramer (Cop #2), John Sencio (Alan), John Fleck (Trick), Conchata Ferrell (Wanda, Nico's Mother [as Conchetta Ferrell]), Brent Briscoe (George, Nico's Stepfather), Louis Elfman (Paint Huffer), Keenan Ratowski (Paint Huffer), Brad Joseph Dubin (Paint Huffer), Dimitri Schell (Paint Huffer), Richard Elfman (Cop with Doughnut), Michelle Csitos (Ulrike Monster Vampire [uncredited]), Francesca Lombardo (Dead Body on Couch [uncredited]), Elizabeth Sampson (Frida Van Helsing [uncredited]).

A vampire posing as a streetwalker angers Count Dracula, who is running a nightclub in L.A. His former protégé, Dallas, is in town as well. The streetwalker picks Dallas as a victim, but they end up falling in love. A vampire hunter named Van Helsing arrives in L.A. and hires the Crips to help him find vampires. Upon being captured, Dallas wants to make a deal to spare Nico and lead the vampire hunters to Dracula.

Mondo Lugosi; U.S., 1987 Documentary; 60 minutes/color, black and white/English; Rhino Video.

Director: Johnny Legend, Jeff Vilencia; *Cast*: Béla Lugosi (Dracula/Himself).

This film chronicles the life and career of Béla Lugosi.

The Monkees (TV Series [1966–1968]), episode "Monstrous Monkee Mash"; U.S., Season 2, Episode 18, 22 January 1968; Comedy, Musical; 30 minutes/color/English/Mono; National Broadcasting Company (NBC), Raybert Productions, Screen Gems Television.

Producers: Bob Rafelson, Bert Schneider, Gerald Shepard, Ward Sylvester; *Writing Credits* Neil Burstyn, David Panich; Director: James Frawley; *Film Editing*: Michael Pozen; Cinematography: Irving Lippman *Original Music*: Stu Phillips; *Art Direction*: Ross Bellah, Phillip Bennett Makeup: Ben Lane; *Special Effects*: Chuck Gaspar *Cast*: Davy Jones (Davy [as David Jones]), Micky Dolenz (Micky), Michael Nesmith (Mike), Peter Tork (Peter), Ron Masak (The Count), Arlene Martel (Lorelei), David Pearl (The Wolfman), James Frawley (Toy Bat [voice] [uncredited]), Valerie Kairys (Girl summoned by wolf howl [uncredited]).

Loreli brings Davy to her uncle Dracula's castle. There he is held prisoner with the wolfman. Davy calls his buddies to the castle to help save him. They all arrive at the castle and hi-jinks ensue.

Monster by Moonlight! The Immortal Saga of "The Wolf Man"; U.S., 1999; Horror/Documentary; 33 minutes/color/English; Universal Studios Home Video.

Producer: David J. Skal; *Writing Credits*: David J. Skal; *Director*: David J. Skal; *Film Editing*: Keith Clark; *Make-Up*: Debbie San Filippo; *Cast*: Rick Baker (Himself), Jan-Christopher Horak (Himself), John Landis (Himself [Host/Narrator]), John W. Morgan (Himself [as John Morgan]), Curt Siodmak (Himself), William T. Stromberg (Himself).

This is a documentary about the *The Wolf Man* films made by Universal Studios, including clips from other movies such as *Abbott & Costello Meet Frankenstein* (1948) and *House of Dracula* (1945).

Monster Force (TV Series [1994]); Canada, 1994; Drama, Comedy/Television, Animation; color/English/Stereo; Lacewood Productions, Universal Cartoon Studios.

Producers: Sheldon S. Wiseman, Gerald Tripp, Kathi Castillo, JoEllyn Marlow, Lee Williams; *Writing Credits*: Darson Hall (4 episodes, 1994) Mary Crawford (3 episodes, 1994) Alan Templeton (3 episodes, 1994) Ken Ross (2 episodes, 1994) Craig Miller (unknown episodes) Marv Wolfman (unknown episodes); *Director*: Chris Schouten; *Original Music*: Edmund Eagan; *Art Direction*: Philip A. Cruden; *Special Effects*: Dimitri Joannides; *Cast*: Philip Akin (Tripp Hansen), Lawrence Bayne (Dr. Reed Crawley), David Hewlett (Lance McGruder), Howard Jerome (Frankenstein), Robert Bockstael (Dracula, Im-Ho-Tep the Mummy), Rob Cowan (Béla the Werewolf), Paul Haddad (The Wolfman), Dean Hagopian (Renfield), Ray Landry, Caroly Larson (Shelley Frank).

A group of teenagers employs high-tech equipment to battle classical monsters and spiritual demons that threaten humanity, including Dracula, The Creature from the Black Lagoon, Im-Ho-Tep the Mummy, and the Werewolf. Some of the members of the Monster Force have more personal reasons for fighting the monsters, while others fight for more altruistic reasons.

Monster Kid Home Movies; U.S., 2005; Horror; color/English; The PPS Group.

Producers: Joseph G. Busam, David C. Phillippi; *Writing Credits*: Tom Abrams (segment "The Gentle Old Madman"), David Colton; *Director*: Robert Tinnell; *Cinematography*: Frank Dietz (segment "Leaves"), Alex Lugones (segment: "Up for Grabs"), Tom Weaver (segment "Up for Grabs"); *Film Editing*: Eric Hampton; *Cast*: Bob Burns (Various Roles ["The Alien," "The Monster"]), David Colton (Narrator [Introduction]), Frank Dietz (Various Roles ["The Lighthouse," "Surprise!," "The Last Omega Man on Earth," "Out of the Frying Pan"]), Kerry Gammill (Various Roles ["Frankenstein Meets the Wolf Man"]), T.Z. Garrison (Hero ["Dracula Meets the Wolf Man," as Jimmy Garrison]), Alex Lugones (The Dead Man ["Up for Grabs"]), Richard Olson (Various Roles ["Caveman Comedy," "Frankenstein and the Wolf Man," "The Monsters," "Dracula's Lab," "Lady Vampire"]), Richard Harland Smith (Hero ["Dracula Must Be Destroyed"]), Mr. Hyde ["Mr. Hyde"]), Jon Weaver (The Gravedigger ["Up for Grabs"]), Randy Olson (Various Roles ["Caveman Comedy"/"Lady Vampire"]).

Moster Kid Home Movies is a collection of several amateur monster and horror productions.

Monster Kids (*Monster Babies* [U.S.]; *Little Monsters* [U.S.]); U.S., 2008; Family, Horror/Animation, Short; 7 minutes/color/English/Stereo; Visionary Cinema.

Producers: Scott Essman (supervising producer), Craig Miller (consulting producer); *Writing Credits*: Scott Essman (charaters), Joseph Fontinos (screenplay); *Director*: Scott Essman; *Film Editing*: Dieter Rozek (supervising film editor); *Original Music*:

Tom Bimmermann; *Art Direction*: Kerry Gammill (character designer), Sidney Ullman (background designer); *Cast*: Robert Collins (Jr. Hyde), Scott Essman (Phantom Kid [voice]), Samantha Ford (Kid Bride), Garou (Wolf Kid [voice]), Robert Stilwell (Invisible Kid), Jonathan Ten broek (Kid Count Dracula), Tyler Ten broek (Kid Frankenstein's Monster).

Dracula Jr. and Kid Frankenstein's Monster both have a crush on Kid Bride. Dracula Jr. uses Kid Frank in his attempts to win the heart of Kid Bride, but Hyde Jr. is two-faced and up to no good.

Monster Mania; U.S., 1997; Horror/Documentary, Television; 62 minutes/color/black and white/English; American Movie Classics (AMC), Fox Television Network, Foxstar Productions, Van Ness Films.

Producers: Brian Anthony, Kevin Burns, David A. Kleiler Jr.; *Writing Credits*: Kevin Burns, Raphael Simon; *Director*: Kevin Burns; *Original Music*: Tom Jenkins; *Make-Up*: Guy Richards (makeup artist, hair stylist); *Cast*: Jack Palance (Host), Cassandra Peterson (as herself [Elvira]).

A documentary about the evolution of the horror film genre, from its silent black and white beginnings at the start of the century to the current day million dollar blockbusters. It features a clip from the 1992 film *Bram Stoker's Dracula*.

Monster Mash; U.S./Italy, 2000; Family, Musical/Animation; 64 minutes/color/English; DiC Entertainment, Radiotelevisione Italiana (RAI), Rai Cinemafiction.

Producers: Pam Arseneau, Alfio Bastiancich, Andy Heyward, Robby London, Michael Maliani, Soon Shin Park (supervising producer); *Writing Credits*: Guido Manuli, Judy Rothman Rofé; *Director*: Guido Manuli; *Original Music*: Jean-Michel Guirao; *Film Editing*: Thierry P. Laurin, Miriam L. Preissel; *Art Direction*: Cullen Blaine, Marcos Borregales, Mike Christian, Maurizio Forestieri, Stefano Gaudiano, Brent Gordon, Scott Heming, Rick Hoberg, Dan Kubat, Fred Miller, Ed Nebres, Bob Nesler, David Pagani, Vincenzo Trippetti, Keith Tucker; *Special Effects*: Park Duk Hyun; *Cast*: Ian James Corlett (voice), Robert O. Smith (voice), Janyse Jaud (Spike/Mom), Jim Byrnes (voice), Patricia Drake (voice), David Sobolok (Frank), Scott McNeil (The Wolfman), French Tickner (voice), Phil Hayes (voice), Tabitha St. Germain (voice), Dave "Squatch" Ward (voice), Phil Trainer (Yorick), David Pavlovitch (uncredited), W. Harlan May (voice), Jason Michas (voice).

The Wolfman, Drac (the vampire), Frankie, Yorick, and Spike/Mom have lost their ability to scare people. They are brought before the Court of Horrors and given one last chance to prove that they are still scary. They must scare the Tinklemeister family, but it proves to be a difficult task.

Monster Mash: The Movie (*Frankenstein Sings* [U.S.]); U.S., 1995; Horror, Comedy, Musical; 82 minutes/color/English.

Producers: Michael Kates, Nathaniel Kramer, Jack Scheider; *Writing Credits*: Sheldon Allman, Bobby Pickett, Mary Shelley [Frankenstein character (uncredited)]; *Director*: Joel Cohen, Alex Sokolow; *Cinematography*: Scott Andrew Ressler; *Film Editing*: Stephen Mirrione; *Original Music*: Bobby Pickett, Joe Troiano, Jeffrey Zahn (as Jeff Zahn); *Make-Up*: Greg Aronowitz (special effects makeup designer), Silvian Knight (makeup department head), Jeff Lewis (special makeup effects artist); *Cast*: Ian Bohen (Scott [Romeo]), Candace Cameron Bure (Mary [Juliet]), Sarah Douglas (Countess Natasha "Nasty" Dracula), John Kassir (Igor), Bobby Picket (Dr. Victor Frankenstein), Adam Shankman (Wolfie), Mink Stole (Wolfie's Mother), Jimmie Walker (Hathaway [as Jimmy Walker]), Anthony Crivello (Count Vladimir Dracula), Linda Cevallos (Dancer #1), Carrie Ann Inaba (Dancer #2), Darly Richardson (Dancer #3), Deron McBee (The Monster), E. Aron Price (Elvis).

Count Vladimir Dracula (Anthony Crivello) is attending a party put on by his friend Dr. Frankenstein (Bobby Pickett). During the party two teenagers, Scott (Ian Bohen) and Mary (Candace Cameron Bure), wander in lost. Dracula is immediately attracted to the girl and spends the rest of the party pursuing her.

Monster Squad (TV Series, U.S., 1976–1977); U.S., 11 September 1976; Horror, Family, Adventure/Television; 30 minutes/color/Mono; D'Angelo-Bullock-Allen Productions.

Producers: R.S. Allen (executive producer [unknown episodes]), Harvey Bullock (executive producer [unknown episodes]), William P. D'Angelo (producer [unknown episodes]); *Director*: Herman Hoffman (unknown episodes), James Sheldon (unknown episodes); *Cast*: Barry Dennen (Mr. Mephisto [1 episode, 1976]), Alice Ghostley (Queen Bee [1 episode, 1976]) Vito Scotti (Albert [1 episode, 1976]), Henry Polic II (Dracula [unknown episodes]), Buck Kartalian (Bruce W. Wolf [unknown episodes]), Mike Lane (Frank N. Stein [unknown episodes]) Fred Grandy (Walter [unknown episodes]).

Wax Museum figures of Dracula, Frankenstein, and Wolf Man are brought to life in a horror museum to fight evil.

The Monster Squad; U.S., 1987; Action, Comedy, Family, Fantasy, Horror; 82 minutes/color/English, German/Dolby; Home Box Office (HBO), Keith Barish Productions, TAFT Entertainment Pictures.

Producers: Keith Barish, Rob Cohen, Peter Hyams, Neil A. Machlis, Jonathan A. Zimbert; *Writing Credits*: Shane Black, Fred Dekker; *Director*: Fred Dekker; *Cinematography*: Bradford May; *Film Editing*: James Mitchell; *Original Music*: Bruce Broughton; *Art Direction*: David M. Haber; *Make-Up*: Katalin Elek, Zoltan Elek (as Zoltan), Matt Rose, John Rosengrant; *Special Effects*: David LeRoy Anderson, Grant Arndt, Grant Arndt, Phil Cory, Eric Fiedler, Alec Gillis, Emilio M. Gonzales, Steven James, David Kindlon, Richard J. Landon, Leonard MacDonald, Lindsay MacGowan, Shane Mahan, Dave Matherly, Hans Metz, Thaine Morris, David Nelson, Steve Patino, Matt Rose, John Rosengrant, Anton Rupprecht, Shannon Shea, Brian Simpson, Wayne Sturm, Ray Svedin, Michiko Tagawa, Jackie Tichenor, Steve Wang, Stan Winston, Tom Woodruff Jr.; *Cast*: Andre Gower (Sean [as André Gower]), Robby Kiger (Patrick), Stephen Macht (Del), Duncan Regehr (Count Dracula), Tom Noonan (Frankenstein), Brent Chalem (Horace), Ryan Lambert (Rudy), Ashley Bank (Phoebe), Michael Faustino (Eugene), Mary Ellen Trainor (Emily), Leonardo Cimino (Scary German Guy), Jon Gries (Desperate Man [as Jonathan Gries]), Stan Shaw (Detective Sapir), Lisa Fuller (Patrick's Sister), Jason Hervey (E.J.), Adam Carl (Derek), Carl Thibault (Wolfman), Tom Woodruff Jr. (Gillman), Michael Reid MacKay (Mummy [as Michael MacKay]), Jack Gwillim (Van Helsing), David Proval (Pilot), Daryl Anderson (Co-Pilot), Robert Lesser (Eugene's Dad), Gwill Richards (Mr. Metzger), Ernie Lively (Night Watchman [as Ernie Brown]), Sonia Curtis (Peasant Girl), Daniel W. Barringer (Squad Room Cop #1 [as Paul Barringer]), Julius LeFlore (Squad Room Cop #2), Jim Stephen (Squad Room Cop #3), Bryan Kestner (Rookie Cop), Denver Mattson (Beefy Cop), Diana Lewis (TV Anchorwoman), Gary Rebstock (TV Anchorman), David Wendel (Army General), Charly Morgan (Vampire Bride with Possom), Phil Culotta (Driver of Coroner Van), Mary Albee (Pantry Girl/Vampire), Brynn Baron (Pantry Girl/Vampire [as Joan-Carrol Baron]), Julie Merrill (Pantry Girl/Vampire), Marianne De Camp (Mrs. Carlsen), Paul Van Camp (Guy in Ground Hog Day), Riad Galayini (Girl in Ground Hog Day [as Riad]), Jake (Pete), Jean-Paul Hellendall (Nerd [uncredited]).

Aided by the other classic monsters of Hollywood, Dracula has returned and plans to rule the world. All that stands between him and world domination is a group of young kids who belong to a club they call "The Monster Clud." Using the diary of Abraham Van Helsing, together they must face the forces of darkness. They are the Monster Squad.

Monster Squad Forever!; 2007, U.S.; 88 minutes/color/English/Stereo; Lions Gate, Red Shirt Pictures.

Producers: Dustin Dean, Michael Felsher, Gary Hertz, Chris Roe; *Director*: Michael Felsher; *Cinematography*: Graeme Potts; *Film Editing*: Michael Felsher; *Original Music*: Bruce Broughton; *Cast*: Ashley Bank (Herself), Bruce Broughton (Himself), Jake Crockett (Himself), James Daisy (Himself), Nick Daisy (Himself), Fred Dekker (Himself), Andre Gower (Himself), Ryan Lambert (Himself), Bradford May (Himself), Tom Noonan (Himself), Duncan Regehr (Himself), Matt Rose (Himself), Steve Wang (Himself), Tom Woodruff Jr. (Himself), Jonathan A. Zimbert (Himself [as Jonathan Zimbert]).

This feature-length documentary examines the cult-classic *Monster Squad*, and includes interviews with writer/director Fred Dekker, and stars of the film like Tom Noonan, Duncan Regehr, Andre Gower, and more.

MonsterFest 2000: The Classics Come Alive; U.S., 2000; Horror; color/English; Universal Studios.

Producer: Marc Juris, Nancy McKenna (executive in charge of production); *Make-Up*: Michael Germain; *Cast*: Linda Blair (Herself/Co-Host), Whoopi Goldberg (Herself—Host).

This film shows clips from classic horror films from the 1930s–1960s, also showing the making of the films and behind-the-scenes footage.

MonsterQuest (TV Series [2007–2009]), episode "Vampires in America"; U.S., Season 2, Episode 11, 6 August 2008; Mystery/Documentary, Television; 45 minutes/color, black and white/English; History Channel.

Producers: Ted Poole; *Writing Credits*: Doug Hajick; *Original Music*: Tom Hambleton *Cast*: Stan Benard (narrator).

This episode investigates the legendary New England vampires of the 1700s, then examines modern-day "living vampires" who claim to have a real craving for blood. Archival footage of the cinematic Dracula is included.

Los Monstruos del terror (*Assignment Terror* [U.S.]; *Dracula Versus Frankenstein* [U.K.]; *Dracula jagt Frankenstein* [West Germany]; *Man Who Came from Ummo, The*; *Operation Terror*; *Operazione terrore* [Italy]); Spain–West Germany–Italy, 1970; Horror, Science Fiction; 84 minutes/color/Spanish/Mono; Eichberg-Film.

Producers: Jaime Prades; *Writing Credits*: Paul Naschy; *Director*: Hugo Fregonese, Tulio Dernichelli, Eberhard Meichsner; *Cinematography*: Godofredo Pachecho; *Film Editing*: Emilio Rodrigues; *Original Music*: Rafael Ferrer-Fito, Franco

Salina; *Make-Up*: Francisco Ramon Ferrer; *Special Effects*: Antonio Molina; *Cast* Michael Rennie (Dr. Odo Warnoff), Karin Dor (Maleva Kerstein), Patty Shepard (Lisa Helga Geissler, Ángel del Pozo (Kirian), Craig Hill (Inspector Tobermann), Paul Naschy (Waldemar Daninsky), Fajda Nicol, Manuel de Blas, Diana Sorel, Peter Damon, Ferdinando Murolo, Gene Reyes, Ella Gessler, Luciano Tacconi.

When their own land faces extinction, aliens come to earth. They reincarnate two scientists and use their knowledge derived from studying earthlings to terrify the inhabitants of the earth by creating situations that prey on human's superstitious beliefs.

Monty Python's Flying Circus (TV Series [1969–1974]), episode "You're No Fun Anymore" (*Gwen Dibley's Flying Circus* [U.K., working title]; *Monty Python* [U.K., new title]; *Monty Python's Flying Circus* [Greece, DVD title]; *Monty Pythonin lentävä sirkus* [Finland]; *Monty Pythons flygande cirkus* [Sweden]; *Monty Pythons flyvende cirkus* [Denmark]; *Os Malucos do Circo* [Portugal]; *Owl-Stretching Time* [U.K., working title]); U.K., Season 1, Episode 7, 30 November 1969; Comedy, Musical, Science Fiction/Television; 30 minutes/color/English/Mono, Stereo; British Broadcasting Corporation (BBC), Python (Monty) Pictures.

Producers: Ian MacNaughton; *Writing Credits*: Graham Chapman, John Cleese, Eric Idle, Terry Jones, Michael Palin, Terry Gilliam; *Director*: Ian MacNaughton; *Cinematography*: Alan Featherstone; *Film Editing*: Ray Millichope; *Make-Up*: Joan Barrett (makeup supervisor); *Cast*: John Cleese (Various Characters), Eric Idle (Various Characters), Graham Chapman (Various Characters), Terry Jones (Various Characters), Terry Gilliam (Various Characters), Michael Palin (Various Characters).

Dracula loses his fangs, which causes him to stop being "fun."

Mother Riley Meets the Vampire (*Dracula's Desire* [undefined]; *Mother Riley Runs Riot* [undefined]; *My Son the Vampire* [U.S.]; *Old Mother Riley Meets the Vampire* [undefined]; *The Robot and the Vampire* [U.S., pre-release title]; *The Vampire and the Robot* [U.S., pre-release title]; *Vampire Over London* [U.S.]); U.K., 1952; Comedy, Horror; 74 minutes/black and white/English/Mono; Fernwood Productions.

Producers: Stanley Couzins, John Gilling; *Writing Credits*: Richard Gordon (story idea, uncredited) Val Valentine; *Director*: Jon Gilling; *Cinematography*: Stanley Pavey (as Stan Pavey); *Film Editing*: Leonard Trumm (as Len Trumm); *Original Music*: Lindo Southworth; *Art Direction*: Bernard Robinson; *Make-Up*: Eric Carter (make-up artist) Betty Lee (hair-stylist); *Cast*: Arthur Lucan (Mrs. Riley), Béla Lugosi (Von Housen), Dora Bryan (Tilly), Philip Leaver (Anton Daschomb), Richard Wattis (Police Constable Freddie), Graham Moffatt Yokel (Graham Moffat), María Mercedes (Julia Loretti), Roderick Lovell (Douglas), David Hurst (Mugsy), Judith Furse (Freda), Ian Wilson (Hitchcock, the butler), Hattie Jacques (Mrs. Jenks), Dandy Nichols (Humphrey's Wife), George Benson (Humphrey the Drunk), Bill Shine (Mugsy's Assistant), David Hannaford (Man Washing Windows), Charles Lloyd Pack (Mr. Pain the Creditor) (as Charles Lloyd-Pack), Cyril Smith (Police Brass), Arthur Brander, (Police Brass), Peter Bathurst (Police Brass), Tom Macaulay (Delivery Driver), Alexander Gauge (Police Constable [uncredited]), John Le Mesurier (uncredited), Laurence Naismith (Policeman at Desk [uncredited]).

The mad scientist and vampire, Von Housen (Béla Lugosi), accidentally sends the robot he is working on to Mother Riley's (Arthur Lucan) home in London. He uses his remote control device to get it back. However, he receives the old Mother Riley along with his robot, and she causes plenty of trouble for Von Housen.

El Mundo de los vampiros (*The World of the Vampires* [U.S.]) Mexico, 1961; Horror; 83 minutes/black and white/Spanish/Mono/35mm; Cinematográfica ABSA.

Producers: Abel Salazar; *Writing Credits*: Alfredo Salazar (adaptation), Jesús Murcielago Velázquez (story), and Raúl Zenteno (story); *Director*: Alfonso Corona Blake; *Cinematography*: Jack Draper; *Film Editing*: Alfredo Rosas Priego (as Alfredo Rosas); *Original Music*: Gustavo César Carrión (as Gustavo Cesar Carreon); *Art Direction*: Javier Torres Torija; *Make-Up*: Elda Loza; *Cast*: Mauricio Garcés (Rodolfo Sabre), Erna Martha Bauman (Leonor Colman), Silvia Fournier (Mirta), Guillermo Murray (Count Sergio Subotai), José Baviera (Sr. Colman), Yolanda Margain, Carlos Nieto, Maricarmen Vela, Alfredo Wally Barrón, Alicia Moreno, Álvaro Matute.

A piano constructed from skulls and bones has the ability to kill vampires.

The Munsters (TV Series) (*Familia Monster, La* [Spain]; *Me hirviöt* [Finland]; *Meet the Munsters* [U.S., working title]; *Monstres, Les* [France]; *Mostri, I* [Italy]; *Munsters, Los* [Argentina]; *Vi monster* [Finland, Swedish title]); U.S., 1964–1966; Comedy, Family/Television; 30 minutes/black and white/English/Mono; Kayro-Vue Productions.

Producers: Joe Connelly (producer, 71 episodes, 1964–1966), Bob Mosher. (producer, 71 episodes, 1964–1966); *Writing Credits*: Joe Connelly (29 episodes, 1964–1966), Bob Mosher (29 episodes,

Al Lewis, left, plays Vladimir "Grandpa Munster" Dracula, along with Yvonne De Carlo as Lily Munster and Fred Gwynne as Herman Munster in the television series *The Munsters* (U.S., 1964–1966).

1964–1966), Dick Conway (12 episodes, 1964–1966), Doug Tibbles (12 episodes, 1965–1966), Tom Adair (11 episodes, 1964–1966), James B. Allardice (11 episodes, 1964–1966), Ed Haas (9 episodes, 1964–1965), Norm Liebmann (9 episodes, 1964–1965), Richard Baer (5 episodes, 1965–1966), Roland MacLane (2 episodes, 1964), Allan Burns (2 episodes, 1965), Chris Hayward (2 episodes, 1965), George Tibbles (2 episodes, 1965); *Director*: Ezra Stone (27 episodes, 1964–1966), Norman Abbott (12 episodes, 1964–1965), Joseph Pevney (11 episodes, 1964–1966), Earl Bellamy (7 episodes, 1964–1965), Lawrence Dobkin (4 episodes, 1964), Jerry Paris (3 episodes, 1965), David Alexander (2 episodes, 1964), Gene Reynolds (2 episodes, 1966); *Cinematography*: Enzo A. Martinelli (23 episodes, 1965–1966), Walter Strenge (14 episodes, 1964–1965), Fred Mandl (10 episodes, 1964–1965), Lionel Lindon (7 episodes, 1964–1965), Monroe P. Askins (4 episodes, 1965), William Margulies (2 episodes, 1965–1966), Jacques R. Marquette (2 episodes, 1965), Bud Thackery (2 episodes, 1965); *Film Editing*: Bud S. Isaacs (59 episodes, 1964–1966), George Ohanian (5 episodes, 1966), Michael R. McAdam (3 episodes, 1965–1966); *Original Music*: Jack Marshall (70 episodes, 1964–1966); *Art Direction*: Henry Larrecq (53 episodes, 1964–1966), Frank Arrigo (7 episodes, 1964–1965), Raymond Beal (3 episodes, 1964–1965), Howard E. Johnson (2 episodes, 1964), John J. Lloyd (2 episodes, 1964); *Make-Up*: Karl Silvera (makeup artist, 71 episodes, 1964–1966), Abe Haberman (makeup artist, 70 episodes, 1964–1966), Michael Westmore (makeup artist, 70 episodes, 1964–1966), Perc Westmore (makeup artist, 70 episodes, 1964–1966), Bud Westmore (makeup artist, 65 episodes, 1964–1966), Larry Germain (hair stylist/makeup artist, 50 episodes, 1964–1966), Virginia Darcy (hair stylist, 18 episodes, 1964–1965); *Special Effects*: Ken Strickfaden (special effects, 1 episode, 1966), Chuck Gaspar (special effects, unknown episodes); *Cast*: in the order of Fred Gwynne (Herman Munster, 72 episodes, 1964–1966), Al Lewis (Grandpa, 72 episodes, 1964–1966), Yvonne De Carlo (Lily Munster, 71 episodes, 1964–1966), Butch Patrick Eddie (Wolfgang Munster, 71 episodes, 1964–1966), Pat

Priest (Marilyn Munster, 57 episodes, 1964–1966), Beverley Owen (Marilyn Munster, 15 episodes, 1964), Bob Hastings (The Raven, 10 episodes, 1964–1966), Mel Blanc (The Raven, 6 episodes, 1964–1966), Chet Stratton (Clyde Thornton, 4 episodes, 1964–1966), Edward Mallory (Jack, 4 episodes, 1964–1965), Harvey Korman (Dr. Leinbach, 3 episodes, 1964–1966), Paul Lynde (Dr. Dudley, 3 episodes, 1964–1965), Pat McCaffrie (Policeman, 3 episodes, 1964–1966), Jane Withers (Fanny Pike, 2 episodes, 1964–1966), Val Avery (Marty, 2 episodes, 1964–1965), Willis Bouchey (Mr. Bradley, 2 episodes, 1965–1966), Irwin Charone (Lester, 2 episodes, 1964–1965), John Hoyt (Barney Walters, 2 episodes, 1964–1965), Henry Beckman ("Leadfoot" Baylor, 2 episodes, 1965), Gene Blakely (Big Leo, 2 episodes, 1965), Marge Redmond (Miss Hazlett, 2 episodes, 1965), Johnny Silver (Blinky, 2 episodes, 1964–1966), Pat Harrington Jr. (Sonny Harkness, 2 episodes, 1964–1965), Frank Maxwell Coach (Roger Denman, 2 episodes, 1965), Bryan O'Byrne (Calvin, 2 epixsodes, 1965), Richard Reeves (Gil Craig, 2 episodes, 1964–1965), Joyce Jameson (Lou, 2 episodes, 1965–1966), Jackie Minty (Jack McGinty, 2 episodes, 1965–1966), Alma Murphy (Susan, 2 episodes, 1965), Bill Quinn (Attendant, 2 episodes, 1965), Walter Woolf King (George Washington, 2 episodes, 1964), (Dennis Cross Policeman, 2 episodes, 1965–1966), Helen Kleeb (The 1st Woman, 2 episodes, 1965–1966), Bella Bruck (Momma, 2 episodes, 1965), Henry Hunter The Mayor, 2 episodes1964–1965), Ronnie Dapo (Roger, 2 episodes, 1965), J. Edward McKinley (Mayor Handley, 2 episodes, 1965), Frank Gardner (Ralph, 2 episodes, 1965–1966), Bob Harvey (The Customer, 2 episodes, 1965–1966), Elsie Baker (Grandma Farber, 2 episodes, 1964–1965), John Fiedler (Mailman, 2 episodes, 1964), John Carradine (Mr. Gateman, 2 episodes, 1965–1966), Claire Carleton (Yolanda Cribbins, 2 episodes, 1964), Gary Owens (Dick Willet, 2 episodes, 1965–1966), Ray Montgomery (Father, 2 episodes, 1965), Michael Ross (The Campus Policeman, (2 episodes, 1964–1966), Vince Williams (2 episodes, 1964–1965), Vito Scotti (Man on Radio, 2 episodes, 1965–1966).

The Munsters is a sitcom about a family of monsters that lives in a human neighborhood. The father, Herman, is similar to Frankenstein's Monster, and his wife, Lily, is a vampire. Grandpa, sporting all-out Lugosi garb, is later revealed as Vladimir "Grandpa" Dracula. Herman and Lily's son, Eddie, is a werewolf.

The Munsters' Revenge; U.S., 1981; Comedy/Television; 96 minutes/color/English/Mono; Universal Pictures.

Producers: Arthur Alsberg (co-producer), Edward Montagne, Don Nelson (co-producer); *Writing Credits*: Norm Liebmann, Ed Haas, Allan Burns, Chris Hayward, Arthur Alsberg, Don Nelson; *Director*: Don Weis; *Cinematography*: Harry L. Wolf; *Film Editing*: Fred Baratta; *Original Music*: Vic Mizzy; *Art Direction*: James Martin Bachman, Curtis A. Schnell (uncredited); *Make-Up*: Karl Silvera, Michael F. Blake (uncredited), Abe Haberman (uncredited); *Special Effects*: Kevin Pike (uncredited) *Cast*: Fred Gwynne (Herman Munster), Al Lewis (Grandpa Munster), Yvonne De Carlo (Lily Munster) (as Yvonne DeCarlo), K.C. Martel (Eddie Munster), Jo McDonnell (Marilyn Munster), Bob Hastings (Phantom of the Opera), Peter Fox (Glen Boyle), Herb Voland (Police Chief Harry Boyle) (as Herbert Voland), Charles Macaulay (Police Commissioner), Colby Chester (Michael), Joseph Ruskin (Paulo), Sid Caesar (Dr. Dustin Diablo), Howard Morris (Igor), Ezra Stone (Dr. Lichtlighter), Michael McManus (Ralph), Sandy Champion (Patrolman Pete) (as Sandy-Alexander Champion), Gary Vinson (Patrolman Larry), Billy Sands (Shorty), Barry Pearl (Warren Thurston), Al White (Prisoner), Thomas Newman (Slim) (as Tom Newman), Anita Dangler (Elvira), Dolores Mann (Mrs. Furnstrom), Hillary Horan (The Girl), Kenny Rhodes (The Boy), Read Morgan (Loader #2), Mickey Deems (Loader #1), Lou Richards (Boyfriend [uncredited]).

The movie begins with the Munsters' trip to a wax museum to visit a display dedicated to their family. They soon discover that the wax replicas are robots that have been stealing from and terrorizing the town. Herman (Fred Gwynne) and Grandpa (Al Lewis) set out to clear their names in time for the family's annual Halloween celebration.

The Munsters' Scary Little Christmas; U.S., 1996; Comedy, Family; 91 minutes/color/English/Stereo; Michael R. Joyce Productions.

Producers: Leslie Belzberg (executive producer), Michael R. Joyce (supervising producer), John Landis, (executive producer), Tony Winley (co-producer); *Writing Credits*: Norm Liebmann (characters), Ed Haas (characters); *Director*: Ian Emes; *Cinematography*: Roger Lanser; *Film Editing*: M. Scott Smith; *Original Music*: Christopher L. Stone; *Special Effects*: Stuart Rowsell (special effects assistant); *Cast*: Sam McMurray (Herman Munster), Ann Magnuson (Lily Munster), Bug Hall (Eddie Munster), Sandy Baron (Grandpa Munster), Mary Woronov (Mrs. Dimwitty), Ed Gale (Larry), Arturo Gil (Lefty), Mark Mitchell (Santa), Jeremy Callaghan (Tom), Elaine Hendrix (Marilyn Munster), John Allen (Mr. Pawlikowski), Noel Ferrier (Door Knocker), Bruce Spence (Mr. Gateman), Kate Fischer (Pretty Girl in Bar), Patricia Howson

(Mrs Matagrano), Dominic Condon (Spooky Onlooker 1), Jonathan Biggins (Spooky Onlooker 2), Alan Zitner (Cop), Daniel Kellie (Glen), Michael Hamilton (Hector Barbieri), Malcolm Mudway (Burly Biker), Donald Cook (Quasimoto, the Hunchback), William Ten Eyck.

Eddie Munster becomes homesick for Transylvania, so the rest of the family gets together to try to make his holiday experience more enjoyable.

The Munsters Today (TV Series) (*The New Munsters* [U.S.]); U.S., 1988–1991; Comedy, Science Fiction/Television; 30 minutes/color/English/Mono; The Arthur Company.

Producers: Bill Rosenthal (story editor [30 episodes, 1988–1990]), Arthur L. Annecharico (executive producer [28 episodes, 1987–1991]), Lloyd J. Schwartz (executive producer [20 episodes, 1987–1991]), Patricia Fass Palmer (supervising producer [17 episodes, 1988–1989]), Bryan Joseph (producer/executive producer [8 episodes, 1988–1989]); *Writing Credits*: Bill Rosenthal (5 episodes, 1988–1990), Noah Taft (4 episodes, 1988–1990), Bryan Joseph (3 episodes, 1988–1989), Lloyd J. Schwartz (2 episodes, 1987–1989); *Director*: Peter Isacksen (8 episodes, 1988–1989), Lee Lochhead (3 episodes, 1988–1989), Doug Rogers (3 episodes, 1988–1989), Bob Claver (2 episodes, 1988–1989), Bruce Bilson, Bonnie Franklin, Dick Harwood, Marlene Laird, Russ Petranto, Jerry Ross; *Original Music*: Bill Fulton, Larry Groupé; *Art Direction*: Jimmy Flores (set construction foreman [8 episodes, 1987–1989]), Andy Jolliff (property assistant); *Make-Up*: David Abbott (makeup department head [13 episodes, 1987–1991]), Gilbert A. Mosko (makeup/makeup department head [10 episodes, 1987–1990]); *Cast*: John Schuck (Herman Munster [31 episodes, 1987–1991]), Lee Meriwether (Lily Munster [31 episodes, 1987–1991]), Jason Marsden (Edward "Eddie" Wolfgang Munster [31 episodes, 1987–1991]), Howard Morton ("Grandpa" Vladimir Dracula [31 episodes, 1987–1991]), Hilary Van Dyke (Marilyn Munster [27 episodes, 1988–1991]).

One of Grandpa's experiments went wrong, and the Munsters woke up in the '80s. Herman looks like Frankenstein's Monster, Lily is a vampire, Eddie is a werewolf, Howard Morton as "Grandpa" is Vladimir Dracula (30 episodes, 1987–1991), and Marilyn looks like a human.

My Life with Count Dracula; U.S., 2003; Documentary; 74 minutes/color/English/Mono; Hungry Jackal Productions.

Producers: Dustin Lance Black, Christopher Hoag; *Writing Credits*: Dustin Lance Black; *Director*: Dustin Lance Black; *Cinematography*: Brian Harris Krinsky; *Film Editing*: Dustin Lance Black; *Original Music*: Christoper Hoag; *Art Direction*: Dustin Lance Black; *Cast*: Forrest J Ackerman (Himself), Dean Devlin (Himself), George Clayton Johnson (Himself), Dr. Donald A. Reed (Himself), Bryan Singer (Himself), Alan White (Himself).

This documentary explores the life of Dr. Donald A. Reed, the founder of Count Dracula Society, the Saturn Awards, and the Academy of Science Fiction, Fantasy & Horror.

Mysterious Journeys (TV Series [2002 and 2007]), episode "The Hunt for Dracula"; U.S., Season 2, Episode 5, 24 October 2007; Documentary, Television; 45 minutes/English/color, black and white; Authentic Entertainment, Inc., Mike Mathis Productions.

Producer: Lauren Lexton, Tom Rogan, Valerie Chow, Megan Peterson, Mona Vasiloiu, Lawrence Williams, David Ballard, Cydney Kaplan; *Writing Credits*: Megan Peterson; *Director*: Megan Peterson; *Cinematography*: Pyongson Yim; *Film Editing*: Kurt Porter; *Original Music*: Scorekeepers Music; *Cast*: Erik Todd Dellums (Narrator), Evan Jonigkeit (Dracula), Andras Balough (Himself), Andrei Nicolau (Himself), Ana Maria Ignat (Herself), Father Nicolae ([of Curtea de Arges] Himself), Bishop Calinic ([of Curtea de Arges] Himself), Adriana Antihi (Herself). Christina Irina (Herself), Alex Priscu (Himself), Gabriel Moisescu (Himself), Paul Vortolomei (Himself).

This televised documentary explores sites in Romania that speak to the country's cultural and historical traditions concerning vampires, the historical Dracula, and Bram Stoker's novel.

Mystery and Imagination (TV Series [1966–1970]), episode "Dracula"; U.K., Season 4, Episode 3, 18 November 1968; Drama, Horror, Mystery/Television; 75 minutes/English/black and white/Mono; Independent Television (ITV).

Producers: Raymond Collier, Jonathan Alwyn (episode producer); *Writing Credits*: Charles Graham (adaptation) Bram Stoker (novel "Dracula"); *Director*: Patrick Dromgoole; *Original Music*: Paul Lewis; *Make-Up*: Don Semmens; *Cast*: Denholm Elliot (Dracula), Susan George (Lucy Weston), Bernard Archard (Dr. Van Helsing), James Maxwell (Dr. Seward), Suzanne Neve (Mina Harker), Corin Redgrave (Jonathan Harker), James Pope (Rowse), Phyllis Morris (Mrs. Perkins), Helena McCarthy (Mrs. Hoskins), Joan Hickson (Mrs. Weston), Hedley Goodall (Swales), Michael Da Costa (Jenkins), Tony Lane (Coachman), Nina Baden-Semper (Vampire), Marie Legrand (Vampire), Valerie Muller (Vampire).

Based on Bram Stoker's classic novel the movie takes place in an asylum in England, with Jonathan Harker telling Dr. Seward and Dr. Van Helsing of the things he saw in Transylvania. Meanwhile, Dracula has bitten Lucy Weston several times, thus turning her into a vampire. Dracula attempts to befriend his victims, in order to build their trust so he can bite their necks. He attacks Mina Harker, Jonathan Harker's wife, but he fails to bite her. Dr. Van Helsing decides to use her in an attempt to trap Dracula.

Mystery in Dracula's Castle; U.S., 1973; Comedy, Horror, Mystery/Television; 91 minutes/color/English/Mono/35mm; Walt Disney Productions.

Producer: Bill Anderson; *Writing Credits*: Sue Milburn; *Director*: Robert Totten; *Cinematography*: Charles F. Wheeler; *Film Editing*: Hugh Chaoupka; *Art Direction*: Malcolm C. Bert, John B. Mansbridge; *Make-Up*: La Rue Matheron, Robert J. Schiffer; *Cast*: Clu Gulager (Keith Raynor), Mariette Hartley (Marsha Booth), Johnny Whitaker (Alfie Booth), Mills Watson (Noah Baxter), John Fiedler (Bill Wasdahl), James T. Callahan (Sheriff Wyndham), Scott C. Kolden (Leonard Booth), Maggie Wellman (Jean Wyndham), Dave Thomson (Count Dracula [as Dave Thompson]), Ben Wrigley (Graverobber).

Leonard and Alfie Booth are out making a horror film using a Dracula-type character, and decide to use an old lighthouse as the castle. Unknown to the young men, two jewel thieves are using the lighthouse for something else, a hideout. The boys' dog takes the necklace, leading the thieves right into the middle of the action.

Nadja; U.S., 1994; Drama, Horror; 93 minutes/black and white/English/Dolby; Kino Link Company.

Producers: Andrew Fierberg, Amy Hobby, David Lynch, Mary Sweeney; *Writing Credits*: Michael Almereyda; *Director*: Michael Almereyda; *Cinematography*: Jim Denault; *Film Editing*: David Leonard; *Original Music*: Simon Fisher-Turner; *Make-Up*: Dina Doll (hair stylist, makeup artist), John Sahag; *Special Effects*: Arthur M. Jolly (special effects), Josh Turi (special effects props); *Cast*: Elina Löwensohn (Nadja), Nic Ratner (Bar Victim), Karl Geary (Renfield), Peter Fonda (Dracula/Dr. Van Helsing), Martin Donovan (Jim), Jack Lotz (Boxing Coach), Galaxy Craze (Lucy), David Lynch (Morgue Receptionist), Isabel Gillies (Waitress), José Zúñiga (Bartender), Bernadette Jurkowski (Dracula's Bride), Jeff Winner (Young Dracula), Sean (Béla), Suzy Amis (Cassandra), Jared Harris (Edgar), Bob Gosse (Garage Mechanic), Rome Neal (Garage Mechanic), Giancarlo Roma (Romanian Kid), Anna Roma (Romanian Mother), Thomas Roma (Romanian Policeman), Aleksander Rasic (Romanian Policeman), Miranda Russell (Lucy's Baby).

Dracula dies by a stake to the heart, and his daughter, Nadja, takes his cremated remains to Brooklyn to visit her brother. Nadja gives some of her blood to her sick brother. In the meantime, people are trying to kill Nadja, so that Dracula will be dead for good.

Nattens engel (*Angel of the Night* [Taiwan/U.S., DVD title]; *Àngel de la nit, L'* [Spain, Catalan title]; *Engel der Finsternis* [Germany]; *Nattens ängel* [Sweden]; *Nuit des vampires, La* [France] *Yön enkeli* [Finland]); Denmark, 1998; Horror; 98 minutes/color/English, Spanish, Danish/Stereo/35mm; Wise Guy Productions.

Producers: Henrik Danstrup (executive producer), Thomas Stegler (producer); *Writing Credits*: Lars Detlefsen, Shaky González; *Director*: Shaky González; *Cinematography*: Jacob Kusk; *Film Editing*: Miriam Nørgaard *Original Music*: Søren Hyldgaard; *Art Direction*: Eva Gøttrup, Mie Sand Sørensen; *Make-Up*: Ingemette Baun Christensen, Kristina Lauritsen, Liana Maj Madsen, Jeanne Müller (hair stylist, makeup artist), Christina Rasmussen (assistant makeup artist, hair stylist), Judy Springer (assistant hair stylist), Mette Strassmann (assistant hair stylist); *Special Effects*: Jesper N. Christiansen (puppeteer), Poul Arne Kring (puppeteer, special effects), Hans Peter Ludvigsen (special effects), Glenn E. Nielsen (special effects); *Cast*: Maria Stokholm (Rebecca [as Maria Karlsen]), Mette Louise Holland (Charlotte), Tomas Villum Jensen (Mads), Svend Johansen (Biskoppen), Claus Flygare (Politimester), Hans Henrik Voetmann (Borgmesteren), Ole Hvidman (Smeden), Karin Rørbeck (Marie), Lise-Lotte Norup (Leilah), Christian Grønvall (Rikard), Beate Bille (Rikards kone), Thomas Bo Larsen (Gary), Nikolaj Coster-Waldau (Frankie), Ulrich Thomsen (Alex), Mads Mikkelsen (Ronnie), Stefano González (Nick/Lumiere), Dennis Dean (Tim/Athos [as Dennis Dean Sølvberg]), Kenneth Carmohn (Stony/Aramis), Lenny Stjernelund (Martin/Porthos), Charlotte Juul (Lucky), Louise Boye (Cecilie), Anette Toftgaard (Sussy), Helle Sørensen (Cindy), Zlatko Buric (Taxachauffør), Miguel Martinez Vasques (Gammel Præst), Timm Mehrens (Monster), Hector Vega Mauricio (Esiah), Erik Holmey (Rico), Janus Nabil Bakrawi (Ricos håndlanger), Teis Bayer (Monster), Marina Bouras (Tanja), Thomas Eje (Boomer), Kasper Gaardsøe (Vred borger & Transvestit), Giada Hansen (Død pige), Henrik Jandorf (Jack), Emilie Schiøtt (Rikards datter), Marie Caroline Schjeldal (Tims kæreste [as Marie Scheldahl]).

The main character, Rebecca, inherits a mansion from her grandmother. She decides to take her best friend and her boyfriend to it to stay the weekend. While they were exploring the crypt, they discover a book that describes the life of a vampire. Eventually they find out that the vampire was Rebecca's great grandfather. Later that night, Rebecca becomes hypnotized and begins to recite an old ritual, which opens her great grandfather's coffin and gives him new life.

Necropolis; Italy, U.K., 1970; Horror, Fantasy; 124 minutes/color/German, French, English, Italian/Mono/35mm. Poli.

Producers: Gianni Barcelloni, Alan Power,; *Writing Credits*: Franco Brocani; *Director*: Franco Brocani (director), Giorgio Monti (first assistant director), Caroline Laure (second assistant director); *Cinematography*: Franco Lecca, Ivan Stoinov (as Ivan Stoynov); *Film Editing*: Ludovica Barbani (as M. Ludovica Barbani); *Original Music*: Gavin Bryars; *Art Direction*: Peter Steifel; *Make-Up*: Alfonso Gola; *Special Effects*: Alfonso Gola; *Cast*: Nicoletta Machiavelli (Nicoletta Macchiavelli), Tina Aumont, Pierre Clementi (Atilla), Paul Jabara, Carmelo Bene, Bruno Corazzari (Frankenstein's monster), Paolo Graziosi, Louis Waldon, Viva (Countess Bathory), Eva Krampen, Mimmo, aldo Mondino, Rada Rassimov, Thomas Rudy (as Thomas Rudi), George Willing (as Georg Willing).

An assortment of frightening, mythical creatures, including, Dracula, vampires, Frankenstein, and witches, among others, inflict evil on the world, including sacrificing virgins, and raising young women to use as sustenance.

Nella stretta morsa del ragno (*And Comes the Dawn ... but colored Red* [International English title]; *Dracula im Schloß des Schreckens* [West Germany]; *Dracula in the Castle of Blood* [International English title]; *E venne l'alba ... ma tinto di rosse* [Italy]; *Edgar Poe chez les morts vivants* [France, reissue title]; *Fantômes de Hurlevent, Les* [France, reissue title]; *Horrible noche del baile de los muertos, La* [Spain]; *In de greep van de spin* [Belgium, video title, Flemish title]; *In the Grip of the Spider* [International English title]; *Prisonnier de l'araignée, Le* [France, reissue title]; *Vampyrernas slott* [Sweden]; *Web of the Spider* [International English title]); France/Italy/West Germany, 1971; Horror; 109 minutes/color/Italian/Mono; Paris-Cannes Productions, Produzione DC7, Terra-Filmkunst.

Producers: Giovanni Addessi; *Writing Credits*: Giovanni Addessi (screenplay revision), Bruno Corbucci, Bruno Corbucci, Giovanni Grimaldi, Giovanni Grimaldi, Antonio Margheriti; *Director*: Antonio Margheriti (as Anthony M. Dawson); *Cinematography*: Guglielmo Mancori (as Memmo Mancori), Sandro Mancori, Silvano Spagnoli; *Film Editing*: Otello Colangeli, Fima Noveck; *Original Music*: Riz Ortolani; *Make-Up*: Maria Luisa Jilli, Angelo Malantrucco (assistant makeup artist), Nicla Palombi, Marisa Tilly (makeup artist, as Maria Luisa Tilli); *Special Effects*: Cataldo Galliano (special effects); *Cast*: Anthony Franciosa (Alan Foster), Michèle Mercier (Elisabeth Blackwood), Klaus Kinski (Edgar Allan Poe), Peter Carsten (Dr. Carmus), Silvano Tranquilli (William Perkins), Karin Field (Julia), Raf Baldassarre (Herbert), Irina Maleeva (Elsie Perkins), Enrico Osterman (Lord Thomas Blackwood), Marco Bonetti (Maurice), Vittorio Fanfoni, Carla Mancini, Paolo GozliNo.

Alan Foster, a journalist, makes a bet that he can spend an entire night at the notoriously haunted Blackwood Castle, but as things would have it, he learns that the rumours of ghosts at the castle are indeed frighteningly true.

Nem As Enfermeiras Escapam; Brazil, 1977; Comedy; 80 minutes/color/Portuguese/Mono; Pheonix Filmes do Brasil.

Producers: Lincoln Bueno, Décio Garcia Nascimento; *Writing Credits*: André José Adler, Hugo Bidet, Lincoln Bueno, Marcos Rey; *Director*: André José Adler; *Cinematography*: A.J. Moreiras; *Film Editing*: Lúcio Braun; *Original Music*: Eduardo Souto Neto, Tavito; *Art Direction*: Waldir Siebert; *Make-Up*: Cecílio Giglioti; *Cast*: Kamal Bacarat, (Enfermeiro), Mário Benvenutti (Diretor do Hospital), Hugo Bidet (Médico), Carlos Bucka (Dracula), Ana Cunha, Sérgio Cunha, Oswaldo D'ávila (Médico), Durval de Souza (Adolfo), Cecílio Giglioti, Sérgio Hingst (Dr. Marhaság), Mário Jorge (Repórter da TV), Viana Júnior (Cacique Machu Paka), Carlos Koppa (Enfermeiro), Christina Kristner (Doutora), Marivalda (Ninfomaníaca), Marta Moyano (Enfermeira), Maria Luiza Muller, Cavagnole Neto (Médico), Armando Paschoallin, Alaide Peyton (Enfermeira), Fernando Reski (Detective, "Carmen Miranda"), Célia Ribeiro, Neide Ribeiro (Enfermeira), Maria do Roccio (Noiva), Sérgio Ropperto (Sádico), Crayton Sarzy (Homem-Galinha), Cleide Singer, José Júlio Spiewak, Marthié Synara.

The New Scooby-Doo Mysteries (TV Series [1984–1985]), episode "Halloween Hassle at Dracula's Castle, Part I"; U.S., Season 1, 27 October 1984; Comedy/Television, Animation; 22 minutes/color/English; Hanna-Barbera Studios.

Producers: Joseph Barbera, William Hanna, Art Scott, George Singer, Iwao Takamoto (creative producer), Kay Wright; *Writing Credits*: Paul Dini; *Director*: Oscar Dufau; *Original Music*: Hoty Curtin *Cast*: Don Messick (Scooby-Doo, Scrappy-Doo), Casey Kasem (Shaggy Rogers), Heather North (Daphne Blake), Maria Frumkin (Velma Dinkley), Frank Welker (Fred Jones).

Scooby and the gang are attending a Halloween party, at which their help soon becomes needed.

The New Scooby-Doo Mysteries (TV Series [1984–1985]), episode "Halloween Hassle at Dracula's Castle, Part II"; U.S., Season 1, 27 October 1984; Comedy/Television, Animation; 11 minutes/color/English/English; Hanna-Barbera Studios.

Producers: Joseph Barbera, William Hanna, Art Scott, George Singer, Iwao Takamoto, Kay Wright; *Writing Credits*: Paul Dini; *Director*: Oscar Dufau; *Original Music*: Hoty Curtin; *Cast*: Don Messick (Scooby-Doo, Scrappy-Doo), Casey Kasem (Shaggy Rogers), Heather North (Daphne Blake), Maria Frumkin (Velma Dinkley), Frank Welker (Fred Jones).

Scooby and the gang have a run-in with Dracula and his monster friends in this Halloween episode.

The New Shmoo (TV Series [1987–1988]), episode "The Return of Dracula"; U.S., episode 11, 16 February 1988; Mystery, Comedy/Animation; 30 minutes/color/English; Hanna-Barbera Studios.

Producers: Art Scott, Alex Lovy; *Writing Credits*: Gene Ayres, Art Browne, Jr., Buzz Dixon, Donald F. Glut, Len Janson, Dale Kirby, Glenn Leopold, Chuck Menville, J. Michael Reaves, Jim Ryan; *Director*: Ray Patterson, Carl Urbano, Oscar Dufau, George Gordon; *Film Editing*: Gil Iverson; *Original Music*: Hoyt Curtin; *Art Direction*: Robert Alvarez, Frank Andrina, Colin Baker, Anne Marie Bardwell, Ed Barge, Bob Bemiller, Robert Bransford, James Brummett, Oliver Callahan, Roger Chiasson, John Conning, Daniel De La Vega, Elaine Despins, Joan Drake, Judith Ann Drake, Gail Finkeldei, Hugh Fraser, Al Gaivoto, Jeff Hall, Bob Hathcock, Fred Hellmich, Bill Hutten, Aundre Knutson, Teresa Loewy, Hicks Lokey, Tony Love, Mauro Maressa, Burt Medall, Tran Vu Minh, Ken Muse, Eduardo Olivares, Margaret Parkes, Lester Pegues, Jr., Harry Rasmussen, Morey Reden, Joel Seibel, Leo Sullivan, Richard Trueblood, Robert Tyler, John Walker, Allen Wilzbach; *Cast*: Frank Welker (Shmoo), Dolores Cantu-Primo (Nita), Chuck McCann (Billy Joe), Bill Idelson (Mickey).

Shmoo is a creature that can turn into any shape that he wants or needs to be. In this episode, Shmoo and the others go to Transylvania to solve the mystery of Count Dracula returning and kidnapping villagers. They discover that Dracula was an actor playing Dracula who was making the missing villagers dig for gold.

Night Bites: Women and Their Vampires; U.S., 2003; Documentary; 60 minutes/color/English.

Producers: Jonathan Blaugrund, Belt Colt, Scott M. Cort, Chris Tragos; *Writing Credits*: Maitland McDonaugh; *Director*: Inbal B. Lessner; *Cinematography*: Yaron Orbach; *Film Editing*: Inbal B. Lessner; *Original Music*: Daniel Lessner; *Make-Up*: Denise Hooper; *Cast*: Marti Noxon (Herself), John Landis (Himself), Elvis Mitchell (Himself), Stephanic Romanov (Herself), Ann Manguson (Herself), Nancy Collins (Herself), David S. Goyer (Himself), Maitland McDonaugh (Herself), Anne Rice (Herself), Shazia (Herself).

This documentary explores the transformation of the vampire's portrayal over time. The vampire has become more and more sexual over time towards women, according to the Women's Entertainment Channel.

Night Court (TV Series [1984–1992]), episode "Death Takes a Halloween"; U.S., Season 8, Episode 5, 26 October 1990; Comedy/Television; 30 minutes/color/English/Stereo; Warner Bros. Studios, Starry Night Productions.

Producers: Kevin Kelton, Fred Rubin, Bob Underwood; *Writing Credits*: Harry Anderson; *Director*: Jim Drake; *Cinematography*: Charles L. Barbee; *Original Music*: Jack Elliott (Composer); *Cast*: Harry Anderson (Judge Harry T. Stone), Melba Englander (Hooker), Brian Kaiser (Werewolf), John Larroquette (Dan Fielding), Doug MacHugh (Dracula), Raf Mauro (Bum), Richard Moll (Nostradamus "Bull" Shannon), Steven J. Oliver (Burglar), Markie Post (Christine Sullivan), Charles Robinson (Mac Robinson), Stephen Root (Spirit of Death), Blanche Rubin (Muriel Brown), Marsha Warfield (Rosalind "Roz" Russell).

A defendant pulled in on a minor charge claims to be the Angel of Death, and says that Harry has to release him. Harry jails him for contempt of court, but begins to feel uncertain as reports come in of people miraculously surviving fatal accidents all over the city. Even more worried is Dan, whose own obituary has appeared in the paper.

Night Gallery (TV Series [1970–1973]), episode "A Matter of Semantics" (*Galería nocturna* [Venezuela]; *Rod Serling's Night Gallery* [U.S.]; *Rod Serling's Wax Museum* [U.S., working title]; *Yöjuttu* [Finland]); U.S., Season 2, Episode 23, 10 November 1971; Mystery, Horror/Television, Short; 2:22 minutes/color/English/Mono; Universal TV.

Producers: Jack Laird, Anthony Redman; *Writing Credits*: Gene R. Kearney (as Gene Kearney); *Director*: Jack Laird; *Cinematography*: Lionel Lindon; *Film Editing*: Jean Jacques Berthelot (as Jean J. Berthelot), David Rawlins; *Art Direction*: Joe Alves (as Joseph Alves Jr.); *Cast*: Monie Ellis (Candy Striper), E.J. Peaker (Nurse), Cesar Romero (Dracula), Rod Serling (Host [as himself]).

In this featurette, Dracula approaches a nurse at a blood bank to procure a "loan."

Night Gallery (TV Series [1970–1973]), episode "A Midnight Visit to the Neighborhood Blood

Bank" (*Galería nocturna* [Venezuela]; *Rod Serling's Night Gallery* [U.S.]; *Rod Serling's Wax Museum* [U.S., working title]; *Yöjuttu* [Finland]); U.S., Season 2, Episode 27, 17 November 1971; Mystery, Comedy, Horror/Television, Short; 1:35 minutes/color/English/Mono; Universal TV.

Producers: Jack Laird; *Writing Credits*: Jack Laird; *Director*: William Hale; *Cinematography*: Lionel Lindon; *Film Editing*: Jean Jacques Berthelot, Larry Lester, David Rawlins; *Original Music*: Art Direction: Joe Alves; *Make-Up*: Bud Westmore; *Cast*: Victor Buono (Vampire), Journey Laird (Intended Victim), Rod Serling (Host [as himself]).

A rather stocky Dracula-type vampire preys on a sleeping young woman in her bedchamber one night after flying through an open window in the form a bat.

Night Gallery (TV Series [1970–1973]), episode "The Devil Is Not Mocked" (*Galería nocturna* [Venezuela]; *Rod Serling's Night Gallery* [U.S.]; *Rod Serling's Wax Museum* [U.S., working title]; *Yöjuttu* [Finland]); U.S., Season 2, Episode 19, 27 October 1971; Mystery, Fantasy, Horror, Thriller/Television; 50 minutes/color/English/Mono; Universal TV.

Producers: Jack Laird; *Writing Credits*: Gene R. Kearney (teleplay [as Gene Kearney]), Manly Wade Wellman (short story "The Devil Is Not Mocked"); *Director*: Gene R. Kearney; *Cinematography*: Lionel Lindon, Leonard J. South; *Film Editing*: David Rawlins, Sam Vitale; *Original Music*: Paul Glass; *Art Direction*: Joe Alves; *Make-Up*: Bud Westmore; *Cast*: Helmut Dantine (General von Grunn), Francis Lederer (Dracula), Hank Brandt (Kranz), Martin Kosleck (Hugo), Gino Gottarelli (Radio Man), Mark de Vries (Machine Gunner), Rod Serling (Host [as himself]).

Nazi soldiers invade the Balkans and attempt to take control of a castle, whose owner turns out to be Count Dracula.

Night Gallery (TV Series [1970–1973]), episode "How to Cure the Common Vampire" (*Galería nocturna* [Venezuela]; *Rod Serling's Night Gallery* [U.S.]; *Rod Serling's Wax Museum* [U.S., working title]; *Yöjuttu* [Finland]); U.S., Season 3, Episode 16, 27 May 1973; Mystery, Fantasy, Horror, Science Fiction, Thriller/Television; 26 minutes/color/English/Mono; Universal TV.

Producers: Burt Astor, Jack Laird, Anthony Redman, Anthony Redman, Herbert Wright; *Writing Credits*: Jack Laird (teleplay); *Director*: Jack Laird; *Cinematography*: Lloyd Ahern, Leonard J. South; *Film Editing*: David Rawlins, Sam Vitale; *Original Music*: Eddie Sauter; *Art Direction*: Joe Alves (as Joseph Alves Jr.); *Cast*: Johnny Brown (Man with Stake), Richard Deacon (Man with Mallet), Rod Serling (Host [as himself]).

This episode concerns a brief story about vampires and the hunters who pursue them. The vampire in this particular vignette is a Dracula-type vampire.

Night of the Ghouls (*Dr. Acula* [U.S., original script title]; *Revenge of the Dead*); U.S., 1959; Horror; 69 minutes/black and white/English/Mono; A Fun Ed Wood Film.

Producers: J.M.A.; Walter Brannon; Anthony Cardoza; Gordon Chesson; J.C. Foxworthy (as Major J.C. Foxworthy, U.S.M.C.R., Ret.]); Paul Marco; Tom Mason; Marg. Usher; Edward D. Wood Jr.; *Writing Credits*: Edward D. Wood Jr.; *Director*: Edward D. Wood Jr.; *Cinematography*: William C. Thompson; *Film Editing*: Edward D. Wood Jr.; *Art Direction*: Kathy Wood; *Make-Up*: Harry Thomas; *Special Effects*: Unknown; *Cast*: Kenne Duncan (Karl/Dr. Acula); Duke Moore (Lt. Daniel Bradford [as "Duke" Moore]); Tor Johnson (Lobo); Valda Hansen (Sheila, the White Ghost); Johnny Carpenter (Capt. Robbins [as John Carpenter]); Paul Marco (Patrolman Paul Kelton); Don Nagel (Sgt. Crandel); Bud Osborne (Mr. Darmoor); Jeannie Stevens (The Black Ghost/Mannequin); Harvey B. Dunn (Henry); Margaret Mason (Martha); Clay Stone (Gigolo); Marcelle Hemphill (Mrs. Maude Wingate Yates Foster); Tom Mason (Wingate Foster's Ghost); James La Maida (Patrolman Hall).

Dr. Acula is a phony medium, accompanied by a fake ghost and a man dressed in rags with horrible scar makeup. He travels around pretending to contact dead relatives but accidentally succeeds once. The newly arisen corpses bury Dr. Acula alive.

Night People; U.K., 2005; Drama; 90 minutes/color/English; Mead Kerr Ltd.

Producers: Claire Kerr; *Writing Credits*: Jack Dickson, Adrian Mead; *Director*: Adrian Mead; Cinematography: Scott Ward; *Film Editing*: Mark Jenkins; *Original Music*: Iain Cook; *Art Direction*: Stephen Bryce; *Make-Up*: Karen Brotherston, Maxine Dallas; *Cast*: Anthony Beselle (Father Matthew), Alastair Bruce (Dracula), Katrina Bryan (Jane), James Bryce (Bald Man), Kellyanne Farquhar (Mary), Frank Gilhooley (Andy), Sandy Grierson (Wizard), Vivienne Harvey (Lizzie), Sean Kane (Yuppie Man), Louise Ludgate (Social Worker), Neil Mackay (Josh), Michael MacKenzie (William), Anthony Martin (David), Alan McCafferty (Stewart), Kirstin Murray (Yuppie Woman), James Paterson (Bradley), Cara Shandley (Kelly), Megan Shandley (Angie), Darren Simpson (Zombie), Jim Sturgeon (Mal), Lily Waterton (Alison).

This film tells the story of five different people (Stewart, Matthew, David, Jane, and a blind man). Each character faces a different challenge, with life-altering decisions hanging in the balance. One character's dilemma involves Alastair Bruce's character, Dracula.

Nightmare: The Birth of Victorian Horror (*Nightmare: The Birth of Horror* [U.K.]); U.K., 1996; Documentary; 60 minutes/color/English.

Writing Credits: Christopher Frayling; *Cast*: Christopher Frayling (Himself/Presenter).

Christopher Frayling discusses Bram Stoker's character Dracula. He explores the novel as he travels across Europe to Castle Dracula.

La Noche de Walpurgis (*A Vámpírok éjjele* [Hungary]; *Blood Moon* [undefined]; *Furie des vampires, La* [France]; *Messe nere della contessa Dracula, Le* [Italy]; *Nacht der Vampire* [West Germany]; *Shadow of the Werewolf* [undefined]; *The Werewolf Versus Vampire Women* [U.S.]; *The Werewolf's Shadow* [undefined]; *Werewolf Shadow* [U.S.]); Spain, 1971; Horror; 85 minutes/color/Spanish/Mono; Plata Films S.A., HIFI Stereo 70 Kg.

Producers: Salvadore Romero; *Writing Credits*: Paul Naschy, Hans Munkel; *Director*: León Klimovsky; *Cinematography*: Leopoldo Villaseñor; *Film Editing*: Antonio Gimeno; *Original Music*: Antón García Abril; *Art Direction*: Gumersindo Andrés; *Make-Up*: José Luis Morales, María Carmen Alberdi (assistant make-up artist), Nuria Paradela; *Special Effects*: Antonio Molina, Juan Díaz; *Cast*: Paul Naschy (Waldemar Daninsky), Gaby Fuchs (Elvira), Barbara Capell (Genevieve Bennett [as Bárbara Capell]), Andrés Resino (Inspector Marcel), Yelena Samarina (Elizabeth Daninsky), José Marco (Pierre), Betsabé Ruiz (Pierre's girl [as Betsabe Sharon]), Barta Barri (Muller), Luis Gaspar (Distraught man), Ruperto Ares, María Luisa Tovar (First female victim), Julio Peña (Dr. Hartwig [coroner]), Patty Shepard (Countess Wandesa Dárvula de Nadasdy [as Paty Shepard]).

Traveling through the French countryside, Elvira and her friend Genevieve search for the lost tomb of a medieval murderess and supposed vampire Countess Wandessa. They come upon the castle of Waldemar Daninsky, who offers an invitation for the women to stay. While Waldemar is showing Elvira the tomb in which the countess supposedly rests, Elvira, by accident, causes the vampire to return to life.

Nocturna (*Granddaughter of Dracula* [undefined]); U.S., 1979; Comedy, Horror; 85 minutes/English/color/Mono; Compass International Pictures.

Producers: Vernon P. Becker (producer [as Vernon Becker]), Nai Bonet, Irwin Yablans; *Writing Credits*: Nai Bonet (story), Harry Hurwitz (writer [as Harry Tampa]); *Director*: Harry Hurwitz (as Harry Tampa); *Cinematography*: Mac Ahlberg; *Film Editing*: Ian Maitland; *Original Music*: Norman Bergen, Reid Whitelaw; *Art Direction*: Steve Davita, Jack Krueger; *Make-Up*: Pamela Jenrette, Gigi Williams; *Cast*: Yvonne De Carlo (Jugula), John Carradine (Dracula), Nai Bonet (Nocturna), Antony Hamilton (Jimmy), Marcus Anthony (Transylvania Character), John Blyth Barrymore (Punk Vampire), Ivery Bell (The Moment of Truth), John Epstein (John), Toby Handman (BSA Member), Norris Harris (The Moment of Truth), Michael Harrison (The Moment of Truth), Frank Irizarry (Disk Jockey), William H. Jones Jr. (The Moment of Truth), Adam Keefe (BSA President), Irwin Keyes (Transylvania Character), Albert Ottenheimer (Dr. Bernstein), Sy Richardson (RH Factor), Thomas Ryan (Policeman), Tony Sanchez (Victim), Al Sapienza (Musician), Jerry Sroka (Musician), Brother Theodore (Theodore), Monica Tidwell (Brenda), Ron Toler (Taxi Driver), Angelo Vignari (BSA Member), A.C. Weary (Musician).

Dracula's granddaughter, Nocturna, is caring for her grandfather, Dracula, when she falls in love with a mortal guitarist, Jimmy, as he plays for the Claret Room at Hotel Transylvania (Castle Dracula). She eventually follows him to New York in an effort to be with Jimmy and become normal. Dracula tries to bring Nocturna back home, and goes to New York with Theodore and stays with his ex, Jugula. Through conflict with Theodore and Dracula, Nocturna stays in New York and becomes mortal with Jimmy at sunrise.

Nohasfrontwo; U.S., 2002; Horror/Short; 9 minutes/black and white/English; Dirt Road Productions.

Producers: Jason Penarelli; *Writing Credits*: Jason Penarelli; *Director*: Jason Penarelli; *Cinematography*: Peter Huntley, Jason Penarelli, Robert Silva; *Film Editing*: Jason Penarelli; *Original Music*: Pauline Laciste, Christopher J. Matalone; *Make-Up*: Christine Bowen (special makeup effects artist); *Special Effects*: Lee Cressey (special effects); *Cast*: Melissa Cyfers (Girl in park), Maria De Los Angeles (Woman in park), Michele Dorantes-Mejia (Maid), Oskar Garcia (Jogger), Michael Healy (Dracula Jr. as a child), Peter Huntley (Dracula Sr.), Christopher J. Matalone (Dracula Jr.), Cynthia Novella (Dracula's Mother), Jamie Waterman (Victim).

Dracula Jr. receives word from his father, Dracula, that he must kill, though he lost his fangs in a childhood golfing accident. Dracula Jr. sets out to be a fearsome killer like his father, but without his fangs, no one respects or fears him at all.

Noroi no yakata: Chi o sû me (*Bloodsucking Eyes* [undefined]; *Bloodthirsty Eyes* [International]; *Dracula's Lust for Blood* [U.S.] *Drakoulas tou Fujiyama, O* [Greece]; *Japula* [undefined]; *Jezioro wampirów*

[Poland]; *Lake of Death* [undefined]; *Lake of Dracula* [U.S.]; *Sangue di Dracula, Il* [Italy]); Japan, 1971; Horror; 82 minutes/color/Japanese/Mono; Toho Company.

Producers: Fumio Tanaka; *Writing Credits*: Ei Ogawa, Masura Takesue; *Director*: Michio Yamamoto; *Cinematography*: Rokuro Nishigaki; *Film Editing*: Hisashi Kondo; *Original Music*: Riichiro Manabe; *Special Effects*: Teruyoshi Nakano; *Cast*: Midori Fujita (Akiko Kashiwagi), Osahide Takahashi (Dr. Saeki Takashi), Sanae Emi (Natsuko Kashiwagi), Shin Kishida (The Vampire) Tadao Fumi, Tadao Futami, Mika Katsuragi, Tatsuo Matsushita, Kei'ichi Noda, Yasuzo Ogawa, Wataru Omae, Hideji Otaki, Suji Otaki, Fusako Tachibana, Kaku Takashina.

A coffin is delivered to a small Japanese village, but the occupant is still alive. The only witness to this gets bitten, and the Vampire terrorizes the village, while a doctor tries to figure the whole thing out.

Nosferatu; France, 2002; Horror/Television, Animation; 60 minutes/color/French/Stereo; Wolfland Pictures.

Producers: Alexandre Brillant; *Writing Credits*: Philippe Druillet; *Director*: Philippe Druillet; *Film Editing*: Jean-Philippe Adande; *Original Music*: Andre Hervee; *Art Direction*: Pierre Meloni (lead graphic designer), Philippe Druillet (storyboards); *Cast*: Jean Rochefort (Nosferatu [voice]).

Nosferatu, eine Symphonie des Grauens (*Nosferatu* [Brazil/Poland/Sweden; U.S., short title]; *Nosferatu le vampire* [Canadian French title/France]; *Die Zwölfte Stunde — Eine Nacht des Grauens* [Austria, recut version]; *Nosferatu — symfonia grozy* [Poland, informal literal title]; *Nosferatu el vampiro* [Spain]; *Nosferatu il vampiro* [Italy]; *Nosferatu the Vampire* [U.S.]; *Nosferatu, a Symphony of Horror;* [undefined]; *Nosferatu, a Symphony of Terror* (undefined); *Nosferatu, o Vampiro* [Portugal]; *Nosferatu, una simfonia del terror* [Spain, Catalan title]; *Terror of Dracula* (undefined); *Upír Nosferatu* [Czechoslovakia]); Germany, 1922; Horror; 94 minutes/black and white/Silent; Jofa-Atelier Berlin-Johannisthal, Prana-Film GmbH.

Producers: Enrico Dieckmann, Albin Grau; *Writing Credits*: Henrik Galeen, Bram Stoker; *Director*:

Max Schreck plays Graf Orlok (a.k.a. Count Dracula) in the earliest surviving *Dracula* film, *Nosferatu, eine Symphonie des Grauens* (Germany, 1922).

F.W. Murnau; *Cinematography*: Fritz Arno Wagner, Günther Krampf (uncredited); *Original Music*: James Bernard, Hans Erdmann, Carlos U. Garza, Timothy Howard, Richard Marriott, Richard O'Meara, Hans Posegga, Peter Schirmann, Bernd Wilden Art direction: Albin Grau; *Cast*: Max Schreck (Graf Orlok), Gustav von Wangenheim (Hutter [as Gustav v. Wangenheim]), Greta Schröder (Ellen Hutter, seine Frau [as Greta Schroeder]), Alexander Granach (Knock, ein Häusermakler), Georg H. Schnel (Westenra — Hutters Freund [as G.H. Schnell]), Ruth Landshoff (Lucy, Westenras Frau), John Gottowt (Professor Bulwer, ein Paracelsianer), Gustav Botz (Professor Sievers, der Stadtartzt), Max Nemetz (Käpitän der Demeter), Wolfgang Heinz (Matrose 1), Albert Venohr (Matrose 2), Eric van Viele (Matrose 3), Karl Etlinger (uncredited), Guido Herzfeld Wirt (uncredited), Fanny Schreck (Krankenschwester im Hospital [uncredited]), Hardy von Francois (Arzt im Hospital [uncredited]), Heinrich Witte (Wärter im Irrenhaus [uncredited]).

Hutter and Ellen are newlyweds who receive news that Hutter is to arrange for Count Orlok's purchase of a home close to the Hutton's house in Bremen. Upon staying with the Count, Hutter is attacked and drained by the Count, but he narrowly escapes. While he is hospitalized, the Count moves into the house close to Hutter and Ellen's. People start to die around the area, and this is blamed to an alleged plague originating from the Count's ship. The "Book of Vampires" instructs Ellen how to rid everyone of the evil vampire.

Nosferatu: Phantom der Nacht (*Nosferatu, vampiro de la noche* [Mexico/Spain]; *Nosferatu* [Argentina]; *Nosferatu— Fantom noci* [Czechoslovakia]; Nosferatu — O Vampiro da Noite [Brazil]; Nosferatu — fantôme de la nuit [France]; Nosferatu — nattens vampyr [Sweden]; *Nosferatu— wampir* [Poland]; *Nosferatu— yön valtias* [Finland] *Nosferatu the Vampyre* [U.S.]; *Nosferatu, o Fantasma da Noite* [Portugal]; *Nosferatu, principe della note* [Italy]); West Germany, 1979; Horror; 107 minutes/color/German/Mono/35mm; Werner Herzog Filmproduktion.

Producers: Werner Herzog, Walter Saxer, Michael Gruskoff, Daniel Toscan du Plantier; *Writing Credits*: Werner Herzog, Bram Stoker; *Director*:

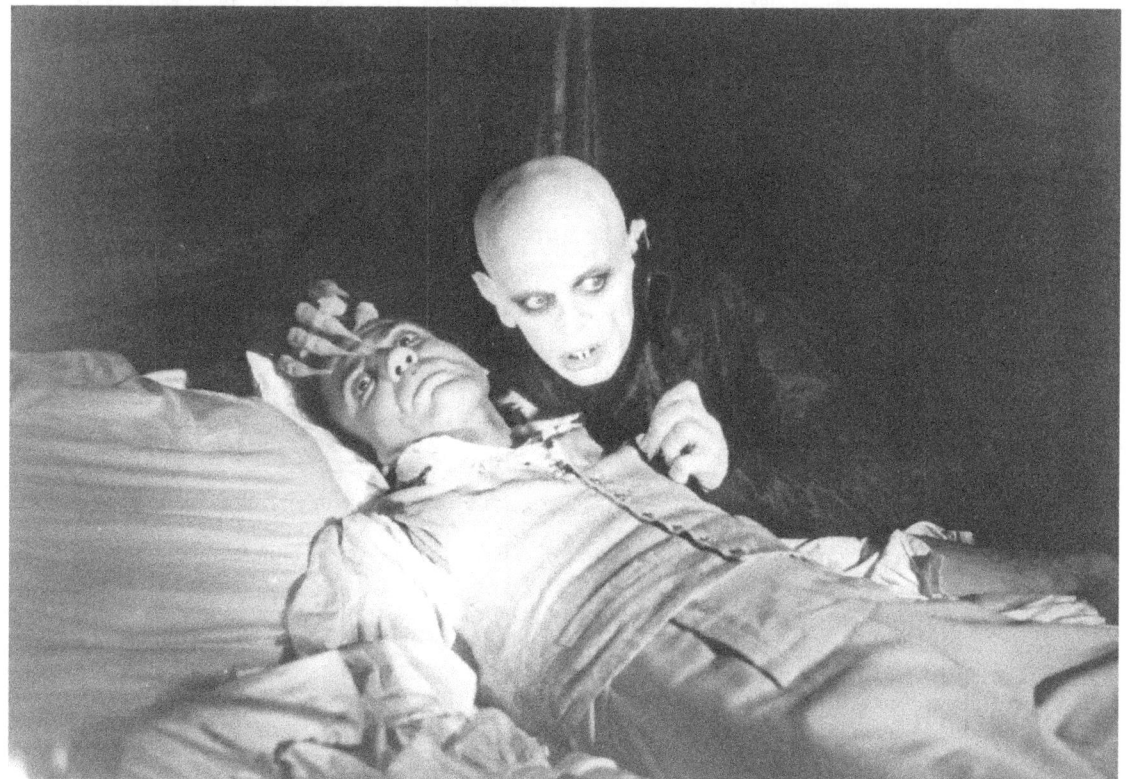

Klaus Kinski, right, plays Dracula opposite Bruno Ganz as Jonathan Harker in *Nosferatu: Phantom der Nacht* (West Germany, 1979).

Werner Herzog; *Cinematography*: Jörg Schmidt-Reitwein; *Film Editing*: Beate Mainka-Jellinghaus; *Original Music*: Popol Vuh; *Art Direction*: Henning von Gierke; *Make-Up*: Dominique Colladant, Reiko Kruk, Ludovic Paris; *Special Effects*: Cornelius Siegel *Cast*: Klaus Kinski (Count Dracula), Isabelle Adjani (Lucy Harker), Bruno Ganz (Jonathan Harker), Roland Topor (Renfield), Walter Ladengast (Dr. Van Helsing), Dan van Husen (Warden), Jan Groth (Harbormaster), Carsten Bodinus (Schrader), Martje Grohmann (Mina), Rijk de Gooyer (Town official) (as Ryk de Gooyer), Clemens Scheitz (Clerk Lo van Hensbergen), John Leddy (Coachman), Margiet van Hartingsveld (Vrouw), Tim Beekman (Coffinbearer), Jacques Dufilho (Captain), Michael Edols (Lord of the manor [uncredited]), Stefan Husar (uncredited), Norbert Losch (uncredited), Johan te Slaa (uncredited), Beverly Walker (Nun [uncredited]).

Newlyweds Jonathan and Lucy Harker's honeymoon is cut short when Jonathan is sent to Transylvania by his employer, Renfield, to sell a house to Count Dracula. Jonathan travels to Transylvania, encounters Dracula, and is bitten by him. He manages to escape Dracula and return home to Lucy. The house Dracula bought happens to be across the street from the Harkers. Dracula begins killing people, but the deaths are attributed to the plague. It is Lucy who manages to distract Dracula until after the sun rises so he cannot escape and is ultimately destroyed.

Nosferatu's Crush; U.S., 2006; Comedy, Horror 93 minutes/color/English; Mystic Night Pictures.

Producers: Mike Burke (Producer); *Writing Credits*: Mike Burke; *Director*: Mike Burke; *Cinematography*: Mike Burke, Sylvia Kovacs; *Film Editing*: Mike Burke; *Original Music*: Peter Lucibelli; *Cast*: Mike Burke (Vladimir Dracula III), Malissa Longo (Rebekah), Lady Altovise (Special Agent Green), Kristy White (Special Agent Kelly), John Gaydos (Tony), Angalisha Marie (Electra/Evil Vampire Woman), Sylvia Kovacs (Eliza), Xaviera Desgrottes (Serena), Katie Kyle Roche (Tara Livingston), Priscilla Jones (Renee), Robert Rickenbaker (Thomas), Mac Gray (Dexter), Chiko Mendez (Leo), Sami Malin (Mel).

While living in 21st century America, Vlad Dracula III is faced with a problem. People are being attacked and killed in his town, and the blame is being placed on his shoulders. Insisting upon his innocence, he decides to get a lawyer and falls in love with her.

Olliver's Adventures (TV Series), episode "What a Pain in the Neck" (*Ollie's Under-the-Bed Adventures* [original title]); Canada, 2002; Family/Television, Animation; 7 minutes/color/English; Collideascope Digital Productions.

Producers: Allison Outhit, Michael-Andreas Kuttner, Steven J.P. Comeau, Beth Stevenson; *Writing Credits*: Edward Kay, Michael Best, George Westerholm, Tara Doyle, Jeffrey Hirschfield, Vicki Grant, Dennise Fordham, Karen Janigan; *Director*: Ron Doucet, Brian Howald; *Film Editing*: Christopher Cooper; *Original Music*: Blain Morris *Cast*: Joanne Miller (Olliver), Glenn Lefchak (Jorge, Trog), Tara Doyle (Tara), Jacqueline Thillaye (Mom, Gertie, Agnes, Larry, Barry), Brian Heighton (Cray), Lex Gigeroff (Cuddle Cubs), Jeremy Webb (Ms. Grumply).

When Olliver and his family attend a fancy restaurant, they notice that their waiter bears an eerie resemblance to Dracula. When Trogg is kidnapped by Dracula, the family discovers that Trogg is in fact modeling the kitchen staff's Halloween costumes.

100 Years of Horror: Blood-Drinking Beings; U.S., 1996; Documentary; 23 minutes/color, black and white/English; Simitar Entertainment.

Producers: Dante J. Pugliese; *Writing Credits*: Ted Newsom, Jeff Forrester; *Director*: Ted Newsom; *Film Editing*: Brian Q. Kelley, Trudi Jo Marie Keck, John D. Johnson; *Cast*: Roy Ward Baker (Himself), Roger Corman (Himself), Robert Cornthwaite (Himself), Christopher Lee (Himself/Host), Ferdy Mayne (Himself), Dick Miller (Himself), Caroline Munro (Herself), Jimmy Sangster (Himself), Brinke Stevens (Herself).

This documentary delves into the blood-sucking characters of past horror films.

100 Years of Horror: The Monster Makers; U.S., 1996; Documentary; 23 minutes/color, black and white/English; Simitar Entertainment.

Producers: Dante J. Pugliese, Ted Newsome; *Writing Credits*: Ted Newsom, Jeff Forrester; *Director*: Ted Newsom; *Film Editing*: Brian Q. Kelley, Trudi Jo Marie Keck, John D. Johnson; *Cast*: Edward Bernds (Himself), Turhan Bey (Himself), John Carradine (Himself), Roger Corman (Himself), Hazel Court (Herself), Richard E. Cunha (Himself), Donald F. Glut (Himself), Hugh M. Hefner (Himself), Gordon Hessler (Himself), Francis Lederer (Himself), Christopher Lee (Host/Narrator), Béla Lugosi Jr. (Himself), Fred Olen Ray (Himself), William Schallert (Himself), D.P. Smith (Himself).

One More Time; U.K., 1970; Comdey, Crime; 92 minutes/color/English/Mono; Chrislaw-TraceMark.

Producers: Milton Ebbins, Sammy Davis Jr., Peter Lawford; *Writing Credits*: Michael Pertwee (screenplay); *Director*: Jerry Lewis; *Cinematography*: Ernest Steward (director of photography); *Film Editing*: Bill Butler; *Original Music*: Les Reed; *Art Direction*: Kenneth Ryan; *Make-Up*: George Frost, Hugh Richards; *Special Effects*: Terry Witherington; *Cast*: Sammy Davis Jr. (Charles Salt), Peter Lawford (Christopher Pepper), John Wood (Figg), Dudley Sutton (Wilson), Maggie Wright (Miss Tomkins), Ester Anderson (Billie [as Esther Anderson]), Percy Herbert (Mander), Anthony Nicholls (Candler), Allan Cuthbertson (Belton), Edward Evans (Gordon), Sydney Arnold (Tombs), Leslie Sands (Inspector Grock), Moultrie Kelsall (Minister), Glyn Owen (Dennis), Lucille Soong (Kim Lee), Cyril Luckham (Magistrate), Bill Maynard (Jenson), David Trevena (Gene Abernathy), Norman Mitchell (Sergeant Smith), Richard Goolden (9th Local), Joanna Wake (Claire Turpington-Mellish), Julian D'Albie (Lord Turpington-Mellish), Gladys Spencer (Lady Turpington-Mellish), Geoffrey Morris (Police Doctor), Norman Pitt (1st Country Gentleman), George McGrath (2nd Country Gentleman), Mischa De La Motte (Maitre D'), Walter Horsbrugh (Clerk of the Court), John Nettles (Dixon), Peter Reeves (Policeman), Juliette Bora (Salt and Pepper Girl), Florence George (Salt and Pepper Girl), Lorraine Hall (Salt and Pepper Girl), Thelma Neal (Salt and Pepper Girl), Amber Dean Smith (Salt and Pepper Girl), Carmel Stratton (Salt and Pepper Girl), Harry (Carey Jr. [uncredited]), Peter Cushing (Dr. Frankenstein [uncredited]), Christopher Lee (Dracula [uncredited]), Jerry Lewis (Bandleader [voice and uncredited]), Richard Loo (uncredited), Nosher Powell (Man [uncredited]).

Sammy Davis Jr. and Peter Lawford play the roles of Charlie Salt and Chris Pepper. Pepper takes the place of his dead brother in a diamond-smuggling operation. The two men are followed through the English countryside by Interpol agents and thieves who are after the stolen gems. Christopher Lee and Peter Cushing make cameo appearances as Dracula and Dr. Frankenstein respectfully.

One of Those Days; U.K., 2008; Comedy/Short; 14 minutes/color/English/Dolby Digital; Memory Box Films, Ltd./Rocket Pictures/Umbrella Entertainment.

Producers: Kate Bleasdale, Kelly Broad, Mark Burton, John Cariss, Alex Hedges, Mark Jones, Ed King Dee Quemby, Tyrone Walker-Hebborn; *Writing Credits*: Mark Burton; *Director*: Hattie Dalton; *Cinematography*: Baz Irvine; *Film Editing*: Michael Parker; *Original Music*: Mark Burton, Willie Dowling; *Make-Up*: Sophie Cox, Karen Dawson, Vicky Ellis, Karen Thomas *Cast*: Joe Absolom (Counter Clerk), Loli Adefope (Person in Queue 1), Jessica Asz (Person in Queue 3), Benjamin Barling (Person in Queue 4), Alexandra Barrois (Person in Queue 5), Diego Bellini (Person in Queue), Meshak Blackman (Person in Queue), Hugh Bonneville (Mr. Burrell), Matt Butcher (Person in Queue), Ashleigh Campbell (Person in Queue), Jack Cariss (Boy in Queue), Terri Caruana (Person in Queue), Claudia Casey (Person in Queue), Douglas Christian (Person in Queue), Laura Clark (Person in Queue), Tara Clark (Person in Queue), Adam Cocker (Angel Steward 3), Peter Coyne (Hitler), Collette Crane (Person in Queue), Karen Criscuolo (Person in Queue), Anita Crisinel (Person in Queue), Joanna David (Jean), Ben Davidson (Person in Queue), Stevie Dawson (Person in Queue), Adam Deacon (Angel Steward 1), Barbara Dehinbo (Person in Queue), D.J. Dehinbo (Person in Queue), Amerjit Deu (Harassed Clerk), Deborah Findlay (Supervisor), Samara Findlayson (Person in Queue), Stuart Frodsham (Person in Queue), Julia Gay (Person in Queue), Tim Gebbels (Preacher), Martin Gentles (Person in Queue), Franki Goodwin (Person in Queue), Katie Groves (Person in Queue), Vicky Hall (Member of Staff), Colin Harriott (Person in Queue), David Harriott (Person in Queue), Martha Harris (Person in Queue), Chris Hession (Person in Queue), Milja Maritta Innila (Person in Queue), Suad Isis Nubia (Person in Queue 2 [as Suad Ali]), Derek Jacob (Howard), Somayeh Jafari (Person in Queue), Caryx Jones (Person in Queue), Mark Jones (Person in Queue), Paddy Keane (Person in Queue), Mary Keh (Person in Queue), Conrad King (Person in Queue), Paul Kirkly (Person in Queue), Mary Keh (Person in Queue), Conrad King (Person in Queue), Paul Kirkly (Person in Queue), Don Klass (Angel Steward 2), Vytautas Laurinaitis (Person in Queue), Vytautas Laurinaitis (Person in Queue), David Lee (Person in Queue), Keiron Lee (Person in Queue), Marilyn Lee (Person in Queue), Stacey Ann Lee (Person in Queue), Jonathan Leney (Person in Queue), Andrea Lowe (Person in Queue), Alli Malone (Person in Queue), Zuzana Manton (Person in Queue), David Margetson (Person in Queue), Larisa Modovina (Person in Queue), Katherine Money (Person in Queue), Alex Moore (Person in Queue), Kacy Moore (Person in Queue), Martin Naylor (Person in Queue), Mike Newell (Person in Queue), Winston Newell (Person in Queue), Arnold Oceng (Angel Steward 4), Deborah Omolade (Person in Queue), Angelee Osborn (Person in Queue), Jessica Osborn (Person in Queue), Ken Otukoya (Person in Queue), Amar Pankhania (Person in Queue), Shirley Pavar (Person in Queue), Freya Pearle (Person in Queue), Linda Peterkopa (Person in Queue), Pedro Pinhal (Person in Queue), Dee Quemby (Person in Queue),

Brenna Rangott (Person in Queue), Matthew Ratcliffe (Person in Queue), Will Rawlings (Person in Queue), Kirt Reddin (Person in Queue), Glen Reidy (Person in Queue), Alistair Rhind (Person in Queue), Holly Rhind (Person in Queue), Sukey Richardson (Person in Queue), Jane Trainer (Heaven Staff Member), John Wheeler (Vlad the Impaler).

Howard Whittham, an innocent and successful Englishman, is refused admittance to Heaven on Judgment Day because he has been confused with Vlad the Impaler. He has to go through several roadblocks to try and clear his name to gain eternal comfort in Heaven.

Onna Kyuketsuki (*The Lady Vampire* [International]; *The Woman Vampire* [International]; *Vampire Man* [International]); Japan, 1959; Horror;78 minutes/black and white/Japanese/Mono; Shintoho Company.

Producers: Mitsugu Okura; Katsuji Tsuda; *Writing Credits*: Katsuyoshi Nakatsu; Shin Nakazawa; Sotoo Tachibana (novel *Chitei-no Binko*); *Director*: Nobuo Nakagawa; *Cinematography*: Yoshimi Hirano; *Original Music*: Hisashi Iuchi; *Art Direction*: Haruyasu Kurosawa; *Cast*: Shigeru Amachi (Shiro Sofue/Nobutaka Takenaka); Keinosuke Wada (Tamio Oki); Junko Ikeuchi (Itsuko Matsummura); Torahiko Nakamura (Shigekatso Matsummura); Hiroshi Sugi (Wada, the butler); Den Kunikata (Hoshino); Masao Takematsu (Dr. Sakakibara).

Set in modern times, this Japansese horror film features an ornately-caped Dracula-type vampire (sporting dark sunglasses).

Operazione paura (*Curse of the Dead* [U.K.]; *Curse of the Living Dead* [U.S.]; *Die Toten Augen* [West Germany]; *Die Toten Augen des Dr. Dracula* [West Germany]; *Don't Walk in the Park* [undefined]; *Kill Baby, Kill* [U.S.]; *Kill Baby ... Kill!* [U.S.]; Mata, Bebe, Mata [Brazil]; *Operation peur* [France]; *Operation Fear* [undefined]); U.S., 1966; Horror; 83 minutes/color/Italian/Mono; FUL Films.

Producers: Luciano Catenacci, Nando Pisani; *Writing Credits*: Romano Migliorini (story & screenplay) Roberto Natale (story & screenplay) Mario Bava (screenplay); *Director*: Mario Bava; *Cinematography*: Antonio Rinaldi, Mario Bava (uncredited); *Film Editing*: Romana Fortini; *Original Music*: Carlo Rustichelli; *Make-Up*: Maurizio Giustini, Marisa Laganga; *Cast*: Giacomo Rossi-Stuart (Dr. Paul Eswai), Erika Blanc (Monica Schuftan), Fabienne Dali (Ruth the sorceress), Piero Lulli (Inspector Kruger), Luciano Catenacci (Karl the burgomeister), Micaela Esdra (Nadienne), Franca Dominici (Martha), Giuseppe Addobbati (Innkeeper), Mirella Panphili (Irena Hollander), Valeria Valeri (Melissa Graps), Giovanna Galletti (Baroness Graps.

Called upon by the local people of a small spooky European village to perform an autopsy on the suicide victim, Dr Eswai and his beautiful assistant, Monica, are unable to explain the strange events happening around them. Like a vampire, the girl haunts the townspeople, and the only one that appears to be able to save them is the witch Fabienne Dali.

La Orgía de los Muertos (*Beyond the Living Dead* [undefined]; *Dans les orgies macabres* [Canada]; *Der Totenchor der Knochenmänner* [West Germany]; *Bestie aus dem Totenreich, Die* [West Germany]; *Bracula the Terror of the Living Dead* [undefined]; *Hanging Woman* [U.S.]; *Kobieta wiesielec* [Poland]; *Orgia dei morti, La* [Italy]; *Orgies macabres, Les* [France]; *Return of the Zombies* [undefined]; *Terror of the Living Dead* [U.S.]; *Hanging Women, The* [U.K.]; *Orgy of the Dead, The* [undefined]; *Zombie 3: Return of the Living Dead* [undefined]; *Zombis återkomst* [Sweden]); Spain, 1973; Horror; 91 minutes/color/Spanish/Mono; Petruka Films.

Producers: Romona Plana; *Writing Credits*: Enrico Colombo, Jose Luis Merino; *Director*: Jose Luis Merino; *Cinematography*: Modesto Rizzolo; *Film Editing*: Sandro Lena; *Original Music*: Francesco De Masi; *Art Direction*: Francesco Di Stefano, Eduardo Torres; *Make-Up*: Julian Ruiz, Bianca Verdirosi; *Cast*: Stelvio Rosi (Stan Cooper), Maria Pia Conte (Nadia Mihaly), Dyanik Zurakowska (Doris Droila), Pasquale Basile (undefined), Gérard Tichy (Professor Leon Droila), Aurora de Alba (Mary), Eleonora Vargas (undefined), José Cárdenas (undefined), Giuliana Garavaglia (Giusy Garr), Carla Mancini (undefined), Alessandro Perrella (undefined), Carlos Quiney (Charles Quiney), Isarco Ravaioli (undefined), Paul Naschy (Igor).

It is 19th century Scotland when a stranger arrives in a small town to claim an inheritance. Suddenly, the stranger begins having evil visions, and the town stumbles upon a crypt full of zombies.

Otra vez Drácula (TV Mini-Series); Argentina, 1970; Horror/Television; 450 minutes (including commercials)/black and white/Spanish/Mono; Canal 9.

Producers: Narciso Ibáñez Menta, Raúl Lecouna, Francisco Tejeira; *Writing Credits*: Horacio S. Meyrialle, Bram Stoker; *Director*: Narciso Ibáñez Menta, Alberto Rinaldi; *Original Music*: Mito García; *Special Effects*: Martín Mendilaharzu; *Cast*: Narciso Ibáñez Menta (Count Dracula/Daniel Carvel), Carlos Muñoz (Professor Fargot), Marta González (Lisa), Graciela Pal (Susana), Susana Campos (Sister), Hector Biuchet (Doctor #1), Inés

Moreno (Nurse), Luisina Brando (Teresa), Rodolfo Morandi (Doctor Krantz), Enrique Talión (Night watchman #1), Lucio Deval (Porter), Marita Battaglia (Wife of the Porter), Jorge Velurtas (Doctor #2), Kim Caram (Virginia), Alejandro Marcial (Commissary), Rey Charol (Negro), Mauricio Monner (Police official), Benigno Ginzo (Braver), Selva Mayo (Vampire woman #1), Max Berliner (Night watchman #2), Walter Korwell (Herbert), Roberto Pieri (Cuidador), Alberto Greco (Neighboring #1), Rubén Tobías (Neighboring #2), Betty Solís (Vampire woman #2), Mario Silver (Enano).

The Passion of Dracula; U.S., 1980; Horror/Televised Theatrical Performance; 100 minutes/color/English; Dracula Theatrical Company, Showtime Theater Productions.

Producers: Burt Dubrow; *Writing Credits*: Bob Hall; *Director*: Bob Hall, David Richmond, Bram Stoker; *Cinematography*: Bob Heller, Frank McSpedon, Joe Sokota; *Film Editing*: Jerry Newman; *Original Music*: Jeff Heritage *Cast*: Christopher Bernau (Dracula), Malachi Throne (Abraham Van Helsing), Brian Bell.

The story takes place in the English countryside at Dr. Sewards's sanitarium. Dracula has slain several girls there. Van Helsing and his band of followers vow to protect a friend of one of the slave girls from being the next victim.

Pathos; U.S., 1997; Comedy; color/English; Mustard Entertainment Group.

Writing Credits: Kevin Abosch; *Director*: Kevin Abosch; *Original Music*: David Norland; *Cast*: Tressa DiFiglia (Doe Eyed Victim), Kevin Fry (Alan), Antoaneta Kolarova (The Masochist), Axel Schill (Count Dracula).

Pehavý Max a strasidlá (*Freckled Max and the Spooks* [International English title]); Czechoslovakia/West Germany, 1987; Comedy; 96 minutes/color/Slovak.

Writing Credits: Jaroslav Dietl, Joachim Hammann, Juraj Jakubisko, Jozef Pastéka, Alan Rune Pettersson; *Director*: Juraj Jakubisko; *Cinematography*: Ján Duris; *Film Editing*: Patrik Pass; *Original Music*: Guido De Angelis; *Art Direction*: Milos Kalina; *Cast*: Martin Hreben (Max), Gerhard Karzel (Albert), Eddie Constantine (Vodník Alojz), Ferdy Mayne (Gróf Dracula), Jacques Herlin (Komorník Igor), Barbara De Rossi (Klára), Viveca Lindfors (Barónka von Frankenstein), Bolek Polívka (Henry), Flavio Bucci (Mr. Talbot), Frantisek Dibarbora, Marie Drahokoupilová (Mrs. Church), Andrej Hryc (Blacksmith), Milan Nedela, Mercedes Sampietro (Elisabeth — the White Lady), Július Satinský, Roman Skamene (Mayor's Son).

Un Petit Garçon silencieux (*Taxi Blanc* [France]); France, 2004; Drama; 90 minutes/color/French; M.F.P.

Producers: Marie-Françoise Mascaro, Valérie Monsauret; *Writing Credits*: Sarah Lévy; *Director*: Sarah Lévy, Geraud Pinaud; *Cinematography*: François Kuhnel; *Film Editing*: Jacqueline Mariani; *Original Music*: Jean-Philippe Goude, Ramon Pipin (as Alain Ranval); *Make-Up*: Florence Eloi, Jacques-Olivier Molon (special makeup effects artist [prosthetic supply]), Annabelle Petit (assistant makeup artist).; *Cast*: Bernard-Pierre Donnadieu (Fédor), Nino Gauzy (Gabriel), Marie Vincent (Hanna), Sophie Mounicot (Edelmann), Franck Gourlat (Alex), Hervé Briaux (Bardouin), Edouard Montoute (Martial), Maher Kamoun (Lucien), Roland Marchisio (Un client hostile), Corinne Masiero (Monique), Hervé Ganem (Dracula), Stéphanie Lagarde (Rosemarie), Lucien Jean-Baptiste (Le médecin de la DDASS), Paul Allio (Le bookmaker), Nathalie Bienaimé (Mapi, la dépanneuse), Patrice Bornand (Oncle Fétide), Eric Bougnon (Président de la commission), Colette Charbonneau (Une passagère), Xing Xing Cheng (La passagère chinoise), Jeanne Delavenay (Infirmière), Tonio Descanvelle (Officier de Police), Jean-Yves Duparc (Un commerçant), Omar Dziri (Le client mélomane), Valérie Even (La mère), Violeta Ferrer (Cliente âgée), Sébastien Knafo (Le client au portable), Laurent Labasse (L'entraîneur), Guillaume Laffly (Un chauffeur), Thierry Laroyene (Psychologue), Sheila O'Connor (L'aide soignante), Stéphane Petit (Bruno, le beau père), Emmanuel Quatra (Educateur), Mireille Roussel (L'assistante sociale), Denis Sebbah (Gynéco), Philippe Spiteri (Le voisin), David Subtil (Le client momie), Corinne Vauvillé (La dame âgée).

Gabriel, a ten-year-old boy who is abused by his parents, becomes silent to the world. A taxi driver is employed to accompany Gabriel around to different institutions and hospitals. Together they form an unlikely bond when the driver teaches him elements of Rugby football, and Gabriel eventually opens up to the taxi driver.

The Phantom Eye (TV Mini-Series) (*Roger Corman's The Phantom Eye* [U.S.]); U.S., 1999; Horror/Television; 60 minutes/color/English/Mono; Concorde-New Horizons.

Producers: Benjamin Carr (producer [as Neal Stevens]), Roger Corman, Marta M. Mobley; *Writing Credits*: Benjamin Carr; *Director*: Gwyneth Gibby; *Cinematography*: Chris Manley; *Film Editing*: Lorne Morris; *Original Music*: David G. Russell; *Make-Up*: Siobhan Carmody, Robert Hall; *Cast*: Roger Corman (Dr. Gorman), Sarah Aldrich (Catherine Winters), David Sean Robinson (Joey

Green), Frank Gorshin (Codger), Frank Kowal (Beulah), François Giroday (Dracula), Lisa Boyle (Bride #1), Bobbie Candler, Dina Cox (Bride #3), David Stifel (High Priest), Brad Cronce (Mummy), Danni Wheeler (Ginny), Linda Porter (Old Woman), Michael J. Anderson (Doll Man/Carl [as Michael Anderson]), Scotti (Roderick Usher), Jonathan Haze (Detective #1), Jude Farese (Detective #2), Timothy Patrick Klein (Society Cad).

This mini-series begins with Gorman (Roger Corman), the head of AMC's Horror Department, sending two interns to locate the missing midnight movie, *The Phantom Eye*. While searching for the movie, they enter a dark cellar and split up to save time. Each door they open inside the cellar leads the two interns into a different horror movie were they play a different character in each. Dr. Gorman is spying on them and tells them they have to survive each horror film or they will die in real live. They also have to find the movie by midnight, or they will be trapped in the horror films forever.

Pink Plasma; U.S., 1975; Comedy/Animation, Short; 6 minutes/color/English/Mono; DePatie-Freleng Enterprises (DFE).

Producers: David H. DePatie, Friz Freleng; *Writing Credits*: John W. Dunn; *Director*: Art Leonardi; *Film Editing*: Rick Steward; *Original Music*: Henry Mancini (Composer: theme "The Pink Panther"); *Cast*: Art Leonardi (Invisible Monster/Laughing Skull/Dracula [voice] [uncredited]).

The Pink Panther stops at a vampire castle to spend the night, thinking it is a lodge. While the panther is sleeping the vampire in the castle, who resembles Dracula, rises from his coffin. He tries to feed on the Pink Panther, and the hilarity ensues.

Il Plenilunio delle vergini (*The Devil's Wedding Night* [U.S.]; *Vierges de la pleine lune, Les* [France]) Italy, 1973; Horror; 80 minutes/color/Italian/Mono/35mm; Virginia Cinematografica.

Producers: Ralph Zucker; *Writing Credits*: Ian Danby (story), Alan M. Harris, Ralph Zucker; *Director*: Luigi Batzella; *Cinematography*: Joe D'Amato; *Film Editing*: Piera Bruni, Gianfranco Simoncelli; *Original Music*: Vasili Kojucharov; *Cast*: Mark Damon (Karl Schiller), Rosalba Neri (La Contessa Dracula [as Sara Bay]), Esmeralda Barros (Lara), Enza Sbordone (Tanya [as Francesca Romana Davila]), Xiro Papas (Il Mostro Vampiro [as Ciro Papas]), Gengher Gatti (L'uomo misterioso [as Alexander Getty]), Giorgio Dolfin (First Villager at Inn [as George Dolfin]), Stefano Oppedisano (Second Villager at Inn [as Stephen Hopper]).

Karl Schiller is in search of the Wagner's Ring of Nibelungen, which is located in Castle Dracula. Franz, Karl's twin brother, warns him that Transylvania is a land of vampires, but Karl proceeds to the castle anyway with an amulet that protects him. On Karl's journey to Castle Dracula, his brother Franz catches up with him and steals his amulet and beats him to the castle. Franz stops in the village before the castle and learns from Tanya, the innkeeper's daughter, that every 50 years on a full moon, "Night of the Virgin Moon," five virgins are called to the castle. Franz ignores this information and rides to the castle anyways and meets Contessa Dominga de Vries and her lesbian housekeeper Lara. Franz forgets his amulet and is seduced by the Contessa and turned into a vampire. On the Night of the Virgin Moon, the Countessa uses the ring to summon 5 virgins and informs Franz that they will be married at the Black Mass. Karl is slow to get to the castle but finally arrives to help his brother. At the mass the Countessa orders Franz, being under the control of the vampires, to kill Tanya, but when she looks in the mirror at Franz, she notices that it is Karl, who then stabs and chops the heads off the vampires.

El Pobrecito Draculín (*Draculin* [West Germany]); Spain, 1977; Horror, Comedy/Television; 95 minutes/color/35mm; Producciones Mezquiriz.

Writing Credits: Luis G. de Blain, Juan Fortuny Mariné, Juan Fortuny Trafaner; *Director*: Juan Fortuny *Cast*: Joe Rígoli (Draculín), Josele Román (Ludgarda), Víctor Israel (Vladimir), Conrado Tortosa "Pipper" (Ivan), Ricardo Palmerola (Laurenz), Joan Borràs (Zacharias), Fernando Rubio (Petronio), Lita Claver (Agatha), Carlos Otero (Bibinsky) *Pudelmützen Rambos* Germany, 2004; Comedy, Action 128 minutes/color/German Sunrise Entertainment; *Director*: Joachen Taubert *Cast*: Christian Bütterhoff (Charly), Yazid Benfeghoul (Pudelmütze), Dolly Buster (uncredited), Jürgen Drews (Himself), Ramona Drews (Herself), Ralf Moeller (uncredited), Harry Wijnvoord (Pfarrer), Frank Zander (Dracula).

Draculin, the last of the celebrated Dracula bloodline, has, after decades of deep sleep, awakened in the present day. Dracula captures Charly's sister, so Charly forms a gang to get her back.

Pumpkin Hill; U.S., 1999; Drama/Short.

Producers: Randi Acton, Randi Acton, Amelia T. Hambrecht Jennifer Peterson; *Writing Credits*: Jennifer Peterson; *Director*: Jennifer Peterson; *Original Music*: Dave Connor; *Cinematography*: Ray Preziosi; *Film Editing*: Kerie Kimbrell, Jennifer Peterson; *Cast*: Kelyn Cain (Sara), Kathleen S. Dunn (Helen), Jay Michael Ferguson (Spence), Mitzi Kapture (Lisa), Gloria LeRoy (Gracie), Ralph P. Martin (Dracula), Aaron Michael Metchik (Alex), Ethan Peck (Joey), Jed Rhein (Ralph).

Joey, an eleven-year-old boy, falls into a deep depression after his best friend Sara is killed. A year later, however, on Halloween night, Sara returns with an important mission: to give Joey the strength and courage to move on with his life.

Puss in Boots (TV Series), episode "Nagagutsu o haita neko no boken"; Japan, 1 April 1992; Adventure, Fantasy, Romance/Television, Animation; 30 minutes/color/Japanese; Enoki Films.

Writing Credits: Charles Perrault, Takashi Yamada; *Director*: Toshifumi Kawase, Hiromichi Matano, Yoshio Suzuki; *Original Music*: Mika Chiba; *Cast*: Banjou Ginga (Minister), Chieko Honda (Arudonsa, Constance, Girl who sells matches, Merusa, Princess Sabrina, Princess Sarah), Chika Sakamoto (Pierre), Hirotaka Suzuoki (Abusan, Jesakku), Kazuhiko Inoue (Torusen), Ryo Horikawa (Ivan), Takehito Koyasu (Jeni), Toshihiko Seki (Christopher).

Put Down the Duckie: A Sesame Street Special (*Sesame Street: Put Down the Duckie—An All-Star Musical Special* [video box title]; *Sesame Street, Special* [TV title]); U.S., 1988; Family, Comedy, Fantasy, Mystery, Musical/Television, Animation; color/English; Children's Television Workshop (CTW), RKO Radio Pictures.

Producer: Lisa Simon, Dulcy Singer; *Writing Credits*: Norman Stiles, Chris Cerf, Cathi Rosenberg-Turow, Mark Saltzman, Nancy Sans, Luis Santeiro; *Director*: Jon Stone; *Original Music*: Tony Geiss; *Cast*: Jim Henson (Kermit the Frog/Ernie [voice]), Kevin Clash (Elmo/Hoots the Owl/Additional Muppets [voice]), Richard Hunt (Placido Flamingo/Additional Muppets [voice]), Jerry Nelson (Pretty Great Performances Announcer/Mr. Johnson/Count Von Count/Additional Muppets [voice]), Frank Oz (Bert/Grover/Cookie Monster [voice]), Caroll Spinney (Big Bird/Oscar the Grouch/Bruno [voice]), Northern Calloway (David), Bob McGrath (Bob Johnson), Linda Bove (Linda), Bill McCutcheon (Uncle Wally), Alison Bartlett (Gina), Emilio Delgado (Luis Rodriguez), Sonia Manzano (Maria Figueroa Rodriguez), Chet O'Brien (Mr. Macintosh), Roscoe Orman (Gordon), Loretta Long (Susan), Martin P. Robinson (Telly Monster [voice]), David Rudman (Additional Muppets [voice]), Phil Donahue (Himself), Martina Navratilova (Herself), Barbara Walters (Herself), Ralph Nader (Himself), Robert MacNeil (Himself), Patti LaBelle (Herself), James Taylor (Himself), Seiji Ozawa (Himself), Carl Banks (Himself), Celia Cruz (Herself), Danny DeVito (Himself), John Candy (Himself), Andrea Martin (Herself), Rhea Perlman (Herself), Paul Reubens (Pee-wee Herman), Madeline Kahn (Herself), Jean Marsh (Herself), Joe Williams (Himself), Paul Simon (Himself), Pete Seeger (Himself), Keith Hernandez (Himself), Mookie Wilson (Himself), Sean Landeta (Himself), Gladys Knight (Herself), Mark L. Ingram (Himself), Karl Nelson (Himself), Jeremy Irons (Himself), Itzhak Perlman (Himself), Gordon Jackson (Himself), Wynton Marsalis (Himself), Jane Curtin (Herself), Maya Angelou (Herself), Pam Arciero (Additional Muppets [voice]), Camille Bonora (Additional Muppets), Fred Garbo Garver (Barkley), William Guest (Himself), Merald Knight (Himself), Ladysmith Black Mambazo (Themselves), Edward Patten (Himself), Bryant Young (Mr. Snuffleupagus [back half]), Kermit Love (Willy [uncredited]).

This broadcast is a pledge-drive special that aired on PBS, featuring new as well as repeat material from the show, including Count von Count.

Pyasa Shaitan; India, 1984; Horror; color/Hindi; Hargobindha Films, Jetspeed Movie Makers.

Producers: J.P. Choudhary, Mrs. Suman L. Mehra, P.A. Puri; *Writing Credits*: Iqbal Durrani, Joginder Shelly; *Director*: Joginder Shelly; *Cinematography*: Deepak Duggal; *Film Editing*: Naresh Malhotra; *Original Music*: Om Prakash Sharma, Master Sonik; *Cast*: Kamal Hassan, Joginder Shelly (as Joginder), Madhu Malhotra, Shobhalata (as Shobha Lata), Beena Banerjee (as Beena), Pappu, Kumar, Rashmi.

This bizarre, almost surreal Bollywood horror film features creepy gags, shameless nudity, and a Dracula-type bloodsucker, who some film posters say is Dracula himself.

Qian li dan qi zhui xiong (*The Lonely Killer* [U.K.]); Hong Kong, 1978; Horror; 71 minutes/color/Cantonese; Dae Yang Films.

Producers: Joseph Lai, E. Charles McBroom, Jim Brown; *Writing Credits*: E. Charles McBroom, Barrie Pattison; *Director*: E. Charles McBroom, John Woo, Tony Elwood; *Cinematography*: *Film Editing*: *Original Music*: *Art Direction*: Gabrielle Wentz; *Make-Up*: *Special Effects*: *Cast*: Michael Alldredge, Geoffrey Binney, Jim Brown (Dracula), Anne Heywood, Michael James, Judith McGrath (as Judy McGrath), George Sewell, Gabrielle Wentz, June Wilkinson, Douglas Wilmer, Yun-Fat Chow, Kong Chu, Danny Lee, Fui-on Shing, Kenneth Tsang, Barry Wong, Parkman Wong, Fan Wei Yee, Sally Yeh, Wing-Cho Yip.

Quantam Leap (TV Series [1989–1993]), episode "Blood Moon—March 10, 1975"; U.S., Season 5, Episode 15, 9 February 1993; Action, Adventure, Drama, Family, Mystery, Science Fiction, Horror/Television; 47 minutes/color/English/Stereo; Belisarius Productions, Universal TV.

Producers: Donald P. Bellisario; *Writing Credits*: Donald P. Bellisario, Toni Graphia, Danielle Alexandra; *Director*: Rob Bowman, Paul Brown, Stuart Margolin, Chris Ruppenthal, John Cullum; *Cinematography*: Henry M. Lebo, Robert Primes; *Film Editing*: Craig Holt, Michael Stern; *Special Effects*: Mark Burnett, Roger Dorney, Scott Milne, William Powloski, Joseph Yanuzzi; *Cast*: Scott Bakula (Dr. Sam Beckett), Dean Stockwell (Admiral Al Calavicci), Ian Buchanan (Victor Drake), Deborah Moore (Claudia [as Deborah Maria Moore]), Shae D'Lyn (Lady Alexandra Corrington), Rod Loomis (Horace, the Butler), Garth Wilton (Detective).

Dracula and Sam swap places to stop his vampiric wife from being sacrificed and having her blood drained.

Quaranta gradi all'ombra del lenzuolo see under **Forty**

Quasimodo d'El Paris; France, 1999; Comedy, Crime; 100 minutes/color/French/DTS (Dolby Digital); Cofimage 10, France 3 Cinéma, Hachette Première, M6 Films, TPS Cinéma, Tentative d'Evasion.

Producers: Bernard Bouix, René Cleitman; *Director*: Patrick Timsit; *Writing Credits*: Jean-François Halin, Victor Hugo, Raffy Shart, Patrick Timsit; *Original Music*: Laurent Petitgirard; *Cinematography*: Vincenzo Marano; *Film Editing*: Catherine Renault; *Make-Up*: Isabel Batista, Vesna Estord, Dominique Galichet, Karina Gruais, Axel Guemraoui, Sarah Guetta key, Philippe Mangin, Margarida Miranda key, Lise Provin, Myriam Roger, Marie-France Thibault, Nathalie Tissier key, Guillaume Tixier; *Special Effects*: Sebastien Alagnon, Philippe Alleton, Rodolphe Chabrier, Pierre Foury, Pierre Hervé, Benoît Lestang, Jean-Yves Orlando, Emmanuel Pitois, Patrick Rouxel, Benoît Squizzato; *Cast*: Patrick Timsit (Quasimodo), Richard Berry (Frollo), Mélanie Thierry (Esméralda/Agnes), Vincent Elbaz (Phoebus), Didier Flamand (Le Gouverneur d'El Paris), Patrick Braoudé (Pierre-Grégoire), Axelle Abbadie (Mme Le Gouverneur), Dominique Pinon (Trouillefou), Albert Dray (Pablo), Doud (Diego), Nicola Pepe (Quasimodo enfant), Tess Indycki (Esméralda enfant), François Levantal (Le psychopathe), Franck Monier (Marc-Antoine), Noëlle Musard (Mme Jackson), Alain Frérot (René), Lolo Ferrari (La fée), Teresa Ovídio (Gudule), Lolo Zazar (Livreur pizzas), Cathy Guetta (La prostituée), Michel B Dupérial (Videur discothèque), Fusto (DJ), Jean-Michel Tinivelli (Dracula), Cécile Peiris (Pouffe Phoebus), Michel Lagueyrie (Armand Pessac), Jean-François Halin (Le conducteur alléché), Rémy Roubakha (Eboueur), Gérard Dufraisse (Vendeur pizzas), Patricia Dinev (Bourgeoise), Jan Rouiller (Spock), Blanca Li (Jolie fille discothèque), Daniel Mauvignier (Frankenstein), Raffy Shart (L'homme au chapeau).

After realizing he might be deformed, a couple leave their son Quasimodo to the town arch-deacon, Frollo. Twenty years later, while living in El Paris, Quasimodo is suspected of numerous murders of women around the town. Jean-Michel Tinivelli plays a character named Dracula.

Read All About It! (TV Series [1979–1980, 1983–1984]), episode "An Evil Smile"; Canada, Season 2, Episode 8, 30 October 1983; Family, Science Fiction; 15 minutes/color/English/Mono; TV Ontario.

Writing Credits: Clive Endersby; *Director*: Jeremy Pollack; *Original Music*: Eric N. Robertson; *Cast*: Lydia Zajc (Lynne Davis), Michael Dwyer (Alex), Edwina Follows (The Book Destroyer), A. Frank Ruffo (Count Dracula), Robert Windsor (Rip Van Winkle).

Lynne and Alex are on their way to find The Book Destroyer when they come across Count Dracula and Rip Van Winkle.

The Real Life of Dracula; Romania, 2005; Documentary, Short; 11 minutes/color/Romanian.

Producers: Raymond Nicolau; *Director*: Raymond Nicolau; *Original Music*: Raymond Nicolau; *Cast*: Ovidiu Mihail Stinga.

This film documents the legendary status of the Dracula character and how it has come to be.

El Retorno de Walpurgis (*Curse of the Devil* [U.S.]; *Die Todeskralle des grausamen Wolfes* [West Germany]; *L'Empreinte de Dracula* [France]; *La Noche de asesino* [Mexico]; *Return of the Werewolf* [International: informal literal title, English title]; *Seytanin laneti* [Turkey, Turkish title]; *The Black Harvest of Countess Dracula* [U.S., video title]; *The Return of Walpurgis* [U.S.]); Spain/Mexico, 1973; Horror; 73 minutes/color/Spanish/Mono/35mm; Producciones Escorpión.

Producers: Ramiro Meléndez, Luis Méndez; *Writing Credits*: Edward Mannix, Paul Naschy (as Jacinto Molina); *Director*: Carlos Aured; *Cinematography*: Francisco Sánchez; *Film Editing*: María Luisa Soriano (as Maruja Soriano); *Original Music*: Antón García Abril; *Make-Up*: Fernando Florido, Dolores García Rey, Esther Gutiérrez; *Special Effects*: Pablo Pérez; *Cast*: Paul Naschy (Waldemar Daninsky/Irineus Daninsky/Werewolf), Fabiola Falcón (Kinga Wilowa), Maritza Olivares (Maria Wilowa), José Manuel Martín (Béla [as José M. Martín]), Eduardo Calvo (Laszlo Wilowa), Mariano Vidal Molina (Roulka [as Vidal Molina]), Ana Farra (Malitza), Fernando Sánchez Polack (Maurice, Waldemar's valet [as Fernando S. Polack]), Inés Morales (Ilona), María Silva (Elizabeth Bathory), Elsa Zabala (Gypsy Witch), Santiago

Rivero, Pilar Vela, José Yepes, Ana Maria Rossie, Sandalio Hernández, Jorge Matamoros, Felicidad Nieto, Eduardo Bea.

Four centuries after a curse was placed on an ancestor, Waldemar Daninsky, under its control, accidentally kills a gypsy while hunting for a wolf. Angry gyp\sys summon Satan and a beautiful mistress to seduce Daninsky. After seducing him, the mistress bites Daninsky on the neck, causing him to become a werewolf at night.

The Return of Count Yorga (*Curse of Count Yorga* [undefined]; *Die Sieben Pranken des Satans* [West Germany]; *Retorno del conde Yorga, El* [Spain]; *The Abominable Count Yorga* [undefined]; *Vampire Story* [Italy]); U.K., 1971; Horror; 97 minutes/color/English/Mono/35mm; Peppertree Productions Inc.

Producers: Michael Macready; *Writing Credits*: Bob Kelljan, Yvonne Wilder; *Director*: Bob Kelljan; *Cinematography*: Bill Butler; *Film Editing*: Laurette Odney, Fabien D. Tordjmann; *Original Music*: Bill Marx; *Art Direction*: Erik L. Nelson; *Make-Up*: Mark Busson; *Special Effects*: Roger George; *Cast*: Robert Quarry (Count Yorga), Mariette Hartley (Cynthia Nelson), Roger Perry (Dr. David Baldwin), Yvonne Wilder (Jennifer Nelson), Tom Toner (the Rev. Thomas, Westwood Orphanage), Rudy De Luca (Lieutenant Madden), Philip Frame (Tommy), George Macready (Professor Rightstat), Walter Brooke (Bill Nelson), Edward Walsh (Brudda, Yorga's Valet), Craig T. Nelson (Sgt. O'Connor [as Craig Nelson], David Lampson (Jason, Ellen's Boyfriend), Karen Ericson (Ellen Nelson [as Karen Huston]), Helen Baron (Mrs. Liza Nelson), Jesse Wells (Mitzi Carthay), Michael Pataki (Joe), Corinne Conley (Witch), Allen Joseph (Michael Farmer, Winner of Costume Party), Peg Shirley (Claret Farmer), Liz Rogers (Laurie Greggs), Paul Hansen (Jonathan Greggs), Marilyn Lovell (Theresa Jordon, Singer [voice]).

In this sequel to *Count Yorga, Vampire*, Count Yorga intends to take a new wife as he continues to prey upon the local community while living by a nearby orphanage.

The Return of Dracula (*Curse of Dracula, The*; *Fantastic Disappearing Man, The* [U.K.]; *Bacio dello spettro, Il* [Italy]); U.S., 1958; Horror, Thriller;

Francis Lederer plays Dracula in *The Return of Dracula* (U.S., 1958).

77 minutes/color/English/Mono; Gramercy Pictures.

Producers: Arthur Gardner, Jules V. Levy; *Writing Credits*: Pat Fielder; *Director*: Paul Landres; *Cinematography*: Jack MacKenzie; *Film Editing*: Sherman A. Rose; *Original Music*: Gerald Fried; *Art Direction*: James Dowell Vance; *Make-Up*: Stanley Smith; *Cast*: Francis Lederer (Count Dracula, posing as Bellac Gordal), Norma Eberhardt (Rachel Mayberry), Ray Stricklyn (Tim Hansen), Jimmy Baird (Mickey Mayberry [as Jimmie Baird]), Greta Granstedt (Cora Mayberry), Virginia Vincent (Jennie Blake), John Wengraf (John Meiermann), Gage Clarke (Doctor Rev. Whitfield), John McNamara (Sheriff Bicknell), Harry Harvey (Station Agent [as Harry Harvey Sr.]), Melvin F. Allen (Mel, the Baggage Clerk [as Mel F. Allen]), Dan Gachman (County Clerk), Hope Summers (Cornelia [scenes deleted]), Robert Lynn (Dr. Paul Beecher), William Fawcett (Eddie, Station Agent [uncredited]), Joseph Hamilton (Man reporting murder at station [uncredited]), Belle Mitchell (Cornelia [uncredited]), Norbert Schiller (Bellack Gordal, the real one [uncredited]), Charles Tannen (Mack Bryant, Dept. of Immigration uncredited]).

Dracula kills and steals the identity of a man traveling to California to visit his relatives. Dracula continues the journey to America in the man's place, where he stays with the man's relatives. Soon, a woman mysteriously dies, and a European police officer shows up suspecting the killer to be Dracula. Dracula chooses his next victim but is thwarted by her boyfriend and killed.

The Return of the Vampire (*El Regreso del Vampiro* [undefined]); U.S., 1944; Horror; 69 minutes/black and white/English/Mono; Colombia Pictures Corporation.

Producers: Sam White, Executive Producer; *Writing Credits*: Randal Faye, Griffin Jay; *Director*: Lew Landers; *Cinematography*: Lewis William O'Connell; *Film Editing*: Paul Borofsky; *Original Music*: Morris W. Stoloff; *Art Direction*: Lionel Banks; *Make-Up*: Clay Campbell; *Special Effects*:

Spanish poster for *The Return of the Vampire* (U.S., 1944), starring Béla Lugosi, who plays Armand Tesla/Dr. Hugo Bruckner.

Cast: Béla Lugosi (Armand Tesla/Dr. Hugo Bruckner), Frieda Inescort (Lady Jane Ainsley), Nina Foch (Niki Saunders), Miles Mander (Sir Frederick Fleet), Roland Varno (John Ainsley), Matt Willis (Andrea Obry), Ottola Nesmith (Elsa) Gilbert Emery (Professor Saunders), Leslie Denison (Lynch), William Austin; Jeanne Bates (Frightened woman [uncredited]); Billy Bevan; Sherlee Collier; George McKay; Donald Dewar.

An English family in 1918 is being hunted by a vampire. The vampire is captured but freed by German bombs in World War II years later. He steals the soul of his old servant, a wolfman, and after disguising himself as an escaped prisoner of war, he sets out to get revenge on the English family.

The Revamping of Dracula; U.S., 2004 Horror/Documentary; 39 minutes/color/English; Universal Studios Home Video.

Producers: Laurent Bouzereau; *Writing Credits*: Laurent Bouzereau; *Director*: Laurent Bouzereau; *Cinematography*: Chris Meagher, Ron Siegel; *Film Editing*: Andy Cohen; *Cast*: John Badham (Himself), Frank Langella (Himself), Béla Lugosi (archive footage), Walter Mirisch (Himself), Kate Nelligan (archive footage), Laurence Olivier (archive footage), Donald Pleasence (archive footage), W.D. Richter (Himself), Edward Van Sloan (archive footage), John Williams (Himself).

This documentary examines Universal's *Dracula* (1979) and includes an interview with Frank Langella, who plays the role of Dracula both in the film and in the Broadway production in 1977.

Revivencial; Brazil, 1989; Comedy; color/Portuguese; Ilusionistas Corporação Artística.

Producers: Moisés Neto, Henrique Amaral (assistant producer); *Writing Credits*: Moisés Neto, Bram Stoker; Director: Moisés Neto; *Cinematography*: Hipólito Soares; *Film Editing*: Moisés Neto, Hipólito Soares *Cast*: Ludi Kadija, Luciana Luciene, Lee Majoris, Emerson Nascimento, Marquesa Primeira e Única, Fernando Tavares.

Riddles of the Dead (TV Series [2003–2005]), episode "Dracula Unearthed"; U.S., 2003; Documentary, Television; 58 minutes/color/English; Hoggard Films.

Original Music: Christopher Moscatiello *Cast*: Mark Benecke (Himself), Leanna Chamish (victim of Dracula).

Part of the *Riddles of the Dead* series on National Geographic Television, "Dracula Unearthed" is a documentary about the historical Dracula and myths of the vampire in literature and film. Dr. Mark Benecke explains the forensic reasons the vampire legends may have developed.

Rinaldó; Hungary, 2003; Action; 83 minutes/color/Hungarian/Dolby Digital; Dinamo.

Producers: János Rózsa; *Writing Credits*: Tamás Tóth; *Director*: Tamás Tóth; *Cinematography*: Péter Szatmári; *Film Editing*: Zsuzsa Csákány, Zsuzsua; *Original Music*: György Selmeczi; *Make-Up*: Ernella Hortobágyi, Brigitta Szabó; *Special Effects*: Laszlo Mates; *Cast*: János Bán (Rezső), Péter Scherer (Mazsola), Lajos Kovács (Garincsa), Bence Mátyássy (Aladár), Zoltán Molnár (Rinaldó), Ádám Rajhona (Rinaldó) (voice), Vilmos Kun (Laci bá), Piroska Molnár (Klári), Péter Andorai (Lajos), Mária Varga (Marika) (as Varga Mari), Vanda Kovács (Jutka), Julcsi Kovács (Évike), Tamás Végvári (Béla), Imre Csuja (Főtörzs), Jenő Kiss (Galambos úr), Norbert Szomora (Karcsika) (as Szomora Norbi), Márta Benkö (Galambosné), Sándor Badár (Bandita), János Horváth (Bandita), Ádám Krum (Bandit), István Hajdu (The Customer) (as Steve Hajdu), Ákos Sinkó (Bandita), Ferenc Miklósi (Bandita), István Rimóczy (Tizedes), József Bagodi (Liftes), György Hunyadkürthy (Dracula, kabinos), Szabolcs Thuróczy (Párbajmester), Szabolcs Jáger (Fekete Gyémánt), Jenő Bodrogi (Gengszter), Gábor Dióssy (Gitáros).

Ripley's Believe It or Not (TV Series [1999–2000]), episode "The Vampire Kit"; Canada, Season 1, Episode 2, 18 July 1999; Family/Television, Animation; 30 minutes/English/color/Mono; Cinar Animation.

Producers: Edward Rohwedder.; *Writing Credits*: Michael O'Mahony; *Director*: Ross Breitenbach, Steve Feld; *Film Editing*: Terence Curren; *Original Music*: Kathie Talbot; *Cast*: Teddy Lee Dillon (Michael Ripley [voice]), Rick Jones (Barker [voice]), Jennifer Morehouse (Samantha Seaver [voice]).

Vlad moves into his cousin the Count's old castle with a plan to scam real estate. The townspeople of Poenari suspect something is wrong when they find a young girl passed out in the town square with just a bite on her neck. With the intention of helping the townspeople out, Rip gets bitten and falls into a coma, and his friend Cyril is transformed into a vampire. It is up to Sam and the Vampire Killing Kit to rid everyone of Vlad and bring peace to the town.

Il Risveglio di Dracula; Italy, 1963; Horror; Italian/color; Malia.

Writing Credits: Roberto Mauri; Director: Umberto Paolessi; *Cast*: Bart Anera, Gill Chadwick, Claudio Ferrari, Paul Gabry, Marta Petrarca, Lino Solari, Enzo TrisoliNo.

Riti, magie nere e segrete orge nel trecento (*Black Magic Rites & the Secret Orgies of the 14th Century* [U.K.]; *Black Magic Rites: Reincarnations* [undefined]; *La Reincarnazione* [undefined]; *Rites, Black Magic and Secret Orgies in the Fourteenth Century* [U.S.]; *The Ghastly Orgies of Count Dracula* [undefined]; *The Horrible Orgies of Count Dracula* [undefined]; *The Reincarnation of Isabel* [undefined]); Italy, 1973; Horror; 98 minutes/color/Italian/Mono/35mm; G.R.P. Cintematografica.

Writing Credits: Renato Polselli; *Director*: Renato Polselli; *Cinematography*: Ugo Brunelli; *Film Editing*: Renato Polselli; *Original Music*: Romolo Forlai, Gianfranco Reverberi; *Art Direction*: Giuseppe Ranieri; *Make-Up*: Marcello Di Paolo, Agnese Panarotto; *Cast*: Mickey Hargitay (Jack Nelson), Rita Calderoni (Isabella/Laureen), Raul Lovecchio (Occultist), Christa Barrymore (Christa), Consolata Moschera (Moschera Consolata), William Darni (Richard Brenton), Max Dorian (undefined), Marcello Bonini Olas (Gerg), Cristina Perrier (undefined), Stefania Fassio (Steffy), Gabriele Bentivoglio (Priest), Vittorio Fanfoni (Fanfoni Vittorio), Anna Ardizzone (undefined), Marisa Indice (undefined), Dunca Balsor (undefined), Tano Cimarosa (scenes deleted).

Satanists are killing virgins in a castle to keep alive Isabella who was burned at the stake in the 14th century. The new owner of the castle is actually Count Dracula and has been waiting 500 years for Isabella, his love, to reincarnate. Isabella is reincarnated and all the vampires go on a killing spree.

The Road to Dracula; U.S., 1999; Documentary, Short; 35 minutes/color/English/Stereo; Universal Studios.

Producers: David J. Skal; *Director*: David J. Skal Writing credits David J. Skal; *Cinematography*: Jay Elkayam, Clay Harrison, Guy Jackson, Wayne Norman; *Film Editing*: Keith Clark Makeup Department Debbie San Filippo; *Cast*: Carla Laemmle (Host), Clive Barker, Bob Madison, David J. Skal, Michael Barsanti, Nina Auerbach, Lokke Heiss, Jan-Christopher Horak, Ivan Butler, John Balderston Jr. (as John Balderston), Béla Lugosi Jr. (as Béla G. Lugosi), Rick Baker, Gary Don Rhodes, Dwight David Frye (as Dwight D. Frye), Scott MacQueen, Lupita Tovar Herself (as Lupita Tovar Kohner), Ronald V. Borst, Richard Gordon.

Filmmakers, writers, and film historians discuss Bram Stoker's prolific character Dracula.

Robot Chicken (TV Series [2005–present]), episode "Nutcracker Sweet"; U.S., Season 1, Episode 2, 27 February 2005; Comedy/Television, Animation; color/English; ShadowMachine Films, Sony Pictures Digital, Stoopid Monkey, Williams Street.

Producers: Matthew Senreich, Seth Green, Michael Lazzo, Keith Crofford, Alexander Bulkley, Corey Campodonico, Tom Root, Douglas Goldstein, Eric Blyler; *Writing Credits*: Mike Fasolo, Seth Green, Matthew Senreich, Tom Root; Douglas Goldstein, Zeb Wells, Jordan Allen-Dutton; *Director*: Douglas Goldstein; *Cinematography*: Bryan Garver; *Film Editing*: Chris McKay; *Original Music*: Michael Suby; *Cast*: Seth Green (Various [voice]), Michael Benyaer (Policeman [voice]), Sarah Michelle Gellar (Princess Allura/Little Girl/Lioness [voice]), Mike Henry (Various [voice]), Dan Milano (Pidge/Hyena/Elian Gonzalez [voice]), Kurtwood Smith (Walt Disney/Lemming/Bodyguard [voice]).

This episode features a brief scene in which many characters, including Dracula, have their testicles smashed in time to the music of the "Nutcracker Suite."

Robot Chicken (TV Series [2005–2009]), episode "Tubba-Bubba's Now Hubba-Bubba"; U.S., Season 3, Episode 15, 1 April 2008; Comedy/Television, Animation; color/English; Shadow Machine Films, Sony Pictures Digital, Stoopid Monkey, Williams Street.

Producers: Eric Blyler, Alexander Bulkley, Corey Campodonico, Keith Crofford, Douglas Goldstein, Seth Green, Michael Lazzo, Tom Root, Matthew Senreich; *Writing Credits*: Mike Fasolo, Douglas Goldstein, Seth Green, Seth Green, Tom Root, Matthew Senreich, Matthew Senreich, Kevin Shinick, Zeb Wells; *Director*: Chris McKay; *Cinematography*: Jeff Gardener; *Film Editing*: Garret Elkins; *Original Music*: Adam Sanborne; *Art Direction*: Ross Shuman; *Cast*: Seth Green (Various [voice]), Mocean Melvin (Ape/Count Dracula/Narrator [voice]), Breckin Meyer (Announcer/First Suspect/Joseph R. Francis/Kid/Pilot/Superman [voice]), Dan Milano (Second Suspect/Voltron Member [voice]), Tom Root (Doctor/Professor [voice]), Kevin Shinick (Commander/Himself/Host [voice]), Mindy Sterling (Chief/Flight Attendant [voice]).

Dracula is a crime fighting hero who can only come out at night. He must interrogate terrorists into telling him on what airplane they have hidden a bomb. During his interrogations he bites and kills them all. He arrives on the plane and saves everyone by getting rid of the bomb, after which he bites them all.

Rockula; U.S., 1990; Comedy, Horror, Musical; 87 minutes/color/English.

Producers: Jefery Levy; *Writing Credits*: Luca Bercovici, Jefery Levy, Chris Ver Wiel; *Director*: Luca Bercovici; *Cinematography*: John Schwartzman; *Film Editing*: Maureen O'Connell; *Original Music*: Hilary Bercovici, Osunlade Makeup: Nina Kent; *Cast*: Dean Cameron (Ralph LaVie), Toni Basil (Phoebe LaVie), Thomas Dolby (Stanley), Tawny Fere (Mona), Susan Tyrrell (Chuck the Bartender), Bo Diddley (Axman), Kevin Hunter (Drunk), Nancye Ferguson (Robin), Rick Zumwalt (Boom Boom), Tamara De Treaux (Bat Dork), Tony Cox (Big Al), Greg Rusin (Elmo), Bill Brochtrup (Roadie), Dean Minerd (Roadie), Sloan Fischer (Cigar Man), Esther Richman (Socialite), Karen Bercovici (Chris), Sacred Johnson (Debutante), Adam Shankman (Driver), Rodney Bingenheimer (Himself), Zan Eisley (Vampire Groupie), Cherra Savage (Vampire Groupie), Aries Hough (Reporter), Luca Bercovici (Pirate Chieftain), Christopher Verwiel (M.C.), Kenya Johnson (Girl), Allan Love (Himself), Shawn Klugman (Punk), Phillip "Fryer" Tuck (Bouncer), Maria Christina Urrea (Miss Tuty), Autumn Kimble (Visiting Kids), Alex Mothersbaugh (Visiting Kids), Scarlett

Rouge (Visiting Kids), Eddie Vail (Surfer), Drew Steele (Surfer), Josef Cannon (Jamie).

Rockula is a vampire who lost the woman he loved centuries ago. She was killed by a pirate with a rhinestone peg leg, wielding a large ham bone. Our hero, the vampire, did nothing to save her. So he is now cursed to watch her be born again in another life, and then watch her die, strangely enough by a pirate with a rhinestone peg leg, wielding you-know-what. Now, in 1990, he has what he suspects to be his last chance to try to save her instead of watching get clubbed over and over again down through the years. In the process, he becomes a rock star.

The Rocky Horror Picture Show (*The Rocky Horror Picture Show* [Argentina/Finland/France/Italy/Spain]; *Festival Rocky de Terror* [Portugal]; *Orgía de horror y locura* [Argentina]); U.K./U.S., 1975; Comedy, Musical; 100 minutes/color/English/Mono/35mm; Twentieth Century–Fox Film Corporation.

Producers: Lou Adler (executive producer), John Goldstone (associate producer), Michael White (producer); *Writing Credits* Richard O'Brien (original musical play), Jim Sharman (screenplay), Richard O'Brien (screenplay); *Director*: Jim Sharman; *Cinematography*: Peter Suschitzky; *Film Editing*: Graeme Clifford; *Original Music*: Richard O'Brien; *Art Direction*: Terry Ackland-Snow; *Make-Up*: Pierre La Roche; *Special Effects*: Colin Chilvers, Wally Veevers; *Cast*: Tim Curry (Dr. Frank-N-Furter — A Scientist), Susan Sarandon (Janet Weiss — A Heroine), Barry Bostwick (Brad Majors — A Hero), Richard O'Brien (Riff Raff — A Handyman), Patricia Quinn (Magenta — A Domestic), Nell Campbell (Columbia — A Groupie [as Little Nell]), Jonathan Adams (Dr. Everett V. Scott — A Rival Scientist), Peter Hinwood (Rocky Horror — A Creation), Meat Loaf (Eddie — Ex Delivery Boy [as Meatloaf]), Charles Gray (The Criminologist — An Expert), Jeremy Newson (Ralph Hapschatt), Hilary Labow (Betty Munroe Hapschatt), Perry Bedden (The Transylvanians), Christopher Biggins (The Transylvanians), Gaye Brown (The Transylvanians), Ishaq Bux (The Transylvanians), Stephen Calcutt (The Transylvanians), Hugh Cecil (The Transylvanians), Imogen Claire (The Transylvanians), Tony Cowan (The Transylvanians), Sadie Corre (The Transylvanians), Fran Fullenwider (The Transylvanians), Lindsay Ingram (The Transylvanians), Peggy Ledger (The Transylvanians), Annabel Leventon (The Transylvanians [as Annabelle Leventon]), Anthony Milner (The Transylvanians), Pamela Obermeyer (The Transylvanians), Tony Then (The Transylvanians), Kimi Wong (The Transylvanians), Gina Barrie (Bridesmaid uncredited), Rufus Collins (The Transylvanians [uncredited]), Petra Leah (Bridesmaid [uncredited]), Frank Lester (Wedding dad [uncredited]), John Marquand (Father [uncredited]), Richard Nixon (Himself) (archive audio: resignation speech) (voice [uncredited]) (archive sound), Koo Stark (Bridesmaid [uncredited]), Henry Woolf (The Transylvanians [uncredited]).

Recently married Brad and Janet decide to take off from Denton, Ohio, but get lost in the rain. They stumble across the castle of Dr. Frank-N-Furter (Dr. Frankenstein meets Dracula), a transvestite scientist who happens to be hosting the annual convention of visitors from the planet Transsexual in the Transylvania galaxy. Frank-N-Furter unveils his creation, named Rocky Horror, and Frank-N-Furter immediately begins making sexual advances towards him. Rocky Horror fears the doctor and rejects his advances. When Frank-N-Furter announces that he is returning to the galaxy Transylvania, Riff Raff the butler and Magenta the maid make clear their own plans. This is an audience participation film.

Roter Tango (*Red Tango* [U.S.]) Germany, 1997; Horror/Short; 15 minutes/color, black and white; German Friends Production GmbH & Co. Medienproduktions KG.

Producers: Nicholas Conradt; *Director*: Henriette Kaiser; *Cinematography*: Martin Farkas; *Film Editing*: Volker Becker Battaglia, Melanie Margalith; *Make-Up*: Birger Laube; *Cast*: Inka Calvi (Sanni), Stefan Gabanyi (Tangospieler), Wilfried Hochholdinger (Regisseur), Dieter Landuris (Dracula), Fanny Landuris (Marie), Nina Petri (Vivian), Johanna Schubert (Klara), Udo Wachtveitl (Gerd)

Sabrina and the Groovie Goolies (TV Series) (*The Groovy Ghoulies and Friends* [U.S., new syndication title]); U.S., 1970–1971; Family/Television, Animation; 60 minutes/color/English/Mono; Filmation Associates.

Producers: Norm Prescott, Lou Scheimer; *Writing Credits*: Bill Danch, Len Janson, Jack Mendelsohn, Chuck Menville, Jim Mulligan, Bob Ogle, Jim Ryan; *Director*: Hal Sutherland; *Film Editing*: Jim Blodgett, Joseph Simon; *Original Music*: Ray Ellis, Ray Ellis, Norm Prescott, Lou Scheimer; *Art Direction*: Don Christensen; *Cast*: Dal McKennon (Salem Saberhagen Spellman), Howard Morris (Franklin "Frankie" Frankenstein/Wolfgang "Wolfie" Wolfman/Orville Mummy/Franklin "Frankie" Frankenstein), John Erwin (Big John Sullivan), Larry Storch (Tom "Drac" Dracula/Fatso), Don Messick (Cousin Ambrose/Harvey Kinkle), Larry D. Mann (Doctor Jeckyll-Hyde/Batso/Boneapart), Jane Webb (Bella Love-Ghostly/Sabrina Spellman/Hagatha/Aunt Hilda/Aunt Zelda).

A witch named Sabrina spends time with the

Groovy Goolies, a rock band that pays homage to classic horror monsters like Dracula, the Wolfman, and Frankenstein, to name just a few. The group spends its time scaring people for fun.

La Saga de Los Dracula (*Dracula Saga* [undefined]; *Dracula: The Bloodline Continues* [undefined]; *Saga of Dracula* [undefined]; *Saga of the Draculas* [undefined]; *Ultimo vampire, L'* [Italy]); Spain, 1972; Horror; color/Spanish/Mono; Profilmes, S.A.

Producers: Ricardo Munoz Suay, Jose Antonio Perez Giner; *Writing Credits*: Emilio Martinez Lazaro (as Lazarus Kaplan), Juan Tebar; *Director*: Leon Klimovsky; *Cinematography*: Francisco Sanchez; *Film Editing*: Antonio Ramirez de Loaysa (as Antonio Ramirez); *Original Music*: Daniel White; *Art Direction*: Gumersindo Andres; *Make-Up*: Miguel Sese; *Special Effects*: Jose Gomez Soria; *Cast*: Narciso Ibáñez Menta (Count Drácula), Tina Sáinz (Berta), Tony Isbert (Hans), Helga Liné (Munia), María Kosty (Xenia [as Maria Kosti]), J.J. Paladino (Gabor), Heinrich Starhemberg (Doctor Karl [as Henry Gregor]), Mimí Muñoz (Mrs. Petruscu), Betsabé Ruiz (Stilla), Elsa Zabala (Mrs. Gastrop), Javier de Rivera (Gert), Ramón Centenero (One-eyed man), José Riesgo (Pepe Riesgo), Ingrid Rabel (Gypsy woman), Manuel Barrera (Gypsy man), Cristina Suriani (Irina), María Luisa Tovar (uncredited), Fernando Villena (uncredited), Luis Ciges (uncredited).

Dracula's granddaughter, who is pregnant, arrives at Dracula's castle with her husband. Dracula is expecting them, because his granddaughter is a vampire, and she's about to add another life to the family tree. The granddaughter's husband, who isn't a vampire, soon finds Dracula's wives that lurk around the castle.

Salem's Lot (TV Mini-Series); U.S., 1979 Horror, Thriller, Drama, Mystery/Television; 112 minutes/color/English/Mono/35mm; Warner Bros. Television.

Producers: Anna Cottle, Richard Kobritz, Stirling Silliphant; *Writing Credits*: Stephen King, Paul Monash; *Director*: Tobe Hooper; Cinematography: Jules Brenner; *Film Editing*: Tom Pryor, Carroll Sax; *Original Music*: Harry Sukman; *Make-Up*: Bette Iverson, Ben Lane, Jack H. Young; *Special Effects*: Frank Torro; *Cast*: David Soul (Ben Mears), James Mason (Richard K. Straker), Lance Kerwin (Mark Petrie), Bonnie Bedelia (Susan Norton), Lew Ayres (Jason Berk), Julie Cobb (Bonnie Sawyer), Elisha Cook Jr. (Gordon "Weasel" Phillips), George Dzundra (Cully Sawyer), Ed Flanders (Dr. Bill Norton), Clarissa Kaye-Mason (Marjorie Glick), Geoffrey Lewis (Mike Ryerson), Barney McFadden (Ned Tebbets), Kenneth McMillan (Constable Parkins Gillespie), Fred Willard (Larry Crocket), Marie Windsor (Eva Miller), Barbara Babcock (June Petrie), Bonnie Bartlett (Ann Norton) Joshua Bryant (Ted Petrie), James Gallery (Father Donald Callahan), Robert Lussier (Deputy Constable Nolly Gardner), Brad Savage (Danny Glick), Ronnie Scribner (Ralphie Glick), Ned Wilson (Henry Glick), Reggie Nalder (Kurt Barlow), Ernest Phillips (Royal Snow).

Based on Stephen King's novel, the film begins with a young novelist returning home to Salem's Lot after many years. Trouble soon arrives to Salem's Lot as well, so he begins to suspect that the source of the trouble may be the eerie old Marsten House that overlooks the town, but what he can't imagine is that a Dracula-type, Orlockian vampire named Mr. Barlow has taken up residence there.

Sangre de vírgenes (*Blood of the Virgins* [U.K.]; *Il Sangue delle vergini* [Italy]) Argentina, 1974; Horror; 72 minutes/color/Spanish.

Producers: Orestes Trucco; *Writing Credits*: Emilio Vieyra; *Director*: Emilio Vieyra; *Cinematography*: Aníbal González Paz; *Film Editing*: Óscar Esparza; *Original Music*: Víctor Buchino; *Special Effects*: Martín Mendilaharzu; *Cast*: Ricardo Bauleo (Tito Ledesma), Susana Beltrán (Ofelia), Gloria Prat (Laura), Walter Kliche (Gustavo), Rolo Puente (Raúl Aguilar), Emilio Vieyra (Comisario Martinez), Mariela Albano, Graciela Mancuso, Justin Martin, Marta Peirano, Orestes Trucco (Man of group with beard).

Though Ofelia is set to marry Eduaurdo, she is in love with Gustavo. Befor their marriage, Gustavo kills Eduaurdo and then turns Ofelia into a vampire. In the present day, a group of kids takes shelter in an old house when their van breaks down. Soon, the women start to disappear, so it is up to the men to find out why.

Santo en el Tesoro de Drácula (*Vampiro y el Sexo, El* [Mexico]; *Santo and Dracula's Treasure* [U.K.]; *Santo in "The Treasure of Dracula"* [U.S.]; *Tesoro de Dracula, El* [undefined]; *Tesoro di Dracula, Il* [Italy]; *Vita sessuale di un vampiro* [Italy]); Mexico, 1969; Action, Adventure, Fantasy, Horror, Thriller; 81 minutes/color, black and white/Spanish/Mono; Cinematografica Calderon SA.

Producers: Guillermo Calderon; *Writing Credits*: Alfredo Salazar; *Director*: Rene Cardona; *Cinematography*: Raul Martinez Solares; *Film Editing*: Jose W. Bustos; *Original Music*: Sergio Guerrero; *Make-Up*: Maria del Catillo; *Special Effects*: Antonio Munoz Ravelo; *Cast*: Santo (Santo, el Enmascarado de Plata), Aldo Monti (Count Dracula), Noelia Noel (Luisa), Roberto G. Rivera (Dr. Kur), Carlos Agosti (Dr. Cesar Supulveda), Alberto Rojas (Perico), Pili Gonzalez (Paquita), Jorge Mondragon (Professor Soler), Gina Morett (Lupe, the maid),

Fernando Mendoza (Professor Van Roth), Jessica Rivano, Javier Rizo, Diana Arriago, Carlos Suarez (Raton), Magali, Victor Manuel Gonzalez, Sonia Aguilar, Guillermo Hernandez (Wrestler X), Paulette, Roberto Y. Palacios (Jose the gardner [uncredited]).

Santo and Dr. Sepulveda invent a time machine that Luisa, Dr. Sepulveda's daughter, uses to travel back to Transylvania during the time of Count Dracula. Luisa gets bitten and is overcome by Dracula's spell. Santo and Dr. Sepulveda must travel back in time to rescue her.

Santo y Blue Demon contra Drácula y el Hombre Lobo (*Blue Demon vs. Dracula and El Hombre Lobo* [undefined]; *Santo & Blue Demon vs. Dracula & the Wolfman* [U.S.]; *Santo and Blue* [undefined]); Mexico, 1973; Horror; 90 minutes/color/Spanish/Mono/35mm; Cinematográfica Calderón S.A.

Producers: Guillermo Calderón (as Guillermo Calderón Stell), Santo (as Santo "El Enmascarado de Plata"); *Writing Credits*: Alfredo Salazar; *Director*: Miguel M. Delgado; *Cinematography*: Rosalio Solano; *Film Editing*: Jorge Bustos; *Original Music*: Gustavo César Carrión; *Cast*: Santo (Santo), Aldo Monti (Drácula), Agustín Martínez Solares, Nubia Martí, María Eugenia San Martín, Alfredo Wally Barrón, Jorge Mondragón, Lissy Fields, Antonio Raxel, Carlos Suárez, Lourdes Bautista, Carlos León, Margarito Luna, Alicia Encinas, Blue Demon (Blue Demon).

When Dracula and the Wolfman return from the dead, it is up to heroic Mexican wrestler, El Santo, and his trusty sidekick, Blue Demon, to save the day.

The Satanic Rites of Dracula (*Count Dracula and His Vampire Bride* [U.S.]; *Diabolische rituelen van Dracula, De* [Belgium]; *Dracula Is Alive and Well and Living in London*; *Dracula Is Dead ... and Well and Living in London, Dracula braucht frisches Blut* [West Germany]; *Dracula och djävulsdyrkarna* [Sweden]; *Dracula vit toujours à Londres* [France]; *Rites of Dracula, Rites satanique de Dracula, Les* [Belgium]; *Ritos Satânicos de Drácula, Os* [Brazil]; *Ritos satánicos de Drácula, Los* [Spain]; *Satanici riti di Dracula, I* [Italy]); U.K., 1973; Horror, Thriller; 87 minutes/color/English/Mono/35mm; Warner Bros. Pictures, Hammer Film Productions.

Producers: Don Houghton, Roy Skeggs; *Writing Credits*: Don Houghton; *Director*: Alan Gibson; *Cinematography*: Brian Probyn; *Film Editing*: Chris Barnes; *Original Music*: John Cacavas; *Art Direction*: Lionel Couch; *Make-Up*: George Blackler, Maude Onslow; *Special Effects*: Les Bowie; *Cast*: Christopher Lee (Count Dracula), Peter Cushing (Prof. Lorrimer Van Helsing), Michael Coles (Insp. Murray), William Franklyn (Torrence), Freddie Jones (Prof. Julian Keeley), Joanna Lumley (Jessica Van Helsing), Richard Vernon (Col. Mathews), Barbara Yu Ling (Chin Yang), Patrick Barr (Lord Carradine), Richard Mathews (John Porter), Lockwood West (General Sir Arthur Freeborne), Valerie Van Ost (Jane), Maurice O'Connell (Hanson), Peter Adair (Doctor), Maggie Fitzgerald (Vampire girl), Pauline Peart (Vampire girl), O'Shannon (Vampire girl), Mia Martin (Vampire girl), John Harvey (Commissionaire), Marc Zuber (Guard #1), Paul Weston (Guard #2), Ian Dewar (Guard #3), Graham Rees (Guard #4).

A undercover agent, Inspector Murray (Michael Coles), escapes from Pellham House of Psychic Examination and tells of seeing a girl sacrificed on an alter. The inspector consults with Prof. Van Helsing (Peter Cushing) about black magic. Inspector Murray, Van Helsing's granddaugter Jessica (Joanna Lumley), and Peter Torrence (William Franklyn) go back the to the Pellham House where they find female vampires living in the basement. Dr. Van Helsing puts the piece together and finds out that the corporation, which was built on the spot were he killed Dracula two years before, is run by a D. D. Denham, who has never been seen in public. Van Helsing confronts D. D. Denham, who is Dracula, and is captured. Dracula orders the capture of Jessica and Insp. Murray with plans to make Jessica is wife and to release a plague to kill all humans.

Saturday Night Live (TV Series [1975–present]), episode "Dracula's Not Gay" (*NBC's Saturday Night* [U.S., complete title]; *SNL* [U.S., informal title]; *Saturday Night* [U.S., first season title]; *The Albert Brooks Show* [U.S., working title]); U.S., Season 20, Episode 3, 14 October 1994; Comedy/Television, Short; 5:32 minutes/color/English/Mono, Stereo; NBC Productions, Broadway Video.

Cast: Kevin Nealon (Male Guest), Janene Garafalo (Female Guest), John Travaolta (Count Dracula), Chris Elliot (Renfield), Michael McKean (Wolfman).

In this sketch, Dracula tries to prove his heterosexuality to two visitors at his castle who think he is gay.

Saturday Night Live (TV Series [1975–present]), episode "The Mirror" (an SNL Digital Short) (*NBC's Saturday Night* [U.S., complete title]; *SNL* [U.S., informal title]; *Saturday Night* [U.S., first season title]; *The Albert Brooks Show* [U.S., working title]); U.S., Season 33, Episode 6, 1 March 2008; Comedy/Television, Short; 2:40 minutes minutes/color/English/Mono, Stereo; NBC Universal Television, Broadway Video, SNL Studios.

Writing Credits: Akiva Schaffer; *Director*: Akiva Schaffer; *Cast*: Ellen Page (girl/sleeper), Andy Samberg (zombie), Will Forte (wolfman), Kristen Wiig (Debbie), Jason Sudeikis (Dracula).

Poster art for *Santo y Blue Demon contra Drácula y el Hombre Lobo* (Mexico, 1973).

First, a girl awakens from a nightmare then goes to her bathroom where she sees a zombie in the mirror, which, in turn, happens to be the nightmare of the zombie, a wolf man, and a woman named Debbie, who is married to Dracula.

Saturday the 14th; U.S., 1981; Comedy, Horror; 75 minutes/color/English/Mono/35mm; New World Pictures.

Producers: Jeff Begun, Julie Corman; *Writing Credits*: Jeff Begun (story), Howard R. Cohen (screenplay); *Director*: Howard R. Cohen; *Cine-*

International poster art for *The Satanic Rites of Dracula* (U.K., 1973).

matography: Daniel Lacambre; *Film Editing*: Kent Beyda, Joanne D'Antonio; *Original Music*: Parmer Fuller; *Art Direction*: Whitney Scott Bain (carpenter), Steve Fiorilla (mask designer); *Make-Up*: R. Christopher Biggs; *Special Effects*: Tony Randel (optical effects supervisor), Joseph Yanuzzi (assistant effects editor); *Cast*: Richard Benjamin (John), Paula Prentiss (Mary), Jeffrey Tambor (Waldemar), Severn Darden (Van Helsing), Kari Michaelson (Debbie), Kevin Brando (Billy), Rosemary DeCamp (Aunt Lucille), Stacy Keach Sr. (Attorney), Nancy Lee Andrews (Yolanda), Carole Androsky (Marge, the Real Estate Broker), Roberta Collins (Cousin Rhonda), Paul "Mousie" Garner (The Major (as Paul Garner), Annie O'Donnell (Annette, the Next Door Neighbor), Thomas Newman (Cousin Phil), Allen Joseph (Uncle Bert), Craig Coulter (Deliveryperson), Renee Braswell (Stuntperson), Elizabeth Charlton Davey (French Maid), Irwin Russo (Truck Driver), Michael Miller (Ernie Muldowney, the Cop), Patrick Campbell (Mailman), Bob Esensten (Attorney Delivering Boxes #1), Stephen Kurzfeld (Attorney Delivering Boxes #2).

An early version of the parodic *Scary Movies* franchise, this film begins with a young child who has stumbled upon an odd book after moving into a Gothic house. The book describes the curse of Saturday the 14th, and after the boy reads it, the book releases a variety of monsters into his house, one of those monsters being Waldemar (or Count Dracula with an assumed named).

Scars of Dracula (*Blizny Drakuli* [Poland]; *Cicatrices de Drácula, Las* [Spain]; *Cicatrices de Dracula, Les* [France]; *Dracula—Nächte des Entsetzens* [West Germany]; *Draculas Blutrausch* [West Germany]; *Draculas märke* [Sweden]; *Gecelerin seytani* [Turkey (Turkish title)]; *Marchio di Dracula, Il* [Italy]; *Vampyrens ärr* [Finland (Swedish title)]; *Vampyyrin arvet* [Finland]); U.K., 1970; Horror; 96 minutes/color/English/Mono/35mm; Hammer Film Productions, EMI Films.

Producers: Aida Young; *Writing Credits*: Anthony Hinds (as John Elder), Bram Stoker; *Director*: Roy Ward Baker; *Cinematography*: Moray Grant; *Film Editing*: James Needs; *Original Music*: James Bernard; *Art Direction*: Scott MacGregor; *Make-Up*: Heather Nurse, Wally Schneiderman; *Special Effects*: Roger Dicken; *Cast*: Christopher Lee (Dracula), Dennis Waterman (Simon Carlson), Jenny Hanley (Sarah Framsen), Christopher Matthews (Paul Carlson), Patrick Troughton (Klove), Michael Gwynn (The Priest), Michael Ripper (Landlord), Wendy Hamilton (Julie), Anouska Hempel (Tania), Delia Lindsay (Alice, burgomaster's daughter), Bob Todd (Burgomaster), Toke Townley (Elderly Waggoner), David Leland (First Policeman), Richard Durden (Second Policeman), Morris Bush (Farmer), Margo Boht (Landlord's Wife), Clive Barrie (Fat Young Man), Olga Anthony (Girl at Party [uncredited]), George Innes (Servant [uncredited]), Nikki Van der Zyl (Sarah Framsen [voice, uncredited]).

Dracula has returned and is once again claiming victims. Paul Carlson, seeking refuge for the night at Dracula's castle, is imprisoned, and Paul's brother and friend go looking for him when they face Dracula and his minions.

Scary America; U.S., 2009; Documentary, 92 minutes/color, black and white/English; POOB Productions, Z-Team Productions.

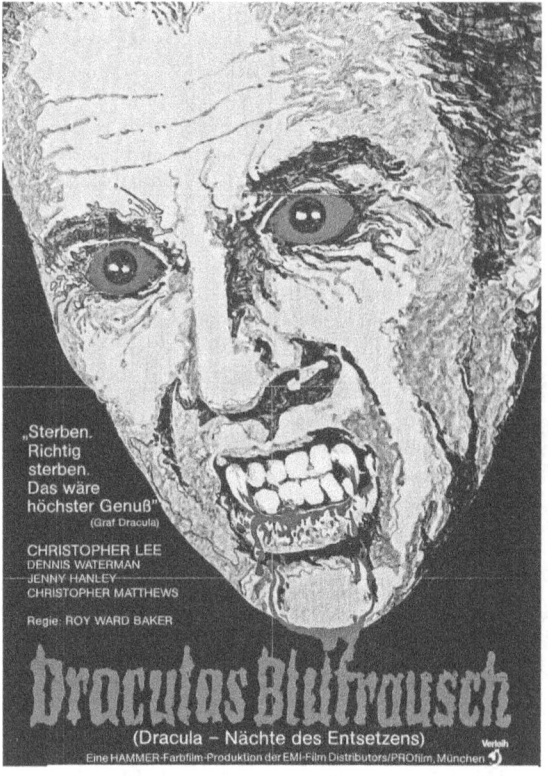

German poster art for *Scars of Dracula* (U.K., 1970).

Producers: Sandy Clark, Michael Monahan; *Writing Credits*: Sandy Clark; *Director*: John E. Hudgens; *Cinematography*: John E. Hudgens; *Film Editing*: John E. Hudgens; *Original Music*: The Moon-Rays *Cast*: Forrest J Ackerman (Himself), Douglas Agosti (Himself/Dr. Shock), Ernie Anderson (Himself/"Ghoulardi" [archive footage]), Curtis Armstrong (Himself), Bob Beidman (Himself/"Carpathian"), Terry Bennett (Himself/"Marvin" [archive footage]), Bob Billbrough (Himself/"Hives the Butler"), Jerry G. Bishop (Himself/"Svengoolie"), John Bloom (Himself), Ken Bramming (Dr. Lucifer [archive footage]), Nicole M. Brooks (Herself), Bob Burns (Himself), P.D. Cacek (Herself/"Moira the Banshee"), Bill "Chilly Billy" Cardille (Himself), George "Gor" Chastain [Himself, Tim Conway (Himself), Lowell Cunningham (Himself), Shane Dallmann (Himself/"Remo D."), Frank J. Dello Stritto (Himself), Jeanne Dietrick (Herself/"Joan E. Cleaver"), John Dimes (Himself/"Dr. Sarcofiguy"), Penny Dreadful (Penny Dreadful [as Danielle Gelehrter]), Richard Dyszel (Himself/"Count Gore DeVol"), Brian Easterling (Himself/"Butch R. Cleaver"), Andrew C. Ely (Himself/"Grimm"), Hart D. Fisher (Himself), Joseph Fotinos (Himself/"Professor Anton Griffin"), Tim Fox (Himself), Neil Gaiman (Himself), Chris Gore (Himself), Billy Hall (Himself), Jeff Hall (Himself [as Jeff "The Sickie" Hall]), Jim Hendricks (Himself/"Commander; U.S."), Timothy Herron (Himself/"Baron Von Wolfstein"), Bob Hinton (Himself/"A. Ghastlee Ghoul"), Barry Hobart (Himself/"Dr. Creep"), Joel Hodgson (Himself), John Kassir (Himself), Adam Kolesm (Himself), Eric Lobo (Himself/"Mr Lobo"), Leonard Maltin (Himself), Russ McCown (Sir Cecil Creepe [archive footage]), Alan F. Milair (Himself/"Dr. E. Nick Witty"), Michael Monahan (Himself/"Doktor Goulfinger"), Joseph Monks (Himself), James Morrow (Himself), Mark D. Newman (Himself/"Dr. Mor B.S."), David Nielsen (Himself), Bob Paulin (Himself), Brittany Paulin (Herself), Mike Price (Himself/"Baron Daemon"), Jimmy Psycho (Himself), John Rinaldi (Himself/"Li'l John"), Tom Savini (Himself), Keven Scarpino (Himself), Chuck Schodowski (Himself/"Big Chuck"), Karen Scioli (Herself/"Stella"), Roberta Solomon (Herself/"Crematia Mortem"), John Stanley (Himself), Ron Sweed (Himself/"The Ghoul"), Patricia Tallman (Herself), Malena Teves (Herself), Jeff Thompson (Himself), Phil Tippett (Himself), Larry Underwood (Himself/"Dr. Gangrene"), Vampira (Herself [as Maila Nurmi]), Len Wein (Himself), Darren Wilhite (Himself), Bob Wilkins (Himself), John Zacherle (Himself/"Zacherley").

From Ghoulardi to Ghoul-A-Go-Go, this documentary examines America's long tradition of horror hosting, following it from its glamorous beginnings, through to its high and low points, as well as its more recent resurgence in an age of cable access and the Internet. Dracula-type vampires, vampiresses, and personalities abound in this documentary.

Schusters Gespenster (TV Mini-Series); West Germany, 1978; Drama, Horror, Mystery/Television; 175 minutes (5 parts)/color/German.

Writing Credits: Klaus-Dieter Lang; *Director*: Bruno Voges; *Cinematography*: Dietrich Lehmstedt; *Cast*: Balduin Baas (Onkel Herbert), Paul Dahlke (Herr Dortelein), Ingrid Froehlich, Kurt Schmidtchen (Eugen Dracula), Karl-Heinz von Hassel, Clara Walbroehl.

The Schuster family inherits a spooky mansion from grandpa. The father, Karl, his wife, son, granny, and uncle, Herbert, do not expect to find the three lurking ghosts who already occupy the house, or the daily visits from Eugen Dracula.

Scooby-Doo and Scrappy-Doo (TV Series [1979–1983]), episode "Who's Minding the Monster?"; U.S., Season 1, Episode 11, 12 November 1983; Horror, Adventure, Family/Television, Animation; 11 minutes/color/English; Hanna-Barbera Studios.

Producers: Joseph Barbera, William Hanna, Art Scott, Iwao Takamoto; *Writing Credits*: Cynthia Friedlob, John Semper; *Director*: Oscar Dufau, George Gordon, Carl Urbano, John Walker, Rudy Zamora; *Film Editing*: Larry C. Cowan; *Cast*: Don Messick (Scooby Doo/Scrappy Doo [voice]), Casey Kasem (Shaggy [voice]), Heather North (Daphne Blake).

Daphne, Scooby, Scrappy, and Shaggy go to investigate reports of monsters in Transylvania. In their investigations, they go under cover and baby sit for the child of Count Dracula. They are also tormented by several monsters.

Scooby-Doo and the Ghoul School; U.S., 1988; Family, Fantasy, Adventure, Mystery/Television, Animation; 90 minutes/color/English; Hanna-Barbera Productions, Wang Film Productions Company, Cuckoo's Nest Studios.
Producers: Joseph Barbera, William Hanna, Bob Hathcock, Bernard Wolf; *Writing Credits*: Glenn Leopold; *Director*: Charles A. Nichols; *Original Music*: Sven Libaek *Cast*: Don Messick (Scooby Doo/Scrappy Doo [voice]), Casey Kasem (Shaggy/Mirror Monster [voice]), Remy Auberjonois (Baxter [voice]), Susan Blu (Sibella Dracula [voice]), Hamilton Camp (Phantom Father [voice]), Jeff Cohen (Grunt [voice]), Glynis Johns (Ms. Grimwood [voice]), Zale Kessler (Daddy Dracula/Frankenstein Senior [voice]), Ruta Lee (Revolta [voice]), Aaron Lohr (Miguel [voice]), Patty Maloney (Tanis the Mummy[voice]), Scott Menville (Tug [voice]), Pat Musick (Elsa Frankensteen [voice]), Bumper Robinson (Jamaal [voice]), Ronnie Schell (Colonel Calloway [voice]), Marilyn Schreffler (Winnie Werewolf [voice]), Andre Stojka (The Grim Creeper/Mummy Daddy [voice]), Russi Taylor (Phantasma the Phantom [voice]), Frank Welker (Matches/Papa Werewolf/Well Dweller [voice]).

Scooby-Doo and the Gang are driving to Miss Grimwood's Finishing School for Girls to be the new coaches. When the Gang arrives at the school, they find out it's not a school for girls but a school for girl ghouls. The students include the daughters of Dracula, Frankenstein, Werewolf and many more. The Gang's goal is to coach the girls for the volleyball match against the undefeated Calloway Military Academy. The plot takes a twist when Revolta plans to kidnap the girls in hope that she will control their fathers. It's up to Scooby-Doo and the gang to rescue the daughters and coach the girls to a victory.

Scooby-Doo and the Reluctant Werewolf; U.S., 1988; Comedy, Family, Thriller, Mystery/Television, Animation; 80 minutes/color/English; Hanna-Barbera Productions.

Producers: Joseph Barbera, William Hanna, Bernard Wolf; *Writing Credits*: Jim Ryan; *Director*: Ray Patterson; *Film Editing*: Mark Bernay *Original Music*: Sven Libaek *Cast*: Don Messick (Scooby-Doo/Scrappy-Doo [voice]), Casey Kasem (Shaggy [voice]), Hamilton Camp (Dracula [voice]), Jim Cummings (Frankenstein/Skull Head/Gengis Kong [voice]), Joan Gerber (Dreadonia/Woman at Store [voice]), Ed Gilbert (Dr. Jeckyll/Mr. Hyde [voice]), Brian Stokes Mitchell (Bonejangles [voice]), Pat Musick (Vanna Pira [voice]), Alan Oppenheimer (Mummy [voice]), Rob Paulsen (Brunch [voice]), Mimi Seaton (Screamer [voice]), B.J. Ward (Googie/Repulsa [voice]), Frank Welker (Crunch [voice]).

Every year, several classical monsters, such as Frankenstein's Monster, the Mummy, and Dr. Jekyl/Mr. Hyde, gather at Count Dracula's castle in Transylvania for the Monster Road Rally. The winner of the race receives the award of Monster of the Year and a trip to Hawaii. A problem occurs when Dracula gets a postcard from Wolfman saying the he has retired and will not be participating in the race. Without the lack of Wolfman, the race is bound to be canceled unless there is another wolfman in the race. The only option is to create a new wolfman. Dracula sends his henchmen to transform Shaggy into a wolfman and to inform him that he is the new wolfman in the race. The only way for Shaggy to rid himself of the curse is to win the race. With many obstacles on the racetrack, Shaggy wins his race and demands to be turned back to human. Dracula refuses to turn him back; but Shaggy and the Gang steal his book, turn Shaggy back to human, and escape from Dracula's castle.

Scooby Doo! Where Are You? (TV Series [1969–1971]), episode "A Gaggle of Galloping Ghosts"; U.S., Season 1, Episode 11, 22 November 1969; Horror, Adventure, Family/Television, Animation; 30 minutes/English/color; Hanna-Barbara Studios.
Producers: Alex Lovy, Lewis Marshall; *Writing Credits*: Larz Bourne, Tom Dagenais; *Director*: Howard Swift; *Cinematography*: Dick Blundell, George Epperson, Charles Flekal, Bill Kotler, Ralph Migliori, Cliff Shirpser, Roy Wade; *Original Music*: David Mook, Ben Raleigh; *Cast*: Nicole Jaffe (Velma Dinkley [voice]), Casey Kasem (Norville "Shaggy" Rogers [voice]), Don Messick (Scoobert "Scooby" Doo (voice)), Frank Welker (Fred "Freddy" Jones [voice]), Stefanianna Christopherson (Daphne Blake [voice]), June Foray (Gypsy Fortune Teller [voice] (uncredited)]).

Scooby and the Gang encounter trouble when they go to investigate a missing jewel case at Franken castle, a gothic mansion which was "imported stone by stone from Transylvania," as explained by Fred. During their investigation, many

Frankenstein-type characters try to stop them, including Dracula and a werewolf.

Scream, Blacula, Scream (*Blacula II, Blacula Is Beautiful, Blacula Lives Again!, Der Schrei des Todes* [West Germany]; *Grite, Blácula, Grite* [Brazil]; *Terror de Blácula* [Portugal]; *The Name Is Blacula*); U.S., 1973; Horror; 96 minutes/color/English/Mono/35mm; American International Pictures, Power Productions.

Producers: Joseph T. Naar; *Writing Credits*: Maurice Jules, Raymond Koenig, Joan Torres; *Director*: Bob Kelljan; *Cinematography*: Isidore Mankofsky; *Film Editing*: Fabien D. Tordjmann; *Original Music*: Bill Marx; *Art Direction*: Alfeo Bocchicchio; *Cast*: William Marshall (Mamuwalde/Blacula), Don Mitchell (Justin), Pam Grier (Lisa), Michael Conrad (Sheriff Dunlop), Richard Lawson (Willis), Lynne Moody (Denny), Janee Michelle (Gloria), Barbara Rhoades (Elaine), Bernie Hamilton (Ragman), Williams (Louis), Van Kirksey (Prof. Walston), Bob Minor (Pimp), Al Jones (Pimp), Eric Mason (Milt), Sybil Scotford (Librarian), Beverly Gill (Maggie), Don Blackman (Doll Man), Elliotte (Prostitute), Dan Roth (Cop), Nicholas Worth (Dennis), Kenneth O'Brien (Joe), Craig Nelson (Sarge), James Payne (Attendant), Richard Washington (Cop), Robert F. Hoy (Cop [as Bob Hoy]), James Kingsley (Sgt. Williams), Anita Bell (Woman).

In attempt to stop Lisa Fortier (Pam Grier) from becoming the leader of a voodoo cult, cult member Willis (Richard Lawson) acquires the bones of and resurrects Prince Mamuwalde (William Marshall), also known as Blacula. Blacula turns Willis into a vampire, and shortly the whole cult is being transformed into vampires. Blacula takes interest in Lisa, believing she is the one that can lift his curse of vampirism. Lisa's lover Justin (Don Mitchell) begins to figure out what is happening and works with the cops to try to stop Blacula. The film ends when Lisa drives an arrow throw the voodoo doll of Blacula that was made for his exorcism.

Scully; U.K., 1984; Comedy 30 minutes/color/English/Mono; Granada Television.

Producers: Steve Morrison; *Writing Credits*: Alan Bleasdale; *Director*: Les Chatfield; *Art Direction*: Anthony Boyle; *Cast*: Gilly Coman, (Marie Morgan [5 episodes, 1984]), Andrew Schofield (Franny Scully (unknown episodes), Ray Kingsley ("Mooey" Morgan [unknown episodes]), Mark McGann (Mad Dog [unknown episodes]), Cathy Tyson (Joanna [unknown episodes]), Richard Burke (Snotty Dog [unknown episodes]), Lucinda Scrivener (Puppy Dog [unknown episodes]), Jean Boht (Gran [unknown episodes]), Kenny Dalglish (as himself [unknown episodes]), Valerie Lilley (Mum [unknown episodes]), David Ross (Steve [unknown episodes]), Gary Bleasdale (Bignall [unknown episodes]), Judith Barker (Mrs. Heath [unknown episodes]), Tom Georgeson (Isaiah [unknown episodes]), Peter Christian (Tony [unknown episodes]), Tony Haygarth (Dracula [unknown episodes]), Jimmy Gallagher (Arthur Scully [unknown episodes]), Paula Jacobs (Florrie [unknown episodes]), Elvis Costello (Henry Scully [unknown episodes]), Angela Catherall (Rita [unknown episodes]), Bruce Grobbelaar (as himself [unknown episodes]), Joey Kaye (Dad [unknown episodes]), Bob Paisley (as Himself [unknown episodes]), Ian St. John (as himself [unknown episodes]).

Sesame Street (TV Series [1969–present]), episode "#4.1" (*rue Sésame* [France]; *Barrio Sésamo* [Spain]; *Les amis de Sésame* [Canada, French title]; *Open Sesame* [New Zealand, new syndication/English title]; *Plaza Sésamo* [Venezuela]; *Seesamitie* [Finland]; *Sesame Street Unpaved* [U.S., syndication title]; *Sesami sutorîto* [Japan, dubbed version]; *Sesamo apriti* [Italy]; *Sesamstraße* [West Germany]; *Sesamstraat* [Netherlands]; *Shalom Sesame* [Israel, Hebrew title]; *Sousami anoixe* [Greece]; *The New Sesame Street* [U.S., new syndication title]; *Ulica sezamkowa* [Poland]); U.S., Season 4, Episode 1, 27 November 1972; Family, Comedy, Fantasy, Musical/Television, Animation; 60 minutes/color/English, Spanish, American Sign Language/Mono, Stereo; Children's Television Workshop (CTW), Henson Associates (HA), Jim Henson Productions, Sesame Workshop.

Producers: Robert Cunniff; *Director*: Jim Henson. *Cast*: Fran Brill (Prairie Dawn/Ursula [voice]), Northern Calloway (David), Emilio Delgado (Luis Rodriguez), Jim Henson (Ernie/Kermit the Frog/Guy Smiley/Granny Fanny Nesselrode/The Baker [voice]), Will Lee (Mr. Harold Hooper), Loretta Long (Susan Robinson), Kermit Love (Willy), Sonia Manzano (Maria Figueroa), Bob McGrath (Bob Johnson), Hal Miller (Gordon Robinson), Jerry Nelson (Farley/Simon Soundman/The Count/Mr. Snuffleupagus/Sam the Robot/Mr. Johnson/Oak Tree/Sun/Teeth/Xavier/Announcer [voice]), Frank Oz (Cookie Monster/Grover/Bert/Cloud/Various Muppets [voice]), Joe Raposo (Singer "Everybody Sleeps" [voice]), Matt Robinson (Roosevelt Franklin [voice]), Caroll Spinney (Big Bird/Oscar the Grouch [voice]), Alex Stevens (The Baker).

This episode features Count von Count, or simply "The Count."

Sesame Street (TV Series [1969–present]), episode "#4.109" (*rue Sésame* [France]; *Barrio Sésamo* [Spain]; *Les amis de Sésame* [Canada, French title]; *Open Sesame* [New Zealand, new syndication/English title]; *Plaza Sésamo* [Venezuela]; *Seesamitie*

[Finland]; *Sesame Street Unpaved* [U.S., syndication title]; *Sesami sutorîto* [Japan, dubbed version]; *Sesamo apriti* [Italy]; *Sesamstraße* [West Germany]; *Sesamstraat* [Netherlands]; *Shalom Sesame* [Israel, Hebrew title]; *Sousami anoixe* [Greece]; *The New Sesame Street* [U.S., new syndication title]; *Ulica sezamkowa* [Poland]); U.S., Season 4, Episode 109, 26 April 1973; Family, Comedy, Fantasy, Musical/Television, Animation; 60 minutes/color/English, Spanish, American Sign Language/Mono, Stereo; Children's Television Workshop (CTW), Henson Associates (HA), Jim Henson Productions, Sesame Workshop.

Producers: Robert Cunniff; *Director*: Jim Henson. *Cast*: Paul Benedict (The Number-Painter), Stockard Channing (Victim of the Number Painter), Cheryl Blaylock (Muppet Performer [voice]), Christopher Cerf (Little Chrissy/Mick Swagger/How-Now-Brown-Cow/Bruce Springbean/Additional voices [voice, uncredited]), Edward G. Christie (Additional Muppets [voice]), Carl Gordon (Mr. Robinson), Paul Hartis (Additional Muppets [voice]), Richard Hunt (Gladys the Cow/Sister Twiddlebug/Sully/Don Music/Two-Headed Monster/Forgetful Jones/Elmo/Leo Monster/Placido Flamingo/Sonny Friendly/Osvaldo the Grouch/Aristotle "Ari" Monster/Shelley Turtle/Flo Bear/Additional Muppets [voice]), Josh LaBove (Grouchkateer (uncredited), Lex Lang (Big Bad Giants/The Devils Advocate/The Loudest Boomingest Announcer Known To Man #1/Tall Man #1/Tall Man #2 [voice, uncredited]), John Lovelady (Rhymie/Additional Muppets [voice]), Peter MacKennan (Additional Muppets [voice, uncredited]), Hal Miller (Gordon Robinson), Howard Morris (Jughead Jones [voice, uncredited]), Jeff Moss (Big Jiffy [voice, uncredited]), Brian Muehl (Barkley/Telly/Grungetta/Pearl/Elmo/Additional Muppets [voice]), Haley Joel Osment (Peter Lane [voice, uncredited]), Marc Petrosino (Additional Muppets), Frank Welker (Additional Voices [voice, uncredited]), Bryant Young (Snuffy), Mark Zeszotem (Additional Muppets [voice]), Linda Bove (Linda), Lisa Buckley (Betty Lou/Additional Muppets [voice]), Alison Mork (Additional Muppets [voice]), Kathryn Mullen (Additional Muppets [voice]), Francesca Rizzo (Little Girl [voice, uncredited]), Caroly Wilcox (Ernie/Additional Muppets [voice]).

This episode features Count von Count, or simply "The Count."

Sesame Street (TV Series [1969–present]), episode "#6.1" (*rue Sésame* [France]; *Barrio Sésamo* [Spain]; *Les amis de Sésame* [Canada, French title]; *Open Sesame* [New Zealand, new syndication/English title]; *Plaza Sésamo* [Venezuela]; *Seesamitie* [Finland]; *Sesame Street Unpaved* [U.S., syndication title]; *Sesami sutorîto* [Japan, dubbed version]; *Sesamo apriti* [Italy]; *Sesamstraße* [West Germany]; *Sesamstraat* [Netherlands]; *Shalom Sesame* [Israel, Hebrew title]; *Sousami anoixe* [Greece]; *The New Sesame Street* [U.S., new syndication title]; *Ulica sezamkowa* [Poland]); U.S., Season 6, Episode 1, 4 November 1974; Family, Comedy, Fantasy, Musical/Television, Animation; 60 minutes/color/English, Spanish, American Sign Language/Mono, Stereo; Children's Television Workshop (CTW), Henson Associates (HA), Jim Henson Productions, Sesame Workshop.

Producers: Robert Cunniff; *Director*: Jim Henson. *Cast*: Northern Calloway (David), Emilio Delgado (Luis Rodriguez), Will Lee (Mr. Harold Hooper), Loretta Long (Susan Robinson), Sonia Manzano (Maria Figueroa), Bob McGrath (Bob Johnson), Roscoe Orman (Gordon Robinson), Caroll Spinney (Big Bird/Oscar the Grouch), Christopher Cerf (Little Chrissy [voice]), Jim Henson (Guy Smiley/Ernie [voice]), Jerry Nelson (The Count/Herry Monster/Rodeo Rosie [voice]), Frank Oz (Bert/Cookie Monster/Grover/Fred the Wonder Horse [voice]), Joe Raposo (Singer "Go Ahead and Touch" and "Frog Struggle Song" [voice]), Matt Robinson (Roosevelt Franklin [voice]), Sheldon Peters Wolfchild (Sheldon Wolfchild American Indian Family).

This episode features Count von Count, or simply "The Count."

Sesame Street (TV Series [1969–present]), episode "#7.15" (*rue Sésame* [France]; *Barrio Sésamo* [Spain]; *Les amis de Sésame* [Canada, French title]; *Open Sesame* [New Zealand, new syndication/English title]; *Plaza Sésamo* [Venezuela]; *Seesamitie* [Finland]; *Sesame Street Unpaved* [U.S., syndication title]; *Sesami sutorîto* [Japan, dubbed version]; *Sesamo apriti* [Italy]; *Sesamstraße* [West Germany]; *Sesamstraat* [Netherlands]; *Shalom Sesame* [Israel, Hebrew title]; *Sousami anoixe* [Greece]; *The New Sesame Street* [U.S., new syndication title]; *Ulica sezamkowa* [Poland]); U.S., Season 7, Episode 15, 19 December 1975; Family, Comedy, Fantasy, Musical/Television, Animation; 60 minutes/color/English, Spanish, American Sign Language/Mono, Stereo; Children's Television Workshop (CTW), Henson Associates (HA), Jim Henson Productions, Sesame Workshop.

Producers: John Stone; *Director*: Jim Henson. *Cast*: Bob Arbogast (Man Getting his Nose Drawn [voice]), Fran Brill (Prairie Dawn [voice]), Northern Calloway (David), Emilio Delgado (Luis/Singer "Three of These Kids"), Jim Henson (Kermit the Frog/Ernie [voice]), Richard Hunt (Sully), Will Lee (Mr. Hooper), Loretta Long (Susan), Shola Lynch (Shola), Sonia Manzano (Maria), Bob

McGrath (Bob), Jerry Nelson (Count von Count/Herry Monster/Biff/Herbert Birdsfoot/The Miller's Daughter/News Flash Announcer [voice]), Roscoe Orman (Gordon), Frank Oz (Bert/Grover/Cookie Monster/Bruce Rumpelstiltskin [voice]), Marilyn Sokol (Betty Lou [voice]), Caroll Spinney (Oscar the Grouch/Big Bird [voice]), Sheldon Peters Wolfchild (Sheldon).

This episode features Count von Count, or simply "The Count."

Sesame Street (TV Series [1969–present]), episode "#7.16" (*rue Sésame* [France]; *Barrio Sésamo* [Spain]; *Les amis de Sésame* [Canada, French title]; *Open Sesame* [New Zealand, new syndication/English title]; *Plaza Sésamo* [Venezuela]; *Seesamitie* [Finland]; *Sesame Street Unpaved* [U.S., syndication title]; *Sesami sutorîto* [Japan, dubbed version]; *Sesamo apriti* [Italy]; *Sesamstraße* [West Germany]; *Sesamstraat* [Netherlands]; *Shalom Sesame* [Israel, Hebrew title]; *Sousami anoixe* [Greece]; *The New Sesame Street* [U.S., new syndication title]; *Ulica sezamkowa* [Poland]); U.S., Season 7, Episode 16, 22 December 1975; Family, Comedy, Fantasy, Musical/Television, Animation; 60 minutes/color/English, Spanish, American Sign Language/Mono, Stereo; Children's Television Workshop (CTW), Henson Associates (HA), Jim Henson Productions, Sesame Workshop.

Director: Jim Henson. *Cast*: Dan Blocker (Himself), Northern Calloway (David/Sluggo the Great), Emilio Delgado (Luis), Joan Gerber (Alice Braithwaite Goodyshoes [voice]), Jim Henson (Ernie/Sinister Sam [voice]), Michael Landon (Himself), Will Lee (Mr. Hooper), Sonia Manzano (Maria), Bob McGrath (Bob), Jerry Nelson (Count von Count/The Amazing Mumford/Herry Monster/Big Barney [voice]), Roscoe Orman (Gordon), Frank Oz (Grover/Bert [voice]), Joe Raposo (Singer [voice]), Caroll Spinney (Big Bird/Oscar the Grouch [voice]).

This episode features Count von Count, or simply "The Count."

Sesame Street (TV Series [1969–present]), episode "#7.17" (*rue Sésame* [France]; *Barrio Sésamo* [Spain]; *Les amis de Sésame* [Canada, French title]; *Open Sesame* [New Zealand, new syndication/English title]; *Plaza Sésamo* [Venezuela]; *Seesamitie* [Finland]; *Sesame Street Unpaved* [U.S., syndication title]; *Sesami sutorîto* [Japan, dubbed version]; *Sesamo apriti* [Italy]; *Sesamstraße* [West Germany]; *Sesamstraat* [Netherlands]; *Shalom Sesame* [Israel, Hebrew title]; *Sousami anoixe* [Greece]; *The New Sesame Street* [U.S., new syndication title]; *Ulica sezamkowa* [Poland]); U.S., Season 7, Episode 17, 23 December 1975; Family, Comedy, Fantasy, Musical/Television, Animation; 60 minutes/color/English, Spanish, American Sign Language/Mono, Stereo; Children's Television Workshop (CTW), Henson Associates (HA), Jim Henson Productions, Sesame Workshop.

Director: Jim Henson. *Cast*: Northern Calloway (David), Judy Collins (The Sad Princess), Emilio Delgado (Luis), Brian Henson (Boy with Seven Nickels), Jim Henson (Kermit the Frog/Ernie/Bad Bart/The Baker [voice]), Richard Hunt (Stuie Monster/Pig #2 [voice]), Bud Luckey (Singer [voice]), Sonia Manzano (Maria), Bob McGrath (Bob), Jerry Nelson (Count von Count/Big Bad Wolf/News Flash Announcer [voice]), Roscoe Orman (Gordon), Frank Oz (Bert/Cookie Monster [voice]), Marilyn Sokol (Marshall Earp [voice]), Caroll Spinney (Oscar the Grouch [voice]), Alex Stevens (The Baker).

This episode features Count von Count, or simply "The Count."

Sesame Street (TV Series [1969–present]), episode "#14.1" (*rue Sésame* [France]; *Barrio Sésamo* [Spain]; *Les amis de Sésame* [Canada, French title]; *Open Sesame* [New Zealand, new syndication/English title]; *Plaza Sésamo* [Venezuela]; *Seesamitie* [Finland]; *Sesame Street Unpaved* [U.S., syndication title]; *Sesami sutorîto* [Japan, dubbed version]; *Sesamo apriti* [Italy]; *Sesamstraße* [West Germany]; *Sesamstraat* [Netherlands]; *Shalom Sesame* [Israel, Hebrew title]; *Sousami anoixe* [Greece]; *The New Sesame Street* [U.S., new syndication title]; *Ulica sezamkowa* [Poland]); U.S., Season 14, Episode 1, 22 November 1982; Family, Comedy, Fantasy, Musical/Television, Animation; 60 minutes/color/English, Spanish, American Sign Language/Mono, Stereo; Children's Television Workshop (CTW), Henson Associates (HA), Jim Henson Productions, Sesame Workshop.

Cast: Harry Belafonte (Himself), Northern Calloway (David), Emilio Delgado (Luis), Giancarlo Esposito (Mickey), Alaina Reed Hall (Olivia (as Alaina Reed), Jim Henson (Ernie/Nature Lover [voice]), Richard Hunt (Two-Headed Monster [voice]), Will Lee (Mr. Hooper), Loretta Long (Susan), Kermit Love (Willy), Sonia Manzano (Maria), Bob McGrath (Bob), Brian Muehl (Rusty [voice]), Jerry Nelson (The Count/Two-Headed Monster [voice]), Chet O"Brien (Mr. Macintosh), Roscoe Orman (Gordon), Frank Oz (Bert [voice]), The Pointer Sisters (Singers "Pinball Number Count #2" [voice]), Martin P. Robinson (Mr. Snuffleupagus [voice]), Marilyn Sokol (Aunt May, the Camp Director), Caroll Spinney (Big Bird/Oscar the Grouch [voice]).

This episode features Count von Count, or simply "The Count."

Sesame Street (TV Series [1969–present]), episode "#14.5" (*rue Sésame* [France]; *Barrio Sésamo* [Spain];

Les amis de Sésame [Canada, French title]; *Open Sesame* [New Zealand, new syndication/English title]; *Plaza Sésamo* [Venezuela]; *Seesamitie* [Finland]; *Sesame Street Unpaved* [U.S., syndication title]; *Sesami sutorîto* [Japan, dubbed version]; *Sesamo apriti* [Italy]; *Sesamstraße* [West Germany]; *Sesamstraat* [Netherlands]; *Shalom Sesame* [Israel, Hebrew title]; *Sousami anoixe* [Greece]; *The New Sesame Street* [U.S., new syndication title]; *Ulica sezamkowa* [Poland]); U.S., Season 14, Episode 5, 26 November 1982; Family, Comedy, Fantasy, Musical/Television, Animation; 60 minutes/color/English, Spanish, American Sign Language/Mono, Stereo; Children's Television Workshop (CTW), Henson Associates (HA), Jim Henson Productions, Sesame Workshop.

Cast: Giancarlo Esposito (Mickey), Jim Henson (Kermit the Frog/Ernie [voice]), Bob McGrath (Bob), Brian Muehl (Rusty [voice]), Jerry Nelson (Count von Count/Big Bad Wolf/Announcer [voice]), Frank Oz (Grover/Bert/Cookie Monster/Pig [voice]), Martin P. Robinson (Mr. Snuffleupagus [voice]), Marilyn Sokol (Aunt May, the Camp Director), Caroll Spinney (Big Bird [voice]).

This episode features Count von Count, or simply "The Count."

Sesame Street (TV Series [1969–present]), episode "#17.1" (*rue Sésame* [France]; *Barrio Sésamo* [Spain]; *Les amis de Sésame* [Canada, French title]; *Open Sesame* [New Zealand, new syndication/English title]; *Plaza Sésamo* [Venezuela]; *Seesamitie* [Finland]; *Sesame Street Unpaved* [U.S., syndication title]; *Sesami sutorîto* [Japan, dubbed version]; *Sesamo apriti* [Italy]; *Sesamstraße* [West Germany]; *Sesamstraat* [Netherlands]; *Shalom Sesame* [Israel, Hebrew title]; *Sousami anoixe* [Greece]; *The New Sesame Street* [U.S., new syndication title]; *Ulica sezamkowa* [Poland]); U.S., Season 17, Episode 1, 18 November 1985; Family, Comedy, Fantasy, Musical/Television, Animation; 60 minutes/color/English, Spanish, American Sign Language/Mono, Stereo; Children's Television Workshop (CTW), Henson Associates (HA), Jim Henson Productions, Sesame Workshop.

Cast: Roscoe Orman (Gordon Robinson), Micki Barnett (Micki), Linda Bove (Linda), Northern Calloway (David Robinson), Kevin Clash (Elmo [voice]), Emilio Delgado (Luis Rodriguez), Phil Donahue (Himself), Jim Henson (Kermit the Frog/Ernie/Little Pig [voice]), Richard Hunt (Little Pig/Two-Headed Monster [voice]), Loretta Long (Susan Robinson), Sonia Manzano (Maria Figueroa Rodriguez), Bill McCutcheon (Uncle Wally), Jerry Nelson (Count von Count/Two-Headed Monster [voice]), Frank Oz (Grover/Bert [voice]), Joe Raposo (Singer "Dressed Up" [voice]), Martin P. Robinson (Mr. Snuffleupagus/Little Pig [voice]), Caroll Spinney (Big Bird/Oscar the Grouch [voice]), Tatyana Ali (Tatyana [uncredited]).

This episode features Count von Count, or simply "The Count."

Sesame Street (TV Series [1969–present]), episode "#19.128" (*rue Sésame* [France]; *Barrio Sésamo* [Spain]; *Les amis de Sésame* [Canada, French title]; *Open Sesame* [New Zealand, new syndication/English title]; *Plaza Sésamo* [Venezuela]; *Seesamitie* [Finland]; *Sesame Street Unpaved* [U.S., syndication title]; *Sesami sutorîto* [Japan, dubbed version]; *Sesamo apriti* [Italy]; *Sesamstraße* [West Germany]; *Sesamstraat* [Netherlands]; *Shalom Sesame* [Israel, Hebrew title]; *Sousami anoixe* [Greece]; *The New Sesame Street* [U.S., new syndication title]; *Ulica sezamkowa* [Poland]); U.S., Season 19, Episode 128, 11 May 1988; Family, Comedy, Fantasy, Musical/Television, Animation; 60 minutes/color/English, Spanish, American Sign Language/Mono, Stereo; Children's Television Workshop (CTW), Henson Associates (HA), Jim Henson Productions, Sesame Workshop.

Cast: Kevin Clash (Elmo/Hoots the Owl [voice]), Emilio Delgado (Luis), Jim Henson (Ernie/Kermit the Frog/Guy Smiley [voice]), Richard Hunt (Placido Flamingo/Two-Headed Monster/Gladys the Cow [voice]), Lillian Hurst (Mrs. Figueroa), Sonia Manzano (Maria), Jerry Nelson (Count von Count/Biff/Two-Headed Monster/Mr. Johnson/Phil Harmonic [voice]), Frank Oz (Grover/Bert [voice]), Caroll Spinney (Big Bird/Oscar the Grouch [voice]), James Taylor (Himself).

This episode features Count von Count, or simply "The Count."

Sesame Street (TV Series [1969–present]), episode "#33.50" (*rue Sésame* [France]; *Barrio Sésamo* [Spain]; *Les amis de Sésame* [Canada, French title]; *Open Sesame* [New Zealand, new syndication/English title]; *Plaza Sésamo* [Venezuela]; *Seesamitie* [Finland]; *Sesame Street Unpaved* [U.S., syndication title]; *Sesami sutorîto* [Japan, dubbed version]; *Sesamo apriti* [Italy]; *Sesamstraße* [West Germany]; *Sesamstraat* [Netherlands]; *Shalom Sesame* [Israel, Hebrew title]; *Sousami anoixe* [Greece]; *The New Sesame Street* [U.S., new syndication title]; *Ulica sezamkowa* [Poland]); U.S., Season 33, Episode 50, 12 April 2002; Family, Comedy, Fantasy, Musical/Television, Animation; 60 minutes/color/English, Spanish, American Sign Language/Mono, Stereo; Children's Television Workshop (CTW), Henson Associates (HA), Jim Henson Productions, Sesame Workshop.

Director: Steve Feldman; *Cast*: Fran Brill (Zoe [voice]), Ruth Buzzi (Suzie Kabloozie [voice]), Kevin Clash (Elmo [voice]), James Gandolfini

(Himself), Eric Jacobson (Bert/Grover [voice]), Alan Muraoka (Alan), Jerry Nelson (Count von Count [voice]), Roscoe Orman (Gordon Robinson), Carmen Osbahr (Rosita [voice]), Marty Robinson (Telly Monster [voice]), David Rudman (Baby Bear/Hero Guy/Cookie Monster [voice]), Caroll Spinney (Big Bird/Oscar the Grouch [voice]), Steve Whitmire (Ernie [voice]).

This episode features Count von Count, or simply "The Count."

Sesame Street (TV Series [1969–present]), episode "#35.4" (*rue Sésame* [France]; *Barrio Sésamo* [Spain]; *Les amis de Sésame* [Canada, French title]; *Open Sesame* [New Zealand, new syndication/English title]; *Plaza Sésamo* [Venezuela]; *Seesamitie* [Finland]; *Sesame Street Unpaved* [U.S., syndication title]; *Sesami sutorîto* [Japan, dubbed version]; *Sesamo apriti* [Italy]; *Sesamstraße* [West Germany]; *Sesamstraat* [Netherlands]; *Shalom Sesame* [Israel, Hebrew title]; *Sousami anoixe* [Greece]; *The New Sesame Street* [U.S., new syndication title]; *Ulica sezamkowa* [Poland]); U.S., Season 35, Episode 4, 2004; Family, Comedy, Fantasy, Musical/Television, Animation; 60 minutes/color/English, Spanish, American Sign Language/Mono, Stereo; Children's Television Workshop (CTW), Henson Associates (HA), Jim Henson Productions, Sesame Workshop.

Cast: Kevin Clash (Elmo/Hoots the Owl [voice]), Eric Jacobson (Grover [voice]), Joey Mazzarino (The Elephant [voice]), Alan Muraoka (Alan), Jerry Nelson (Count [voice]), Roscoe Orman (Trash Gordon), Carmen Osbahr (Rosita [voice]), Frank Oz (Bert/Cookie Monster [voice]), Natalie Portman (Natalie), David Rudman (Baby Bear [voice]), Caroll Spinney (Big Bird/Oscar [voice]), Matt Vogel (Big Bird [voice]), Steve Whitmire (Ernie [voice]), Venus Williams (Herself).

This episode features Count von Count, or simply "The Count."

Sesame Street (TV Series [1969–present]), episode "#37.1" (*rue Sésame* [France]; *Barrio Sésamo* [Spain]; *Les amis de Sésame* [Canada, French title]; *Open Sesame* [New Zealand, new syndication/English title]; *Plaza Sésamo* [Venezuela]; *Seesamitie* [Finland]; *Sesame Street Unpaved* [U.S., syndication title]; *Sesami sutorîto* [Japan, dubbed version]; *Sesamo apriti* [Italy]; *Sesamstraße* [West Germany]; *Sesamstraat* [Netherlands]; *Shalom Sesame* [Israel, Hebrew title]; *Sousami anoixe* [Greece]; *The New Sesame Street* [U.S., new syndication title]; *Ulica sezamkowa* [Poland]); U.S., Season 37, Episode 1, 14 August 2006; Family, Comedy, Fantasy, Musical/Television, Animation; 60 minutes/color/English, Spanish, American Sign Language/Mono, Stereo; Children's Television Workshop (CTW), Henson Associates (HA), Jim Henson Productions, Sesame Workshop.

Writing Credits: Tony Geiss; *Director*: Emily Squires; *Cast*: Fran Brill (Zoe/Prairie Dawn/Det. Olivia Benson [voice]), Tyler Bunch (Prince Cha-Cha Charming [voice]), Ruth Buzzi (Suzie Kabloozie [voice]), Leslie Carrara (Abby Cadabby/Sleeping Beauty [voice]), Kristin Chenoweth (Ms. Noodle), Kevin Clash (Elmo/Hoots [voice]), Vinny DeGennaro (Fireman), Emilio Delgado (Luis Rodriguez), Larry Goldstein (Larry), Bill Irwin (Mr. Noodle), John Legend (Himself), Sonia Manzano (Maria Figueroa Rodriguez), Joey Mazzarino (Det. Elliot Stabler [voice]), Jerry Nelson (Count [voice]), Martin P. Robinson (Snuffleupagus/Capt. Donald Cragen [voice]), David Rudman (Cookie Monster/Det. John Munch [voice]), Caroll Spinney (Big Bird/Oscar the Grouch [voice]).

This episode features Count von Count, or simply "The Count."

Sesame Street (TV Series [1969–present]), episode "#38.2" (*rue Sésame* [France]; *Barrio Sésamo* [Spain]; *Les amis de Sésame* [Canada, French title]; *Open Sesame* [New Zealand, new syndication/English title]; *Plaza Sésamo* [Venezuela]; *Seesamitie* [Finland]; *Sesame Street Unpaved* [U.S., syndication title]; *Sesami sutorîto* [Japan, dubbed version]; *Sesamo apriti* [Italy]; *Sesamstraße* [West Germany]; *Sesamstraat* [Netherlands]; *Shalom Sesame* [Israel, Hebrew title]; *Sousami anoixe* [Greece]; *The New Sesame Street* [U.S., new syndication title]; *Ulica sezamkowa* [Poland]); U.S., Season 38, Episode 2, 14 August 2007; Family, Comedy, Fantasy, Musical/Television, Animation; 60 minutes/color/English, Spanish, American Sign Language/Mono, Stereo; Children's Television Workshop (CTW), Henson Associates (HA), Jim Henson Productions, Sesame Workshop.

Producers: Tim Carter, April Chadderdon, Kevin Clash, Melissa Dino, Todd E. James, Benjamin Lehmann, Carol-Lynn Parente, Rebecca Rosa, Crystal Whaley; *Writing Credits*: Lou Berger, Judy Freudberg, Molly Boylan, Annie Evans, Christine Ferraro, Tony Geiss, Emily Perl Kingsley, Joey Mazzarino, Luis Santeiro, Belinda Ward, John Weidman; *Director*: Kevin Clash, Ken Diego, Victor DiNapoli, Dean Gordon, Tom Guadarrama, Ted May, Joey Mazzarino, Lisa Simon, Emily Squires, Nadine Zylstra; *Film Editing*: Selbern Narby, Chris Reinhart, John Tierney; *Original Music*: Christopher Cerf (as Chris Cerf), Tony Geiss, Stephen Lawrence, Jeff Moss, John Pizzarelli, Sam Pottle, Mark Radice, Joe Raposo, Mike Renzi, Earl Rose, Russell Velazquez; *Art Direction*: Mike Pantuso, Bob Phillips; *Make-Up*: Jane DiPersio (as Jane Di Persio), Jackie Payne; *Cast*: Alan Muraoka (Alan),

Roscoe Orman (Gordon), Loretta Long (Susan), Christopher Knowings (Chris Robinson [as Chris Knowings]), Caroll Spinney (Oscar [voice]), Pam Arciero (Muppet), Heather Asch (Muppet), Jennifer Barnhart (Muppet), Fran Brill (Muppet), Tyler Bunch (Muppet), Leslie Carrara (Abby Cadabby [voice]), Kevin Clash (Elmo [voice]), Bruce Connelly (Muppet [as R. Bruce Connelly]), Melissa Creighton (Muppet), Stephanie D'Abruzzo (Muppet), Ryan Dillon (Muppet), Eric Jacobson (Muppet), Peter Linz (Muppet), Lara MacLean (Muppet), Noel MacNeal (Muppet), Amanda Maddock (Muppet), Jim Martin (Muppet), Joey Mazzarino (Horatio Elephant/Murray Monster/Stinky the Stinkweed [voice]), Paul McGinnis (Muppet), Jerry Nelson (Count von Count [voice]), Carmen Osbahr (Muppet), Frank Oz (Muppet), Martin P. Robinson (Muppet), David Rudman (Cookie Monster [voice]), Matt Vogel (Muppet), Steve Whitmire (Muppet [voice]), Bryant Young (Muppet), Norah Jones (Herself [archive footage]), Fred Newman (Himself), Christopher Cerf (Singer [voice]), Michele Mariana (Cecille [voice]), Bill Irwin (Mr. Noodle [uncredited]), Logan Kulick ([uncredited]), Matt Lauer (Himself [uncredited]).

This episode features Count von Count, or simply "The Count."

Sesame Street (TV Series [1969–present]), episode "The Bookaneers" (*rue Sésame* [France]; *Barrio Sésamo* [Spain]; *Les amis de Sésame* [Canada, French title]; *Open Sesame* [New Zealand, new syndication/English title]; *Plaza Sésamo* [Venezuela]; *Seesamitie* [Finland]; *Sesame Street Unpaved* [U.S., syndication title]; *Sesami sutorîto* [Japan, dubbed version]; *Sesamo apriti* [Italy]; *Sesamstraße* [West Germany]; *Sesamstraat* [Netherlands]; *Shalom Sesame* [Israel, Hebrew title]; *Sousami anoixe* [Greece]; *The New Sesame Street* [U.S., new syndication title]; *Ulica sezamkowa* [Poland]); U.S., Season 38, Episode 1, 13 August 2007; Family, Comedy, Fantasy, Musical/Television, Animation; 60 minutes/color/English, Spanish, American Sign Language/Mono, Stereo; Children's Television Workshop (CTW), Henson Associates (HA), Jim Henson Productions, Sesame Workshop.

Producers: Tim Carter, April Chadderdon, Kevin Clash, Melissa Dino, Todd E. James, Benjamin Lehmann, Carol-Lynn Parente, Rebecca Rosa, Crystal Whaley; *Writing Credits*: Lou Berger, Judy Freudberg, Molly Boylan, Annie Evans, Christine Ferraro, Tony Geiss, Emily Perl Kingsley, Joey Mazzarino, Luis Santeiro, Belinda Ward, John Weidman; *Director*: Kevin Clash, Ken Diego, Victor DiNapoli, Dean Gordon, Tom Guadarrama, Jim Martin, Ted May, Joey Mazzarino, Lisa Simon, Emily Squires, Nadine Zylstra; *Film Editing*: Selbern Narby, Chris Reinhart, John Tierney; *Original Music*: Christopher Cerf (as Chris Cerf), Tony Geiss, Stephen Lawrence, Jeff Moss, John Pizzarelli, Sam Pottle, Mark Radice, Joe Raposo, Mike Renzi, Earl Rose, Russell Velazquez; *Art Direction*: Pete Ortiz, Mike Pantuso, Bob Phillips; *Make-Up*: Jane DiPersio (as Jane Di Persio), Jackie Payne; *Cast*: Alan Muraoka (Alan), Pam Arciero (Muppet), Heather Asch (Muppet), Jennifer Barnhart (Muppet), Fran Brill (Muppet), Tyler Bunch (Muppet), Leslie Carrara (Abby Cadabby [voice] [as Leslie Carrara-Rudolph]), Kevin Clash (Elmo [voice]), Bruce Connelly (Muppet [as R. Bruce Connelly]), Melissa Creighton (Muppet), Stephanie D'Abruzzo (Muppet), Ryan Dillon (Muppet), Eric Jacobson (Muppet), Peter Linz (Muppet), Lara MacLean (Muppet), Noel MacNeal (Muppet), Amanda Maddock (Muppet), Jim Martin (Muppet), Joey Mazzarino (Murray Monster [voice]), Paul McGinnis (Muppet), Jerry Nelson (The Count [voice]), Carmen Osbahr (Muppet), Frank Oz (Cookie Monster [voice]) (archive footage), Martin P. Robinson (Muppet), David Rudman (Muppet), Caroll Spinney (Oscar [voice]), Matt Vogel (Muppet), Steve Whitmire (Muppet [voice]), Brian Williams (Himself), Bryant Young (Muppet), Lexine Bondoc (Lexine [uncredited] [archive footage]), Chris Brown (Himself [uncredited]), Tina Fey (Bookaneer Captain [uncredited]), Bill Irwin (Mr. Noodle [uncredited]).

This episode features Count von Count, or simply "The Count."

Sesame Street (TV Series [1969–present]), episode "Elmo & Zoe's Hat Contest" (*rue Sésame* [France]; *Barrio Sésamo* [Spain]; *Les amis de Sésame* [Canada, French title]; *Open Sesame* [New Zealand, new syndication/English title]; *Plaza Sésamo* [Venezuela]; *Seesamitie* [Finland]; *Sesame Street Unpaved* [U.S., syndication title]; *Sesami sutorîto* [Japan, dubbed version]; *Sesamo apriti* [Italy]; *Sesamstraße* [West Germany]; *Sesamstraat* [Netherlands]; *Shalom Sesame* [Israel, Hebrew title]; *Sousami anoixe* [Greece]; *The New Sesame Street* [U.S., new syndication title]; *Ulica sezamkowa* [Poland]); U.S., Season 39, Episode 8, 22 August 2008; Family, Comedy, Fantasy, Musical/Television, Animation; 60 minutes/color/English, Spanish, American Sign Language/Mono, Stereo; Children's Television Workshop (CTW), Henson Associates (HA), Jim Henson Productions, Sesame Workshop.

Producers: Johanna Egger, Alison Folino; *Writing Credits*: J. Milligan; *Film Editing*: Meghann Artes; *Art Direction*: Russell Zambito; *Cast*: David Beckham (Himself), Fran Brill (Zoe [voice]), Tyler Bunch (Jack the Boss [voice]), Leslie Carrara (Abby Cadabby [voice]), Kevin Clash (Elmo [voice]),

Stephanie D'Abruzzo (Liz Lemon [voice]), Bill Irwin (Mr. Noodle [archive footage]), Eric Jacobson (Grover [voice]), Christopher Knowings (Chris), Loretta Long (Susan), Joey Mazzarino (Murray Monster [voice]), Khalid Moultrie (Traction Jackson [voice]), Alan Muraoka (Alan), Jerry Nelson (The Count/Tornado [voice]), Roscoe Orman (Gordon), Carmen Osbahr (Ovejita [voice]), Frank Oz (Grover [voice]), Leon Redbone (Singer [voice]), Martin P. Robinson (Telly [voice]), Caroll Spinney (Oscar/Big Bird [voice]), Lillias White (Singer "Not Alive" [voice] [archive footage]).

This episode features Count von Count, or simply "The Count."

Sesame Street (TV Series [1969–present]), episode "Little Furry Red Monster Parade" (*rue Sésame* [France]; *Barrio Sésamo* [Spain]; *Les amis de Sésame* [Canada, French title]; *Open Sesame* [New Zealand, new syndication/English title]; *Plaza Sésamo* [Venezuela]; *Seesamitie* [Finland]; *Sesame Street Unpaved* [U.S., syndication title]; *Sesami sutorîto* [Japan, dubbed version]; *Sesamo apriti* [Italy]; *Sesamstraße* [West Germany]; *Sesamstraat* [Netherlands]; *Shalom Sesame* [Israel, Hebrew title]; *Sousami anoixe* [Greece]; *The New Sesame Street* [U.S., new syndication title]; *Ulica sezamkowa* [Poland]); U.S., Season 35, Episode 6, 12 April 2004; Family, Comedy, Fantasy, Musical/Television, Animation; 60 minutes/color/English, Spanish, American Sign Language/Mono, Stereo; Children's Television Workshop (CTW), Henson Associates (HA), Jim Henson Productions, Sesame Workshop.

Cast: Jennifer Barnhart (Gladys [voice]), Fran Brill (Zoe [voice]), Ruth Buzzi (Suzie Kabloozie [voice]), Desiree Casado (Gabi), Kevin Clash (Elmo/Mel [voice]), Ángel Corella (Himself), Stephanie D'Abruzzo (Curly Bear [voice]), Olamide Faison (Miles Robinson), Jim Henson (Ernie [voice]) (archive footage), Bill Irwin (Mr. Noodle), Eric Jacobson (Grover [voice]), Sonia Manzano (Maria Figueroa Rodriguez), Joey Mazzarino (Narf/Big Foot/Tomato/Stinky the Stinkweed [voice]), Phil McGraw (Himself), Alan Muraoka (Alan), Jerry Nelson (The Count [voice]), Roscoe Orman (Trash Gordon), Carmen Osbahr (Rosita [voice]), Frank Oz (Bert [voice]) (archive footage), Martin P. Robinson (Telly Monster [voice]), David Rudman (Baby Bear/Cookie Monster [voice]), Caroll Spinney (Big Bird/Oscar [voice]), Steve Whitmire (Ernie [voice]).

This episode features Count von Count, or simply "The Count."

Sesame Street (TV Series [1969–present]), episode "Miles Babysits" (*rue Sésame* [France]; *Barrio Sésamo* [Spain]; *Les amis de Sésame* [Canada, French title]; *Open Sesame* [New Zealand, new syndication/English title]; *Plaza Sésamo* [Venezuela]; *Seesamitie* [Finland]; *Sesame Street Unpaved* [U.S., syndication title]; *Sesami sutorîto* [Japan, dubbed version]; *Sesamo apriti* [Italy]; *Sesamstraße* [West Germany]; *Sesamstraat* [Netherlands]; *Shalom Sesame* [Israel, Hebrew title]; *Sousami anoixe* [Greece]; *The New Sesame Street* [U.S., new syndication title]; *Ulica sezamkowa* [Poland]); U.S., Season 31, Episode 21, 31 January 2000; Family, Comedy, Fantasy, Musical/Television, Animation; 60 minutes/color/English, Spanish, American Sign Language/Mono, Stereo; Children's Television Workshop (CTW), Henson Associates (HA), Jim Henson Productions, Sesame Workshop.

Cast: Ruth Buzzi (Ruthie/Suzy Kabloozy/Additional Voices [voice]), Desiree Casado (Gabriella "Gaby" Rodriguez), Kevin Clash (Elmo/Hoots the Owl/Baby Natasha/Benny the Bunny/Wolfgang the Seal/The Duck/Kingston Livingston III/Grand-high-Triangle-Lover/Mel/Additional Muppets [voice]), Emilio Delgado (Luis Rodriguez), The Goo Goo Dolls (Themselves), Jerry Nelson (The Announcer/Fat Blue/Herbert Birdsfoot/Sherlock Hemlock/Herry Monster/Farley/Amazing Mumford/Frazzle/Simon Soundman/Snuffy Snuffleupagus/Brother Twiddlebug/Sam the Robot/The Count/Biff/Rodeo Rosie/Genie/Two-Headed Monster/Fred the Wonderhorse/Jarome/Leonard Wolf/Additional Muppets [voice]), Imani Patterson (Miles Robinson), Jessica Peters (Jessica), Martin P. Robinson (Snuffy Snuffleupagus/Slimey/Telly/Dickie Tick/Monty/Frazzle/Old MacDonald/Elephant/Additional Muppets [voice]), David Rudman (Athena/Baby Bear/Davey Monkey/Little Chrissy/Humphrey/Chicago Lion/Two-Headed Monster/Cookie Monster/Additional Muppets [voice]), Caroll Spinney (Big Bird/Oscar the Grouch/Bruno/Granny Bird/Lefty/Bennett Snerf [voice]), Michael Jeter (Mr. Noodle's Brother, Mr. Noodle [uncredited]), Andrea Martin (Wanda the Fairy/Additional Voices [voice, uncredited])

This episode features Count von Count, or simply "The Count."

Sesame Street (TV Series [1969–present]), episode "Sleepy Grouchy" (*rue Sésame* [France]; *Barrio Sésamo* [Spain]; *Les amis de Sésame* [Canada, French title]; *Open Sesame* [New Zealand, new syndication/English title]; *Plaza Sésamo* [Venezuela]; *Seesamitie* [Finland]; *Sesame Street Unpaved* [U.S., syndication title]; *Sesami sutorîto* [Japan, dubbed version]; *Sesamo apriti* [Italy]; *Sesamstraße* [West Germany]; *Sesamstraat* [Netherlands]; *Shalom Sesame* [Israel, Hebrew title]; *Sousami anoixe* [Greece]; *The New Sesame Street* [U.S., new syndication title]; *Ulica sezamkowa* [Poland]); U.S., Season 38, Episode 9, 29 August 2007; Family, Comedy,

Fantasy, Musical/Television, Animation; 60 minutes/color/English, Spanish, American Sign Language/Mono, Stereo; Children's Television Workshop (CTW), Henson Associates (HA), Jim Henson Productions, Sesame Workshop.

Producers: Tim Carter, April Chadderdon, Kevin Clash, Melissa Dino, Todd E. James, Benjamin Lehmann, Carol-Lynn Parente, Rebecca Rosa, Crystal Whaley; *Writing Credits*: Lou Berger, Judy Freudberg, Molly Boylan, Annie Evans, Christine Ferraro, Tony Geiss, Emily Perl Kingsley, Joey Mazzarino, Luis Santeiro; *Director*: Kevin Clash, Ken Diego, Victor DiNapoli, Dean Gordon, Tom Guadarrama, Ted May, Joey Mazzarino, Lisa Simon, Emily Squires; *Film Editing*: Selbern Narby, Chris Reinhart, John Tierney; *Original Music*: Christopher Cerf (as Chris Cerf), Tony Geiss, Stephen Lawrence, Jeff Moss, John Pizzarelli, Sam Pottle, Mark Radice, Joe Raposo, Mike Renzi, Earl Rose; *Art Direction*: Mike Pantuso, Bob Phillips, Pete Ortiz; *Make-Up*: Jane DiPersio (as Jane Di Persio), Jackie Payne; *Cast*: Sonia Manzano (Maria), Roscoe Orman (Gordon), Alison Bartlett (Gina [as Alison Bartlett O'Reilly]), Pam Arciero (Grungetta [voice]), Heather Asch (Muppet), Jennifer Barnhart (Muppet), Fran Brill (Zoe/Prairie Dawn/Grouch [voice]), Tyler Bunch (Muppet), Leslie Carrara (Abby Cadabby/Grouch [voice]), Kevin Clash (Elmo [voice]), Bruce Connelly (Muppet [as R. Bruce Connelly]), Melissa Creighton (Muppet), Stephanie D'Abruzzo (Muppet), Ryan Dillon (Muppet), Eric Jacobson (Muppet), Peter Linz (Muppet), Lara MacLean (Muppet), Noel MacNeal (Muppet), Amanda Maddock (Muppet), Jim Martin (Muppet), Joey Mazzarino (Murray Monster [voice]), Paul McGinnis (Muppet), Jerry Nelson (The Count [voice]), Carmen Osbahr (Rosita [voice]), Frank Oz (Cookie Monster/Grover [voice] [archive footage]), Martin P. Robinson (Telly Monster/Slimey [voice]), David Rudman (Grouch [voice]), Caroll Spinney (Oscar [voice]), Matt Vogel (Grouch [voice]), Steve Whitmire (Muppet [voice]), Bryant Young (Muppet), Chundo (Professor Chundo, segment "Ten O'Clock Scholar" [uncredited] [archive footage]), Harvey Fierstein (Himself) [uncredited]), Bill Irwin (Mr. Noodle [uncredited]), Howie Mandel (Himself) [uncredited]), William Wegman (Narrator (segment "Ten O'Clock Scholar" [voice] [uncredited] [archive footage]).

This episode features Count von Count, or simply "The Count."

Sesame Street (TV Series [1969–present]), episode "Telly's New Shoes" (*rue Sésame* [France]; *Barrio Sésamo* [Spain]; *Les amis de Sésame* [Canada, French title]; *Open Sesame* [New Zealand, new syndication/English title]; *Plaza Sésamo* [Venezuela]; *Seesamitie* [Finland]; *Sesame Street Unpaved* [U.S., syndication title]; *Sesami sutorîto* [Japan, dubbed version]; *Sesamo apriti* [Italy]; *Sesamstraße* [West Germany]; *Sesamstraat* [Netherlands]; *Shalom Sesame* [Israel, Hebrew title]; *Sousami anoixe* [Greece]; *The New Sesame Street* [U.S., new syndication title]; *Ulica sezamkowa* [Poland]); U.S., Season 39, Episode 2, 12 August 2008; Family, Comedy, Fantasy, Musical/Television, Animation; 60 minutes/color/English, Spanish, American Sign Language/Mono, Stereo; Children's Television Workshop (CTW), Henson Associates (HA), Jim Henson Productions, Sesame Workshop.

Producers: Kevin Clash, Benjamin Lehmann; *Cast*: Fran Brill (Zoe [voice]), Leslie Carrara (Abby Cadabby [voice]), Desiree Casado (Gabi), Kevin Clash (Elmo [voice]), Lorena Feijóo (Herself), Lorna Feijoo (Herself), Neil Patrick Harris (The Fairy Shoeperson), Eric Jacobson (Grover [voice]), Joey Mazzarino (Murray Monster [voice]), Jerry Nelson (The Count [voice]), Carmen Osbahr (Ovejita [voice]), Martin P. Robinson (Telly Monster/Book [voice]), Steve Whitmire (Ernie [voice]).

This episode features Count von Count, or simply "The Count."

Sesame Street Jam: A Musical Celebration; U.S., 1994; Family, Comedy, Fantasy, Musical/Television; 60 minutes/color/English/Dolby Digital 2.0 Stereo; Children's Television Workshop (CTW), The Jim Henson Company.

Producer: Arlene Sherman, Karin Young Shiel; *Writing Credits*: Sara Compton, Judy Freudberg, Jeff Moss, Luis Santeiro, Norman Stiles; *Director*: Mustapha Khan (as Mustapha Kahn), Jon Stone; *Original Music*: Christopher Cerf, Stephen Lawrence, Joe Raposo; *Cast*: Caroll Spinney (Big Bird/Oscar the Grouch [voice]), Martin P. Robinson (Telly Monster [voice]), Fran Brill (Prairie Dawn [voice]), Jerry Nelson (The Count/The Amazing Mumford/Herry Monster/Biff [voice]), Kevin Clash (Elmo/Natasha/Hoots the Owl [voice]), David Rudman (Chicago Lion/Humphrey/Davey Monkey [voice]), Joey Mazzarino (Joey Monkey [voice] [as Joe Mazzarino]), Pam Arciero (Muppet Performer [voice]), James J. Kroupa (Muppet Performer [voice] [as James Kroupa]), Noel MacNeal (Muppet Performer [voice]), Bryant Young (Muppet Performer [voice]), Richard Hunt (Gladys the Cow [voice] [archive footage]), Frank Oz (Bert/Grover/Cookie Monster [voice]), Jim Henson (Ernie/Kermit the Frog/Guy Smiley [voice] [archive footage]), Alison Bartlett (Gina Jefferson), Annette Calud (Celina), Savion Glover (Savion), Angel Jemmott (Angela), Sonia Manzano (Maria), Bob McGrath (Bob), Jou Jou Papailler (Jamal), Ladysmith Black Mambazo

(Special Guests), En Vogue (Special Guests), Christopher Cerf (Little Chrissy [voice]), Cooley Jackson (Grover).

Count von Count appears, along with other celebrated Sesame Street characters, in this musical extravaganza.

Sesame Street Stays Up Late! (*Sesame Street Celebrates Around the World* [VHS/DVD title]); U.S., 1993; Family, Comedy, Fantasy, Musical/Television, Animation; 60 minutes/color/English; Children's Television Workshop (CTW), The Jim Henson Company.

Producer: Nina Elias-Bamberger; *Writing Credits*: Lou Berger; *Director*: Chuck Vinson; *Cast*: Ivy Austin (Tita [voice]), Alison Bartlett (Gina), Fran Brill (Prairie Dawn/Zoe [voice]), Kevin Clash (Elmo/Cousin Pepe/Elmonosuke/Wolfgang the Seal [voice]), Savion Glover (Savion), Joey Mazzarino (MNN Logo Purple Monster [voice]), Jerry Nelson (Count [voice]), Olivia Oguma (Young Girl (from New York City), Carmen Osbahr (Rosita [voice]), Frank Oz (Bert/Grover/Cookie Monster/Uncle Hank [voice]), Martin P. Robinson (Telly/Mrs. Grouch/Snuffy [voice]), David Rudman (Baby Bear/MNN Logo Orange Monster [voice]), Caroll Spinney (Big Bird/Oscar [voice]), Lily Tomlin (Ernestine), Steve Whitmire (Ernie [voice]).

Count von Count appears along with other celebrated Sesame Street characters in this 1993 New Years special broadcast.

Shadow of the Vampire (*Sombra del vampiro* [Argentina/Columbia/Spain]; *Ombre du vampire* [Canada/France]; *A Sombra do Vampiro* [Portugal]; *Burned to Light* [U.S.]; *Ngao payabat peesat amata* [Thailand]; *Ombra del vampire* [Italy]; *Shadow of the Vampire* [Germany] *Umbra vampirului* [Romania]; *Xixuegui De Yingzi* [China]); U.S., 2000; Horror, Drama; 92 minutes/color, black and white/English/Dolby SR/35mm; Saturn Films (presents), Long Shot Pictures (producer [as Long Shot Films]), BBC Films (in association with), Delux Productions (in association with), Luxembourg Film Fund (produced in association with) (as Film Fund Luxembourg), Pilgrim Films Ltd. (produced in association with), Shadow of the Vampire, Metrodome Films (uncredited).

Producers: Paul Brooks, Nicolas Cage, Jimmy de Brabant (co-producer), Norman Golightly, Alan Howden, Richard Johns (co-producer), Jeff Levine, Orian Williams; *Writing Credits*: Steven Katz; *Director*: E. Elias Merhige; *Cinematography*: Lou Bogue; *Film Editing*: Milly Ellis, John Heath, George Korin; *Original Music*: Martin Astle, Christopher Austin, Dan Jones, Elizabeth Purnell, Jon Trotter, Nicholas Whiting; *Art Direction*: Chris Bradley (as Christopher Bradley); *Special Effects*: Philippe Lebreton, Patrick Rappard, Edward Wiessenhaan, Harrie Wiessenhaan, Rick Wiessenhaan, Jim Davey; *Cast*: John Malkovich (Murnau), Willem Dafoe (Schreck), Udo Kier (Grau), Cary Elwes (Wagner), Catherine McCormack (Greta), Eddie Izzard (Gustav), Aden Gillett (Galeen), Nicholas Elliott (Paul), Ronan Vibert (Muller), Sophie Langevin (Elke), Myriam Muller (Maria), Milos Hlavac (Innkeeper), Marja-Leena Junker (Innkeeper's Wife), Derek Kueter (Reporter 1), Norman Golightly (Reporter 2), Patrick Hastert (Reporter 3), Sascha Ley (Drunken Woman), Marie-Paule von Roesgen (Old Woman), Jean-Claude Croes (Murnau's Crew), Christophe Chrompin (Murnau's Crew), Graham Johnston (Murnau's Crew), Brian Williams (Murnau's Crew).

While silent German horror film is in production, strange things begin to occur around the set. The director wants the film to be so great that he casts an actual vampire as the lead role.

Shaitani Dracula; India, 2006; Horror/Adult; color/Hindi.

Producers: Harinam Singh; *Director*: Harinam Singh; *Writing Credits*: Harinam Singh; *Cinematography*: Bhawarlal Verma; *Cast*: Harinam Singh (Dracula), Ramesh Goel, Janardhan Mishra, Vivek Kanhaiya, Anil Nagrath, Vinod Tripathi.

Dracula and his minions begin harassing some campers in order for Dracula to seduce some of the young ladies for dinner.

Shaman King (TV Series 2003–2005), episode "Vampire Ambush"; Japan, Season 2, Episode 10, 20 November 2004; Action, Family/Television, Animation; 30 minutes/color/Japanese, English; Television Tokyo, NAS, Xebec.

Producers: Alfred R Kahn, Norman J. Grossfield, Kara Krupnick, Sherene Sharp; *Writing Credits*: Jay Bacal, Barton Bishop, Alan Kingsberg, Jim Malone, Mark Ryan; *Director*: Seiji Mizushima; Cinematography: Katsutoshi Hirose; *Film Editing*: Yayoi Otake; *Original Music*: Toshiyuki Omori, Joel Douek (English version); *Art Direction*: Toshihisa Koyama; *Cast*: Oliver Wyman (Boris Tepes Dracula III [as Pete Zarustica]), Marco Balzarotti (Boris Tepes Dracula III [voice, Italian cast]), Marc Thompson (En Tao/Additional Voices), Wayne Grayson (Tokegeroh/Additional Voices), Michael Sinterniklaas (Trey Racer), Amy Palant (Millie), Sam Riegel (Faust VIII), Andrew Rannells (Len "Lenny" Tao), Nicole Dooley (Jun Tao), Sebastian Arcelus (Yoh Asakura), Dan Green (Lee Pai Long/Silva), Yui Horie (Iron Maiden Jeanne), Bella Hudson (Lyserg Diethel), Veronica Taylor (Tamra "Tammy"), Eric Stuart (Marco), Sean Schemmel (Amidamaru/Rio).

The Shaman learns the powers of the undead to compete in the Grand Shaman King tournament.

Shaman King (TV Series [2003–2005]), episode "Winged Destroyers"; Japan, Episode 36, 13 March 2003; Fantasy, Action/Television, Animation; 30 minutes/English, color/Japanese; Television Tokyo, NAS, Xebec.

Cast: Oliver Wyman (Boris Tepes Dracula III [as Pete Zarustica]), Marco Balzarotti (Boris Tepes Dracula III [voice, Italian cast]), Marc Thompson (En Tao/Additional Voices), Dan Green (Lee Pai Long/Silva), Wayne Grayson (Tokegeroh/Additional Voices), Michael Sinterniklaas (Trey Racer), Amy Palant (Millie), Sam Riegel (Faust VIII), Andrew Rannells (Len "Lenny" Tao), Nicole Dooley (Jun Tao), Sebastian Arcelus (Yoh Asakura), Yui Horie (Iron Maiden Jeanne), Pete Zarustica (Mortimer "Morty" Oyamata), Bella Hudson (Lyserg Diethel), Veronica Taylor (Tamra "Tammy"), Eric Stuart (Marco).

The Shamans attend the theater to watch a movie when suddenly Rio is bitten by a Dracula-type vampire names Boris Tepes Dracula III.

Si Popeye, atbp (*Pop-eye Atbp* (Philippines [English title]); Philippines, 1972; Comedy; color/Filipino, Tagalog; Sine Pilipino.

Producers: Douglas Quijano; *Writing Credits*: Douglas Quijano; *Director*: Ishmael Bernal, Elwood Perez, Joey Gosiengfiao; *Cast*: Ariel Ureta (Popeye), Aurora Pijuan (Olive Oyl), Orestes Ojeda (Dracula/The Prince of Darkness), Celia Rodriguez (Lady of Darkness), Gina Pareno, Maricru del Gallego.

Silver Scream; U.S., 2003; Comedy, Horror, Musical; 91 minutes/color/English/Digital; It Came From Planet X.

Producers: April Monique Burril (as April Burril), Jimmyo Burril, Justin Alvarez (co-producer), Jennifer Hessler (co-producer [as Jen Hessler]); *Writing Credits*: Jimmyo Burril; Director: Jimmyo Burril; *Cinematography*: Jimmyo Burril; *Film Editing*: Jimmyo Burril; *Original Music*: James M. Taylor; *Art Direction*: April Monique Burril (as April Burril); *Make-Up*: Jimmyo Burril, April Monique Burril (as April Burril), Jennifer Hessler (as Jen Hessler), Beth Hillyard; *Special Effects*: Jimmyo Burril; *Cast*: Justin Alvarez (George DeMarco), Andy Wentsel (Tobe Freeling), Kristen Hudson (Shelley Freeling), David R. Calhoun (Mr. Friedkin) (as David Calhoun), Jimmyo Burril (The Count), April Monique Burril (Clamidia/Babysitter/Witch #1/Dancer [as April Burril]), Nicolette le Faye (Clitorice/Lagoon Girl #1/Babysitter), Lauren Stevenson (Chastity/Gore-Gore Girl), Jen Brill (Witch #2/Lagoon Girl #2/Dancer), Jennifer Hessler (Witch #3/Popcorn Girl) (as Jen Hessler), Lanie Carlson (Gypsy Fortune Teller [as Lanie Carlson-Limz]), Tammy Crisp (Dancer), Katie Hutchinson (The Bride/Dancer), Walt DeBell (Slasher/Zombie), Belle Gaskin (Babysitter/Dancer), Katie Taylor (The Vampiress), Launa Dixon (Dancer), Alan Martineck (Slasher), Michael Valentine (Renfield), Mike Eaves (The Monster), Naheed Mirza (Dancer), Alec Joseph (Dancer) (as Alec Penrod), Arthur E. Pittman Jr. (Slasher/Zombie [as Art Pittman]), Al Rush (Slasher/Zombie), John Sollers (Slasher), James M. Taylor (Guy getting popcorn), Lauren Weaver (Dancer), Lilly Burril (Babysitter Kid), Jessie Hutchinson (Babysitter Kid), Josh Hutchinson (Babysitter Kid), Dean Arnold (Babysitter Kid), Eric Arnold (Babysitter Kid), Lilly Jade Lim (Babysitter Kid), Sherni Alavarez (Extra), Liz Burril (Extra), Melvin Burril (Extra), Mike Bernando (Extra), Beth Cochran (Extra), Chad Collier (Extra), Jennifer DeBell (Extra), Jeremy Elliot (Extra), Amber-Lynn Elliot (Extra), Nori Elliot (Extra), Nikki Florea (Extra), Ariel Gibson (Extra), Doug Hansen (Extra), Warren Hansen (Extra), Tara Hardy (Extra), Jessica Hessler (Extra), Beth Hillyard (Extra), Jen Jackson (Extra), Steward Jackson (Extra), Ariel Jicha (Extra), Michael Knavev (Extra), Katie Lofland (Extra), Larry G. Lim (Extra), Aaron Martinek (Extra), Dave McClintock (Extra), Jose Perez (Extra), Richard Pope (Extra), Brian Pritchard (Extra), Lionel Rouzic (Extra), Claire Rush (Extra), Steven Silva (Extra), Brad Smoley (Extra), Anne Stieberg (Extra), Tim Wann (Extra), Liam Ward (Extra), Barbara Weaver (Extra), Tom Weaver (Extra), Randall Wentsel (Extra), Cydney Wentsel (Extra), Matthew Wetherell (Extra), Samuel Wightman (Extra), Bethany Willis (Extra), Beth Winter (Extra) Katy Woods (Extra), Thomas Wynn (Extra), Jane Wynn (Extra), Charlie Wyse (Extra), Chi Yan (Extra), Anthony Starcher (Vagrant [Biloxi scenes]), Matthew Maurer (Cashier [Biloxi scenes]), Patricia Causey (Sidewalk Crowd), Alyssa DiLorenzo (Sidewalk Crowd), Patrick DiLorenzo (Sidewalk Crowd), Sharon DiLorenzo (Sidewalk Crowd), Tommy DiLorenzo (Sidewalk Crowd), Allison Garner (Sidewalk Crowd), Ashley Ingraham (Sidewalk Crowd), Kaylyn Ladner (Sidewalk Crowd), Johnny Langford (Sidewalk Crowd).

While gathered at a theater that is about to be closed down, three friends are sucked into a magical realm. The realm is ruled by a vampire called The Count who recruits two of the friends to save his magical realm, the theater, and their friend Shelley (Kristen Hudson). The friends must go through different horror movies to complete their task while being chased by the villain Mr. Friedkin.

The Simpsons (TV Series [1989–present]), episode "All's Fair in Oven War"; U.S., Season 16, Episode 2, 1 November 2004; Comedy, Family/Television, Animation; 30 minutes/color/English; 20th Century–Fox Television.

Producers: James L. Brooks, Alexander Duke, Matt Groening, Sam Simon; *Writing Credits*: Matt Groening, James L. Brooks, Sam Simon; *Director*: Mark Kirkland; *Original Music*: Danny Elfman; *Cast*: Dan Castellaneta (Homer Simpson [voice]), Julie Kavner (Marge Simpson [voice]), Nancy Cartwright (Bart Simpson [voice]), Yeardley Smith (Lisa Simpson [voice]), Hank Azaria (Moe Szyslak/Chief Wiggum/Apu/Comic Book Guy/Cletus/Prof. Frink/Others [voice]), Harry Shearer (voice), James Caan (Himself [voice]), Thomas Pynchon (Himself [voice]), Marcia Wallace (Edna Krabappel [voice]), Pamela Hayden (Milhouse Van Houten/Rod Flanders/Others [voice]), Tress MacNeille (voice), Russi Taylor (voice), Karl Wiedergott (voice).

Homer buys Marge a new kitchen, and Marge likes cooking in the new kitchen so much that she attends the Ovenfresh Bakeoff. During one scene, a clip from the fake film "Blacula Meets Black Dracula" can be seen briefly.

The Simpsons (TV Series [1989–present]), episode "Brawl in the Family"; U.S., Season 13, Episode 7, 6 January 2002; Comedy, Family/Television, Animation; 30 minutes/color/English; 20th Century–Fox Television, Grace Films.

Producers: James L. Brooks, Matt Groening, George Meyer, Sam Simon, Marc Wilmore; *Writing Credits*: Matt Groening, James L. Brooks, Matt Groening, Sam Simon, Joel H. Cohen; *Director*: Matthew Nastuk; *Original Music*: Danny Elfman; *Cast*: Dan Castellaneta (Homer Simpson/Krusty the Clown/Dracula/Rich Texan/Groundskeeper Willie/Grampa [voice]), Julie Kavner (Marge Simpson [voice]), Nancy Cartwright (Bart Simpson/Nelson Muntz/Todd Flanders [voice]), Yeardley Smith (Lisa Simpson [voice]), Hank Azaria (Chief Wiggum [voice]), Pamela Hayden (Milhouse [voice]), Jane Kaczmarek (Judge Constance Harm [voice]), Delroy Lindo (Gabriel [voice]), Tress MacNeille (Woman/Amber [voice]), Harry Shearer (Montgomery Burns/Strom Thurmond/Bob Dole/Kent Brockman/Principal Skinner/Ned Flanders/Lenny [voice]), Karl Wiedergott (Additional Voices [voice]).

After a social services officer brings the Simpson family together, its newfound happiness becomes threatened when a cocktail waitress Homer married in Las Vegas appears at the door. Count Dracula makes an appearance with the Springfield Republican Party.

The Simpsons (TV Series [1989–present]), episode "Sideshow Bob Roberts"; U.S., Season 6, Episode 5, 9 October 1994; Comedy, Family/Television, Animation; 30 minutes/color/English/Stereo; 20th Century–Fox Television.

Producers: Joseph A. Boucher, James L. Brooks, Jonathan Collier, Greg Daniels, Matt Groening, Al Jean, Colin A.B.V. Lewis, J. Michael Mendel, George Meyer, George Meyer, David Mirkin, Bill Oakley, Richard Raynis, Mike Reiss, Jace Richdale, Phil Roman, David Sacks, Richard Sakai, Bill Schultz, Mike Scully, David Silverman, Sam Simon, Ken Tsumura, Josh Weinstein, Michael Wolf; *Writing Credits*: Bill Oakley, Josh Weinstein; *Director*: Mark Kirkland; *Original Music*: Alf Clausen; *Cast*: Dan Castellaneta (Homer Simpson/Grampa/Barney Gumble/Krusty the Klown/Groundskeeper Willie/Mayor Quimby/Hans Moleman/Sideshow Mel/Others [voice]), Julie Kavner (Marge Simpson/Patty Bouvier/Selma Bouvier/Others [voice]), Nancy Cartwright (Bart Simpson/Nelson Muntz/Todd Flanders/Ralph Wiggum/Kearney/Others [voice]), Yeardley Smith (Lisa Simpson [voice]), Hank Azaria (Moe Szyslak/Chief Wiggum/Apu/Comic Book Guy/Cletus/Prof. Frink/Others [voice]), Harry Shearer (Montgomery Burns/Waylon Smithers/Ned Flanders/Kent Brockman/the Rev. Lovejoy/Principal Skinner/Dr. Hibbert/Rainer Wolfcastle/Others [voice]), Barry Hansen (Himself [voice] [as Dr. Demento]), Kelsey Grammer (Sideshow Bob [voice]), Phil Hartman (Lionel Hutz/Troy McClure [voice]), Larry King (Himself [voice]), Marcia Wallace (Mrs. Krabappel [voice]), Henry Corden (Fred Flintstone [voice]), Pamela Hayden (Others [voice]).

After Sideshow Bob gets released from prison, he runs for mayor on the Republican ticket and defeats "Diamond" Joe Quimby, Springfield's long-term mayor. But an informant surfaces and informs Bart and Lisa that Sideshow Bob rigged the election. Now it is up to Bart and Lisa to reveal Sideshow Bob as the scoundrel he is. Count Dracula appears with the Springfield Republican Party.

The Simpsons (TV Series), episode "Treehouse of Horror IV"; U.S., Season 5, Episode 5, 28 October 1993; Comedy/Television, Animation; 30minutes/color/English/Dolby; 20th Century–Fox Television (as "20th Television").

Producers: James L. Brooks, Jonathan Collier (producer, as Cracklin' Jack Collier), Greg Daniels (co-producer, as Gravedancing Greg Daniels), Matt Groening, Al Jean (consulting producer, as Avuncular Al Jean), Harold Kimmel (supervising producer, as Harold "Help! I'm Alive!" Kimmel), David Mirkin (executive producer, as Damned

David Mirkin), Frank Mula (supervising producer, as Unfriendly Frank Mula), Bill Oakley (supervising producer, as The Late Bill Oakley), Conan O'Brien (supervising producer, 30 NBC" O'Brien, as Conan '12), Mike Reiss (consulting producer, as Meshuggeh Mike Reiss), David Richardson (supervising producer, as Depressed David Richardson), Gerry Richardson (producer, as Inimaginative Gerry Richardson), Jace Richdale (co-executive producer, as Horribly Jaded Jace Richdale), David Sacks (producer, as David "The Unfriendly Ghost" Sacks), David Silverman (producer, as Depravid David Silverman), Sam Simon,, John Swartzwelder (producer, as Scary John Swartzwelder), Josh Weinstein (supervising producer, as The Estate of Josh Weinstein); *Writing Credits*: Matt Groening (creator), James L. Brooks (developer), Matt Groening (developer), Sam Simon (developer), Bill Canterbury (staff writer, as Bilious Bill Canterbury), David X. Cohen (staff writer, as Discurteous David Cohen), Stephen Vincent Benet (play), Bill Canterbury (written by, as Bilious Bill Canterbury), Greg Daniels (written by, as Greg "It's Aliiive!" Daniels), Dan McGrath (written by, as Disfigured Dan McGrath), Bill Oakley (written by, as The Late Bill Oakley), Conan O'Brien (writer, as Watch Conan O'Brien), Josh Weinstein (written by, as The Estate of Josh Weinstein); *Director*: David Silverman (as David "Dry Bones" Silverman); *Film Editing*: Tim Long; *Original Music*: Danny Elfman (composer: theme "The Simpsons"), Chris Ledesma (music editor); *Art Direction*: Lucas Gray (prop designer); *Cast*: Dan Castellaneta (Homer Simpson [voice] [as Dysfunctional Dan Castellaneta]), Julie Kavner (Marge Simpson [voice] [as Jooooolie Kavner]), Nancy Cartwright (Bart Simpson [voice] [as Nasty Nancy Cartwright]), Yeardley Smith (Lisa Simpson [voice] [as Scabby Yeardley Smith]), Hank Azaria (Moe Szyslak, Chief Wiggum, Apu, Comic Book Guy, Cletus, Prof. Frink, Others [voice] [as Boo! Boo! Scare Ya Hank Azaria]), Harry Shearer (Montgomery Burns, Waylon Smithers, Ned Flanders, Kent Brockman, the Rev. Lovejoy, Principal Skinner, Dr. Hibbert, Rainer Wolfcastle, Others [voice] [as Frighticious Harry Shearer]), Phil Hartman (Lionel Hutz [voice] [as Phil Hart-on-the-Stick Man]), Pamela Hayden (Milhouse Van Houten, Jimbo [voice] [as Pamela Hacksaw Hayden]), Russi Taylor (Martin Prince, Uter [voice] [as Rancid Russi Taylor]), Frank Welker (The Gremlin [voice] [as Dr. Frankenwelker]).

Mr. Burns plays as Dracula, visually imitating the Columbia picture directed by Francis Ford Cappola.

The Simpsons (TV Series [1989–Present]), episode "Treehouse of Horror XVI," segment "I've Grown a Costume on Your Face"; U.S., Season 17, Episode 4, 6 November 2005; Family, Comedy/Television, Animation; 30 minutes/color/English/Dolby; Gracie Films, 20th Century–Fox Television, Film Roman Productions.

Producers: James L. Brooks, Alexander Duke, Matt Groening, Rick Polizzi (animation producer), Sam Simon; *Writing Credits*: Matt Groening (creator), James L. Brooks, (developer), Matt Groening, (developer), Sam Simon (developer); *Director* David Silverman; *Film Editing*: Kurtis Kunsak; *Original Music*: Alf Clausen; *Cast*: Dan Castellaneta (Homer Simpson/Grampa/Barney Gumble/Krusty the Klown/Groundskeeper Willie/Mayor Quimby/Hans Moleman/Sideshow Mel/Others [voice]), Julie Kavner (Marge Simpson/Patty Bouvier/Selma Bouvier/Others [voice]), Nancy Cartwright (Bart Simpson/Nelson Muntz/Todd Flanders/Ralph Wiggum/Kearney/Others [voice]), Yeardley Smith (Lisa Simpson [voice]), Hank Azaria (Moe Szyslak/Chief Wiggum/Apu/Comic Book Guy/Cletus/Prof. Frink/Others [voice]), Harry Shearer (Montgomery Burns/Waylon Smithers/Ned Flanders/Kent Brockman/the Rev. Lovejoy/Principal Skinner/Dr. Hibbert/Rainer Wolfcastle/Others [voice]), Tress MacNeille (Jimbo Jones/Agnes Skinner/Others [voice]), Pamela Hayden (Milhouse Van Houten/Rod Flanders/Others [voice]), Russi Taylor (Martin Prince/Others [voice]), Karl Wiedergott (Additional Voices [voice]), Terry Bradshaw (Himself [voice]), Terry Greene, Dennis Rodman (Himself [voice]).

In this segment, the citizens of Springfield dress in Halloween costumes for a local contest. Also entering the contest is a real-life wicked witch, who in fact wins. However, after she reveals her true identity (as an actual witch), the judges disqualify her and take away her prize. To take revenge, she turns everyone at the contest into the actual figures portrayed by their costumes. Mistaken for Blacula by Mayor Quimby, Dr. Hibbert is dressed as Dracula.

The Simpsons (TV Series [1989–present]), episode "You Kent Always Say What You Want"; U.S., Season 18, Episode 22, 20 May 2007; Family, Comedy/Television, Animation; 30 minutes/color/English; Gracie Films, 20th Century–Fox Television.

Producers: James L. Brooks, Matt Groening, Ron Hauge, Tim Long, Bill Odenkirk, Rick Polizzi, David Silverman, Sam Simon, Marc Wilmore; *Writing Credits*: James L. Brooks, Matt Groening, Tim Long, Sam Simon; *Director*: Matthew Nastuk; *Film Editing*: Kurtis Kunsak; *Original Music*: Alf Clausen; *Cast*: Dan Castellaneta (Homer Simpson/Hans Moleman/Mayor Quimby/Barney Gumble/Tooth Decay/Squeaky Voiced Teen/Grampa

Simpson/Arnie Pye/Newshound/Krusty/Sideshow Mel/Mr. Teeny/Rich Texan/Count Dracula [voice]), Julie Kavner (Marge Simpson/Patty Bouvier/Selma Bouvier [voice]), Nancy Cartwright (Bart Simpson/Miss Springfield/Girl in pool #2/Girl in pool #4/Girl in pool #5/Dentist #2/Rod Flanders/Children in audience/Nelson Muntz/Stripper #3 [voice]), Yeardley Smith (Lisa Simpson [voice]), Hank Azaria (Snake/Chief Wiggum/Chinese #2/Chinese #3/Asian dentist/Phineas Q. Butterfat/Comic Book Guy/'Landing Strip' announcer/Teenager boy [voice]), Harry Shearer (Gum Disease/Principal Seymour Skinner/Kent Brockman/Ned Flanders/Birch Barlow/Mr. Burns/Rainier Wolfcastle [voice]), Ludacris (Himself [voice] (as Chris "Ludacris" Bridges), Maurice LaMarche (Fox announcer/Chinese #1/Chinese #4/Leprechaun [voice]), Pamela Hayden (Girl in pool #6/Dentist's assistant/Children in audience/Stripper #2 [voice]), Tress MacNeille (Girl in pool #1/Dentist #1/Mother/Lindsey Naegle/Stripper #1/Teenager girl [voice]), Maggie Roswell (Girl in pool #3/Helen Lovejoy [voice]), Karl Wiedergott (voice).

Kent Brockman is fired from his post as a news anchor, so he and Lisa use the Internet to expose the Fox News Conspiracy. Count Dracula also makes another appearance.

Son of Dracula (*Hijo de Drácula, El* [Argentina/Spain]; *Draculan poika* [Finland, TV title]; *Draculas son* [Sweden]; *Figlio di Dracula, Il* [Italy]; *Filho de Drácula, O* [Brazil, TV title]); U.S., 1943; Horror; 80 minutes/black and white/English/Mono; Universal Pictures.

Producers: Ford Beebe, Donald H. Browne, Jack J. Gross (uncredited); *Writing Credits*: Curt Siodmak (as Curtis Siodmak), Eric Taylor; *Director*: Robert Siodmak; *Cinematography*: George Robinson; *Film Editing*: Saul A. Goodkind (as Saul Goodkind); *Original Music*: Werner R. Heymann (uncredited), Charles Previn (uncredited), Frank Skinner (uncredited); *Art Direction*: John B. Goodman, Martin Obzina; *Make-Up*: Emmy Eckhardt (uncredited), Jack P. Pierce (uncredited); *Special Effects*: John P. Fulton (uncredited); *Cast*: Robert Paige (Frank Stanley), Louise Allbritton (Katherine Caldwell), Evelyn Ankers (Claire Caldwell), Frank Craven (Doctor Brewster), J. Edward Bromberg (Professor Lazlo), Samuel S. Hinds (Judge Simmons), Adeline De Walt Reynolds (Madame Zimba) (as Adeline DeWalt Reynolds), Pat Moriarty (Sheriff Dawes) (as Patrick Moriarty), Etta McDaniel (Sarah), George Irving (Colonel Caldwell), Lon Chaney Jr. (Count Dracula [as Lon Chaney]), Charles Bates (Tommy Land [uncredited]), Joan Blair (Mrs. Land [uncredited]), Jess Lee Brooks (Stephen) (the Valet [uncredited]), Cyril Delevanti (Dr. Peters) (the Coroner [uncredited]), Robert Dudley (Jonathan Kirby, Justice of the Peace [uncredited]), Ben Erway (Deputy Shooting at Frank [uncredited]), Robert Hill (Deputy Shooting at Frank [uncredited]), Sam McDaniel (Andy) (Servant Who Greets Dracula [uncredited]), George Meeker (Part Guest [uncredited]), Jack Rockwell (Jack) (Deputy [uncredited]), Walter Sande (Mac) (Deputy [uncredited]), Emmett Smith (Servant [uncredited]).

Katherine Caldwell, one of two daughters of New Orleans plantation owner Colonel Caldwell, invites Hungarian Count Alucard to the U.S. Colonel Caldwell dies soon after Alucard's arrival, leaving his estate to Katherine, and his money to his other daughter, Claire. Katherine marries Alucard, rejecting her long-time boyfriend Frank Stanley, who confronts the couple and tries to shoot Alucard; the bullets go through the Count's body and hit Katherine, appearing to kill her. Frank consults Professor Brewster, who visits the Caldwell estate and finds Alucard with a living Katherine; Frank confesses to Katherine's murder, and a Sheriff's inspection of the estate turns up Katherine's corpse. Frank is sent to jail. Baffled, Brewster notices that Alucard is Dracula spelled backwards, and the recently arrived Hungarian Professor Lazlo suspects vampirism when a boy's body turns up drained of blood. A vampiric Katherine visits Frank in jail, professes her love, and they attempt to work together to destroy Alucard.

Son of Dracula (*Count Downe* [U.K.]; *Young Dracula* [undefined]); U.S., 1974 Horror, Comedy, Musical; 90 minutes/color/English/Mono.

Producers: Tim Gross, Ringo Starr, Tim Van Relim; *Writing Credits*: Jennifer Jayne (as Jayne Fairbank); *Director*: Freddie Francis; *Cinematography*: Norman Warwick; *Film Editing*: Ringo Starr Derek York; *Original Music*: Paul Buckmaster; *Art Direction*: Andrew Sanders; *Make-Up*: Jill Carpenter; *Cast*: Harry Nilsson (Count Downe), Ringo Starr (Merlin, the Magician), Dennis Price (Van Helsing), Suzanna Leigh (Amber), Freddie Jones (Dr. Frankenstein), Peter Frampton (Musician), Keith Moon (Musician), John Bonham (Musician), Rosanna Lee (Girl), David Bailie (Brian), Morris Bush (Monster), Shakira Caine (Housekeeper, as Shakira Baksh), Ricki Farr (Musician), Bobby Keyes (Musician), Nita Lorraine (Gorgon Woman), Skip Martin (Igor), Dan Meaden (Count Dracula), Rachelle Miller (Club Hostess), Beth Morris (Wendy), Jim Price (Musician), Jenny Runacre (Woman in Black), Leon Russell (Musician), Klaus Voormann (Musician), Hedger Wallace (Vampire), Lorna Wilde (Countess Dracula), Derek Woodward (Werewolf).

The son of Count Dracula and Baron Frankenstein are both in line to be crowned King of the Netherworld. Merlin the Magician is the mentor of Count Downe, son of Dracula, and is going to crown the King. A beautiful human, Amber, captures the heart of Count Downe.

La Sorella di Satana (*Asimenios vrykolakas* [Greece]; *Il lago di Satana* [Italy]; *Revenge of the Blood Beast* [undefined]; *Satan's Sister* [undefined]; *She Beast* [U.S.]; *Sister of Satan* [undefined]; *The She-Beast* [undefined]); U.K./Italy/Yugoslavia, 1966; Horror; 74 minutes/color/English/Mono.
Producers: Paul Manlansky, Michael Reeves; *Writing Credits*: Michael Reeves; *Director*: Michael Reeves; *Cinematography*: Gioacchino Gengarelli; *Film Editing*: Nira Omri *Original Music*: Ralph Ferraro (U.S. version), Paul Ferris; *Make Up*: David Pollack *Cast*: Barbara Steele (Veronica), John Karlsen (Count von Helsing), Ian Ogilvy (Philip), Mel Welles (Ladislav Groper), Jay Riley (Police Lieutenant), Richard Watson (Truck Driver), Edward B. Randolph (Man on Scooter), Peter Grippe (Policeman), Lucretia Love (Groper's Niece), Tony Antonelli (Policeman), Kevin Welles (Boy in Flashback), Woody Welles (Boy at Cockfight).

A young woman is involved in a car accident while driving along side a lake. The car plunges into the water, and her body is possessed by the vengeful spirit of an 18th-century witch who was killed by local Transylvanian villagers. Philip, the young woman's lover, seeks the help of a certain von Helsing, the elderly descendant of the man who slayed the infamous Count Dracula.

Space (TV Mini-Series) (*James A. Michener's Space* [undefined]); U.S., 1985 Drama/Television; 125 minutes (total)/color/English/Mono/35mm; Dick Berg-Stonehenge Productions.
Producers: Richard Berg, Martin Manulis, Allan Marcil; *Writing Credits*: Richard Berg (as Dick Berg), James Michener, Stirling Silliphant; *Director*: Lee Philips, Joseph Sargent; *Cinematography*: Héctor R. Figueroa (episode 1, 5–6), Gayne Rescher (episodes 2–4); *Original Music*: Miles Goodman; *Special Effects*: Gary D. Bierend, Paul Corbould, Ricky Farns, Martin Gutteridge, Garth Inns; *Cast*: James Garner (Sen. Norman Grant), Susan Anspach (Elinor Grant), Beau Bridges (Randy Claggett), Blair Brown (Penny Hardesty Pope), Buce Dern (Stanley Mott), Melinda Dillon (Rachel Mott), David Dukes (Martin Scorcella/Leopold Strabismus), Harry Hamlin (John Pope), Barbara Sukowa (Leisel Kolff), Michael York (Dieter Kolff), Ralph Bellamy (Paul Stidham), Roscoe Lee Browne (Farquar), Martin Balsam (Sen. Glancey), James Sutorius (Finnerty), Stephanie Faracy (Debbie Dee Claggett), G.D. Spradlin (Tucker Thomas), Wolf Kahler (Funkhauser), Jennifer Runyon (Marcia Grant), David Spielberg (Skip Morgan), Bert Remsen (Ed Specktor), Maggie Han (Cindy Rhee), Clu Gulager (Victor Hardesty), Dick Anthony Williams (Gawain Butler), Les Lannom (Larry Penzos), Scotch Byerley (Harry Jensen), James Edgcomb (Ed Cater), Lawrence Lott (Timothy Bell), Richard Partlow (Charles Lee), Jonathan Goldsmith (Raf Perry), Christina Pickles (Mrs. McKellar), Gerald Hiken (Prof. Anderson), Murphy Dunne (Lt. Wiles), Michael Talbott (Tom Savage), Peter Nelson (Millard Mott), Richard Pierson (Roger), Charles Tyner (Dracula), Barbara Bingham (Cluny Bell), Christine Dickinson (Gloria Cater), Jeanne Langer (Inger Jensen), Annie O'Neill (Sandra Lee), Donald Craig (Newsman), Robby Weaver (Sam Cottage), Julie Phillips (Ronnie), Alan Fudge (Pomfret), Lia Sargent (Mia Portnoy), Sue String (Sally Quint), Michael Cochrane (Wing Cmdr. Blount), Stephen Jenn (Hans Brenner), Gary Kasper (Brother), Bill Morey (Dean Robert Hawkins), Shane Rimmer (Gen Quigley), Sheila Ruskin (Lt. Constance Hall-Tipping), Michael Sheard (Himmler), Eleanor Zee (Mrs. Griffin), Mary Jackson (Frankie), Richard Delmonte (Ramirez), Walter Mathews (Jennings), Burke Byrnes (FBI Agent), Nancy Abramson (School Secretary), Jim Antonio (Levering), Ivan Bonar (Harry Crampton), Jack Garner (Flight Operations Officer), Bill Sorrells (Col. Boyd), Jack Thibeau (Capt. Penscott), Howard Mann (Lawyer/Tycoon), Bob McLean (Newsman), Richard X. Slattery (Navy Captain), Vernon Weddle (Burgess), Kenneth White (Expert), Richard Gordon (CapCom), James Avery (Jean-Marie), Lizabeth Pritchett (Esther Glancey), Woody Eney (TV Science Consultant), Marya Morgan (Anchorwoman), Laurence Luckinbill (Narrator), Gale Baker (U.S.O Dancer), Burton Collins, Thomas F. Duffy (Brad), Dyanne Thorne (Entertainer), Marcus Olah Sr. (Pilot [uncredited]), William A. Purcell (Extra [uncredited]).

Space is a fictional story about the lives of members of the United States space program during the space race with the Soviet Union, between the end of World War II and the Apollo program in the 1970s. The mini-series features a character named Dracula.

Sphinx — Geheimnisse der Geschichte (TV Series [1994–2009]), episode "Die Vampirprinzessin"; Germany, 2007; Documentary, Television; 52 minutes/color, black and white/German/Dolby Digital; ZDF, Arte.
Writing Credits: Klaus T. Steindl, Andreas Sulzer; *Director*: Klaus T. Steindl, Andreas Sulzer; *Cinematography*: Hubert Doppler; *Film Editing*: Michaela Müllner; *Original Music*: Peter Wolf.

Researchers investigate the historical sources on vampirism that Bram Stoker may have used when writing *Dracula*, particularly less familiar sources like the 18th century Austrian princess Eleonore von Schwarzenberg.

Spider-Man and His Amazing Friends (TV Series [1981–1986]), episode "Transylvanian Connection"; U.S., Season 3, Episode 2, 1983; Action, Family, Fantasy/Television, Animation; 22 minutes/English/color/Mono; Marvel Productions, Mihahn (in association with), DePatie-Freleng Enterprises.
Producers: David H. DuPatie, Lee Gunther, Dennis Marks; *Writing Credits*: Jack Mendelsohn *Original Music*: Johnny Douglas (as John Douglas); *Cast*: Kathy Garver (Firestar/Angelica Jones [voice]), Dan Gilvezan (Spider-Man/Peter Parker [voice]), Frank Welker (Iceman/Bobby Drake [voice]).

Outside of a dance, Angelica is lured by a stranger, and then hypnotized. Spider-Man and Iceman follow to find that the stranger is Dracula. The plane is on its way to Dracula's home, Transylvania, and defeat a werewolf and Frankenstein in order to get Angelica back.

Spider-Woman (TV Series [1979]), episode "Dracula's Revenge"; U.S., Season 1, Episode 10, 26 August 1979; Action, Family, Fantasy/Television, Animation; 30 minutes/color/English; DePatie-Freleng Enterprises.
Producers: David H. DePatie, Friz Freleng, Lee Gunther; *Writing Credits*: Stan Lee, Jeffery Scott; *Original Music*: Eric Rogers; *Cast*: Joan Van Ark (Jessica Drew/Spider-Woman [voice]), Bruce Miller (Jeff Hunt [voice]), Bryan Scott (Billy Drew [voice]), Lou Krugman (Police Chief [voice]), Larry Carroll (Detective Miller [voice]), John H. Mayer (voice), Vic Perrin (voice), Ilene Latter (voice), Tony Young (voice), Karen Machon (voice), John Milford (voice), Dick Tufeld (Narrator [voice]).

Dracula is awakened from his deep slumber and vows revenge against all mortals. He then wakes Frankenstein and the Wolfman. Spider-woman finds herself up against a force of slaves created by Dracula, The Wolfman, and Frankenstein.

SpongeBob SquarePants (TV Series [1999–present]), episode "Graveyard Shift/Krusty Love"; U.S., Season 3, Episode 13, 6 September 2002; Comedy, Fantasy/Television, Animation; 30 minutes/color/English/Stereo; Nicktoons Productions.
Producers: Paul Tibbitt (supervising producer); *Writing Credits*: Stephen Hillenburg, Derek Drymon, Stephen Hillenurg, Mr. Lawrence, Jay Lender, Mark O'Hare, Kent Osborne, Dan Povenmire, William Reiss; *Director*: Jay Lender; *Film Editing*: Lynn Hobson; *Art Direction*: Nicholas R. Jennings; *Cast*: Tom Kenny (SpongeBob SquarePants/Narrator/Woman/Waiter [voice]), Rodger Bumpass (Squidward Tentacles [voice]), Bill Fagerbakke (Patrick Star [voice]), Clancy Brown (Mr. Eugene H. Krabs [voice]), Mary Jo Catlett (Mrs. Poppy Puff [voice]), Dee Bradley Baker (Richard/Customer 40/Customer 6 [voice]), Max Schreck (archive footage from *Nosferatu* [uncredited]).

SpongeBob and Squidward have to work the nightshift at the Krusty Krab after Mr. Krabs (Clancy Brown) decides to stay open 24 hours. Strange things keep happening throughout the night. They have scary customers, green ooze drips from the walls, and the lights keep flicking on and off. They find out it was Nosferatu (Max Schreck), a.k.a. Dracula, standing in the corner flipping the switch up and down.

The Steve Allen Show (TV Series [1956–1960]), episode "2.35" (*The Steve Allen Plymouth Show* [U.S.]; *Show de Steve Allen, El* [Venezuela]); U.S., Season 2, Episode 35, 16 June 1957; Comedy/Television; 60 minutes/black and white/English/Mono; National Broadcasting Company.
Writing Credits: Don Hinkley; *Cast*: Steve Allen (Himself/Host), Don Adams (Himself), Edie Adams (Herself), Dayton Allen ("Why Not Man"), Gabriel Dell (Count Dracula [as Gabe Dell]), Herbert Hartig, Skitch Henderson (Himself Bandleader/Sidney Ferguson), Peggy King (Herself), Don Knotts (Mr. Morrsion), Louis Nye (Gordon Hathaway), Tom Poston ("Man Who Can't Remember His Name"), Gene Rayburn (Announcer), Dale Robertson (Himself), John Cameron Swayze (Himself).

Gabriel Dell appears as Dracula on the show.

The Steve Allen Show (TV Series [1956–1960]), episode "5.3" (*Show de Steve Allen, El* [Venezuela]; *The Steve Allen Plymouth Show* [U.S., new title]); U.S., Season 5, Episode 3, 12 October 1959; Comedy/Television; 60 minutes/black and white/English/Mono; National Broadcasting Company.
Writing Credits: Don Hinkley; *Cast*: Steve Allen (Himself/Host), Les Brown (Himself/Conductor), Gene Rayburn (Himself/Announcer): Gabriel Dell (Count Dracula [as Gabe Dell]), Pat Harrington Jr. (Guido Panzini), Cal Howard (Announcer), Crystal Joy (Herself/Singer), The King Sisters (Themselves), Don Knotts (Himself), Lee Marvin (Himself), Louis Nye (Himself).

Gabriel Dell appears as Dracula on the show.

The Steve Allen Show (TV Series [1956–1960]), episode "5.14" (*Show de Steve Allen, El* [Venezuela]; *The Steve Allen Plymouth Show* [U.S., new title]); U.S., Season 5, Episode 14, 11 January 1960; Comedy/Television; 60 minutes/color/English/Mono; National Broadcasting Company.

Writing Credits: Don Hinkley; *Cast*: Steve Allen (Himself/Host), Tony Bennett (Himself), Les Brown (Himself), Gabriel Dell (Count Dracula [as Gabe Dell]), Les Brown and His Band of Renown (Themselves), Jayne Meadows (Herself), Louis Nye (Frankenstein's Monster), Caroline Richter (Comedian).

Gabriel Dell appears as Dracula on the show.

Sundown: The Vampire in Retreat; U.S., 1990; Comedy, Horror, Western; 104 minuets/color/English/Dolby; Vestron Pictures.

Producers: Dan Ireland, Jack Lorenz, Jefferson Richard; *Writing Credits*: John Burgess, Anthony Hickox; *Director*: Anthony Hickox; Cinematography: Levie Isaacks; *Film Editing*: Christopher Cibelli; *Original Music*: Richard Stone; *Art Direction*: Fernando Altschul; *Make-Up*: Rene Bresee, Katie Douthit, Tony Gardner, Tony Gardner, Larry Hamlin, Cheryl Markowitz (as Cheryl Ann Markowitz), Beatrice Marot, Michael Burnett; *Special Effects*: Jim Braverman (as "Diamond" Jim Braverman), Frank Furlong, Steve Greene, Jenny Hall, Hal Miles, Brian D. Veatch, Damien Veatch, Rex Whitney; *Cast*: David Carradine (Jozek Mardulak/Count Dracula), Morgan Brittany (Sarah Harrison), Bruce Campbell (Robert Van Helsing), Jim Metzler (David Harrison), Maxwell Caulfield (Shane), Deborah Foreman (Sandy White), M. Emmet Walsh (Mort Bisby), John Ireland (Ethan Jefferson), Dana Ashbrook (Jack), John Hancock (Quinton Canada), Marion Eaton (Anna Trotsberg), Dabbs Greer (Otto Trotsberg), Bert Remsen (Milt Bisby), Sunshine Parker (Merle Bisby), Helena Carroll (Madge), Elizabeth Gracen (Alice), Christopher Bradley (Chaz), Kathy MacQuarrie Martin (Burgundy), Jack Eiseman (Nigel), George 'Buck' Flower (Bailey), Erin Gourlay (Juliet Harrison), Vanessa Pierson (Grewdolyn Harrison), Brendan Hughes (James), Gerardo Mejía (Pucci), Mike Najjar (Ramon), Phillip Simon (Pierre), Chris Caputo (Dan, the Bodyguard [as Christopher Caputo]), Dean Cleverdon (Vampire #1), Jay Bernard (Vampire #2), Stuart Cohn (Vampire #3), Phillip Esposito (Tom "Redneck" Pryor), Larry Barsky (Vampire [uncredited]).

In a small desert town called Purgatory located in the American west lives a cluster of vampires. They wear special sunblock and large sombreros to protect themselves from the sunlight, and drink synthetic blood. David Carradine plays Jozek Mardulak (i.e. Count Dracula).

The Super Mario Bros. Super Show! (TV Series [1989–1991]), episode "Bats in the Basement/Mario and the Beanstalk"; U.S., Season 1, Episode 8, 13 September 1989; Fantasy, Family, Action/Television, Animation; 15 minutes/color/English; DiC Entertainment, Sei Young Animation Co., Ltd.

Producers: John Grusd; *Writing Credits*: George Atkins; *Director*: Steve Binder, John Grusd, Dan Riba; *Original Music*: Eric Allaman, Shuki Levy, Haim Saban; *Art Direction*: Hervé Bédard, Royce Mathew; *Cast*: Lou Albano (Mario "Jumpman" Mario), Harvey Atkin (King Bowser Koopa/Mushroom Mayor/Tryclyde/Sniffet) (voice), Jeannie Elias (Princess Peach Toadstool/Shyguy) (voice), John Stocker (Toad/Mouser #1/Koopa Troopa/Beezo/Flurry) (voice), Danny Wells (Luigi Mario), Robert Bockstael (Mouser #2) (voice) (credit only), Greg Morton (voice) (credit only), Dorian Joe Clark (voice) (credit only), Joyce Gordon (voice) (credit only), Rob Cowan (voice) (credit only), Greg Swanson (voice) (credit only), Denise Pidgeon (voice) (credit only), Diane Fabian (voice) (credit only), Marilyn Lightstone (voice) (credit only), Paulina Gillis Sprite/Additional Voices (voice) (credit only), Marla Lukofsky (voice) (credit only), Jim Ward (Count Zoltan Dracula).

Based on the popular video game, this series follows the adventures of Mario and Luigi as they help Princess Toadstool rid their land of the evil King Bowser and his band of goons. This particular episode features Mario and Luigi fighting Count Zoltan Dracula as they investigate bats in a basement.

The Super Mario Bros. Super Show! (TV Series [1989–1991]), episode "Count Koopula"; U.S., Season 1, Episode 18, 27 September 1989; Family, Fantasy, Action, Adventure/Television, Animation; 14 minutes/color/English/Mono; DiC Enterprises.

Producers: Steve Binder, Andy Heyward, Robby London, John Grusd, Troy Miller, Keiren Kasun, Lisa Rosales, Jack Spillum; *Writing Credits*: Phil Harnage; *Director*: Dan Riba; *Film Editing*: Karen Rosenbloom, Donald P. Zappala; *Original Music*: Eric Allaman, Shuki Levy, Haim Saban; *Art Direction*: Hervé Bédard, Royce Mathew; *Special Effects*: Kexx Singleton; *Cast*: Lou Albano (Mario "Jumpman" Mario), Harvey Atkin (King Bowser Koopa/Mushroom Mayor/Tryclyde/Sniffet [voice]), Jeannie Elias (Princess Peach Toadstool/Shyguy [voice]), John Stocker (Toad/Mouser #1/Koopa Troopa/Beezo/Flurry [voice]) Danny Wells (Luigi Mario), Robert Bockstael (Mouser #2 [voice]), Greg Morton (voice), Dorian Joe Clark (voice), Joyce Gordon (voice), Rob Cowan (voice), Greg Swanson (voice), Denise Pidgeon (voice), Diane Fabian (voice), Marilyn Lightstone (voice), Paulina Gillis (Sprite/Additional Voices), Marla Lukofsky (voice).

Luigi and Mario seek refuge in the vampire Count Koopula's castle in Turtlevania. There they must keep Princess Peach (Jeannie Elias) from being turned into a vampire by the evil Count as well as fight off his many minions.

Taiho shichauzo (TV Series [1996–1997]), episode "40" (*You're Under Arrest* [International English Title]; *Équipières de choc* [French]; *Están Arrestados* [Spanish]; *Estás Arrestado!!* [Spanish]; *Quedes dentingut, Sei in arresto!* [Italian]; *Taiho Shichauzo* [Japanese]); Japan, 1997; Action, Comedy/Television, Animation; 46 minutes/color/Japanese, English; Studio DEEN.

Producers: Hiroyuki Fukumoto, Tetsuo Gensho, Kazunori Noguchi; *Writing Credits*: Kôsuke Fujishima, Akemi Omode, Kazuhisa Sakaguchi, Michiru Shimada, Sho Tokimura, Keiko Watanabe, Michiko Yokote; *Director*: Kazuhiro Furuhashi; *Cinematography*: Mitsunobu Yoshida; *Film Editing*: Seiji Morita; *Original Music*: Yasunori Iwasaki, Kô Ôtani (as Koh Ohtani); *Cast*: Takehiro Murozono (Dracula), Haruka Naruzaki (Guide), Kazuya Ichijou (Gasmask Man), Takayasu Usui (Wolfman), Tetsuya Sakai (Fry Man), Yuu Hatto (50 cm Head Man).

Tales from the Darkside (TV Series [1984–1988]), episode "The Circus"; U.S., Season 3, Episode 1, 28 September 1986; Fantasy, Horror, Thriller/Television; 30 minutes/color/English/Mono/35mm; Laurel Entertainment Inc.

Producers: Jerry Golod, George A. Romero, Richard P. Rubinstein, Jan Saunders, William Teitler; *Writing Credits*: George A. Romero; *Director*: Michael Gornick; *Cinematography*: Jon Fauer; *Film Editing*: Scott Vickrey; *Original Music*: Ken Mazur; *Make-Up*: Gigi Williams; *Special Effects*: James Chai (special effects makeup assistant), Ed French (special effects makeup), David Scott Gagnon (special effects); *Cast*: Ed French (Creature/Vampire), William Hickey (Dr. Nis), Kevin O'Connor (Bragg), Jacques Sandulescu (Nanoosh), David Thornton (Werewolf).

Interestingly referred to as a "succubus" during the episode (a "succubus" being the female equivalent to the male "incubus," each being a sort of "dream vampire" but nonetheless distinctly gendered), the "Creature/Vampire" who appears here in Dr. Nis's circus displays the repulsive *Nosferatu*-type physical features of Orlock/Dracula, coupled with the more refined opera attire of the Universal/Hammer Dracula's cape, both features suggestive that this un-dead attraction is a Dracula-type character. However, it is not until the "Creature/Vampire" appears in context with the circus' other monster attractions (i.e. a mummy, a werewolf, a Frankenstein-type reanimated corpse) that the Dracula nuances far exceed suggestion.

Tales from the Darkside (TV Series [1984–1988]), episode "My Ghostwriter — The Vampire"; U.S., Season 3, Episode 14, 1 February 1987; Fantasy, Horror, Thriller/Television; 30 minutes/color/English/Mono/35mm; Laurel Entertainment Inc., Tribune Entertainment.

Producers: T. J. Castronova (supervising producer), Anthony Santa Croce, Christopher T. Welch; *Writing Credits*: Scott Edelman, Peter O'Keefe; *Director*: Frank De Palma; *Cinematography*: Joseph Urbanczyk; *Film Editing*: William Flicker; *Original Music*: Ken Mazur; *Art Direction*: Gene Abel; *Make-Up*: Tyler Smith; *Special Effects*: Joe LaPenna; *Cast*: Jeff Conaway (Peter), Roy Dotrice (Vampire Count Draco), Jillie Mack (Jayne), Paul Sparer (Narrator).

A vampire approaches a writer and asks him to write his life story, in return for being made immortal. The writer does so and when he becomes famous, the vampire returns and wants a share of the profits.

Tales from the Darkside (TV Series [1984–1988]), episode "Strange Love"; U.S., Season 2, Episode 21, 11 May 1986; Fantasy, Horror/Television. Fantasy, horror, thriller/Television; 30 minutes/color/English/Mono/35mm; Laurel Entertainment Inc., Tribue Entertainment

Producers: Jerry Golod, George A. Romero, Richard P. Rubinstein, Jan Saunders, William Teitler; *Writing Credits*: Edithe Swensen; *Director*: Theodore Gershuny; *Cinematography*: Karen Grossman; *Film Editing*: Edmund Ferrell, Derek Parsons; *Original Music*: Irwin Fisch; *Art Direction*: Gene Abel; *Make-Up*: Tyler Smith; *Special Effects*: Tyler Smith; *Cast*: Harsh Nayyar (Edmund Alcott), Marcia Cross (Marie Alcott), Patrick Kilpatrick (Dr. Philip Carrol), Paul Sparer (Narrator).

A vampire couple is dancing one night when the wife breaks her leg. A doctor is called and when he is finished with the wife, the two vampires hold him captive. Over time the female vampire falls in love with the doctor and turns him into a vampire as well.

Tales of the Wizard of Oz (TV Series [1961]), episode "The Reunion"; U.S., February 1961; Comedy, Fantasy, Family/Television, Animation; 5 minutes/color/English; Rankin Bass Productions, Crawley Films.

Producers: Arthur Rankin Jr., Jules Bass, Larry Roemer, Antony Peters, Bernard Cohen; *Writing Credits*: Arthur Rankin Jr.; *Director*: Bernard Cohen; *Cast*: Carl Banas (Dandy Lion), James Duhan (The Wizard of Oz), Larry D. Mann (Rusty the Tin Woodman, Witch), Bernard Cohen (Munchkins), Alfie Scoop (Socrates the Scarecrow).

Frankie Dracula, Velma Vellan, and the Wicked Witch of the West attend their 50th class reunion from the Oz School for Sorcerers. They talk about the days when they picked on Little Woo-Woo, and to their surprise, he grew up to be the Wizard of Oz.

A Taste of Blood (*The Secret of Dr. Alucard*); U.S., 1967; Horror; 117 minutes/color/English/Mono; Creative Film Enterprises Inc..

Producers: Herschell Gordon Lewis, Sidney J. Reich; *Writing Credits*: Donald Stanford; *Director*: Herschell Gordon Lewis; *Cinematography*: Andy Romanoff; *Film Editing*: Richard Brinkman; *Original Music*: Larry Wellington; *Cast*: Bill Rogers (John Stone), Elizabeth Wilkinson (Helene Stone), William Kerwin (Dr. Hank Tyson [as Thomas Wood]), Lawrence Tobin (Det. Crane), Ted Schell (Lord Gold), Otto Schlessinger (Dr. Howard Helsing), Eleanor Vaill (Hester Avery), Gail Janis (Vivian), Herschell Gordon Lewis (The Limey Seaman/Voice of Baron Khron [as Seymour Sheldon]), Judy Waterberry (Ida, the maid), Dolores Carlos (Sherri Morris), Roy Collodi (Delivery Man), Karl Stoeber (Man walking dog), Thomas Rowland (Detective), Sidney J. Reich (Arthur Morris [as Sidney Jaye]), Barrie Walton (Telephone Operator), Cal Bowman (Hank's golfing friend), Doug Weston (Police photographer), Jake R. Pawlson (Policeman), Bill Kozak (Man running from tomb).

Businessman John Stone becomes a vampire after drinking two old bottles of brandy sent to him from Europe. Stone then travels to England to kill the descendants of Van Helsing while being pursued by a Howard Helsing, a distant relative of the man famous for killing Dracula.

Taste the Blood of Dracula (*Blodsmak* [Sweden]; *Dracula, paholaisen lähettiläs* [Finland]; *Messa per Dracula, Una* [Italy]; *Paholaisen lähettiläs* [Finland]; *Poder de la sangre de Drácula, El* [Spain]; *Prueba la sangre de Drácula* [Argentina (cable TV title)]; *Sangue de Drácula, O* [Brazil]; *Une messe pour Dracula* [France]; *Wie schmeckt das Blut von Dracula?* [West Germany]); U.K., 1970; Horror, Romance; 95 minutes/color/English/Mono/35mm; Hammer Film Productions.

Producers: Aida Young; *Writing Credits*: Anthony Hinds (as John Elder), Bram Stoker; *Director*: Peter Sasdy; Cinematography: Arthur Grant; *Film Editing*: Chris Barnes; *Original Music*: James Bernard; *Make-Up*: Gerry Fletcher; *Special Effects*: Brian Johnson (as Brian Johncock), Terry Schubert (uncredited), Mike Tilley (uncredited); *Cast*: Christopher Lee (Dracula), Geoffrey Keen (William Hargood), Gwen Watford (Martha Hargood), Linda Hayden (Alice Hargood), Peter Sallis (Samuel Paxton), Anthony Higgins (Paul Paxton [as Anthony Corlan]), Isla Blair (Lucy Paxton), John Carson (Jonathon Secker), Martin Jarvis (Jeremy Secker), Ralph Bates (Lord Courtley), Roy Kinnear (Weller), Michael Ripper (Inspector Cobb), Russell Hunter (Felix), Shirley Jaffe (Betty — Hargood's Maid), Keith Marsh (Father), Peter May (Son), Reginald Barratt (Vicar), Madeline Smith (Dolly [as Maddy Smith]), Lai Ling (Chinese girl [as Chai Ling]), Malaika Martin (Snake girl), Amber Blare (Bordello Girl [uncredited]), Vicky Gillespie (Bordello Girl [uncredited]), June Palmer (Redhead Prostitute [uncredited]).

Four men attempt to bring Count Dracula back to life through a ceremony of drinking his blood. Three men refuse to drink the blood; the fourth man who does drink the blood is transformed into Dracula. Dracula then proceeds to carry out his revenge on the three men who abandoned the ceremony by means of killing their children.

Tempi duri per i vampiri (*Agárrame ese vampiro* [Spain]; *Hard Times for Dracula* [undefined]; *Hard Times for Vampires* [undefined]; *My Uncle the Vampire* [undefined]; *Schlechte Zeiten für Vampire* [West Germany]; *Temps sont durs pour les vampires, Les* [France]; *Uncle Was a Vampire* [undefined]); Italy/France, 1959; Comedy, Horror; 85 minutes/color/Italian; CEI.

Producers: Mario Cecchi Gori, Adriano De Micheli, Joseph E. Levine, Antonio Sarno; *Writing Credits*: Edoardo Anton, Mario Cecchi Gori, Marcello Fondato, Renato Rascel, Steno (as Stefano Vanzina), Edoardo Anton, Sandro Continenza, Dino Verde, Steno (as Stefano Vanzina); *Director*: Steno; *Cinematography*: Marco Scarpelli; *Film Editing*: Eraldo Da Roma; *Original Music*: Renato Rascel, Armando Trovajoli; *Art Direction*: Andrea A. Tomassi; *Make-Up*: Gustavo Sisi, Eligio Trani; *Cast*: Renato Rascel (Baron Osvaldo Lambertenghi), Sylva Koscina (Carla), Lia Zoppelli (Letizia), Kai Fischer (Lellina), Franco Scandurra (Prof. Stricker), Carl Wery, Antje Geerk, Federico Collino, Susanne Loret, (Susan) (American tourist), Angelo Zanolli, Antonio Mambretti, Ivana Gilli, Franco Giacobini, Fiorella Ferrero, Leonardo Porzio.

Baron Osvaldo Lambertenghi is forced to sell his ancient castle to become a hotel. Once sold, he stays on the property working as a bellboy. One day, his uncle shows up and turns out to be a vampire. After he is bitten and turned into a vampire by his uncle, he proceeds to attack and suck the necks of female guests staying at the hotel.

Tendre Dracula (*Grande trouille, La* [France]; *Tender Dracula, or Confessions of a Blood Drinker* [U.S.]; *Tendre Dracula*, [Canada]; *The Big Scare* [U.S.]) France, 1974; Fantasy, Horror; 98 minutes/color/French/Mono; AMLF.

Director: Pierre Grunstein; *Original Music*: Karl-Heinz Schäfer; *Make-Up*: Alain Folgoas; *Cast*: Peter Cushing (MacGregor), Nathalie Courval (Madeleine), Miou-Miou (Marie), Bernard Menez (Alfred), Stéphane Shandor (Boris [as Stephan Shandor]), Percival Russel (Abélard, le serviteur), Alida

Valli (Héloïse), Julien Guiomar (Le producteur), Brigitte Borghese (La secrétaire du producteur [as Brigitte De Borghese]).

Two writers take their girlfriends with them on a trip to a castle while researching an actor who has performed the role of a vampire in many films. The longer they spend at the castle, the possibility of the actor being an actual vampire seems more real.

Teta (TV Series) (*Frankenstein's Aunt* [undefined]; *Frankensteins Tante* [West Germany]; *La tante de Frankenstein* [France]; *La tia de Frankenstein* [Spain]; *Los monstruos de Transilvania* [Spain]); Austria/West Germany/France/Czechoslovakia/Spain/Italy, 1987; Family, Comedy, Fantasy/Television; 25 minutes/color/Slovak; Ceskoslovenská Televize Bratislava, Films du Sabre, France 3 (FR 3), MR Filmproduktion, Radiotelevisione Italiana, Slovenská filmová tvorba Koliba (SFT), Televisión Española (TVE).

Producers: Kurt J. Mrkwicka; *Writing Credits*: Jaroslav Dietl, Joachim Hammann, Juraj Jakubisko, Alan Rune Pettersson, Mary Shelley, Bram Stoker; *Director*: Juraj Jakubisko; *Cinematography*: Ján Duris, Juraj Jakubisko, Ján Piroh; *Film Editing*: Patrik Pass; *Original Music*: Guido De Angelis, Maurizio De Angelis; *Art Direction*: Lubor Cencak; *Special Effects*: Willi Neuner, Karl-Heinz Bochnig, Uli Nefzer; *Cast*: Viveca Lindfors (Hannah von Frankenstein [7 episodes, 1987]), Martin Hreben (Max [7 episodes, 1987]), Gerhard Karzel (Albert [7 episodes, 1987]), Barbara De Rossi (Klara [7 episodes, 1987]), Eddie Constantine (Alois — Water Spirit [7 episodes, 1987]), Flavio Bucci (Talbot — Werewolf [7 episodes, 1987]), Ferdy Mayne (Count Dracula [7 episodes, 1987]), Mercedes Sampietro (Elisabeth — the White Lady [7 episodes, 1987]), Jacques Herlin (Igor [7 episodes, 1987]), Andrej Hryc (Schmied [7 episodes, 1987]), Roman Skamene (Hans — Mayor's Son [7 episodes, 1987]), Tilo Prückner (Sepp [6 episodes, 1987]), Marie Drahokoupilová (Mrs. Karch [5 episodes, 1987]), Milan Lasica (Teacher [5 episodes, 1987]), Bolek Polívka (Henry Frankenstein [4 episodes, 1987]), Gail Gatterburg (Bertha [4 episodes, 1987]), Sancho Gracia (Investigating judge [2 episodes, 1987]), Ales Furundarena (unknown episodes).

Tetsuwan Atom (TV Series [1963–1966], episode "Vampire Vale" (*Astro Boy* [U.S.]; *Mighty Atom* [International]); Japan, 1964; Action, Adventure, Family/Television, Animation; 30 minutes/black and white/Japanese; Tezuka Productions, Mushi Productions, Video Promotions, Inc.

Producers: Osamu Tezuka; *Writing Credits*: Osamu Tezuka, Fred Ladd; *Director*: Osamu Tezuka, Fred Ladd (English version); *Film Editing*: Pablo Zavalo; *Original Music*: Tatsuo Takai; *Cast*: Billie Lou Watt (Astro Boy [English voice]), Cliff Owen (Dr. Elefun [English voice]), Gilbert Mack (Mr. Pompus [English voice]).

One night, two travelers named Tick and Tock become lost in the mountains of Europe. They eventually find themselves in a deserted town called Tran"smell"vania, whose windows are covered with crosses and garlic. Tick and Tock end up taking refuge in a nearby castle where they are attacked by what appears to be a Dracula-type vampire.

The Thirst: Blood Wars (*Blood Wars* [U.S., DVD title]; *The Thirst* [U.S., working title]); U.S., 2008; 90 minutes/color/English/Dolby Surround Sound; Psycho Studios, In-Motion Pictures, MEB Entertainment.

Producers: Mark Burman, Marco Antonio Cuadros, A.J. Draven, Stephanie Lemelin, Scott Pearlman, Eric Ricart, Tom Shell; *Writing Credits*: Ramesh Thadani; *Director*: Tom Shell; *Cinematography*: Howard Wexler; *Film Editing*: Andrew Bentler; *Make-Up*: Jeffrey S. Farley, Debra Martinez, Isabelle Murray, Joy Shulman; *Cast*: Tony Todd (Julien), A.J. Draven (Will Hawkins), Jason Connery (Claudius), Allison Lange (Jayne), America Olivo (Amelia), Owiso Odera (Rico), Rini Bell (Ashley), Cameron Zeidler (Darren), Nick Holmes (Jason Pierce), Stephanie Lemelin (Laurie), Mark Ryan (Reeve), Bill Doyle (Titus), Jarrad Hewett (Aldren), C. Thomas Howell (Jed), Mark Holton (Earl), Jonathan Durante (Tommy), Cyd Schulte (Sister 1 [as Cydne Schulte]), Mary Votava (Sister 2), Tiffany McFarland (Sister 3), Zachary Ray Sherman (Victor), Peter Looney (Homeless Man [as Peter Loony]), Marci Holmes (Mystery Girl), Mark Burman (Prof. Potatohead), Joy Shulman (Surprised Girl [uncredited]).

Will, a laid-back college student, gets caught up in a war between vampires and a group of warlocks called Sentries. But after he is bitten by a seductive vampiress, he is forced to have to choose sides. Tony Todd plays a Dracula-type vampire master.

30 Days of Night; U.S., 2007; Horror, Thriller; 113 minutes/color/English/Dolby Digital; Columbia Pictures, Dark Horse Entertainment, Ghost House Pictures.

Producers: Ted Adams, Joseph Drake, Aubrey Henderson, Nathan Kahane, Mike Richardson, Sam Raimi, Chloe Smith, Robert G. Tapert; *Writing Credits*: Steve Niles, Stuart Beattie, Brian Nelson, Ben Templesmith; *Director*: David Slade; *Cinematography*: Jo Willems; *Film Editing*: Art Jones; *Original Music*: Brian Reitzell; *Cast*: Josh Hartnett (Sherrif Eben Oleson), Melissa George (Stella Oleson), Danny Huston (Marlow), Ben Foster (The Stranger), Mark Boone Junior (Beau Brower), Mark Rebdall (Jake Oleson), Amber Sainsbury (Denise), Manu Bennett (Deputy Billy Kitka),

Megan Franich (Iris), Joel Tobeck (Doug Hertz), Elizabeth Hawthorne (Lucy Ikos), Nathaniel Lees (Carter Davies), Craig Hall (Wilson Bulosan), Chic Littlewood (Isaac Bulosan), Peter Feeney (John Riis), Min Windle (Ally Riis), Camille Keenan (Kirsten Toomey), Jack Walley (Peter Toomey), Elizabeth McRae (Helen Munson), Joe Dekkers-Reihana (Tom Melanson), Scott Taylor (Paul Jayko), Grant Tilly (Gus Lambert), Pua Magasiva (Maleki Hamm), Jared Turner (Aaron), Kelson Henderson (Gabe), John Wraight (Adam Colletta), Dayna Porter (Jeannie Colletta), Kate Butler (Michelle Robbins), Patrick Kake (Frank Robbins), Thomas Newman (Larry Robbins), Rachel Maitland-Smith (Gail Robbins), Abbey-May Wakefield (Little Girl Vampire), John Rawls (Zurial), Andrew Stehlin (Arvin), Tim McLachlan (Archibald), Ben Fransham (Heron), Kate Elliott (Dawn), Allan Smith (Khan), Jarrod Martin (Edgar), Sam La Hood (Strigoi), Jacob Tomuri (Seth), Kate O'Rourke (Inika), Melissa Billington (Kali), Aaron Cortesi (Cicero), Matt Gillanders (Daeron), Jay Saussey (Doug's Wife).

An isolated Alaskan town is plunged into darkness for a month each year when the sun sinks below the horizon, after which, the town is attacked by a bloodthirsty gang of vampires whose aim is to drain and destroy the entire town. Leading the vampires is Marlow, a Dracula-type vampire. Only the small town's husband-and-wife Sheriff team stands between the last few survivors and certain destruction.

This Darkness: The Vampire Virus (*The Darkness* [U.S., DVD box title]; *Vamps* [undefined]); U.S., 2003; Horror; 106 minutes/color/English.

Producers: Dylan O'Leary; *Writing Credits*: Dylan O'Leary; *Director*: Dylan O'Leary; *Cinematography*: John McLeod; *Film Editing*: Chris Cook; *Cast*: David Everritt (Tarquin the Vampire), Jenevieve Frank (Rally), Amanda Cook (Dr. Mary Kmai), Sean Bennett (Dr. Bob), Son Nguyen (FBI Agent Sean Nguyen), Dylan O'Leary (Dr. Van Helsing VII), John McLeod (Ronder), Ron Little (Master Little), Eli Born (Eli), Tony Malachi (Tony), Mitch Roberts (Dean Jones), Dr. Terry Prewitt (Wedding Minister), Rachel Barevich, Amanda Cherry (Amanda (as Amanda Ratchford), Carley Quina (Carley), Jaimee Cooley (Cheerleader (as Jamiee Cooley), Chad Wosniak (Tom the Surfer), Nathan Beene (Lab Assistant), Jonah Criswell (Lab Assistant), Chris Anderson (Dr. Van Helsing VI), Travis Macks, Taylor Biggs, Laurie Biggs, Heather Mott (Vampire), Paul Travitsky (Vampire), Adam Moon (Vampire), Michael (Vampire), Matt Lacy (Vampire), Mama Trish (Vampire), Constantine Varazo (Vampire), Lance Brannon (Vampire), Mario Cieri (Vampire), Blake Hardin (Vampire from Ron Little Martial Arts), Rob Mercieri (Vampire from Ron Little Martial Arts), Chad Beck (Vampire from Ron Little Martial Arts), Seth Joyner (Vampire from Ron Little Martial Arts), Arron Smith (Vampire from Ron Little Martial Arts), Ryan Farrell (Vampire from Ron Little Martial Arts), Vincent Woodruff (uncredited).

When genetic engineer Dr. Van Helsing VII discovers the secret to immortality, no sooner is he confronted by real life vampires. The Lord of the Undead (a.k.a. Dracula), orders Van Helsing to fashion him a bride or suffer his wrath. A battle between the two sides soon begins when a young female starts working at his lab.

3-2-1 (TV Series [1978–1987]), episode "The Magic of Merlin"; U.K., Season 8, 16 November 1985; Family/Television; 60 minutes/color/English; Yorkshire Television (YTV).

Producers: John Bartlett, Derek Burrell-Davis, Philip Casson, Mike Goddard, Terry Henebery, Graham Wetherell; *Director*: Ian Bolt, David Millard, Paddy Russell, Philip Casson; *Cinematography*: Phil Knockton; *Original Music*: Johnny Pearson; *Make-Up*: Hazel Burridge; *Cast*: Ted Rogers (Himself/Host), Caroline Munro (Hostess), Jeremy Connor, Kenneth Connor, (Merlin), Chris Emmett, Aimi MacDonald (Marilyn Monroe), Jon Pertwee (Dracula).

Three's Horrible: Part 1; U.S., 2008; Comedy/Short, Animation; 2 minutes/English/color.

Writing Credits: Stephen A. Brooks; *Director*: Stephen A. Brooks; *Original Music*: Stephen A. Brooks *Cast*: Stephen A. Brooks (Dracula/Wolfman/Frank).

This short introduces the humorous and strained relationship between Dracula, Frankenstein's monster, and the Wolf-Man as they all live together in an apartment.

Tiempos duros para Drácula; Spain/Argentina, 1976; Comedy; color/Spanish; Aitor & Espacio.

Writing Credits: Jorge Darnell; *Director*: Jorge Darnell; *Cinematography*: Teodoro Escamilla; *Original Music*: Adolfo Waitzman; *Cast*: José Lifante (Drácula), Alberto Fernández de Rosa, María Noel, Miguel Ligero, Alba Múgica, Adolfo Linvel, Luis Politti, Joaquín Roa, Alfonso De Grazia, Sally Acuña, Luis Barboo, Carmen Carrión, Saturno Cerra, Coco Fossati, Adelco Lanza, Antonio Mayans, (J. Antonio Mayans), Alfonso Pícaro, Odile Pons (Odille Pons), Mirna Quesada, Beatriz Savón.

Dracula is experiencing a rough period in his life. His health is not well and his finances are stretching thin. Now, his castle has been made open to the public, denying him the serenity and rest he desires.

Titeuf (TV Series), episode "Pépé Dracula"; France, Season 1, Episode 57, April 2001; Family/Television, Animation; 7 minutes/color/French; France Animation, Glénat, Canal J, France 3, SMEC.

Writing Credits: Nathalie Reznikoff, Zep; *Director*: Daniel Duda; *Original Music*: Didier Ledan, Joseph Refalo; *Cast*: Donald Reignoux (Titeuf, Hugo), Thierry Ragueneau (Le père de Titeuf), Danièle Hazan (La mère de Titeuf, L'institutrice), Caroline Pascal (Nadia), Sabrina Leurquin (Manu, Dumbo), Vincent Ropion (François).

While visiting their grandfather, Titeuf and Manu happen upon a set of dentures in a glass of water. If the dentures belong to grandfather, then Titeuf and Manu fear that he may be some sort of Dracula.

To Die For (*Bram Stoker's To Die For* [U.S., DVD box title]; *Drácula — Pacto de Sangue* [Brazil]; *Dracula: The Love Story* [undefined]; *Dracula: The Love Story to Die For* [U.S., DVD title]; *Passion sanglante* [Canada, video title] [French title]; *Sang et passion* [France]; *Tödliche Lippen* [West Germany]; *Tappava himo* [Finland]; *Vampiri* [Italy]); U.S., 1988; Horror, Romance, Thriller; 94 minutes/color/English/35mm; Arrowhead Productions.

Producers: Lee Caplin, Greg H. Sims, Barin Kumar, Edward Oleschak; *Writing Credits*: Leslie King; Director: Deran Sarafian; *Cinematography*: Jacques Haitkin; *Film Editing*: Dennis Dolan; *Original Music*: Cliff Eidelman; *Art Direction*: Gregory Oehler; *Make-Up*: Jerrie Werkman, Sherry Mixon; *Special Effects*: John Carl Buechler (as John Buechler), John Criswell, Michael Deak, Michael Deak, John Foster, Greg Johnson, Timothy Ralston, Wayne Toth; *Cast*: Brendan Hughes (Vlad Tsepsh), Sydney Walsh (Kate Wooten), Amanda Wyss (Celia Kett), Scott Jacoby (Martin Planting), Micah Grant (Mike Dunn), Duane Jones (Simon Little), Steve Bond (Tom), Remy O'Neill (Jane), Al Fann (Lt. Williams), Philip Granger (Detective Bocco), Lloyd Alan (Rich), Julie Maddalena (Paula Higgins), Eloise DeJoria (Girl at Party) (as Eloise Broady), Cate Caplin (Michelle), Ava Fabian (Franny), Dean Anthony (Ben), Fred Waugh (Bum), Bill Handy (Dump Truck Driver), Richard C. Sarafian (Bartender), Sharon Mullings (Woman on Yacht), Jim Ladd (Radio DJ) (voice) Bill Riback (Comedian) (voice), Ben Bray (Vampire), Lance Slaton (Delivery Guy), Devorah Valins (Female Victim [uncredited]).

Real estate agent Kate Wooten falls in love with a client to whom she sold an old isolated castle. She discovers that the client is the vampire Vlad Tsepsh, whose nemesis Tom is seeking revenge on Vlad for stealing his lover 100 years earlier.

Topo Gigio (TV Series [1988–1989]), episode "Gigio and Vampire" (*Yume Miru Topo Gigio* [Japan]; *Die Weltraum-Maus* [Germany]); Japan, 1988 Family/Television, Animation; 25 minutes/color/Japanese; Nippon Animation Co.

Producers: Koichi Motohashi; *Writing Credits*: Noboru Ishiguro, Chiyu Tadaoki; *Director*: Shigeo Koshi, Noboru Ishiguro; *Original Music*: Nobuyoshi Koshibe; *Art Direction*: Shuichi Ishibashi.

Gigio and his friends watch a horror movie about Dracula on TV. Afterwards, Alner tells his friends that vampires are real, and that a few were even spotted in the old ruined castle up in the hills near Santa Catalina. It turns out Alner is right.

Topo Gigio — No Castelo do Conde Drácula; Brazil, 1987; Family/Television, Animation; 45 minutes/color/Portuguese; Rede Bandeirantes.

Director: Pedro Siaretta; *Cast*: Marthus Mathias, Samanta Monteiro.

Activating a time machine by accident, Samantha sends Topo Gigio to Dracula's Castle, where Topo turns into a little vampire.

Train Ride to Hollywood (*Night Train*); U.S., 1975; Comedy, Musical, Fantasy; 89 minutes/color/English/Stereo; Todd-AO Studios/Billy Jack Enterprises, Crystal Jukebox Film Corp.

Producers: Michael Payne; *Writing Credits*: Dan Gordon; *Director*: Charles R. Rondeau; *Cinematography*: Al Francis; *Film Editing*: James T. Heckert; *Original Music*: Pip Williams; *Art Direction*: Philip M. Jefferies; *Cast*: Willis Draffen Jr. (Himself), Charles Love (Himself), Charles McCormick (Himself), Harry Williams (Himself), Michael Payne (Eric), Guy Marks (Humphrey Bogart), Jay Robinson (Dracula), Jay Lawrence (Rhett Butler/Clark Gable), Phyllis Davis (Scarlett O'Hara), Roberta Collins (Jean Harlow), Bill Oberlin (W.C. Fields), John Myhers (Sheik), Tracy Reed (Stupid bimbo), Gerri Reddick (Rhythm Professor), Peter Ratray (Nelson Eddy), Ann Willis (Jeanette MacDonald), Elliot Robins (The Godfather/Marlon Brando/The Wild One), Peter Gonneau (Assistant Producer/Godson/Peter Lorre), Jack DeLeon (News reporter), Jessamine Milner (Benny), Burt Mustin (George), Jimmy Lennon Sr. (Himself), Bob Westmoreland (Referee), Don Dandridge (Doctor), Whitey Hughes (Killer Fewakki).

Harry Williams, a member of a band called Bloodstone, is about to go on stage for a concert when he is hit on the head. The rest of the movie is his dream. The band members change into conductors on a train filled with characters and actors from the 1930s, such as Dracula, played by Jay Robinson, and Scarlett O'Hara. The singing conductors are obliged to solve a mystery.

Transylmania; U.S., 2009; Comedy, Horror; 92 minutes/color/English/SDDS, Dolby SR, Dolby

Digital, DTS; Film Rock, Hill & Brand Entertainment.

Producers: Radu Badica, Nicholas Bonavia, Aaron L. Gilbert, Sanford Hampton, Edward Jarzobski, Michael Long, Scott Nell, Viorel Sergovici, Kim Swartz, Jor Van Kline; *Writing Credits*: Patrick Casey, Worm Miller; *Director*: David Hillenbrand, Scott Hillenbrand; *Cinematography*: Viorel Sergovici *Film Editing*: Dave O'Brien; *Make-Up*: Miruna Panaitescu; *Special Effects*: Petre Constantin, Larry Fioritto, Vincent J. Guastini, Mircea Cristian Nicolae, Marian Pisau, Jor Van Kline, Dean Welch, Valeriu Zamfir.

A spoof on previous vampire and horror films, this film follows some college students who do a semester abroad in Romania, where they soon realize that if too much partying does not kill them first, the vampires just might. Several characters and character names pay homage to previous *Dracula* films.

Transylvania 6-5000 (*Notte in Transylvania, Una* [Italy]; *Transilvânia—Hotel do Outro Lado do Mundo* [Brazil]); U.S., 1985; Comedy, Horror; 93 minutes/color/English/Mono; Balcor Film Investors.

Producers: Thomas H. Brodek, Arnie Fishman, Paul Lichtman, Glenn Neufeld, Mace Neufeld; *Writing Credits*: Rudy De Luca; *Director*: Rudy De Luca; *Cinematography*: Tomislav Pinter (as Tom Pinter); *Film Editing*: Harry Keller; *Original Music*: Ira Hearshen, Lee Holdridge, Alfi Kabiljo (as Alfie Kabiljo); *Art Direction*: *Make-Up*: Halid Redzebasic (as Halid Redzebastic); *Special Effects*: Ellis Burman Jr. (as Ellis Burman), Marijan Karoglan (as Marijan Kuroglan), Branko Repalust, Bob Williams; *Cast*: Jeff Goldblum (Jack Harrison), Joseph Bologna (Dr. Malavaqua), Ed Begley Jr. (Gil Turner), Carol Kane (Lupi), Jeffrey Jones (Lepescu), John Byner (Radu), Geena Davis (Odette), Michael Richards (Fejos), Donald Gibb (Wolfman), Norman Fell (Mac Turner), Teresa Ganzel (Elizabeth Ellison), Rudy De Luca (Lawrence Malbot), Inge Apelt (Madame Morovia), Bozidar Smiljanic (Insp. Percek), Petar Buntic (Hunyadi), Dusko Valentic (Twisted man), Ksenia Prohaska (Mummy [as Ksenija Prohaska]), Sara Grdjan (Laura Ellison), Nada Abrus (Uta [as Nada Arbus]), Visnja Babic (Peasant girl [as Visnja Konigskneght]), Slobodan Milovanovic (Front guard), Vida Jerman (Rear guard), Vjenceslav Kapural (Jailer [as Venco Kapural]), Thomas H. Brodek (Bandleader).

In a story that draws heavily from Shelley's and Stoker's works, two tabloid writers receive evidence of a Frankenstein's Monster and travel to a somewhat modernized Transylvania to investigate. While there, they discover many of the other classic staple monsters as well.

Transylvania Twist; U.S., 1989; Comedy, Horror; 90 minutes/color/English/Mono; Concord Productions Inc.

Producers: Alida Camp, Roger Corman; *Writing Credits*: R.J. Robertson, Jim Wynorski; *Director*: Jim Wynorski; *Cinematography*: Zoran Hochstätter; *Film Editing*: Nina Gilberti; *Original Music*: Chuck Cirino; *Art Direction*: Beth Elliott; *Make-Up*: Dean Gates, Desne J. Holland, Dean Jones, Starr Jones, Angela Moos, Angela Moos, Sunyata Palmer, Tricia Sawyer, Cristina Patterson Ceret (uncredited); *Special Effects*: Michael Clark, Joe Earle, Howie Rogue, Neil Smith; *Cast*: Robert Vaughn (Lord Byron Orlock), Teri Copley (Marissa Orlock), Steve Altman (Dexter Ward), Ace Mask (Victor Von Helsing), Angus Scrimm (Stefen), Steve Franken (Hans Hoff), Vinette Cecelia (Laverne), Monique Gabrielle (Patty) (Patricia), Howard Morris (Marinas Orlock), Jay Robinson (Uncle Ephram), Lenny Juliano (Maxie Fields), Joe Lerer (Hans Downe), Clement von Franckenstein (Hans Hoff), R.J. Robertson (Hans Phull), Arthur Roberts (Hans N. Fritz), Toni Naples (Maxine), Frazer Smith (Slick Lambert), Becky LeBeau (Rita), Stu Nahan (Sports Announcer), Jack Behr (Director), Kelli Maroney (Hannah), Michael Chieffo (Ed Norton Look-Alike), Jon Locke (Mr. Sweeney), Magda Harout (Peasant Woman), Deanna Lund (Teacher), Brinke Stevens (Betty Lou), Harriet Harris (Granny), Michael Vlastas (James Vasvolakas), Art Hern (Willoughby).

In this horror spoof, a young man and his girlfriend travel to Transylvania to find a book entitled "The Book of All Evils." This book is 200 years old and belonged to a vampire named Lord Byron Orlock. The book contains an apocalyptic spell, and because of this evil, the book must be destroyed.

A Trip with Dracula; U.S., 1970; Underground Film.

Twins of Evil (*Djävulens dotter* [Sweden]; *Drácula y las mellizas* [Spain]; *Draculan kaksoset* [Finland]; *Draculas Hexenjagd* [West Germany]; *Draculas dotter* [Sweden]; *Figlie di Dracula, Le* [Italy]; *Paholaisen kaksoset* [Finland]; *Pirun kaksoset* [Finland]; *Sévices de Dracula, Les* [France]; *The Evil Twins* [U.K.]; *The Gemini Twins* [undefined]; *The Virgin Vampires* [U.K., pre-release title]; *Twins of Dracula* [undefined]; U.K., 1971; Horror, Drama; 87 minutes/color/English/Mono/35mm; Hammer Film Productions, The Rank Organisation (presents).

Producers: Harry Fine, Michael Style; *Writing Credits*: Tudor Gates, Sheridan Le Fanu; *Director*: John Hough; *Cinematography*: Dick Bush; *Film Editing*: Spencer Reeve; *Original Music*: Harry Robertson; *Art Direction*: Roy Stannard; *Make-Up*:

George Blackler, Pearl Tipaldi, John Webber; *Special Effects*: Jack Mills, Bert Luxford (uncredited); *Cast*: Inigo Jackson (Woodman), Judy Matheson (Woodman's Daughter), Peter Cushing (Gustav Weil), Harvey Hall (Franz), Alex Scott (Hermann), Shelagh Wilcocks (Lady in Coach), Madeleine Collinson (Frieda Gellhorn), Mary Collinson (Maria Gellhorn), Kathleen Byron (Katy Weil), Roy Stewart (Joachim), Luan Peters (Gerta), Damien Thomas (Count Karnstein), Dennis Price (Dietrich), Maggie Wright (Alexa), Katya Wyeth (Countess Mircalla), David Warbeck (Anton Hoffer), Isobel Black (Ingrid Hoffer), Kirsten Lindholm (Young Girl at Stake), Peter Thompson (Gaoler), Roy Boyd (Dying Man [uncredited]), Maxine Casson (Schoolgirl [uncredited]), Vivienne Chandler (Schoolgirl [uncredited]), Doreen Chanter (Schoolgirl [uncredited]), Irene Chanter (Schoolgirl [uncredited]), George Claydon (Midget [uncredited]), John Fahey (Puritan [uncredited]), Kenneth Gilbert (Puritan [uncredited]), Derek Glynne-Percy (Puritan [uncredited]), Cathy Howard (Girl on Tomb [uncredited]), Jason James (Puritan [uncredited]), Sebastian Graham Jones (Puritan [uncredited]), Jackie Leapman (Schoolgirl [uncredited]), Janet Lynn (Schoolgirl [uncredited]), Annette Roberts (Schoolgirl [uncredited]), Bill Sawyer (Puritan [uncredited]), Peter Stephens (Member of the Brotherhood [uncredited]), Garth Watkins (Chief Priest [uncredited]).

Following the death of their parents, the Gellhorn twins, Maria and Frieda, journey from Vienna to Karnstein in order to live with their uncle, Gustav Weil, who heads the Brotherhood, a vigilante group trying to stamp out vampirism. One evening when Frieda has had enough of Uncle Gustav, she sneaks out of the house and finds herself in the clutches of Count Karnstein (Damien Thomas), who turns her into a vampire. A Dracula-type vampire also makes an appearance.

U.F.O. U.K., 1993; Comedy, Science Fiction; 79 mintues/color/English; George Forster, PolyGram Filmed Entertainment.

Producers: Peter Smith, Simon Wright; *Writing Credits*: Roy "Chubby" Brown, Richard Hall, Simon Wright; *Director*: Tony Dow; *Cinematography*: Paul Wheeler; *Film Editing*: Michael John Bateman, Geoff Hogg; *Art Direction*: Martyn John; *Make-Up*: Julie Van Praag; *Special Effects*: Alan Whibley; *Cast*: Roy "Chubby" Brown (Himself), Sara Stockbridge (Zoe), Amanda Symonds (Ava), Roger Lloyd-Pack (Solo, as Roger Lloyd Pack), Shirley Anne Field (Supreme Commander), Sue Lloyd (Judge), Diran Shah (Genghis Khan), Kenny Baker (Casanova), Rusty Goffe (Henry VIII), Anthony Georghiou (Dracula), James Culshaw (Man), Sheila Gill (Old Woman), Paul Sarony (Journalist), Ben Aris (Doctor), Laura Jackson (Guard), Robbie Dee (Band Member), Claire Robinson (Band Member), Jenny Michelmore (Receptionist), Ken MacDonald (Plumber), Walter Sparrow (Old Codger), Alan Bodenham (Milkman), Shaun Curry (Barman), Jean Warren (Sheena), Mike Hallett (Snooker Player), Sam Britchford (Dancer), Isabel Rua-Hunt (Dancer), Alex Avenall (Dancer), Karen Holle (Dancer), Mandy Miller (Dancer), Natalie George (Dancer).

Roy "Chubby" Brown, a chauvinistic comedian, is kidnapped by a group of 25th century feminists after watching him from a distant galaxy, and he is to be put on trial for his horrid jokes. Dracula makes an appearance.

Ultimate Super Heroes, Vixens, and Villains (TV Series [2005]), segment "Ultimate Super Villains"; U.S., Season 1, Episode 3, 28 May 2005; Fantasy, Horror/Documentary, Television; 60 minutes/color, black and white/English/Mono; Prometheus Entertainment, Fox Television Studios, Van Ness Films.

Producers: Kevin Burns, Scott Hartford (senior producer), Kim Sheerin (co-executive producer), Gary Simson, Steven Smith (supervising producer), Lisa Van Eyssen; *Writing Credits*: Gary Simson, Steven Smith, Steven Smith; *Film Editing*: Kevin Benson, Troy Bogert, John W. Richardson; *Special Effects*: Patrick Sheehan (digital compositor); *Cast*: Vivica A. Fox (Herself), Ben Affleck (Himself), Bryan Singer (Herself), George Lucas (Himself), Harrison Ford (Himself), Hugh Jackman (Himself), James Earl Jones (Himself), Jessica Alba (Herself), Kirsten Dunst (Herself), Mike Myers (Himself), Stan Lee (Himself), Steven Spielberg (Himself), Adam West (Narrator).

This segment examines the top comic book evildoers, including Dracula.

Universal Horror; U.K., 1998; Horror/Television, Documentary; 95 minutes/color, black and white/Stereo; Photoplay Productions.

Producers: Peter Langs, Patrick Stanbury; *Director*: Kevin Brownlow; *Film Editing*: Kevin Brownlow, Sherief M. Hassan; *Original Music*: James Bernard; *Cast*: Kenneth Branagh (Narrator), Forrest J Ackerman (Himself), Turhan Bey (Himself), Ray Bradbury (Himself), Jim Curtis (Himself), Curtis Harrington (Himself), Adolf Hitler (Himself [archive footage]), Rose Hobart (Herself), Gloria Jean (Herself), James Karen (Himself), Boris Karloff (Himself [archive footage]), Sara Karloff (Herself [daughter of Boris Karloff]), Carla Laemmle (Herself), Fritz Lang (Himself [archive footage]), Rouben Mamoulian (Himself [archive footage]), Curt Siodmak (Himself), David J. Skal

(Himself), Gloria Stuart (Herself), Lupita Tovar (Herself), Fay Wray (Herself).

This documentary explores the era of horror movies created by Universal Studios. It uses a basic starting point of Béla Lugosi's *Dracula*, but mentions some older titles as well. Although the documentary is centered around Universal Studios, it makes note of titles from other companies such as MGM and Warner Brothers. Many Dracula titles are included.

Urusei Yatsura (TV Series [1981–1986]), episode "What a Dracula!"; Japan, Season 2, Episode 6, 12 May 1982; Comedy, Science Fiction/Television, Animation; 23 minutes/color/Japanese; Studio Pierrot, AnimEigo.

Producers: Takao Inoue, Yuji Nunokawa; *Writing Credits*: Kazunori Ito, Shoo Hisaichi; *Director*: Mamoru Oshii, Junji Nishimura (assistant director); *Original Music*: Anzai Fumitaka, Zazado Shinsuke; *Special Effects*: Abe Goo; *Cast*: Fumi Hirano (Lum), Toshio Furukawa (Ataru Moroboshi), Kaneta Kimotsuki (Count Dracula).

In this episode, Dracula is in love and tries to court Lum, the beautiful alien from outer space who has her own problems as it is, as she tries to help high school student Ataru, the main protagonist of the show who also likes Lum.

Vampira (*Folle histoire de vampiror, La* [France]; *Old Drac* [U.S.]; *Old Dracula* [U.S.]; *Temps sont durs pour Dracula, Les* [France]; *Vampira — en tjej på bettet* [Sweden]; *Vampira — piru hampaissa* [Finland]); U.K., 1974; Comedy, Horror; 88 minutes/color/English/Mono/35mm; World Film Services.

Producers: Jack Wiener; *Writing Credits*: Jeremy Lloyd; *Director*: Clive Donner; *Cinematography*: Anthony B. Richmond; *Film Editing*: Bill Butler; *Original Music*: David Whitaker; *Make-Up*: Philip Leakey, Christopher Tucker; *Cast*: David Niven (Count Dracula), Teresa Graves (Countess Vampira), Peter Bayliss (Maltravers), Jennie Linden (Angela), Nicky Henson (Marc), Linda Hayden (Helga), Bernard Bresslaw (Pottinger), Cathie Shirriff (Nancy), Andrea Allan (Eve), Veronica Carlson (Ritva), Minah Bird (Rose), Christopher Sandford (Milton), Freddie Jones (Gilmore), Frank Thornton (Mr. King), Aimi MacDonald (Woman in Hotel Room), Patrick Newell (Man in Hotel Room), Kenneth Cranham (Paddy, the Delinquent), Carol Cleveland (Jane, the Delinquent's Victim), Luan Peters (Pottinger's Secretary), Marcia Fox (Air Hostess), David Rowlands (Drunk), Ben Aris (Policeman), Nadim Sawalha (Airline Representative), Hoima McDonald ("Playboy" Bunny), Nicola Austin ("Playboy" Bunny) (as Nicola Austine), Penny Irving ("Playboy" Bunny), James Payne (Taxi driver at airport [uncredited]).

Dracula seeks to revive his long lost love Vampira. In order to resurrect her, he takes blood from several Playboy Bunnies living in his mansion, one of which is black. The excess pigmentation from the Black Playboy Bunny turns Vampira into a black woman, and Dracula must deal with his love's new appearance.

Las Vampiras (*The Vampire Girls* [U.S., video box title]; *The Vampires* [U.K.]) Mexico, 1969; Horror, Action; 91 minutes/color/Spanish/Mono; Filmica Vergara S.A.

Producers: Jesús Fragoso Montoya (as Jesús Fragoso), Luis Enrique Vergara; *Writing Credits*: Federico Curiel Adolfo Torres Portillo; *Director*: Federico Curiel; *Cinematography*: Alfredo Uribe; *Film Editing*: Juan José Munguía; *Original Music*: Gustavo César Carrión *Cast*: John Carradine (Bronos), Mil Mascaras, María Duval, Maura Monti, Marta Romero, Pedro Armendáriz Jr., Sergio Beauregard, Sara Benítez, Joe Carson, Rossy Ceballos, Felipe del Castillo, Manuel Garay, Nathanael León, Adolfo Magaldi, Elsa Maria, Jessica Munguía, Juan Ortiz Hernandez, Dagoberto Rodríguez.

The Count sends his vampire brides out to transform new vampires. However, his plan is stopped cold when a wrestler comes to save the day.

Vampire Blues (*Blues del Vampire, Los* [DVD title, Spain]; *Vampire Sex — Lady Dracula 3* [Germany]; *Vampyr Blues* [VCD title, Spain]); U.S., 1999; Horror; 91 minutes/color/English/Stereo; One-Shot Productions.

Producers: Kevin Collins, Peter Evanko (as Peter J. Evanko), Hugh Gallagher, Karen Wong; *Writing Credits*: Kevin Collins, Jesus Franco (as Jess Franco); *Director*: Jesus Franco (as Jess Franco); Cinematography: Raquel Cabra; *Film Editing*: Juan Jose Villar; *Original Music*: Jesus Franco, Brian D. Horrorwitz, Randy Manos, Daniel White; *Make-Up*: Eva Salcedo (makeup artist, as Eva I. Salcedo); *Special Effects*: Joaquin Phre, Juan Jose Villar; *Cast*: Rachel Sheppard (Rachel Crosby), Analia Ivars (Countess Irina von Murnau), Lina Romay (Marga, the Gipsy), Jesus Franco (The Merchant), Pedro Temboury (The Guitarist), Jessica Luo (Rachel Crosby [voice]), Leyora Zuberman (Countess Irina von Murnau [voice]).

Countess Irina von Murnau seduces the young Rachel Crosby through her dreams. Rachel's subconscious leads her to an old house on a hill overlooking the town. She finds out the house belongs to the woman of her dreams, Countess Irina von Murnau. The Countess finds Rachel attractive and uses her powers of seduction to bite Rachel. After Rachel leaves the Countess she meets a gypsy named Marga. The Gypsy helps Rachel defeat the Countess.

Vampire City (*Vampire City Episode I — Rock 'N Roll Vampires from Hell* [Austria]); Austria, 2009; Horror; 71 minutes/color/English/Dolby Digital; WildRebel Productions.

Producers: Wolf Morrison, Jeff Taylor; *Writing Credits*: Wolf Morrison; *Director*: Wolf Morrison; *Cinematography*: Bob Czerny, Julia Jellen, Wolf Morrison, Guenther Rubik; *Film Editing*: Wolf Morrison; *Original Music*: Wolf Morrison; *Art Direction*: Franz Zimmermann (set designer); *Make-Up*: Verena Wehr; *Special Effects*: John T. Tyler; *Cast*: Wolf Morrison (Count Dracula/Robert Van Helsing), Birgit Waite (Vampire Queen [as Biggie Waite]), Christian Gassler (Morlock), Sofia Soul (Pia), Franziska Doppel (Isabelle), Robert Cerny (Wild Vampire), Robert Czerny (Wild Vampire), Guenther Kubik (Waiter), Christina Breit (Princess), Viktoria Stoifl (Vampire Girl), Andrea Schmidt (Vampire Girl), David Braune (Actor in Movie), Melanie Breit (Vampire Girl), Renee Chantalle (Glenda), Humungus (Guest), Johnny Lapitz (Actor in Movie), Herbie Smith (Actor in Movie), Silvia Welich (Actress in Movie).

The search for his father's murderer leads Robert Van Helsing to Vienna. There he meets Dracula and the beautiful girls Pia and Isabelle. Together they fight against the evil Vampire Queen and her lover Morlock who are plotting to rule the world.

Le Vampire déchu (*Der Gefallene Vampir* [Austria/Germany]; *Béla Lugosi — Dracula's Dubbelganger* [Netherlands]); France/Romania/Austria/Germany/Netherlands, 2007; Documentary; 52 minutes/color, black and white/English, French, German; AVRO Television.

Producers: Susanne Biermann, Razvan Georgescu, Franz Grabner, Olaf Grunert, Maijke Huijbregts (as Marijke Huijbregts), Ramona Iepan, Heike Lettau, Nicoleta Mocanu, Claudia Nedelcu, Carl Schmitt (as Carl Schmidt), Cecile Thomas; *Writing Credits*: Florin Iepan, Ramona Iepan, Calin Meda; *Director*: Florin Iepan; *Cinematography*: Alfred Schupler, Cosmin Tiglar, Rafael Vasilcin; *Film Editing*: Wolfgang Lehmann; *Original Music*: Tavi Iepan, Remus Rujinski; *Cast*: Béla Lugosi (Himself/Dracula [archive footage]), Carroll Borland (Herself [archive footage] [as Carol Borland]), Lon Chaney (Himself [archive footage]), Clark Gable (Himself [archive footage]), Otilia Hedesan (Herself), Boris Karloff (Himself [archive footage]), Béla Lugosi Jr. (Himself), Péter Müller (Himself), Gary Don Rhodes (Himself [as Gary D. Rhodes]), Helen Richman (Herself), István Szabó (Himself), Dorothy West (Herself [archive footage]).

Vampire Hookers (*Cemetery Girls* [U.S.]); Philippines/U.S., 1978; Comedy, Horror; 82 minutes/color/English; Capricorn Three/Cosa Nueva.

Producers: Robert E. Waters; *Writing Credits*: Howard R. Cohen; *Director*: Cirio H. Santiago; *Cinematography*: Johnny Araojo, Ricardo Remias; *Original Music*: Jaime Mendoza-Nava; *Art Direction*: Laida Lim-Perez; *Cast*: John Carradine (Richmond Reed, vampire), Bruce Fairbairn (Tom Buckley), Trey Wilson (Terry Wayne), Karen Stride (Cheris).

John Carradine stars as Richmond Reed, a Dracula-type vampire who needs fresh blood to survive. He therefore deceptively disguises his captured women as prostitutes as a means to find new sources of blood, a strategy that works well to ensnare unfortunate sailors looking for a good time while their ships are docked in the Philippines.

The Vampire Hunters Club; U.S./Canada, 2001; Comedy, Horror/Short; 30 minutes/color/English/Mono; Doodle Barnett Productions, Irena Belle Films.

Producers: Whitney Scott Bain, Buddy Barnett, Kathe Duba-Barnett, Edward L. Plumb; *Writing Credits*: Buddy Barnett, Kathe Duba-Barnett, Edward L. Plumb; *Director*: Donald F. Glut; *Cinematography*: Stephen Rocha; *Film Editing*: Lindsey Jackson; *Original Music*: Bill Noland; *Make-Up*: Ashley Gardner, Lorraine Martin, Corrie Mendes, Corrie Milsted, Jennifer Pitt; *Cast*: John Agar (Reggie), William Smith (Johnny), Bob Burns (Bob), Forrest J Ackerman (Forry), David Donham (Nigel), Daniel Roebuck (Dracula), Dina Vernon (Tina), Sam Aaron (Young Bob), Mary Woronov (Receptionist), Nikki Fritz (Vampire Waitress), Steven Lekowicz (Young Reggie), Nick Bennett (Young Forry), Mink Stole (Vampire Woman), Carla Laemmle (Elder Vampire), John Pepe (Young Johnny), Chuck Williams (Mongo), Conrad Brooks (Conrad), Carel Struycken (Host Vampire), Monica Kim (Debbie), Belinda Balaski (Vampire Mother), Brinke Stevens (Brinke), James Keane (Jonathan White), Thom Mathews (Henry Pratt), Deborah Dutch (Rhoda Pratt), R.A. Mihailoff (Doorman), Titus Moede (Heart Hungry Man), Gunther Jenson (Bodyguard), Irwin Keyes (Obnoxious Dancer), Del Howison (Del), Jennifer Rawlings (Casmir), Natalie Farrey (Vampire Daughter), Molly Murphy (Suicide Girl), David J. Skal (Bart Barlow), Brad Linaweaver (Werewolf), John Norris (Marty), Dan Campbell (Scared Vampire), Andrea Gaspar (Tall Vampire), Violet Lake (Tall Vampire), Shelly Littlefeather (Coffin Vampire), Janna Bossier (Archer Vampire), Regan D'-Lynn (Punk Vampire), Shawna Baca (Flower Seller), Katrina Gourley (Belly Dancer), Lisa Armstrong (Dancer), Lisa Elaine Bailey (Dancer), Amber Leigh Alderman (Office vampire), Mayra Gomez (Office Vampire), Jennifer Mann (Fortune

Teller), Michael Copner (Vampire), Marta Dobrovitz (Nosferatu Vampire), Donna Wieczorkowski (Thermamin Player), Connie O. Barnett (Alley vampire), Lance Mitchell (Vampire), Spider Subke (Vampire), Mary Angello (Balloon making vampire [as Mary Bewitz]), Steve Rivera (Alley vampire), Amanda Jordan (Montage Vampire At Wall), Erin McKeever (Montage Angry Vampire), Erica P. Hanson (Montage Seductive Vampire), Buddy Barnett (Arguing Man), Kathe Duba-Barnett (Arguing Woman), Kimmie Fadem (Montage hippie vampire), Ashley Gardner (Vampire Daughter two), Diane King (Silhouette Vampre).

This short tells the story of a group of young hunters searching for a vampire who has bitten a member's girlfriend. They spend the majority of their lives searching for the Dracula-type character. The short parodies many older horror films and character stereotypes.

Vampire in Brooklyn (*Brooklyn Vampiri* [Turkey]; *Um Vampiro no Brooklyn* [Brazil]; *Un vampire à Brooklyn* [France]; *Vámpír Brooklynban* [Hungary]; *Vampire à Brooklyn* [Canada]; *Vampiro a Brooklyn* [Italy]; *Vampiro em Brooklyn* [Portugal]; *Vampiro suelto en Brooklyn, Un* [Spain]; *Wampir w Brooklynie* [Poland]); U.S., 1995; Comedy, Horror; 100 minutes/color/English/Dolby Digital; Eddie Murphy Productions, Paramount Pictures.

Producers: Stuart M. Besser, Dixie J. Capp, Jeffrey Fenner, Mark Lipsky, Marianne Maddalena, Eddie Murphy, Ray Murphy Jr.; *Writing Credits*: Eddie Murphy, Vernon Lynch, Charles Q. Murphy (as Charles Murphy), Michael Lucker, Chris Parker (as Christopher Parker); *Director*: Wes Craven; *Cinematography*: Mark Irwin; *Film Editing*: Patrick Lussier; *Original Music*: J. Peter Robinson; *Art Direction*: Cynthia Kay Charette (as Cynthia Charette), Gary Diamond; *Make-Up*: Bernadine M. Anderson, David LeRoy Anderson, Karrie Aubuchon, Howard Berger, John Bisson, Evan Campbell, Marietta Carter-Narcisse (as Marie Carter), Jean Pierre Durand, Jeff Edwards, Erin Haggerty, Rob Hinderstein, William Howard, Erma Kent, Robert Kurtzman, Robert Maverick, Gregory Nicotero, Douglas Noe, Brian Rae, Shannon Shea, Richard Snell, Mark Tavares, Wayne Toth, Toy Van Lierop, Henrik von Ryzin; *Special Effects*: Gary D. Bierend, Peter Chesney (as Peter M. Chesney), Tom Chesney, Michel Gagné, Donn Markel, Edward T. Reiff Jr., Karl Nettmann (uncredited); *Cast*: Eddie Murphy (Maximilian/Preacher Pauty/Guido), Angela Bassett (Def. Rita Veder), Allen Payne (Detective Justice), Kadeem Hardison (Julius Jones), John Witherspoon (Silas Green), Zakes Mokae (Dr. Zeko), Joanna Cassidy (Capt. Dewey), Simbi Khali (Nikki, Rita's Roomate), Messiri Freeman (Eva, Julius' Girl), Kelly Cinnante (Policewoman Photographer), Jsu Garcia (Anthony) (as Nick Corri), W. Earl Brown (Thrasher), Ayo Adeyemi (Bartender), Troy Curvey Jr. (Choir Leader), Vickilyn Reynolds (Mrs. Brown), William Blount (Deacon Brown), Joe Costanza (Bear), John LaMotta (Lizzy), Marcelo Tubert (Waiter at Caprisi's), Nick DeMauro (Kitty Caprisi), Jerry Hall (Woman in Park), Mark Haining (Man in Park), Wendy Robie (Zealot at Police Station), Alyse Mandel (Policewoman), Larry Paul Marshall (Greeter at Church), Vince Micelli (Checkers Player), Oren Waters (Singer), Carlton Davis (Singer), Clive Ross (Singer), Michael Hyde (Singer), Maxine Waters Willard (Singer), Josef Powell (Singer), Roy Galloway (Singer), Carmen Carter (Singer), Julie Waters Tillman (Singer), Carmen Twillie (Singer), Ray Combs (Game Show Host), Andrew DePalma (Joey [uncredited]), Mitch Pileggi (Tony the Hitman [uncredited]), Ken Tipton (Thug [uncredited]).

Maximilian, a Dracula-type vampire, finds himself in Brooklyn searching for a half vampire named Rita. He is the last of his kind and would like Rita to help repopulate the vampire species. His plan turns out to be a little more complicated then he thought. Being a half vampire Rita can decide whether she wants to be a vampire or stay human. Maximilian makes many unsuccessful attempts to charm Rita into becoming a vampire.

The Vampire Interviews; U.S., 1994; Documentary, 50 minutes/color, black and white/English/Mono; Heidelberg Films.

Producers: Richard Foos, Bill Kelley, Ted Newsom, Arny Schorr; *Director*: Ted Newsom; *Film Editing*: Ray Baden, Keith Fernandes, Tom Reichlin; *Make-Up*: Lydia V. Duffy; *Cast*: Roy Ward Baker (Himself), Nick Bougas (Himself), Veronica Carlson (Herself), John Carradine (Himself [archive footage]), Michael Carreras (Himself), Peter Cushing (Himself [archive footage]), Joe Dante (Himself), Freddie Francis (Himself), Christopher Lee (Himself), Béla Lugosi (Himself [archive footage]), Joan Marlowe (Joan), Ferdy Mayne (Himself), Douglas McFerran (Himself), Caroline Munro (Herself), Amanda Osborne (Herself).

This documentary is an in-depth look at fictional and non-fictional vampires, both in film and in real life.

Vampire Secrets; U.S., 2006; Documentary, Television; 100 minutes/color/English; Indigo Films, Jeff Margolis Productions.

Producers: M. Frank, Eileen Rivera, Luke H. Sauer, Diana Zaslaw; *Writing Credits*: Josh Rosen; *Director*: Diana Zaslaw; *Cinematography*: Yoram Astrakham, Adam Vardy; *Art Direction*: Anna Noel

Rockwell; *Make-Up*: Lisamarie Costabile, Michael Peterson; *Cast*: Corey Burton (Narrator [voice]), Deborah Rombaut (Demon Woman), Adrian Balbontin (Gaspard Robilette), Danielle Barcena (Young Virgin #1), Joe Bardellini (Hungarian Soldier), Christa Bella (Elizabeth Bathory reenactment), Veronica Belmont (Virgin #5), Chris Carlone (Hungarian Soldier), Jeffery Davis (vampire), Jeff De Lucio-Brook (Hungarian Farmer), Vern Dorethy (Vampire Roleplayer), Ralpha Filice (Grandfather), Ronna Foote Malson (Victim), Justin Rodgers Hall (vampire), Thais Harris (Katherine Ramsland), Dan Higgins (James Spalding), Lisa Konczal (Nobel Virgin), Byron Lambie (Hungarian Farmer), George Mauro (Bram Stoker), Jennifer Stoker (Vampire Roleplayer), Lyndsey Nelson (Susan Walsh), Woody Purdy (Vampire Roleplayer), Jack Sale (Rod Ferrell), Jay Sayles (Hungarian Ax Soldier), Scot Serby (Vampire Roleplayer), Peter Stack (Ficzko), Brittany Sunderland (Vampire Roleplayer), Ray Thomas (Vampire Roleplayer), Tony Timmer (Vampire Roleplayer), Nick Toka (Vampire Roleplayer), Scott Updegrave (Richard Wendorf), April Vancelette (Farmer's Wife), Kari Wishingrad (Bathory Chambermaid), Christopher C. Wright (Vampire Roleplayer).

This A&E/History Channel documentary examines the history of vampire legends.

Vampirella; U.S., 1996; Horror, Science Fiction; 82 minutes/color/English/Ultra Stereo/35mm; Concorde-New Horizons, Showtime Networks, Sunset Films International.

Producers: Forrest J Ackerman, Mark Patrick Carducci, Roger Corman, Paul Hertzberg, Angela Plasschaert (producer [as Angela Baynes]), Jim Wynorski; *Writing Credits*: Forrest J Ackerman, Gary Gerani; *Director*: Jim Wynorski; *Cinematography*: Andrea V. Rossotto; *Film Editing*: Richard Gentner, Robert L. Goodman (recut), Jud Pratt; *Original Music*: Joel Goldsmith; *Art Direction*: Vincent Reynaud; *Make-Up*: Wendy Robin; *Special Effects*: Peter Cappadocia; *Cast*: Talisa Soto (Vampirella), Roger Daltrey (Vlad/Jamie Blood), Richard Joseph Paul (Adam Van Helsing), Brian Bloom (Demos), Corinna Harney (Sallah), Rusty Meyers (Quinn), Lee de Broux (Lt. Walsh), Tom Deters (Traxx), Jack Zavorak (Captain Stryker), Lenny Juliano (Carlos), Anne Howard (Stepmother), Angus Scrimm (High Elder), Tyde Kierney (Adam's Father), David B. Katz (Forry Ackerman), Robert Clotworthy (Professor Steinman), John Landis (Astronaut #1 [Beard]), John Terlesky (Astronaut #2 [Stubble]), Toru Nagai (Mr. Nakamuchi), Jay Kessler (Remirez), Jeff Jay (Archie), Eric Randell (Matheson), Peggy Trentini (Vampire Girl #1), Antonia Dorian (Vampire Girl #2), Bret Davidson (Mr. Maurice), Patrick J. Statham (Drakulon Guard), Scott Stevensen (Purge Operative), John Oshima (Purge Operative), Anthony Hansen (Big Vampire), Thomas Case (Dark Vampire), Michael Harris (Drakulon Elder), Hilary Halbert (Red Headed Vampire), Forrest J Ackerman (Club Patron [uncredited]), Gary Gerani (Council Vampire [uncredited]), Jeremy Settles (Limo Driver [uncredited]), Jay So (Alien Soldier [uncredited]), Peter Spellos (Robot voice [uncredited]), Jim Wynorski (TV News Anchor [uncredited]).

Loosely based on the comic book by Forrest J Ackerman, this film features a sexy, scantily-clad vampiress named Ella who comes to Earth from the planet Drakulon in pursuit of her father's killer, an outlaw vampire named Vlad (a.k.a. Dracula). After a long period of deep hibernation in space, Ella teams up with Adam Van Helsing, great-grandson of Dracula's nemesis.

Vampires; U.S., 1994; Documentary; 90 minutes/color, black and white/English; Atlantic Coast Entertainment, SLC Productions, Inc.

Producer: S.C. Lewanowicz; *Writing Credits*: Victor Monteagudo; *Director*: S.C. Lewanowicz; *Make-Up*: Rita Clayton, Jodie Johnston. *Cast*: David Myler (Host), Mitchell Bourg (vampire), Katrina Williams (vampire victim), Donna Hames (interview recreation), Amy Bush (interview recreation), Eileen land (interview recreation), erik Schoaff (character voice), Bill Greenley (character voice), Brittney Jewel (character voice).

This documentary explores the history of vampires in myth as well as in criminal cases. Vlad Dracula and Elizabeth Bathory are also examined.

El Vampiro sangriento (*Count Frankenhausen* [U.S.]; *The Bloody Vampire* [U.S.]); Mexico, 1962; Horror; 110 minutes/black and white/Spanish/Mono/35mm; Tele Talia Films/Internacional Sono Film S.A.

Producers: Rafael Pérez Grovas, K. Gordon Murray. *Writing Credits*: Miguel Morayta; *Director*: Miguel Morayata; *Cinematography*: Raúl Martínez Solares; *Film Editing*: Gloria Schoemann; *Original Music*: Luis Hernández Bretón; *Make-Up*: Esperanza Gómez, Armando Meyer; *Special Effects*: Juan Muñoz Ravelo; *Cast*: Begoña Palacios (Anna Cagliostro), Erna Martha Bauman (Countess Eugenia Frankenhausen), Raúl Farell (Dr. Riccardo Peisser), Bertha Moss (Frau Hildegarde), Pancho Córdova (Justus — as Francisco A. Cordova), Antonio Raxel (Count Valsamo de Cagliostro) Enrique Lucero (Lazaro), Lupe Carriles (Lupe, the innkeeper), Nathanael León (Torture Chamber Master [uncredited]).

El Vampiro Teporocho; Mexico, 1989; Comedy, Horror; 90 minutes/color/Spanish; Laguna Films.

Producers: Luis Bekris; *Writing Credits*: Luis Bekris, Antonio Orellana, Rafael Villaseñor Kuri; *Director*: Rafael Villaseñor Kuri; *Cinematography*: Agustín Lara Alvarado; *Film Editing*: Maximino Sánchez Molina (as Max Sánchez); *Original Music*: Carlos Torres; *Cast*: Pedro Weber "Chatanuga," Charly Valentino, Humberto Herrera, Gabriela Goldsmith, Rebeca Silva, Guillermo de Alvarado (as Guillermo de Alvarado "Condorito"), Raúl Alberto, Patricia Alvarado, Carlos Cantú, José Luis Caro (as José Luis Carol), Ernesto Casillas, Rafael Fernández, Barbara Fox, Tito Guillén, Gina Leal, Gabriela Ríos, Laura Tovar, Mário Zebadúa (as Mário Zebadúa "El Colocho").

Three adventurous scientists discover the body of Count Dracula, which has been pierced by a stake. Fearing that Dracula might reanimate, the scientists place his body in a rocket and launch it into space. However, the plan backfires when the rocket instead lands in Mexico City where Dracula joins a group of "teporochos."

¡Vampiros en La Habana! (*Vampires in Havana* [U.S.]; *Krieg der Vampire* [West Germany]); Cuba/Spain/West Germany, 1985; Comedy/Animation; 69 minutes/color/Spanish/Mono; Instituto Cubano del Arte e Industrias Cinematograficos (ICAIC).

Writing Credits: Ernesto Padron, Juan Padron; *Director*: Juan Padron; *Cinematography*: Julio Simoneau; *Cast*: Manuel Marin, Margarita Aguero, Frank Gonzalez, Irela Bravo (voice), Carlos Gonzalez (voice), Mirella Giullot (voice), Krikor Melikyan (voice), Juan Padron (voice), Christine Schnell (voice: German version), Carmen Solar (voice).

A scientist invents a potion that allows vampires to be able to live under the rays of the sun. When the word gets out to the vampires of the world, they fly to Cuba to gain control of the potion. It becomes a battle between the American and the Eastern European vampires. A trumpet player is the scientist's nephew and holds the formula for the elixir.

Vampiros Lesbos (*Das Mal des Vampirs* [West Germany, working title]; *Im Zeichen der Vampire* [West Germany, working title]; *Lesbian Vampires* [undefined]; *Lesbian Vampires: The Heiress of Dracula* [undefined]; *Schlechte Zeiten für Vampire* [West Germany, working title]; *Signo del vampiro, El* [undefined]; *The Heiress of Dracula* [undefined]; *The Heritage of Dracula* [undefined]; *The Sign of the Vampire* [undefined]; *The Strange Adventure of Jonathan Harker* [undefined]; *The Vampire Women* [undefined]; *Vampiras, Las* [Spain, cut version]; *Vampire lesbos* [France]; *Vampiros Lesbos* [France]; *Vampyros Lesbos: Die Erbin des Dracula* [West Germany]); West Germany/Spain, 1971; Horror; 89 minutes/color/German/Mono; CCC Telecine.

Producers: Artur Brauner, Karl Heinz Mannchen; *Writing Credits*: Jaime Chávarri, Jaime Chávarri, Jesus Franco, Bram Stoker (uncredited); *Director*: Jesus Franco; *Cinematography*: Manuel Merino; *Film Editing*: Clarissa Ambach; *Original Music*: Jesus Franco (as David Khune), Manfred Hübler (as Manfred Hubler), Sigi Schwab (as Siegfried Schwab); *Cast*: Ewa Strömberg (Linda Westinghouse), Soledad Miranda (Countess Nadine Carody) (as Susann Korda), Andrés Monales (Omar) (as Victor Feldman), Dennis Price (Dr. Alwin Seward), Paul Muller (Dr. Steiner), Heidrun Kussin (Agra), Michael Berling (Dr. Seward's Assistant), Beni Cardoso (Dead Woman [uncredited]), Jesus Franco (Memmet [uncredited]), José Martínez Blanco (Morpho [uncredited]).

Linda is a young American lawyer in Istanbul. While she sleeps, she has nightmares in which she is molested by a sexy woman from whom she is unable to escape. When she arrives on an island off the Turkish coast, her worst dreams come to life.

Vampyres (*Blood Hunger* [undefined]; *Daughters of Dracula* [U.S., reissue title]; *Filhas de Drácula, As* [Brazil]; *Hijas de Drácula, Las* [Spain]; *Ossessione carnale* [Italy]; *Satan's Daughters* [undefined]; *Vampiras, As* [Portugal]; *Vampyres, Daughters of Dracula* [undefined]; *Vampyres: Daughters of Darkness* [U.S.]); U.K., 1974; Horror; 87 minutes/color/English/Mono; Lurco Films.

Producers: Brian Smedley-Aston; *Writing Credits*: D. Daubeney, José Ramón Larraz (uncredited), Thomas Owen; *Director*: José Ramón Larraz (as Joseph Larraz); *Cinematography*: Harry Waxman; *Film Editing*: Geoff R. Brown; *Original Music*: James Kenelm Clarke (as James Clark); *Make-Up*: Colin Arthur; *Cast*: Marianne Morris (Fran), Anulka Dziubinska (Miriam, as Anulka), Murray Brown (Ted), Brian Deacon (John), Sally Faulkner (Harriet), Michael Byrne (Playboy), Karl Lanchbury (Rupert, Margaret Heald (Receptionist), Gerald Case (Estate Agent), Bessie Love (American Lady), Elliott Sullivan (American Man).

A lesbian vampire couple uses an old mansion as a place to terrorize and kill passing travelers. They pretend to be hitchhikers, and then seduce the men that are willing to drive them to the old house. When the American, Harriet, attempts to fight back, they team up against her. The Dracula theme is evidenced, in part, through the red and black cloak that the blonde vampire wears.

Van Helsing (*Van Helsing* [Canada/Czech Republic/France/Germany/Slovakia/Spain/Turkey]; *Kallarai Manithan* [India]; *Van Helsing— O Caçador* de Monstros [Brazil]; *Van Helsing: Cazador de monstruos* [Venezuela]; *Van Helsing: El cazador de monstruos* [Argentina]); U.S., 2004; Action, Adventure, Horror, Fantasy, Thriller; 132 minutes/color/English/SDDS, DTS, Dolby Digital; Universal Pictures, Carpathian Pictures, Stillking Films, The Sommers Company.

Producers: Bob Ducsay, Sam Mercer, David Minkowski, Artist W. Robinson, Stephen Sommers, Matthew Stillman; *Writing Credits*: Stephen Sommers; *Director*: Stephen Sommers; *Cinematography*: Allen Daviau; *Film Editing*: Bob Ducsay, Kelly Matsumoto, Jim May; *Original Music*: Alan Silvestri; *Art Direction*: Steve Arnold, Keith P. Cunningham, Giles Masters, Tony Reading, Jaromír Svarc.; *Make-Up*: Ozzy Alvarez, Anthony Allen Barlow, Colleen Callaghan, Greg Cannom, Ken Culver, Justin Ditter, Jirí Farkas, Nathan Franson, Will Huff, Stephen Kelley, John Kim, Mary Kim, Natasha Ladek, Steve LaPorte, Angela Levin, Douglas Noe, Ruzena Novotna, Alexei O'Brien, Michael O'Brien, Mimi Palazon, James Parr, Michael Peterson, Lee Romaire, Brian Sipe, Nena Smarz, Vasilios Tanis, Keith VanderLaan, Milan Vlcek, Brian Wade, Gabriel De Cunto (uncredited), Nancie Marsalis (uncredited); *Special Effects*: Peter Abrahamson, Ryan Arndt, Steve Austin, Anthony Allen Barlow, David Blitstein, Peter A. Chevako, Jerry Constantine, Garry Cooper, Barry Crane, Steve Cremin, Michael Del Rossa, John J. Downey, Matt Downey, Ante Dugandzic, Gary Elmendorf, Manuel S. Epstein, Ron Epstein, Christian Eubank, Jack Firman, Damian Fisher, Scott R. Fisher, Thomas L. Fisher, John Fleming, Ronald D. Goldstein, Chris Hampton, David Heron, Ray Hoffman, Thomas R. Homsher, Mike Hyrman, Garth Inns, Dominik Janda, Joe Judd, Nick Karas, Jay King, Bruce Y. Kuroyama, Kristen Lobstein, Roland Loew, Joe Love, Miroslav Miclik, Bruce Minkus, Michael O'Brien, Katrissa "Kat" Peterson, Bryan Phillips, Pavel Policar, Edward T. Reiff Jr., Jim Rollins, Terry Sandin, John Shea, Robert L. Slater, Leo Leoncio Solis, Christopher A. Suarez, Keith VanderLaan, Brian Van Dorn, Mario Vanillo, Andy Weder, Douglas D. Ziegler, Arthur G. Schlosser (uncredited); *Cast*: Hugh Jackman (Van Helsing), Kate Beckinsale (Anna Valerious), Richard Roxburgh (Count Vladislaus Dracula), David Wenham (Carl), Shuler Hensley (Frankenstein's Monster), Elena Anaya (Aleera), Will Kemp (Velkan), Kevin J. O'Connor (Igor), Alun Armstrong (Cardinal Jinette), Silvia Colloca (Verona), Josie Maran (Marishka), Tom Fisher (Top Hat), Samuel West (Dr. Victor Frankenstein), Robbie Coltrane (Mr. Hyde), Stephen Fisher (Dr. Jekyll), Dana Moravková (Barmaid), Zuzana Durdinova (Opera Singer), Jaroslav Vízner (Gendarme), Marek Vasut (Villager), Samantha Sommers (Vampire Child), Dorel Mois (Dracula's Ball Performer), Marianna Mois (Dracula's Ball Performer), Laurence Racine (Dracula's Ball Performer), Patrice Wojciechowski (Dracula's Ball Performer), Kacie Borrowman (Dwerger [uncredited]), Ryan James (Villager [uncredited]), Martin Klebba (Dwerger [uncredited]), Allison Queal (Dwerger [uncredited]).

Infamous monster hunter Gabriel Van Helsing is sent to Transylvania to help Anna, the last of the Valerious family, defeat the powerful Count Dracula. Her family is doomed by an ancient curse to never enter heaven if they do not destroy this unstoppable vampire. As Count Dracula will do anything to bring his offspring to life, Van Helsing finds out the unimaginable secret to stopping this evil villain.

Van Helsing Chronicles; U.S., 1997; Science Fiction, Horror/Television; Jim Henson Company.

Producers: Javier Grillo-Marxuach; *Writing Credits*: Javier Grillo-Marxuach; *Director*: Geoffrey Sax; *Cinematography*: Paul Elliott *Cast*: Dan Gauthier (Christian Van Helsing), Teri Polo (Helena Harker), Chris Williams (Officer Denton [uncredited]).

Van Helsing: The Man and the Monsters; U.S., 2004; Documentary, 60 minutes/color/English/Stereo; New Wave Entertainment Television.

Producers: Lisa Blond, Joy Lissandrello, Paul Apel, Alan Baral, Gabrielle M. Fasulo, Wendy Lamb, Elizabeth Imus-Clark; *Writing Credits*: Joy Lissandrello; *Cast*: Hugh Jackman (Interviewee), Kate Beckinsale (Interviewee), Samuel West (Interviewee), Stephen Sommers (Interviewee), David Wenham (Interviewee), Richard Roxburgh (Interviewee), Shuler Hensley (Interviewee), Kevin O'Connor (Interviewee), Will Kemp (Interviewee), R. A. Rondell (Interviewee), Ben Snow (Interviewee), Elena Anaya (Interviewee), Josie Maran (Interviewee), Silvia Colloca (Interviewee), Christian Alzmann (Interviewee), Greg Cannom (Interviewee), Justin Peed (Narrator).

This documentary takes a behind-the-scenes look at the 2004 movie "Van Helsing," with clips and interviews with the cast and crew. The documentary also focuses on some of the myths surrounding Dracula, Werewolves, and other monsters featured in the film.

Vanpaia hosuto (TV Series) (*Bloodhound: Vampire Gigolo* [U.S.]; *Vampire Host* U.S., literal English title]); Japan, 2004; Comedy, Horror, Action/Television; 25 Minutes/color/Japanese; TV Tokyo (Japan), Bandai Entertainment (U.S.).

Directors: Hitoshe One, Michizo Kito and Seiya Nishikawa; *Cast*: Minako Koukai (Rion Kanou), Yurie Kojima (Shiho Aiga), Satoshi Matsuda (Suou).

Rion, a young lady, is searching for her best friend, ShiNo. Along the way, she encounters Suou, a gigolo. Suou works at a club, Kranke Haus, and happens to be a Dracula-type vampire, one, however, loves garlic and doesn't fear crosses nor daylight.

Vem var Dracula (*Pajakt efter Dracula* [Romanian]; *Auf den Spuren Draculas* [Germany (DVD title)]; *Dracula's Transylvania* [undefined]; *In Search of Dracula* [U.S. (literal English title)]; *The Legend of Dracula* [undefined]); Sweden, 1975; Horror/Documentary; 81 minutes/color/English/Mono; Aspekt Telefilm-Produktion GmbH.

Producers: Alvar Domeij, Calvin Floyd; *Writing Credits*: Radu Florescu, Yvonne Floyd, Raymond McNally; *Director*: Calvin Floyd; *Cinematography*: Anders Bodin, Tony Forsberg, Gunnar Larsson; *Original Music*: Calvin Floyd; *Cast*: Tor Isedal (Narrator), Christopher Lee (Himself/Vlad Tepes/Count Dracula).

Investigating the vampire legend and the 15th century Romanian ruler Vlad ("The Impaler") Dracula (played by Christopher Lee), this documentary uses paintings, books, early films, and historical reenactments to explore this historical figure.

Vlad; U.S., 2003; Horror, Thriller; 98 minutes/color/English/Dolby Digital; Quantum Entertainment.

Producers: William J. Booker, Pamela Vlastas, Dina Burke, Nick Mandracken, John Remark, Frank DeMartini, Tony Shawkat, Michael P. Flannigan; *Writing Credits*: Michael D. Sellers; Director: Michael D. Sellers; *Cinematography*: Viorel Sergovici; *Film Editing*: Joel Bender; *Original Music*: Brian Mitchell; *Art Direction*: Iulian Bostanaru, Ioana Corciova; *Make-Up*: Clara Tudose, Edwina Voda, Mircea Voda, Alexis Walker; *Special Effects*: Liviu Lungu, Adrian Popescu, Iosif Vasile (as Horia Vasile); *Cast*: Billy Zane (Adrian), Paul Popowich (Jeff Meyer/Husband), Kam Heskin (Alexa Meyer), Nicholas Irons (Justin/Knight), Brad Dourif (Radescu), Francesco Quinn (Vlad Tepes), Monica Davidescu (Linsey), Iva Hasperger (Ilona), Emil Hostina (Mircea), Guy Siner (Ilie Mircea Stoian) (Claudiu), Andreea Macelaru (Stefana) (as Andrea Macelaru), Alin Panc (Petre), Alexandra Velniciuc (Andrea), Zoltan Butuc (Grandfather), John Rhys-Davies (Narrator), Anca-Ioana Androne (Widow), Adrian Pintea (Iancu de Hunedoara), Claudiu Bleont (Vlad II), Ioan Ionescu (Mircea Drakula), Catalin Rotaru (Young Vlad), Cristian Popa (Radu cel Frumos), Vasile Albinet (Romanian soldier), Alex Revan (Slayer).

Four college graduate students embark on an adventure through the Carpathian Mountains in Romania. One of the students possesses a necklace that will bring Vlad Dracula back to life if it reaches Poenari. If Vlad is revived he will bring untold destruction and mayhem with him.

Vlad Tepes (*Vlad the Impaler: The True Life of Dracula* [U.S.]; *Wahre Leben des Fürsten Dracula, Das* [Germany]); Romania, 1979; Horror; 114 minutes/color/Romanian/Mono; Real Video International/Romanian Film Company.

Producers: Lidia Popita; *Writing Credits*: Mircea Mohur; *Director*: Doru Nastase; *Cinematography*: Aurel Kostrachievici; *Original Music*: Tiberiu Olah; *Art Direction*: Pisau Pitrecia; *Special Effects*: Popesu Aurel; *Cast*: Stefan Sileanu, Ernest Maftei, Emanoil Petrut, Teofil Vilcu, Constantin Codrescu, Constantin Barbulescu, Basile Cosman, Ion Marinescu, Kovacs Gyorgy, Vadasz Zoltan, Petre Georghiu-Doli, Mihai Paladescu.

This film is a biography of Vlad Dracula, a Romanian hero and defender who faught the Turks and, through his favorite method of murder, earned the nickname "Vlad the Impaler."

Vlad the Impaler: The True Story of Dracula; Canada, 2002; Documentary, Television; 51 minutes/color/English/Dolby, HiFi Sound; TMW Media Group, C21ETV/Canadian Learning TV and Access TV.

Producers: George Angelescu; *Writing Credits*: George Angelescu; *Director*: George Angelescu; *Film Editing*: George Angelescu; *Original Music*: Eugen Baboi, Valeriu Apan; *Art Direction*: Maria Eremia-Baboi; *Cast*: Garth Collins (Narrator), George Angelescu (Vlad's Voice).

In this documentary, Garth Collins explores the myth of Dracula and compares the popular vampire to the infamous historical figure Vlad Dracula.

The Vulture's Eye; U.S., 2004; Horror; 95 minutes/color/English/DD2; Brain Damage Films.

Producers: Tom Basham, Diane Park, Christopher Sciurba, Frank Sciurba; *Writing Credits*: Frank Sciurba; *Director*: Frank Sciurba; *Original Music*: Christopher Sciurba; *Art Direction*: Tom Basham; *Make-Up*: Alec Negri; *Cast*: Brooke Paller (Lucy), Anne Flosnik (Mina), Jason King (Arthur), Fred Iacovo (Quincy), Paul Zacheis (Van Helsing), James Nalitz (Count Klaus Vogel), Joseph Reo (Jack), Joel Pollard (Dan Renfield), Eve Young (Phyllis Renfield), Tammy Farwell (Marci), Garett Farwell (Estate Hand), Sandy Lisiewski (Hedwig), Ava Ann Vrooman (Vogel's Wife #1), Kim Cogle (Vogel's Wife #2).

Lucy and her friends enjoy riding horses in the peaceful rolling hills of the Virginia countryside. On a solo horse ride, Lucy falls from her horse. She is "rescued" by her new neighbor, the Foreign

Count "Klaus Vogul." The count becomes obsessed by the sultry Lucy and all of her friends. As Lucy starts behaving strangely and becomes ill, an old-time Southern Doctor is called in to diagnose and treat her. As the Doctor intervenes, Count Vogul attempts to lure them into a wave of living death. Will they all fall prey to the Count's perverse plans? Remember, when death starts looking good, you're staring into the "Vulture's Eye."

Wake, Rattle and Roll (TV Series [1990–1992]), segment "Monster Tails"; U.S., 1990; Comedy/Television, Animation; 30 minutes/color/English; Hanna-Barbera Studios.

Producers: William Hanna and Joseph Barbera; *Writing Credits*: Unknown; *Director*: Unknown; *Cast*: Tim Curry (Ronald Chump), Charlie Adler (Catula/Igor Jr), Frank Welker (Frankenhound/Mumfrey), Pat Musick (Elsa/Angel), Jonathan Winters (Dr. Heckell/Mr. Snide).

This four-part cartoon segment is about some very famous monster pets, including Dracula's cat, Catula, and Frankenstein's Monster's dogs, Frankenhound and Elsa. They get into all kinds of wacky situations with the help of their caretaker, a hunchback flat-top geek named Igor Jr.

Walpurgis Nacht; U.S., 2004; Horror/Short; 7 minutes/black and white/English/Mono/16mm.

Producers: David Kruschke; *Writing Credits*: David Kruschke Bram Stoker; *Director*: David Kruschke; Cinematography: David Kruschke; *Film Editing*: David Kruschke; *Original Music*: David Korgan; *Art Direction*: Matt Jones; *Make-Up*: Kendra Johnson.

Based on Bram Stoker's "Dracula's Guest," this short follows the story of a British man who goes sightseeing in Eastern Germany. He discovers more than he bargained for, as he is surrounded by vampires. Though the film doesn't feature Dracula himself, the man is surrounded by female vampires from Dracula's castle.

Waxwork (*Figury z wosku* [Poland]; *Illusione infernale* [Italy]; *Museu de Cera* [Portugal]; *Reise zurück in der Zeit* [West Germany]; *Waxwork: Museo de cera* [Spain]); U.S./West Germany, 1988; Comedy, Horror; 95 minutes/color/English/Dolby; Vestron Pictures.

Producers: Staffan Ahrenberg, Gregory Cascante, Julian Forbes, Dan Ireland William J. Quigley, Eyal Rimmon, Mario Sotela; *Writing Credits*: Anthony Hickox; *Director*: Anthony Hickox; *Cinematography*: Gerry Lively; *Film Editing*: Christopher Cibelli; *Original Music*: Roger Bellon; *Art Direction*: Peter Marangoni; *Make-Up*: Ian Brown, Mark Coulier, Dave Elsey, Steve Hardie, Steve Hardie, Alan Hedgcock, Paul Jones, Dave Keen, Nina Kraft; *Special Effects*: Ray Beetz, Lou Carlucci, Jeff Frink, Steve Galich, Bob Keen, Joe Knott, Patrick Tantalo, Cliff Wallace; *Cast*: Zach Galligan (Mark), Jennifer Bassey (Mrs. Loftmore), Joe Baker (Jenkins), Deborah Foreman (Sarah), Michelle Johnson (China), David Warner (Waxwork Man), Eric Brown (James), Clare Carey (Gemma), Buckley Norris (Lecturer), Dana Ashbrook (Tony), Micah Grant (Johnathan), Mihaly "Michu" Meszaros (Hans) (as Mihaly "Michu" Mesza), Jack David Walker (Junior) (as Jack David Warner), John Rhys-Davies (Werewolf), Nelson Welch (Elderly Man), Miles O'Keeffe (Count Dracula), Christopher Bradley (Stephan), Tom McGreevey (Charles) (as Tom MacGreevey), Irene Olga López (Maid), Charles McCaughan (Inspector Roberts), Julian Forbes (Police Driver), Edward Ashley (Professor Sutherland), Kendall Conrad (Girl in Pyramid), Patrick Macnee (Sir Wilfred), J. Kenneth Campbell (Marquis de Sade), Anthony Hickox (English Prince), Staffan Ahrenberg (French Guard), Gabriella Dufwa (Courtesan), Gary M. Bettman (Mark's Grandfather), James D.R. Hickox (Werewolf Killer's Assistant), Candi (Dracula's Butler) (as Candy), James Lincoln (Dracula's Man Servant), Merle Stronck (Vampire Girl #1), Joanne Russell (Vampire Girl #2), Ann Sophie Noblet (Vampire Girl #3), Paul Badger (Mummy), Eyal Rimmon (Egyptian Boy), Kim Henderson (Marquis de Sade Girl #1), Hilary English (Marquis de Sade Girl #2), Nicole Seguin (Marquis de Sade Girl #3), Carolyn Bray (Marquis de Sade Girl #4), Henrietta Folkeson (Marquis de Sade Girl #5), Dan Ireland (Zombie #1) (scenes deleted), Karen Schaffer (Zombie #2), Leonard Pollack (Zombie #3), Bruce Barlow (Zombie #4), Cliff Wallace (Zombie #5), Dave Elsey (Zombie #6), Gerry Lively (Sir Wilfred's Butler), Steven Santamaria (Taxi Driver).

After being invited to a waxwork museum, Mark and his friends go to see the new display. They are surrounded by wax sculptures of horrifying figures, one being Dracula himself. When his friends go missing, he realizes they are all in great danger. They are victims living out scenes in which they will ultimately be killed by these wax sculptures.

Waxwork II: Lost in Time; U.S., 1992; Comedy, Horror; 104 minutes/color/English/Dolby; Electric Pictures, Contemporary Films, Lost In Time Productions.

Producers: Nancy Paloian, Mario Sotela; *Writing Credits*: Anthony Hickox; *Director*: Anthony Hickox; *Cinematography*: Gerry Lively; *Film Editing*: Christopher Cibelli; *Original Music*: Steve Schiff; *Art Direction*: John Chichester; *Make-Up*: Dave

Chagouri, Mark Coulier, Richard Darwin, Shaune Harrison, Paul Jones, Bob Keen, Bob Keen, Fiona Leech, Beatrice Marot, Martin L. Mercer, Ian Morse, Stephen Norrington, Steve Painter, Martin Parnal, Lisa Marie Rosenberg, Rudy Sotomayor, Paul Spateri, Paul Spateri, Gary J. Tunnicliffe, Bernard H. Wood; *Special Effects*: Glenn Campbell, Bob Keen, Kevin Francis "Boomer" McCarthy, Casey Quinn, G. Bruno Stempel, Lynda Weinman; *Cast*: Zach Galligan (Mark Loftmore), Monika Schnarre (Sarah Brightman), Martin Kemp (Baron Von Frankenstein), Bruce Campbell (John Loftmore), Michael Des Barres (George), Jim Metzler (Roger), Sophie Ward (Elenore), Marina Sirtis (Gloria), Billy Kane (Nigel), Joe Baker (The Peasant), Juliet Mills (The Defense Lawyer), John Ireland (King Arthur), Patrick Macnee (Sir Wilfred), David Carradine (The Beggar), Alexander Godunov (Scarabis), George "Buck" Flower (Sarah's Stepfather), Jack Eiseman (Cabbie), James D.R. Hickox (Polansky), Buckley Norris (Judge), Paul Hampton (Prosecution), Stanley Sheff (Speaker for Jury), John O'Leary (Herr Vogel), Erin Breznikar (Wise), Elisha Shapiro (Felix), Stefanos Miltsakakis (Frankenstein's Monster), Maxwell Caulfield (Mickey), Erin Gourlay (Ghost Girl), Bryan Travis Smith (Peasant Boy), Steve Matteucci (Master's Guard), Guy J. Louthan (Master's Officer), Kate Murtagh (The Matron), Eyal Rimmon (Chief Worshipper), Shanna Lynn (Panther Girl), Anthony Hickox (King's Officer), Piers Plowden (King's Guard), Harrison Young (James Westbourne), Ivan Markota (Press Man), Marie Foti (Press Woman), Frank Zagarino (Zombie Killer #1), Martin C. Jones (Zombie Killer #2), Darryl Pierce (Zombie Killer #3), John Breznikar (Mark's Father), Lisa Oestreich (Mark's Mother), Brent Bolthouse (Cabbie #2), Caron Bernstein (The Master's Girl), Gerry Lively (Lead Prisoner), Yanko Damboulev (Lead Prisoner), Jim Silverman (Lead Prisoner), Paul Madigan (Lead Prisoner), Kim Henderson (Party Babe), Treasure Little (Party Babe), Lisa Jay (Party Babe), Elizabeth Nottoli (Party Babe), Márcia Santos Rocha (Party Babe), Felicia Hernández (Party Babe), Crystal Calderoni (Party Babe), Bob Keen (Mad Monk), Chris Breed (King's Announcer), Emile Gladstone (The Jester), Gregory G. Woertz (Zombie Killer), Michael Viela (Dr. Jekyll), Ilona Margolis (Zombie Killer), Martin L. Mercer (Lead Zombie), Dorian Langdon (Romero), John Mushroom Mappin (Argento), Jonathan Breznihar (Shelly), Mark Courier (Scott), Robert Kass (Hitchcock), Steve Painter (Nosferatu), Drew Barrymore (Vampire Victim #1), Hadria Lawner (Vampire Victim #2), Paul Jones (The Hand), Alex Butler (Jack the Ripper), Yolanda Jilot (Lady of the Night), Godzilla (Himself), Rick Kleber (Torturer/Dungeon Master [uncredited]), Laurie Rose (Belly Dancer [uncredited]).

Winter with Dracula; U.K., 1971; Documentary; 30 minutes/color; Polonius Film Services, Border Films.

Director: John Dooley.

This documentary is a travelogue of Romania that briefly references Vlad Dracula.

Wolfster, Part 1: The Curse of the Emo Vamp; U.S., 2006; Horror, Comedy; 80 minutes/color/English.

Producers: Amanda Burgess, Cathy Rudzinski; Director: Steve Rudzinski Writing credits: Steve Rudzinski; *Film Editing*: Steve Rudzinski; *Cast*: in the order of credits Brad Bendis (Smart Vampire), Amanda Burgess (Lois), Henrique Couto (Dracula), Jessie Deep (Beth), Nic Pesante (Deacon Sloan), Steve Rudzinski (Dave/Wolfster), Christine Schwesinger (Jess), Shawn Shelpman (Nathan Sloan), Keegan Teel (Barry), Jeff Waltrowski (Awesome Vampire).

This film is a spoof about a man named Dave who is chosen by a vampire to be his pet werewolf. When this vampire begins reading his bad poetry halfway through the spell, it causes Dave to be able to keep his free will and control his werewolf transformations. There is another side-effect to Dave's transformation: he realizes that he is in a movie.

The World of Hammer (TV Series [1994]), episode "Christopher Lee"; U.K., Season 1, Episode 11, 21 October 1994; Documentary, Television; 25 minutes/English/color, black and white/Stereo; Best of British Films and Television Production, Hammer Film Productions.

Producers: Robert Sidaway, John Thompson; *Writing Credits*: Ashley Sidaway, Robert Sidaway; *Director*: Robert Sidaway; *Original Music*: Brian Bennett; *Cast*: Oliver Reed (Narrator).

This documentary examines Christopher Lee, famous for his role as Dracula.

The World of Hammer (TV Series [1994]), episode "Costumers"; U.K., Season 1, Episode 13, 4 November 1994; Documentary, Television; 25 minutes/English/color, black and white/Stereo; Best of British Films and Television Production, Hammer Film Productions.

Producers: Robert Sidaway, John Thompson; *Writing Credits*: Ashley Sidaway, Robert Sidaway; *Director*: Robert Sidaway; *Original Music*: Brian Bennett; *Cast*: Oliver Reed (Narrator).

This documentary examines the costumers of Hammer Films and includes scenes with Dracula.

The World of Hammer (TV Series [1994]), episode "Dracula and the Undead"; U.K., Season 1, Episode

2, 19 August 1994; Documentary, Television; 25 minutes/English/color, black and white/Stereo; Best of British Films and Television Production, Hammer Film Productions.

Producers: Robert Sidaway, John Thompson; *Writing Credits*: Ashley Sidaway, Robert Sidaway; *Director*: Robert Sidaway; *Original Music*: Brian Bennett; *Cast*: Oliver Reed (Narrator).

This documentary examines Dracula and the undead in Hammer Films productions.

The World of Hammer (TV Series [1994]), episode "Hammer"; U.K., Season 1, Episode 12, 28 October 1994; Documentary, Television; 25 minutes/English/color, black and white/Stereo; Best of British Films and Television Production, Hammer Film Productions.

Producers: Robert Sidaway, John Thompson; *Writing Credits*: Ashley Sidaway, Robert Sidaway; *Director*: Robert Sidaway; *Original Music*: Brian Bennett; *Cast*: Oliver Reed (Narrator).

This documentary provides an overview of Hammer Film's production portfolio, including scenes from *Dracula* films.

The World of Hammer (TV Series [1994]), episode "Mummies, Werewolves and the Living Dead"; U.K., Season 1, Episode 8, 30 September 1994; Documentary, Television; 25 minutes/English/color, black and white/Stereo; Best of British Films and Television Production, Hammer Film Productions.

Producers: Robert Sidaway, John Thompson; *Writing Credits*: Ashley Sidaway, Robert Sidaway; *Director*: Robert Sidaway; *Original Music*: Brian Bennett; *Cast*: Oliver Reed (Narrator).

This documentary examines mummies, werewolves, and the living dead in Hammer Films productions.

The World of Hammer (TV Series [1994]), episode "Peter Cushing"; U.K., Season 1, Episode 1, 12 August 1994; Documentary, Television; 25 minutes/English/color, black and white/Stereo; Best of British Films and Television Production, Hammer Film Productions.

Producers: Robert Sidaway, John Thompson; *Writing Credits*: Ashley Sidaway, Robert Sidaway; *Director*: Robert Sidaway; *Original Music*: Brian Bennett; *Cast*: Oliver Reed (Narrator)

This documentary examines Peter Cushing, famous for his role as Dr. Van Helsing in *Dracula*.

The World of Hammer (TV Series [1994]), episode "Vamp"; U.K., Season 1, Episode 4, 1 September 1994; Documentary, Television; 25 minutes/English/color, black and white/Stereo; Best of British Films and Television Production, Hammer Film Productions.

Producers: Robert Sidaway, John Thompson; *Writing Credits*: Ashley Sidaway, Robert Sidaway; *Director*: Robert Sidaway; *Film Editing*: Ashley Sidaway; *Original Music*: Brian Bennett.

This documentary examines Hammer Films's female vampires, including clips from *Brides of Dracula* and *Dracula: Prince of Darkness*.

Yami no teio kyuketsuki Dracula (*Dracula* [International English Title]; *Dracula: Sovereign of The Damned*; *Tomb of Dracula*); Japan, 1980; Horror/Television, Animation; 89 minutes/color/Japanese/Mono; Harmony Gold/Toei Animation Company.

Writing Credits: Bram Stoker, Marv Wolfman, Gene Colan, Tom Palmer; *Director*s: Akinori Nagaoka, Minoru Okazaki (as Robert Barron); *Original Music*: Seiji Yokoyama, Michael Bradley, Stephen Wittmack.

In this Japanese adaptation of the classic American *The Tomb of Dracula* comic book series began by Marvel Comics in 1972, which is based on the characters originally developed by Bram Stoker in *Dracula*, Dracula bursts into a Satanic ceremony in present-day Boston where the ritualists mistake him for a manifestation of Satan. Dracula abducts a woman named Delores from the ceremony before she can be sacrificed. Overcome with love for the woman, Dracula finds himself unable to drink her blood. The two make a life together and have a child who they name Janus. In the meantime, wheelchair-ridden Hans Harker and crossbow-wielding Rachel Van Helsing recruit Frank Drake, one of Dracula's present-day descendants, in order to form a vampire-hunting team. Out of revenge, the Satanists then kill Janus, who is later divinely resurrected. Meanwhile, Satan strips Dracula of that power which he gave him: his vampirism, thus forcing Dracula on a quest to find another vampire who might restore his vampire powers.

Yi yao O.K. (*A Bite of Love* [Hong Kong: English title]; *Yat aau O.K.* [Hong Kong: Cantonese title]); Hong Kong, 1990; Comedy, Horror; 94 Minutes/color/Cantonese/Dolby/35mm.

Producers: Dickson Poon, Stephen Shin; *Writing Credits*: Siu-keung Cheng, Tony Leung Hung-Wah; *Director*: Stephen Shin; *Cinematography*: Siu-keung Cheng; *Film Editing*: Wing-ming Wong; *Original Music*: Ting Yat Chung, George Lam; *Cast*: Norman Chu (Fung), Shiu Hung Hui (Duke Lee's Butler), Rosamund Kwan (Anna), Kan-Wing Tsang (Mr. Tsang).

A vampire is repulsed by the thought of killing in order to stay alive. He becomes the local blood bank's best customer. However, when the bank runs out of blood, he must take a hard look at his situation.

Yin ji (*Kung Fu from Beyond the Grave* [undefined]); Hong Kong, 1982; Action, Horror, Adventure; 90 minutes/color/Cantonese; The Eternal Film Company.

Cast: Billy Chong (Chun Sing), Lieh Lo (Kam Tai Fu), Sai Aan Dai (Black Magician), Mien Fang (Old Fang [as Fong Min]), Sha-fei Ouyang (Chun Sing's mother), Alan Chui (Rebellious Reign).

Sai Aan Dai is a black magician bent on stirring up evil. Billy Chong is here to kill the master, Lieh Lo, after receiving a message from his father that he must take revenge. Alan Chui, who shows up in semi-comedic fight scenes. Chui and Chong then take on Sai Aan Dai, who conjures Dracula to help him.

Yogi's Treasure Hunt (TV Series [1985–1987]), episode "Countdown Drac"; U.S., Season I, Episode 3, 16 September 1985. Comedy, Family, Adventure/Television, Animation; 30 minutes/color/English; Hanna-Barbera Studios.

Producer: William Hanna, Joseph Barbera, Bob Hathcock, Jeff Hall; *Director*: Oscar Dafau, Tony Love, Rudy Zamora, Bill Hutton, Alan Zaslove, Ray Patterson, *Film Editing*: Gil Iverson; *Original Music*: Hoyt Curtain; *Art Direction*: Bob Alvarez, Bob Goe, Bill Hutton, Rick Leon, Tony Love, Tim Walker, Irv Spence; *Cast*: Daws Butler (Yogi Bear/Huckleberry Hound/Super Snooper/Blabber Mouse/QuickDraw McGraw/Snagglepuss/Augie Doggie [voice]), Don Messick (Boo Boo/Ranger Smith/Muttley [voice]), Gary Owens (Narrator [voice]), Arnold Stang (Top Cat [voice]), John Stephenson (Doggie Daddy [voice]), Paul Winchell (Dick Dastardly [voice]).

Yogi and friends go to a castle in Transylvania to search for Countdown Drac's long lost treasure, which turns out to be some fellow ghouls, including Frankenstein's Monster, who can help improve Drac's musical band.

You Wish (TV Series [1997]), episode "Halloween"; U.S., Season 1 Episode 6, 31 October 1997; Comedy/Television; 30 minutes/color/English.

Producers: Mitchell Bank, Susan Estelle Jansen, Andrew Nicholls, Jeff Sherman, Darrell Vickers; *Writing Credits*: Michael Craven, Michael Jacobs, Susan Estelle Jansen, Heather MacGillvray, Linda Mathious, Daniel Paige, Sue Paige, Steve Pepoon, David Silverman, Stephen Sustarsic; *Director*: Jeff McCracken; *Original Music* Ray Colcord; *Special Effects*: Ted Rae; *Cast*: John Ales (Genie), Harley Jane Kozak (Gillian Apple), Jerry Van Dyke (Grandpa Max), Alex McKenna (Mickey Apple), Nathan Lawrence (Travis Apple), Sylvain Cecile (Frankenstein's Monster), Larry Cedar (The Mummy), Mark DeCarlo (Cable Repairman), Andrew Masset (Dracula), Kente Scott (Kid), Spencer Vrooman (Matt), Jordan Zucker (Cleopatra [uncredited]).

Young Dracula (TV Series); U.K., 2006–2008; Comedy, Family/Television; 25 minutes/color/English; BBC Wales.

Producers: Mia Jupp; *Writing Credits*: Joe Williams (writer, 6 episodes, 2006–2008), Max Allen (writer, 4 episodes, 2006–2008), Michael Lawrence (writer, 2 episodes, 2006), Danny Robins (writer, 2 episodes, 2006); *Director*: Joss Agnew (11 episodes, 2006–2008), Craig Lines (3 episodes, 2007–2008); *Cinematography*: Sarah Bartles-Smith; *Original Music*: Nick Lloyd; *Make-Up*: Bethan Jones, Steve Williams (makeup designer); *Special Effects*: Colin Newman; *Cast*: Gerran Howell (Vladimir Dracula), Care Thomas (Ingrid Dracula), Keith-Lee Castle (Count Dracula), Simon Ludders (Renfield), Craig Roberts (Robin Branaugh), Terence Maynard (Mr. Van Helsing), Terry Haywood (Jonathon Van Helsing), Lucy Borja-Edwards (Chloe Branaugh), Aneirin Hughes (Graham Branaugh), Andy Bradshaw (Zoltan), Beth Robert (Elizabeth Branaugh), Ben McGregor (Ian Branaugh), Luke Bridgeman (Paul Branaugh), Harry Ferrier (Will Clarke), Jo-Anne Knowles (Mina Van Helsing), Donna Grant (Magda Westenra), Ciaran Joyce (Boris Dracula), Philip Brodie (Ivan Dracula), Dafydd Emyr (Mr. Perkins), Betsan Llwyd (Mrs. Harker), Madeleine Rakic-Platt (Olga Dracula), Richard Elfyn (Grand High Vampire).

The Dracula family (Vlad, his dad The Count, and his sister Ingrid) have to move from Transylvania to a normal small town in Britain.

Young-guwa heubhyeolgwi dracula (*Young-gu and Count Dracula* [English title]); South Korea, 1992; Action, Family, Horror; 67 minutes/color/Korean.

Producers: Cun-beom Kim; *Writing Credits*: Deok-gyun Jang; *Director*: Hyung-rae Shim; *Cinematography*: Myeong-ui Shin; *Film Editing*: Dongchun Hyeon; *Original Music*: Cheol-hyeok Lee; *Cast*: Hyung-rae Shim (Young-gu), Jong-cheol Yang, Seong-woo Oh, Sung-dae Park, Jae-mi Oh.

The Young Indiana Jones Chronicles (TV Series [1992–1993]), episode "Transylvania, January 1918"; U.S., Season 2, Episode 22, 21 August 1993; Action, Adventure, Family/Television; 45 minutes/color/English, Italian, Icelandic/Dolby; Lucasfilm, Paramount Television, Amblin Entertainment.

Writing Credits: Jonathan Hensleigh; *Director*: Dick Maas, Carl Schultz; *Cinematography*: David Tattersall; *Film Editing*: Edgar Burckse; *Original Music*: Curt Sobel; *Art Direction*: Ricky Eyres; *Make-Up*: Thomas R. Burman (as Tom Burman), Bari Dreiband-Burman (as Bari Burman), Katerina

Erbanova, Eva Vytlelová; *Special Effects*: David Beavis; *Cast*: Sean Patrick Flanery (Indiana Jones), George Hall (Dr. Henry "Indiana" Jones, Jr.), Bob Peck (General Targo), Keith Szarabajka (Colonel Waters), Simone Bendix (Maria), Paul Kynman (Nicholas Hunyadi), Sam Kelly (Dr. Franz Heinzer/Capt. Adolf Schmidt), Alan Polonsky (Agent McCall), Michael Mellinger (Paretti), William Roberts (Stanfill), William Armstrong (The Major), Steven Hartley (Agent Picard), Anne Tirard (Tarot Reader), Petr Svárovský (Venetian Policeman), David Gilliam (Agent Thompson), Petr Jákl (German General), Jiri Kraus (French General), Lee Norris (Kid #1), Grady Bowman (Kid #2, as Grady McCloud Bowman), Darwin Brandis (Kid #3).

Old Indiana Jones tells a story about a missson to Transylvania on a Halloween night.

Yûreiyashiki no kyôfu: Chi o suu ningyô (*Legacy of Dracula*; *Bloodsucking Doll*; *Chi o suu ningyô* [Japan (short title)]; *Fear of the Ghost House: Bloodsucking Doll* [U.S.]; *The Ghost Mansion's Horror: A Bloodsucking Doll*; *The Night of the Vampire*; *The Vampire Doll*); Japan, 1970; Horror; 85 minutes/color/Japanese/Mono; Toho Company.

Producers: Fumio Tanaka, Tomoyuki Tanaka; *Writing Credits*: Hiroshi Nagano, Ei Ogawa; *Director*: Michio Yamamoto; *Cinematography*: Kazutami Hara; *Film Editing*: Koichi Iwashita; *Original Music*: Riichiro Manabe; *Special Effects*: Teruyoshi Nakano (special effects director); *Cast*: Yukiko Kobayashi (Yuko Nonomura), Kayo Matsuo (Keiko Sagawa), Yôko Minakaze (Shido Nonomura, The Mother), Atsuo Nakamura (Kazuhiko Sagawa), Akira Nakao (Hiroshi Takagi, The Friend), Jun Usami (Dr. Yamaguchi), Jun Hamamura (Official), Sachio Sakai (Taxi Driver), Ginzô Sekiguchi, Itaru Takashima.

A boy disappears after visiting his girlfriend's grave, causing his sister Keiko and her boyfriend to follow his trail to his girlfriend's ancestral home. There they discover supernatural horrors and the danger of the Vampire Doll.

Zinda Laash (*Dracula in Pakistan* [U.S.]; *The Living Corpse* [International English title]); Pakistan, 1967; Crime, Horror; 103 minutes/black and white/Urdu/Mono/35mm.

Producers: Abdul Baqi, Hafiz Chaudhry, Qaim Hussain; *Writing Credits*: Naseem Rizwani, Khwaja Sarfraz; *Director*: Khwaja Sarfraz; *Cinematography*: Nabi Ahmed, Raza Mir; *Original Music*: Tassadaque Hussain; *Cast*: Ala-Ud-In (Parvez), Asad Bukhari (Dr. Aqil Harker [as Asad]), Cham Cham, Latif Charlie, Deeba (Shabnam), Habib (Aqil's Brother), Baby Najmi, Nasreen (Vampire bride), Rehan (Professor Tabani/Dracula), Sheela, Yasmine (Shirin), Munwar Zarif.

Professor Tabani, a mad scientist, drinks an eternal life-giving potion he concocted in his laboratory but is turned into a vampire instead. When Dr. Aqil pays the professor a visit, Tabani sees a picture of Aqil's wife Shabnam. He then turns Aqil into a vampire then pursues Shabnam to make her his bride. Aqil's brother discovers the grave of the vampire and his brother at Tabani's castle, and kills his brother in order to free his soul. Tabani suceeds at turning Shabnam into a vampire, and once she is turned, she tries to lure her young niece away. Aqil's brother is all that stands in the way of this vampire curse.

Zora la vampiera (*Zora the Vampire International* [English title]); Italy, 2000; Comedy; 105 minutes/color/Italian; Virginia Produzioni.

Producers: Vittorio Cecchi Gori, Matteo De Laurentiis, Marco Scaffardi, Carlo Verdone; *Writing Credits*: Antonio Manetti, Marco Manetti; *Director*: Antonio Manetti, Marco Manetti; *Cinematography*: \Federico Schlatter; *Film Editing*: Federico Maneschi; *Original Music*: Skratch DJ Gruff, Squarta; *Make-Up*: Vincenzo Cardella, Simone Gregoris; *Special Effects*: Tiberio Angeloni, Franco Galiano, Rosario Prestopino, Francesco Sabelli; *Cast*: Toni Bertorelli (Conte Dracula), Micaela Ramazzotti (Zora), Raffaele Vannoli (Servo) (as Lele Vannoli), Chef Ragoo (Zombie), Carlo Verdone (Commissario Damiani), Ivo Garrani (Prete), G. Max (Lama), Tormento (Cianuro), Selen (Vampira), Juliet Esey Joseph (Vampira), Marco Manetti (Bue), Sandro Ghiani (Cuccureddu), Massimo De Santis (Tossico), Alessia Barela (Tossica), Elda Alvigini (Ragazza Piercing), Marco Forieri (Tipo segaligno), Michael Maser (Peloso), Turi (Rocco), Erika Savastani (Michelina), Rude MC (Rude), James Senese (Compagno di Napoli), Lampadina (Rasta) (as Lampadread), Lori Bofta (Dafne) (as Lory Bofta), Roberta Modigliani (Giornalista), Tommaso Ausili, Fabio Ferri (Ventura), Macromarco, Valerio Mastandrea (Nicola Speranza), Tomas Milian, Massimo Pittarello (Poliziotto), Letizia Sedrick (Ragazza Africana), Cor Veleno, Matteo Villani.

Dracula travels to Italy in pursuit of the beautiful Zora.

PART II
Dracula in Adult Film

Introduction —
I Want to Suck Your...:
Dracula in Pornographic Film

Laura Helen Marks

There is a certain inevitability to pornographic representations of vampirism; the overtly sexual nature of vampire mythology lends well to a pornographic medium, as the metaphor of sexual deviancy and lust present in vampire lore is rendered literal in the pornographic film. Dracula, in particular, has been a consistent presence throughout the adult feature's relatively short lifespan, perhaps embodying the ultimate pornographic figure: "an elegant and seductive count who preys not only upon the bodies of men and women, but also on the very *being* of his victims, transforming them into creatures as sexually monstrous as himself."[1] The mythos and iconography of Dracula has invited a multitude of pornographic interpretations since the sexploitation flicks of the 1960s and the first hardcore features of the early–1970s.[2]

David J. Hogan has noted that Béla Lugosi's Dracula has become "a figure of parody, not simply of vampirism, but of predatory heterosexuality,"[3] and indeed it is worth noting the number of pornographic adaptations of the Dracula myth that are comedies or parodies of mainstream films. However, the Dracula of the porn world is not exclusively heterosexual or male, with a number of porn films utilizing the Dracula legend to invert or subvert traditional approaches to the original Stoker tale. Furthermore, the iconography of Dracula and vampirism can be seen as offering an interesting resolution to sexual conflict. As Franco Moretti has noted of the original Stoker novel, "Dracula ... liberates and exalts sexual desire. And this desire attracts but — at the same time — frightens."[4] This sexual tension can be seen in the majority of pornographic vampire films, particularly in motifs such as Dracula as pimp, and BDSM[5] films. Drawing on the novel's underlying queer sexualities, porn filmmakers have incorporated the Dracula character, and vampirism in general, into films that cover a spectrum of audience and sexual preference.

Censorship and the Stag Film

Before the feature length hardcore films of the late twentieth century, "stag" films circulated amongst men's groups and fraternity houses, the earliest of these films dating back to around 1910.[6] These graphic one-reel films were primitive: short, silent, and often lacking in narrative coherence.[7] Stags were made during

14th February, 1958

J. Nicholls, Esq.,
British Board of Film Censors,
Soho square,
W.1.

My dear John,

Just a few general observations on "horror pictures".

These pictures get an 'X' Certificate which immediately bars everybody under sixteen years of age from seeing them.

The 'X' Certificate also means that approximately 800 cinemas who call themselves family houses will not book the pictures.

The horror audience is a very specialised one and many people who go to "'X' for sex" pictures will not go to see a horror film.

Naturally those who do go to see horror films expect to see something out of the ordinary, although quite often the horror mis-fires and they laugh at it.

With the very poor state our industry is in it would be a terrible thing if the horror addicts go to see horror pictures and there is no horror in them, in other words, we will lose this audience.

There has always been a horror audience since movies began and nobody has ever been the worse for it.

"DRACULA" is acknowledged the grandaddy of them all and as you know, has been made at least a dozen times.

The specialised audience who will go to see "DRACULA" will expect thrills but the cuts that you are asking us to make, in our opinion, are taking every thrill out of the picture, in fact it is not as horrific as any of the past "DRACULA'S" and we cannot believe that that is your intention.

We have once again to-day resubmitted the three reels that you have objected to and I am seeing you at 4.15 this afternoon to discuss this matter.

Kind regards,

Yours sincerely,

J. CARRERAS,
DIRECTOR.

A letter from James Carreras of Hammer Films to John Nicholls of the British Board of Film Censors concerning the release of *Dracula* (1958; *Horror of Dracula* [U.S.]) (courtesy John Edgar Browning).

an era of tight censorship thanks to the Comstock law, a federal law enacted in 1873 that banned "obscene, lewd, or lascivious" materials from being sent in the mail. As a result, stags were screened illegally, and enjoyed a thriving underground trade amongst men. It appears that during this period there were no stag films that featured Dracula or vampire iconography, possibly due to the stags' lack of narrative structure. Having said that, stag films are difficult to track down, and there may well be a long forgotten Dracula stag film lurking in someone's private collection.[8]

It was not until the landmark *United States v. Roth* obscenity trial of 1957, known as the *Roth* decision, that pornographic film took on the narrative styles of more mainstream Hollywood fare. The *Roth* decision is key to the evolution of pornography: Justice Brennan affirmed the Comstock law, yet significantly revised it by concluding that a work is legally obscene if it is "utterly without redeeming social importance" as judged by "local community standards."[9] One consequence of this ruling was the publication of several banned works of literature, such as D. H. Lawrence's *Lady Chatterley's Lover*; another consequence was the popularization of the softcore sexploitation film, and eventually the hardcore pornographic feature film.

The Golden Age

As Eric Schaefer has shown, the sexploitation movie thrived during the 1960s alongside hardcore shorts, known as "beaver films," which were essentially legal stags. At the same time, documentaries with sexual content, known as "white coaters," were being screened under the guise of having educational value.[10] During this period, the pseudo-documentaries *Sexy Probitissimo* (1963) and *Kiss Me Quick* (1964) had fleeting appearances of Dracula iconography, while sexploitation flicks *Dracula, the Dirty Old Man* (1969) and *Sex and the Single Vampire* (1970) brought Dracula into the fictional narrative world of softcore sexploitation. By the turn of the decade, however, hardcore features emerged in theaters, most notably *Deep Throat* (1972), which is commonly perceived as signaling the beginning of the "golden age" of porn. The golden age is generally regarded as "the period between the early 1970s and the mid–1980s"[11] in which hardcore pornographic films were being screened in theaters, often to mainstream audiences, and the medium took on a degree of credibility and "chic."[12] The introduction of the hardcore feature signals, in part, a response to the legal demand that sexually graphic material have redeeming social importance, and filmmakers were sure to create scripts that would deter the censors.[13] A popular narrative device from the earliest stages of the feature was to mimic Hollywood genres. As Linda Williams notes, "the new 'porno'" strove to position itself as simply a "genre among other genres."[14] "As if to insist on this fact," Williams goes on, "hard-core narratives went about imitating other Hollywood genres with a vengeance, inflecting well-known titles and genres with an X-rated difference."[15] With this in mind, it is instructive to note the number of Dracula-themed porn movies that are parodies of Hollywood productions.

Dracula appears to have been a popular protagonist for hardcore porn narratives from the very beginning of the golden age, debuting in the pre–*Deep Throat* feature *Dracula and the Boys* (1969). Not only is *Dracula and the Boys* a landmark film in terms of the emergence of the hardcore feature, but it also stands out as the very first homosexual vampire film, emphasizing the idea that Dracula and vampirism enable articulations of alternative sexualities much in the same way as Hollywood had been attempting metaphorically up until this time. In his study of queer sexuality in monster movies, *Monsters in the Closet*, Harry M. Benshoff speaks to this trend in Hollywood horror films, arguing, "For the better part of the twentieth century, homosexuals, like vampires, have rarely cast a reflection in the social looking-glass of popular culture. When they are seen, they are often filtered through the iconography of the horror film: ominous sound cues, shocked reaction shots, or even thunder and lightning."[16] In monster movies, Benshoff contends, homosexuality is symbolically coded as monstrous: "Both movie monsters and homosexuals have existed chiefly in shadowy closets, and when they do emerge from those proscribed places into the sunlit world, they cause panic and fear."[17] Indeed, homosexual Draculas, while fewer in number than their heterosexual counterparts, have been a consistent presence throughout the lifespan of hardcore and softcore adult film, a medium that seems to have afforded the homosexual vampire a degree of humanity.[18] Following *Dracula and the Boys* came 1973's *Dragula*, the 1983 effort *Gayracula*, and later, 1988's softcore *Love Bites*.

Also during this initial period we see the trope of conflation of different bodily fluids, as seen in 1976's *The Bride's Initiation* in which Dracula's lifesource is semen. Ostensibly a heterosexual hardcore feature, this narrative choice indicates the queer potential of Dracula and vampire-themed storylines. The ending of the film, in which Dracula consumes a man's semen and subsequently declares his love for the male victim, further emphasizes this queer potential.

Dracula continued to be a popular subject of hardcore throughout the remainder of the golden age, with quality efforts such as *Dracula Exotica* (1981) being filmed on 35mm, along with detailed scripts and attention to acting. The transition from film to video in the mid–1980s is often regarded as contributing to the demise of quality hardcore feature productions, yet interestingly Dracula appears to have survived the steady decline in plot-driven hardcore.

Film to Video

With the introduction of the VCR to U.S. households, the porn industry went through a change almost as significant as that of the revision of obscenity law. With home entertainment now an option, porn theater attendance decreased significantly, while porn consumption increased. Meanwhile, porn production went up, porn film budgets went down, and fewer and fewer narrative-driven hardcore features were being produced.[19] In 1990, 1 percent of U.S. households owned a VCR; by 1997, VCRs could be found in 85,500,000 U.S. homes.[20]

Alongside these technological advances, other elements of socio-sexual life were being impacted, as Chuck Kleinhans notes: "This development [in technology] was concurrent with changes in the sociopolitical environment, such as a new wave of sexual image censorship, changes in sexual practices and ideologies due to the AIDS crisis, and the increased public visibility of previously stigmatized sexualities such as sadomasochism."[21] These concurrent changes can be seen in subtle shifts in porn production, such as an increase in gonzo porn,[22] as well as a proliferation of sexual categories in the adult film trade, thanks in part to lowered production budgets and increased access to media.

While cultural analysts, and popular media, have regarded the introduction of video to be the downfall of hardcore features,[23] the presence of vampire- and Dracula-themed porn seems unabated. Indeed, vampirism and Dracula seem to match well with BDSM and fetish porn, with Dracula's castle, dungeon, dark attire, and violent sexuality seemingly tailor-made for BDSM films. *Bizarre's Dracula I and II*, and *Dracula's Dungeon*, all produced in 1995, tapped into the fetishistic potential of the original Dracula tale, featuring dominance and submission in the dungeons of castles.

Throughout the late–1980s and early–1990s, gay adult film continued to draw on vampire mythology for inspiration, with notable entries including the softcore *Love Bites* (1988), and the hardcore efforts *Dragula, Queen of Darkness* (1996) and *Ultimate Reality* (1996). *Love Bites* in particular has been lauded for revising Hollywood representations of queerness "in an attempt to draw out or exorcise the monster from the queer."[24] Benshoff argues that *Love Bites* "rewrites generic imperatives from a gay male point of view and (somewhat refreshingly) allows both Count Dracula and his servant Renfield to find love and redemption with modern-day West Hollywood gay boys."[25]

The Night Boys (1991) is another important entry into the canon, not for its filmmaking but for the emergence of the first African American character in a gay vampire porn movie; it was only four years earlier that the first African American Dracula appeared in hardcore, in 1987's *Lust for Blackula*, inspired by 1972's blaxploitation-horror *Blacula*. Not only does *Lust for Blackula* cash in on the original cult classic, but it taps into what was then a burgeoning and thriving market for black porn; a market that has only increased, yet without a particular proliferation of African American vampire films.[26] A notable recent African American Dracula, however, can be seen in 2008's *The Accidental Hooker*.

It is also around this time that lesbian vampires and female Draculas seem to have caught on in the porn world. Dracula of the 1990s video porn is no longer exclusively a dominant male seducer, with characters such as Countess Draculust in the hardcore film *Out For Blood* (1990). It is around this time, also, that lesbian vampires take center stage. *Cunt Dykula* is an intriguing entry: not porn, per se, but rather a comedy short produced for a queer film festival, cashing in on the sexual connotations of the original Count. It is the softcore world, however, that the lesbian vampire thrives and presides over the narrative. Starting around the late-1990s, a massive amount of vampire and Dracula-themed softcore was produced. Being softcore, these films can be sold on mainstream sites such as Amazon and retain a high level of narrative in spite of their low budget. In 2000, *Mistress of Seduction* and *Hot Vampire Nights* feature predatory lesbian vampires as the protagonist. Vamparina in *Mistress* is Dracula's daughter, seeking revenge against the reincarnated Van Helsing, while in *Hot Vampire Nights* Mina is the aggressor, seeking out beautiful women on the streets of Miami. This trend in redressing the balance, admittedly for erotic appeal, has endured, and in recent years the number of these softcore productions has only increased.

It would be a mistake, however, to assume that the introduction of video obliterated the mainstream heterosexual hardcore feature, and certainly Dracula remained an enduring presence during this period with productions such as *Ejacula, la vampira* (1992), *Ejacula 2* (1995), and *Dracula* (1994), all of which were fairly low budget.

The Digital Era

With the popularization of the Internet in the late–1990s, the porn industry underwent another significant shift both in production and consumption practices.[27] If the introduction of video led to reduced budgets and fewer narrative-driven features, the internet encouraged pornographic websites and porn sold by the scene, leading in part to a further decline in feature films, as well as a fast-growing online porn industry.[28] Indeed, the pornographic allure of vampire mythology is alive and well online, with websites such as VampireErotica.net, VampirePorn.net, and XXXHorror.com. Vampirism has also persisted as an inspiration for hardcore and softcore filmmakers outside of the web-based industry, with a continued trend in softcore lesbian vampire films, as well as a select but significant group of filmmakers attempting to produce high quality feature films in the face of an industry comprised predominantly of specialist, amateur, or gonzo productions.

The most prevalent use of vampirism in adult film during this period is in the softcore industry, particularly in the output of Frontline Entertainment and Seduction Cinema, both of whom have their movies available on mainstream websites. In the same vein as the softcore films of the late–1990s, these films position lesbian women at the forefront of the narrative, with female Draculas in *The Erotic*

Rites of Countess Dracula (2001), *Countess Dracula's Orgy of Blood* (2004), *Sexy Adventures of Van Helsing* (2004)—which also features a female Van Helsing—and *G-String Vampire* (2005).

While Kleinhans argues that the transition from film to video has resulted in the minimization of sets, costumes, and locations, he allows that the lack of such quality has prompted some filmmakers to use their big budget as a selling point.[29] *Draculya: The Girls Are Hungry* (2006), for example, announces on its cover that the film is shot on location in a real European castle and a fifteenth century dungeon. In addition, *Draculya* is a fetish feature, as is 2008's *Graf Dracula's Bissige Saftfotzen*, continuing the BDSM trend in vampire porn noted of the 1990s. With regard to more mainstream efforts, *Dark Angels 2* (2005) and *The Accidental Hooker* (2008), while not big budget by Hollywood standards, are recent efforts to construct quality, narrative-driven hardcore, suggesting that developments in technology have not completely erased a market for features, nor deterred filmmakers from taking advantage of the sexual nature of vampire mythology.

Outside of feature films, the legend of Dracula, in particular the oral connotations of this legend, has been used to market compilation DVDs such as *Count Spermula* (2005) and *Count Suckula* (2008). This type of DVD consists of scenes from previous films; the content of these particular compilations have nothing to do with Dracula, but put an emphasis on fellatio, as do similar compilations with vampiric titles slapped on the cover as a marketing strategy, such as the *Cum Vampires* series.

Finally, it should be noted that aside from occasional fluctuations in fad, or shifts in production style according to technological progression (or regression, depending on your perspective), Dracula and his vampiric minions have been a consistent source of inspiration for hardcore and softcore filmmakers regardless of budget or script. The appeal of vampiric porn films appears to rest in the intersection of sexuality and danger, played out symbolically in the original novel and subsequent Hollywood adaptations. In the majority of the pornographic films cited, Dracula figures as a kind of orchestrator of sexual abandon, providing a fantastical and sexually free space within a real and conflicted world. Whether in complex narrative adaptations, invocation of the Dracula brand for oral-themed compilations, or simply through the use of a cheap Dracula cape, the relationship between pornographic film and Dracula mythology is consistent and enduring in the face of all manner of industry, technological, and audience changes.

Notes

1. Harry M. Benshoff, *Monsters in the Closet: Homosexuality and the Horror Film* (Manchester: Manchester University Press, 1997), 19.
2. It is instructive to briefly define "hardcore" and "softcore" pornographic film. As Linda Williams succinctly explains in *Screening Sex* (Durham, NC: Duke University Press, 2008), hardcore is "explicit, unsimulated" while softcore is "simulated, faked" (64). In addition, the term "pornography" is often invoked yet rarely defined. Again, Williams' definition, in *Hard Core: Power, Pleasure, and the Frenzy of the Visible* (Berkeley: University of California Press, 1989) is simple and useful: "the visual (and sometimes aural) representation of living, moving bodies engaged in explicit, usually unfaked, sexual acts with a primary intent of arousing viewers" (30). What is useful about this definition is the way in which it allows for moments in pornography that are *not* intended to arouse viewers. A limitation of the definition is that it does not allow for animated films—films that do not involve "living ... bodies"—to be classified as pornographic.
3. David J. Hogan, *Dark Romance: Sexuality in the Horror Film* (Jefferson, NC: McFarland, 1986), 140.
4. Franco Moretti, "A Capital *Dracula*" in *Dracula*, by Bram Stoker, ed. Nina Auerbach and David J. Skal (New York: Norton, 1997), 439.
5. Compound abbreviation for Bondage and Discipline, Dominance and Submission, Sadism and Masochism.
6. Williams, *Hard Core*, 61.
7. Williams, *Hard Core*, 60.
8. There have been efforts to chart the history of the stag film, most notably in Williams' chapter

on the subject in *Hard Core*, 58–92. See also Al Di Lauro and Gerald Rabkin's effort, *Dirty Movies: An Illustrated History of the Stag Film, 1915–1970* (New York: Chelsea House, 1976), and Alex de Renzy's 1970 documentary, *A History of the Blue Movie*.

9. Williams, *Hard Core*, 88.

10. Eric Schaefer, "Gauging a Revolution: 16mm Film and the Rise of the Pornographic Feature," in *Porn Studies*, ed. Linda Williams (Durham, NC: Duke University Press, 2004), 370–371.

11. Schaefer, "Gauging a Revolution," 371.

12. See Ralph Blumenthal's "Pornochic; 'Hardcore' Grows Fashionable — and Very Profitable," which offers a contemporary reflection on this important period of pornographic film. *New York Times*, January 21, 1973, 28–32.

13. It is critical to note that this is only one component of why porn features developed as they did. Schaefer's essay "Gauging a Revolution" offers an insightful analysis of the various contributing factors.

14. Williams, *Hard Core*, 120.

15. Williams, *Hard Core*, 120.

16. Benshoff, *Monsters in the Closet*, 1–2.

17. Benshoff, *Monsters in the Closet*, 2.

18. For many, gay porn offered a revolutionary visibility to an emerging community in the 1970s. The 2008 documentary *Wrangler: Anatomy of an Icon* covers this topic through the charting of the career of gay porn star Jack Wrangler. Also see Williams' analysis of the 1971 gay porn film, *Boys in the Sand*, in which she asserts, "Gay pornography would prove a crucial aspect of [the] ability for homosexuals to be themselves," yet cautions that this view of gay porn as simply "the throwing off of repression" is an overly simplistic way of looking at pornography. *Screening Sex*, 143.

19. Chuck Kleinhans, "The Change from Film to Video Pornography: Implications for Analysis," in *Pornography: Film and Culture*, ed. Peter Lehman (New Brunswick, NJ: Rutgers University Press, 2006), 157.

20. Kleinhans, "The Change from Film to Video Pornography," 157.

21. Kleinhans, "The Change from Film to Video Pornography," 154.

22. "Gonzo" porn, as described by Tricia Devereaux, wife of gonzo founder John "Buttman" Stagliano, "can take on several different forms" but with one specific feature in common: the acknowledgment, either by cameraman, director, or performer, of the fact that they are filming a movie. Lawrence C. Ross, *Money Shot: Wild Days and Lonely Nights Inside the Black Porn Industry* (New York: Thunder's Mouth Press, 2007), 274.

23. Kleinhans quotes industry insiders such as actor Joey Silvera, and Jeremy Stone's introduction to the *Adam Film World Guide* to express the widely held perception that the introduction of video, and by extension the internet, has led to a decrease in overall film quality. Kleinhans quotes Stone as saying that "the essence of erotic filmmaking has been reduced to its most basic form" and that this means "more emphasis on the visual and sexual imagery, and less thought given to established filmmaking philosophy." Kleinhans, "The Change from Film to Video Pornography," 155–156.

24. Benshoff, *Monsters in the Closet*, 286.

25. Benshoff, *Monsters in the Closet*, 286.

26. Apart from essays that condemn racist portrayals and demeaning racialized images in porn, such as Daniel Bernardi's recent "Interracial Joysticks: Pornography's Web of Racist Attractions," in *Pornography: Film and Culture*, ed. Peter Lehman (New Brunswick, NJ: Rutgers University Press, 2006) and Patricia Hill Collins' chapter on the subject in *Black Feminist Thought: Knowledge, Consciousness, and the Politics of Empowerment*, Second Edition (New York: Routledge, 2000), very little has been written about the black porn industry. A recent book, *Money Shot* by Lawrence C. Ross Jr., while not a scholarly contribution, provides a much-needed inside look and raises some important questions.

27. For a discussion of viewing practices in relation to internet porn, see Zabet Patterson's "Going Online," in *Porn Studies*, ed. Linda Williams (Durham, NC: Duke University Press, 2004), 104–123.

28. See Matt Richtel's article, "Lights, Camera, Lots of Action: Forget the Script" for a perspective on why porn features are in decline. *New York Times*, July 7, 2009.

29. Kleinhans, "The Change from Video to Film Pornography," 159.

Filmography

The Accidental Hooker; U.S., 2008; Thriller, Horror/Adult (Hardcore); 129 minutes/color/English/Dolby Digital Surround 5.1; Wicked Pictures.

Producers: Mark Nicholson; *Writing Credits:* Jon Bitton; *Director:* Brad Armstrong; *Cinematography:* Francois Clousot; *Film Editing:* Eddie Door; *Original Music:* Groove Addicts; *Art Direction:* Rod Hopkins; *Make-Up:* Shelby Stevens & Flick; *Special Effects:* Eddie Door; *Cast:* Kaylani Lei (Silvia), Devon Lee, Jennifer Dark, Mikayla, Shyla Stylez, Victoria Sin, Barrett Blade, Barry Scott, Brad Armstrong, Chris Cannon, Deep Threat (Vladdy), Derrick Pierce, Marcus London (Michael), Niko, Tommy Gunn.

A documentary film crew interviews a prostitute, Silvia, for a film about escorts. As Silvia tells her story, her tale is told via flashbacks, detailing her immersion in high-class prostitution. Silvia becomes a prostitute by "accident"—she meets an internet date whom she spends the night with, and wakes up to find money by the side of the bed. From this point, Silvia decides to continue having sex for money. Her next client is the dark and seductive Vladdy. At the end of the interview, Silvia reveals she is a vampire, and that her story of becoming a prostitute is in reality also that of becoming a vampire.

Les Avaleuses (*Bare Breasted Countess* [cut version]; *Caldo corpo di femmina, Un* [Italy]; *La Comtesse aux seins nus* [France]; *La Comtesse noire* [France, cut version]; *Entfesselte Begierde* [West Germany, video]; *Erotic Kill* [U.S.]; *Erotikill* [West Germany]; *Erotikill—Lüsterne Vampire im Spermarausch* [Germany, DVD]; *Erotikiller* [Italy, video, cut version]; *Female Vampire*; *Insatiable Lust* [France, X-rated version]; *Jacula*; *Lüsterne Vampire im Spermarausch* [Germany]; *La Mujer vampire* [Argentina]; *Sicarius—the Midnight Party*; *The Black Countess*; *The Last Thrill*; *The Loves of Irina*; *Verentahrima morsian* [Finland]; *Yacula*); France/Belgium, 1973; Horror/Adult (Erotica); 82 minutes/color/French/Mono/35mm; Eurociné, Général Films.

Producers: Marius Lesoeur, Pierre Quérut; *Writing Credits:* Gérard Brisseau, Jesus Franco (as J.P. Johnson); *Director:* Jesus Franco (as J.P. Johnson); *Cinematography:* Jesus Franco (as Joan Vincent); *Film Editing:* Jesus Franco (as P. Querut); *Original Music:* Daniel White; *Cast:* Lina Romay (Countess Irina Karlstein), Jack Taylor (Baron Von Rathony), Alice Arno (Irina's servant), Monica Swinn (Princess de Rochefort), Jesus Franco (Dr. Roberts), Luis Barboo (Irina's Manservant), Jean-Pierre Bouyxou (Dr. Orloff), Raymond Hardy (Hotel Masseur), Anne Watican (Anna, a journalist), Gilda Arancio (victim in the wall[uncredited]), Roger Germanes (Irina's first victim [uncredited]), Ricardo Vázquez (uncredited).

Countess Irina Karlstein, a mute suffering from the curse of her vampire ancestors, goes from victim to victim, making love to them and taking their life at the point of their orgasm. Irina's murders arouse the suspicions of Dr. Roberts, who investigates the deaths with the help of his friend Dr. Orloff.

The Bizarre Cage #3; Japan, 2001; Horror, Thriller/Animation, Adult (Fetish); 30 minutes/color/Dolby Digital 2.0 Surround; NuTech Digital, Pink Pineapple, Studio Kuma.

Producers: Omiya Saburo, Show Kumabe; *Writing Credits:* Shibata Nekoru (scenario); *Director:* Konno Sei.

The third and final installment in the series, this chapter finds Tamami still imprisoned and subjected to "the Dracula" Inouye's perversions. After realizing their friend Tamami is missing, Saito and Kazuko go to Dracula's castle to save her.

Bizarre's Dracula; U.S., 1995; Horror/Adult (Hardcore, Fetish); 50 minutes/color/English; Bizarre Video.

Writing Credits: Wolfgang Smyth; *Director:* Wolfgang Smyth; *Cinematography:* Johnny Stecchino; *Original Music:* Neil B. Formie; *Cast:* Luc Wylder (Dracula), Barbara Reilly (as Ariana)

(Mina), Anna Malle, Summer Cummings (Girl with Broom), Ivy English, Nicole London (Blonde Slave Girl), Scott Baker (Jon), Mitch Rabida (The Bald Servant), Hank Armstrong (Spanking Master).

Jon and his wife are lured into the world of vampires; Jon discovers his penchant for dominance, while his wife develops a taste for blood. Meanwhile, Dracula seduces Mina, turning her from a young woman into a vampire submissive.

Bizarre's Dracula II; U.S., 1995; Horror/Adult (Hardcore, Fetish); 52 minutes/color/English; Bizarre Video.

Writing Credits: Wolfgang Smyth; *Director:* Wolfgang Smyth; *Cinematography:* Johnny Stecchino; *Cast:* Luc Wylder (Dracula), Barbara Reilly (as Ariana), Anna Malle, Summer Cummings, Ivy English, Nicole London, Scott Baker (Jon), Mitch Rabida (The Bald Servant), Hank Armstrong.

This sequel finds Dracula still holding Mina as one of his many slaves. The film follows Dracula as he tortures the slaves in his dungeon, and at his club for an audience of spectators, where he encases Mina's entire body in hot wax for the pleasure of the crowd.

The Bride's Initiation; U.S., 1976; Horror/Adult (Hardcore); 67 minutes/color/English/Mono/35mm.

Producers: Duncan Stewart; *Writing Credits:* Jerry Sheldon; *Director:* Duncan Stewart; *Cinematography:* Roberto Raphael; *Film Editing:* Gordon Craig; *Cast:* Marc Brock (Dracula), Tony Marshall, Steve Morgan, Jack O'Brien, Bonna Quigley, George Croder, Mona Robbins, Cammy Young, Judy Sanders, Bill Harris, Walter Flartz, John Seeley, Gail Ward, Luke Spencer, Dona Cord, Jack Birch (James the Chauffeur [uncredited]), Carol Connors (Miss Richmond [uncredited]).

A recently married couple are kidnapped and taken to Dracula's castle where they are seduced in order for Dracula to obtain his life source: semen. Meanwhile, the Count has spotted a woman named Carol, decides he must have her, and has her brought to him. The bride's parents hire a detective, who is subsequently drained of his semen for the Count's consumption; after consuming the semen, the Count declares his love for the detective.

Brides of Countess Recula; U.S., 1999; Adult; 97 minutes/color/English; Mondo Family.

Director: Col Robert Schaffner, W B Schaffner; *Cast:* Ariel, Big Dick Franco Rocketboy, Billy Bagg, Bridgette Powerz, Bruno, Chante, Divine Stein, Donita, Frankenchrist, Janos Skorzeny, Jay Strange, Jennifer Leigh, Jorge Strange, Lisa Labia, Melinda Strange, Nick Dagger, Pie Dog Savage, Rok Wolfstein, Sue Johnson, Tex.

Brooke West Collection; U.S., 2006; Adult (Hardcore), Compilation; 120 minutes/color/English; Alpha Blue Productions.

Cast: Brooke West.

This film compiles classic Brooke West scenes, including one in which her partner is Dracula.

Buffy the Vampire Layer; U.S., 1996; Horror/Adult (Hardcore); 79 minutes/color/English; CDI.

Writing Credits: Gene Ross (as W. Bosley DeLongprez); *Director:* Jack Stephen; *Cast:* Kristi Myst (Buffy), Michael Hurt, Zasu Knight, Lancaster Merrin, Alex Metro, Mila (Madam Duda), Randi Rage, Sahara Sands, Jack Stephen, Kyle Stone, Randi Storm.

Evil Count Hymie "The Impaler" Draculwitz summons Buffy to Transylvania.

Cathula; U.K., 2001; Horror/Adult (Hardcore); 93 minutes/color/English/Video; Pumpkin Films.

Director: Phil Barry; *Cast:* Cathy Barry (Cathula), Frazer Fox, Angel Long, Laura Michaels, Geoff Pearce, Paul Plenty, Jane Whitehouse, Phil Barry (Man with Cut Finger [uncredited]).

After finding an amulet, a young girl is led to Cathula's castle. Cathula awakens, and sets her plan in motion: to turn the world into sex-crazed vampires.

Cathula 2: Vampires of Sex; U.K., 2004; Horror/Adult (Hardcore); 142 minutes/color/English; Pumpkin Films.

Director: Phil Barry; *Cast:* Autumn, Cathy Barry (Cathula), Phil Barry (Marnish), Dave Courtney (The Devil), Donna-Marie, Frazer Fox, Angel Long, Laura Michaels (as Laura Ranger), Geoff Pearce, Paul Plenty, Alex Stone, Ian Tate, Michelle Thorne, Jane Whitehouse.

Cathula is searching for an ancient book belonging to an ancient clan of vampires. With the help of her servant, Marnish, Cathula embarks on a journey that sees her engage in various sexual scenarios.

Count Erotica, Vampire (*Count Erotico — Vampire* [U.S. DVD title]); U.S., 1975; Horror, Comedy/Adult (Hardcore); 33 minutes/color/English/Mono; Lobo Films.

Writing Credits: Hans Klepper; *Director:* Tony Teresi; *Cinematography:* Ron Pitts; *Cast:* Antona Morell (Count Erotica), Joy Winters, Robin Tate, Phil Craig, D.G. Cole, Anna Busch, Keith Erickson.

Count Erotica refuses to come out of his coffin, forcing the perpetually aroused Mrs. Erotica to pursue and seduce sex partners, starting with the family freak.

Count Spermula; U.S., 2005; Adult (Hardcore), Compilation; 240 minutes/color/English; Vivid.

Cast: Cherokee, Briana Banks, Kay London, Sana Fey, Tia Bella, Heather Hunter, Kira Kener, Dee, Johnni Black, Julia Ann, Roxanne Hall, Jessica Darlin, Devon, Kate Moore, Taylor Hayes, Sunny, Anastasia Blue, Carolina, Jessica Drake, Sydnee Steele, Gwen Summers, Angelica Sin, Alana Evans, Tasha Hunter.

"The Count's hungry, sexy minions prowl the night searching for victims to suck ... and it ain't blood they're after... The Count will show you loads of fun and a Howling good time!!! She loves 'The Seed of Evil' in her face!!!" This film compiles Vivid sex scenes from previous productions, with an emphasis on oral sex.

Count Suckula; U.S., 2008; Adult (Hardcore), Compilation; 240 minutes/color/English; Wicked Pictures.

Cast: jessica drake, Nicole Sheridan, Chloe, Kylie Ireland, Voodoo, TT Boy, Tyler Knight, Mia Smiles, Alexa Rae, Kaylynn, Tina Tyler, Crystal Wilder, Exotica, Kirsten Price, Carmen Hart, Delilah Strong, Kirsty Waay, Nikki Lynn, Kayla Paige, Pason, Jay Huntington, Jasmine Lynn, TJ Cummings, Heidi Maybe, Leanni Lei, Tommy Gunn, Evan Stone, Randy Spears, Peter North, Chris Cannon, Alex Sanders, Brad Armstrong, Jonathan Morgan, Barrett Blade, Randy West, Ian Daniels, Joey Ray.

"21 Wicked sex scenes to sink your teeth into!!!" This film compiles Wicked Pictures sex scenes from previous productions, with an emphasis on oral sex.

Countess Dracula's Orgy of Blood; U.S., 2004; Horror/Adult (Softcore); 86 minutes/color/English/Dolby Digital; Frontline Entertainment.

Producers: Donald F. Glut, Daniel J. Mullen, Kimberly A. Ray; *Writing Credits:* Donald F. Glut; *Director:* Donald F. Glut; *Cinematography:* Gary Graver; *Film Editing:* Dean McKendrick; *Original Music:* Terry Huud (as Peter Damien); *Make-Up:* Mark Bedell, Rick Bongiovanni, Glori-Anne Gilbert, Mindy Krejci, Stefanie Owens, Greyson R. Wolf; *Special Effects:* Mark Bedell, John Carl Buechler, Mindy Krejci; *Cast:* Paul Naschy (Padre Jacinto), Glori-Anne Gilbert (Diana), Arthur Roberts (Lord Ruthven), Danielle Petty (Roxanne) (as Kennedy Johnson), Eyana Barsky (Martine), Tony Clay (Count Dracula), Del Howison (Renfield), Jana Thompson (Valerie), Lolana (Lilith), Belinda Gavin (Anne), Mark Bedell (Dumas), Jason Peters (Mal), Marina Yaloyan (Natasha), Bella Diona (Hooker #1), Olga Hammerstein (Hooker #2), Whayne Jerome-Clayton (Bouncer), Dawn McMahan (Kandi), Joe Baisur (Frugal Street John), Allen G. Krakalik (Bartender), Tango Perlita (Hooker), Cindy Greene (Hooker), Paul Guay ("A List" Strip Club Patron), Donald F. Glut ("A List" Strip Club Patron [as Don Glut]), Richard Dyszel (Count Gore De Vol), Tony Malanowski ("A List" Strip Club Patron [as Skip Malanowski]).

Inspired by "The Vampyre" (1819) by Dr. John Polidori, this sequel to *The Erotic Rites of Countess Dracula* (2001) sees the vampiric Lord Ruthven brought back to life in the 21st century by Countess Dracula. Having been cursed so he cannot drink blood, Ruthven discovers he can drink blood if filtered through another vampire. So, revives his evil lesbian sister, Diana, to stalk prey for him. Now resurrected, the siblings pursue the resurrection of Roxanne, a woman they had both stalked as prey over a century ago.

Cunt Dykula; U.S., 1993; Horror, Comedy/Short; 5 minutes/color, black and white/English.

Producers: Lisa Kühne; *Writing Credits:* Lisa Kühne; *Director:* Lisa Kühne; *Cinematography:* Lisel; *Original Music:* Front 242, Girls in the Nose, Lisa Kühne (as Lisa); *Cast:* Lupé (Cunt Dykula), Lisa Kühne (Victim).

This film is a parody of a lesbian safe-sex public service announcement, part of "She's Safe"—a program of lesbian safe-sex videos. A solitary woman stands in a park as a Dracula-type figure approaches, preparing to bite her neck. The girl fends off the attacker by holding up a safe-sex diagram.

Dark Angels 2: Bloodline; U.S., 2005; Horror/Adult (Hardcore); 114 minutes/color/English/2.0 Dolby Digital; Digital Sin, New Sensations Video, Original Sin Films.

Producers: Scott Taylor; *Writing Credits:* Nic Andrews; *Director:* Nic Andrews; *Cinematography:* Nic Andrews; *Film Editing:* Nic Andrews; *Original Music:* Derik Andrews; *Special Effects:* Al Magliochetti; *Cast:* August (Draken's First Victim), Barrett Blade (Draken), Dillon Day (Jack Cross), Destiny Deville (Trailer Whore), Tommy Gunn (Eddie), Ron Jeremy (Diner Manager), Karina Kay (Paula), Mike Lane (Diner Patron), Shelby Lane (Diner Patron), Sunny Lane (Jesse), David Lord (Bum) (as David Crawford), Monica Mayhem (Petra), Kirsten Price (anon) (as Kristen Price), Evan Stone (Quinn), Chris Webber (S.W.A.T. Team Leader), Tyler Wood (Mike).

A group of vampires, led by Draken, uses zombies to seek out a special type of blood that the vampires need in order to thrive. Having found a girl, Jesse, with the sought-after blood type, Draken and his vampires pursue her. Meanwhile, she finds refuge with her protector, Jack Cross.

Doracula (*Dracula ga Neratteru* [Japan]); Japan; Adult (Hardcore); 59 minutes/color/Japanese; Shy Kikaku.

Cast: Ari.

Dracula (*Böse, Das; Dracula XXX*); Italy, 1994; Horror/Adult (Hardcore); 80 minutes/color/English (dubbed); Plum Productions, Colmax.
Director: Mario Salieri; *Cinematography:* Bruno De Sisti; *Film Editing:* Clemente del Duca; *Cast:* Selene, Joy Karins, Simona Valli, Deborah Wells, Maeva, Draghixa, Tanya La Riviere, Dalila, Manuela Simone, Nicoletta Astori, John Walton (as Jolth Walton), Ron Jeremy, Jean-Yves Le Castel (as Joe Calzone), Eric Vincent, Franck David, Richard Voisin (as Richard Voicin), Roberto Malone, Don Fernando, John Sanders, Michael Hart.

Vlad the Impaler unsuccessfully attempts to make his wife flee a Turkish invasion of Romania. Vlad is killed, while his wife is kidnapped and tortured until she will submit herself sexually to the sultan. Her suicide, on top of Vlad's grave, reawakens Vlad, who returns to take vengeance.

Dracula and the Boys (*Does Dracula Really Suck?* [U.S.]); U.S., 1969; Horror/Adult (Hardcore); color/English/Mono; Merrick International Films.
Director: Laurence Merrick.

This hardcore gay vampire film is the first openly homosexual vampire film ever produced.

Dracula Exotica (*Dracula Erotica* [Australia]; *Love at First Gulp*); U.S., 1981; Horror, Comedy/Adult (Hardcore); 100 minutes/color/English/Mono/ 35mm; Entertainment Ventures (EVI), TVX Video, VCA Pictures.
Producers: Zora Coast, Shaun Costello (as K. Schwartz), Bill Milling (as Dexter Eagle); *Writing Credits:* Shaun Costello (as K. Schwartz); *Director:* Shaun Costello (as Warren Evans); *Cinematography:* William de Main; *Film Editing:* Robert Luttrell; *Original Music:* Allan Gerber; *Art Direction:* Steve Finken (as Steve Finkin); *Make-Up:* Maryanne Guar (as Mary Ann Guar); *Cast:* Jamie Gillis (Count Dracula), Samantha Fox (Surka/Sally Lancu), Vanessa del Rio (Vita Valdes), Eric Edwards (Big Bird) (as Erik Edwards), Roger Caine (Sgt. Wilmo Blick) (as Mark Dexter), Gordon G. Duvall (Renfrew), Bobby Astyr (Anatole), Murray Bukofski (Chikopnik), Alba Bonn (Castle Guide), Leigh Hope (Hunter Graduate), Terry Yule (Gilda Glad), Carol Markoe (Shopping Bag Lady), Inez de Falla (Flamenco Dancer), Denise Sloan (Vampire Wife #1), Diana Sloan (Vampire Wife #2), Herschel Savage (Morgue Attendant) (as Joel Kane), Donald Blank (Pimples), Christine De Shaffer (Medieval Partygoer [uncredited]), Ron Hudd (Eric—Smuggler in Blue Shirt [uncredited]), Ron Jeremy (Juggling Medieval Partygoer [uncredited]), Tony Mansfield (Sadistic Partygoer in Vest [uncredited]), Ashley Moore (Paco—Smuggler with Mustache [uncredited]), Dave Ruby (Smuggler in Sleeveless Shirt [uncredited]), Robin Sane (Medieval Partygoer [uncredited]), Marc Valentine (Medieval Partygoer in Belt [uncredited]), Randy West (Medieval Partygoer in Vest [uncredited]), Marlene Willoughby (Medieval Partygoer with Apple [uncredited]).

After Count Dracula rapes his virgin lover at the end of a night of drunken revelry, the girl's subsequent suicide prompts Dracula to commit suicide and curse himself to be one of the undead for all time. 400 years later, Dracula decides to move to America for a change of lifestyle. Once there, the "F.I.B." are quickly on his trail, led by Sally, who is startlingly reminiscent of Dracula's lost love.

Drácula mascafierro; Mexico, 2002; Comedy, Horror/Adult; 75 minutes/color/Spanish; Producciones Potosi S.A.
Producers: Juan Cruz; *Director:* Victor Manuel Castro; *Cinematography:* Salvador Cerecero; *Cast:* Roberto Guzmán, Jorge Aldama, Gary Rivas, Liliana Perez, Siena Perez, Lety Uri, Mário Zebadúa.

Flaco Guzman is hotel owner/vampire who lures his women customers into the hotel, where he bites them and turns them into vampires as well. Flaco starts to draw attention from other coworkers, and one asks him as to what his secret to getting so many women is, not knowing his evil ways.

Dracula Meets the Outer Space Chicks; U.S., 1967; Film Co. Independent.

Dracula Sucks (*Dracula's Bride* [undefined] [X-rated version]; *Dracula ... ti succhio* [Italy]; *Kaftes erotikes nyhtes tou Drakoula* [Greece]; *La novia de Drácula* [Venezuela]; *Liebling, du beißt so gut* [West Germany]; *Lust at First Bite* [undefined]; *The Coming of Dracula's Bride* [U.S.]); U.S., 1979; Horror, Comedy/Adult (Hardcore); 108 minutes/color/English/Mono/16mm (negative format), 35mm (printed film format); First International Pictures, M R Productions.
Producers: Scott Brody, David E. Emerich, David Kern, Darryl Marshak (as Darryl A. Marshak), Nettie Peña; *Writing Credits:* Darryl Marshak (as Darryl A. Marshak), Phillip Marshak (as David J. Kern), T. Bell, William Margold, Mitch Morrill; *Director:* Phillip Marshak (as Phillip A. Marshak); *Cinematography:* Hanania Baer; *Film Editing:* Nettie Peña; *Original Music:* Lionel Thomas; *Make-Up:* Rhavan Briggs (as Rahavan B. Briggs), Martin L. Dorf, Phillis Ellis, Priscilla Morales; *Special Effects:* Richard King; *Cast:* Jamie Gillis (Dracula), Annette Haven (Mina), John Leslie (Dr. Arthur Seward), Serena (Lucy Webster), Reggie Nalder (Dr. Van Helsing [as Detlef van Berg]), Kay Parker (Dr. Sybil Seward), John Holmes (Dr. John Stoker), Mike Ranger (Dr. Peter Bradley), Paul Thomas (Jonathan Harker), Richard Bulik (Richard Renfield) (as McGoogle Schlepper), Pat

Poster for *Dracula Sucks* (U.S., 1979).

Dracula, The Dirty Old Man; U.S., 1969; Comedy, Horror/Adult (Sexploitation); 80 minutes/color/English/Mono/35mm.

Producers: William Edwards, Clifton Bowen; *Writing Credits:* William Edwards; *Director:* William Edwards; *Cinematography:* William G. Troiano; *Film Editing:* Ludwig Moner; *Art Direction:* X.O. Vangam; *Make-Up:* Tony Tierney; *Cast:* Vince Kelley (Alucard), Ann Hollis (Ann), Libby Caculus (Marge), Joan Pickett (Joan), Billy Whitman (Jackal-Man), Sue Allen (Carol), Adarraine (Susn), Ron Scott (Bob), Bob Whitton (Station Attendant), Rebecca Reynolds (Stranded Girl).

Dracula has a new slave, Dr. Irving Jekyll, who has been turned into a half-man, half-jackal creature. Dracula demands that Jekyll lure young females to Dracula's Los Angeles cabin so that he may get at their blood.

Dracula's Dungeon; U.S., 1995; Horror/Adult (Hardcore, Fetish); 60 minutes/color/English/Video; London Video, HOM.

Cast: K.C. Dylan, Isadora Rose, Alexis Payne, Diva.

Countess Dracula pursues, seduces, and tortures beautiful women in the dungeons of her castle.

Draculya: The Girls Are Hungry; U.S., 2006; Horror/Adult (Hardcore, Fetish); 120 minutes/color/English/Digital Stereo; Pirate Fetish Machine, Private DVD, Pure Play Media.

Director: Susi Medus; *Cast:* Ellen Saint (Szoliali; Katrina's Lover), Julie Silver (Orphan; Draculya), Liliane Tiger (Countess Hilona; Elszebel; 1st Executioner), Lucy Love (Katrina), Natalli Di Angelo (Cemetery Vamp), Nikki Sun (2nd Motorcycle Vamp), J.J. (Count Budway Drakowisky, 2nd Executioner), Dillon (Count Brasov), Vanessa (1st Motorcycle Vamp), Rudy (Gyorgy Drakowisky).

Two beautiful 1880s Carpathian women prey on the sexual desires of men and women, feeding off of them after the victim's climax.

Dragula; U.S., 1973; Horror, Comedy/Adult (Hardcore); English/color/Mono.

Director: Jim Moss, Andy Milligan (uncredited); *Cinematography:* Andy Milligan; *Cast:* Calvin Cul-

Manning (Irene Renfield), David Lee Bynum (Jarvis), Seka (Nurse Betty Lawson), Martin L. Dorf (Martin), George Lee (Singing Cowboy), Renee Andre (Hand Maiden), Slavica (Hand Maiden), Kurt Sjoberg (Hitler), Ken Yontz (Patient [as Ken Michaels]), Nancy Hoffman (Patient), Mitch Morrill (Patient), William Margold (Henry [as Bill Margold]).

Two siblings discover an underground tomb beneath the sanatorium they run, where Dracula has been resting. He awakens and goes on the rampage, seducing and having his way with a series of beautiful women. Van Helsing visits the sanatorium and begins to suspect that his arch nemesis is loose. Meanwhile, Dracula seeks out Mina for his bride.

ver (as Casey Donovan), Calvin Holt, Walter Kent, Jan Wallman, John Wallowitch, Hal Borske (uncredited), Joe Downing (Dragula [uncredited]).

In this film Dracula has two sons who are complete opposites. One is a softer guy who everyone loves while the other is a dominant power seeking alpha-male. It is a homosexual vampire movie where the brothers are against each other.

Dragula, Queen of Darkness; U.S., 1996; Horror/Adult (Hardcore); 90 minutes/color/English; He-She Studios.

Cast: Bram Stroker.

This film offers four unrelated scenes featuring transsexual vampires.

Ejacula, la vampira; Italy/U.S., 1992; Horror/Adult (Hardcore); 92 minutes/color/English/Dolby Digital 2.0/; VCA.

Producers: Mario Pollak; *Director:* Alessandro del Mar (as Max Bellocchio); *Cast:* Tonisha Mills, Lynn Lemay, Patricia Kennedy, Carolyn Monroe, Lois Ayers, Beatrice Sall, Vivian, Elisabeth, Allessandra, Rocco Siffredi (Ejacula), Ron Jeremy (as Reinfeld Ronfeld), Joey Silvera, JP Armand, Richard Voisin, Giancarlo Bini, Yves Baillard.

Mills and Siffredi play two vampires living together in their castle, served by their hunchbacked servant (Ron Jeremy). After being found out by repairmen, the vampires receive a series of visitors whom they seduce and then turn into vampires, leading to a vampire orgy. Their servant harvests the semen for the vampire masters to complete a vampire ceremony. The film ends on a cliffhanger as a man (Joey Silvera) shows up at the door.

Ejacula 2; U.S., 1995; Horror/Adult (Hardcore); 90 minutes/color/English/Dolby Digital 2.0; VCA.

Director: Alessandro del Mar (as Max Bellocchio); *Cast:* Tonisha Mills, Patricia Kennedy, Lynn Lemay, Lois Ayers, Florance, Carolyn Monroe (as Caroline Monroe), Cristina, Lucia, Elisabetta Baruy, Vivien, Babette, Rocco Siffredi (Ejacula), Ron Jeremy, Viocin, Max Bellocchio, Giancarlo Bini, Ralph Scott.

Having harvested semen for his vampire ceremony, Ejacula must find a virgin to complete the ritual in this sequel to *Ejacula*. Luckily, a man and his new virgin bride (Joey Silvera and Babette) have arrived at the castle on their honeymoon. After a series of seductions, the film culminates in an orgy involving all cast members. However, Ejacula and his minions do not realize that vampire hunters have been waiting for them to get distracted so the hunters can strike.

Emmanuelle the Private Collection: Emmanuelle vs. Dracula; U.S., 2004; Horror/Adult (Softcore), Television; 87 minutes/color/English/Mono; Biouw Beleggingen B. V., Click Productions Inc., Oranton Ltd.

Producers: Todd Allen, Jakob Hausman, Yamie Philippi, Alain Siritzky; *Writing Credits:* Rolfe Kanefsky (as Rafael Glenn), Emmanuelle Arsan; *Director:* KLS; *Cinematography:* Anne Etheridge; *Original Music:* Ray Arthur Wang (as RAW); *Art Direction:* Anne Bauer; *Make-Up:* Katie Custer, Amelle Lapu, Jorge Palmeira, Anca Palmschi, Kristy Pieratt, Claudia Tarbac; *Special Effects:* Josef Tousseau; *Cast:* Natasja Vermeer (Emmanuelle), Beverly Lynne (Mary), Kelsey Heart (Susn) (as Kelsey), Molinee Green (Lucy) (as Mollie Green), Valerie Baber (Jennifer), Ernesto Perdomo (The Dark One), Marcus DeAnda (Dracula), Luke Anthony (Bruce), Kaya Redford (Arthur), Tais Ferrari, Florentina Alecu, Gabriela Pena, Aurelian Ciocîrlie, Titus Patrascu, Adrian Boureanu, George Laurentiu, Christina Mihai, Stefania Sition Ruset, Florentina Olaru, Alexandra Constantin, Cornelia Anitei, Brîndus Nicole Mutoiu, Georgiana Danila, Tania Cucoreanu, Oana Mihaela Ciocîrlie, Monica-Maria Benegui, Anca-Floriana Ionitete, Alina Maria Cumpana, Andreea Rusu, Stefania Silion, Fabiola Soares, Ellen Chaves, Vazconcelos de Aguiar.

Dracula happens upon a slumber party, attended by the eponymous Emmanuelle who quickly discovers that Dracula aims to have sex with the party girls, thereby turning them into vampires.

The Erotic Rites of Countess Dracula (*Scarlet Countess* [U.S. Working Title]); U.S., 2001; Horror/Adult (Softcore); 80 minutes/color/English/Stereo; Frontline Entertainment.

Producers: Stuart DesBrisay, Kevin M. Glover, Edward L. Plumb; *Writing Credits:* Donald F. Glut; *Director:* Donald F. Glut; *Cinematography:* Stephen Rocha; *Film Editing:* Dean McKendrick; *Art Direction:* Eddie Cacho; *Make-Up:* Dan Frye; *Cast:* Brick Randall (Scarlet), William Smith (Count Dracula), Del Howison (Renfield), Meredith Rinehart (Tiffany), Nicole Liberty-Whitlock (Vicki), Julia Anna Thurman (Shado), Luther Robinson (Skyler), Charlie (Wet Dream Girl), Shea Alexander (Maggie the Waitress), Joan Marlowe (Josie the Bartender), Jason Peters (Nightclub Masher), Tony Clay (Radio Announcer), Utaka Ito (Chinatown Hooker), Alexander Lehr (Hippie Couple), Boyana Zietlow (Hippie Couple), Greg Webb (Music Video Cameraman), Christine Brooks (Park Hooker), Tina Lee (Park Hooker), Stacy Michaels (Park Hooker), Wesley Burnett (Chauffeur), Brenda Garcin Brick (Paparazzi), Allen G. Krakalik (Photographer), Edward L. Plumb (Bookstore Customer), Bill Warren (Man on Street), Max & Tucker (Children of the Night), Gio Banderas (Scarlet Countess Dancer), Darlene Rae Brickes

(Scarlet Countess Dancer), Jason Ryan Hall (Scarlet Countess Dancer), Amanda Maria Lee (Scarlet Countess Dancer), Sandra Martinez (Scarlet Countess Dancer), Miguel Montalvo (Scarlet Countess Dancer), Rafael Nunez (Scarlet Countess Dancer), William Pappas (Scarlet Countess Dancer).

After being attacked and rendered undead by Count Dracula in 1966, wannabe rock star Scarlet Brooks curses her existence as a vampire until, thirty-five years later, she orders her servant, Renfield, to drive a stake through her heart. Unable to do it, Renfield discovers that Scarlet can be made mortal again by drinking the blood of three willing virgins. Scarlet seeks out and seduces three beauties, making love to them, and finally drinking their blood. However, life as a mortal proves to be an even worse situation requiring an erotic solution.

Poster for *Gayracula* (U.S., 1983).

From Dusk 'til Porn; U.K., 2004; Horror, Comedy/Adult (Hardcore); 156 minutes/color/English; Relish.

Director: Hazza B'Gunne; *Cast:* Angel Dark, Sarah O'Neil, Janca (Venetia), Lucy Rush (Prostitute), Cheryl, Avalon, Kat Varga, Claudia (DI Nurmi), Mark Sloan (Jon Harker), Pascal White (Gladys the Inhaler) Steve Hooper (DI Topperov), Vincent Van Goth (Makepeace), Blake Death (Headcase).

Protagonist Jon Harker informs police of the strange things that have been happening to him since meeting Venetia in a Soho nightclub, told via flashback. Jon meets Venetia, a vampire tired of her life in the dark, and invites her back to his flat where they have sex, following which Venetia bites him on the neck. Their union has angered the other vampires, and Jon is taken to Glad the Inhaler by heavies, Makepeace and Headcase, in order to ascertain if he has been fully vampirized, while Venetia pleads for Jon's life. Jon is able to escape to the police after being sent by Glad to murder a prostitute as a way of testing his potential as a vampire. At the end of Jon's police interview, DI Nurmi seduces both Jon and Topperov, but then the men notice she is starting to act rather strange.

Gayracula; U.S., 1983; Horror/Adult; 83 minutes/color/English; HIS Video

Producers: Terry LeGrand; *Writing Credits:* Laurei I. Lee, Dorothee Psaw; *Director:* Roger Earl; *Cinematography:* David Scott, Gregg Welles; *Film Editing:* Russell Moore, Brandon Ryan; *Original Music:* Rand Bohn; *Art Direction:* Rand Bohn; *Make-Up:* Michael Harris; *Cast:* Tim Kramer (Gaylord Young), Steve Collins (The Marquis de Suede), Rand Remington (Boris), Randal Butler (Randy), Michael Christopher (Delivery Boy), Ray Medina (Ray), Max Montoya (Backroom Guy) (as Max Cooper), Doug Weston (Blood Bank Donor), Douglas Poston (Blood Bank Guy), Davin McNeil (Gavin) (as David McNeil).

A farm boy is seduced and turned into a vampire by the Marquis de Suede. Centuries later, the boy, now Count Gaylord, is prowling the streets of Los Angeles, still seeking vengeance against de Suede. In the meantime, he is able to find all the young male flesh he desires, with the help of his manservant.

Graf Dracula's Bissige Saftfotzen (*Count Dracula's Snappish Juicecunts* [English title]); Germany, circa 2008; Horror/Adult (Hardcore); 90 minutes/color/German; Herzog Video Productions.

Director: Henry Hidden, M. Alexander; *Cast:* Sabrina, Jack Hammer, Gina Blonde, Asia Blondi, Kasia Laska, Maria Magdalena.

Count Dracula and his lusty vampires indulge in their thirst for blood and sex in Dracula's lair. Meanwhile, a vampire hunter is sneaking around the castle attempting to resist the charms of Dracula's vampiric beauties.

G-String Vampire; U.S., 2005; Horror/Adult (Softcore); 64 minutes/color/English; Seduction Cinema.

Producers: Michael Raso (as Michael Beck); *Director:* Sean Thornton; *Cinematography:* Charlie Brewster; *Film Editing:* John Bacchus; *Original Music:* Don Mike; *Cast:* Barbi Leigh (Janet Turner), Chante Bey (Countess Dracula), Angel Marie Taylor (Helen Wells — Accountant), Tracy Rose (Jill), Katrina Raey (Lt. Jenkins) (as Samantha), Katie Ann Taylor (Dancer #1), Brittany Prada (Dancer #2), Jennifer (Controller).

Janet Turner is a special agent for an organization that destroys vampires, working undercover in a Miami strip club where she believes there is a vampire infiltration. Countess Dracula has already seduced two of the dancers into the legions of the undead, and Turner is worried she may be outmatched.

The Horny Vampire; U.S., 1971; Horror, Comedy/Adult (Hardcore); 45 minutes/color/English/Mono.

Director: Ray Dennis Steckler (as Sven Christian); *Cast:* Jerry Deloney (The Vampire [as Victor Alexander]).

Count Dracula's relative wanders around Las Vegas in cape and tie, attempting to master the art of picking up women.

Hot Vampire Nights; U.S., 2000; Horror/Adult (Softcore); 57 minutes/color/English; Innisfree Pictures, Seduction Cinema.

Producers: Will Danahur, Travis McGee, James Monk, Michael Raso; *Writing Credits:* Charlton Byrnes; *Director:* Sean Thornton (as Will Danahur); *Cinematography:* Charlie Brewster; *Film Editing:* Carmilla Karnstein; *Original Music:* Peter Vincent; *Cast:* Shelly Jones (Mina, the Lesbian Vampire), Allegra (Mina's Victim #4), Dominique (Mina's Victim #2), Katelyn Gold (Mina's Victim #3), Beth Linhart (Mina's Victim #1), Anita Hayes (Bobbi Harker — WBLD Late-Night Hostess).

Lesbian vampire Mina cruises the streets of Miami for hot young women to satisfy her sexual appetites.

House on Bare Mountain (*Colline du désir, La* [Belgium/French]; *Monstres et les nues, Les* [Belgium/French]; *Night on Bare Mountain* [undefined]; *Vampire érotique, Le* [France/French]; U.S., 1962; Comedy/Adult (Sexploitation); 62 minutes/color/English/Mono/35mm; B and M productions.

Producers: Wes Bishop, Bob Cresse; *Writer:* Denver Scott; *Director:* Lee Frost, Wes Bishop; *Cinematography:* Gregory Sandor; *Film Editing:* Gary Lindsay; *Original Music:* Pierre Martel; *Make-Up:* Harry Thomas (special makeup effects artist); *Cast:* Bob Cresse (Granny Good), Laura Eden (Prudence Bumgartner/Badge N0.261), Ann Myers (Sally), AngelaWebster (Honey), Warren Ames (Frankenstein), Jeffrey Smithers (Dracula), William Engesser (Krakow, the Werewolf).

Wolfman, Dracula, and Frankenstein invade a girls' school in the mountains after spying on their oft-nude exploits.

Kiss Attack; U.S., 2008; Horror, Science Fiction/Adult (Hardcore); 90 minutes/color/English/Dolby Digital; Adam & Eve Productions.

Director: Carlos Batts; *Cast:* Sasha Grey, April Flores, Claudia Rossi, Sarah Vandella, Penny Flame (as Penny), Claire Adams, Alex Gonz, Mikey Butders, Christian.

After years of slumber, Vlad Drakul spawns five beautiful but deadly daughters in order to continue his reign of terror. Each daughter will use her particular deadly power to seduce men and enslave the world. Vlad hires an alchemist, Mr. Experiment, to protect his daughters, but Mr. Experiment's son, VMMX, grows jealous of the attention his father pays to the girls. VMMX vows to destroy Vlad's daughters, and creates the Fleshers (specially bred assassins) to achieve his goal.

Kiss Me Quick! (*Dr. Breedlove* [undefined]; *Dr. Breedlove or How I Learned to Stop Worrying and Love* [undefined]; *Embrasse-moi vite! Belgium* [French title]; *Kiss Me Quick U.S.* [alternative spelling]; *Vie sexuelle de Frankenstein, La* [France]); U.S., 1964; Comedy, Science Fiction/Adult (Sexploitation); 70 minutes/color/English/Mono; Fantasy Films, Inc.

Producers: Max Gardens (as Seymour Tuchus) Harry H. Novak (as Seymour Tuchus); *Writing Credits:* Bethel Buckalew (uncredited); *Director:* Bethel Buckalew (as Seymour Tuchus); *Cinematography:* László Kovács (as Lester Kovacs); *Cast:* Max Gardens (Dr. Breedlove/The Grand Glom, as Manny Goodtimes), Frank A. Coe (Sterilox/Frankenstein Monster, as Fattie Beltbuckle), Natasha (Boobra), Jackie De Witt (Kissme, as Jackie), Bibi (Barebra), Claudia Banks (Hotty Totty, as Claudia), Althea Currier (Gertie Tassle, as Althea), Donna (Gigi String), Lucky (Lotta Cash), Pat Hall (Gina Catchafanni, as Pat) rest of cast listed alphabetically: Robyn Hilton Girl (uncredited).

The mad Dr. Breedlove, whose creations include Dracula, Frankenstein's Monster, and a mummy, helps Sterilox, an asexual alien, to find the perfect woman to accompany him back home to his galaxy.

Love Bites; U.S., 1988; Horror, Comedy/Adult (Softcore); 70 minutes/color/English; Pride Video Productions.

Producers: Kevin M. Glover; *Writing Credits:* Kevin M. Glover; *Director:* Marvin Jones; *Cinematography:* Ron Hamill; *Original Music:* Steve Bonino; *Cast:* Kevin M. Glover (The Count), Bernard Barnes Jarvis (Manfield), Christopher Ladd (Leslie), Tom Wagner (Jake Hunter), Erich Lange.

"After 347 years of one night stands, the Count has fallen in love ... with a man!" Jake Hunter, vampire killer, travels to Hollywood along with his sidekick to face The Count. However, on arriving, Jake discovers a handsome hunk rather than the monstrous vampire he was expecting, and a romance blossoms.

Lust for Dracula; U.S., 2004; Horror/Adult (Softcore); 90 minutes/color/English; Seduction Cinema.

Producers: Michael Raso, Rick Van Meter; *Writing Credits:* Tony Marsiglia (as Anthony Marsiglia); *Director:* Tony Marsiglia (as Anthony Marsiglia); *Cinematography:* Dang Lenawea; *Film Editing:* Tony Marsiglia (as Anthony Marsiglia); *Original Music:* Don Mike; *Cast:* Darian Caine (Dracula), Misty Mundae (Mina Harker), Julian Wells (Jonathan Harker), Andrea Davis (Sara), Shelly Jones (Abigail Van Helsing), Casey Jones (Beth)

Mina is desperate to conceive a child as a way of bringing her and her husband, Jonathan, closer together. When she discovers she cannot conceive, Mina turns to the evil and seductive Dracula for help. Meanwhile, Mina's sister Abigail has come to visit, with lustful intentions toward Mina's husband.

Lust of Blackula; U.S., 1987; Horror/Adult (Hardcore); 77 minutes/color/English.

Producers: Jason Dralon; *Writing Credits:* Jennings Halis; *Director:* Barry Morrison; *Film Editing:* Maria Logan; *Original Music:* P.S. Nolan; *Cast:* Dominique, F.M. Bradley (Alacard), Nina DePonca (as Jane Daville), Ron Jeremy (Barry), Donna N. (as Donna-Anne), Ray Victory, Ebony Ayes (Charmine) (as Ebony Eyes), Melba Cruz (as Lacy Logan).

This pornographic blaxploitation twist on the Dracula story features Blackula, who roams the night to seduce women, feeding on their sexual fluids rather than blood.

The Mad Love Life of a Hot Vampire; U.S., 1971; Horror/Adult (Hardcore); 50 minutes/color/English.

Director: Ray Dennis Steckler (as Sven Christian); *Art Direction:* De Sade; *Cast:* Jim Parker (Count Dracula), Carolyn Brandt (Elaina — Wife of Dracula) (as Jane Bond), Rock Heinrich (Hunchback), Will Long, Greta Smith, Fritz King, Kim Kim, Ken Moore, Sam.

Dracula roams Las Vegas pimping out vampire prostitutes to unsuspecting victims in order to collect their blood. Meanwhile, Van Helsing helps his friend Bill unravel the mystery of his sister's death, which leads them to discover Dracula and try to kill him.

Mistress of Seduction (*Dracula's Dirty Daughter* [U.S. DVD title]); U.S., 2000; Horror/Adult (Softcore); 80 minutes/color/English/NTSC; E.I. Independent Cinema, Seduction Cinema.

Producers: Chet Bennett, Michael Raso (as Michael Beckerman); *Writing Credits:* Michael Pacitto; *Director:* Michael Pacitto; *Cinematography:* Pete Schuermann; *Film Editing:* Pete Schuermann; *Original Music:* Motor Dolls, DJ Gratcher; *Art Direction:* Jon Eberhardt; *Special Effects:* Milko Davis; *Cast:* Alysabeth Clements (Vamparina), Gentle Fritz (Corina), Thomas Martwick (John), Justiz Donaldson (Matt), Josh Dirmish (Pat), Michelle Tebow (Tanya), Kellie Brown (Kristal), Diane Skiba (Mercedes), Jim Prange (Professor Steele), Jack Leeper (Dorrman), Jeff Haxton (Jimmy), Duane Clements (Bartender), Colin Smith (Mr. Buckner), Robert Samuelson (Himself), Jack Ray (Student), Stacy Storer (Student), Heather Trippleton (Student), Matt Jersey (Hot Tarts Patron), Bari Brenner, Flame, Lori Masters

For centuries, Vamparina, the seductive daughter of Count Dracula, has searched for the reincarnated soul of Van Helsing, her father's killer. Vamparina has also spent much of this time seducing young, beautiful women, and believes she has found Van Helsing's soul in the body of a college student. Now she must decide whether they will be lovers or enemies.

The Naked World of Harrison Marks (*Alastomat hunajapupuni* [Finland]; *The Dream World of Harrison Marks* [U.S.]); U.K., 1965; Fantasy, Comedy/Documentary, Adult; 84 minutes/color/English; Harrison Marks Productions.

Producers: George Harrison Marks, Harry Reuben; *Writing Credits:* Terry Maher (screenplay), George Harrison Marks (screenplay), Jim McDonald (screenplay), William Templeton (commentary); *Director:* George Harrison Marks; *Cinematography:* Len Harris; *Film Editing:* Jim Connock; *Original Music:* John Hawksworth (as Johnny Hawksworth); *Art Direction:* Tony Roberts; *Make-Up:* Dorrie Hamilton; *Cast:* George Harrison Marks (Himself), Chris Bromfield, Deborah DeLacey

(Herself), Valentine Dyall (Narrator) (voice), Beryl Gilchrist (Narrator) (voice), Jutka Goz (Herself), Pamela Green (Herself), Ken Hayes, Robyn Hilton (Herself), Annette Johnson (Herself), Jerry Lorden, Toni Harrison Marks (Herself) (as Toni Burnett), Derek Nichols, Vera Novak (Herself), June Palmer (Herself), Molly Peters (Herself), David Roberts, Stuart Samuels (Various), Christine Williams (Herself).

This documentary-style exploration into the day to day life of Harrison Marks offers a glimpse into the behind the scenes activities on the set. In the film, several of Harrison Marks's fantasies are played out in the form of what the public perceives him to be. In one of these fantasies, Harrison Marks plays the role of Count Dracula.

The Night Boys; U.S., 1991; Horror/Adult (Hardcore); 70 minutes/color/English.

Producers: Gino Colbert; *Writing Credits:* Edward Lee; *Director:* Gino Colbert.

Count Vladimir has his servant, Ivan, lure young men into the Count's mausoleum in order to satisfy the Count's sexual appetites. The Count seduces the young men and turns them into his slaves. Of note for being the first gay vampire porn to feature African Americans.

Nightmare at Elm Manor; U.K., 1961; Horror/Short, Adult; 4:57 minutes/black and white/Silent.

Producer: Harrison Marks; *Director:* Harrison Marks; *Cinematography:* Harrison Marks; *Cast:* June Palmer (hotel guest), Stuart Samuels (*maître d'hôtel*/vampire).

A woman stays at the old Elm Manor hotel where she dreams of being chased naked around the upper and lower floors by the *maître d'hôtel*, who now resembles a caped Dracula-type vampire with stand-up collar and tuxedo.

Out for Blood; U.S., 1990; Horror/Adult (Hardcore); 84 minutes/color/English/Mono; Vivid Entertainment.

Director: Paul Thomas; *Cast:* Tori Welles (Countess Draculust), Racquel Darrian, Randy Spears, Kelly Royce, Cheri Taylor (as Serry Taylor), Eric Price, Nick Random, Tantala Ray (as Tantala), Dizzy Blonde, Alex Horn, Derrick Lane, Jennifer Stewart, Chaz Vincent.

Plan 69 from Outer Space; U.S., 1993; Science Fiction, Horror, Comedy/Adult (Hardcore); 84 minutes/color/English; Caballero Control Corporation Home Video (CCC).

Producers: Jimmy Houston; *Writing Credits:* Edward D. Wood Jr.; *Director:* Frank Marino; *Cinematography:* Frank Marino; *Film Editing:* Maurice de la Rue; *Make-Up:* Lisa Gibson; *Special Effects:* Ken Hunt; *Cast:* Dyanna Lauren (Dyanna, the beautiful rocket scientist), Celeste (Melanie, another beautiful rocket scientist), Peter North (Major Biff Bummer, the hero-type pilot), Beatrice Valle (Miss Iva Honeypot, the willing co-pilot), Woody Long (Platsko, the evil space alien), Blake Palmer (Vek, the inept space alien), Brad Armstrong (Zombie in Dracula costume), Fifi Bardot (Nude crew member in shower), Frank Marino (Narrator).

In this film, alien mad scientists quench their carnal needs.

Sex and the Single Vampire; U.S., 1970; Horror/Adult (Softcore, Sexploitation); 55 minutes/color/English/Mono; Alpha Blue Archives, Something Weird Video.

Producers: Wolfgang Klutzman; *Writing Credits:* F.N. Spelling; *Director:* Modunk Phreezer; *Cinematography:* Jose Wrecks; *Film Editing:* Phil Meditor; *Original Music:* Sigfried von Wanghunt; *Make-Up:* Kristine; *Cast:* John Holmes (Count Spatula/Bella Donna), John Dullaghan (Rod Hammer) (as John Dullahan), L.G. Allard (Lance Slot), Jesse Moreno (Pete Bandaido), Sandy Dempsey (Ruby) (as Sanday Dempsey), Stephanie Sarver (Tina), Kathy Hilton (Doris) (as Cathy Hilton), Lu Tomeny (Marcee), Chocolat Mousse (Mouse).

Count Spatula, living in a run-down old house, is interrupted by a group of swingers who break into Spatula's home, hoping to have sex in a haunted house.

Sexy Adventures of Van Helsing; U.S., 2004; Horror, Comedy/Adult (Softcore); 88 minutes/color/English; E.I. Independent Cinema, Seduction Cinema

Producers: Michael Raso; *Writing Credits:* John Bacchus, Helen Black, Clancy Fitzsimmons, Bruce G. Hallenbeck, Michael Raso (as Michael Beckerman), Max Von Diesel; *Director:* Max Von Diesel; *Cinematography:* John Paul Fedele (as John Fedele); *Film Editing:* Brian McNulty; *Original Music:* Pink Delicates, Michael Roszhart; *Make-Up:* Paige Davis (Makeup Artist); *Cast:* Erika Smith (Wilhelmina Van Helsing), Darian Caine (Countess Dracula), A.J. Kahn (Philomenia), Isadora Edison (Klownie), Andrea Davis (Hottie), Bob MacKay (Uncle Abe), Tatiana Stone (Duey), Jessica Abbott (Smokin'), Tracy Rose (Maiden #1), Misty Mundae (Maiden #2), Barbi Leigh (Maiden #3) (as Barbie Leigh), Katrina Raey (Maiden #4), Angel Marie (Maiden #5), John Samuel Jordan (Mark), Justin Wingenfeld (Clem the Waiter), Kay Kirtland, Eric Loeffler (Man #1), Dave Marmo (Man #2), Bennigan Feeney (Mr. Conservative), Caitlin Ross (Mrs. Conservative), Tom Cikoski (Mr. Pesser).

Van Helsing, great granddaughter of the legendary vampire killer, must find and kill Countess

Dracula before she seduces and kills more women. Having found Dracula in her lair, Van Helsing instead makes a deal that requires her to seek out virgins for Dracula. Van Helsing sets about securing the only certain virgins: lesbians.

Sexy Proibitissimo (*Sexy Proibito* [Italy]; *Danse du désir, La* [Belgium/French]; *Onko seksi kiellettyä?* [Finland]; *Prohibited Sex* [U.S.]; *Super Sexy Interdit* [France]; *Sexy Interdit* [France]); Italy, 1963; Documentary, Adult; 63 minutes/color/Italian; Films Marbeuf.

Producers: Gino Mordini; Directors: Osvaldo Civirani, Marcello Martinelli; *Original Music:* Coriolano Gori; *Cast:* Carol Carter, Joan Clair, Dominique, Corinne Fontaine, Rita Himalaya, Violeta Montenegro, Joanna Negulesco, Leonor Rainer, Bud Thompson, Maureen Verrich.

This documentary examines the history of the striptease. In one particular scene, Dracula enters the bedroom of a stripper, whom he intends to feed on. But before he can do so, she begins to remove her close, so he watches instead.

Spermula (*L'amour est un fleuve en Russie* [France, working title]); France, 1976; Science Fiction, Comedy/Adult (Softcore); 103 minutes/color/French/Mono; 5 Continents, Film and Co.

Producers: Bernard Lenteric; *Writing Credits:* Charles Matton; *Director:* Charles Matton; *Cinematography:* Jean-Jacques Flori; *Film Editing:* Isabelle Rathery, Sarah Taouss-Matton (as Sarah Matton); *Original Music:* José Bartel; *Art Direction:* Sarah Taouss-Matton (as Sarah Matton); *Cast:* Dayle Haddon (Spermula), Udo Kier (Werner), François Dunoyer (Tristan), Jocelyne Boisseau (Cascade), Ginette Leclerc (Gromana), Isabelle Mercanton (Blanche), Georges Géret (Grop), Radiah Frye (Ruth), Angela McDonald (Gilda), Suzannah Dijan (Diamant), Myriam Mézières (Bonne), Karin Petersen (Sala), Valérie Bonnier (Liberte), Sylvie Matton (Sylvie) (as Sylvie Meyer), Diana Chase (Diana), Christian Chevreuse (Cardinal), Hervé Hallf (Pierre), Alain Flick (Choupetit), Benny Luke (Luc), Gérard Tardy (Petit Curé), Roxiane De Montaignac (Roxiane), Dominique Basquin (Dominique), Maud Darsy (La Vieille Dane), Marie-France (Rita), Joan Kohler (Joan), Aline Ruat (Caline), Céline La Frenière (Celine), Annette Deweger (Annette), Viveka Grey (Marie-Jo), Vibeke Knudsen (Natacha) (as Natacha Knudsen), Francis Rignault (Francis), Piéral, Eva Ionesco (uncredited).

Planet Spermula, home of the Spermulites, is facing destruction. The Spermulites decide to transform themselves into beautiful women, go to Earth, and suck the semen out of the men who live there. This makes the men lazy and unable to procreate, leaving the path clear for the Spermulites to take over Earth. However, one of the Spermulites did not successfully transform.

Star Virgin; U.S., 1979; Comedy, Science Fiction/Adult (Hardcore); 78 minutes/color/English/Mono; Treetop Production.

Producers: Jason W. Mayall, Howard Ziehm (as Linus Gator); *Writing Credits:* Humphry Knipe; *Director:* Howard Ziehm (as Linus Gator); *Original Music:* Nisan Eventoff; *Cinematography:* Thomas Jaques; *Film Editing:* Jeff Rosen; *Makeup Department:* Tony Lambe; *Special Effects:* Jason W. Mayall; *Cast:* Kari Klark (Space Virgin), Kevin Thompson (Mentor), Tracy Walton (Eve), Rocky Johnson (Adam), J.C. Phillips (Snake), Jeanette Harlow (Prissy, Dracula's Guest), Chris Bloom (Percy, Prissy's Escort), Tricky Dicky (Igor), Johnny Harden (Dracula), Terri Dolan (Cheerleader (as Trisha Cole), Hillary Summers (Cheerleader (as Judy Ziehm), Lisa Curry (Cheerleader), Anne Magle (Cheerleader (as Anna Karenya), Dundis Bloor (Coach Madhouse, Dayton Plowboys), Mike Ranger (Roger Starstruck, Plowboy QB), Tantala Ray (Snake Dancer (as Darcy Nicholas), Pandora Box (Waitress), Brian Flynn (Customer), Zen Kitty (Dancer), Brenda Leggs (Dancer).

Space Virgin is the last of her very sexual species. Confused by her sexual desires, she turns to her personal robot to explain where she is and what is happening to her. Through a series of vignettes, her robot teachers her about the planet Earth and its history, including even Dracula.

Suckula; U.S., 1973; Horror, Comedy/Adult (Hardcore); 54 minutes/color/English.

Cast: Keith Erikson.

A journalist reports on vampiric happenings in Los Angeles. Suckula sports a necktie rather than a tuxedo, and there also appears a vampire named Rodney Alucard III, who is a direct descendant of Count Dracula.

Titanic 2000 (*Scary Sexy Disaster Movie* [U.S. new title]; *Vampire of the TITanic* [U.S. trailer title]); U.S., 1999; Horror, Comedy/Adult (Softcore); 85 minutes/color/English/Video; E.I. Independent Cinema, Seduction Cinema.

Producers: John Paul Fedele (as John P. Fedele), Michael Raso (as Michael L. Raso); *Writing Credits:* Clancy Fitzsimmons, Joe Ned, Michael Raso; *Director:* John Paul Fedele; *Cinematography:* Timothy Healy; *Film Editing:* Frank Terranova; *Special Effects:* Frank Terranova (digital effects); *Cast:* Tammy Parks (Vladimina), Tina Krause (Shari O'Kari), Elizabeth Cintron (Molly Black), David Fine (Mr. Blatent), Bob MacKay (Chimes/Edmund), Jasi Cotton Lanier (Second Victim [as

Rozanne Michaels]), Suzanne Lenore (1st Victim), Michael R. Thomas (Eegor/Captain Skimmer), Jacob Bogert (Mareem), Zachary Winston Snygg (Winslow [as Zachary Snygg]), Jeffrey Faoro (Mr. Smythe/Second Mate [as Jeff Faoro]), Joseph Prussak (Mr. Pidant [as Joe Prussak]), Peter O'Hara (Mr. Felon), Pete Jacelone (Mr. Pissington), William Hellfire (Beaner/Ralph/Guitar Player [as Bill Hellfire]), Joey Smack (Drummer), Misty Mundae (Bass Player), Paige Turner (Party Girl), John Link (Willy), John Paul Fedele (Glitter Bolan [as John Fedele]), Jon Fidelli (Mr. Visper), Mickey Ovum (Mr. Bushsmell [as Mikey Ovum]), Mike Raso (First Mate), J. Feefifofumdeli (Third Mate), Zippy (Clown), Fred Mekeel (Sir Leonardo of DiCaprio), Nathan Lanman (Guy in Hallway), Kyle LaFerrera (Arm Wrestler), Matthew Scott (Extra), Jennifer O'Keefe (Extra), Dean Paul (Extra), Erik Maietta (Extra), Sare Marrero (Extra), Melissa Phillips (Extra), Cindy Wright (Extra), Scot Isakoff (Extra), Brenda A. Trotsky (Extra), David Husbands (Extra), Dee Kaye (Extra), Djonaj (Extra), Christine McCaffrey (Extra), Mike Scillia (Extra), Dennis Peterson (Extra), Frank McGlynn (Extra), Angela Sapone (Extra), Margo G. McKeel (Extra), Nice Nice (Extra), Moth Man (Extra), Erin Ashley Scillia (Extra), Tracey Messel (Extra), Violet Violence (Extra), Benny the Stain (Extra), Richard Alfred Semator (Extra), Greg Ziemba (Extra), Demoness Ipek (Extra), Salvatore Lopresti (Extra), Liz Molinski (Extra).

Vladimina, a beautiful but deadly lesbian vampire, has been stowed aboard the Titanic 2000. With the help of her henchmen, Vladimina prowls around the ship looking for a woman she can seduce and render her soulmate.

A Touch of Sweden (*Pastries* [X-rated version]); U.S., 1971; Adult (Sexploitation, Hardcore); 59 minutes/color/English/Mono; Cricket Films.

Director: Joseph F. Robertson; *Cast:* Uschi Digard (Sherry Bignurse [as Ushi Digart]), Starlyn Simone (Margie Lovenurse [as Michelle Combe]), Sandy Dempsey (Virgin Virginia), Ray Sebastian III (Dr. Tom Drill/Mr. D), Jack Buddliner (Dr. Bob Dart [as Barney Bosnick]), Peggy Church (Sally Pretty), Al Ward (Skater Hangup), Maria Arnold (The I'm Late Date [as Marie Arnold]), Wayne Chapman (The Hospital Angel), Rhonda Illif (The Floor Girl), Norman Fields (Elmer Marks [as Norm Fields]), John Keith (The Bottle Freak [as Pat O'Connor]), Barbara Mills (Millie Goodnurse), Sandy Carey (Selma Sweetnurse), Jack King (Fat Peter Horn), Liz Wolfe (Sunset Anne), Con Covert (Marion Transvest [as Con Convert]), Becky Jones (Mrs. Tranvest), Chuck Smith (Gorilla Hop), Ron Darby (Rodney Morton Stuart III [uncredited]), Christopher Geoffries (Pat, the film producer [uncredited]), John Paul Jones (Insert guy [uncredited]), Levi Richards (Rocky Nichols [uncredited]), Joseph F. Robertson (Cecil/Bum [uncredited]).

Sherry Bignurse relates tales of sexy American adventures to a Swedish friend, including a sexual escapade with Count Dracula on his boat. Originally a softcore sexploitation film, *A Touch of Sweden* was edited to include hardcore inserts and rereleased as *Pastries*.

Ultimate Reality; U.S., 1996; Horror, Science Fiction/Adult; (Hardcore); 76 minutes/color/English; Minotaur, Studio 2000.

Producers: John Travis, Scott Masters; *Writing Credits:* Tyler Adams; *Director:* Ross Cannon.

This is a gay porn movie about a cybersex CD-ROM that allows participants to indulge in their fantasies. Each scene is a different man's fantasy, each replicating a classic horror tale, including the werewolf, the Phantom of the Opera, Frankenstein, and Dracula.

Vampire; U.K., 1963; Horror/Short, Adult; black and white/Silent; Kamera Productions.

Producer: Harrison Marks, Tony Roberts; *Cinematography:* Harrison Marks, Tony Roberts; *Cast:* Harrison Marks (Count Dracula III), Wendy Luton (Carmilla).

Count Dracula III uses a pendant to entrance a young naked woman and lead her out of her bedroom to his lair, where he turns her into a vampire. When sunrise comes, Dracula retreats to his coffin. Suddenly, sunlight beams through a window and throws the shadow of a cross onto the woman's body, returning her to human form. She then plunges a wooden stake into the heart of the sleeping Dracula, then awakens to find herself back in her own bed clutching the Dracula's pendant.

Vampire Vixens; U.S., 2003; Horror, Comedy/Adult (Softcore); 78 minutes/color/English; E.I. Independent Cinema, Seduction Cinema.

Producers: Michael Raso; *Writing Credits:* John Bacchus; *Director:* John Bacchus; *Cinematography:* Giorgy Benaskovich (as Giorgyorgy Benaskovich); *Cast:* Tina Krause (Dracoola) (as Mia Copia), A.J. Khan (Diane Shelton) (as AJ Khan), John Paul Fedele (Wally Van Helsing) (as John Fedele), Darian Caine (Dottie), Misty Mundae (Sherry), Elizabeth Hitchcock (Sandy), Zachary Winston Snygg (Eugene Reinfield [as Zack Snygg]), Michael R. Thomas (The Boss [as Michael Thomas]), Jonathan Doe (Al Siegfried), Bob MacKay (Rick Roy [as Bob MacKay]), Katie Jordan (Margaret [uncredited]).

In this sequel to *Vampire's Seduction*, Dracoola

enlists Eugene, a nerdy delivery boy, to help her find and seduce female victims. Meanwhile, Wally Van Helsing — business executive turned vampire slayer, and great-great-grandson of the famous Van Helsing — is hatching a plan to kill her.

Vampires; U.S., 2007; Horror/Adult (Hardcore); 147 minutes/color/English; Rodnievision.

Director: Rodney Moore; *Cast:* Jamie Tyler, Mandy Luxx, Jack Vegas, Franco Del Toro, Caroline Pierce, Rodney Moore, Lee Stone, Veronica Jett, Rebecca Linares, Barry Scott, Aiden Starr, Leah Jaye.

This film features six loosely connected vampire sex scenes, including "Countess Caroline's Revenge" in which Jack Vegas captures the dreaded Countess, who seduces men, drains them of their fluids, and castrates her victims with her mouth. Waiting for Dr. Van Helstromm to arrive and take the Countess away, Jack becomes her latest victim.

Vampire's Seduction (*Vampiresas* [Venezuela]); U.S., 1998; Horror, Comedy/Adult (Softcore); 140 minutes/color/English; E.I. Independent Cinema, Seduction Cinema, Brain Escape Pictures.

Producers: Michael Raso (as Michael Beckerman); *Writing Credits:* John Bacchus; *Director:* John Bacchus; *Cinematography:* Alan Spence, Frank Terranova; *Film Editing:* John Granata, David Taylor; *Cast:* Tina Krause (Dracoola), Paige Turner (Dr. Lesbian), Kiki Michaels (Sexy Business Woman), Dawn Monacco (Patient), Debbie Rochon (Waitress Mary), Chelsea Mundae (Mrs. Seltzer) (as Daisy), Janie (Patty), Jenna (Gidget), Michael Devin (Pizza Boy Sal), Zachary Winston Snygg (Ex-Heisman Winner) (as Zack Snygg), Hans Rasmussen (Frankenstein), John Paul Fedele (Wally).

Dracula's daughter, Dracoola, must walk the earth for eternity, so she chooses to spend her time seducing beautiful lesbians.

Vamps (*Deadly Dreamgirls*; *Vamps: Deadly Dreamgirls*; *Vampiresas* [Venezuela]); U.S., 1995; Horror/Adult (Softcore); 90 minutes/color/English/Mono; B+ Productions.

Producers: Mark Burchett, Michael D. Fox; *Writing Credits:* Mark Burchett, Michael D. Fox; *Director:* Mark Burchett, Michael D. Fox; *Cinematography:* Jeff Barklage; *Film Editing:* Michael D. Fox; *Original Music:* Jeff Dunn, Steve Gatch, Aaron Mahoney; *Make-Up:* J.D. Bowers; *Special Effects:* Dave Molloy; *Cast:* Jennifer Huss (Heather), Paul Morris (Seamus), Jenny Wallace (Tasha), Amber Newman (Randi), Stacey Sparks (Tabitha), Charles Cooper (Max), Rob Calvert (Larry), Tamika Hoffman (Angel), Susn Foreman (Trixie), Ed Belarski (Jason), Ozell Large (Sergeant Grant), Sean Nielsen (Keith), Mark Burchett (The Vampire Busters) Jack Carpenter (The Vampire Busters/Bar Patron), Steve Gatch (Count Hackula/Bar Patron), Karen Stolle (Vanna the Vampire), Sharon Gloff (Barmaid), Michelle Volkart (Barmaid), Stephanie Browning (Bar Patron), Dave Meyers (Bar Patron), Joyce McNutt (Diner Waitress), Kevin Becker (Queen's Servant), Lorissa McComas (The Vampire Queen)

A young priest, Father Seamus, is talked into attending a strip club where, unbeknownst to him, the strippers are all vampires. After striking up a friendship with Heather, an old classmate who is stripping at the club for the first time that night, Seamus tries to stop the vamps from turning Heather into one of the undead.

PART III

Dracula in Video Games

Introduction —
Vampire Bytes and Digital Draculas
Timothy Dodd Alley

One seldom has to look far (just over one's shoulder?) to recognize Dracula's omnipresence in popular culture. According to author David J. Skal, Dracula has been "a literary Victorian sex nightmare, a stock figure of theatrical melodrama, a movie icon, trademark, cuddle toy, swizzle stick, and breakfast cereal."[1] One could go on extensively about where the Count has been seen last — while running an errand or watching a television commercial. It comes as little surprise then that inevitably he should penetrate the realm of digital gaming as well. The particular focus of this section concerns Dracula's presence within the narrative framework of the popular video game, which Browning and Picart have meticulously researched and cataloged. These video game titles feature Dracula as anything from a lead character to a mere cameo appearance and reveal just how Dracula has evolved in the game world from a pixilated blip on a screen to a vivid, three-dimensional construction. Now, players even have the opportunity to literally take a swing at him with Nintendo Wii's recent *Castlevania Judgement*. In a digital world where players can vicariously become protagonists who battle antagonists, Count Dracula's prominence as an undying villain in popular culture makes him the perfect candidate for game character casting.

Dracula's initial integration into video games started with the boom of the Nintendo Entertainment System (hereafter NES). Beginning in the mid–1980s, the NES became a hit with game players in the United States thanks to its affordability and "rapid contraction in Europe and the USA."[2] The most popular title to be released during the Nintendo explosion was *Super Mario Brothers* (1985). In this particular game, the premise was simple and familiar: a male protagonist overcomes obstacles and minions in order to reach a "big boss." After destroying the "big boss," the protagonist is rewarded with victory. In the case of *Super Mario Brothers*, the lead character, Mario, must strive to defeat a large dragon-like creature named Koopa in order to liberate a captive princess, thereby earning her affection.

With that, the opportunity to be a hero was readily available to any NES console owner. Game developers could simply fill in the roles of hero and villain with any figure deemed desirable by the players. Naturally, with Count Dracula figuring prominently, and unfailingly, in popular culture, the game franchise known as *Castlevania* was born in 1986. The game's protagonist, Simon Belmont, is a vampire hunter who ventures into the castle of Count Dracula where Belmont must overcome horror cliché obstacles such as bats, rats, and wolves. This leads to the final confrontation with "big boss" Count Dracula, whose defeat means victoriously completing the video game.

The success of *Castlevania* spawned a Dracula-based franchise that still breathes today. However, where did games such as *Castlevania* find inspiration for their widely familiar narrative structuring? To understand this, it is helpful to briefly discuss the ideas of classical horror storytelling, and why they work so well when applied to the realm of video gaming. Some of the most memorable horror stories were first told through the film medium. Films such as *Frankenstein*, *The Mummy*, and, of course, *Dracula*, are narratives, among many others, that focus on the binary conflict between good and evil. However, the villainous monsters portrayed in such stories are born of alterity, or "otherness." Author Gregory Waller refers to these monsters (our "others") as external creatures who bring with them an "imported evil."[3] The character of Count Dracula is no exception: he is inhuman, his abode is a distantly located castle, and he threatens to disturb the normalcy enjoyed by protagonist characters.

Whether or not early NES players understood video game titles like *Castlevania* purely in terms of some sort of external horror is mistakenly reductionist. However, video game consumers were certainly familiar with the concept of villainous outsiders, and the urgency to stop them in order to restore normalcy. This idea was not only present in classic horror films, but in classic literary titles aimed specifically at children, such as *Little Red Riding Hood* or *Hansel and Gretel*. It seemed inevitable then that studios would create video game titles in which game players could, at last, become the central character from a horror movie or a storybook, and ensure any monstrous threat is vanquished. When King Koopa transports from another world to kidnap a damsel in distress in *Super Mario Brothers*, gamers can empathize with Mario on his journey to achieve a happy ending. Likewise, in glimpsing Dracula's presence in popular culture, it is clear that players would enjoy the opportunity to travel to a spooky, distantly located castle in the shoes of Simon Belmont and have the opportunity to defeat one of fiction's most notorious evildoers in the game *Castlevania*.

Riding the success of the NES and the *Castlevania* title, game company Konami followed with the sequel *Castlevania II: Simon's Quest* (1987), in which we observe the popular filmic tradition that the villain Count Dracula has returned and is (un)alive and kicking. In fact, in this particular installment, the protagonist, Simon Belmont, must collect physical parts of Dracula in order to remove a curse and ultimately defeat the vampire once more to conquer the game. *Castlevania III: Dracula's Curse* (1989), also released for the NES, served as a prequel to the growing franchise, following the Belmont ancestry and their struggles to thwart Dracula's agenda of spreading darkness throughout Europe.

After these initial *Castlevania* titles were developed for the NES through the late-1980s, the series continued as newer videogame platforms developed. Although the *Castlevania* series followed in the footsteps of other ubiquitous titles for the NES, one may also note parallels between the *Castlevania* franchise and the classic *Dracula* film titles produced throughout prior decades. While many videogame titles were almost certainly produced with profit and quick release in mind, the narratives of the *Castlevania* sequels tended to mirror the same premise behind *Dracula* films, which allowed these narratives to cultivate a loyal fanbase. Of the more memorable *Dracula* films were those released from Hammer Studios in the United Kingdom, featuring Christopher Lee in the title role. These films in particular thrived on the idea that Count Dracula could be resurrected again and again, from sequel to sequel. Christopher Lee's portrayal of Dracula was, according to Skal, "an anti-authoritarian authority figure, a destabilizing force who could always be depended upon to subvert the stuffy status quo and bring vampire excitement into corseted, middle-class lives. In film after film Lee's ever-more ingenious resurrections were typically greeted with wild applause by his fans."[4] With a villain who could not die, studio executives and video game developers had an unlimited supply of concepts.

Video game developer Konami would go on to do for its gaming fans what Hammer did for its horror fans. With home gaming becoming a lucrative industry by the late–1980s, players began wanting more when they discovered a video game title that was both challenging and fun. Count Dracula, whose reputation for resurrections preceded him, was a fitting character for a digital game world in which both villains and heroes could be constantly reanimated from the dead. In the case of *Castlevania*, Count Dracula was resurrected for one sequel after another to appease fans who yearned for more chances to defeat one of horror's greatest monsters.

Castlevania's monopoly on the *Dracula* franchise ended when video game platforms competing with the NES began putting out their own video game titles by the early-1990s. The early-1990s saw the release of *Bram Stoker's Dracula* (1993) for the Super NES and Sega gaming consoles. This particular title was adapted from the popular film released from Columbia Pictures a year earlier. While the film received tepid reviews, it was a box office success, taking in $82.5 million domestically in the United States and $192.5 million worldwide.[5] Hence, with the success of the film came the release of the video game of the same title, a tradition that continues in the video gaming world even today. Another notable title came with *Dracula Unleashed* (1993), made for the Sega and PC platforms. A follow-up to Bram Stoker's tale, this title utilized video clips to narrate a story in which the brother of Quincy Morris, Alexander, teams up with Van Helsing to help protect a village and Alexander's love interest from the fangs of Dracula, who is, of course, still alive. With the box office success of Columbia's picture in 1992, the video game titles featuring Dracula that directly followed appeared to be timely releases in response to the "Dracula fever" that was only then just beginning to flourish again.

Throughout the 1990s, the *Castlevania* series began to see releases in one platform after another. The start of the 2000s began to put out a slew of video game titles that referenced the legendary character. One such title, *Dracula: The Resurrection*, was released for the Playstation in 2000. That same year, Dimension Films attempted to resurrect the Count in *Dracula 2000*, which featured the then up-and-coming Gerard Butler in the title role. The parallel releases of these film and video game titles around the same time may have been another attempt to capitalize on a popular theme, as seen in the early-1990s. A similar parallel release came with *Van Helsing* in 2004, which was inspired by the film of the same title released from Universal that same year.

Another critical issue to consider, in light of video game releases featuring Dracula, is the popularity of the "survival horror"[6] genre, one in which the *Resident Evil* series features prominently. Throughout the 2000s, other video game titles followed with *Dracula 2: The Last Sanctuary* (2001) and comic book creator Todd McFarlane's *Evil Prophecy* (2004), which may have been a response to survival horror titles, narratives that are in essence interactive horror films that give players the opportunity to become immersed in terrifying worlds. These horror video games would become so popular that even "Hollywood decided to capitalize on this video game adrenaline rush" by creating film adaptations of survival horror video game titles that were, ironically, inspired by horror film aesthetics in the first place.[7] With the success of survival horror narratives, again it is no surprise that Count Dracula should be included amongst the slew of survival horror villains who were central components in these chilling game worlds. With time, moviegoers and Hollywood have become more and more acclimated to video game technology, and this will inevitably continue to support the prominence of video game film spin-offs, as well as video game adaptation films, like *Resident Evil*, as the film medium merges closer and closer with the video game medium.

Notes

1. David J. Skal, *Hollywood Gothic* (New York: Faber and Faber, 2004), 4.
2. John Kirriemuir, "A History of Digital Games," in *Understanding Digital Games*, eds. Jason Rutter and Jo Bryce (Thousand Oaks, CA: Sage, 2006), 27.
3. Gregory Waller, *American Horrors* (Chicago and Urbana: University of Illinois Press, 1987), 3.
4. Skal, 265.
5. Skal, 278.
6. For further discussion, see Richard J. Hand, "Proliferating Horrors: Survival Horror and the Resident Evil Franchise," in *Horror Film: Creating and Marketing Fear*, Ed. Steffen Hantke (Jackson: University Press of Mississippi, 2004), 117–134.
7. Dodd Alley, *Gamers and Gorehounds: The Influence of Video Games on the Contemporary American Horror Film* (Saarbrucken: VDM Verlag Dr. Muller, 2007), 44.

Video Gameography

Akumajô Dorakiyura: Yami no juin (*Castlevania: Curse of Darkness* [U.S.]); Japan, 2005; Horror, Action, Adventure/Video Game; XBox (Microsoft), PS2 (Sony)/RPG, 3D; color/Japanese and English/Dolby; Konami.

Producers: Koji Igarashi (as IGA), Shigeharu Umezaki, Eiren Chong, Masanori Kobayashi, Kumiko Ogawa, Ken Ohara; *Writing Credits:* Koji Igarashi (as IGA); *Director:* Takashi Takeda; *Original Music:* Michiru Yamane; *Art Direction:* Shinichiro Shimamura; *Audio Direction:* Michiru Yamane; *Creative Direction:* Makoto Suda; *Programming:* Shuichi Hirohara; *Cast:* Takahiro Yoshimizu (Hector [voice: Japanese version]), Moriya Endo (Isaac [voice: Japanese version]), Yasunori Masutani (Trevor Belmont [voice: Japanese version]), Tetsuo Sakaguchi (Saint Germain [voice: Japanese version]), Yukitoshi Hori (Zead [voice: Japanese version]), Mahito Ôba (Dracula/Narrator [voice: Japanese version]), Tomoko Fujino (Julia Laforeze [voice: Japanese version]), Masaharu Satô (Death [voice: Japanese version]), Steve Blum (Dracula [voice: English version] [uncredited]), Adam D. Clark (Saint Germain [voice: English version] [uncredited]), Dorothy Elias-Fahn (Jula Laforeze [voice: English version] [uncredited]), Crispin Freeman (Hector [voice: English version] [uncredited]), Michael McConnohie (Narrator [voice: English version] [uncredited]), Liam O'Brien (Isaac/Death/Zead [voice: English version] [uncredited]), Steve Staley (Trevor Belmont [voice: English version] [uncredited]).

The player controls Hector, Dracula's former Devil forgemaster, as he fights back the curse left on Europe after Dracula's latest defeat. Hector can craft familiars to aid him as he fights the late vampire lord's servants.

Akumajo Dorakyura: Jajimento (*Castlevania: Judgement* [U.S.]); U.S., 2008; Action/Video Game; Wii (Nintendo)/one-vs-one 3D fighting; color/Japanese and English; Konami.

Producers: Koji Igarashi (as IGA), Hideki Kuraku, Katsunori Okita, Yusaku Toyoshima; *Director:* A.S. Minakata, Yuta Kobayashi (Eighting Co. Ltd.), Masaru Matsumoto (Gemba Inc.); *Cast:* Kenichi Suzumura (Additional Voices [Japanese version]), Mamoru Miyano (Additional Voices [Japanese version]), Hiroshi Kamiya (Additional Voices [Japanese version]), Houko Kuwashima (Additional Voices [Japanese version, as Hoko Kuwashima]), Katsuyuki Konishi (Additional Voices [Japanese version]), Yûko Sanpei (Additional Voices [Japanese version]), Takashi Kondô (Additional Voices [Japanese version]), Ami Koshimizu (Additional Voices [Japanese version]), Jôji Nakata (Additional Voices [Japanese version, as Johji Nakata]), Miyu Matsuki (Additional Voices [Japanese version]), Kôichi Sakaguchi (Additional Voices [Japanese version, as Kouichi Sakaguchi]), Sayaka Ohara (Additional Voices [Japanese version]), Masaya Onosaka (Additional Voices [Japanese version]), Hiroshi Shirokuma (Additional Voices [Japanese version]), Gideon Emery (Trevor Belmont [voice: English version, uncredited]), Alessandro Juliani (Grant DaNasty [voice: English version, uncredited]), Yuri Lowenthal (Alucard [voice: English version, uncredited]), Michelle Ruff (Maria/Shanoa [voice: English version, uncredited]), Patrick Seitz (Count Dracula [voice: English version, uncredited]), Keith Silverstein (Simon Belmont [voice: English version, uncredited]), Ezra Weisz (Aeon [voice: English version, uncredited]).

Galamoth sends the Time Reaper 10,000 years into his past, which takes him close to modern times, to assassinate Dracula and allow Galamoth to take the thrown. Sensing this, time-protector Aeon gathers 13 heroes and villans from Castlevania's timeline to decide who will defeat the Time Reaper and save the timeline.

Akumajo Dracula (*Demon Castle Dracula's* [Translated Japanese Title]; *Castlevania* [U.S.]; *Haunted Castle* [remake]; *Vampire Killer* [remake]; *Super Castlevania IV* [remake]; *Castlevania Chronicles/Akumajo Dracula X68000* [remake]); Japan, 1986;

Horror, Action-Adventure)/Video Game; Family Computer Disk System (Nintendo), Nintendo Entertainment System (Nintendo), Commodore 64 (Commodore International), Commodore Amiga (Commodore–Amiga Inc.), PC MS-DOS (IBM), PC Microsoft Windows (Windows), Game Boy Advance (Nintendo), AT&T Wireless mMode Network (AT&T), WiiVirtual Console (Nintendo), Arcade (Konami), MXS2 (Microsoft), PS2 (Sony), SNES (Nintendo), Sharp X68000 (Sharp corporation)/3rd person, 2D platformer; color/Japanese and English; Konami.

Writing Credits: Vram Stoker; *Director:* Trans Fishers; *Original Music:* Kinuyo Yamashita (as James Banana); *Cast:* Christopher Bee (Dracula), Belo Lugosi (Death), Boris Karloffice (Frankenstein), Love Chaney Jr. (Mummy Man), Barber Sherry (Medusa), Mix Schrecks (Vampire Bat), Love Chaney (Hunch Back), Green Stranger (Fish Man), Cafebar Read (Armor), Andre Moral (Skeleton), Jone Candies (Zombie), Simon Belmondo (The Hero).

Dracula rises from the dead every century and must be stopped by the Belmont family before he can terrorize Europe. This time the player takes Simon Belmont inside Dracula's castle to defeat skeletons, bats, and other monsters with his family's whip to eventually slay Dracula once more.

Akumajô Dracula: Shikkoku taru zensôkyoku (*Akumaj Dracula: Dark Night Prelude* [original title]; *Castlevania: Legends* [United States]); Japan, 1997; Action-Adventure/Videogame; black and white/Japanese/Stereo; Game Boy (Nintendo)/Side-Scrolling Adventure; Konami.

Producer: Hiroyuki Fukui; *Director:* Kouki Yamashita; *Art Direction:* Kazunobu Uchida; *Audio Direction:* Youichi Iwata, Kaoru Okada; *Programming:* Yoshiteru Yamaguchi.

Story: Dracula has transformed from a human to a being that can control all evil and begins to send undead armies to conquer the world. The player controls Sonia, a girl that can sense supernatural beings and fight with a whip, to fight through Dracula's castle to fight the great evil. Sonia develops a relationship with Alucard, Dracula's prodigal son, during the game.

Akumajô Dracula: The Arcade (*Castlevania: The Arcade* [United States]); Japan, 2009; Horror, Action/Video Game; free-standing arcade/shooter; color/Japanese; Konami.

The player can choose to fight with guns, whip, or magic and fight through Dracula's Castle. Enemies include Death, a few dragons, and Dracula.

Akumajô Dracula: The Medal; Japan, 2008; Gambling/Video Game; Japanese "medal game" machine/slots; color/Japanese; Konami.

This is a Castlevania-themed electronic slot machine where different combinations provoke actions from Castlevania characters. Hearts earned can be used for boss fights leading up to a fight with Dracula, but medals earned are not redeemable for money, but may be used for prizes and more plays.

Akumajô Dracula: Ubawareta Kokuin (*Castlevania: Order of Ecclesia* [United States]); United States, 2008; Action-Adventure/Video Game; Nintendo DS (Nintendo)/2D platformer, Role-Playing Game; color/Japanese, English; Konami

Producer: Koji Igarashi (as IGA), Katsunori Okita; *Director:* Moriemon; *Original Music:* Michiru Yamane, Yasuhiro Ichihashi; *Audio Direction:* Yasuhiro Ichihashi; *Creative Direction:* Hiroto Yamaguchi; *Programming:* Shutaro; *Cast:* Houro Kuwashima (voice), Toshihiro Seki (voice), Kouji Ishii (voice), Ryo Tatsuura (voice), Norio Wakamoto (voice), Masaru Suzuri (voice), Umeka Shoji (voice), Eri Yasui (voice).

Searching for a way to stop Dracula without the help of the Belmonts, who have gone missing, the order of Ecclesia begins a ritual to use Shanoa's, the player character's, power of Dominus. A rouge agent steals important scrolls during the ritual, and Shanoa must hunt them down to be able to stop Dracula.

Akumajo Dracula X: Chi no Rondo (*Castlevania: Rondo of Blood* [informal title]; *Castlevania: Dracula X Chronicles* [remake]); Japan, 1993; Horror, Action-Adventure/Video Game; TurboGrafx CD (Hudson Soft and NEC), PSP (Sony), Wii Virtual Console (Nintendo)/3rd person, 2D platformer; color/Japanese, German, and English; Konami.

Producer: Y. Yamada; *Director:* Toru Hagihara (as T. Hagihara); *Cast:* Hans Gunther Claude (Narrator [voice]), Atsuko Honda (Annette [voice]), Jin Horikawa (Richter Belmont [voice]), Hiroya Ishimaru (Count Dracula [voice]), Hiromi Murata (Tera [voice]), Youko Teppozuka (Maria Renard [voice]), Akie Yamada (Iris [voice]).

Ritcher Belmont's fiancée has been kidnapped by Dracula. The player controls Ritcher as he bashes his way through Dracula's minions with his whip so he can defeat the vampire lord.

Akumajô Dracula X: Gekka no yasukyôoku (*Castlevania: Symphony of the Night* [United States]; *Dracula X: Nocturne in the Moonlight* [Japan: English title]; *Nocturne in the Moonlight*); Japan, 1997; Action-adventure/Videogame; PlayStation (Sony), Sega Saturn (Sega), Xbox 360 (Microsoft), PlayStation Portable (Sony)/2D platformer, Role-Playing Game; color/Japanese; Konami.

Producers: Toru Hagihara, Kazumi Kitaue; *Writing Credits:* Koji Igarashi (as Kouji Iga), Toshiharu

Furukawa; *Director:* Toru Hagihara; *Original Music:* Michiru Yamane; *Programming:* Gagensai. F, Toru Hagihara, Koji Igarashi (as Kouji Iga), Kousuke Iwakura; *Cast:* Robert Belgrade (Alucard/Adrian Tepes [voice]), Kimberly Forsythe (Maria Renard [voice]), Michael Gough (Richter Belmont [voice] [as Michael G]), Scott McCulloch (Count Vlad Dracula [voice]), Dennis Falt (Death [voice]), Jeff Manning (Shaft [voice] [as Jeffrey Manning]), Barbara Whitlow (Lisa Farenheights [voice]), Alison Lester (Succubus [voice]), Ryôtarô Okiayu (Alucard [voice]), Norio Wakamoto (Dracula [voice: Japanese version]), Kiyoyuki Yanada (Richter Belmont [voice: Japanese version]), Chisa Yokoyama (Maria [voice: Japanese version]).

Dracula has risen from the grave again along with his castle, and Alucard awakens from his hibernation. The player takes control of the prodigal son Alucard to once again restore the balance of good and evil by slaying Dracula.

Akumajō Dracula XX (*Castlevania: Vampire's Kiss* [Europe]; *Akumajō Dorakyura Daburu Ekkusu* [Japan]; *Castlevania: Dracula X* [United States]); Japan, 1995; Horror/Video Game; SNES (Nintendo)/Side-scrolling platformer; color/Japanese; Konami.

Producer: Kuniaki Kinoshita; *Director:* Kouki Yamashita; *Art Direction:* Ashenden; *Programming:* A.S. Minakata, Ogawa.

Dracula has been resurrected by a dark cult and kidnaps to women to draw out the Belmont bloodline. The player controls Ritcher Belmont as he fights through Dracula's castle to save his hostage lover and the other girl.

Akumajo Special: Boku Dracula-kun! (*Kid Dracula* [United States re-release]); Japan, 1990 (1993); Action-Adventure/Video Game; Nintendo (Nintendo), Game Boy (Nintendo)/Platformer; color/ Japanese, English; Konami.

Director: Shirou Murata; *Art Direction:* (Nobuaki Matsumoto); *Audio Direction:* Shinji Tasaka, Satoko Minami, (Akiko Itoh); *Programming:* Shirou Murata, Etsunobu Ebisu, Yasuhiro Yamamoto, (Yukari Hayano).

This is a parody of Konami's *Castlevania* series in which the player plays the part of a young Dracula. The player must fight around Dracula's castle to prevent the evil demon Garamos from wrecking it.

Akumajou Densetsu (*Legend of Demon Castle* [Translated Japanese Title]; *Castlevania III: Dracula's Curse* [United States]); Japan, 1990; Horror, Action-Adventure/Video Game; NES (Nintendo), Wii Virtual Console (Nintendo)/3rd person, 2D platformer; color/Japanese, English; Konami.

Director: H. Akamatsu; *Programming:* H. Akamatsu, Yasuo Okuda.

Dracula has amassed an army to destroy all life on Earth, and it has been left to the Belmont clan to stop him. Trevor Belmont, his Belmont's sacred family whip, and various companions fight through the castle and its monstrous inhabitants to slay Dracula.

Akumajou Dracula: Circle of the Moon (*Castlevania* [Europe]; *Castlevania: Circle of the Moon* [United States]); Japan, 2001; Horror, Action-Adventure/Video Game; Game Boy Advance (Nintendo)/3rd person, 2D platformer; color/Japanese, English/Stereo; Konami.

Producers: Koji Horie (Ko-G), Keita Kawaminami, Etsunobu Ebisu, Shigeharu Umezaki; *Original Music:* Hiroshi Mitsuoka Sotaro Tojima; *Audio Direction:* Takeshi Iwakiri.

Dracula has returned and threatens to spread evil throughout the land. Players assume the role of Nathan Graves, using his whip and other equipment to battle through Dracula's castle in search of the Count.

Akumajou Dracula: Gallery of Labyrinth (*Castlevania: Portrait of Ruin* [United States]); Japan, 2006; Action-Adventure/Video Game; Nintendo DS (Nintendo)/2D platformer; color/Japanese, English; Konami.

Producers: Koji Igarashi (as IGA), Hirotaka Ishikawa; *Writing Credits:* Koji Igarashi, Hiroto Yamaguchi, Shutaro; *Director:* Satoshi Kushibuchi; *Original Music:* Yuzo Koshiko, Michiru Yamane; *Engineering/Technical Direction:* Sumiko Shindo (YOU AND ME); *Art Direction:* Takanobu Mizuno; *Audio Direction:* Tetsushi Takahashi; *Creative Direction:* Hiroto Yamaguchi; *Programming:* Shutaro; *Cast:* Takahiro Sakurai (voice), Yumi Kakazu (voice), Mariko Suzuki (voice), Yasuhiro Tokuyama (voice), Kohei Fukuhara (voice), Hisao Egawa (voice), Nokio Wakamoto (voice).

A vampire artist is using his paintings to capture the power of Dracula's castle, and Jonathan Morris and a young witch named Charlotte Aulin (played alternatively by the player) are trying to stop him. In the course of events Dracula is resurrected and must be slain again.

Akumajou Dracula: Sougetsu no Juujika (*Demon Castle Dracula: Cross of the Blue Moon* [Japan title]; *Castlevania: Dawn of Sorrow* [United States]; *CV: DoS* [abbreviation]); Japan, 2005; Action-Adventure/Video Game; Nintendo DS (Nintendo), Java ME for mobile phones (Java)/Role-Playing Game; color/Japanese, English; Konami.

Producers: Koji Igarashi (as IGA), Shigeharu Umezaki; *Writing Credits:* Koji Igarashi (as IGA);

Director: Satoshi Kushibuchi; *Original Music:* Michiru Yamane; *Engineering/Technical Direction:* Sumiko Shindo; *Art Direction:* Jun Kawagoe; *Audio Direction:* AKT; *Creative Direction:* Hiroto Yamaguchi; *Programming:* Shutaro; *Cast:* Hikaru Midorikawa (Soma Cruz [voice]), Ryoutarou Okiayu (voice), Tetsu Inada (voice), Ao Takahashi (voice), Yuka Shioyama (voice), Hidehiko Kaneko (voice), Takahiro Fujimoto (voice).

A year after *Aria of Sorrow*'s events, Soma remains his "good-aligned" self and believes he has lost his powers. But after an attack by some monsters, Soma defeats them with the powers he acquired from Dracula and afterwards heads out to dispose of a cult wanting to use him to resurrect the vampire lord.

Atic Atac; U.K., 1983; Horror, Adventure/Video Game; Sinclair ZX Spectrum (Sinclair Research Ltd.)/Top-down fighter, maze; colors/English; Ashby Computers and Graphics Ltd.

Producers: Tim Stamper, Chris Stamper; *Art Direction:* Tim Stamper, Carol Ward; *Programming:* Chris Stamper, John Lathbury.

Based on the children's ITV show *Knightmare*, this game gives players the option of playing as a fighter, wizard, or surf who, after falling through a trapdoor, must then fight his way out of a labyrinthine castle. Many archetypal monsters, like Dracula, appear and are scarcely beatable, though Dracula fails to re-appear after the player finds a cross.

The Awesome Adventures of Victor Vector & Yondo: The Vampire's Coffin (*Victor Vector 1* [informal name]); 1993; Horror, Adventure/Video Game; Macintosh (Apple Inc.), Windows 3.x (Microsoft)/Puzzle; color/English; Sanctuary Woods, Inc.

In this educational puzzle game that teaches vampire folklore, Victor Vector and his dog travel back in time to collect Dracula's coffin for The Museum of Fantastic Phenomena. They must get around all manner of undead creatures to reach the Count's resting place.

The Brides of Dracula; United States, 1991; Horror, Action-Adventure/Video Game; Amiga (Amiga), Atari ST (Atari)/2D platformer; color/English; Toast Dept./Gonzo Games.

Two players compete against each other as either Van Helsing or Dracula to navigate enemies and hazards and collect items to defeat the other. Helsing must find 13 weapons and bring them to his shed while Dracula searches to turn 13 fair maidens and store them in coffins.

Castlevania (*Castlevania 64* [common title and differentiation from original *Castlevania*]; *Akumajō Dorakyura Mokushiroku* [Japan]; *Dracula 3D* [in-development name]; *Dracula 64* [in-development name]); United States, 1999; Horror, Action-Adventure/Video Game; Nintendo 64/3D platformer, combat; color/English, Japanese; Konami

Producers: Kazuhiro Namba, Etsunobu Ebisu, Shigeharu Umezaki, Yuji Shibata; *Director:* Yuji Shibata; *Original Music:* Masahiko Kimura, Motoaki Furukawa, Mariko Egawa; *Art Direction:* Takashi Kakuta; *Audio Direction:* Tomoya Tomita; *Creative Direction:* Tomohiro Morisawa (chief designer); *Programming:* Hiroshi Shibata (chief programmer); *Cast:* Andrew Hankinson (Reinhardt Schneider [voice]), Bianca Allen (Carrie Fernandez [voice]), Harald Gjerd (Malus [voice]), Scott McCulloch (Narration).

Humanity's wickedness has again resurrected Dracula, who is disguised as the boy Malus while the vampiric Gilles de Rais pretends to be the "real" Dracula. The player can assume the role of either Reinhardt Schneider, heir to the Belmont clan, or the magical Carrie Fernandez, while fighting through Dracula's servants to put his evil back to sleep.

Castlevania: Akatsuki no Minuet (*Castlevania: Minuet of Dawn* [Japan title]; *Castlevania: Gyôgetsu no enbukyoku* [Japan, alternate spelling] *Castlevania: Aria of Sorrow* [United States]; *CV: AoS* [abbreviation]); United States, 2003; Action-Adventure/Video Game; Game Boy Advanced (Nintendo), Java ME for mobile phones (Java)/RPG; color/Japanese, English; Konami.

Producers: Koji Igarashi (as IGA), Kenichiro Honda; *Writing Credits:* Koji Igarashi (as IGA); *Director:* Junichi Murakami; *Original Music:* Michiru Yamane, Takashi Yoshida, Soshiro Hokkai; *Audio Direction:* Soshiro Hokkai; *Programming:* Shutaro; *Cast:* Hikaru Midorikawa (Soma Cruz [voice]), Hiroko Takahashi (voice), Osamu Ryutani (voice), Tetsu Inada (voice).

In 2035, Soma Cruz and several others, each of whom turn out to have special powers, are drawn into an eclipse and find themselves in a castle. Soma eventually discovers that although Dracula is truly dead, one of them is his reincarnation, inheriting his powers as well.

Castlevania: Bloodlines (*Vampire Killer* [Japan]; *Castlevania: The New Generation* [Europe]); United States. 1994; Horror, Action-Adventure/Video Game; Sega Genesis (Sega)/Platformer; color/Japanese, English; Konami.

Producer: Tomikazu Kirita; *Director:* Yutaka Haruki; *Audio Direction:* Michiru Yamane; *Programming:* Hanaten, Takeda, Kenichiro Horio, Koji Komata, Hidenari Inamura, Atsushi Fujio, Osamu Kasai.

Drolta Tzuentes and Elizabeth Bartley cause the

assassination of Franz Ferdinand to throw Europe into war and use the souls to resurrect Count Dracula. Now John Morris, descendant of the Belmont clan, and Eric Lecarde, whose girlfriend had been turned, fight to stop the resurrection ceremony.

Castlevania: Byakuya no Concerto (*Castlevania: Concerto of Midnight Sun* [Japan title]; *Castlevania: Hakuya no kyôsôkyoku* [Japan, alternate spelling] *Castlevania: Harmony of Dissonance* [United States]; *CV:HoD* [abbreviation]); Japan, 2002; Action-Adventure/Video Game; Game Boy Advanced (Nintendo)/2D RGP, platformer; color/Japanese, English; Konami.

Producer: Koji Igarashi (as IGA); *Writing Credits:* Koji Igarashi (as IGA); *Director:* Takeda Takeshi; *Original Music:* Michiru Yamane; *Audio Direction:* Soshiro Hokkai.

Juste Belmont goes to a castle, Dracula's castle, to rescue a kidnapped friend and happens to meet another from you had blanked out after gathering Dracula's remains to break a curse. Juste fights through the castle, re-gathers the remains, and defeats the spirit of Dracula possessing the second friend.

Castlevania: Lament of Innocence (*CV: LoI* [common abbreviation]; *Castlevania* [Japan and Europe]; United States, 2003; Horror, Action-Adventure/Video Game; PlayStation 2 (Sony)/RPG, combat; color/English, Japanese; Konami.

Producers: Koji Igarashi (as IGA), Yutaka Maseba, Haruyo Kanesaku, Kenichiro Honda; *Original Music:* Michiru Yamane; *Creative Direction:* Shinichiro Shimamura; *Programming:* Takashi Takeda; *Cast:* Nobutoshi Kanna (Additional Voices [Japanese version, as Nobutoshi Canna]), Hidekatsu Shibata (Additional Voices [Japanese version]), Yumi Tôma (Additional Voices [apanese version]), Haruko Kitahama (Additional Voices [Japanese version]), Hiroshi Kamiya (Additional Voices [Japanese version]), Yukimasa Kishino (Additional Voices [Japanese version]), Nobuhiko Kazama (Additional Voices [Japanese version]), Masaharu Satô (Additional Voices [Japanese version]), Melissa Fahn (Sara Trantoul [voice: English version, uncredited]), Crispin Freeman (Mathias Cronqvist [voice: English version, uncredited]), Wendee Lee (Succubus [voice: English version, uncredited]), Michael McConnohie (Narrator/Rinaldo Gandolfi [voice: English version, uncredited]), Mary Elizabeth McGlynn (Medusa [voice: English version, uncredited]), Liam O'Brien (Joachim Armster [voice: English version, uncredited]), Jamieson Price (Walter Bernhard [voice: English version, uncredited]), Dave Wittenberg (Leon Belmont [voice: English version, uncredited]), Tom Wyner (Death [voice: English version, uncredited]), Matt Lagan (drama actor), Eric Bossick (drama actor), Amy Colyer (drama actor), Antun Percic (drama actor), Keiji Hasegawa (action actor), Keiichi Ishiyama (action actor).

This is the first in both the *Castlevania* chronology and in the story of Dracula, the infamous whip, and the Belmont family curse. After the death of his wife, Mathias Cronqvist becomes angry at God and arranges for his companion's wife to be kidnapped by the King of the Vampires. Leon Belmont, the player's character, must fight with a whip to save his wife and slay the King, but the whole thing is an elaborate plot to allow Mathias to become ruler himself and later take the name "Dracula."

Castlevania: Legacy of Darkness (*Akumajou Dracula Mokushiroku Gaiden: The Legend of Cornell* [Japan]; United States, 1999; Horror, Action-Adventure/Video Game; Nintendo 64 (Nintendo)/3D platformer; color/English, Japanese; Konami.

Producers: Etsunobu Ebisu, K. Namba, Shigeharu Umezaki; *Writing Credits:* Takeo Yakushiji, Koichi Yagi; *Director:* Yuji Shibata; *Original Music:* Masahiko Kimura; *Art Direction:* Tomohiro Morisawa; *Audio Direction:* Tomoya Tomita; *Cast:* John Nuzzo (as Cornell[voice]), Takashi Bratcher (as Henry [Boy] [voice]), Scott McCulloch (as Narration)

This game contains four stories. In the first the player controls the werewolf Cornell who must rescue his little sister by fighting through Dracula's castle, and the second features a demon slayer, Hank, who rescues more children from Dracula. The other two stories take place 8 years later and are remakes of Castlevania 64 with the characters Reinhardt Schneider and Carrie Fernandez.

Castlevania: Order of Shadows; 2007; Action-Adventure/Video Game; Java Platform, Micro Edition (Java, on mobile phones)/2D Role-Playing Game, combat; color/English; Upstart Games/Konami Mobile.

Producer: James Bradbury; *Writing Credits:* Koji Igarashi (as IGA); *Director:* Victor Rodriguez; *Engineering/Technical Direction:* Alex Lewis, Ken Lui; *Art Direction:* Tyrone Rodriguez; *Audio Direction:* Vincent Diamante.

In this *Castlevania* side-story, Desmond Belmont attempts to stop an evil cult that continuously attempts to resurrect Dracula.

Chapolim x Drácula: Um Duelo Assustador; 1993; Horror, Action/Video Game; Sega Master System (Sega)/2D platformer; color/Portuguese; Sega/Tec Toy.

Based on the 1986 game *Ghost House* and Mexican television series *El Chapulín colorado*, this game features the character Chapolim, who is going to solve the problem of Transylvania's starving vampire population by reducing their numbers. Chapolim must find keys to unlock the vampire's coffins before he can defeat the five on each level. This game was created by "hacking" *Ghost House* with permission.

Conker's Bad Fur Day (*Twelve Tales: Conker 64* [1998 United States Press Release Name]; *Conker's BFD* [Abbreviated Title]; *Conker: Live & Reloaded* [Xbox remake]); United States, 2001; Action-Adventure/Video Game; Nintendo 64 (Nintendo), Xbox (Microsoft)/3D platformer; color/English/Dolby Surround; Rare.

Producer: Chris Seavor; *Writing Credits:* Chris Seavor, Robin Beanland; *Director:* Chris Seavor; *Original Music:* Robin Beanland; *Art Direction:* Don Murphy; *Audio Direction:* Robin Beanland; *Creative Direction:* Chris Seavor; *Cast:* Chris Seavor (Conker T. Squirrel, Birdy, Gargoyle, Gregg the Grim Reaper, Counta Conkula "Batula" Squirrel, Panther King, Beetles, Wayne, Wasps, Mr. King Bee, Franky, Boss, Professor, Ugas, Bugga the Knut, Rock Creatures, Male Villagers, Monk, Squirrel Army, Weasels, Private Rodent, Ron, Reg, Haybot, Boiler, Imps, Jack, Burt, Marvin, Tediz, Mr. Barrel, Baby Fangy, Dragon God, Cash, Carl, Quentin, Buggerlugs The Bull, Guards, Sarge, Louise Ridgeway (Berri, Mrs. Queen Bee, Sunflower, Jugga, others [all voice]), Chris Marlow (The Great Mighty Poo [voice]).

Player controls the anthropomorphic squirrel Conkers while the game explains how he went from a drunken stupor to being "king of all the land." One area in the game features a castle with a Dracula parody, Count Conkula. This N64 game has received a rating of M15+.

The Count; United States, 1981; Horror, Adventure/Video Game; Apple II Plus (Apple Computer, Inc.), Atari 8-bit (Atari), Commodore 64 (Commodore), TI-99/4A (Texas Instruments), TRS-80 (Tandy Corporation), VIC-20 (Commodore), ZX Spectrum (Sinclair Research Ltd.), Internet Browser/Text-based; color (varies by system)/English; Adventure International.

Producer: Scott Adams; *Writing Credits:* Scott Adams; *Director:* Scott Adams; *Programming:* Scott Adams.

The player's character wakes up on a brass bed one night in the Count's castle. The player has three game days to avoid attack and collect items to defeat Dracula with. An enhanced version with illustrations came out in 1982 for the Atari 8-bit.

Dracula; United States, 1982; Horror, Action/Video Game; Intellivision (Mattel)/2D side-scroller; color/English; Imagic.

Programming: Alan Smith.

Dracula, the player's character, must walk the streets at night to feed on people and return to his tomb by sunrises. Constables, wolves, and hawks will attempt to stop the vampire's feeding.

Dracula (Bram Stoker's Dracula); United States, 1993; Horror/Video Game; MS-DOS (Microsoft), Amiga (Amiga), Game Boy (Nintendo), Game Gear (Sega), Genesis (Sega), NES (Nintendo), SEGA CD (Sega), SEGA Master System (Sega), SNES (Nintendo)/1st person adventure on MS-DOS or side-scrolling fighter on the others; color/English; Probe Software Ltd., Psygnosis Limited, Traveller's Tales Ltd./Sony Imagesoft.

Producers: Mike Simpson, Tony Beckwith, Richard Robinson; *Director:* Mike Simpson, Tag Turner (as Tag); *Original Music:* Phil Morris, Jeroen Tel; *Cast:* (Sega CD version): Jeff Bramfitt (Van Helsing), Lee Carus-Wescott (Harker/Dracula), Nicky Carus-Wescott (Brides), Neil Thompson (Renfield).

Based on *Bram Stoker's Dracula* (1992), this game features Jonathan Harker as the player, who must escape from Dracula's Castle, return to London, and stop the Count from terrorizing the city.

Dracula 3 — The Path of the Dragon (*Dracula 3: Адвокат дьявола* [Russia], *Dracula 3: La Voie du Dragon* [France], *Drácula 3: La Senda del Dragón* [Spain], *Dracula 3 — Der Pfad des Drachen* [Germany]); Belgium/France, 2008; Horror, Adventure/Video Game; Computer (Windows)/1st person, puzzle; color/English/Stereo; Kheops Studio/MC2-Microïds.

Producer: Catherine Peyrot; *Original Music:* Yan Volsy; *Director:* Benoît Hozjan; *Engineering/Technical Direction:* Stéphane Petit; *Art Direction:* Frank Letiec; *Creative Direction:* Alexis Lang; *Programming:* Frédéric Jaume, Wilfried Hinault, Stéphane Petit, Jordane Suarez; *Cast:* David Gasman (voice), Jodie Forrest (voice), Sharon A. Mann (voice), Paul Bandey (voice), Douglas Rand (voice), Eddie Crew (voice)

A supposedly saintly woman in Transylvania has been beautifying people, and Father Arno Moriani has been sent to investigate. After marks are found on a corpse, the player, as Moriani, must seek out clues of Dracula's current existence. This is the sequel to Dracula: The Resurrection.

Dracula Densetsu (*Castlevania: The Adventure* [United States]); Japan, 1989; Action-Adventure/Video Game; Game Boy (Nintendo)/2D platformer; Monochrome/Japanese, English; Konami.

Art Direction: Kouichi Kimura, Nobuya Nakazato; *Audio Direction:* Shigeru Fukutake, Hidehiro Funauchi, Norio Hanzawa; *Programming:* Masato Maegawa, Yoshiaki Yamada.

Dracula has risen from the grave and is bent on revenge against the Belmont Clan. The player takes Christopher Belmont and his whip into Dracula's Castle to put the vampire back to rest.

Dracula Densetsu II (*Castlevania II: Belmont's Revenge* [United States]; *Castlevania: The Adventure II* [United States, unofficial, to avoid confusion with *Castlevania II: Simon's Quest*]); Japan and United States, 1991; Action-Adventure/Video Game; Game Boy (Nintendo)/2D platformer; Monochrome/Japanese, English; Konami.

Art Direction: Kouichi Kimura; *Audio Direction:* Hidehiro Funauchi; *Programming:* Toru Hagihara, Yukari HayaNo.

Dracula comes out of hiding fifteen years after he is defeated by Christopher Belmont, captures the hero's son, and turns the son into a monster. Christopher and his family's whip must face Dracula and the castle once again to save his son.

Dracula II: Noroi no fûin (*Castlevania II: Simon's Quest* [United States]; *Dracula II: The Accursed* Seal [Translated Japanese Title]; *Legend of Dracula II, Simon's Quest Watch Game* [remake]; *LCD Simon's Quest* [remake]); Japan, 1987; Horror, Action-Adventure/Video Game; Nintendo (Nintendo), Wii (Nintendo), individual handheld (Tiger Electronics), wrist watch game (Tiger Electronics)/3rd person, platformer; color/Japanese, English; Konami.

Director: H. Akamatsu (Invicibility); *Original Music:* Kenichi Matsubara; *Staff Members:* H. Akamatsu (Invincibility), Iwasa (Permanence), N. Togakushi (Philosophy), Kawanishi (Masterpiece), Hatano (Sensitivity), Terashima (Excellence), Kuwahara (Ambivalence), Higasa (Flourish), Ohyama (Admiration), Murata (Superiority), Kenichi Matsubara (Synchronism), Konami (Circumstance).

Simon Belmont is cursed after defeating Dracula earlier in the *Castlevania* the series. The only cure is to collect and burn the 5 scattered parts of Dracula's body.

The Dracula Files; United States, 2009; Horror, Action-Adventure/Video Game; Windows, Nintendo DS, Wii/1st person; color/English; TechFront Studios/eGames, Inc.

A hundres years have passed since Dracula's defeat, and now he has returned as the evil Vladimir Draco. Only the Harker and Van Helsing family descendants can put an end to his thirst for blood and revenge. These descendants face off against werewolves, vampires, and dark spirits, and in the process find holy relics to fend off the undead.

Dracula in London; United States, 1988; Horror, Action-Adventure/Video Game; Dos, Windows 3.x (Microsoft, 1993 re-release)/Turn-based adventure; color/English; SDJ Enterprises, Inc.

Original Music: Scott Laytham; *Engineering/Technical Direction:* Gary Barg; *Art Direction:* Steven D. Jones; *Audio Direction:* Scott Laytham; *Programming:* Steven D. Jones.

Dracula has come to London just like the classic story, and 6 of the humans in the original *Dracula*, controlled by one person or 6 different people, have different skills to help stop the Count. The player must hunt clues around London and make difficult decisions in hopes of saving London and the members of the party.

Dracula the Undead; United States, 1991; Horror/Video Game; Atari Lynx (Atari)/3rd person, Interactive Story; color/English; Atari/Hand Made Software, Ltd.

Writing Credits: Bram Stoker

Controlling Jonathan Harker, the player explores Dracula's castle to assess the Count's threat to the world and eventually confronts the vampire. A digital Bram Stoker narrates the story.

Dracula Twins (Дети Дракулы [Russian]); World, 2006; Horror, Action/Video Game; PC (Microsoft)/3rd person, side-scrolling platformer; color/English, Russian; Nerlaska, Legendo/Legendo.

Producer: Björn Larsson, Alberto De Hoyo Nebot; *Writing Credits:* Björn Larsson; *Director:* Björn Larsson; *Original Music:* Alexander Röder; *Art Direction:* Joe Sharp, Rob Sharp; *Audio Direction:* Björn Larsson; *Creative Direction:* Björn Larsson; *Programming:* Alberto De Hoyo Nebot.

Dracula has been captured by the vampire hunter Dr. Lifelust, who plans to use Dracula's blood to live forever. The player controls either Drac or Dracana, Dracula's son and daughter respectively, through various levels to save their father.

Dracula Unleashed; United States, 1993; Horror/Video Game; Computer (DOS, Macintosh), SEGA CD (SEGA)/FMV Adventure; color/English; ICOM Simulations, Inc./SEGA, Viacom.

Producers: Ken Tarolla, David Marsh, Kent Russell; *Writing Credits:* Anthony Sherman, Andrew Greenberg, William Bridges; *Original Music:* Byte-Size Sound; *Director:* Mike Plant; *Art Direction:* Greg Stiever; *Programming:* Fred Allen; *Cast:* Jay Nickerson (Arthur Holmwood), John Arthur Olson (Dr. Van Helsing), Bill Williamson (Alexander Morris), Kathleen Russell, Louis Markert, Nichole Pelerine, Tim McGivern.

Ten years after the events in *Dracula*, Quincey Morris's brother Alexander travels to London to investigate his brother's death. New accounts of a vampire attacking women start to crop up, and the player, as Alexander, must search London for clues before his new love is turned into a vampire.

Dracula: Crazy Vampire; United States, 2001; Action/Video Game; Game Boy color (Nintendo)/2D platformer; color/English; Planet Interactive/DreamCatcher Interactive, Cyro Interactive.

Producer: Claire Meddas; *Director:* Isabelle Thorin; *Original Music:* Mark Cooksey; *Art Direction:* Fouzar Alcala, Julien Grycan; *Creative Direction:* Jean-Luc Nanchino, Alexis Kaliky; *Programming:* Alain Boisrame.

The player controls a chibi Dracula via top down view as the vampire seeks to unite 11 vampires against a Great Inquisitor Torquemada. Dracula must avoid sunlight and enemies as well as fight classic monsters like the Mummy, Wolfman, and the Swamp Thing.

Dracula: The Days of Gore; United States, 2007; Action/Video Game; PC (Microsoft)/1st person, 3D, shooter; color/English; Wolfgroup/IncaGold.

In the 19th century Dracula is the true ruler behind the kings of Europe, and his empire is fueled by the blood of the innocent. The player takes the role of a detective and member of an ancient order of knights as he investigates a strange series of murders tracing back to Dracula.

Dracula 2: The Last Sanctuary (*Dracula II: Die letzte Zufluchtsstätte* [Germany]; *Drácula: El último santuario* [Spain]; *Dracula 2: The Last Place of Refuge* [U.K.]; *Dracula 2: Posledni utociste* [Czech Republic]; *Drácula 2: O Último Santuário* [Brazil]; *Dracula 2: Ostatnie Sanktuarium* [Poland]; *Dracula 2: L'Ultimo Santuario* [Italy]; *Dracula 2: Le Dernier Sanctuaire* [France]; *Dracula 2: Die letzte Zufluchtsstätte* [Germany]; *Dracula 2* [Belguim]); France, 2000; Horror/Video Game; Macintosh (Apple), PlayStation (Sony), Windows (Microsft)/1st person point-and-click, Puzzle-solving; color/English; Canal+Multimédia, France Télécom Multimédia, index+/DreamCatcher Interactive Inc., Cyro Interactive.

Producer: Frédéric Locca; *Writing Credits:* Jacques Simian, Francois Villard; *Original Music:* Laurent Parisi; *Programming:* Francois Villard; *Cast:* Herbert Flack (Dracula [voice]), Tamar Baruch (Mina, Dorko [voices]), Guy Van Der Hofstadt (Jonathan [voice]), Doude Van Herwijnen (Hopkins, Seward, Viorel, Bill, Pibody [voices]).

In this sequel to *Dracula: The Resurrection*, Jonathan Harker, the player, follows Dracula form London to Transylvania to save Jonathan's wife Mina.

Dracula: The Resurrection (*Dracula: Zmartwychwstanie* [Polish]; *Dracula Resurrection* [German]; *Drácula Resurección* Spanish]; *Dracula: La risurrezione* [Italian]; *Drácula (a ressurreição)* [Portuguese]; *Drácula* [Brazilian]); United States, 2000; Horror, Adventure/Video Game; Computer (Windows, Macintosh) PlayStation (Sony)/Puzzle; color/English; Canal+Multimédia, France Télécom Multimédia, index+/DreamCatcher Interactive Inc.

Producer: Vincent Berlioz; *Writing Credits:* Jacques Simian, Francois Villard; *Original Music:* Laurent Parisi; *Director:* Jacques Simian; *Programming:* Philippe Bouet, Francois Villard; *Cast:* Francoise Blanchard (Mina, Dorko [voices]), Marie-Christine Dara (Barina, Zalina [voices]), Lorenzo Pancino (Micha, Viorel, Iorga, Goran [voices]), Cyrille Artaux (Jonathan Harker [voice]), Joel Zafarano (Dracula [voice]).

Seven years after the events of *Dracula*, Mina becomes ill and travels under a strange compulsion to Transylvania where Dracula is inexplicably restored. As Jonathan Harker, the player must follow her and find a way into Dracula's castle to save Harker's wife.

Dracula: Origin (Охотник на Дракулу [Russia]; *Drákula: Zrození* [Czech]; *Dracula: Początek* [Poland]); United States, 2008; Horror-Adventure/Video Game; Computer (Windows)/3rd person, puzzle; color/English/Stereo; Frogwares Game Development Studio/The Adventure Company.

Producers: Mike Adams, Dan Dawang, George Chastain Jr.; *Original Music:* Resnick Enterprises; *Director:* Byron Gaum; *Art Direction:* Jay Kinsella; *Audio Direction:* Todd Resnick; *Creative Direction:* Esther Sucre; *Cast:* Kevin Delaney (Abraham Van Helsing, Dracula [voice]), Sarah Ripard (voice), Ralph Lister (voice), Paul Rogan (voice), Ben Hurst (voice), David Lodge (voice).

Dracula has learned of a ritual to bring his beloved, a suicide, back to life and plans to use Mina to complete the ritual. As Van Helsing, the player must find and stop Dracula from completing the ritual.

Dracula's Secret (*Het Geheim van Dracula*; *Drakulas Hemlighet*; *Dracula: Le Mystère du château*); Canada, 1996; Horror, Adventure/Video Game; Macintosh (Apple Inc.), Windows (Microsoft), Windows 3.x (Microsoft)/Puzzle; color/English, French, Dutch, and Swedish; Corel Corporation, KLA Visual Productions Ltd./Future Endeavors, Inc.

Writing Credits: Lee Atkinson, Vic Atkinson; *Director:* Lee Atkinson; *Original Music:* Jack Blyth, Gen Digital Soundtrack Design Ltd.; *Art Direction:* Kathi Atkinson; *Creative Direction:* Vic Atkinson; *Programming:* Duane Phillips, Alexander Martin, Nickolai Buwalda, Richard V. Woodend; *Cast:* Rick Jones (voice), Nancy Neilson (voice), Ron Henry (voice), Jack Blyth (voice), Bob Johnson (voice).

Dracula has invited the player over to his castle

to search for a hidden secret. The player must solve puzzles to assemble Dracula's Coat of Arms while being taunted by the vampire.

Dráscula: El Vampiro (*Dráscula: The Vampire Strikes Back*); Spain, 1996; Horror, Adventure/Video Game; DOS/Puzzle; color/Spanish; Alcachofa Soft S.L./Digital Dreams Multimedia.

Producers: Mario de Luis Garcia, Carlos Doral; *Writing Credits:* Fernando Lancha, Emilio de Paz; *Original Music:* Emilio de Paz; *Engineering/Technical Direction:* Juan Fernández; *Art Direction:* Miguel Angel Manrique; *Programming:* Emilio de Paz; *Cast:* Alfredo Cernuda (voice), Vicente Redondo (voice), Germán Yepes (voice), M. José del Moral (voice), Emilio de Paz (voice), Santiago Lancha (voice), Martín de Paz (voice), Fernando Lancha (voice).

John Hacker, the player character, is sent from Britain to speak with Count Dráscula. There he meets a woman who gets kidnapped by Dracula, and Mr. Hacker has to rescue her in a comedic adventure.

The Elder Scrolls IV: Oblivion (*Oblivion* [common name]); United States, 2006; Action, Adventure/Video Game; PlayStation 3 (Sony), Windows (Microsoft), Xbox 360 (Microsoft)/RPG; color/English; Bethesda Game Studios/2K Games, Bethesda Softworks LLC, Ubisoft Entertainment.

Producers: Gavin Carter, Craig Lafferty, Todd Howard, Ashley Cheng, Emma Timms; *Writing Credits:* Ted Peterson, Michael Kirkbride; *Original Music:* Jeremy Soule; *Art Direction:* Matthew Carofano, Christiane Meister, Istvan Pely; *Creative Direction:* Ken Rolston; *Programming:* Guy Carver, Craig Walton; *Cast:* Patrick Stewart (Emperor Uriel Septim VII [voice]), Sean Bean (Emperor Martin Septim [voice]), Terence Stamp (Mankar Camoran [voice]), Lynda Carter (Female Nords/Female Orcs [voice]), Jeff Baker (Haskill [voice]), Bari Biern (Golden Saint Warrior [voice]), Jonathan Bryce (Male Argonians/Male Khajiits/Male Nords/Male Orcs [voice]), Ralph Cosham (Jauffre/Vincent Valtieri/Male Bretons [voice]), Catherine Flye (Female Bretons/Female Imperials [voice]), Gayle Jessup (Female Redguards [voice]), Wes Johnson (Lucien Lachance/Dremora/Arena Announcer/The Prophet/Pelinal Whitestrake/Sheogorath/Hirrus Clutumnus/Herdir/The Gray Fox/Male Imperials [voice]), Michael Mack (Baurus/Owyn/Redguard Males [voice]), Elisabeth Noone (Female Argonians/Female Khajiits [voice]), Craig Sechler (High Chancellor Ocato/Falcar/Alval Uvani/Faelian/The Adoring Fan/Male Dunmer/Male Altmer/Male Bosmers [voice]), Linda Kanyon (race voices).

Oblivon's story revolves around a royal assassination, a lost Imperial heir, demon incursions, and the fate of the player's character to have a role in the events. Some of the quests in the game take the player to Janus Hassildor, the vampiric Count of Skingrad whose castle resides on a wooded hill and separated from the city of Skingrad. This count dresses in regal clothing and robe, and some of the quest involving him include getting rid of a party of vampire slayers and a quest to cure his wife (as well as yourself) of vampirism.

Eternal Knights 2; Japan; Gambling/Video Game; Japanese "medal game" machine/Role-Playing Game; color/Japanese; Konami.

In this medal game, players create teams of RPG-style characters and either complete dungeons or fight competitively to earn medals. These medals are redeemable for more plays or prizes. *Eternal Knights 2* has *Castlevania*-inspired vampire hunter characters and a Dracula enemy.

Evolution Skateboarding; United States, 2002; Sport/Video Game; PlayStation 2 (Sony) and GameCube (Nintendo)/Skatebording; color/English; Konami.

Producer: Madoka Yamauchi; *Director:* Madoka Yamauchi; *Audio Direction:* Satoru Okubo; *Programming:* Akihiko Shimizu, Jyunji Maruhashi, Hirotaka Hosokawa.

In this game, players choose a character, do stunts with a skateboard, earn points, and do sidequests. This game includes an unlockable Simon Belmont character and a *Castlevania* level in which Dracula is featured.

Fantomu Bureibu (*Phantom Brave* [United States]; *Phantom Brave: We Meet Again* [United States, Wii version]); Japan, 2004; Action, Adventure/Video Game; PlayStation 2 (Sony), Wii (Nintendo)/Tactical RPG; color/Japanese and English; Nippon Ichi Software Inc./NIS America, Inc., KOEI Co., Ltd.

Producers: Sohei Niikawa, Koichi Kitazumi, Haru Akenaga; *Writing Credits:* Sohei Niikawa, Shinichi Ikeda; *Director:* Keith Arem, Shinichi Ikeda, Yoshitsuna Kobayashi; *Original Music:* Tenpei Sato; *Cast:* Osamu Hosoi (Persimmon, Canary [voice, Japanese version]), Yui Itsuki (Castile [voice, Japanese version]), Steve Kramer (Fake Raphael, Additional VoicesJunji Majima (Raphael [voice, Japanese version]), Hironori Miyata (Count Malt, Cauldron, President Hogg [voice, Japanese version]), Kaori Mizuhashi (Marona [voice, Japanese version]), Takashi Nagasako (Sprout, Ringmaster Hamm [voice, Japanese version]), Miki Narahashi (Narration [voice, Japanese version]), Hiro Shimono (Ash [voice, Japanese version]), Brian Silva (Fox, Lierre, Royal Employee Ringmaster Ham,

Bully, Circus Member [voices]), Kosuke Toriumi (Walnut, Murasaki [voices, Japanese version, as Kohsuke Toriumu]), Miho Yamada (Sienna [voice, Japanese version]), Steve Blum (Walnut [voice, English version, uncredited]), Sandy Fox (Marona [voice, English version, uncredited]), Crispin Freeman (Raphael [voice, English version, uncredited]), Barbara Goodson (Laharl [voice, English version, uncredited]), Lex Lang (Ash [voice, English version, uncredited]), David Lodge (Sprout [voice, English version, uncredited]), Mary Elizabeth McGlynn (Pisa [voice, English version, uncredited]), Lara Jill Miller (Castille [voice, English version, uncredited]), Liam O'Brien (Additional Voices [voices, English version, uncredited]), Bob Papenbrook (Count Malt, Cauldron, President Hogg, Island Elder [voices, English version, uncredited]), Kirk Thornton (Ringmaster Hamm [voice, English version, uncredited]), Dave Wittenberg (Persimmon, Canary [voices, English version, uncredited]).

Marona, an orphan girl, attempts to follow in her parent's bounty hunter work with the help of their old companion, now a phantom. Eventually they encounter and set out to defeat an evil creature that threatens to conquer the world. A hidden boss in the game is Count Vyers (from the first Disgaea game), who speaks with an Eastern European-esque accent and wears a red and black outfit with a wing-shaped cloak; this Count's fangs, long dark hair, and other similarities reveal his Dracula-inspired heritage.

Ganbare Goemon 2: Kiteretsu Shogun Magginesu; Japan, 1993; Action/Video Game; Super Nintendo (Nintendo), Wii Virtual console (Nintendo)/2D platformer; color/Japanese; Konami.

Goemon must stop General Magginesu and his army of bunny-men from westernizing Japan. There is an unlockable *Castlevania* level containing Simon Belmont and what must be Dracula as the boss.

Gegege No Kitaro: Fukkatsu! Tenma Daiou; Japan, 1993; Horror, Action/Video Game; Super Nintendo (Nintendo)/2D platformer, fighter; color/Japanese; Bandai.

Writing Credits: Shigeru Mizuki.

Inspired by Shigeru Mizuki's *Gegege no Kitarō* (manga series first published in the late 1950's), this game follows Kitaro (and a companion in 2-player mode), who scrolls through the levels and defeats groups of enemies and mini-bosses using various attacks until the level's boss monster appears. Then he must defeat the boss (Dracula is a boss in chapter 3), possibly rescue a companion, and then continue on to the next level.

Gegege no Kitaro: Gyakushuu! Youkai Daichisen; Japan, 2003; Horror, Action/Video Game; Playstation (Sony)/2D Platformer; color/Japanese; Konami.

Writing Credits: Shigeru Mizuki; *Cast:* Rika Matsumoto (Kitarō), Kazuo Kumakura (Medama Oyaji), Nachi Nozawa (Nezumi-Otoko), Yuko Miyamura (Neko Musume), Junko Hori (Sunakake Babaa), Takanobu Hozumi (Konaki Jijii), Kenichi Ogata (Ittan Momen), Kousei Tomita (Nurikabe), Junpei Takiguchi (Nurarihyon), Akio Ōtsuka (Dracula), Michitaka Kobayashi (Back Beard), Seizō Katō (Giga)

Inspired by Shigeru Mizuki's *Gegege no Kitarō* (manga series first published in the late 1950s), this game follows Kitaro, who scrolls through the levels while fighting various Eastern monsters, as well as a few Western ones like Dracula.

Gegege no Kitarō: Youkai Dai Makyou (*Ninja Kid* [United States]); Japan, 1986; Horror, Action-Adventure/Video Game; Nintendo (Nintendo)/2D platformer; color/Japanese and English; Tose/Bandai

Writing Credits: Shigeru Mizuki.

The original game involved the ghost boy Kitaro using various projectile attacks to defeat Yokai and stop an attack on the humans. The American version removes all references to the manga/anime, turned Kitaro into a nameless ninja, and replaced Japanese monsters with film monster like Frankenstein's monster and Dracula. The goal in *Ninja Kid* is to complete the eight challenges of Shangri-La, which involves defeating the monsters.

Ghost House (*Chapolim x Dracula: Um Duelo Assastador* [South America]; United States, 1986; Horror, Action/Video Game; Sega Master System (Sega)/2D platformer; color/English; Sega.

Young Mick, the player character, must battle through traps and monsters in Count Dracula's Mansion to recover the family jewels he just inherited. Mick must find keys, open up coffins of five Draculas on each level, and slay the Draculas to advance.

Gokujō Parodius! ~Kako no Eikō o Motomete~ (*Ultimate Parodius ~Pursue the Glory of the Past~* [United States]; *Fantastic Journey* [Europe]); Japan, 1994; Action/Video Game; Super Nintendo (Nintendo)/scrolling shooter; color/Japanese, English/Stereo; Konami.

Producer: Shigeharu Umezaki; *Director:* Nobuhiro Matsuoka; *Audio Direction:* Keroppi Inoue, Nobuyuki Akena; *Programming:* Nobuhiro Matsuoka, Masatsugu Nagata, Hidenao Yamane, Chacha Yoshida.

A parody of Konami's popular *Gradius*, this

game has the player choose one of several characters to fly across the stage and shoot humorous enemies with. One of the playable characters is Dracula-Kun/Kid-Dracula from a *Castlevania* parody.

Goosebumps: Escape from Horrorland; United States, 1996; Horror/Video Game; Windows (Microsoft)/Interactive Story; color/English; DreamWorks Interactive L.L.C.

Director: Lawrence Guterman; *Original Music:* Andy Garfield; *Cast:* Glynis Barber (Mrs. Morris), Jeff Bennett (Pumpkins [voice]), Mark Caso (Werewolf), Tatum Marie Fjersted (Lizzy Morris), Eric Gavriluk (Zombie #2), Jeff Goldblum (Dracula), Nadine Grycan (Suzy-Q), Robert Joy (Madison Storm/Stump), Eric Lloyd (Clay), J.P. Manoux (Squat), Tracey McAlister (Zombie #3), Walter Phelan (Mummy/Zombie), Dennon Rawles (Vampire Dancer #1), Isabella Rossellini (Lady Cadaver), Neil Ross (Riddle Wall/Horus [voice]), Charles Martin Smith (Renfield), Judy Tenuta (Hannah Black), Sue Thoma (Vampire Dancer #2), Steve Valentine (Scarecrow/Stretch), Scott Walters (Zombie #4), David Wells (Mr. Morris), Adam Wylie (Luke Morris).

This is a sequel to *One Day at Horrorland*, in which the player and his friends Lizzy, Luke, and Clay must escape again from the evil theme park. The player must confront classic monsters like the Mummy, Wolfman, and Dracula before escaping.

Goosebumps HorrorLand; United States, 2008; Horror, Adventure/Video Game; Nintendo DS (Nintendo), Wii (Nintendo), and PlayStation 2 (Sony)/Minigames; color/English; Gusto Game/Scholastic, Inc.

In this game based on R.L. Stine's *Goosebumps Horrorland* series, the player's young character and character's friends are trapped in an evil amusement park and want to escape. One of the themed areas is Vampire Village, and it contains Dracula-type vampires.

In the Wake of Vampire (*Master of Darkness* [United States]); Japan, 1992; Horror, Action-Adventure/Video Game; Game Gear (Sega), SEGA Master System (Sega)/2D platformer; color/Japanese, English; SIMS Co., Ltd./Sega.

Director: Sats King; *Art Direction:* Super Punch; *Audio Direction:* Fumi, Yoko Wada (Nasubi); *Creative Direction:* Sats King; *Programming:* Super Punch, Yen.

The player plays as psychologist Ferdinand Social after the character finds out that Jack the Ripper's murders have actually been committed by Dracula. In a game reminiscent of *Castlevania*, he must fight through various monsters, minions, and locations to eventually defeat the murderous Count.

Jikkyō Oshaberi Parodius: forever with me; Japan, 1996; Action/Video Game; PlayStation (Sony), Sega Saturn (Sega)/scrolling shooter; color/Japanese; Konami.

Producers: Shigeharu Umezaki, Kuniaki Kinoshita; *Director:* Nobuhiro Matsuoka; *Audio Direction:* Kazuhiko Uehara; *Programming:* Nobuhiro Matsuoka.

This is a paraody of the *Gradius* series in which the player chooses a character, flies through multiple game levels, and shoots at humorous enemies. This particular version is a port of *Jikkyō Oshaberi Parodius* and contains Dracula-Kun and Kid-Dracula as unlockable characters.

King's Quest II: Romancing the Throne (*KQ2* [abbreviation]); United States, 1985; Action-Adventure/Video Game; Amiga (Amiga), Apple II (Apple Inc.), Apple IIgs (Apple Inc.), Atari ST (Atari), DOS, PC Booter (Microsoft)/Interactive Fiction; color/English; Sierra On-Line, Inc.

Writing Credits: Roberta Williams, Annette Childs; *Original Music:* Al Lowe; *Programming:* Jeff Stephenson, Chris Iden.

King Graham is searching for a queen and has decided on a maiden in a faraway land who is trapped in a quartz tower locked by three keys. In his quest, King Graham comes across the deadly Dracula.

Konami Wai Wai Racing Advance (*Konami Krazy Racers* [United States]); Japan, 2001; Sports/Video Game; Game Boy Advanced (Nintendo)/Racing; color/Japanese and English; Konami.

Producers: Etsunobu Ebisu, Keita Kawaminami, Shigeharu Umezaki; *Director:* Toyokazu Nonaka; *Art Direction:* Toyokazu Nonaka, Shouichi Maekawa, Chieko Tobioka; *Audio Direction:* Sotaro Tojima; *Programming:* Hiroshi Shibata, Jun'ichi Taniguchi, Ken Yokota; *Cast:* Hayap (voice), Bikke (voice), Chisa Matsuda (voice), Kouzou Nakamura (voice), Sotaro Tojima (voice).

In this game, the player chooses a chibi (sometimes referred to as "super deformed") character, races around a track with other characters, and collects coins to buy items. A chibi of the *Castlevania* Dracula is available as a character.

Konami Wai Wai World; Japan, 1988; Action-Adventure/Video Game; Nintendo (Nintendo), mobile phones/2D platformer, Scrolling shooter; color/Japanese; Konami.

This game plays similarly to *Castlevania* and features unlockable characters from various Konami games. There is a Castlevania level in which Simon Belmont III can be unlocked, and Dracula is the level's boss.

LCD Symphony of the Night; United States, 1998; Action/Video Game; LCD Tiger Handheld (Tiger

Electronics)/2D platformer; color/English; Tiger Electronics/Konami.

Dracula is resurrected by his wizard Shaft, and Dracula's son Alucard, the play character, sets off to stop his father's evil plans. This is an individual handheld remake of *Akumajō Dracula X: Gekka no Yasōkyoku* (*Castlevania: Symphony of the Night*).

Makai Senki Disugaia (*Disgaea: Hour of Darkness* [United States]; *Disgaea: Afternoon of Darkness* [PSP rerelease]; *Makai Senki Disgaea: Makai no Ouji to Akai Tsuki* [PSP rerelease, Japan]; *Disgaea DS* [DS rerelease, United States]); Japan, 2003; Comedy, Adventure/Video Game; PlayStation 2 (Sony), PSP (Sony), Nintendo DS (Nintendo)/Tactical Role-Playing Game; color/Japanese, English; Nippon Ichi Software Inc/Atlus U.S.A., Inc., NIS America, Inc., KOEI Co., Ltd.

Producers: Sohei Niikawa, Kohichi Kitazumi; *Writing Credits:* Sohei Niikawa; *Director:* Yoshitsuna Kobayashi; *Original Music:* Sohei Niikawa (lyrics), Tenpei Satō; *Engineering/Technical Direction:* Yuzuru Nakayama; *Audio Direction:* Kentaro Furusyo; *Creative Direction:* Yoshitsuna Kobayashi; *Programming:* Yoshitsuna Kobayashi; *Cast:* Kaori Mizuhashi (Laharl [voice: Japanese version]), Tomoe Hanba (Etna [voice: Japanese version]), Yûko Sasamoto (Flonne [voice: Japanese version]), Junji Majima (Prinny Squad, Seraph Lamington [voices: Japanese version]), Chihiro Suzuki (Mid-Boss, Vyers [voice: Japanese version]), Nobuo Tobita (Captain Gordon [voice: Japanese version]), Chiwa Saito (Jennifer [voice: Japanese version]), Yurika Ochiai (Thursday [voice: Japanese version]), Kosuke Toriumi (Kurtis [voice: Japanese version, as Koshsuke Toriumi]), Tomomichi Nishimura (General Carter [voice: Japanese version]), Hironori Miyata (Archangel Vulcanus [voice: Japanese version]), Sandy Fox (Flonne [voice: English version, uncredited]), Grant George (King Krychevskoy, "Dark Adonis," Prinny Squad, Don Juaquin [voices: English version, uncredited]), Barbara Goodson (Laharl [voice: English version, uncredited]), Michael McConnohie (Captain Gordon, Maderas [voices: English version, uncredited]), Bob Papenbrook (Archangel Vulcanus, Thursday, General Carter [voices: English version, uncredited]), Jamieson Price (Seraph Lamington, Narration, Kurtis [voices: English version, uncredited]), Yukari Tamura (Angel Class, Catgirl Class [voices: Japanese version, uncredited]), Amanda Winn Lee (Etna [voice: English version, uncredited]).

Two years after Demon Overlord King Krichevskoy has died, his son Laharl is awakened by his disrespectful vassal Etna. Prince Laharl and Etna (and later the angel Flonne) set off to claim Laharl's title of Overlord form the other upstart demons, and there first target is the castle of Count Vyers (named Mid-boss by Laharl). Vyers, who calls himself the Dark Adonis, speaks with an Eastern European-esque accent, and wears a red and black outfit with a wing-shaped cloak; this Count's fangs, long dark hair, and other similarities reveal his Dracula-inspired heritage.

Makai Senki Disugaia Surī (*Disgaea 3: Absence of Justice* [United States]); Japan, 2008; Comedy, Adventure/Video Game; PlayStation 3 (Sony)/Tactical Role-Playing Game; color/Japanese, English; Nippon Ichi Software Inc./NIS America, Inc., Square Enix.

Producers: Sohei Niikawa, Kohichi Kitazumi, Ryoji Yamuse; *Writing Credits:* Kaori Shinmei, Sohei Niikawa, Haruo Sotozaki; *Director:* Masahiro Yamamoto, Haruo Sotozaki; *Original Music:* Sohei Niikawa, Tenpei Satō; *Art Direction:* Haruo Sotozaki, Kazuo Ebisawa; *Creative Direction:* Masahiro Yamamoto, Yoshimori Yamamoto; *Programming:* Masahiro Yamamoto; *Cast:* Laura Bailey (Raspberyl [voice, English version]), Akiko Hasegawa (Sapphire Rhodonite [voice, Japanese version]), Hiromi Hirata (Mao [voice, Japanese version]), Natsuki Kousaka (Asuka Cranekick [voice, Japanese version]), Gorou Kubota (Geoffery [voice, Japanese version]), Keiichi Kuwabara (Mr. Champloo [voice, Japanese version]), Vic Mignogna (Mao [voice, English version]), Lara Jill Miller (Kyoko Needleworker [voice, English version]), Liam O'Brien (Master Bigstar [voice, English version]), Toshihiro Okubo (Super Hero Auram [voice, Japanese version]), Michelle Ruff (Salvatore the Great [voice, English version]), Chiwa Saitou (Raspberyl [voice, Japanese version]), Stephanie Sheh (Sapphire Rhodonite [voice, English version]), Hiro Shimono (Almaz [voice, Japanese version]), Arai Shizuka (Kyoko Needleworker [voice, Japanese version]), Christopher Corey Smith (Mr. Champloo [voice, English version]), Chihiro Suzuki (Master Bigstar [voice, Japanese version]), Dave Wittenberg (Geoffery/Super Hero Auram [voice, English version]), Miho Yamada (Salvatore the Great [voice, Japanese version]).

Mao, a demon and son of the Overlord, attends underworld academy where honor students skip class and delinquents do all their homework. His attempts to gain power and overthrow his father pull him through a variety of adventures and complications. One teacher there is Count Vyers (from the first *Disgaea* game) who speaks with an Eastern European-esque accent and wears a red and black outfit with a wing-shaped cloak; this Count's fangs, long dark hair, and other similarities reveal his Dracula-inspired heritage.

Makai Senki Disugaia Tsū (*Disgaea 2: Cursed Memories* [United States]; *Makai Senki Disgaea 2*

Portable [rerelease for PSP, Japan]; *Disgaea 2: Dark Hero Days* [rerelease for PSP, United States]); Japan, 2006; Comedy, Adventure/Video Game; PlayStation 2 (Sony), PSP (Sony)/Tactical Role-Playing Game; color/Japanese, English; Nippon Ichi Software Inc./NIS America, Inc., KOEI Co., Ltd.

Producers: Sohei Niikawa, Kohichi Kitazumi; *Writing Credits:* Sohei Niikawa; *Director:* Haruo Sotozaki, Shinichi Ikeda; *Original Music:* Sohei Niikawa, Tenpei Satō; *Engineering/Technical Direction:* Yuzuru Nakayama; *Art Direction:* Kazuo Ebisawa, Haruo Sotozaki; *Creative Direction:* Masahiro Yamamoto, Shinichi Ikeda; *Programming:* Masahiro Yamamoto; *Cast:* Hikaru Midorikawa (Adell [voice, Japanese version]), Yukari Tamura (Rozalin [voice, Japanese version]), Tomoe Hanba (Etna [voice, Japanese version]), Junji Majima (Prinny, Masked Man [voices, Japanese version]), Hiro Shimono (Taro [voice, Japanese version]), Kaori Mizuhashi (Hanako, Overlord Laharl [voices, Japanese version]), Chihiro Suzuki (Tink [voice, Japanese version]), Kana Ueda (Yukimaru [voice, Japanese version]), Takehito Koyasu (Fubuki, Usagi [voices, Japanese version]), Rokurô Naya (Dad [voice, Japanese version, as Rokurou Naya]), Eriko Hara (Mom [voice, Japanese version]), Nobuyuki Hiyama (Axel [voice, Japanese version]), Takashi Nagasako (Director [voice, Japanese version]), Yûko Sasamoto (Masked Woman, Fallen Angel Flonne [voices, Japanese version, as Yuuko Sasamoto]), Norio Wakamoto (Overlord Zenon [voices, Japanese version]), Richard Epcar (Overlord Zetta, Prism Orange [voices, English version, uncredited]), Grant George (Axel, King Krychevskoy, Dark Adonis [voices, English version, uncredited]), Barbara Goodson (Laharl, Axel's little brother, Axel's mother [voices, English version, uncredited]), Steve Kramer (Dad, Prism Purple [voices, English version, uncredited]), Lex Lang (Overlord Zenon, Invincible Hero, Old Man Geo [voices, English version, uncredited]), Wendee Lee (Rozalin, Taro [voices, English version, uncredited]), David Lodge (Masked Man, Kurtis [voices, English version, uncredited]), Michael McConnohie (Captain Gordon [voice, English version, uncredited]), Mary Elizabeth McGlynn (Mom, Elenor [voices, English version, uncredited]), Lara Jill Miller (Yukimaru [voice, English version, uncredited]), Jamieson Price (Usagi, Prism Indigo [voices, English version, uncredited]), Derek Stephen Prince (Director, Prism Green, Pizza Delivery Man [voices, English version, uncredited]), Michelle Ruff (Etna [voice, English version, uncredited]), Stephanie Sheh (Hanako [voice, English version, uncredited]), Shiloh Strong (Adell [voice, English version, uncredited]), Kirk Thornton (Fubuki, Sammy, Prism Red [voices, English version, uncredited]), Dave Wittenberg (Tink, Prism Yellow [voices, English version, uncredited]).

Adell is the only human left on his world after a demon Overlord's curse turns everyone else into demons, so he makes it his mission to break the curse. Dark Adonis Vyers the hidden boss of an unlockable stage, but is assumed to just be the mid-boss. Count Vyers, a character from the first Disgaea, speaks with an Eastern European-esque accent and wears a red and black outfit with a wing-shaped cloak; this Count's fangs, long dark hair, and other similarities reveal his Dracula-inspired heritage.

McFarlane's Evil Prophecy (*Evil Prophecy*); United States, 2004; Action/Video Game; PlayStation 2 (Sony); color/English; Konami.

Producers: Kenichiro Imaizumi, Todd McFarlane; *Writing Credits:* Jean Eyestone, Kenichiro Imaizumi, Hitoshi Matsuda; *Director:* Kazuhiko Takata; *Original Music:* Jesper Kyd.

A prophecy predicts an age of darkness, and when the dead start rising from the grave, a group of expert monster hunters is called together. The hunters must fight monsters like Dracula, the Mummy, Frankenstein's Monster, and werewolves, as well as slightly less classic beings like sea monsters and a voodoo queen.

New International Track & Field; Japan, 2008; Sports/Video Game; Nintendo DS (Nintendo)/Olympiad; color/Japanese, English; Sumo Digital/Konami.

Producers: Pat Phelan, Tony Allen; *Engineering/Technical Direction:* Paul Porter; *Art Direction:* David Blewett (lead artist), Simon Bradley, Sean Millard; *Audio Direction:* John Broomhall; *Creative Direction:* Darren Mills; *Programming:* James Graves.

Players choose a character from a selection of eighteen (including Simon Belmont), use the DS stylus to compete in various track and field events, and even cheer (literally) to give the character a boost. Dracula is an archery target.

NightHunter; 1988; Horror, Action-Adventure/Video Game; Amiga (Amiga), Amstrad CPC (Amstrad), Atari ST (Atari), DOS, ZX Spectrum (Sinclair Research Ltd.)/2D platformer; color/English; Ubi Soft Entertainment Software.

Original Music: Christian Morel Bahler; *Art Direction:* Patrick Daher; *Creative Direction:* Olivier Marty; *Programming:* Nick Fitzsimons, Olivier Marty.

In this particular game, it is Dracula who is a controlled character, and he can morph into a bat and werewolf as he searches for magical objects to spread chaos around the world. Van Helsing and other vampire hunters are out to defeat the Count, and being out when the sun rises means instant death.

Operation Darkness; Japan, 2007; Action-Adventure/Video Game; XBox 360 (Microsoft)/RPG; color/Japanese/Dolby Digital; Success/Atlus.

Producers: Ken Ogura, Shinichi Suzuki, Takato Yoshinari; *Writing Credits:* Ken Ogura; *Director:* Hisakazu Masubuchi; *Engineering/Technical Direction:* Masaki Abe, Eiji Takaki; *Art Direction:* Shusaku Chamoto; *Audio Direction:* Tetsuro Sato; *Cast:* Tesshô Genda (Additional Voices [voice: Japanese version]), Kazuhiko Inoue (Additional Voices [voice: Japanese version]), Hiroshi Kamiya (Additional Voices [voice: Japanese version]), Jûrôta Kosugi (Additional Voices [voice: Japanese version]), Takehito Koyasu (Additional Voices [voice: Japanese version]), Toshiyuki Kusuda (Additional Voices [voice: Japanese version]), Masakazu Morita (Additional Voices [voice: Japanese version]), Takamasa Oohashi (Additional Voices [voice: Japanese version]), Akio Ôtsuka (Additional Voices [voice: Japanese version]), Asami Sanada (Additional Voices [voice: Japanese version]), Miyuki Sawashiro (Additional Voices [voice: Japanese version]), Naomi Shindô (Additional Voices [voice: Japanese version]), Troy Baker (Additional Voices [voice: English version] [uncredited]), Clayton Chan (Zombie/Alp [voice: English version] [uncredited]), Zach Hanks (Narrator [voice: English version] [uncredited]), Kyle Hebert (Additional Voices [voice: English version] [uncredited]), Megan Hollingshead (Additional Voices [voice: English version] [uncredited]), Lex Lang (Lewis Canton/Additional Voices [voice: English version] [uncredited]), Mela Lee (Additional Voices [voice: English version] [uncredited]), Wendee Lee (Elisa Van Helsing/Additional Voices [voice: English version] [uncredited]), Yuri Lowenthal (Edward Kyle/Additional Voices [voice: English version] [uncredited]), Michael McConnohie (Additional Voices [voice: English version] [uncredited]), Vic Mignogna (Additional Voices [voice: English version] [uncredited]), Daran Norris (Keith Miller/Alexander Vlado/Additional Voices [voice: English version] [uncredited]), Liam O'Brien (Jude Lancelot/Herbert East/Additional Voices [voice: English version] [uncredited]), Jamie Ortiz (American Soldier #3 [voice: English version] [uncredited]), Tara Platt (Carmilla/Additional Voices [voice: English version] [uncredited]), Jamieson Price (Frank Gaunt [voice: English version] [uncredited]), Derek Stephen Prince (Adolf Hitler/Jack the Ripper/Additional Voices [voice: English version] [uncredited]), Michelle Ruff (Additional Voices [voice: English version] [uncredited]), Jason Ruper (American Soldier #4 [voice: English version] [uncredited]), Douglas Rye (Additional Voices [voice: English version] [uncredited]), Patrick Seitz (Additional Voices [voice: English version] [uncredited]), Stephanie Sheh (Cordelia Blake/Additional Voices [voice: English version] [uncredited]), Spike Spencer (Additional Voices [voice: English version] [uncredited]), Paul St. Peter (James Gallant [voice: English version] [uncredited]), Karen Strassman (Leona [voice: English version] [uncredited]), Jessica Straus (Cynthia Rivele [voice: English version] [uncredited]), Kirk Thornton (Additional Voices [voice: English version] [uncredited]), Dave Wittenberg (Heinrich Himmler/Additional Voices [voice: English version] [uncredited]), Dan Woren (Additional Voices [voice: English version] [uncredited]).

The player must lead a British team of supernaturals against the Nazis in World War II. Nazi supernatural threats such as dragons and a team of vampires trying to resurrect Dracula are encountered during gameplay.

Pachislot Akumajō Dracula; Japan, 2008; Gambling/Video Game; Japanese Pachinko machine/Pachinko; color/Japanese.

The player buys small metal balls (if within a Pachinko palor) and inserts the balls into a "plinko"-like machine. If a ball goes through the central gate, an electronic slot spins and offers the player a chance to win more balls (which can sometimes be exchanged for prizes). This particular machine also awards players with a series of cut scenes creating a Castlevania story featuring Dracula.

Phantomas 2 (*Vampire* [U.K.]); 1986; Science Fiction, Action-Adventure/Video Game; Amstrad CPC (Amstrad), Commodore 64 (Commodore), ZX Spectrum (Sinclair Research Ltd.), MSX (Microsoft)/2D platformer; color/English; Dinamic Software/Codemasters.

Programming: Emilio Pablo Salgueiro Torrado.

The hero of the first *Phantomas* has returned from outer space to stop Count Dracula's reign of terror. The player, as the hero, must find various items to unlock areas while fighting Dracula's henchman; obtain a stake, hammer, and cross; and have a final showdown with Dracula using a "laser bolt and jet-pack thrusters."

Quackshot (*Alive! Donald Duck: Georgia Ou no Hihou* [Japan]); United States, 1991; Action-Adventure/Video Game; Genesis (SEGA)/3rd-person, side-scrolling, platform; color/English/Stereo; SEGA/SEGA.

Producer: Emirin; *Writing Credits:* Walt Disney; *Original Music:* Kamiya Studio; *Art Direction:* Takashi Thomas Yuda; *Audio Direction:* BO; *Creative*

Direction: Emirin; *Programming:* Muimui, Momonga Momo, M-Ohmori, Yamai, Ryuu, Tatsuyan.

Donald Duck (playable character) and his nephews find a treasure map and visit various places around the world to look for clues while using various wacky weapons. One world zone is Transylvania, where the player must enter the infamous castle for a boss battle with Count Duckula.

Realm of the Undead; 1984; Action/Video Game; ZX Spectrum (Sinclair Research Ltd)/maze; color/English; Express Programmes Company.

Programming: R. J. Yorke.

The player must navigate through maze versions of Dracula's garden, dungeon, and coffin-chambers while collecting garlic, a stake, and a hammer. Tarantulas, bats, zombies, and the Count himself must be avoided before collecting the items to slay Dracula.

Runescape; U.K., 2001; Fantasy/Video Game; Computer running Java/MMORPG; color/English; Jagex.

Director: Andrew G; *Engineering/Technical Direction:* Nick T; *Art Direction:* Joe R; *Audio Direction:* Ian T; *Creative Direction:* Alex J.

In this game, the player creates a character in a virtual world online with other player characters, defeats monsters, and completes quests. One quest is to defeat Count Draynor (who is outfitted in Dracula-type garb) using a killing blow with a hammer and wooden stake.

Rusty; Japan, 1993; Action-Adventure/Video Game; PC98 (NEC Corporation)/2D platformer; color/Japanese; C-lab.

Producer: Masayosi Koyama; *Writing Credits:* Naota Niida; *Director:* Naoto Niida; *Original Music:* Masahiro Kajihara, Kenichi Arakawa, Ryu Takami; *Programming:* Naoto Niida; *Cast:* Mieko Kato (voice), Ryoko Sano (voice), Tomoko Kato (voice), Junichi Nishiyama (voice), Masayoshi Koyama (voice), Yoshihiro Ohta (voice), Kuniyoshi Takazawa (voice).

Rusty, the player character, must fight through a castle to save what seems to be several women of her village and then defeat Dracula. This game has been (with very good reason) dubbed as a *Castlevania* clone, but *Akumajo Dracula X: Rondo of Blood*, the game it most closely resembles, came out three months after *Rusty* did. It is possible that *Rusty* had some ties to Konami during development but for some reason did not receive a *Castlevania* title.

Snatcher (*Snatcher: CD ROMantic* [Turbo CD title]); Japan, 1988; Science Fiction, Action-Adventure/Video Game; MSX (Microsoft), PlayStation (Sony), SEGA CD (Sega), SEGA Saturn (Sega), TurboGrafx CD (NEC)/Interactive Fiction, Shooter; color/Japanese and English; Konami.

Producers: Tomikazu Kirita, Yutaka Haruki; *Writing Credits:* Hideo Kojima, Mitsuhiro Togo, Jeremy Blaustein; *Director:* Yoshinori Sasaki; *Original Music:* Konami Kukeiha Club; *Art Direction:* Satoshi Kushibuchi; *Programming:* Masahiko Saito; *Cast:* Jeff Lupetin (as Gillian Seed; Snatcher), Lucy Childs (as Metal Gear; Female Employee), Jim Parks (as Random Hajile; Napoleon; Jean Jack Gibson; Ivan Rodorigez), Ray Van Steen (as Benson Cunningham; Harry Benson; Elijah Modnar; Chin Shu Oh; Narrator; Ramen Guy), Susan Mele (as Jamie Seed; Fortune Teller), Kimberley Harne (as Mika Slayton), Lynn Foosaner (as Katrina Gibson; Lisa; Telephone Operator).

The player takes the role of Gillian Seed, an amnesiac officer of the special JUNKER task force responsible for rooting out the human-replacing Snatchers. In a strip club scene in the Sega CD version of the game, two characters in the foreground are Dracula and Simon Belmont from Konami's *Castlevania* series. The main characters have a short discussion about the other game.

Transylvania; United States, 1982; Horror, Adventure/Video Game; Amiga (Amiga), Apple II (Apple Inc.), Atari 8-bit (Atari), Atari ST (Atari), Commodore 64 (Commodore), DOS, Macintosh (Apple Inc.)/text-based; color/English; Penguin Software, Inc.

Programming: Antonio Antiochia.

King John the Good is looking for someone to save his daughter Princess Sabrina, and the player's character volunteers to search the woods of Transylvania. There he finds vampires, goblins, a werewolf who is hunting him, and Dracula.

Transylvania II: The Crimson Crown (*The Crimson Crown* [common title]; *Further Adventures in Transylvania* [subtitle]); United States, 1985; Horror, Adventure/Video Game; Amiga (Amiga), Apple II (Apple Inc.), Atari ST (Atari), Commodore 64 (Commodore), DOS, Macintosh (Apple Inc.)/text-based; color depends on system/English; Polarware.

Writing Credits: Antonio Antiochia; *Programming:* Antonio Antiochia.

King John the Good is dead, and Vampire Lord Drakul has stolen the magic crown to become king. The player's character sets off with magic-using Princess Sabrina and the royal Crown Prince Erik to stop Drakul's evil plan.

Vampire Night (*Xixuegui zhi Ye* [China]); Japan, 2000; Horror, Action/Video Game; Arcade, PlayStation 2 (Sony)/FPS; color/Japanese, English; Wow Entertainment Inc., Namco Limited, SEGA/Namco Hometek Inc.

Producer: Yasuhiro Noguchi.

Albert and Michel, the player characters, are two half-vampire vampire hunters who seek to destroy the Dracula-type Count Auguste and all vampires for good. 1 or 2 players use special "gun-controllers" to direct their in-game bullets towards the various vampires and monsters that try to stop the quest.

Vampire's Empire; United States, 1988; Horror, Action/Video Game; Amiga (Amiga), Atari ST (Atari), Commodore 64 (Commodore), MSX (Microsoft), ZX Spectrum (Sinclair Research Ltd)/2D platformer; color/English; Magic Bytes/DigiTek Software, Gremlin Graphics Software Ltd., Dro Soft.

Original Music: Georg Brandt; *Art Direction:* Bernard Morell, Stefan Rissmann; *Programming:* Gisbert Siegmund, Jörg Prenzing, Michael Oelze.

Doctor Van Helsing, the player character, is attempting to rid the world of Count Dracula while only armed with mirrors and a light beam. Bats, snakes, and coffins must be avoided while the doctor slays the vampires.

A Vampyre Story: Chapter One (*A Vampyre Story: Кровавый роман* [Russia]; *A Vampyre Story* [common title]); Germany, 2008; Horror, Adventure/Video Game; Macintosh (Apple Inc.), Windows (Microsoft)/Puzzle; color/German, Russian, English; Autumn Moon Entertainment LLC/Crimson Cow.

Producers: Amy Tiller, William V. Tiller; *Writing Credits:* William V. Tiller, Dave Harris, William L. Eaken; *Director:* William V. Tiller; *Original Music:* Pedro Macedo Camacho; *Engineering/Technical Direction:* Jory K. Prum; *Art Direction:* James Almeida; *Programming:* Geoff Goldberg; *Cast:* Celine Fontanges (German voice of: Mona), Tetje Mierendorf (German voice of: Froderick), Bernd Stephan (German voice), Michael Grimm (German voice), Monty Arnold (German voice), Kristina von Weltzien (German voice), Helgo Liebig (German voice), Frank Felicetti (German voice), Reent Reins (German voice), Nicolas König (German voice), Agnes Regan (German voice), Jennifer Böttcher (German voice), Hennes Bender (German voice), Guido Zimmermann (German voice), Rebecca Schweitzer (English voice of: Mona de Laffite, Mina Stoker, Shannon O'Doherty), Jeremy Koerner (English voice of: Froderick), Molly Benson (English voice of: Woman of Low Moral Fiber), David Boyle (English voice of: Milton T. Meininger, Band Leader, Constable Bud Crane, Constable Lou Crane, Constable Otto Van Pelt), Gavin Hammon (English voice of: Monsignor Calvin), Suzanne Henry (English voice of: Gina Martinelli, Jersey Lady), Melissa Hutchinson (English voice of: Pyewacket), Liz Mamorsky (English voice of: Madam Strigoi), Amy Rubinate (English voice of: Barb the Iron Maiden), Brian Sommer (English voice of: Balcu, Shrowdy Von Kiefer, Shrodwy Ghost), Tim Talbot (English voice of: Edgar Raven, Rufus the Gargoyle, Frankie the Rat, Ozzy the Gargoyle), Sam O'Byrne (English voice of: Siegfried and Roy Stoker).

Several years before the game begins, the opera singer Mona de Laffite has been turned by the diminutive Dracula Baron Shrowdy von Kiefer and abducted to his castle in Draxsylvania. After Shrowdy is killed one day, Mona takes a chance and tries to escape, the player guiding her along the path to freedom.

Van Helsing (United States, 2004; Horror, Action-Adventure)/Video Game; XBox (Microsoft), PS2 (Sony)/3rd person shooter; color/English/Dolby; Saffire Corporation/Vivendi Universal Games, Inc.

Producers: William Oertel, Nathan Whitman; *Director:* John Slowsky; *Original Music:* Steve Kutay, Michael A. Reagan, Tom Zehnder, Cris Velasco; *Art Direction:* Walter Park; *Audio Direction:* Rick Bradshaw; *Programming:* Joel Barber; *Cast:* Hugh Jackman (Van Helsing [voice] [archive footage]), Richard Roxburgh (Dracula [voice] [archive footage]), Will Kemp (Velkan/The Wolf Man [voice]), Kevin J. O'Connor (Igor [voice] [archive footage]), Shuler Hensley (The Frankenstein Monster [voice] [archive footage]), Alun Armstrong (Cardinal Jinette [voice] [archive footage]), Silvia Colloca (Verona [voice]), Josie Maran (Marishka [voice] [archive footage]), Kathryn Cressida (Aleera [voice] [archive footage] [as Kat Cressida]), Mandy Steckelberg (Anna [voice] [archive footage]), Fred Tatasciore (Valerious [voice] [archive footage]), Bob Joles (Hyde [voice] [archive footage]), Ivo Nanov (Villager [voice] [archive footage]), Courtenay Taylor (Additional Voices [voice]), Jenna Macari (Villager [voice] [archive footage]), James Horan (Villager [voice] [archive footage]), Neil Kaplan (Villager [voice] [archive footage]), Robin Atkin Downes (Additional Voices [voice] [archive footage]), Angie Jaree (Singer [voice] [archive footage]), David Wenham (Carl/Karl [voice] [archive footage]), Steve Wilcox.

The legendary Dr. Van Helsing, the player character, travels throughout Transylvania fighting monsters like the wolfman, Mr. Hyde, Frankenstein's Monster, and finally, Dracula.

Vlad Tepes Dracula (*Dracula: Reign of Terror* [alternate title]; *Dracula: Le Guerrier des Carpates* (*Dracula: The Warrior of Carpathians*) [Canada]); United States, 1997; Historical Fiction/Video Game; Windows (Microsoft)/Battle strategy; color/English and French; ComputerHouse GBG AB/SoftKey Multimedia Inc.

Producers: Peter Pettersson, Mikael Östberg; *Original Music:* Carl Hansson; *Art Direction:* Per Simonsson; *Audio Direction:* Carl Hansson; *Programming:* Peter Pettersson, Erik Möller; *Cast:* Jim Georgiades (voice), Carl Hansson (voice), Per Simonsson (voice), Thomas Backman (voice).

The Turkish armies have been sweeping across Eastern Europe and claiming lands for their empire. It is the player's goal to rebuild the army of Vlad Tepes Dracula and reclaim his lost lands.

Wai Wai World 2: SOS! Parsley Jō (*Wai Wai World 2: SOS!! Parsley Castle* [United States]); Japan, 1991; Action-Adventure/Video Game; Nintendo (Nintendo)/2D platformer, scrolling shooter, driving, puzzle; color/Japanese, English; Konami.

A parody of previous Konami games and characters, the player character is a robot with the ability to transform into various Konami characters in order to save the princess of Konami world. Simon Belmont III is one of the usable characters, and Dracula makes an appearance as a normal enemy in Simon's level.

PART IV

Dracula in Comic Books

Introduction —
The Darker Cape: Dracula, Vampires, and Superheroes in Comics

Mitch Frye

While Dracula and his fellow bloodsuckers have seldom featured prominently in popular comics, their presence in the background has been both enduring and entertaining. Industry self-regulations forbade vampires from appearing in works by Marvel, DC, and the other major publishing houses from 1954 to 1971, but these restrictions have been lifted for decades, allowing Dracula-inspired works to carve out a respectable niche for themselves in the larger market. Nevertheless, horror comics in general have historically struggled against competition from works in the superhero genre, because the industry's most prominent publishers devote the bulk of their resources to titles featuring big name heroes.[1] In some cases, vampires have been assimilated into the bombastic textual terrain of the costumed crime-fighter. Marvel and DC, for instance, have embraced the Dracula mythos as part of their mainstream continuity. In other cases, creators have had the freedom to invent original tales unhindered by ongoing plots in other titles. Independent publishers like Dark Horse and IDW have sought to profit from the continuing popularity of vampire stories by offering writers and artists this sort of creative freedom. Scott McCloud's comments on alternative storytelling in the comics format apply especially well to the endurance of vampire comics: "Against a sea of superheroes other genres held on. And still do today."[2]

Moving Pictures and Funny Books

Vampires have walked among superheroes in comics since the 1930s. One of Batman's earliest adversaries was the Mad Monk, a hooded vampire who battled the Caped Crusader in two issues of *Detective Comics* from 1939. Creators Bob Kane and Bill Finger modeled Batman's own costume in part on Dracula's cape and cowl combo. Because of this apparent nod to Bram Stoker's work and its contribution to Batman's prominent role in comics history, one may be tempted to regard the author's influence on the medium as an exciting intersection of gothic literature and pop art. The reality is that cinema has been more directly responsible for the presence of Dracula and his blood-brethren in comics. In the history of comic book vampire stories, we see the symbiotic relationship between two industries: film and comics. Kane and Finger's conceptualization of the Batman costume as a heroic take on Dracula's attire relied not on Stoker's 1897 text but instead on Universal's 1931 film starring Béla Lugosi, and this preference for cinematic influence over literary allusion has subsequently defined the cultural parameters of the comic book vampire.

Vampires have generally played a very small part in the story continuity maintained by Batman's publisher, DC Comics. Aside from a few pseudo-vampiric characters (for instance, Brother Blood, the Teen Titans villain) and alternate reality tales (including Doug Moench and Kelly Jones's *Batman & Dracula: Red Rain*), the Dracula legend has been used rather sparingly by DC writers. Perhaps this is because the world of DC Comics is colorful and cartoonish, a decidedly inhospitable environment for gothic storytelling. On the other hand, their darker Vertigo imprint has published a handful of vampire stories in the *Preacher* and *Bite Club* titles.

DC's primary competitor, Marvel Comics, has always touted itself as the grittier of the two, so naturally Marvel has found more opportunity to employ vampire motifs. In 1971, Marvel incorporated two vampiric characters into their fictional universe. In *Amazing Spider-Man* #101, writer Roy Thomas introduced Michael Morbius, a scientist who accidentally turned himself into a pseudo-vampire when he tried to cure himself of a fatal disease with an infusion of bat blood. While not strictly a textbook vampire, Morbius displayed many of the essential traits (blood-thirst, fangs, the ability to fly, etc.). The *Tomb of Dracula* title, published in the early-1970s and stylistically indebted to Hammer's vampire movies, brought the real thing—Dracula himself—into the Marvel Universe. While the series' writing was never first-rate, its art (supplied by comics legend Gene Colan) certainly was. This mixture of awkward plotting and provocative visuals has led comics critic Douglas Wolk to describe *Tomb* as "the cheap, strong stuff ... a genre comic—not a twist on vampire horror, but a straight-up, lustily and faithfully executed vampire story."[3] While *Tomb* cannot be praised for its storytelling innovations, it must be given due credit for fully incorporating vampire fiction into mainstream comics. The series established that Stoker's Dracula character would continue to impact the fictional lives of Marvel superheroes for years to come. Characters from Spider-Man to Captain Britain have since battled the likes of Count Dracula and Morbius in the comics, and Marvel has preserved these stories within its continuity canon. DC, on the other hand, has either retconned their own, allowing future writers to ignore them, or labeled them as "Elseworlds" tales, which are regarded independently from happenings in the DC Universe proper.

It is also worth noting that Marvel has created the most popular vampire hunter since Stoker's own Van Helsing. In 1973, *Tomb of Dracula* debuted a new hero, Blade the Daywalker, to function as the title's occasional protagonist. One suspects that writer Marv Wolfman derived his inspiration for the African American vampire hunter from the blaxploitation films of the 1970s. Blade first appeared in comics three years after *Shaft* hit theaters and one year after *Blacula* inverted the Eurocentric norms of the original *Dracula* story. Thus, Blade is essentially a comic book pastiche of Shaft and Blacula, bearing a name reminiscent of the former and possessing the vampiric associations of the latter. Over the character's thirty-odd year history, he has become the most recognizable African American hero in mainstream comics. Others—like Black Goliath, Luke Cage, and the Falcon— have retained a cult status, but Blade alone has moved beyond the comics medium into film and television. He has transcended his blaxploitation roots in a way that has eluded these other characters, who remain mired in what Jeffrey A. Brown has called the "limited stereotype" of the form.[4] Yet despite Blade's popularity, it can hardly be said that vampire stories represent a significant portion of what Marvel publishes in its comics or produces in its films.

If the superheroic preoccupations of mainstream comics writers have prevented them from more fully utilizing the Dracula mythos, writers for the indie publishers have certainly picked up their slack. In the past two decades, independent companies such as Dark Horse and IDW in particular have made names for themselves by offering readers dark alternatives to the typical superhero story. Dark Horse's *Hellboy*, *BPRD*, and *The Goon* ongoing titles regularly feature stories about vampires and other supernatural creatures of the night. In the early-2000s, IDW's Alaskan vampire tale *30 Days of Night* became an overnight sensation, first as a bestselling comic series and, later, as a feature film. Ben Templesmith, the artist whose frenetic style helped make the series a massive success, went on to illustrate a new edition of the *Dracula* novel, which was published by IDW in 2009.

Indie publishers have also cornered the market on film adaptations, a genre in which the motion picture industry displays an even greater control over the depiction of vampires in comics than it normally does. In adapting films for serial adaptation in the comics medium, artists and writers will often take some liberties with the script, but the plot is nevertheless predetermined, and the story itself must be read separately from the ongoing events in the publisher's continuity.

Douglas Wolk identifies this type of series as a misuse of the comics form: "When comics try to be *specific* movies or novels, they are indeed unsuccessful. Comics adaptations of movies are pointless cash-ins at best — movies that don't move, with inaccurate drawings of the actors and scenery. Why would anyone but an obsessive want to look at that?"[5]

Nevertheless, a few of these projects are notable. For example, Topps' 1992 adaptation of *Bram Stoker's Dracula* features relatively early art from Mike Mignola, who would go on to create the aforementioned *Hellboy* franchise. Also, Now Comics' adaptation of *Fright Night* offered new stories set within the world of the movie franchise.

Obviously, other media besides film have impacted the comic book vampire, albeit to a lesser extent. Marvel currently publishes *Anita Blake: Vampire Hunter*, a title based on Laurel K. Hamilton's bestselling fiction series, and IDW has seen partial success with Konami's *Castlevania* video game franchise. When the popular *Buffy the Vampire Slayer* television program went off the air after seven seasons, series creator and pop culture icon Joss Whedon decided to produce future seasons in the comic book format. History, too, has proven to be a source of inspiration for the vampire comic genre; Topps published a *Vlad the Impaler* mini-series in 1993 to explore the historical character hinted at in the Coppola film. But perhaps the greatest impetus for the publication of vampire stories in comic books has come, ironically, from the U.S. government's attack on the medium.

Suppression and Resurgence

In the late-1940s, psychiatrist Frederic Wertham began his assault on the comic book industry, claiming that comics contributed significantly to juvenile delinquency. Other activists had previously sought to make the same point, but Wertham's scientific demeanor and humanistic approach achieved more credibility than the strategies of his religious-minded predecessors. He published a series of articles on the subject of comics and delinquency in popular magazines. These eventually became the basis of his 1954 book *The Seduction of the Innocent*. Wertham's critique of fascist, sexist, racist, and sadistic elements in comics was damning, especially to post–World War II parents keen on stamping out anti–American sentiment. He argued that comics foster "distrust for democratic law."[6] Moreover, Wertham singled out the Dracula-inspired Batman title as a "homosexual and anti-feminine" work; he described the cohabitation of Batman and Robin as a "wish dream of two homosexuals living together."[7] Aside from these scattershot attacks on the superhero genre, the funny books that received the greater part of his vitriol were comics of crime and horror, such as those published by Entertaining Comics (more commonly known as EC Comics).

Following the public outcry resulting from Wertham's scare tactics, a U.S. Senate subcommittee formed and called a hearing on the comics industry.

Senators and psychiatrists spent several days humiliating industry representatives. William Gaines, publisher of EC Comics, was harshly questioned regarding his company's graphic horror titles. The subcommittee took special interest in a *Haunt of Fear* story that concerned a werewolf boy taken in by vampire foster parents who try to kill him. The investigators asked Gaines what effect he thought the story would have on actual foster children; for good measure, they also asked him if he believed in vampires.[8] This line of questioning, equal parts witch hunt and nonsequitur, succeeded in making the industry's representatives look like irresponsible monsters. As a result, the committee achieved two of its major goals. First, the industry's self-regulating Comics Code Authority (CCA) was established in 1954 to censor sex, violence, and subversive themes in comic books. Second, EC, publisher of *Vault of Horror, Crypt of Terror,* and *Haunt of Fear,* ceased publication of these books to focus on less controversial genres. Vampires and other supernatural creatures were prohibited from appearing in CCA-approved titles, and egregious violence no longer had a place in the medium, so the heyday of horror comics had ended.

This led to the rise of the comparatively tamer superhero genre, which had previously faced stiff competition from crime and horror titles but now found itself more capable of adapting to the new regulations than its competitors. Such books remained relatively tame until DC and Marvel began bucking CCA standards in the late-1960s and early-1970s, when the industry closed ranks and its leaders met to liberalize the outdated regulations. While the prohibitions on sex remained firmly in place, the 1971 revisions allowed for more violence and for the return of supernatural entities to the medium.[9] As noted earlier, Marvel immediately capitalized on this loosening of restrictions by deploying a number of vampire characters and stories. The publisher clearly recognized that its readers were eager to receive supernatural tales, having been starved of them for two decades by censorship and suppression. Its *Tomb of Dracula* title served as an homage to the EC horror comics of the 1950s, though the code still prevented them from indulging in the gore that had made those publications so infamous.

Realizing there was a market for violent books that bypassed CCA approval, Marvel and other publishers offered unrated magazine titles as alternatives to their regulated mainstream comics. These magazines were generally larger than the standard comic format, and they were often published in black and white. In addition to fantasy magazines like *Conan* and vigilante titles like *The Punisher*, Marvel introduced a handful of horror books in the mid–1970s. Many of these paid homage to the Universal monsters of Hollywood's past, and several starred Dracula himself. Such titles included *Dracula Lives, Monsters Unleashed,* and *The Legion of Monsters.* Though the writers assigned to these books were often the same people writing stories for Marvel and DC's CCA-approved material, it is clear for a number of reasons that the monster magazines of the 1970s were geared towards a post-pubescent readership. First, the books lacked color illustrations, which the child psychiatrists of Wertham's day held to be a major draw for young readers. Second, the stories in the magazines starred monsters that had been popularized in the 1950s, so the ideal reader for such works would be at least in his or her twenties. Third, the magazines cost approximately three times as much as regular comics and were not as widely available as mainstream titles, which could often be purchased on spinner racks in convenience stores and supermarkets. This manner of targeted marketing foreshadowed the future of comics publishing.

While publishers of modern comics continue to self-regulate their titles through the CCA, graphic violence, sexual innuendo, and supernatural elements are no longer forbidden by the code. A considerable number of comics bypass these lax standards entirely and are published with no regard to the code whatsoever. Today, the majority of fans are grownups, thanks to a set of restrictions that have little to do with censorship and a lot to do with economics. Modern comics are relatively pricey and available only in specialty stores, so — like the horror magazines of the 1970s — they are geared towards nostalgic adults. The industry has become far more receptive to mature content, and, as a result, the sequential art format proves to be an increasingly appropriate vehicle for vampire stories indebted to the Dracula mythos, even if these are vastly outnumbered by tales of superheroes and their derring-do. Creators like Steve Niles, Mike Mignola, and Eric Powell continue to refine the art of horror writing in a medium still saddled with superheroic conventions.

Notes

1. The years 1949 to 1954 constitute the only period in the history of comics publishing that horror comics have outranked superhero books in popularity. See David Hajdu's *The Ten-Cent Plague: The Great Comic Book Scare and How It Changed America* (New York: Picador, 2008) for a full discussion of the factors that allowed the genre to prosper uncensored for half a decade.

2. Scott McCloud, *Reinventing Comics: How Imagination and Technology Are Revolutionizing an Art Form* (New York: HarperCollins, 2000).

3. Douglas Wolk, "*Tomb of Dracula*: The Cheap, Strong Stuff," *Reading Comics: How Graphic Novels Work and What They Mean* (Cambridge, MA: Da Capo, 2007), 321–23.

4. Jeffrey A. Brown, *Black Superheroes, Milestone Comics, and Their Fans* (Jackson: University Press of Mississippi, 2001), 4.

5. Wolk, "What Comics Are and What They Aren't," *Reading Comics*, 13.

6. Frederic Wertham, *The Seduction of the Innocent* (New York: Rinehart, 1953), 96.

7. Wertham, *Seduction of the Innocent*, 190–91.

8. Bradford W. Wright, *Comic Book Nation: The Transformation of Youth Culture in America* (Baltimore: Johns Hopkins University Press, 2001), 165–68.

9. Amy Kiste Nyberg, *Seal of Approval: The History of the Comics Code* (Jackson: University of Mississippi Press, 1998), 139–42.

Comics Listing

Action Planet Comics (1996–1998). No. 1–2 (Action Planet), No. 3 (Image), Giant-Size Special No. 1. Action Planet/Image. b&w.

Adventures into Terror. No. 6 (Oct. 1951), No. 18 (Apr. 1953). Marvel/Atlas. color.

Adventures into the Unknown. No. 29 (March 1952). American Comics Group. color.

The Adventures of Jerry Lewis. No. 83 (1964). DC.

The Adventures of Olivia. No. 3 (Fall 1991). Jabberwocky. b&w. Adult. Magazine.

Alf Annual. No. 2 (1989). Marvel.

Amazing Heroes. No. 11 (1982), No. 164 (May 1, 1989). Fantagraphics. Portfolio.

Amora. No. 1 (Apr. 1991). Eros Comics. b&w/color. Adult.

Anton's Collected Drek Featuring Wendy Whitebread. 2nd Expanded Ed. No. 3 (1994). Eros Comix/Eros GraphicAlbums. Adult. b&w. Rpt. in 3rd Ed. (1995) and 4th Ed. (1997). color.

Amazing Spider-man. Giant-Size No. 1 (July 1974). Marvel. color.

Anything Goes! No. 3 (Mar. 1986). Fantagraphics Books. b&w/color.

Archie. No. 123 (Nov. 1961). Archie Comics.

Archie Giant Series Magazine. No. 571 (Sep. 1987). Archie Comics. color.

Archie's Double Digest Magazine. No. 49 (Nov. 1990). Archie Comics. color.

Archie's Madhouse. No. 8 (Oct. 1960.), No. 21 (Sep. 1962.), No. 29 (Oct. 1963.), No. 43 (Oct. 1965). Archie Comics.

Army of Darkness (2005–2007). No. 8–11. Dynamite Entertainment.

Army of Darkness: Ash Vs. The Classic Monsters (and More) ("Ash Vs. Dracula"). No. 8–11 (2006). Dynamite Entertainment. color.

ARRGH! (1974–1975). No. 1–2, No. 4–5. Marvel. color.

The Art of Neal Adams. No. 2 (1977). Sal Quartuccio. b&w.

Avengers (1963–1996). Vol. 1. No. 118, Annual No. 16. Marvel. color

The Avengers. No. 2 (Sep. 29, 1973), No. 44 (July 20, 1974). Marvel. U.K. color.

The Bash Street Kids Summer Special (1998). D.C. Thomson. U.K. color.

Batman & Dracula (2002). No. 1 (One-Shot). Panini. Germany. color.

Batman and Dracula: Red Rain (1991). No. 1–1A (Trade Paperback, Softcover/Hardcover). DC. color.

Batman and Dracula: Red Rain (1991). No. 1. Titan. U.K. Trade Paperback. color.

Batman and Dracula: Red Rain (1991). No. 1. Warner Books. Trade Paperback. color.

Batman: Nosferatu (1999). No. 1. DC. Trade Paperback.

The Beano. No. 2318 (20 Dec 1986), No. 2358 (Sep. 26, 1987), No. 2615 (Aug. 29, 1992), No. 2844 (Jan. 18, 1997), No. 2869 (July 12, 1997), No. 2988 (Oct. 23, 1999), No. 2989 (Oct. 30, 1999). DC Thomson. U.K. Magazine. color.

The Beano Book. No. 59 (1999). D.C. Thomson. U.K. Hardcover.

Beano Comic Library (1982–1995). No. 35, No. 132. DC Thomson. U.K..

The Beezer and Cracker (1956–1993). No. 1140 (Nov. 19, 1977), No. 1267 (Apr. 26, 1980), No. 1656 (Oct. 10, 1987), No. 1659 (Oct. 31, 1987), No. 1661 (Nov. 14, 1987), No. 1675 (Feb. 20, 1988), No. 1679 (Mar. 19, 1988), No. 1680 (Mar. 26, 1988), No. 1682 (Apr. 9, 1988), No. 1685 (Apr. 30, 1988), No. 1691 (June 11, 1988), No. 1692 (June 18, 1988), No. 1694 (July 2, 1988), No. 1695 (July 9, 1988), No. 1697 (July 23, 1988), No. 1701 (Aug. 20, 1988), No. 1708 (Oct. 8, 1988), No. 1710 (Oct. 22, 1988), No. 1737 (Apr. 29, 1989), No. 1784 (Mar. 24, 1990). D.C. Thomson. U.K. Magazine. color.

The Beezer and Topper. No. 108 (Oct. 10, 1992), No. 111 (Oct. 31, 1992). D.C. Thomson. U.K. Magazine. color.

The Beezer Book (1996). D.C. Thomson. U.K. Hardcover.

The Beezer Summer Special (1991). D.C. Thomson. U.K. Magazine.
Before the Fantastic Four: The Storms (2000). No. 1–3. Marvel.
Beowulf Dragon Slayer. No. 4 (1975). DC. color.
The Best of Buster Monthly (Sep. 1987). IPC Magazines/Fleetway. b&w. Magazine.
The Best of Drag Cartoons. No. 1 (1968), No. 2 (1969). Rex Publishing Company. b&w. Rpt. Magazine.
The Best of National Lampoon. No. 3 (1972). National Lampoon, Inc. b&w. Rpt. Magazine
The Best of Whizzer and Chips (Jan. 1989). Fleetway. U.K. Magazine.
The Best of Whoopee! (Sep. 1985.), (Nov. 1985.), (Dec. 1985). IPC Magazines. U.K. Magazine.
Big Bad Blood of Dracula (1991). No. 1–2. Apple. b&w.
Big Bang Comics. Vol. 2., No. 16 (Jan. 1998). Image.
The Big Book of Bad (1998). Factoid Books/Paradox Press. b&w. Anthology. Oversize format.
The Big Comic. No. 3 (July 9–22, 1988), No. 4 (July 23–Aug. 5, 1988), No. 16 (Jan. 7–20, 1989), No. 18 (Feb. 4–17, 1989), No. 27 (June 10–23, 1989), No. 28 (June 24/July 7, 1989), No. 29 (July 8–21, 1989), No. 33 (Sep. 2–15, 1989), No. 34 (Sep. 16–29, 1989), No. 36 (Oct. 14–27, 1989), No. 37 (Oct. 28/Nov. 10, 1989), No. 42 (Jan. 6–19, 1990), No. 50 (Apr. 28/May 11, 1990), No. 52 (May 26/June 8, 1990), No. 53 (June 9–22, 1990), No. 54 (June 23/July 6, 1990), No. 56 (July 21/Aug. 3, 1990), No. 61 (Sep. 29–Oct. 12, 1990), No. 66 (Dec. 8–21, 1990), No. 93 (Dec. 21, 1991/Jan. 3, 1992), No. 95 (Jan. 18–31, 1992), No. 105 (June 6–19, 1992), No. 106 (June 30–July 3, 1992), No. 134 (July 17–30, 1993), No. 167 (Nov. 4, 1994). Fleetway. U.K. b&w. Magazine.
The Big Comic Holiday Special (1998). Fleetway. U.K.
Billy Joe Van Helsing: Redneck Vampire Hunter. No. 1 (Dec. 1994). Alpha Productions. b&w.
Black Cat Mystery. No. 34 (Apr. 1952). Harvey Comics.
Bizarre Adventures (1981–1983). No. 33. Marvel. Magazine.
Blade (2006). No. 1. Marvel. color
Blade: The Vampire Hunter (1994–1995). No. 1–3, 8, 10. Marvel. color.
Blood of Dracula (1987–1990). No. 1–20. Apple.
Blood of the Innocent (1986). No. 1–4, and Preview (1985). Warp Graphics.
Bloodstone (2001–2002). No. 1–2, 4. Marvel.
The Blood Sword. No. 4 (Nov. 1988). Jademan Comics.
Boris Karloff: Tales of Mystery. No. 85 (Oct. 1978). Gold Key.

Bram Stoker's Dracula (1992–1993). No. 1, 1A–1B, 2–4; No. 1, 1A (Trade Paperback). Topps. Movie Adaptation. color.
Bram Stoker's Dracula. (1980). Delacorte Press. Hardcover (dj). Trade Paperback. Large format.
Bram Stoker's Dracula (1980). Heineman. U.K. Hardcover (dj).
Bram Stoker's Dracula (1993). Titan. U.K. Trade Paperback..
Bram Stoker's Dracula (1993). Topps. Trade Paperback.
Bram Stoker's Dracula (1993). Topps/Diamond Comics Distributors. Trade Paperback.
Bram Stoker's Dracula (1993). Topps. Star Edition. Trade Paperback.
Bride of Heavy Metal (1985). HM Communications. Trade Paperback.
Burger King Kids Club Adventures. Vol. 8, No. 7 (1997). Promotional give-away.
Buster. (Mar. 27, 1976), (Nov. 13, 1976), (Nov. 20, 1976), (Dec. 4, 1976), (Dec. 12, 1976), (Dec. 25, 1976), (Jan. 1, 1977), (Jan. 15, 1977), (Jan. 29, 1977), (Feb. 5, 1977), (Feb. 26, 1977), (Mar. 5, 1977), (Sep. 10, 1977), (Sep. 17, 1977), (Oct. 1, 1977), (Oct. 15, 1977), (Oct. 22, 1977), (Mar. 24, 1984) (July 7, 1984), (Oct. 13, 1984), (May 18, 1985), (July 6, 1985), (May 3, 1987), (May 30, 1987), (June 6, 1987), (June 13, 1987), (June 20, 1987), (June 27, 1987), (July 4, 1987), (July 11, 1987, (July 18, 1987), (July 25, 1987), (Aug. 1, 1987), (Aug. 8, 1987), (Aug. 15, 1987), (Aug. 22, 1987), (Aug. 29, 1987), (Sep. 5, 1987), (Sep. 12, 1987), (Sep. 19, 1987), (Sep. 26, 1987), (Oct. 3, 1987), (Oct. 10, 1987), (Oct. 17, 1987), (Oct. 24, 1987), (Oct. 31, 1987), (Nov. 7, 1987), (Nov. 14, 1987), (Nov. 21, 1987), (Nov. 28, 1987), (Dec. 5, 1987), (Dec. 12, 1987), (Dec. 19, 1987) , (Dec. 26, 1987), (Jan. 2, 1988), (Jan. 9, 1988), (Jan. 16, 1988), (Jan. 23, 1988), (Jan. 30, 1988), (Feb. 6, 1988), (Feb. 13, 1988), (Feb. 20, 1988), (Feb. 27, 1988), (Mar. 5, 1988), (Mar. 12, 1988), (Mar. 19, 1988), (Mar. 26, 1988), (Apr. 2, 1988), (Apr. 9, 1988), (Apr. 16, 1988), (Apr. 23, 1988), (Apr. 30, 1988), (May 7, 1988), (May 14, 1988), (May 21, 1988), (May 28, 1988), (June 4, 1988), (June 11, 1988), (June 18, 1988), (June 25, 1988), (July 2, 1988), (July 9, 1988), (July 16, 1988), (July 23, 1988), (July 30, 1988), (Aug. 6, 1988), (Aug. 13, 1988), (Aug. 20, 1988), (Aug. 27, 1988), (Sep. 10, 1988), (Sep. 17, 1988), (Sep. 24, 1988), (Oct. 1, 1988), (Oct. 29, 1988), (Nov. 5, 1988), (Nov. 12, 1988), (Nov. 19, 1988), (Nov. 26, 1988), (Dec. 3, 1988), (Dec. 10, 1988), (Dec. 24, 1988), (Jan. 7, 1989), (Jan. 14, 1989), (Jan. 21, 1989), (Feb. 4, 1989), (Feb. 11, 1989), (Feb. 25, 1989), (Mar. 4, 1989), (Mar. 11, 1989), (Mar. 18, 1989), (Mar. 25, 1989), (Apr. 1, 1989), (Apr.

8, 1989), (Apr. 15, 1989), (Apr. 22, 1989), (Apr. 29, 1989), (May 6, 1989), (May 13, 1989), (May 20, 1989), (June 3, 1989), (June 10, 1989), (June 17, 1989), (June 24, 1989), (July 1, 1989), (July 8, 1989), (July 15, 1989), (July 22, 1989), (July 29, 1989), (Aug. 5, 1989), (Aug. 12, 1989), (Aug. 26, 1989), (Sep. 2, 1989), (Sep. 9, 1989), (Sep. 16, 1989), (Sep. 23, 1989), (Sep. 30, 1989), (Oct. 21, 1989), (Oct. 28, 1989), (Nov. 4, 1989), (Nov. 11, 1989), (Nov. 25, 1989, (Dec. 2, 1989), (Dec. 9, 1989), (Dec. 16, 1989), (Dec. 23, 1989), (Dec. 30, 1989), (Jan. 6, 1990), (Jan. 13, 1990), (Jan. 20, 1990), (Jan. 27, 1990), (Feb. 3, 1990), (Feb. 10, 1990, (Feb. 17, 1990), (Feb. 24, 1990), (Mar. 10, 1990), (Mar. 17, 1990), (Mar. 31, 1990), (Apr. 7, 1990), (Apr. 14, 1990), (Apr. 21, 1990), (Apr. 28, 1990), (May 5, 1990), (May 12, 1990), (May 19, 1990), (June 2, 1990), (June 9, 1990), (June 16, 1990), (June 23, 1990) (July 7, 1990, (July 14, 1990), (July 21, 1990), (July 28, 1990), (Aug. 4, 1990), (Aug. 11, 1990), (Aug. 18, 1990), (Aug. 25, 1990), (Sep. 1, 1990), (Sep. 8, 1990), (Sep. 15, 1990), (Sep. 22, 1990), (Sep. 29, 1990), (Oct. 13, 1990), (Oct. 20, 1990), (Nov. 3, 1990), (Nov. 10, 1990), (Nov. 17, 1990), (Nov. 24, 1990), (Dec. 8, 1990), (Dec. 15, 1990), (Dec. 22, 1990), (Jan. 5, 1991), (Jan. 12, 1991), (Jan. 19, 1991), (Feb. 2, 1991), (Feb. 9, 1991), (Feb. 16, 1991), (Feb. 23, 1991), (Mar. 2, 1991), (Mar. 9, 1991), (Mar. 16, 1991), (Mar. 30, 1991), (Apr. 6, 1991), (Apr. 13, 1991), (Apr. 20, 1991), (Apr. 27, 1991), (May 4, 1991), (May 11, 1991, (May 18, 1991), (May 25, 1991), (June 1, 1991), (June 8, 1991), (June 22, 1991), (June 29, 1991), (July 6, 1991), (July 13, 1991), (July 20, 1991), (July 27, 1991), (Aug. 3, 1991), (Aug. 10, 1991), (Aug. 17, 1991), (Aug. 24, 1991), (Aug. 31, 1991), (Sep. 7, 1991), (Oct. 12, 1991), (Nov. 10, 1991), (Nov. 17, 1991), (May 30, 1992), (June 13, 1992), (July 4, 1992), (Aug. 15, 1992), (Aug. 29, 1992), (Sep. 5, 1992), (Sep. 12, 1992), (Sep. 26, 1992), (Oct. 17, 1992), (Oct. 24, 1992), (Oct. 31, 1992), (Nov. 7, 1992), (Nov. 21, 1992), (Dec. 5, 1992), (Dec. 12, 1992), (Dec. 19, 1992), (Jan. 2, 1993), (Jan. 9, 1993), (Jan. 23, 1993), (Feb. 20, 1993), (May 1, 1993), (May 8, 1993), (May 29, 1993), (June 5, 1993), (June 19, 1993), (July 10, 1993), (July 17, 1993), (Aug. 21, 1993), (Sep. 4, 1993), (Oct. 16, 1993), (Oct. 30, 1993), (Dec. 4, 1993), (Dec. 11, 1993), (Dec. 25, 1993), (Jan. 21, 1994), (Feb. 11, 1994), (March 18, 1994), (April 8, 1994), (May 6, 1994), (May 27, 1994), (July 22, 1994), (Aug. 5, 1994), (Aug. 26, 1994), (Sep. 23, 1994), (Oct. 28, 1994), (Dec. 17–29, 1994). IPC/Fleetway. U.K. b&w.; all color from Apr. 14, 1990. Magazine.

Buster Classics. No. 7 (Aug. 1996). IPC/Fleetway. U.K.

Buster Comic Library. No. 21 (1985). IPC/Fleetway. U.K.

Buster and Monster Fun Holiday Special. Multiple Issues c.1980–1989. IPC/Fleetway. U.K.

Buster and Monster Fun Spring Special. (c.1982). IPC/Fleetway. U.K.

The Buster Book (1983), (1989), (1990), (1994). Fleetway. U.K. Hardcover Annual.

Buster Fortnightly. No. 12 (June 23, 1995), No. 16 (Aug. 18, 1995), No. 20 (Oct. 13, 1995), No. 21 (Oct. 27, 1995), No. 23 (Nov. 24, 1995), No. 24 (Dec. 8, 1995), No. 33 (Apr. 12, 1996), No. 43 (Sep. 3, 1996), No. 76 (Dec. 9, 1997), (Dec. 9–Dec. 22, 1998), No. 120 (Aug. 4–Aug. 17, 1999), (Sep. 1–Sep. 14, 1999), (Oct. 13–Oct. 26, 1999), (Oct. 27–Nov. 9, 1999), No. 127 (Nov. 10–Nov. 23, 1999). IPC/Fleetway. U.K.

The Buster Holiday Special (1983). IPC. U.K. Magazine b&w.

Called from Darkness. No. 1–1a (1997). Anarchy Bridgeworks. b&w.

Captain America (1968–1996). Vol. 1, No. 253. Marvel.

Car Toons. No. 25 (Oct. 1965), No. 61 (Oct. 1971), No. 79 (Oct. 1974). Petersen. Magazine.

Castle of Horror (1978). No. 1. Portman. U.K. Anthology. b&w. Magazine

Cavewoman: One-Shot Special. No. 1 (July 2000). Basement Comics.

Cheval Noir. No. 4 (Feb. 1990). Dark Horse. Anthology. b&w. Movie tie-in.

Chiller Pocket Book (1980–1982). No. 1–8, 10–14, 16–17, 19–28. Marvel. U.K. Anthology. Rpt.

Chilling Monster Tales. Vol. 1, No. 1 (1966). M. M. Publishing, Ltd.

Christopher Lee's Treasury of Terror (1966). Pyramid Books. b&w. Mass market. Trade Paperback.

Classic Horror Tales (previously *Horror Tales*) (1976). Vol. 8, No. 1–3. Magazine. Eerie Publications.

Classic Horror Tales (previously *Horror Tales*) (1977). Vol. 9, No. 4–5. Magazine. Eerie Publications.

The Collector's Dracula. No. 1 (1993), No. 2 (1994). Millennium. Anthology. b&w/color.

Comics to color 1992. Golden, Western Publishing Company. Trade Paperback. Coloring book/Activity book.

Comix International (1975). No. 2. Warren Publishing Co. Magazine.

The Complete Crumb Comics. Vol. 1 (1987). Fantagraphics Books. Anthology. Trade Paperback. Rpt.

The Complete Foo! (1980). Bijou Publishing. Rpt.

The Complete Sally Forth (1998). Fantagraphics Books. Rpt. Oversize Format. Anthology. Trade Paperback.

Conan Saga. No. 18 (Oct. 1988), No. 31 (Nov. 1989). Marvel. Anthology. b&w. Magazine.

Cor!! Comic Annual (1977). IPC Magazines. U.K. Hardcover.

Count Duckula (1988–1991). No. 1–15. Marvel.

Count Duckula (1989–1990). No. 1–32. Celebrity Publications. U.K. Magazine.

Count Duckula (1992). No. 1–5. London Editions Magazines/Fleetway. U.K. Magazine.

Count Duckula Annual (1989). Marvel. U.K. Hardcover.

Count Duckula Annual (1990), (1991). Egmont. U.K. Hardcover.

Count Duckula Winter Special (1988). Marvel. U.K.

The Cougar (1975). No. 1. Atlas Seaboard.

Cracked Annuals. Biggest Greatest Cracked. No. 1 (1965), King-Sized Cracked No. 3 (1969), Biggest Greatest Cracked No. 5 (1970), Biggest Greatest Cracked No. 9 (1973), Biggest Greatest Cracked No. 10 (1974), Super Cracked No. 7 (1974), King-Sized Cracked No. 9 (Fall 1975), Super Cracked No. 9 (Spr. 1976), Biggest Greatest Cracked No. 13 (Fall 1978), Extra Special Cracked No. 3 (Win. 1979), Extra Special Cracked No. 4 (Win. 1980), Super Cracked No. 14 (Fall 1980), Super Cracked No. 18 (Fall 1982), Super Cracked No. 19 (Win. 1983), Extra Special Cracked No. 9 (Win. 1986), Biggest Greatest Cracked No. 21 (Fall 1986) Major Magazines. Anthology. b&w. Magazine.

Cracked Blockbuster. No. 7 (Win. 1993/1994), No. 10 (Sum. 1996). Glove Communications. Anthology. b&w. Magazine.

Cracked Collector's Edition. No. 8 (1975), No. 17 (1977), (Sep. 1978), (Feb. 1980), (July 1980), (Sep. 1981), (Feb. 1982), (Sep. 1982), (Feb. 1983), (May 1983), (Feb. 1984), (July 1984), (Feb. 1985), No. 68 (Nov. 1986), No. 71 (July 1987), No. 72 (Sep. 1987), No. 73 (Jan. 1988), No. 75 (July 1988), No. 87 (July 1991), No. 92 (Sep. 1992), No. 96 (Sep. 1993). Major Magazines. Anthology. b&w. Magazine.

Cracked Digest. No. 2 (Jan. 1987). Major Magazines. Anthology. b&w. Rpt. Magazine. Small format.

Cracked Magazine. No. 2 (May 1958), No. 8 (Mar. 1959), No. 32 (Nov. 1963), No. 35 (Apr. 1964), No. 36 (June 1964), No. 37 (July 1964), No. 38 (Aug. 1964), No. 40 (Nov. 1964), No. 43 (May 1965), No. 50 (Mar. 1966), No. 52 (June 1966), No. 55 (Sep. 1966), No. 56 (Nov. 1966), No. 90 (Jan. 1971), No. 94 (Aug. 1971), No. 107 (Mar. 1973), No. 121 (Nov. 1974), No. 132 (May 1976), No. 133 (July 1976), No. 138 (Dec. 1976), No. 154 (Oct. 1976), No. 155 (Nov. 1976), No. 165 (Dec. 1979), No. 167 (Mar. 1980), No. 215 (Oct. 1985), No. 216 (Nov. 1985), No. 217 (Jan. 1986), No. 221 (Aug. 1986), No. 224 (Nov. 1986), No. 229 (Aug. 1987), No. 232 (Nov. 1987), No. 240 (Nov. 1988), No. 250 (Dec. 1989), No. 254 (July 1990), No. 261 (Mar. 1991), No. 272 (July 1992), No. 280 (May 1993), No. 304 (Dec. 1995), No. 323 (Jan. 1998), No. 350 (Dec. 2000). Major Magazines. Anthology. b&w. Magazine.

Cracked Magazine. Byblos No. 10. U.K. Anthology. b&w. Satire. Magazine.

Cracked Monster Party. No. 1 (July 1988), No. 2 (Oct. 1988), No. 4 (Apr. 1989), No. 5 (July 1989), No. 6 (Oct. 1989), No. 7 (Nov. 1989), No. 8 (Jan. 1990), No. 9 (Aug. 1990), No. 10 (Oct. 1990), No. 11 (Jan. 1991), No. 12 (Apr. 1991), No. 14 (Oct. 1991), No. 15 (Jan. 1992), No. 16 (Apr. 1992), No. 17 (Aug. 1992), No. 18 (Oct. 1992), No. 19 (Jan. 1993), No. 20 (Apr. 1993), No. 21 (Aug. 1993), No. 22 (Win. 1993), No. 23 (Spr. 1994), No. 24 (Sum. 1994), No. 25 (Fall 1994), No. 26 (Win. 1994), No. 27 (Spr. 1995), No. 28 (Sum. 1995), No. 29 (Fall 1995), No. 30 (Win. 1995/96), No. 31 (Spr. 1996), No. 32 (Sum. 1996), No. 33 (Fall 1996), No. 34 (Win. 1996/97), No. 35 (Spr. 1997), No. 37 (Fall 1997), No. 38 (Win. 1997/98), No. 39 (Spr. 1998), No. 40 (Sum. 1998), No. 41 (Fall 1998), No. 42 (Win. 1998/99), No. 43 (Spr. 1999), No. 44 (Sum. 1999), No. 45 (Win. 1999/2000), No. 46 (Spr. 2000). Globe Communications. Anthology. b&w. Satire. Magazine.

Cracked Summer Special. No. 1 (1991), No. 3 (1993), No. 5 (1995). Globe Communicatons. Anthology. b&w. Magazine.

Cracked's for Monsters Only. No. 1 (Nov. 1965), No. 3 (Nov. 1966), No. 4 (Mar. 1967), No. 7 (Apr. 1969). Major Magazines, Inc. b&w. Anthology. Satire. Magazine.

Cracked's for Monsters Only Annual. (Nov. 1966) and (1967). Major Magazines. Anthology. b&w. Magazine. Rpt.

Cracker. No. 57 (Feb. 14, 1976). D.C. Thomson. U.K. Magazine.

Crazy Comics. No. 3 (Feb. 1954). Marvel/Atlas. Anthology. Satire. Magazine.

Crazy Magazine. No. 1 (Oct. 1973), No. 1a Rpt. (Sum. 1975), No. 6 (Aug. 1974), No. 17 (May 1976), No. 18 (June 1976), No. 22 (Jan. 1977), No. 26 (June 1977), No. 33 (Jan. 1978), No. 37 (May 1978), No. 47 (Feb. 1979), No. 54 (Sep. 1979), No. 57 (Dec. 1979), No. 63 (June 1980), No. 64 (July 1980). Marvel. Anthology. b&w. Magazine.

Creepsville. No. 4 (1991), No. 5 (1992). Go-Co Comics. Anthology. b&w.

Creepy (1964–1983). No. 5, No. 7–10, No. 27, No. 31, No. 39, No. 46–48, No. 50–51, No. 55, No. 74, No. 111–112, No. 144, Yearbook 1968 (Magazine). Warren Publishing Corp.

Creepy. No. 7 (1974) and No. 8. Murray. Australia. b&w. Magazine.
Creepy, The Best of (1971). No. 1 (Trade Paperback). Grossett & Dunlap.
Creepy: The Classic Years (1991). No. 1 (Trade Paper Back). Harris Publications.
Crossfire. No. 22 (June 1987). Eclipse.
Cryptic Tales (1987). No. 1. Showcase. b&w
The Curse of Dracula (Mini-Series) (1998). No. 1–3; No. 1 (Rpt. as trade paperback in 2005). Dark Horse.
Daffy Duck. No. 92 (Feb. 1975). Gold Key.
Dampyr (2005). No. 1. Italy.
The Dandy. D.C. Thomson. U.K. Anthology. Magazine. No. 2333 (Aug. 9, 1986), No. 2353 (Dec. 27, 1986), No. 2367 (Apr. 4, 1987), No. 2368 (Apr. 11, 1987), No. 2369 (Apr. 18, 1987), No. 2370 (Apr. 25, 1987), No. 2371 (May 2, 1987), No. 2372 (May 9, 1987), No. 2373 (May 16, 1987), No. 2374 (May 23, 1987), No. 2375 (May 30, 1987), No. 2376 (June 6, 1987), No. 2377 (June 13, 1987), No. 2378 (June 20, 1987) No. 2379 (June 27, 1987), No. 2380 (July 4, 1987), No. 2381 (July 11, 1987), No. 2382 (July 18, 1987), No. 2383 (July 25, 1987), No. 2384 (Aug. 1, 1987), No. 2385 (Aug. 8, 1987), No. 2386 (Aug. 15, 1987), No. 2393 (Oct. 3, 1987), No. 2394 (Oct. 10, 1987), No. 2397 (Oct. 31, 1987), No. 2400 (Nov. 21, 1987), No. 2413 (Feb. 20, 1988), No. 2428 (June 4, 1988), No. 2429 (June 11, 1988, No. 2466 (Feb. 25, 1989), No. 2482 (June 17, 1989), No. 2502 (Nov. 4, 1989), No. 2512 (Jan. 13, 1990), No. 2521 (Mar. 17, 1990), No. 2528 (May 5, 1990), No. 2529 (May 12, 1990), No. 2536 (June 30, 1990), No. 2542 (Aug. 11, 1990), No. 2554 (Nov. 3, 1990), No. 2559 (Dec. 8, 1990), No. 253 (Jan. 5, 1991), No. 2616 (Jan. 11, 1992), No. 2622 (Feb. 22, 1992), No. 2664 (Dec. 12, 1992) , No. 2683 (Apr. 24, 1993), No. 2686 (May 15, 1993), No. 2721 (Jan. 15, 1994), No. 2783 (Mar. 25, 1995), No. 2786 (Apr. 15, 1995), No. 2803 (Aug. 12, 1995), No. 2844 (May 25, 1996), No. 2861 (Sep. 21, 1996), No. 2942 (Apr. 11, 1998), No. 2973 (Nov. 14, 1998), No. 2977 (Dec. 12, 1998).
The Dandy Book (1992), (1994). D.C. Thomson. U.K. Anthology. Hardcover.
Dandy Comic Library. No. 64 (1985). D.C. Thomson. U.K. Anthology. Pocket format.
Deadbeats. No. 30 (May 1998). Claypool Comics. b&w.
Dead Souls. No. 1–3 (2008–2009). Seraphemera Books. b&w.
Deadtime Stories. No. 1 (Nov. 1987). New Comics Group. Anthology. b&w.
Detective Comics. No. 671 (Feb. 1994). DC. Batman Series.
Dinosaurs for Hire. No. 2 (June 1988), No. 3 (Aug. 1988). Eternity. b&w.
Disney Adventures. Vol. 8. No. 11 (Sep. 1998). Buena Vista Publishing. Small format. Magazine.
D.P.7. No. 15 (Jan. 1988). Marvel.
The Darkness Vs. Eva: Daughter of Dracula (2008). No. 1–4. Dynamite Entertainment.
Dark Wars: The Tale of Meiji Dracula (2008). No. 1 (One-Shot, Trade Paperback). b&w. Del Rey/Ballantine Books.
The Defenders (1972–1986). No. 95, No. 95A. Marvel.
Der Prinz der Nacht (2002–2003). No. 1–6. Yves Swolfs. Softcover.
Doctor Strange (1988–1996). Vol. 3. No. 37. Marvel.
Death Dreams of Dracula (1991–1992). No. 1–4. Apple.
Diary of a Vampire: Young Dracula (1998) No. 1. (Trade Paperback). Caliber.
Doctor Strange: Master of the Mystic Arts (1974–1987). No. 14 (May 1976, rpt. in *Super Spider-Man with the Super-Heroes* No. 185 [1976]), No. 14a, No. 58 (Apr. 1983, rpt. in *Doctor Strange versus Dracula: The Montesi Formula* [2006]), No. 59 (June 1983, rpt. in *Doctor Strange versus Dracula: The Montesi Formula* [2006]), No. 60 (Aug. 1983, rpt. in *Doctor Strange versus Dracula: The Montesi Formula* [2006]), No. 61 (Oct. 1983, rpt. in *Doctor Strange versus Dracula: The Montesi Formula* [2006]), No. 62 (Dec. 1983, rpt. in *Doctor Strange versus Dracula: The Montesi Formula* [2006]). Marvel.
Dr. Strange: Sorcerer Supreme. No. 6 (Aug. 1989), No. 8 (Oct. 1989), No. 9, No. 10 (Nov. 1989), No. 15, No. 37 (Jan. 1992). Marvel.
Doctor Strange Vs. Dracula: The Montesi Formula (2006). No. 1 (Trade Paperback). Marvel.
Don Martin Magazine (1994). No. 2 (1994). Welsh Publishing Group. Anthology. Magazine.
Doomsday Album. No. 13–14. (c.1970s). Murray. Australia. b&w. Magazine.
Doorway to Nightmare. (n.d. possibly 1981). Murray. Australia. b&w. Magazine.
Dracula (1984). Academic Industries. Trade Paperback. b&w. Rpt. Mass Market Paperback (Rpt. of *Dracula* [Pendulum Press, 1973]).
Dracula (1984). American Guidance Services. Trade Paperback. b&w. Rpt. Mass Market Paperback (Rpt. of Dracula [Pendulum Press, 1973]).
Dracula (1966). No. 1 (Trade Paperback). Ballantine Books.
Dracula (1984). Catalan Communications. Trade Paperback. Large format.
Dracula (1984). (Spanish edition of Dracula [Catalan Communications, 1984]). Spain. Avagraf/Toutain Editor.

Dracula (1989–1990). No. 1–1A (Second Printing), 2–4. Eternity. b&w.

Dracula (1990). Eternity (Malibu). Trade Paperback. b&w. (Rpt. Dracula/Eternity mini-series).

Dracula (1994). Gateway Educational Products. Trade Paperback. b&w. Rpt.

Dracula (1981). Happy House Books. Trade Paperback. b&w. Rpt.

Dracula (1975). Manor. Mass Market Paperback. b&w. Rpt.

Drácula. Biblioteca. Grandes Del Co'mic. Pleneta DeGostini.

Dracula (1993). N0.1 (One-Shot, Trade Paperback). Titan. U.K..

Dracula. No. 1–10. Dark Horse International. U.K. Anthology. Magazine.

Dracula (1972–1973). No. 1–12. New English Library. U.K.. Anthology. Magazine.

Dracula (1962–1973). No. 1–8: No. 1 (Oct./Dec. 1962, Rpt. in *Universal Pictures Presents Dracula—The Mummy & Other Stories* [1963]), No. 2 (Nov. 1966, Rpt. as No. 6), No. 3 (Feb. 1967, Rpt. as No. 7), No. 4 (Mar. 1967, Rpt. as No. 8), No. 6 (July 1972), No. 7 (Oct. 1972), No. 8 (July 1973). Dell (Dracula and Al Ulysses series).

Dracula (1972). No. 1 Warren Publishing Corp. Magazine. (One-Shot).

Dracula (1974). No. 1. Power Records. (book-and-record set; Rpt. *Tomb of Dracula* No. 19).

Dracula (1973). No. 1. Now Age Illustrated Classic. One-Shot, Trade Paperback. b&w. Pendelum Press.

Dracula. By Victor G. Ambrus. Trade Paperback. Oxford-New York: Oxford University Press, 1981 (Rpt. in 1982).

Dracula (1981). Peter Haddock Publishing. U.K. b&w. Rpt.

Dracula (1980). Starstream Products. b&w. Rpt.

Dracula (c.1963). Thorpe & Porter. U.K.. b&w. Anthology.

Dracula (1962). Top Sellers. U.K.

Dracula (1972). No. 1–6 (New English Library, 1970–1971.). Warren Publishing Company. Anthology. b&w. Magazine.

Dracula Annual (1974). No. 1–12 (New English Library). New English Library. U.K. Rpt. Trade Paperback. Anthology. Magazine.

Dracula. No. 1–13. Newton. Australia. b&w. Rpt.

Dracula (1973). Now Age Books. Trade Paperback. b&w. Rpt.

Dracula (1981). Oxford-New York: Oxford University Press. (Rpt. in 1982.). Trade Paperback.

Dracula (1973). Pendulum Press (Picture Classics). Trade Paperback. b&w. (Rpt. by Now Age Books [1973], by Marvel Classics Comics [1976], by Starstream Products [1980], by Happy House Books [1981], by Peter Haddock [1981], by Academic Industries [1984], by American Guidance Services [1994]).

Dracula (1981). Peter Haddock. U.K. Rpt. b&w.

Dracula (1974). No. 15 (1974). Power Records.

Dracula (1980). Starstream Products. Rpt. b&w.

Dracula. (n.d. possibly 1963). Thorpe & Porter. U.K. Rpt. b&w. Anthology.

Dracula. No. 1 (1962). Top Sellers. U.K.

Dracula (2006). No. 1 (Graphic Novel/Softcover). Puffin Graphics.

Dracula (2005). No. 1 (Softcover). Del Rey.

Dracula (1970–1972). Warren Publishing Company. Anthology. b&w. Hardcover.

Dracula Annual (1971, 1974). New English Library. U.K. Rpt. Trade Paperback. Anthology.

Dracula Annual. No. 1 (Jan. 1976), No. 4 (1974.), No. 6 (1974), No. 5 (1974). Newton. Australia. b&w. Rpt.

Dracula: Asylum Novel. Dark Horse. Graphic Novel.

Dracula: A Symphony in Moonlight and Nightmares (1992). No. 1 (Trade paperback, Softcover, Hardcover). NBM.

Dracula: A Symphony in Moonlight and Nightmares (1986.). Marvel Comics. Hardcover. Large format.

Dracula: A Symphony in Moonlight and Nightmares (1986). Marvel Comics. Trade Paperback. Large format.

Dracula: A Symphony in Moonlight and Nightmares (1993). NRM Publishing. Hardcover. Large format.

Dracula: A Symphony in Moonlight and Nightmares (1993). NRM Publishing. Trade Paperback. Large format.

The Dracula Chronicles (Mini-Series) (1995). No. 1–3. Topps.

Dracula Comics Special. No. 1 (1974, Rpt. in *The House of Hammer* No. 6 (1976) and Rpt. in *The House of Hammer* No. 1 (1976)). Quality Communication. U.K. b&w. Rpt. Anthology. Magazine.

Dracula in Hell (1992). No. 1 (Jan. 1992), No. 2 (Mar. 1992). Apple. b&w.

Dracula Lives (1973–1975). No. 1–13. Marvel. Magazine.

Dracula Lives (1974–1976; 1982). No. 1 (1973), No. 2 (1973, Rpt. in *Dracula Lives Annual* (1975), Rpt. in *Dr. Strange, Sorcerer Supereme* No. 10 (1989), No. 3 (Oct. 1973, Rpt. in *Dracula Lives Annual* (1975) and *Dracula Lives Annual* (1975), No. 4 (Jan 1974, Rpt. in *Dracula Lives Annual* (1975) and *Journey into Unknown Worlds* No. 29 (1954)), No. 5 (Mar. 1974, Rpt. in *Stoker's Dracula* No. 1 (2004) and *Dracula Lives Annual* (1975), No. 6 (May 1974, Rpt. in *Stoker's*

Dracula No. 1 (2004) and Rpt. in *Dracula Lives Annual* (1975), No. 7 (July 1974, Rpt. in *Stoker's Dracula* No. 1 (2004), No. 8 (Sep. 1974, Rpt. in *Stoker's Dracula*. No. 1 (2004), No. 9 (Nov. 1974), No. 10 (Jan. 1975), No. 11 (Mar. 1975), No. 12 (May 1975), No. 13 (July 1975) No. 14–87; Summer Special No. 1. Marvel. U.K.. Anthology. b&w. Magazine.

Dracula Lives. Vol. 2. No. 1 (Mar 1974). Cadence Comics Publications. Canada. b&w. Magazine.

Dracula Lives. No. 1 (Oct. 26, 1974), No. 2 (Nov. 2, 1974), No. 3 (Nov. 9, 1974), No. 4 (Nov. 16, 1974), No. 5 (Nov. 23, 1974), No. 6 (Nov. 30, 1974), No. 7 (Dec. 7, 1974), No. 8 (Dec. 14, 1974), No. 9 (Dec. 21, 1974), No. 10 (Dec. 28, 1974), No. 11 (Jan. 4, 1975), No. 12 (Jan. 11, 1975), No. 13 (Jan. 18, 1975), No. 14 (Jan. 25, 1975), No. 15 (Feb. 1, 1975), No. 16 (Feb. 8, 1975), No. 17 (Feb. 15, 1975), No. 18 (Feb. 22, 1975), No. 19 (Mar. 1, 1975), No. 20 (Mar. 8, 1975) No. 21 (Mar. 15, 1975), No. 22 (Mar. 22, 1975), No. 23 (Mar. 29, 1975), No. 24 (Apr. 5, 1975), No. 25 (Apr. 12, 1975), No. 26 (Apr. 19, 1975), No. 27 (Apr. 26, 1975), No. 28 (May 3, 1975), No. 29 (May 10, 1975), No. 30 (May 17, 1975, No. 31 (May 24, 1975), No. 32 (May 31, 1975), No. 33 (June 7, 1975), No. 34 (June 14, 1975), No. 35 (June 21, 1975), No. 36 (June 28, 1975), No. 37 (July 5, 1975), No. 38 (July 12, 1975), No. 39 (July 19, 1975), No. 40 (July 26, 1975), No. 41 (Aug. 2, 1975), No. 42 (Aug. 9, 1975), No. 43 (Aug. 16, 1975), No. 44 (Aug. 23, 1975), No. 45 (Aug. 30, 1975), No. 46 (Sep. 6, 1975), No. 47 (Sep. 13, 1975), No. 48 (Sep. 20, 1975), No. 49 (Sep. 27, 1975), No. 49 (Sep. 27, 1975), No. 50 (Oct. 4, 1975), No. 51 (Oct. 11, 1975), no 52 (Oct. 18, 1975), No. 53 (Oct. 25, 1975), No. 54 (Oct. 25, 1975), No. 55 (Nov. 8, 1975), No. 56 (Nov. 15, 1975), No. 57 (Nov. 22, 1975), No. 58 (Nov. 29, 1975), and No. 59 (Dec. 6, 1975). Marvel Comics International. U.K. Anthology. b&w. Rpt. Magazine.

Dracula Lives. No. 11 (Dec. 1975). Newton. Australia. b&w. Rpt. Anthology. Magazine.

Dracula Lives. No. (1978), No. 2 (1979), No. 3 (1979), No. 4 (Jan. 1974). Yaffa. Australia. b&w. Rpt. Anthology. Magazine.

Dracula Lives Annual. No. 1 (Sum. 1975, Rpt. *Dracula Lives!* #2 (1973).), No. 5 (1974), No. 4 (1974), No. 3 (1973), No. 6 (1974), No. 2, 1973)). Marvel Comics. b&w. Rpt. Magazine.

Dracula Lives Featuring the Legion of Monsters. No. 60 (Dec. 13, 1975), No. 61 (Dec. 20, 1975), No. 62 (Dec. 27, 1975), No. 63 (Jan. 3, 1976), No. 64 (Jan. 10, 1976), No. 65 (Jan. 17, 1976), No. 66 (Jan. 24, 1976), No. 67 (Jan. 31, 1976), No. 68 (Feb. 7, 1976), No. 69 (Feb. 14, 1976), No. 70 (Feb. 21, 1976), No. 71 (Feb. 28, 1976), No. 72 (mar. 6, 1976), No. 73 (Mar. 13, 1976), No. 74 (Mar. 20, 1976), No. 75 (Mar. 27, 1976), No. 76 (Apr. 3, 1976), No. 77 (Apr. 10, 1976), No. 78 (Apr. 17, 1976), No. 79 (Apr. 24, 1976), No. 80 (May 1, 1976), No. 81 (May 8, 1976), No. 82 (May 15, 1976), No. 83 (May 22, 1976), No. 84 (May 29, 1976), No. 85 (June 5, 1976), No. 86 (June 9, 1976), and No. 87 (June 16, 1976). Marvel Comics International. U.K. b&w. Anthology. Rpt. Magazine.

Dracula Lives Special. No. 1 (1976). World Distributors. U.K. Anthology. Rpt. Trade Paperback.

Dracula: Lord of the Undead (Mini-Series) (1998). No. 1 (Dec. 1998), No. 2 (Dec. 1998), and No. 3 (Dec. 1998). Marvel.

Dracula Meets Jesus (1992). Meg Smith/Gekko Party Productions. b&w.

Dracula: Return of the Impaler (Mini-Series) (1993). No. 1 (July 1993), No. 2 (July 1993), No. 3 (Mar. 1994), and No. 4 (Oct. 1994). Slave Labor Graphics.

Dracula: Return of the Impaler. Slave Labor Graphics. b&w.

Dracula '79 (1979). Warren. One-Shot. Rpt. Magazine.

Dracula Sucks. Dolphin. Fumette. Adult. Magazine.

Dracula Summer Special. No. 1 (1982). Marvel. U.K. b&w. Anthology. Magazine.

Dracula: The Illustrated Novel of Horror (1990). No. 1. Malibu.

Dracula: The Impaler (1991). No. 1 (1991). (One-Shot). Comax Productions. b&w.

Dracula: The Lady in the Tomb (1991). No. 1 (Jan. 1991). Eternity Comics. b&w.

Dracula: The Suicide Club (1992). No. 1 (Aug. 1992), No. 2 (Sep. 1992), No. 3 (Oct. 1992), No. 4 (Nov. 1992). Adventure Comics (Eternity). b&w.

Dracula 3-D (1992). No. 1. 3-D Zone.

Dracula 3-D. No. 1 (1992). The 3-D Zone. Rpt./Revised.

Dracula's Revenge (2004). No. 1–2. IDW.

Dracula versus Zorro. No. 1 (1993) and No. 2 (1993, Rpt. in *Dracula vs. Zorro* [1998]). Topps Comics.

Dracula: Vlad the Impaler (1993). No. 1 (Feb. 1993), 1A, No. 2 (Mar. 1993), No. 3 (Apr. 1993). Topps. Polybagged.

Dracula Vs. Capone (2006). No. 1. Silent Devil Comics.

Dracula vs. the Grad. No. 1 (July 1998). Dreamland Comics. b&w. Anthology.

Dracula Versus King Arthur (2005–2006). No. 1–2, 2A, 3–4. Silent Devil.

Dracula Versus Zorro (1993). No. 1–2. Topps.

Dracula Versus Zorro: The Complete Saga (1994). Vol. 2 No. 1. (Graphic Album) Topps.

Dracula Versus Zorro (1998). No. 1–2. (Topps Reprints). Image.

Dracula vs Zorro. No. 1 (Sep. 1998) and No. 2 (Oct. 1998). b&w. Rpt. Image.

Dracula vs Zorro. No. 1 (Apr. 1994). Topps. Trade Paperback. Rpt.

Dracula's Daughter. No. 1 (Sep. 1991, partial reprint in *Anton's Collected Drek* [1974]). Eros Comix. b&w. Adult.

Dracula's Spinechillers (1982). Annual. Suron Enterprises/World International Publishing. Hardcover. Anthology. Large format.

Draculina. No. 31 (Oct. 1997). Draculina Publishing Co. Magazine.

Draculina. No. 1 (1993). Draculina Publishing. b&w. Adult.

Draculina's Cozy Coffin. No. 1 (1994), No. 2 (1994), No. 3 (1995), No. 4 (1996). Draculina Publishing. b&w. Anthology. Adult.

Drag Cartoons. No. 6 (Aug. 1964), No. 7 (Sep. 1964), No. 8 (Oct. 1964), No. 9 (Nov. 1964), No. 10 (Dec. 1964), No. 11 (Jan. 1965), No. 12 (Feb. 1965), No. 13 (Mar. 1965), No. 14 (Apr. 1965), and No. 15 (May 1965, Rpt. in *Toth "One for the Road"* (2000). The Millar Company. Anthology. b&w. Magazine.

Dr. Strange Vs. Dracula (1994). No. 1. Marvel.

Duckula. London Editions Magazines/Fleetway. U.K. Television tie-in. Magazine.

Duckula Summer Special (1991). London Editions Magazines/Fleetway. U.K. Television tie-in. Magazine.

Eagle. No. 136 (Oct. 27, 1984), No. 258 (Feb. 28, 1987), No. 259 (Mar. 7, 1987), No. 260 (Mar. 14, 1987), No. 261 (Mar. 21, 1987), No. 262 (Mar. 28, 1987), No. 263 (Apr. 4, 1987), No. 264 (Apr. 11, 1987), No. 265 (Apr. 18, 1987), No. 266 (Apr. 25, 1987), No. 267 (May 2, 1987), No. 268 (May 9, 1987), No. 269 (May 16, 1987), No. 270 (May 23, 1987), No. 271 (May 30, 1987), No. 272 (June 6, 1987), No. 273 (June 13, 1987), No. 274 (June 20, 1987), No. 275 (June 27, 1987), No. 276 (July 4, 1987), No. 277 (July 11, 1987), No. 328 (July 2, 1988), No. 329 (July 9, 1988), No. 330 (July 16, 1988), No. 331 (July 23, 1988), No. 332 (July 30, 1988), No. 333 (Aug. 6, 1988), No. 334 (Aug. 13, 1988), and No. 335 (Aug. 20, 1988). IPC Magazines Ltd. U.K. b&w.

Echo of Future Past (1984–1986). No. 1 (1984), No. 2 (1984), No. 3 (Nov. 1984), No. 4 (Feb. 1985), No. 5 (Apr. 1985). Continuity Comics.

Eerie. No. 12 (Aug. 1953, Rpt. as *Dracula 3-D* [1992]). Avon Periodicals.

Eerie (1965–1983). No. 11 (Sep. 1967, Rpt. in *Famous Monsters of Filmland* No. 48 [1968]), No. 16 (July 1968), No. 24 (Nov. 1969), No. 40 (June 1972, Rpt. in #51), No. 46 (Mar. 1973), No. 48 (June 1973), No. 50 (Aug. 1973), 93, No. 124 (Sep. 1981), and125. Warren Publishing Corp. Magazine.

Eerie. No. 7 (1974) and No. 11. Murray. Australia. b&w. Rpt. Anthology.

The Electric Company Magazine. No. 69 (Oct. 1980). Children's Television Workshop. Magazine.

Elson's Presents. No. 3 (1981). Elson's-DC. Anthology. Rpt.

Elvira: Mistress of the Dark (1993–Current). No. 13 (May 1994, Rpt. as *Elvira: Mistress of the Dark: Double Delights* [2000]), No. 14 (June 1994), No. 18 (Oct. 1994), No. 27 (July 1995), No. 47 (Mar. 1997), No. 48 (Apr. 1997), No. 49 (May 1997), No. 50 (June 1997), No. 51 (July 1997), No. 56 (Dec. 1997), and No. 63 (July 1998). Leonia, NJ : Claypool Comics (U.S.)

Elvira: Mistress of the Dark. Claypool Comics. b&w. Rpt. Trade Paperback.

Essential Tomb of Dracula (2003–Current). N0.1, 1A–1B, 2, 2A, 3–4. Marvel.

Essential X-Men. Vol. 3 (1998). Marvel. Trade Paperback. Rpt.

Eternal Romance. No. 1 (Feb. 1977). Best Destiny. b&w. Anthology.

Evil Ernie vs The Movie Monsters (March 1997). Chaos! Comics.

Famous Monsters of Filmland (1958–1983). No. 29 (July 1964), No. 32 (Mar. 1965), No. 48 (Feb. 1968), and No. 50 (July 1968). Warren Publishing. Magazine.

Fandom's Finest Comics (1997). Hamster Press. Trade Paperback. Anthology.

Fang. No. 1 (1991). Tangram. b&w. Anthology.

Fanhunter: Dracula Returns (c.1995). Forum. One-Shot.

Fantastic Fears. No. 10 (Nov./Dec. 1954, Rpt. in *Weird* Vol. 1, No. 11 [1966]), Ajax/Farrell. Precode horror. Anthology. Four Star Publications, Inc.

Fantastic Four. Vol. 1, No. 30 (Sep. 1964). Marvel.

Fantastic Four (1998–2003). Vol. 3. No. 36 (Dec. 2000). Marvel.

Fast Forward. No. 120 (Jan. 1–7, 1992). BBC Magazines. U.K. Magazine.

Fantomen (1992). Vol. 43, No. 11. Egmont.

Femforce in the House of Horror. No. 1 (1989). AC Comics. b&w.

The Flintstones (Hanna-Barbera) (1962–1970). No. 33 (1966). Gold Key.

Foo! No. 2 (Oct. 1958). Animal Town Comics. Anthology.

For Monsters Only (1965–1972). No. 1–9, Annual 1967. Major Magazines Inc. Magazine.

Forbidden Mad (Oct. 1984). Warner Books. b&w. Anthology. Mass market. Trade Paperback.

The Frankenstein/Dracula War. No. 1 (Feb. 1995). Topps Comics.

Frankie's Frightmare. No. 1 (Oct. 1991). Cat's Paw Comics. b&w. Satire. Anthology.

Frantic. Vol. 2, No. 1 (Feb. 1959). Pierce Publishing Corporation. b&w. Satire. Magazine.

Fright (1975). No. 1 (Aug. 1975). Atlas Seaboard.

Fright. No. 12 (July 1989). Eternity. b&w. Rpt. Anthology.

Fright Night. No. 14 (Dec. 1989, Rpt. [3-D] in *Fright Night 3-D* [1992]) and No. 15 (Jan. 1990, Rpt. in *Fright Night 3-D* [1992]). Now Comics.

Fright Night 3-D. No. 1 (June 1992). Now Comics. Rpt.

Funny Fortnightly. No. 1 (Mar. 29/Apr. 7, 1989), No. 5 (May 20/June 2, 1989), No. 7 (June 17–30, 1989), No. 9 (July 15–28, 1989), No. 10 (July 29/Aug. 11, 1989), No. 11 (Aug. 12–25, 1989), No. 12 (Aug. 26/Sep. 8, 1989), and No. 19 (Dec. 2/Dec. 15, 1989). IPC. U.K. b&w. Anthology. Satire. Magazine.

Funny Monthly. Dec. 1990, Jan. 1991, Feb. 1991, Apr. 1991. IPC. U.K. b&w. Anthology. Magazine.

Geeksville. No. 2 (1999). 3 Finger Prints. b&w.

Generation X (1994–2001). No. 1 (1998). Annual 1998. Marvel.

Get Lost. No. 2 (Apr./May 1954). MikeRoss Publications. Anthology.

Ghost Rider (1973–1983). Vol. 1 or Vol. 2, No. 48., No. 43 (Apr. 1980), No. 82 (Feb. 1997), No. 83 (Mar. 1997), No. 84 (Apr. 1997), No. 85 (May 1997). Marvel.

Ghosts of Dracula (1991). No. 1 (Sep. 1991), No. 2–5. Eternity.

Ghouls. No. 1 (Jan 1989). Eternity. b&w. Anthology.

Giant Cracked (July 1979, Oct. 1979 July 1983). Major Magazines. b&w. Anthology. Magazine.

Giant Size Action Planet Halloween Special. No. 1 (1998). Action Planet. Anthology. Oversize format.

Giant-Size Chillers (June 1974). No. 1. Marvel.

Giant-Size Dracula (Previously *Giant-Size Chillers* Vol. 1) (1974). No. 2 (Sep. 1974, Rpt. in *Tomb of Dracula. Omnibus Vol. 1* [2008]), No. 3 (Dec. 1974, Rpt. from *Spellbound* #22 [1954], Rpt. in *Tomb of Dracula. Omnibus Vol. 1* [2008]), No. 4 (Mar. 1975, Rpt. from *Adventures into Terror* No. 6 [1951]), No. 5 (June 1975, Rpt. from *Journey into Mystery* #2 [1952]). Marvel.

Giant-Size Man-Thing (1973–1975). No. 5 (Aug. 1975). Marvel.

Giant-Size Spider-Man. No. 1 (July 1974), No. 31 (June 1976). Marvel.

Graphic Classics: Bram Stoker (2007). Eureka Productions. Graphic Novel.

Gray Morrow's Private Commissions. No. 1 (Jan. 1992). Forbidden Fruit. b&w. Adult.

Grimm's Ghost Stories. No. 56 (Oct. 1980). Dell. Anthology.

Gruft Von Dracula, Die (2005–Current). No. 1–11 (hard cover), No. 1–11 (Trade Paperback). Panini. Germany.

Halloween Megazine. No. 1 (Dec. 1996). Marvel. Rpt.

Halls of Horror Presents Dracula Comics Special (1982). No. 1. Quality Communications/Periodicals. U.K.. Magazine.

Happy Hour at Casa Dracula. Marta Acosta.

Haunted Tales. No. 21. Murray. Australia. b&w. Rpt. Anthology.

The Haunt of Horror (1973). No. 2. Marvel. Digest Size.

Heavy Metal's Dracula (2005). No. 1. Heavy Metal. One-Shot, Hardcover.

Heavy Metal. Heavy Metal. Vol. 9, No. 9 (Dec. 1985) and vol. 17, No. 4 (Sep. 1). b&w/color. Fantasy. Anthology. Magazine.

Hellsing (2003–Current). No. 1–7. Dark Horse. Trade Paperback/Manga.

Hellsing (2004–Current). No. 1–2. Panini. Germany.

Helsing. No. 1 (1998). Caliber Comics. b&w.

Helsing: Dawn of Armageddon. No. 1 (1999). Caliber Comics. b&w. Rpt.

Herbie. No. 20 (1966). ACG. Satire. Anthology.

The History of Grendel: Grendel Tales (1993). Dark Horse. Rpt.

Hoot. No. 18 (Feb. 22, 1986), No. 25 (Apr. 12, 1986), No. 26 (Apr. 19, 1986), No. 27 (Apr. 26, 1986), No. 29 (May 10, 1986), No. 49 (Sep. 27, 1986), and No. 50 (Oct. 4, 1986). D.C. Thomson. U.K. Magazine.

Horror Monsters. No. 6 (Fall 1963). Charlton Publications, Inc. Magazine.

Horror of Dracula and Curse of Frankenstein (1964). No. 1. Warren Publishing.

Horror Tales (1970–1974). Vol. 2, No. 3–4, Vol. 3, No. 5–6, Vol. 4, No. 1, No. 3–5, No. 6, Vol. 5, No. 1–2, No. 4–5, Vol. 6, No. 5. Eerie Publications. Magazine.

Hot 'N Cold Heroes. No. 1 (1990) and No. 2 (1990). Sword in Stone Productions/A+ Comics. b&w. Anthology.

The House of Hammer (later *Hammer's Hall of Horror*). No. 1 (May 1976, Rpt. in No. 20), No. 4 (Aug. 1976, Rpt. in No. 24), No. 6 (Dec. 1976, Rpt. in No. 24), No. 18 (Mar. 1978, Rpt. in *Echo of Future Past* No. 1–5 [1984–85]), No. 21 (June 1978), No. 24 (1982), No. 27 (1983), and No. 28 (1983). General Book Distribution. U.K./Quality Communications, Ltd. U.K. b&w. Monster Movie. Magazine.

Howard the Duck (1979–1981). No. 5. Marvel. Magazine.

How Sick Can You Get (June 1974). Zebra Books. b&w. Anthology. Mass Market Trade Paperback.

Illegal Aliens (Sep. 1992). Eclipse. b&w.

Illustrated Classex. No. 1 (Dec. 1991). Comic Zone Productions. b&w. Anthology. Adult.

The Illustrated Dracula (1975). No. 1. Manor Books. One-Shot. Softcover.

Informania: Vampires. London: Walker Books, 1998. Hardcover.

Informania: Vampires. Cambridge, MA: Candlewick Press, 2000. Trade Paperback.

Informania: Vampires. London: Walker Books, 2000. Trade Paperback.

Impaler (2006–2007). No. 1–4. Image.

International Insanity. No. 1 (July 1976). Phi Publishing Company. b&w. Anthology. Magazine.

Invaders (1975–1979). Vol. 1, No. 9. Marvel.

It's Science with Dr. Radium Special (1989). Slave Labor Graphics. b&w.

Jackpot Comics. No. 19 (Sep. 8, 1979). IPC. U.K. Magazine.

Jacula (1968–1982, 1982–1984). Vol. 1 (327 issues). Vol. 2, 129 Rpts. Studio Giolitti. Erregi/Ediperiodici. Italy.

Jademan Collection. No. 2 (1990). Jademan. Hong Kong. b&w. Anthology.

Journey into Fear (1951–1954; July 1952). No. 8 and No. 21 (Jan. 1955). Superior Publishers Limited. Canada.

Journey into Mystery. No. 2 (Dec. 1972, Rpt. in *Masters of Terror* No. 1 [1975]). Marvel.

Journey into Unknown Worlds. No. 27 (May 1954, Rpt. in *Vampire Tales* No. 10 [1975]), No. 29 (July 1954). Atlas.

Jughead. No. 295 (Dec. 1979).

Knockabout. No. 14 (1988). Knockabout Publications. U.K. b&w. Anthology. Magazine. Adult.

Krazy Comic. No. 1 (Oct. 16, 1976). Fleetway. U.K. Magazine.

Lady Dracula (1995). No. 1–2. Fantaco/Tundra.

Lady Dracula. No. 1 (1995). Media International/FantaCo Enterprises. b&w. Adult.

Laff Time Cartoon Annual (1968). Crestwood Publishing. b&w. Magazine.

Laugh Comics Digest. No. 61 (Nov. 1985) and No. 102 (Aug. 1992). Archie Comics Publications.

Lawbreakers Always Lose. No. 4 (Oct. 1948). Marvel.

Legend: Horror Classics. No. 1, No. 2, No. 5. Legend Publishing. U.K. Magazine.

The Legend of Dracula. Innervision.

Legion of Monsters (1975). No. 1. Marvel. Anthology. b&w. Magazine.

Lennon's Behold the Cartoons of Dracula. Dublin: Sceptic Tank Press, 1997. Trade Paperback.

Life Sucks (2008). A First Second Production.

Little Book of Horror: Dracula (2005). No. 1. IDW. Hardcover.

Little Archie. No. 125 (Dec. 1977). Archie.

Little Dracula (1992). No. 1–3. Harvey.

Little Monsters. No. 6 (Oct. 1966, Rpt. in No. 18) and No. 18 (Sep. 1972, Rpt. in No. 6). Gold Key.

Little Monsters. No. 18 (Sep. 1972). Whitman. Rpt.

Look In (occasionally spelled *Look-In*). No. 39 (Sep. 24, 1988), No. 2 (Jan. 7, 1989), No. 3 (Jan. 14, 1989), No. 4 (Jan. 21, 1989), No. 5 (Jan. 28, 1989), No. 9 (Feb. 25, 1989), No. 11 (Mar. 11, 1989), No. 49 (Dec. 3, 1988), No. 51 (Dec. 17, 1988), No. 2 (Jan. 7, 1989), No. 10 (Mar. 4, 1989), No. 11 (Mar. 11, 1989), No. 14 (Apr. 1, 1989), No. 29 (July 15, 1989), No. 30 (July 22, 1989), No. 38 (Sep. 16, 1989), No. 47 (Nov. 18, 1989), No. 48 (Nov. 25, 1989), No. 49 (Dec. 2, 1989), No. 1 (Jan. 6, 1990), No. 2 (Jan. 13, 1990), No. 3 (Jan. 20, 1990), No. 4 (Jan. 27, 1990), No. 5 (Feb. 3, 1990), No. 6 (Feb. 10, 1990), No. 7 (Feb. 17, 1990), No. 8 (Feb. 24, 1990), No. 9 (Mar. 3, 1990), No. 10 (Mar. 10, 1990), No. 11 (Mar. 17, 1990), No. 12 (Mar. 24, 1990), No. 13 (Mar. 31, 1990), No. 14 (Apr. 7, 1990). TV Times. U.K. Magazine.

Look In Television Annual (1990). TV Times. U.K. Hardcover.

Love Bites (1991). No. 1–3. Eros Comix/Fantagraphic Books. b&w. Anthology. Adult.

Love Journal. OUR/Toytown. Anthology.

Mad (1952–Current). No. 68 (Jan. 1962), No. 85 (Mar. 1964), No. 138 (Oct. 1970), No. 199 (June 1978, Rpt. in *Mad Super Special* No. 45 [1983]; *Forbidden Mad* [1984]), No. 213 (Mar. 1980, Rpt. in *Mad Super Special* No. 57 [1986]; *Mad-Duds* [1987]), No. 221 (Mar. 1981, Rpt. in *Mad Super Special* No. 56 [1986]; *Mad Blasts* [1988]), No. 277 (Mar. 1988, Rpt. in *Mad Super Special* No. 102 [1988]), No. 319 (June 1993, Rpt. in *Mad XL* No. 4 [2000]), No. 363 (Nov. 1997, Rpt. in *Mad XL* No. 19 [2003]), and No. 228 (Apr. 1981, Rpt No. 228 [Apr. 1981]). E.C. Anthology. b&w. Magazine.

Mad (1977–1994). No. 373. Suron Ent./London Ed./Fleetway. U.K. Magazine.

Mad Blasts (Oct. 1988). Warner Books. b&w. Rpt. Anthology. Mass Market Trade Paperback.

The Mad Book of Horror Stories, Yecchy Creatures, and Other Stuff (1986). Warner Books. b&w. Anthology. Mass Market Trade Paperback.

Mad Brain Ticklers, Puzzlers, and Lousy Jokes (July 1986). Warner Books. b&w. Anthology. Mass Market Trade Paperback.

Mad Duds (June 1987). Warner Books. b&w. Rpt. Anthology. Mass Market Trade Paperback.

Mad House Annual. No. 8 (1970/71). Radio Comics.

Mad House Comics. No. 100 (Nov. 1975), No. 105 (Nov. 1976), No. 109 (Sep. 1977), No. 115 (Feb. 1979), No. 118 (Oct. 1979), and No. 119 (Feb. 1980). ArchieEnterprises. Satire. Anthology.

Mad Lobsters and Other Abominable Housebroken Creatures (Nov. 1986). Warner Books. b&w. Mass market. Trade Paperback.

A Mad Look at the Future (May 1978). Warner Books. b&w. Anthology. Mass Market Trade Paperback.

Mad Monster Party. No. 1 (Sep. 1967). Dell.

Mad Monster Party. No. 1 (1999). Black Bear Press. b&w. Rpt.

Mad Special/Mad Super Special. No. 12 (1973), No. 45 (Win. 1983), No. 56 (Fall 1986), No. 57 (Win. 1986), No. 99 (Early Fall 1994), and No. 102 (Mar. 1995). E.C. Publications. b&w. Anthology. Rpt. Magazine.

Mad XL (May 1982). No. 4 (July 2000). EC Publications. b&w. Magazine.

Mad's Al Jaffee Freaks Out. Warner Books. Mass Market Trade Paperback.

Madhouse Comics Digest. No. 2 (1976). Radio Comics. Digest.

The Man Called Nova. No. 23 (Jan. 1978). Marvel.

The Many Ghosts of Dr. Grave. No. 44 (Jan. 1974). Charlton Comics. Anthology.

Marvel Age. No. 45 (Dec. 1986), No. 68 (Nov. 1988), No. 105 (Oct. 1991). Marvel.

Marvel Bumper Comic. No. 3 (Oct. 29, 1988). Marvel. U.K. Anthology.

Marvel Classics Comic: Dracula (1976–1978). No. 9. Marvel

Marvel Collection. No. 1 (1976) and No. 2 (1975). Marvel. U.K. Anthology. Rpt.

Marvel Comic. No. 330 (Jan. 24, 1979), No. 331 (Jan. 31, 1979), No. 332 (Mar. 7, 1979), No. 333 (Mar. 14, 1979), No. 334 (Mar. 21, 1979), No. 337 (Apr. 11, 1979), No. 338 (Apr. 18, 1979), No. 339 (Apr. 25, 1979), No. 340 (May 2, 1979), No. 341 (May 9, 1979), No. 342 (May 16, 1979) No. 343 (May 23, 1979), No. 344 (May 30, 1979), No. 345 (June 6, 1979), No. 346 (June 13, 1979), No. 347 (June 20, 1979), No. 348 (June 27, 1979), No. 349 (July 4, 1979), and No. 350 (July 11, 1979). Marvel. U.K. Anthology. Rpt.

Marvel Comics Presents (1988–1995). No. 64 (1990) and No. 77–79. Marvel.

Marvel Fanfare (1982–1991). Vol. 1, No. 42 (Feb. 1989), No. 45 (Aug. 1989). Marvel.

Marvel Madhouse. No. 40 (Mar. 1982). Marvel Comics. U.K. Anthology.

Marvel Preview (1975–1980). No. 3, 12, 16. Marvel. b&w. Magazine.

Marvel: Shadows and Light (1997). No. 1. Marvel.

Marvel Team-Up (1997–1998). Vol. 3, No. 7 and No. 36 (Aug. 1975). Marvel.

Marvel Winter Special 1988. No. 1 (1988). Marvel. U.K. Rpt.

Maxwell Madd and His Wrestling Women. No. 1 (1989). Outside Comics. b&w.

Megaton Man: Hardcopy. No. 1 (Feb. 1999). Image. b&w.

Megaton Man vs. Forbidden Frankestein (aka *Bizarre Heroes,* No. 16). No. 1 (Apr. 1996). Fiasco Comics.

Midnight Graffiti (June 1988). Kilimanjaro Corporation. b&w. Magazine.

The Mighty World of Marvel featuring The Incredible Hulk and Dracula Lives. No. 105 (Oct. 5, 1974), No. 199 (July 21, 1976), No. 260 (Sep. 21, 1977). Marvel Comics International. U.K. b&w. Anthology. Rpt. Magazine.

Misty. No. 35 (Sep. 30, 1978). IPC/Fleetway. U.K.

Misty Annual (1979, 1980, 1983, 1984). IPC/Fleetway. U.K.

Monkey Business. No. 3 (1993). Parody Press. Satire. Anthology.

The Monster Frankenstein (becomes *The Frankenstein Monster*) (1973–1975). No. 7 (Nov. 1973, Rpt. in *Essential Monster of Frankenstein* No. 1 [2004]) and No. 8 (Jan. 1974, Rpt. in *Essential Monster of Frankenstein* #1 [2004]). Marvel.

Monster Fun. No. 1 (June 14, 1975), No. 2 (June 21, 1975), No. 3 (June 28, 1975), No. 4 (July 5, 1975), No. 5 (July 12, 1975), No. 6 (July 19, 1975), No. 7 (July 26, 1975), No. 8 (Aug. 2, 1975), No. 9 (Aug. 9, 1975), No. 10 (Aug. 16, 1975), No. 11 (Aug. 23, 1975), No. 12 (Aug. 30, 1975), No. 13 (Sep. 6, 1975), No. 14 (Sep. 13, 1975), No. 15 (Sep. 20, 1975), No. 16 (Sep. 26, 1975), No. 17 (Oct. 4, 1975), No. 18 (Oct. 11, 1975), No. 19 (Oct. 18, 1975), No. 20 (Oct. 25, 1975), No. 21 (Nov. 1, 1975), No. 22 (Nov. 8, 1975), No. 23 (Nov. 15, 1975), No. 24 (Nov. 22, 1975), No. 25 (Nov. 29, 1975), No. 26 (Dec. 6, 1975), No. 27 (Dec. 13, 1975), No. 28 (Dec. 20, 1975), No. 29 (Dec. 27, 1975), No. 30 (Jan. 3, 1976), No. 31 (Jan. 10, 1976), No. 32 (Jan. 17, 1976), No. 33 (Jan. 24, 1976), No. 34 (Jan. 31, 1976), No. 35 (Feb. 7, 1976), No. 36 (Feb. 14, 1976), No. 37 (Feb. 21, 1976), No. 38 (Feb. 28, 1976), No. 39 (Mar. 6, 1976), No. 40 (Mar. 13, 1976), No. 41 (Mar. 20, 1976), No. 42 (Mar. 27, 1976), No. 43 (Apr. 3, 1976), No. 44 (Apr. 10, 1976), No. 45 (Apr. 17, 1976), No. 46 (Apr. 24, 1976), No. 47 (May 1, 1976), No. 48 (May 8, 1976), No. 49 (May 15, 1976), No. 50 (May 22, 1976), No. 51 (May 29, 1976), No. 52 (June 5, 1976), No. 53 (June 12, 1976), No. 54 (June 19, 1976), No. 55 (June 26, 1976), No. 56 (July 3, 1976), No. 57 (July 10, 1976), No. 58 (July 17,

1976), No. 59 (July 24, 1976), No. 60 (July 31, 1976), No. 61 (Aug. 7, 1976), No. 62 (Aug. 14, 1976), No. 62 (Aug. 14, 1976), No. 63 (Aug. 21, 1976), No. 64 (Aug. 28, 1976), No. 65 (Sep. 4, 1976), No. 66 (Sep. 11, 1976), No. 67 (Sep. 18, 1976), No. 68 (Sep. 25, 1976), No. 69 (Oct. 2, 1976), No. 70 (Oct. 9, 1976), No. 71 (Oct. 2, 1976), No. 72 (Oct. 23, 1976), No. 73 (Oct. 30, 1976). IPC. U.K. b&w. Anthology. Magazine.

Monster Fun Annual (1977–1984). IPC. U.K. Hardcover.

Monster Fun Summer Special (1976). IPC. U.K.

Monster Howls. Humor Vision. No. 1 (Dec. 1966). b&w. Magazine.

Monster Hunters. No. 5 (Apr. 1976, abridged version Rpt. in *Hot'n Cold Heroes* #2 (1990). Charlton.

Monster Hunters. Ser. 3, No. 7. Murray. Australia. b&w. Rpt. Anthology.

Monster Scene. No. 1 (Mar. 1991). Avalon Fine Arts. b&w. Magazine.

The Monster Times. No. 41 (May 1975) and No. 46 (Mar. 1976). The Monster Time Publishing Co. Large Format. Magazine.

Monster World. No. 9 (July 1966). Warren Publishing. b&w. Magazine.

Monster Wars: Magdalena Vs. Dracula (Mini-Series) (2005). No. 1, 1B–1M. Image.

More Fun Comics (previously *New Fun Comics*). No. 7 (January 1936). National Periodical Publications (DC).

More Fun Comics (previously *New Fun Comics*). No. 8 (February 1936). National Periodical Publications (DC).

Mr. T Versus Dracula (2008). Mohawk Media.

Ms. Marvel (1977–1979). No. 14. Marvel.

Munden's Bar Annual. No. 1 (Apr. 1988). First. Anthology.

The Munsters. No. 1 (Jan. 1965). Gold Key Comics. Anthology.

The Munsters. No. 1 (Aug. 1997). TV Comics. b&w.

The Munsters Collected Edition (1998). No. 1 (1997). TV Comics. b&w. Rpt. Trade Paperback.

Mysterious Adventures. Vol. 1, No. 4 (1979). Story Comics. Anthology.

Mystery Comics Digest. No. 25 (Sep. 1975). Gold Key. Anthology. Digest.

National Lampoon. Vol. 1, No. 20 (Nov 1971, Rpt. in *The Best of National Lampoon* No. 3 [1972]). AC DC Comics.

Negative Burn: An Anthology. No. 30 (1995). Caliber. b&w. Anthology.

New Fun: The Big Comic Magazine (a.k.a. *New Fun Comics*) (October 1935). No. 6. National Periodical Publications (DC).

Nightmare. No. 9 (Oct. 1972), No. 15 (Oct. 1973, Rpt. in *Vampyres* No. 2 [1988]), No. 17, No. 19 (June 1974), No. 21. Skywald Publications. Magazine.

The Nightmare Annual. No. 1 (1972). Skywald Publishing Corp. b&w. Anthology. Magazine.

Nightmare Yearbook (1974). No. 1. Skywald Publications. Magazine.

Nightmare. No. 9. Page. Australia. b&w. Rpt. Anthology.

Night's Children Vampyr! No. 4 (1994). Millennium Publications. b&w.

Nightstalkers (1992–1994). No. 11, No. 17 (Mar. 1994), and 18. Marvel.

The Night Walker. No. 1 (1993). Fleetway. U.K.

Nightlinger. No. 1 (1993). Gauntlet Comics/Caliber Press. b&w.

Nosferatu (1991). No. 1 (May 1991), No. 2. Run Tome Comics.

Nosferatu-Plague of Terror. No. 1 (May 1991). Millennium Publications. b&w.

Not Brand Echh. No. 3 (Oct. 1967), No. 10 (Oct. 1968), No. 11 (Dec. 1968). Marvel. Anthology.

Nova Girls Fun House. No. 1 (1991). MN Designs Productions.

Nutty. D.C. No. 43 (Dec. 6, 1980), No. 58 (Mar. 21, 1981), No. 62 (Apr. 18, 1981), No. 72 (June 27, 1981), No. 91 (Nov. 7, 1981), No. 149 (Dec. 18, 1982), No. 150 (Dec. 25, 1982), No. 155 (Jan. 29, 1983), No. 156 (Feb. 5, 1983), No. 161 (Mar. 12, 1983), No. 193 (Oct. 22, 1983), No. 201 (Dec. 17, 1983), No. 207 (Jan. 28, 1984), No. 214 (Mar. 17, 1984), No. 215 (Mar. 24, 1984), No. 231 (July 14, 1984), No. 232 (July 21, 1984), No. 233 (July 28, 1984), No. 234 (Aug. 4, 1984), No. 235 (Aug. 11, 1984), No. 236 (Aug. 18, 1984), No. 237 (Aug. 25, 1984), No. 238 (Sep. 1, 1984), No. 239 (Sep. 8, 1984), No. 240 (Sep. 15, 1984), No. 241 (Sep. 22, 1984), No. 242 (Sep. 29, 1984), No. 243 (Oct. 6, 1984), No. 244 (Oct. 13, 1984), No. 245 (Oct. 20, 1984), No. 246 (Oct. 27, 1984), No. 247 (Nov. 3, 1984), No. 248 (Nov. 10, 1984), No. 249 (Nov. 17, 1984), No. 250 (Nov. 24, 1984), No. 251 (Dec. 1, 1984), No. 252 (Dec. 8, 1984), No. 253 (Dec. 15, 1984), No. 254 (Dec. 22, 1984), No. 255 (Dec. 29, 1984), No. 274 (May 11, 1985), No. 282 (July 6, 1985), No. 283 (July 13, 1985), No. 285 (July 27, 1985), No. 286 (Aug. 3, 1985), and No. 290 (Aug. 31, 1985). Thomson. U.K. Anthology. Magazine.

The Occult Files of Doctor Spektor. No. 1, No. 5 (Dec. 1973), No. 8 (June 1974), No. 25 (1973).

Official Handbook of the Marvel Universe (1985–1988). Vol. 2, No. 17. Marvel.

Official Handbook of the Marvel Universe: Horror (2005). No. 1. Marvel.

Panic. No. 2 (Nov. 1958). Panic Publications. b&w. Anthology. Magazine.

Pater Dracula (2003). Weissblech Comics. Germany.
Penthouse. Vol. 4, No. 13 (Sep. 1973). Penthouse International. Adult. Magazine.
Penthouse Wicked Wanda (1975). Penthouse International. Tpb. Adult.
Peter Porker, The Spectacular Spider-Ham. No. 13 (Jan. 1987). Marvel.
The Phantom (1992–1993). No. 5. Wolf Publishing.
Planet of the Apes and Dracula Lives. No. 88 (June 23, 1976), No. 89 (June 30, 1976), No. 90 (July 7, 1976), No. 91 (July 14, 1976), No. 92 (July 21, 1976), No. 93 (July 28, 1976), No. 97 (Aug. 25, 1976), No. 98 (Sep. 1, 1976), No. 99 (Sep. 8, 1976), No. 102 (Sep. 29, 1976), No. 103 (Oct. 6, 1976), No. 104 (Oct. 13, 1976), No. 105 (Oct. 20, 1976), . 106 (Oct. 27, 1976), No. 108 (Nov. 10, 1976), No. 109 (Nov. 17, 1996), No. 109 (Nov. 17, 1996), No. 110 (Nov. 24, 1976), No. 111 (Dec. 1, 1976), No. 112 (Dec. 8, 1976), No. 114 (Dec. 22, 1976), No. 120 (Feb. 2, 1977), No. 121 (Feb. 9, 1977), and No. 122 (Feb. 16, 1977). Marvel Comic International. U.K. b&w. Anthology. Rpt. Magazine.
Planet of Vampires (1975). No. 2. Atlas Seaboard.
Playboy. Vol. 25, No. 9 (Sep. 1978). Playboy Press. Adult. Magazine.
Plug Comic. No. 3 (Oct. 8, 1977). D.C. Thomson. U.K. Magazine.
Post Halloween Left Over Monster Thanksgiving Special. No. 1 (1998). Blind Wolf Comics. b&w. Anthology.
Previews. No. 1 (1998). Thorby Comics.
Prez (1973–1974). No. 4. DC.
Psycho (1971–1975). No. 3, No. 6, 7, No. 8, 9–11, 13–14, 17, 19, 21, 24, Annual 1972. Skywald Publications. Australia. b&w. Rpt. Anthology. Magazine.
Psycho (197[1]–197[5]). No. 2. Skywald Publications. France/Canada. Magazine.
Psycho. No. 6. Yaffa. Australia. b&w. Rpt. Anthology.
Psycho Annual. No. 1 (1972). Skywald Publishing Corp. b&w. Rpt. Anthology. Magazine.
Psycho: The 1974 Fall-Special (1974). Skywald Publishing Corp. b&w. Rpt. Anthology. Magazine.
Pulse of Darkness. No. 3 (1989) and No. 4 (1990). Opal Press. Australia. b&w.
Purgatori: The Dracula Gambit (2000). No. 1, 1A (Centennial Premium Edition), No. 3 (Dec. 1998, Rpt. in *Purgatori Collected Edition* #2 (2000)), and No. 7 (Apr. 1999, Rpt. in *Purgatori Collected Edition* No. 4 [2000]). Chaos! Comics. One-Shot.
Purgatori: The Dracula Gambit (Chaos! Comics Deutschland Imprint) (1998). No. 1, 1A. MG Publishing. One-Shot.
Purgatori: The Dracula Gambit Sketchbook (2000). No. 1. Chaos! Comics. One-Shot.
Purgatori Collected Edition. No. 2 (June 2000) and No. 4 (Aug. 2000). Chaos! Comics.
Purgatori: Goddess Rising. No. 1 (July 1999). Chaos! Comics.
Quack! No. 7 (June 1976). Star Reach Production.
Red Circle Sorcery. No. 10 (Dec. 1974, Rpt. in *The Collector's Dracula* No. 2 [1994]). Red Circle.
The Renegade. No. 1 (Oct. 1993). Studio S Productions. b&w.
Renfield. No. 1 (1994). Caliber Press. b&w.
Renfield: A Tale of Madness (1994–1995). No. -1, 1, 1A, 2, 3, No. 1. Caliber Comics. b&w. Trade Paperback.
Requiem Chevalier Vampire (2005–2008). Nickel Editions. color.
Requiem Der Vampirritter (2003–2008). Kult Editions.
Requiem for Dracula (1993). No. 1. Marvel. One-Shot. color.
Requiem Vampire Knight (2003–2009). Heavy Metal. color.
Requiem Vampire Knight (2009). Heavy Metal. Rpt. Trade Paperback. color.
Requiem Vampire Knight (2009). Panini Comics. Rpt. Trade Paperback. color.
Richie Rich & Casper. No. 9 (Dec. 1975), No. 21 (Dec. 1977). Harvey Comics.
Richie Rich Vault of Mystery. No. 2 (Jan. 1975). Harvey Comics.
Ripley's Believe It or Not! No. 26 (June 1971). Gold Key.
Ripley's Believe It or Not: Cruelty. No. 1 (June 1993). Schanes Products.
Le Rituel de la mort (*Dracula le vampire* Series) (1980). Artima. France. color.
Rockin' Bones. No. 2 (June 1992). New England Comics Press. b&w. Anthology.
The Rook. No. 10 (Aug. 1981). Warren.
Saban's Mighty Morphin Power Rangers. Vol. 1, No. 1 (Dec. 1994, Rpt. in *Saban's Mighty Morphin Power Rangers Graphic Album* No. 1 [1995]). Hamilton Comics.
Saban's Mighty Morphin Power Rangers Graphic Album. No. 1 (1995). Hamilton Comics.
Sabrina: The Teen-Age Witch. No. 1 (Apr. 1971). Archie. Anthology.
Sally Forth. No. 4 (1994). Eros Comics/Fanatagraphic Books.
Savage Action. No. 6 (Apr. 1981). Marvel. U.K. Rpt.
Savage Return of Dracula (1992). No. 1. Marvel. One-Shot.
Savage Sword of Conan (1974–1995). No. 26. Marvel. b&w. Sword and Sorcery Anthology. Magazine.
The Savage Sword of Conan. No. 24 (Oct. 1979).

Marvel. U.K. b&w. Sword and Sorcery Rpt. Anthology. Magazine.

Scarlet in Gaslight: An Adventure in Terror (1987–1988). No. 1–4, No. 1. Eternity/Malibu. b&w. Trade Paperback.

Scarlet in Gaslight (1990). Eternity Comics. b&w. Trade Paperback.

Scarlet in Gaslight (1996). Caliber Comics. b&w. Rpt. Trade Paperback.

Scary Monsters Magazine. No. 16 (Sep. 1995). Dennis Druktenis. b&w. Magazine.

Scary Monsters Magazine Yearbook: Monster Memories. No. 7 (1999). Dennis Druktenis. b&w. Magazine.

Scary Tales (1975–1984). No. 1. Charlton Comics.

Scooby Doo Mystery Comics. No. 25 (June 1974). Gold Key.

Scooby-Doo: The Mystery Card Caper. No. 1 (2000). Hanna Barbera. Small Format.

Scooby Doo ... Where Are You! (1976). Annual. Brown Watson. U.K. Hardcover. Anthology.

Scream (1973–1975). No. 1 (Aug. 1973, Rpt. in *Fright* No. 4 (1988)), No. 3 (Dec. 1973), No. 4 (Feb. 1974), No. 10 (Oct. 1974, Rpt. in *Vampyres* No. 1 [1988]), No. 11 (Feb. 1975). Skywald Publications. b&w. Anthology. Magazine.

Scream! (1984). No. 1–15. Holiday Special 1985, Holiday Special 1986. Fleetway (AP/IPC). U.K..

The Shadow of Dracula. Happy Face Productions.

Scream. No. 2, No. 6, and No. 7. Page. Australia. b&w. Rpt. Anthology.

Scream! No. 1 (Mar. 24, 1984), No. 2 (Mar. 31, 1984), No. 3 (Apr. 7, 1984), No. 4 (Apr. 14, 1984), No. 5 (Apr. 21, 1984), No. 5 (Apr. 21, 1984), No. 7 (May 5, 1984), No. 8 (May 12, 1984), No. 9 (May 19, 1984), No. 10 (May 26, 1984), No. 11 (June 2, 1984), No. 12 (June 9, 1984), No. 13 (June 16, 1984), No. 14 (June 23, 1984), and No. 15 (June 30, 1984). IPC Magazines. U.K. b&w. Anthology.

Scream! Holiday Special (1985–1986). IPC Magazines. U.K. b&w. Anthology.

Screen Monsters. No. 2 (Nov. 1992). Comic Zone Productions. b&w.

Secrets of Haunted House. No. 32 (Jan. 1981, Rpt. in *Elson's Presents* No. 3 [1981]). DC. Anthology.

The Sexy Dick. No. 1417 (1972). Golden Newcomics. b&w. Adult.

Shiver and Shake (Mar. 9, 1974). IPC. U.K. b&w. Anthology. Magazine.

Shiver and Shake Annual (1977, 1981, 1985, and 1986). IPC. U.K. Anthology. Trade Paperback.

Sick. Vol. 6, No. 1 [41] (Dec. 1965), vol. 9, no 2 [66] (Mar. 1969), vol. 14, No. 1 [97] (Mar. 1974), vol. 15, No. 14 [105] (Aug. 1975), vol. 17, No. 114 (Mar. 1977), vol. 19, No. 129 (Oct. 1979). Crestwood Publications, then Pyramid Publications, then Charlton. b&w. Anthology. Magazine.

Silver Blade (1987–1988). No. 6–7. DC.

Silver Surfer Vs. Dracula (1994). No. 1 (1993). Marvel. One-Shot. Rpt.

Sin Comics. No. 1 (Dec. 1993). Black Eye Productions. b&w.

666: The Mark of the Beast. No. 9, No. 13–17 (1993), and No. 18 (1994). Fleetway. Anthology.

Smash. No. 128 (July 13, 1968). Oldhams Press. U.K. Magazine.

Spider-Man Annual (1976). Marvel. U.K.

Spider-Man Comics Weekly. No. 542 (July 27, 1983). Marvel. U.K.

Spider-Man Team-Up (1995–1996). No. 6 (Mar. 1996). Marvel.

Spider-Man Unlimited. No. 20 (May 1998). Marvel.

Spiderman Vs./Versus Dracula (1994). No. 1 (1993). Marvel. One-Shot

Spider-Woman. No. 32 (Nov. 1980). Marvel.

Spidey Super Stories. No. 7 (Apr. 1975), No. 11 (Aug. 1975), and No. 14 (Dec. 1975). Marvel.

Spike Vs. Dracula (2006). No. 1, 1A–1E, 2, 2A–2D, 3, 3A–3D, 4, 4A–4D, 5, 5A–5D. IDW.

Spoof (1970–1973). No. 1 (Oct. 1971) and No. 4 (Mar. 1973). Marvel.

Spooks'n'Monsters Howling Funny Joke Book (1990). Ladybird. U.K.

Star Comics Magazine. No. 8 (Feb. 1988). Marvel. Satire. Anthology. Digest.

Star Trek. No. 4 (July 1980). Marvel.

Stoker's Dracula (Mini-Series) (2004–2005). No. 1–4; No. 1. Marvel. Hardcover.

Strike the Sot! A Wizard of Id Collection (1988). Kansas City–New York: Andrews & McMeel. Trade Paperback.

Super DC Giant. No. S-19 (Oct./Nov. 1970). DC. Rpt.

Super Funnies. No. 2 (Mar. 1954). Superior Comics. Canada. Satire. Anthology.

Superman (1939–1986, 2006–Current). Vol. 1, No. 344, vol. 2, No. 70 (Aug. 1992). DC.

Superman. No. 344 (Feb. 1980). Whitman Canada. Rpt.

Superman: The Man of Steel. No. 14 (Aug. 1992). DC.

Superman's Pal the New Jimmy Olsen (previously *Superman's Pal Jimmy Olsen*) (1954–1974). No. 142–143. DC.

The Supernaturals. No. 3 (Dec. 1998). Marvel.

Super Spider-Man. No. 178 (July 7, 1976), No. 182 (Aug. 4, 1976), No. 183 (Aug. 11, 1976), No. 184 (Aug. 18, 1976), No. 185 (Aug. 25, 1976), No. 295 (Oct. 4, 1978), No. 296 (Oct. 11, 1978), and No. 297 (Oct. 18, 1978). Marvel, U.K.

Sur les Traces de Dracula (2006). No. 1–5. Casterman. France.

Suspense. No. 7 (March 1951). Marval/Atlas.

Sword of Dracula (2003). No. 1–6. Image.
Sword of Dracula (2005). No. 1. Trade Paperback. Image Reprints. IDW
Sword of Dracula (Color Edition) (2005). Vol. 2, No. 1. Digital Webbing.
Tales Calculated to Drive You Bats. No. 1 (Nov. 1961), No. 2 (Jan 1962), No. 3 (Mar. 1962). Archie. Anthology.
Tales Calculated to Drive You Bats. No. 1 (1966). Radio Comics. Anthology. Rpt.
Tales from the Tomb (1969). Vol. 1, No. 7, Vol. 2. No. 2, 4–6 (1970), vol. 3. No. 3, 5–6 (1971), vol. 4. No. 1–2, 4–5 (1972), vol. 5. No. 1, 3, 6 (1973). Eerie Publications. Magazine.
Tales of Horror-Dracula (1975–1976). No. 1–14. Annual 1. Special Issue (mid–1976). Newton. Gredown. Australia. b&w. Rpt. Anthology.
Tales of the Multiverse: Batman — Vampire (2007). DC. Trade Paperback.
Tales of Voodoo (1970–1974). Vol. 2, No. 1 (Feb. 1969), vol. 3. No. 2–4 (1970), vol. 4, No. 6 (1971), vol. 5, No. 2–5 (1972), vol. 6, No. 1–3, 5 (1973), and vol. 7, No. 1–3 (1974). Eerie Publications. Magazine.
Tales to Tremble By (1984). World International Publishing. U.K. Anthology. Hardcover.
Tales Too Terrible to Tell (1989–1993). No. 2. New England Comics Press.
Tentacles of Terror. No. 1. Gredown. Australia. b&w. Rpt. Anthology.
Terreur de Dracula (1975–1976). No. 1–3 (Rpt. from *Dracula Lives!*) Marvel. France.
Terrors of Dracula (1979–1981). Vol. 1. No. 1–5, vol. 2, No. 1–4 (1980), and vol. 3, No. 1–2 (1981). Modern Day Periodicals. b&w. Anthology. Magazine.
Terror Tales (1970–1978). Vol. 2. No. 2–4, vol. 3, No. 1 (1971), vol. 4, No. 6–7 (1972), vol. 5, No. 1, 3, (1973), vol. 6, No. 1, 4 (1974), vol. 7, No. 1, 3–4 (1976), vol. 9, No. 2, 4 (1978). Eerie Publications. Magazine.
The Thing. No. 19 (Jan. 1985). Marvel.
Thor. No. 332 (June 1983) and No. 333 (July 1983). Marvel.
Thrills & Chills (1994–1996). No. 1–No. 18 (1996). Scholastic. Magazine.
The Tick's Big Halloween Special. No. 1 (Oct. 2000). NEC Press. b&w.
The Titans. No. 24 (Apr. 3, 1976) and No. 36 (June 23, 1976). Marvel. U.K. b&w.
Tomb of Dracula (1979). No. 1–4 Yaffa Publishing Group. Australia.
Tomb of Dracula (Mini-Series) (2004). No. 1–4 Marvel.
Tomb of Dracula (1972–1979) No. 1 (Rpt. in *Dracula* (Newton Comics, 1975), No. 2–10, No. 10A (*Blade* [1998] film give-away), No. 11–25, No. 25A (1994 Reprint), No. 26–43, No. 43A, No. 44, No. 44A, No. 45, No. 45A, No. 46, No. 46A, No. 47, No. 47A, No. 48–57, No. 57A, No. 58, No. 58A, No. 59, No. 59A, No. 60, No. 60A, No. 61–70. Marvel.
Tomb of Dracula (1979–1980) No. 1–6. Magazine
Tomb of Dracula (Mini-Series) (1991–1992). No. 1–4. Marvel.
Tomb of Dracula: Halloween Megazine (1996) No. 1. Marvel. One-Shot.
La Tomba di Dracula (1991–1992). Vol. 1. No. 1, vol. 2, No. 1 (1992). Edizioni Star Comics (Marvel Comics). Italy. One-Shot.
Le Tombeau de Dracula (1970s). No. 1–68. Édition Héritage. Montréal, Canada. b&w.
Topps Comics Presents (1993). No. 0 (1993). Topps. b&w. Anthology.
Toth "One for the Road" (2000). San Francisco: Auad Publishing. Trade Paperback.
Trash. No. 2 (June 1978), No. 3 (Aug. 1978). Trash Publishing Co. b&w. Anthology. Magazine.
Trash Comics. N.p. b&w. Adult.
La Tumba de Dracula (1976). No. 18 (reprint of No. 8 ToD). Producciones Hernandez Medina. Mexico.
TV Century 21 Annual (1967). Century 21 Publishing & City Magazines. U.K. Hardcover.
TV Comic. No. 1079 (Aug. 19, 1972), No. 1236 (Aug. 23, 1975), No. 1280 (June 26, 1976). Polystyle. U.K. Large format.
TV Times. Vol. 134, No. 9 (Feb. 25–Mar. 3, 1989). Independent Television Publications. U.K. Large format. Magazine.
TV 21. No. 181 (July 6, "2068"— in fact, 1968) and No. 191 (Sep. 14, "2068"–actually, 1968). City Magazines. U.K.
TV 21 Annual (1969). Century 21 Publishing & City Magazines. U.K. Hardcover.
The Twilight Zone (1962–1982). No. 18 (Nov. 1966), No. 66. Gold Key/Marvel. Anthology.
Twist. No. 1 (1987). Kitchen Sink Comix. b&w. Anthology. Adult.
Two on a Guillotine. Dell.
2000 AD. No. 800 (Sep. 12, 1992). IPC-Fleetway. U.K. Magazine.
The Uncanny X-Men (1963–Current). No. 159 (July 1982, Rpt. as *X-Men Classic* No. 63 [1991] and in *Essential X-Men* Vol. 3 [1998]), Annual and No. 6. Marvel.
The Unexpected. No. 199 (June 1980). DC. Horror. Anthology.
Universal Monsters Cavalcade of Horror (2006). No. 1. Dark Horse. Trade Paperback.
Universal Monsters: Dracula (1991). No. 1. Dark Horse. Softcover.
Universal Monsters: Dracula (Peter Pan Records)

(Mini-Series) (1975). No. 2, King-Size No. 1. Power Records (book-and-record set).

Universal Pictures Presents: Dracula, the Mummy, Plus Other Stories (1963). No. 1 (Sep./Nov. 1963). Dell. Anthology.

Unknown Worlds. No. 55 (Apr./May 1967). ACG/Best Syndicated Features. Anthology.

Vamperotica. No. 1 (1996). Brainstorm. b&w. Rpt. Trade Paperback. Anthology. Adult.

Vampire! No. 6. G. R. Carr. Australia. b&w. Anthology. Magazine.

Vampire Jokes and Cartoons: "A Comedy of Terrors" (1974). Pyramid Books. Mass Market Trade Paperback. b&w.

Vampirella (1969–1983). No. 16, 18 (Aug. 1972), No. 19 (Sep. 1972), No. 20 (Oct. 1972), No. 21 (Dec. 1972), No. 22 (Mar. 1973), No. 39 (Jan. 1975), No. 40 (Mar. 1975), No. 41 (Apr. 1975), No. 43 (June 1975), 81 (Sep. 1979), No. 85 (Mar. 1980), No. 100 (Oct. 1981). Warren Publishing Corp. Magazine.

Vampirella. No. 1 (Nov. 1992), No. 2 (Feb. 1993), No. 3 (Mar. 1993), No. 4 (July 1993), No. 5 (Nov. 1993). Series 3. Harris.

Vampirella (1970). No. 10, No. 11, No. 13, No. 20, No. 27, No. 28, and No. 29. Murray. Australia. b&w. Anthology. Magazine.

Vampirella Classic. No. 4 (Aug. 1995). Harris. Rpt.

Vampirella: Commemorative Edition. No. 1 (Nov. 1996). Harris. Rpt.

Vampirella/Dracula: The Centennial (1997). No. 1 (Oct. 1997), No. 1A–1B, No. 2. Harris.

Vampirella: The Dracula War! (1993). No. 1, 1A–1B. Harris.

Vampirella/Dracula & Pantha Showcase. No. 1 (Aug. 1997). Harris.

Vampirella: Horror Classics. No. 1 (2000). Harris. Hardcover. Rpt. Anthology.

Vampirella of Drakulon. No. 2 (Mar. 1996), No. 3 (May 1996). Harris. Rpt.

Vampire Tales (1973–1975). No. 1 (Aug. 1973), 5 (June 1974), 6 (Aug. 1974), 8 (Dec. 1974), and 9 (Feb. 1975), . Marvel. b&w. Magazine.

Vampirella: Sad Wings of Destiny. No. 1 (1996). Harris.

Vampirella: 25th Anniversary Special. No. 1 (1996). Harris. Rpt. Anthology.

Vampirella: Transcending Time and Space (1992). Harris. b&w. Rpt. Anthology. Trade Paperback.

Vampirella vs. The Cult of Chaos (1996). Harris. b&w. Rpt. Trade Paperback.

Vampiric Jihad (1991). No. 1. Apple Comics.

Vampiric Jihad (1992). Apple Comics. b&w. Rpt. Trade Paperback.

Vampyres. No. 1 (Sep. 1988), No. 2 (Dec. 1988), and No. 4 (July 1989). Eternity Comics. b&w. Rpt. Anthology.

Vampyres (1991). Malibu Graphics. b&w. Rpt. Trade Paperback. Anthology.

Vegas Knights. No. 1 (July 1989). Pioneer.

Vicious. No. 1 (1994). Brainstorm Comics. b&w. Horror. Anthology.

Vision and the Scarlet Witch (1985–1986). Vol. 2, No. 5. Marvel.

Visions. No. 4 (1994). Caliber Press. b&w.

Wacko. No. 2 (Apr. 1981). Ideal Publishing Co. b&w. Satire. Magazine.

Walt Disney's Goofy Adventures. No. 17 (Oct. 1991). Walt Disney Publications. Anthology.

Walt Disney's Uncle Scrooge. No. 313 (Sep. 1998). Bruce Hamilton.

Warp Graphics Annual. No. 1 (1986). Warp Graphics.

Waxwork. No. 1 (Nov. 1988). Blackthorne. b&w.

Waxwork 3-D. No. 1 (Fall 1988). Blackthorne. 3-D.

Wedding of Dracula (1993). No. 1 (One-Shot) Marvel.

The Wedding of Dracula. No. 1 (Jan. 1992). Marvel. Rpt.

Weird (1966–81). Vol. 1. No. 11 (1966), vol. 3, No. 1, 5 (1968), vol. 5, No. 2, 4 (1970), vol. 7, No. 1, 3, 6 (1972), vol. 8, No. 7 (1973), vol. 11, No. 4 (1976), vol. 12, No. 2 (1977), vol. 14, No. 1 (1979), vol. 16, No. 1 (1981). Eerie Publications. Magazine.

Weird Mysteries. No. 46. Murray. Australia. b&w. Rpt. Anthology.

Weird Mystery Tales (1972–1975). No. 14 (Oct./Nov. 1974). DC.

Weird Tales of the Macabre (1975). No. 2 (Mar. 1975). Seaboard Publications. b&w. Anthology. Magazine.

Weird Vampire Tales (1979). Vol. 3, No. 1, 3–4. Modern Day Periodicals. Magazine.

Weird Vampire Tales (1981). Vol. 5, No. 2. Modern Day Periodicals. Magazine.

Weird War Tales (1971–1983). No. 18 (Oct. 1973) and No. 107 (Jan. 1982). DC.

Werewolf by Night (1972–1977). Vol. 1, No. 15 (Mar. 1973), 19 (July 1974). Marvel.

What If...? (1989–1998). Vol. 2, No. 24 (Apr. 1991), No. 37. Marvel.

Where Creatures Roam. No. 4 (Jan. 1971). Marvel. Anthology.

Whizzer and Chips (Oct. 18, 1969–Oct. 27, 1990). IPC Magazines. U.K. Magazine.

Whizzer and Chips Holiday Special (1970–1991). IPC Magazines. U.K. Magazine.

Whizzer and Chips Presents Junior Rotter Holiday Special (1986). IPC Magazines. U.K. Hardcover.

Whoopee! No. 9 (May 4, 1974), No. 18 (July 6, 1974). IPC Magazines. U.K. b&w. Anthology. Magazine.

Whoopee! Book of Frankie Stein (1977). IPC Magazines. U.K. b&w. Anthology. Large format.

Whoopee! Monthly (Apr. 1993). Fleetway. U.K. b&w. Anthology. Magazine.

Winnipeg Free Press Canada's Leading Comic Section (Oct. 30, 1975). Sunday comics supplement to the daily *Winnipeg Free Press.*

Witches' Tales (1970). Vol. 2, No. 4, vol. 4, No. 2 (1972), vol. 5, No. 1–2, 4–6 (1973), vol. 6, No. 1–2 (1974), vol. 7, No. 1 (1975). Eerie Publications. Magazine.

The Witching Hour! No. 34 (Sep. 1973). DC.

Wolff and Byrd, Counselors of the Macabre. No. 7 (June 1995), No. 13 (Oct. 1996), and No. 14 (Feb. 1997). Exhibit A Press. b&w.

Wolff & Byrd: Counselors of the Macabre (1996). Vol. 2. Exhibit A Press. b&w. Rpt. Trade Paperback. Anthology.

Wow! No. 1 (June 5, 1982), No. 4 (June 26, 1982), No. 6 (July 10, 1982), No. 10 (Aug. 7, 1982), No. 14 (Sep. 4, 1982), No. 18 (Oct. 2, 1982), No. 20 (Oct. 16, 1982), No. 27 (Dec. 4, 1982), No. 30 (Dec. 25, 1982), No. 31 (Jan. 1, 1983), No. 33 (Jan. 15, 1983), No. 34 (Jan. 22, 1983), No. 36 (Feb. 5, 1983), No. 38 (Feb. 19, 1983), No. 41 (Mar. 12, 1983), No. 43 (Mar. 26, 1983), No. 45 (Apr. 9, 1983), No. 51 (May 21, 1983), No. 52 (May 28, 1983), No. 54 (June 11, 1983), and No. 56 (June 25, 1983). IPC Magazines. U.K. b&w.

Wow! Holiday Special (1985). IPC Magazines. U.K. b&w.

X-Men Classic. No. 63 (Sep. 1991). Marvel.

X-Men Vs. Dracula (1993). No. 1 (Dec. 1993). Marvel. One-Shot.

X-Men: Apocalypse Vs. Dracula (2006) No. 1–4 Marvel

Yikes. No. 2 (May 1998). Alternative Press. Small format.

Yosemite Sam and Bugs Bunny (1970–1980). No. 6, No. 7 (Apr. 1972). Gold Key.

Young Dracula (1992). No. 1–3. Caliber.

Young Dracula (1994). Caliber Press. Rpt. b&w. Trade Paperback.

Young Dracula: Prayer of the Vampire (1999). No. 1–5. Boneyard Press. b&w.

Japanese Manga

Akumaj Dorakyura: Yami no Juin (*Castlevania: Curse of Darkness*). Volume 1. Written by Kou Sasakura. Translated by Ray Yoshimoto. Japan: Konami Digital Entertainment Co. (2005). Publishers: Toyko Pop (2008). 172 pages.

Hellsing. Written by Kohta Hirano. Translated by Duane Johnson. Lettering by Wilbert Lacuna. U.S. Publisher (English-language version): Dark Horse and Digital Manga Publishing (2003–2009). 10 volumes.

Hipara-Kun (*Hipira: The Little Vampire*). Written by Katsuhiro Otomo. Illustrated by Shinji Kimura. Japan: Shufu-to-Seikatsu Sha Ltd (2002). U.S. Publishers: Dark Horse (2005). Trans. Kumar Sivasubramanian. French Publisher: Casterman. 1 volume. 28 pages. color.

Vanpaia. Written and illustrated by Yuki Takahashi. Japan: Hakusensha. Serialized in Bessatsu Hana to Yume. Seven Seas Entertainment (2009). 2 volumes. 360 pages.

Yorugata Aijin Senmonten—Blood Hound. By Kaori Yuki. Japan: Hakusensha. Manga (2003–2004).

Afterword

Ian Holt

As co-writer of *Dracula: The Un-Dead*, I have spent 20 years researching the historical Dracula, Bram Stoker's Count Dracula and Bram Stoker himself. Many times during those years, the task of locating sources of any considerable interest was arduous, to say the least. Thanks to Browning and Picart, this task has just become decidedly easier.

The historical overlap between the fifteenth-century Prince Vlad Dracula III and Bram Stoker's Victorian count has always been shrouded in mystery and conjecture. The first two Western scholars to bring light to the subject were my mentors, professors Raymond T. McNally and Radu Florescu, in their best-selling work of nonfiction, *In Search of Dracula* (1972). These professors scoured Europe and Russia for 10 years, hunting down scraps of information to complete their groundbreaking work, a task that was, at times, overwhelming and backbreaking. I once asked Professor Florescu what compelled him to take on such a monumental research project, aside from the more obvious reasons, like his Romanian heritage and that he is believed to be Prince Dracula's last known descendent. In the end, he simply said, "It was time, and someone had to do it." The same, I feel, can be said here for Browning and Picart's work.

Responding to the fanatical popularity of Stoker's vampire in media culture over the past century, the late Professor McNally—"Ray"—always used to say, "The old count

Ian Holt, Dracula documentarian and co-author of the Stoker family-sanctioned sequel, *Dracula: The Un-Dead* (photograph by Jan Cobb).

really knew how to put the show in the business." Since Béla Lugosi's iconic image first appeared on movie screens across America in 1931, Dracula and vampires have endured as dominant, inescapable images and personalities of mass culture. Dracula is everywhere, from our Halloween costume shops to cereal boxes on our breakfast tables, to children's television shows. He has been revived time and again in all manner and caliber of movies, television series, novels and comic books. Dracula and vampires are hotter today than ever before, and in the wake of their success, they have imparted to us a legacy of literally thousands of incarnations for fans to sift through. Many of these incarnations we remember as children, or as teenagers, and the impressions they left have been endearing ones. Sifting through the wealth of Dracula material out there is daunting, almost impossible, which underscores the feat of Browning and Picart's painstaking work.

For the researcher whose livelihood depends upon it, or the hardcore fan, or the newcomer looking to catch up, Browning and Picart's book is one-stop shopping. I can't tell you how excited I am that someone has finally attempted to compile nearly every film, broadcast, comic book, and video game in which Dracula, or his likeness, has appeared. Even someone like me who prides himself on having seen or read everything to do with Dracula has to admit that some material has inevitably fallen between the cracks. For me, and many others I'm sure, this catalog is the ultimate bucket list.

Unlike Dracula, we humans do not live forever, which is unfortunate because it would take at least that long for someone to sift through everything in this book. Many fancy the idea of traveling the world and seeing incredible sites. As crazy as it sounds, for me, it's a personal challenge to read and see everything to do with Dracula. Until now, I thought that task would be almost impossible to achieve in a single lifetime. However, I realize now that it would have been at least two lifetimes without the aide of this widely accessible resource.

Dracula and vampire fans are in general extremely well-versed in the genre and have

Right: Castle Ambras, near Innsbruck, Austria, houses an oil portrait of Prince Vlad Dracula, painted in the late fifteenth century or early sixteenth century, as part of the original collection of Ferdinand II (courtesy Kunsthistorisches Museum, Vienna).

wide and varied tastes. This is why among the numerous lectures on Prince Dracula and Stoker's novel that I have given at various times and places, the most difficult part is not the lecture itself actually, but rather when I invite the audience to ask questions, of which they are very capable with every conceivable variation. Lecturing on vampires and answering questions are not exactly what I would recommend to the ill-prepared. Professors McNally and Florescu, who between them had 80 years of experience, would still get nervous about someone from the audience asking questions they could not answer. Now, with Browning and Picart's book safely hidden (and open) behind the lectern with me, I hardly think I'll be stumped again.

Appendix 1.
Dracula in Print: A Checklist

Robert Eighteen-Bisang and
J. Gordon Melton

It is no longer necessary to make a case for the importance of Bram Stoker's macabre fairy tale. More than a century after its initial publication, *Dracula* has been recognized as one of the greatest horror stories ever written.[1] The novel has not only generated countless books, plays and movies but laid the foundation for new generations of vampires — including Anne Rice's *Interview with the Vampire*, Joss Whedon's *Buffy, the Vampire Slayer* and Stephenie Meyer's *Twilight*. The fact that *Dracula* has not been out of print since it was first published in 1897 testifies to its popular appeal.

This essay provides readers with a summary of the creation of the novel and offers a checklist of important editions.[2] After extensive research, Eighteen-Bisang and Melton compiled a definitive three-volume Dracula/vampire bibliography, *Dracula: A Century of Editions, Adaptations and Translations*,[3] to which the following material adds crucial updates.

Dracula was published by Archibald Constable and Company of 2 Whitehall Gardens, London, in 1897. The first edition was preceded by an early draft, a typescript and a contract for a novel entitled *The Un-Dead*, while four post-textual documents enriched our appreciation of the many layers of meaning]hidden in the text. Revised editions that furnish the source text for other publications came out in 1899 (Doubleday), 1901 (Constable), 1912 (Rider) and 1927 (Doubleday).

Bram Stoker's Notes for Dracula

Following Bram Stoker's death in 1912, early notes for *Dracula* and other personal effects were auctioned at Sotheby, Wilkinson and Hodge in London on July 7, 1913. These papers are now in the custodianship of the Rosenbach Museum and Library in Philadelphia, which acquired them in 1970.

Bram Stoker's Original Foundation Notes & Data for His "Dracula" consists of 124 pages of early research and plot notes that have been divided into three sections: handwritten notes on the plot; handwritten research notes; and typed research notes (which include maps and photographs). These papers show the development of the plot from early, often unrecognizable pastiches of people, places and events to a nine-page calendar that includes most of the familiar story that has been told and retold for more than a century.

Notes testifies to Bram Stoker's extensive planning and research. Dates on some of the pages prove that he had started working on *Dracula* by March 1890 and continued writing and revising it until (at least) 1896.

These documents received little attention until 1979 when Raymond McNally and Radu Florescu announced that they had "discovered" them in their annotated edition of Bram Stoker's opus.[4] Twenty-nine years later, Robert Eighteen-Bisang and Elizabeth Miller published a scholarly edition of the *Notes*.[5] *Bram Stoker's Notes for Dracula* includes photo-facsimiles and transcriptions of every page of notes with an introduction, a conclusion, appendices and indices. We now know that two early segments were jettisoned. The first part was to be an exchange of letters between Count Dracula and his lawyers in England; the second, a record of Jonathan Harker's fateful trip to Munich on his way to Transylvania — including a night at the opera, a visit to a museum and mysteries in a "dead-house" (i.e., a morgue). Notes about a "snow storm" with a "wolf" form the basis of "Dracula's Guest," which was published in 1914. Stoker's initial cast of characters differed widely from his final selection: the Count had two servants, a deaf mute woman and a silent man; Lucy was engaged to Dr. Seward; a man named Brutus became Quincey P. Morris; while three deleted characters (a German philosopher and historian, a scientist, and a detective) were amalgamated as the redoubtable Professor Abraham Van Helsing.

Notes tells us that the story was set in 1893, and furnishes a list of many works the author consulted. His most important non-fiction sources were William Wilkersons' article "An Account of the Principalities of Wallachia and Moldavia" (1820)—where, we assume, he found the name "Dracula"—and Emily Gerard's "Transylvanian Superstitions," which was published in 1885. Contrary to popular belief, Stoker never set foot in Transylvania.

The Un-Dead

The manuscript for *Dracula* was not among the material that had been sold at Sotheby's in 1913 and, until recently, it was assumed to have been irretrievably lost or destroyed. In the spring of 1977 a sheaf of yellowing type-written papers was discovered in a trunk in rural Pennsylvania. The text had been cut and pasted together numerous times, and was peppered with corrections in pen and blue pencil. The smudged, grubby title page bore the title "The Un-dead" and the author's name, "Bram Stoker." Further investigation revealed that this was the long-lost manuscript for the world's best-known vampire novel.

After passing through several hands, the typescript was acquired by John McLaughlin, the proprietor of the Book Sail in Orange, California, who offered it for sale in the *The Undead: The Book Sail's 16th Anniversary Catalogue* in 1984. It is described as:

The Un-Dead (later *Dracula*). "Original typed manuscript, ribbon copy, on the rectos of 529 pages, varying in size between 8½" × 10" to 14½" ... Bram Stoker's original manuscript, with his extensive annotations, corrections and revisions in holograph, including a hand-written title page and bearing his autographed inscription 26 times."

No offer matched his (undisclosed) minimum bid but Christie's in New York auctioned the typescript on April 17, 2002 and, eventually, sold it to a private collector for $941,000.

Most pages bear at least three distinct sets of pagination: one typed and two in ink in Stoker's hand. This suggests the existence of previous typescripts, or, at the very at least, a drastic rearrangement of the people, places and events in the novel. The typed set of numerals and one of the handwritten sets are crossed out. The final numbered sequence commences with page 3—which is preceded by Stoker's prefatory note and the first unnumbered page of text—and continues (with irregularities) to page 541. The text differs from that of the first edition in various ways. A few changes and corrections are apparent, and several references to one of the first two chapters ("Dracula's Guest") were deleted. The most important change is the deletion of two paragraphs that followed the sentence: "The castle of Dracula now stood out against the red sun and every stone of its broken battlements was articulated against the light" (Chapter 27). The "missing" passage describes a series of cataclysmic events, including an earthquake, that destroyed Castle Dracula after his death. This episode underscores the fact that the Count was a sorcerer who maintained his domain through magical means. This is in keeping with folklore, which usually sees vampires as demons or sorcerers.

Leslie S. Klinger transcribed most of the "missing" passages in *The New Annotated Dracula*, which was published by W. W. Norton in 2008.

Dracula: or, the Un-Dead

The only extant copy of Bram Stoker's play, *Dracula: or, the Un-Dead*, is located in the British Library. It consists of at least two proof copies of *Dracula* that were cut and pasted unto large sheets of paper, with stage directions and interlocutory text scribbled in Bram Stoker's hasty, often illegible hand.

Prior to the publication of the novel, a five-act play was presented to establish its copyright. *Dracula: or The Undead* was performed for a small group of employees and passers-by at the Lyceum Theatre on May 18, 1897. The cast was drawn from the theater's supporting ranks, with an actor named "Jones" (probably Whitworth Jones) playing the part of Count Dracula. All of the major characters were included, while the account of the Demeter was read by a character called "Coastguard."

The play opens "Outside Castle Dracula" where Jonathan Harker summarizes the preceding material as he stands at the entrance. Dracula has more dialogue than he does in the novel, for much of what is attributed to Harker in the first four chapters is voiced by the Count in the dramatic reading. In contrast, the scene where Harker is "seduced" by three vampire women is reduced to the following dialogue:

1ST WOMAN: Go on! You are first and we shall follow; yours is the right to begin.

2ND WOMAN: He is young and strong; there are kisses for us all.

Lengthy segments of the script follow the novel verbatim. Most important speeches remain intact, including lengthy monologues by Swales and Van Helsing. In contrast, the conclusion is surprisingly abrupt. As the hunters and gypsies converge, it reads:

Horsemen fight with gypsies and Morris and Harker throw box from cart and prise it open. Count seen. Fades away as knives cut off his head. Sunset falls on the group.

The novel refers to Dracula's method of execution obliquely—"I shrieked as I saw it [Jonathan's Kukri knife] shear through the throat; while at the same moment Mr. Morris's bowie knife plunged into the heart" (p. 388)—but the play tells us that the Count was decapitated.

The fact that two early versions of the text are more explicit than the novel about Dracula's "final" death is puzzling. The possibility that Stoker had a sequel in mind lends credence to Roger Sherman Hoar's claim that "Stoker told me he planned to bring Dracula over to America in another story" (cited in Peter Haining, ed., *Shades of Dracula*, p. 135).

The entire play and a detailed commentary are presented in Sylvia Sunshine's *Dracula: or, the Un-Dead*, which was published by Pumpkin Books, 1997. It includes an introduction with an account of the first performance at the Lyceum Theatre, along with photographs of the theatre, the original cast, and the opening page of *Dracula* in Stoker's hand.

Bram Stoker's Contract for "The Un-Dead"

Bram Stoker drew up an undated, handwritten "Memorandum of Agreement" for a novel titled "The Un-Dead." His publisher revised and typed up this agreement, and both parties signed it on the 20th of May 1897. The contract specified what royalties the author would receive and provided for a colonial edition (or editions). When the novel appeared in bookstores, the title had been changed to *Dracula*— the memorable, emphatic name of its main character. We do not know if this change was made by the author or an editor, but "the decision was fortuitous — the one-word title itself, the three sinister syllables that crack and undulate on the tongue, ambiguous, foreign, and somehow alluring, was certainly a component of the book's initial and continued mystique" (David Skal, *Hollywood Gothic*, p. 22).

Archibald Constable & Co.

The first Constable edition of *Dracula* is described as: Westminster [London]: Archibald Constable and Company, 1897. [ix], 390 p. hb. with yellow binding, red lettering & a red rule. The first edition and early reprints state "1897" on their title pages, but do not carry a statement of edition. Their copyright pages say "Copyright, 1897, in the United States of America, according to an Act of Congress, by Bram Stoker. All rights reserved."

The exact date of its release is a matter of contention; dates as divergent as May 26th and June 24th have been put forth. However, there is no doubt that Constable re-printed *Dracula* three or four times in 1897. The first printing that stated the date of publication was the "fifth edition" of "1898." Hence, earlier editions must be differentiated by any advertisements that follow the text. Presentation copies are assumed to be examples of the first edition, first state. All of them have an embossed stamp on the title page: "Presented by Archibald Constable & Co." while pages [391] and [392] are blank. The second edition is assumed to be the variant with an advertisement for *The Shoulder of Shasta* on page [392] (but no additional ads). The third and fourth editions have numerous advertisements, while the fifth, sixth and seventh state the edition and year of publication on their title pages. Each edition has multiple states with variations in the number and content of advertisements.

Colonial Editions

From the middle of the nineteenth century, colonial editions were distributed to four areas: Africa, Australia, Canada, and India. They provided publishers with an additional, early source of profit, and allowed countries that did not have a large enough population to support a local publishing industry opportunities to enjoy the latest popular literature. There are at least two colonial editions of *Dracula*. In 2002, Robert Eighteen-Bisang found a copy of "Hutchinson's Colonial Library Edition of *Dracula*," which had been distributed in Australia, and announced this *rara avis* to the world. This edition was printed from the same plates as the domestic (Constable) edition and bears the same printer's colophon. The only differences are its blood-red binding, gilt lettering, title page (which reads: "Hutchinson & Co." and "1897") and copyright page ("This edition is issued for circulation in India and the British Colonies only"). This may be the "true first" edition. Another colonial edition that was printed by Hutchinson and

Doubleday & McClure

New York: Doubleday & McClure Co., 1899. [x], 378 p. hb. with brown, pictorial binding. Cover: (Dracula's castle against a setting sun).

The first American edition corrects some typographic errors and makes a small but important change in chapter four. When Dracula tells his "Brides" that they can feed on Jonathan Harker the following night, the Constable edition says, "To-morrow night, to-morrow night, is yours!" [p. 51] but Doubleday contends that Dracula intends to feed on him to: "To-night is mine. Tomorrow night is yours!" [p. 51]. This is the only instance of a male vampire feeding on another man.

Constable's Abridged Edition

Westminster: Archibald Constable and Company, 1901. 144 p. tr. pb. Cover (a line-drawing by Nathan shows Dracula with bat-like wings crawling down the wall of his castle as Jonathan Harker looks on in amazement). Double columns of text, p. 11–138.

An abridged version of *Dracula* was issued in 1901. The revised text deletes or abridges many of the lengthy descriptions and conversations that dominate the text, and corrects a few errors in the first edition. The fact that Stoker himself made these changes affords scholars a unique, stereoscopic view into the author's original intentions.

Bram Stoker's Preface to the Icelandic Edition

Bram Stoker wrote an original Preface for an abridged edition of *Dracula* that was published in Iceland in 1901 under the Title *Makt Myrkanna [The Power of Darkness]*. His new introduction linked the novel with Jack the Ripper, who butchered (at least five) prostitutes in the slums of Whitechapel in 1888.

1901–1912

The novel's popular appeal has increased the value of early editions, which are avidly sought out by a wide variety of collectors.

New York: A. Wessels Company, 1901. [x], 378 p. hb. The title page says: "Special Limited Edition." There are variant bindings, but the most common has a tan background w. a red & green garland, green lettering & a green rule. One variant has Wessels' imprint on the title page but says: bound by Coop-Clark in Toronto was discovered in Canada.

"Grosset & Dunlap" on the spine. NUC lists a paperbound edition but no copy is extant.

New York: Doubleday, Page & Co., 1902. [x], 378 p. hb. w. red binding & an inlay of Dracula, a bat and a wolf. Rpt. 1904. Variant: green binding. Rpt. 1904.

New York: Doubleday, Page & Company, 1903. [x], 378 p. hb. w. green marbled boards. Crowned Masterpieces of Modern Fiction. Special Subscription Edition.

Westminster: Archibald Constable & Co. Ltd., 1904. [viii], 390 p. hb.

The eighth edition was published in three decorative bindings: a. dark black-blue cloth w. a reddish-orange decoration running down the left side; title in gilt; b. black cloth w. red lettering & a petal design. Variant: Petal Design; red cloth w. black lettering.

William Rider & Son

In 1912, William Rider & Son obtained the domestic rights to *Dracula*. Their edition reset the text and corrected most of the errors that had crept into the Constable edition. The Rider text became the primary source for new editions and reprints in England and the colonies.

London: William Rider & Son, Limited, 1912. viii + 404 p. hb. (red binding with an embossed, decorative cover & gilt lettering on the spine). dj. (Halloway's magnificent, color dust jacket shows the Count crawling head-first down the wall of his castle; a phoenix motif is embedded in the folds of his cloak). Popular edition. Price: 1s Net. Note: The title page of the first Rider edition says, "Ninth edition" in recognition of Constable's hardbound editions of 1897 to 1904.

1913

Garden City, NY: Doubleday, Page & Company, 1913. [x], 378 p. hb. Rpt. 1917, 1919, 1920, 1924 & 1927.

Dracula's Guest

Two years after Stoker's death, his widow, Florence, brought out the first book in a proposed three-volume set of her husband's short fiction. She claimed that the title story was "a hitherto unpublished episode from *Dracula* ... [that] was originally excised due to the length of the book." The story, "Dracula's Guest," has been reprinted in dozens of anthologies. At the outset Jonathan Harker's visit to Transylvania, he becomes lost in a snowstorm near Munich and, eventually, encounters a vampiress and a werewolf.

Dracula's Guest: And Other Weird Stories. London: George Routledge & Sons, Ltd., 1914. vii, 200 p. hb. dj. (by Handworth; a supine Jonathan Harker is protected by a wolf). Contents: "Preface" by Florence A. L. Bram Stoker." "Dracula's Guest." Rpt. 1914 to 1935, 13th edition. The first American edition was not published until 1937. The first paperbound editions were issued by Arrow, 1966, and Zebra, 1978.

1913–1919

Dracula: A Horror Story. New York: W. R. Caldwell, n.d. [circa 1918]. 378 p. hb. dj. (a plain wrapper). frontis. International Adventure Library Series. Three Owls Edition. Caldwell's edition boasts the first frontispiece.

London: William Rider & Son, Limited, 1918. viii, 404 p. tr. pb. 12th edition. Rider's Cheap Fiction Series.

1920s

London: William Rider & Son, Limited, 1921. viii, 404 p. hb. w. green, decorative binding. dj. 14th edition.

Garden City, NY: Doubleday, Page & Company, 1924. [x], 378 p. hb. w. red Leather binding. dj. The Lambskin Library Series No. 5.

The Argosy: The World's Best Stories. London (June 1926–February 1927) 10 pt. Mrs. Florence A. L. Bram Stoker wrote a "Foreword" to the novel's first serial publication.

Garden City, NY: Doubleday, Page & Company, 1927. [ix], 354 p. hb. w. brown binding, black lettering & a black border. Cover (says: "Dracula" and "Bram Stoker"), dj. Doubleday's new, re-typeset edition of *Dracula* became the source of subsequent American editions.

London: Rider & Co., 1927. viii, 404 p. hb. w. green, decorative binding. dj. 16th edition.

Doubleday, Doran & Company

Doubleday revised and re-typeset *Dracula* in 1928. This edition, which broke the text into smaller paragraphs, became the source of American reprints by Doubleday and other companies.

Garden City, NY: Doubleday, Doran & Company, Inc., 1928. ix, 354 p. hb. dj.

Garden City, NY: Garden City Publishing Company, Inc., 1928. [ix], 354 p. hb. dj. (green lettering on a yellow background w. Dracula in a tuxedo, top hat and cloak). Sun Dial Library Series. This edition, with its stylish dust jacket, was the source of the first Modern Library edition which was published four years later.

New York: Grosset & Dunlap, n.d. [1928]. [i–ix], 354 p. hb. w. a pictorial dj. (a large head with prominent feminine eyes looming over a sleeping blond woman). Back panel of dj. says: "Did you see the play...?" Rpt.

1930s

New York: Grosset & Dunlap Publishers, n.d. [1930]. [i–ix], 354 p. hb. dj. (yellow eyes menace a sleeping brunette woman). Jr. frontis. plate (Béla Lugosi) & 3 plates of photographs from Universal Pictures' adaptation of 1930. First movie tie-in edition. First Béla Lugosi edition. Rpt.

London: Rider & Co., 1931. viii, 404 p. dj. (this is the first of three rare variants of Halloway's dust jacket; his drawing is enclosed in a white border, while "Dracula," "Bram Stoker" and "Punch says: — The very weirdest of weird tales" are printed in red). 19th edition. Rider & Co. published an undated variant, while a variant with an illustrated title page was issued by "The House of Rider."

New York: Modern Library, 1932. (xii) [418] p. hb. (in flexible "balloon cloth"). dj. (red title & black lettering on a white background w. Dracula in a tuxedo, top hat and cloak). ML #31. Rpt. n.d. The Modern Library purchased the Sun Dial Library from Doubleday in 1930. ML published new editions of *Dracula* in 1941, 1966, 1978, 1996 and 2001, which features an introduction by Peter Straub.

The Horror Omnibus. New York: Grosset & Dunlap, n.d. [c. 1935.] [viii], 354 p. hb. dj. Contents: *Dracula*. After *Dracula* entered the public domain in 1962, it appeared in a variety of omnibuses.

1940s

Dracula: A Horror Story. New York: Editions for the Armed Services, Inc., n.d. [1944]. 448 p. tr. pb. Oblong format. #L 25. Rpt. n.d. [1945]. #851. These editions were distributed free of charge to soldiers stationed overseas during World War II.

London, New York, Melbourne, Sydney, Cape Town: Rider and Company, n.d. [1947]. 335 p. hb. dj. (a fiendish face emerging from a dark background; dj. says: "More than a million copies sold"). Rpt. n.d. [1949].

New York: Pocket Books, 1947. 409 p. pb. Cover (a caricature of Béla Lugosi hovers over a sleeping woman). Text: "Dracula: the most famous horror story ever told." The first mass-market paperback edition of *Dracula*.

1950s

London: Arrow Books, 1954. 336 p. tr. pb. Cover (a fiendish face emerging from a dark background — from Rider's edition of 1947). Arrow was Rider's paperbound imprint. It reprinted *Dracula* with many different, often gory, covers in: 1954, 1958, 1959, 1962, 1965, 1967, 1969, 1970, 1971, 1973, 1974 and 1979.

New York: Permabooks, 1957. 376 p. pb. Cover (a woman is menaced by a stylized hand). This was the first edition of *Dracula* to omit copyright notice of 1897.

New York: Permabooks, 1958. 376 p. pb. Cover (photograph; Christopher Lee and Melissa Stribling). Movie tie-in edition.

Garden City, NY: Garden City Books, n.d. [1959]. ix, 354 p. hb. dj. (by Ben Feder; a line-drawing of a heavily mustachioed Dracula). Book club edition. Rpt. n.d. Rpt. n.d.

1960s

Dracula entered the public domain in 1962 — just as the mass market, paperback revolution was taking the publishing industry by storm. By 1965 most publishers realized that the novel had entered the public domain. Many of the first wave of new editions are now collector's items:

New York: Signet Books, 1965. 382 p. pb. Signet Classic Series. Cover (a stylized bat/skull). Text: "A Masterpiece of Gothic Horror — The Nightmare Story of the Dread Master of the Undead" The New American Library continues to issue new editions/covers to this day.

New York: Airmont Publishing Company, Inc., 1965. 317 p. pb. Airmont Classic Series CL 72. Abridged for grades 7 and up. "Bram Stoker, Introduction" by Robert A. W. Lowndes, p. 1–5.

New York: Dell Books, March 1965. 416 p. pb. Laurel Leaf Library Series. Cover (by Paul Davies; a profile of a blue-faced Dracula with long white hair and a prominent mustache in an oval).

New York: The Limited Editions Club, 1965. xiv, 410 p. hb. illus. w. wood engravings by Felix Hoffman; some color. In slipcase. 1500 signed & numbered copies. With an introduction by Anthony Boucher. The first deluxe edition of *Dracula* was reissued by Heritage Press and Easton Press — which both published more than one variation — in different bindings.

New York: Pyramid Books, 1965. 352 p. pb. Cover (Dracula and a bat against a white background).

London: Jarrolds, 1966. 336 p. hb. dj. "Publisher Note" [by Richard Dalby. Rpt. 1970, 1972. This edition is part a uniform set that includes: "Dracula's Guest," *The Jewel of Seven Stars*, *The Lady of the Shroud* and *The Lair of the White Worm*.

1970s

Contemporary scholarly interest in *Dracula* began in the 1970s, following Raymond McNally and Radu Florescu's best-selling *In Search of Dracula* (1972). Their pioneering study linked the fictional Count Dracula with a fifteenth-century warlord who had been called "Dracula" (the "Son of Dracul") before earning the name "Vlad Tepes" ("Vlad the Impaler") in battle. The theory that Stoker's literary creation was based on Vlad has been discredited, but the belief that Count Dracula was a real person has entrenched itself as one-of-things-everybody-knows-about-vampires. The first annotated editions of the text in 1975 and 1979 set the tone for future scholarly editions.

New York: Dodd, Mead & Co., 1970. [viii], 430 p. hb. dj. frontis. & illus. (plates). Edited by James Nelson.

New York: Magnum Easy Eye/Lancer Books, 1970. 558 p. pb. The first large-print edition.

New York: Scholastic Book Services, 1971. 462 p. pb. Abridged by Nora Kramer. Rpt. 1975 & n.d.

The Annotated Dracula. New York: Clarkson N. Potter, 1975. [xxii], 362 p. hb. dj. frontis. [plate] & photographs w. illus. by Satty. Edited by Leonard Wolf. Rpt. 1976. tr. pb. Revised: *The Essential Dracula*, 1993. Leonard Wolf's *Dreams of Dracula* (1972) explored the Count's impact on popular culture. He broke new ground again with the first scholarly, annotated edition of Dracula.

The Illustrated Dracula. New York: Drake, 1975. [iv], 184 p. hb. dj. illus. w. photographs. Rpt. tr. pb.

New York: A Jove Book, 1979. 352 p. pb. Cover (Frank Langella). Movie tie-in edition.

The Essential Dracula: A Completely Illustrated & Annotated Edition of Bram Stoker's Classic Novel. New York: Mayflower Books, 1979. 320 p. hb. dj. illus. w. photographs. Edited by Raymond McNally & Radu Florescu. Rpt. 1993. The editors restored the missing chapter, "Dracula's Guest," and dropped tantalizing hints about the author's original intentions. For example, he had considered the titles: "The Un-Dead" and "The Dead Un-Dead" before deciding on *Dracula*. Moreover, his vampire, who was once called "Count Wampyr," initially resided in Styria (the home of Joseph Sheridan LeFanu's Carmilla). However, their work left many questions unanswered.

1980s

New trade paperback editions of *Dracula* were designed for classrooms, colleges and other readers who wanted text with larger print than mass market paperbacks. These books set a new trend that has continued until the present day. They not only explain the text but highlight issues in history, literature, psychology, sociology, etc. that were being explored by scholars. Oxford University Press, which brought out the first such edition, has continued to reprint and update it.

New York: Bantam Books, 1981. [xxiv], 402 p. pb. Edited by George Stade. Bantam Classic Series. Rpt.

Oxford and New York: Oxford University Press, 1983. [xxviii], 380 p. tr. pb. Edited by Andrew Norman Wilson. Rpt.

London: Blackie, 1988. 379 p. hb. dj. & illus. by Charles Keeping. Rpt.

New York: Tor, 1989. [xiii], 368 p. pb. Edited by R. L. Fisher. Rpt.

1990s

The 1990s saw a variety of new editions of *Dracula* as publishers rushed to cash in on the publicity that surrounded the centennial of the first publication in 1897 and the release of Francis Ford Coppola's movie *Bram Stoker's Dracula*.[6]

London: Pan Books, 1992. [xii], 382 p. pb. Cover (a gargoyle). illus. with an insert of photographs. Introduction by Leonard Wolf. Movie tie-in edition.

London: A Signet Book, 1992. [xii], 382 p. pb. Cover (a gargoyle). illus. with an insert of photographs. Introduction by Leonard Wolf. Movie tie-in edition.

London: J. M. Dent; Richmond, VT: Charles E. Tuttle, 1993. [xviii], 402 p. pb. Edited by Marjorie Howes.

London and New York: Penguin Books, 1993. xl, 520 p. tr. pb. Penguin Classics Series. Edited by Maurice Hindle. Rpt.

Ware, Hertfordshire, U.K.: Wordsworth Classics, 1993. [iv], 312 p. hb. (illustrated boards) & dj. Rpt. pb.

Dracula: The Definitive Edition. New York: Barnes & Noble, 1996. [xxxii], 427 p. hb. dj. illus. by Edward Gorey. Edited by Marvin Kaye. 3 states: lettered, numbered and trade.

Peterborough, ON, Canada: Broadview Press, 1997. 493 p. tr. pb. Edited by Glennis Byron. Broadview Literary Texts Series.

New York: W. W. Norton & Company, 1997. [xiv], 488 p. tr. pb. Norton Critical Editions Series. Edited by Nina Auerbach and David J. Skal.

Dracula Unearthed. Westcliff-on-the-Sea, Essex, U.K.: Desert Island Books, 1998. 512 p. hb. dj. Edited by Clive Leatherdale. This edition, which is full of insights into Victorian England, adds the day of the week at the beginning of each entry. Revised: 2006. tr. pb.

The 21st Century

Boston [and] New York: Bedford/St. Martin's, 2002. [xvi], 622 p. hb. dj. Edited by John Paul Riquelme. Case Studies in Contemporary Criticism Series.

New York: Pearson Longman, 2008. [xviii], 494 p. tr. pb. Edited by Richard Appelbaum. A Longman Annotated Edition for Developing College Readers.

Bram Stoker's Dracula. San Diego, CA: IDW, 2009. 444 p. hb. illus. by Ben Templesmith.

The POD Revolution

In the 1990s, advances in printing and the digitalization of text fostered a new industry — print on demand books. Advances in technology allowed publishers to print books as they were needed, eliminating the need for large print runs and expensive warehouses. These advances created a new type of vanity press that welcomed authors who could not find standard publishers for their work. Other publishers brought out an array of "classic" titles (i.e., books that were out of copyright) but continued to sell. Of course, *Dracula* was, and will remain, one of the foremost of such titles. Ironically, a few editions with small print runs from ephemeral publishers may become collectors' items.

The epitome of Print-on-Demand editions of *Dracula* may be variations by Customized Classics (*http://www.customizedclassics.com/*), which offers customers one-of-a-kind copies of the text with the names of the major characters — Dracula, Abraham Van Helsing, Jonathan Harker, and Mina Murray — replaced by any name the customer wants. If they choose a new name for Dracula, this name also becomes the title of the novel.

Adaptations and Translations

In addition to the text, the modern era has been besieged by adaptations of *Dracula* in media, from stage, radio, cinema, television, records, and audio recordings, to CDs, DVDs, and comic books. There are even *Dracula* coloring books!

There are about 75 adaptations in the following formats: Juvenile editions of *Dracula* introduce the Count to a younger market than that for which the novel was originally intended. Abridged versions of the story omit the most erotic and gory scenes, and often carry age-appropriate illustrations. Many juvenile adaptations are ESL (English-as-a-second-language) readers. In some cases, these texts print the English beside that of the reader's first language. On the other end of the spectrum, there are adaptations of *Dracula* with sexually-explicit content. The first of these books was *The Adult Version of Dracula*, in 1970.

During the first half of the 20th century, *Dracula* was translated into French, German,[7] Italian, and Spanish. There are different translations in each of these languages, and at least one edition in 50 other languages. *Dracula* was translated into Chinese in 1999. An abridged edition was published in the People's Republic of China in 2002, and the complete text followed two years later.

Conclusion

Changes in the publishing industry from the late 1880s to the present day — including one of the first typewritten manuscripts — are reflected in the numerous editions of *Dracula* that have appeared during this time. At the dawn of the present century, more and more editions are available on CD-ROMs, DVD's and the internet. Only time will tell what form *Dracula* will take in the future.

Notes

1. "After their first appearance in nineteenth century England, three [works] quickly became classic tales of terror, the modern equivalent of myths: Mary Shelley's Frankenstein, Robert Louis Stevenson's Dr. Jekyll and Mr. Hyde, and Bram Stoker's Dracula." Martin Tropp, *Images of Fear: How Horror Stories Helped Shape Modern Culture (1818–1918)* (Jefferson, NC: McFarland, 1990), 1.

2. J. Gordon Melton has posted a preliminary list of every English-language edition of *Dracula*, under the title "All Things Dracula" at *http://www.cesnur.org/2003/dracula/*.) In addition, Bob and Melinda Hayes have posted pictures and descriptions of their editions of *Dracula* at *http://isd.usc.edu/~melindah/Stoker/dracthum.htm*).

3. Robert Eighteen-Bisang and J. Gordon Melton, *Dracula: A Century of Editions, Adaptations and Translations: Part One; English Language Editions* (Santa Barbara, CA: Transylvanian Society of Dracula, 1998).

4. Raymond McNally and Radu Florescu, eds., *The Essential Dracula: A Completely Illustrated and Annotated Edition of Bram Stoker's Classic Novel* (New York: Mayflower, 1979).

5. Bram Stoker, *Bram Stoker's Notes for* Dracula: *A Facsimile Edition*, Annotated and Transcribed by Robert Eighteen-Bisang and Elizabeth Miller (Jefferson, NC: McFarland, 2008).

6. Caveat emptor: *Bram Stoker's Dracula* by Fred Saberhagen and James V. Hart is the novelization of Coppola's movie, rather than Bram Stoker's text.

7. The first German edition, published in 1908, is significant, for it is the only translation of the complete text that emerged during Stoker's lifetime.

Appendix 2.
Film, Television, and Video Game Chronology

1921
Drakula halála (Hungary/Austria)

1922
Nosferatu, eine Symphonie des Grauens (Germany)

1928
Dracula/Garden of Eden (USA)

1931
Dracula (USA)
Drácula (USA)

1932
Boo (USA)

1933
Hollywood on Parade No. A-8 (USA). Documentary
Mickey's Gala Premier (USA). Animation

1935
Mark of the Vampire (USA)

1936
Dracula's Daughter (USA)

1939
Gandy Goose in G-Man Jitters (USA). Animation

1943
Son of Dracula (USA)

1944
Gandy Goose in Ghost Town (USA). Animation
House of Frankenstein (USA)
Return of the Vampire (USA)
The Vampire Interviews (USA) Documentary

1945
House of Dracula (USA)
Mighty Mouse: Mighty Mouse Meets Bad Bill Bunion (USA). Animation

1946
The Jail Break (USA). Animation

1948
Bud Abbott and Lou Costello Meet Frankenstein (USA)

1952
Mother Riley Meets the Vampire (U.K.)

1953
Drakula Istanbul'da (Turkey)

1954
El Fantasma de la opereta (Argentina)
Haram alek (Egypt)

1956

Black Inferno (USA)
Matinee Theatre, episode "Dracula" (USA). Television

1957

Blood of Dracula (USA)
The Steve Allen Show, episode "2.35" (USA). Television

1958

Dracula (U.K.)
The Return of Dracula (USA)

1959

Drakoulas & Sia (Greece)
Night of the Ghouls (USA)
Onna Kyuketsuki (Japan)
The Steve Allen Show, episode "5.3" (USA). Television
Tempi duri per i vampiri (Italy/France)

1960

The Brides of Dracula (U.K.)
The Steve Allen Show, episode "5.14" (USA). Television

1961

Akui ggot (South Korea)
El Mundo de los vampiros (Mexico)
Nightmare at Elm Manor (U.K.). Adult
Tales of the Wizard of Oz, episode "The Reunion" (USA). Television/Animation

1962

Dragstrip Dracula (USA)
House on Bare Mountain (USA). Adult
El Vampiro sangriento (Mexico)

1963

Escala en Hi-Fi (Spain)
Merrie Melodies, episode "Transylvania 6-5000" (USA). Television/Animation
Mga Manugang ni Drakula (Philippines)
Il Risveglio di Dracula (Italy)
Sexy Proibitissimo (Italy). Documentary/Adult
Tetsuwan Atom, episode "Vampire Vale" (Japan). Television/Animation
Vampire (U.K.). Adult

1964

Batman Dracula (USA)
Il Castello dei morti vivi (Italy)
Kiss Me Quick! (USA). Adult
Kulay Dugo ang Gabi (Philippines/USA)
The Munsters (USA). Television

1965

The Beatles, episode "Misery" (U.K.). Television/Animation
Doctor Who, episode "The Executioners" (U.K.). Television
Doctor Who, serial "The Chase," episode "Journey into Terror" (U.K.). Television
Get Smart, episode "The Wax Max" (USA). Television
The Naked World of Harrison Marks (U.K.). Documentary/Adult

1966

Billy the Kid Versus Dracula (USA)
Chappaqua (USA/France)
Doom of Dracula (USA)
Dracula (USA)
Dracula: Prince of Darkness (U.K.)
Emotion: densetsu no gogo=itsukamita Dracula (Japan)
Gilligan's Island, episode "Up at Bat" (USA). Television
Ibulong mo sa hangin (Philippines)
Operazione paura (Italy)
La Sorella di Satana (Italy)

1967

El Barón Brakola (Mexico)
Batman Fights Dracula (Philippines)
Dark Shadows 1840 Flashback (USA). Television
Dr. Terror's Gallery of Horrors (USA)
Dracula Meets the Outer Space Chicks (USA). Adult
Dracula's Wedding Day (USA)
The Fearless Vampire Killers; or, Pardon Me, but Your Teeth Are in My Neck (USA/U.K.)
El Imperio de Drácula (Mexico)
Mad Monster Party? (USA). Animation
A Taste of Blood (USA)
Zinda Laash (Pakistan)

1968

Dracula Has Risen from the Grave (U.K.)
Hay que matar a Drácula (Argentina)
The Inspector, episode "Transylvania Mania" (USA). Television/Animation

Kaibutsu-Kun (Japan). Animation
Kyuketsuki Gokemidoro (Japan)
La Marca del Hombre-lobo (Spain)
The Monkees, episode "Monstrous Monkee Mash" (USA). Television
Mystery and Imagination, episode "Dracula" (U.K.). Television

1969

Blood of Dracula's Castle (USA)
Carry on Christmas (U.K.)
Dracul cu scripca (Romania). Documentary
Dracula and the Boys; aka Does Dracula Really Suck? (USA). Adult
Dracula, The Dirty Old Man (USA). Adult
Drakulita (Philippines)
Dugo ng Vampira (Philippines)
The Magic Christian (U.K.)
Malenka (Spain/Italy)
Men of Action Meet Women of Drakula (Philippines)
Monty Python's Flying Circus, episode "No Fun Anymore" (U.K.). Television
Santo en El tesoro de Dracula (Mexico)
Scooby Doo! Where Are You?, episode "A Gaggle of Galloping Ghosts" (USA). Television/Animation
Las Vampiras (Mexico)

1970

Ashes of Doom (Canada)
Bela Lugosi Scrapbook (USA)
El Conde Drácula (Spain/West Germany/Italy/Liechtenstein)
Count Yorga, Vampire (USA)
Dracula's Baby (USA)
Cuadecuc, vampir (Spain). Documentary
Every Home Should Have One (U.K.)
Guess What Happened to Count Dracula (USA)
House of Dark Shadows (USA)
Jonathan (West Germany)
Los Monstruos del terror (Spain, West Germany, Italy)
Necropolis (Italy/U.K.)
One More Time (U.K.)
Otra vez Drácula (Argentina). Television
Sabrina and the Groovie Goolies (USA). Television/Animation
Scars of Dracula (U.K.)
Sex and the Single Vampire (USA). Adult
Taste the Blood of Dracula (U.K.)
A Trip with Dracula (USA)
Yûreiyashiki no kyôfu: Chi o suu ningyô (Japan)

1971

El Águila Descalza (Mexico)
Batuta ni Dracula (Philippines)
Capulina Contra los Vampiros (Mexico)
El Conde Mácula (Spain). Animation
Countess Dracula (U.K.)
Dracula Vs. Frankenstein (USA)
The Electric Company (USA). Television
El Fang-Dango (USA)
Gebissen wird nur nachts (West Germany)
The Hilarious House of Frightenstein (Canada). Television
The Horny Vampire (USA). Adult
The House That Dripped Blood (U.K.)
Hrabe Drakula (Czechoslovakia)
The Mad Love Life of a Hot Vampire (USA). Adult
Nella stretta morsa del ragno (Italy)
Night Gallery, episode "The Devil Is Not Mocked" (USA). Television
Night Gallery, episode "A Matter of Semantics" (USA). Television
Night Gallery, episode "A Midnight Visit to the Neighborhood Blood Bank" (USA). Television
La Noche de Walpurgis (Spain)
Noroi no yakata: Chi o sû me (Japan)
The Return of Count Yorga (U.K.)
A Touch of Sweden (USA). Adult
Twins of Evil (U.K.)
Vampiros Lesbos (West Germany/Spain)
Winter with Dracula (U.K.). Documentary

1972

The ABC Saturday Superstar Movie, episode "Daffy Duck and Porky Pig Meet the Groovie Goolies" (USA). Television/Animation
The ABC Saturday Superstar Movie, episode "The Mad, Mad, Mad Monsters" (USA). Television/Animation
Blacula (USA)
Dracula A.D. 1972 (U.K.)
Drácula contra Frankenstein (Spain)
La Fille de Dracula (France)
Go for a Take (U.K.)
El Gran amor del conde Drácula (Spain)
La Saga de los Dracula (Spain)
Sesame Street, episode "#4.1" (USA). Television/Animation
Si Popeye, atbp

1973

The Addams Family, episode "The Fastest Creepy Camper in the West" (USA). Television/Animation
Les Avaleuses (France/Belgium). Adult
Ceremonia Sangrienta (Spain/Italy)
Dororon Emma-Kun (Japan). Television/Animation
Dracula (Canada). Television
Dracula (U.K.). Television

Dragula (USA). Adult
Drakula Goes to R.P. (Philippines)
Fem døgn i august (Norway)
Mystery in Dracula's Castle (USA). Television
Night Gallery, episode "How to Cure the Common Vampire" (USA). Television
La Orgía de los muertos (Spain)
Il Plenilunio delle vergini (Italy)
El Retorno de Walpurgis (Spain/Mexico)
Riti, magie nere e segrete orge nel trecento (Italy)
Santo y Blue Demon contra Drácula y el Hombre Lobo (Mexico)
The Satanic Rites of Dracula (U.K.)
Scream, Blacula, Scream (USA)
Sesame Street, episode "#4.109" (USA). Television/Animation
Suckula (USA). Adult

1974

Benyamin kontra Drakula (Indonesia)
Blood (USA)
Blood for Dracula (Italy)
Chi o suu bara (Japan)
The Dracula Business (U.K.). Documentary
Kara boga (Turkey)
The Legend of the 7 Golden Vampires (Hong Kong/U.K.)
Sangre de vírgenes (Argentina)
Sesame Street, episode "#6.1" USA. Television/Animation
Son of Dracula (USA)
Tendre Dracula (France)
Vampira (U.K.)
Vampyres (U.K.)

1975

Il Cav. Costante Nicosia demoniaco, ovvero: Dracula in Brianza (Italy)
Count Erotica, Vampire (USA). Adult
Deafula (USA)
Las Alegras Vampiras de Vögel (Spain)
Pink Plasma (USA). Animation
The Rocky Horror Picture Show (U.K./USA)
Sesame Street, episode "7.15" (USA). Television/Animation
Sesame Street, episode "7.16" (USA). Television/Animation
Sesame Street, episode "7.17" (USA). Television/Animation
Train Ride to Hollywood (USA)
Vem Var Dracula (Sweden). Documentary

1976

The Bride's Initiation (USA). Adult
Dracula père et fils (France)
40 gradi all'ombra del lenzuolo (Italy)
Historical Dracula, Facts Behind the Fiction (USA/Romania). Documentary
Monster Squad (USA). Television
Spermula; L'amour est un fleuve en Russie France (France). Adult
Tiempos duros para Drácula (Spain/Argentina)

1977

Count Dracula (U.K.). Television
Halloween with the New Addams Family (USA). Television
El Jovencito Dracula (Spain)
Li san jiao wei zhen di yu men (Hong Kong)
McCloud, episode "McCloud Meets Dracula" (USA). Television
Nem As Enfermeiras Escapam (Brazil)
El Pobrecito Draculín (Spain). Television

1978

Alucarda, la hija de las tinieblas (Mexico)
Challenge of the SuperFriends, episode "Attack of the Vampire" (USA). Television/Animation
Doctor Dracula (USA)
Dracula's Dog (USA)
Hyakumannen chikyû no tabi: Bandâ bukku (Japan). Television/Animation
Lady Dracula (West Germany)
Qian li dan qi zhui xiong (USA). Adult
Schusters Gespenster (West Germany). Television
Vampire Hookers (Philippines/USA)

1979

B.J. and the Bear, episode "A Coffin with a View" (USA). Television
Count Dracula, The True Story (Canada). Documentary
The Curse of Dracula (USA). Television
Dracula (USA/U.K.)
Dracula Bites the Big Apple (USA)
Dracula Sucks (USA, Canada/Australia). Adult
Graf Dracula beißt jetzt in Oberbayern (West Germany)
The Halloween That Almost Wasn't (USA). Television
Love at First Bite (USA)
Nocturna (USA)
Nosferatu: Phantom der Nacht (West Germany)
Salem's Lot (USA). Television
Spider-Woman, episode "Dracula's Revenge" (USA). Television/Animation
Star Virgin (USA). Adult
Vlad Tepes (Romania)

1980

Buck Rogers in the 25th Century, episode "Space Vampire" (USA). Television
Les Charlots contre Dracula (France)
Drácula, Uma História de Amor (Brazil). Television
The Drak Pack (USA). Television/Animation
Fade to Black (USA)
The Fonz and the Happy Days Gang, episode "The Vampire Strikes Back" (USA). Television/Animation
Gorp (USA)
Les Jeux de la Comtesse Dolingen de Gratz (France)
Kaibutsu-kun (Japan). Animation
Last Rites (USA)
Mama Dracula (Belgium)
The Passion of Dracula (USA). Televised Theatrical Performance
Yami no teio kyuketsuki Dracula (Japan). Television/Animation

1981

The Count (USA). Video Game
La Dinastía de Dracula (Mexico)
Dracula Exotica (USA). Adult
Mr. and Mrs. Dracula (USA). Television
The Munsters' Revenge (USA). Television
Saturday the 14th (USA)

1982

ABC Weekend Specials, episode, "Bunnicula, The Vampire Rabbit" (USA). Television/Animation
Banquete das Taras (Brazil)
Buenas Noches, Señor Monstruo (Spain)
Darakula (Philippines)
Don Dracula (Japan). Television/Animation
Dracula (USA). Video Game
Ghost in the Water (U.K.). Television
The Great Bear Scare (USA). Television/Animation
Kwansukui Dracula (South Korea)
Sesame Street, episode "#14.1" (USA). Television/Animation
Sesame Street, episode "#14.5" (USA). Television/Animation
Transylvania (USA). Video Game
Urusei Yatsura, episode "What a Dracula!" (Japan). Television/Animation
Yin ji (Hong Kong)

1983

Atic Atac (U.K.). Video Game
O Drakoulas ton Exarheion (Greece)
Gayracula (USA). Adult
Hungarian Dracula (Hungary). Television
Hysterical (USA)
Inspector Gadget, episode "Haunted Castle" (USA). Television/Animation
Read All About It!, episode "An Evil Smile" (Canada). Television
Scooby-Doo and Scrappy-Doo, episode "Who's Minding the Monster?" (USA). Television/Animation
Spider-Man and His Amazing Friends, episode "Transylvanian Connection" (USA). Television/Animation

1984

The New Scooby-Doo Mysteries, episode "Halloween Hassle at Dracula's Castle, Part I" (USA). Television/Animation
The New Scooby-Doo Mysteries, episode "Halloween Hassle at Dracula's Castle, Part II" (USA). Television/Animation
Pyasa Shaitan (India)
Realm of the Undead. Video Game
Scully (U.K.)

1985

Countdown Dracula (USA). Television
Dracula, the Great Undead (USA). Documentary
Fracchia Contro Dracula (Italy)
Hello Dracula (Hong Kong)
King's Quest II: Romancing the Throne (USA). Video Game
Kyûketsuki hantâ D (Japan). Animation
Lugosi: The Forgotten King (USA). Television/Documentary
Sesame Street, episode "#17.1" (USA). Television/Animation
Space (USA). Television
3-2-1, episode "The Magic of Merlin" (U.K.). Television
Transylvania II: The Crimson Crown (USA). Video Game
Transylvania 6-5000 (USA)
¡Vampiros en La Habana! (Cuba). Animation

1986

Defenders of the Earth, episode "Dracula's Potion" (USA). Television/Animation
Gegege no Kitarō: Youkai Dai Makyou (Japan). Video Game
Ghost Busters, episode "Shades of Dracula" (USA). Television/Animation
Ghost House (USA). Video Game
Home to Roost, episode "Open House" (U.K.). Television
Phantomas 2 (Country?). Video Game

Tales from the Darkside, episode "The Circus" (USA). Television
Tales from the Darkside, episode "Strange Love" (USA). Television

1987

The Comic Strip (USA), segment, "The Mini-Monsters." Television/Animation
Dracula II: Noroi no fûin (Japan). Video Game
Ghost Fever (USA)
Lust of Blackula (USA). Adult
The Mini-Monsters: Adventures at Camp Mini-Mon (USA). Television/Animation
Mondo Lugosi (USA). Documentary
Pehavý Max a strasidlá (Czechoslovakia/West Germany)
Tales from the Darkside, episode "My Ghostwriter-The Vampire" (USA). Television
Teta (Austria/West Germany/France/Czechoslovakia/Spain/Italy). Television
Topo Gigio-No Castelo do Conde Drácula (Brazil). Television/Animation

1988

Count Duckula (USA). Television/Animation
Dracula in London (USA). Video Game
Dracula's Widow (USA)
Friday the 13th: The Series, episode "The Baron's Bride" (USA). Television
Konami Wai Wai World (Japan). Video Game
Love Bites (USA). Adult
The Munsters Today (USA). Television
The New Shmoo, episode "The Return of Dracula" (USA). Television/Animation
NightHunter (Country?). Video Game
Put Down the Duckie: A Sesame Street Special (USA). Television/Animation
Scooby-Doo and the Ghoul School (USA). Television/Animation
Scooby-Doo and the Reluctant Werewolf (USA). Animation
Sesame Street, episode "#19.128" (USA). Television/Animation
Snatcher (Japan). Video Game
To Die For (USA)
Topo Gigio, episode "Gigio and Vampire" (Japan). Television/Animation
Vampire's Empire (USA). Video Game
Waxworks (USA/West Germany)

1989

Alfred Hitchcock Presents, episode "Night Creatures" (USA). Television
Dracula Densetsu (Japan). Video Game
Dracula Live from Transylvania (USA). Television/Documentary
Fangs! A History of Vampires in the Movies (USA). Documentary
Fright Night Part 2 (USA)
Revivencial (Brazil)
The Super Mario Bros. Super Show!, episode "Bats in the Basement/Mario and the Beanstalk" (USA). Television/Animation
The Super Mario Bros. Super Show!, episode "Count Koopula" (USA). Television/Animation
Transylvania Twist (USA)
El Vampiro Teporocho (Mexico)

1990

Akumajo Dracula (Japan). Video Game
Akumajo Special: Boku Dracula-kun! (Japan). Video Game
Akumajou Densetsu (Japan). Video Game
Attack of the Killer Tomatoes, episode "Spatula, Prinze of Dorkness" (USA). Television/Animation
Bandh Darwaza (India)
Dracula: The Series (USA). Television
Garfield and Friends, episode "Count Lasagna" (USA). Television/Animation
Geung see yee saang (Hong Kong)
Grampa's Monster Movies (USA). Television
Gravedale High (USA). Television/Animation
Night Court, episode "Death Takes a Halloween" (USA). Television
Out for Blood (USA). Adult
Rockula (USA)
Sundown: The Vampire in Retreat (USA)
Wake, Rattle and Roll, segment "Monster Tails" (USA). Television/Animation
Yi yao O.K. (Hong Kong)

1991

The Brides of Dracula (USA). Video Game
Captain N: The Game Master, episode "Return to Castlevania" (USA). Television/Animation
Dark Shadows: Behind the Scenes (USA). Documentary
Dark Shadows: Music Videos (USA). Documentary
Dark Shadows' Scariest Moments (USA). Documentary
Dark Shadows 25th Anniversary Tribute (USA). Documentary
Dracula: A Cinematic Scrapbook (USA). Documentary
Dracula Densetsu II (Japan/USA). Video Game
Dracula the Undead (USA). Video Game
Ernest Le Vampire (France). Television
Kamitsukitai/Dorakiyura yori ai-0 (Japan)

Little Dracula (USA). Animation
The Night Boys (USA). Adult
Quackshot (USA). Video Game
Wai Wai World 2: SOS! Parsley Jō (Japan). Video Game

1992

Blood Lines: Dracula—The Man, the Myth, the Movies (USA). Documentary
Bram Stoker's Dracula (USA)
Buffy the Vampire Slayer (USA)
Dracula: Fact or Fiction (USA). Documentary
Dracula in the Movies (USA). Documentary
Draculito, mon Saigneur (Germany). Animation
Ejacula, la vampira (Italy/USA). Adult
In Living Color, episode "Bram Stoker's Wanda" (USA). Television
In the Wake of Vampire (Japan). Video Game
Khooni Dracula (India)
Making Bram Stoker's Dracula (USA). Television/Documentary
Puss in Boots, episode "Nagagutsu o haita neko no boken" (Japan). Television/Animation
Waxwork II: Lost in Time (USA)
Young-guwa heubhyeolgwi dracula (South Korea)

1993

Akumajo Dracula X: Chi no Rondo (Japan). Video Game
Animaniacs, episode "Draculee, Draculaa/Phranken-Runt" (USA). Television/Animation
The Awesome Adventures of Victor Vector & Yondo: The Vampire's Coffin. Video Game
Breakfast with Dracula (Italy/USA)
Chapolim x Drácula: Um Duelo Assustador. Video Game
Cunt Dykula (USA). Adult
Dark Shadows: Bloopers (USA). Documentary
Dracula (USA). Video Game
Dracula Mon Amour (France)
Dracula Rising (USA)
Dracula Unleashed (USA). Video Game
Ganbare Goemon 2: Kiteretsu Shogun Magginesu (Japan). Video Game
Gegege No Kitaro: Fukkatsu! Tenma Daiou (Japan). Video Game
Quantam Leap, episode "Blood Moon — March 10, 1975" (USA). Television
Rusty (Japan). Video Game
Sesame Street Stays Up Late! (USA). Television/Animation
The Simpsons, episode "Treehouse of Horror IV" (USA). Television/Animation
U.F.O. (U.K.)
The Young Indiana Jones Chronicles, episode "Transylvania, January 1918" (USA). Television

1994

Animaniacs, episode "Randy Beaman's Pal #6" (USA). Television/Animation
Castlevania: Bloodlines (USA). Video Game
Children of Dracula (USA). Documentary
Dracula (Italy). Adult
Dracula aema (South Korea)
Flesh and Blood: The Hammer Heritage of Horror (USA/U.K.). Documentary
Gokujō Parodius! -Kako no Eikō o Motomete- (Japan). Video Game
Monster Force (Canada). Television/Animation
Nadja (USA)
Saturday Night Live, episode "Dracula's Not Gay" (USA). Television
Sesame Street Jam: A Musical Celebration (USA). Television
The Simpsons, episode "Sideshow Bob Roberts" (USA). Television/Animation
Vampires (USA). Documentary
The World of Hammer, episode "Christopher Lee" (U.K.). Television/Documentary
The World of Hammer, episode "Costumers" (U.K.). Television/Documentary
The World of Hammer, episode "Dracula and the Undead" (U.K.). Television/Documentary
The World of Hammer, episode "Hammer" (U.K.). Television/Documentary
The World of Hammer, episode "Mummies, Werewolves and the Living Dead" (U.K.). Television/Documentary
The World of Hammer, episode "Peter Cushing" (U.K.). Television/Documentary
The World of Hammer, episode "Vamp" (U.K.). Television/Documentary

1995

Akumajō Dracula XX (Japan). Video Game
Bizarre's Dracula (USA). Adult
Bizarre's Dracula II (USA). Adult
Casualty, episode "Trials and Tribulations" (U.K.). Television
Chickula: Teenage Vampire (USA)
Dark Shadows: Vampires and Ghosts (USA). Documentary
Dracula III: Legacy (USA)
Dracula's Dungeon (USA). Adult
Ejacula 2 (USA). Adult
Hercules: The Legendary Journeys, episode "Darkness Visible" (USA). Television
Here Come the Munsters (USA). Television
Mina and the Count (1995–2003). Television/Animation
Monster Mash: The Movie (USA)
Vampire in Brooklyn (USA)
Vamps: Deadly Dreamgirls (USA). Adult

1996

Buffy the Vampire Layer (USA). Adult
Dark Shadows 30th Anniversary Tribute (USA). Documentary
Dracula's Secret (Canada). Video Game
Draculina Video Magazine (USA). Documentary
Dragula, Queen of Darkness (USA). Adult
Drácula: El Vampiro (Spain). Video Game
Elmo Saves Christmas (USA). Animation
Elmo Says Boo (USA). Animation
Frankenstein and Me (Canada)
Goosebumps: Escape from Horrorland (USA). Video Game
In Search of Dracula with Jonathan Ross (U.K.). Television/Documentary
Jikkyō Oshaberi Parodius: forever with me (Japan). Video Game
Karmina (Canada)
Macabre Pair of Shorts (USA)
The Munsters' Scary Little Christmas (USA)
Nightmare: The Birth of Victorian Horror (U.K.). Documentary
100 Years of Horror: Blood-Drinking Beings (USA). Documentary
100 Years of Horror: The Monster Makers (USA). Documentary
Ultimate Reality (USA). Adult
Vampirella (USA)

1997

Akumajô Dracula: Shikkoku taru zensôkyoku (Japan). Videogame
Akumajô Dracula X: Gekka no yasukyôoku (Japan). Videogame
Animaniacs — Spooky Stuff (USA)
Blood Suckers (USA)
Brácula Condemor II (Spain)
The Creeps (USA)
Dark Shadows Resurrected: The Video (USA). Documentary
Dracula: The True Story (USA). Documentary
Fraiser, episode "Halloween" (USA). Television
Lexx (Canada). Television
Lugosi: Hollywood's Dracula (USA). Documentary
The Mark of Dracula (USA)
Monster Mania (USA). Television/Documentary
Pathos (USA)
Roter Tango (Germany)
Van Helsing Chronicles (USA). Television
Vlad Tepes Dracula (USA). Video Game
You Wish, episode "Halloween" (USA). Television

1998

Elmopalooza (USA). Television/Animation
Everybody Loves Raymond, episode "Halloween Candy" (USA). Television
Evil of Dracula (USA). Animation
LCD Symphony of the Night (USA). Video Game
Macaroni tout garni (Canada)
Meitantei Conan, episode "Dracula Murder Case: Part 1" (Japan). Television/Animation
Meitantei Conan, episode "Dracula Murder Case: Part 2" (Japan). Television/Animation
Modern Vampires (USA)
Nattens engel (Denmark)
Universal Horror (U.K.). Television/Documentary
Vampire's Seduction (USA). Adult

1999

The Adventures of Elmo in Grouchland (USA). Animation
The Adventures of Young Indiana Jones: Masks of Evil (USA)
Brides of Countess Recula (USA). Adult
Castlevania (USA). Video Game
Castlevania: Legacy of Darkness (USA). Video Game
Cinderelmo (USA). Television/Animation
Dark Shadows: Video Scrapbook (USA). Documentary
Drácula (Argentina). Television
Dracula (India)
Dracula in Vegas (USA)
Monster by Moonlight! The Immortal Saga of "The Wolf Man" (USA). Documentary
The Phantom Eye (USA). Television
Pumpkin Hill (USA)
Quasimodo d'El Paris (France)
Ripley's Believe It or Not, episode "The Vampire Kit" (Canada). Television/Animation
The Road to Dracula (USA). Documentary
Titanic 2000 (USA). Adult
Vampire Blues (USA)

2000

Banpaia hantâ D (Japan/Hong Kong/USA). Animation
Bud Abbott and Lou Costello Meet the Monsters! (USA)
Buffy the Vampire Slayer, episode "Buffy vs. Dracula" (USA). Television
Call Him Jess (Spain). Documentary
Dark Prince: The True Story of Dracula (USA). Television
Dracula: A Chamber Musical (Canada). Television
Dracula: The Resurrection (USA). Video Game
Dracula 2: The Last Sanctuary (France). Video Game
Dracula 2000 (USA)
Hot Vampire Nights (USA). Adult

In Search of History: The Real Dracula (USA). Television/Documentary
Mistress of Seduction (USA). Adult
Monster Mash (USA/Italy). Animation
MonsterFest 2000: The Classics Come Alive (USA)
Sesame Street, episode "Miles Babysits" (USA). Television/Animation
Shadow of the Vampire (USA)
Vampire Night (Japan). Video Game
Zora la vampiera (Italy)

2001

Akumajou Dracula: Circle of the Moon (Japan). Video Game
Aqua Teen Hunger Force, episode "Bus of the Undead" (USA). Television/Animation
Bara no Konrei ~ Mayonaka ni Kawashita Yakusoku (Japan)
The Bizarre Cage #3 (Japan). Animation/Adult
The Breed (USA/Hungary)
Cathula (U.K.). Adult
Chair (USA). Documentary
Conker's Bad Fur Day (USA). Video Game
Dracula: Crazy Vampire (USA). Video Game
The Erotic Rites of Countess Dracula (USA). Adult
Heroes of Horror (USA). Documentary
Herushingu (Japan). Television/Animation
The Horror of Hammer (USA). Documentary
Inside Television's Greatest: Addams Family & The Munsters (USA). Documentary
Karmina 2 (Canada)
Konami Wai Wai Racing Advance (Japan). Video Game
Runescape (U.K.). Video Game
Titeuf, episode "Pépé Dracula" (France). Television/Animation
The Vampire Hunters Club (USA/Canada)

2002

All My Children, episode "Episode dated 31 October 2002" (USA). Television
Il Bacio di Dracula (Italy/Germany). Television
The Baskervilles (Canada). Television
Behind the Fame: The Munsters/Addams Family (USA). Television/Documentary
Boris Karloff and Bela Lugosi (France). Television/Animation
Castlevania: Byakuya no Concerto (Japan). Video Game
Cyberchase, episode "Castleblanca" (Canada). Television/Animation
Dracula mascafierro (Mexico). Adult
Dracula: Pages from a Virgin's Diary (Canada). Ballet
Dracula the Impaler (Romania)
Dracula Unearthed (USA). Documentary
Evolution Skateboarding (USA). Video Game
La Fiancée de Dracula (France)
The Impaler: A Biographical/Historical Look at the Life of Vlad the Impaler, Widely Known as Dracula (Canada). Television/Documentary
Killer Barbys Vs. Dracula (Spain)
Magnificent Obsessions (Canada). Documentary
Nohasfrontwo (USA)
Nosferatu (France). Television/Animation
Olliver's Adventures, episode "What a Pain in the Neck" (Canada). Television/Animation
Sesame Street, episode "#33.50" (USA). Television/Animation
SpongeBob SquarePants, episode "Graveyard Shift/Krusty Love" (USA). Television/Animation
Taiho shichauzo (Japan). Television
Vlad the Impaler: The True Story of Dracula (Canada). Television/Documentary

2003

AFI's 100 Years ... 100 Heroes & Villains (USA). Documentary
Alucard (USA)
Birth of the Vampire (USA)
Bloodlines: The Dracula Family Tree (USA). Television/Documentary
Castlevania: Akatsuki no Minuet (USA). Video Game
Castlevania: Lament of Innocence (USA). Video Game
Codename: Kids Next Door, episode "Operation S.P.A.N.K." (USA). Television/Animation
Dracula II: Ascension (USA)
Dracula's Bram Stoker (Ireland). Television/Documentary
Duck Dodgers, episode "I'm Going to Get You, Fat Sucka" (USA). Television/Animation
Galgali familywa Dracula (South Korea)
Gegege no Kitarō: Gyakushuu! Youkai Daichisen (Japan). Video Game
Hallow's End (USA)
The League of Extraordinary Gentlemen (USA/Germany/Czech Republic/U.K.)
Lucy en Miroir (France)
Makai Senki Disugaia (Japan). Video Game
Mas vampiros en La Habana (Cuba/Spain). Animation
Matantei Loki Ragnarok, episode "Dorakyura Jyou no Wana" (Japan). Television/Animation
My Life with Count Dracula (USA). Documentary
Night Bites: Women and Their Vampires (USA). Documentary
Riddles of the Dead, episode "Dracula Unearthed" (USA) Television/Documentary
Rinaldó (Hungary)

Shaman King, episode "Winged Destroyers" (Japan). Television/Animation
Silver Scream (USA)
This Darkness: The Vampire Virus (USA)
Three's Horrible: Part 1 (USA). Animation
Vampire Vixens (USA). Adult
Vlad (USA)

2004

Adventures of Young Van Helsing: The Quest for the Lost Scepter (USA)
Aqua Teen Hunger Force, episode "Little Brittle" (USA). Television/Animation
Biography, episode "Bram Stoker" (USA). Television/Documentary
Blade: Trinity (USA)
Cathula 2: Vampires of Sex (U.K.). Adult
Countess Dracula's Orgy of Blood (USA). Adult
Dracula 3000 (Germany/South Africa)
Drum bun — Jo utat! (Hungary/Germany/Switzerland)
Emmanuelle the Private Collection: Emmanuelle vs. Dracula (USA). Television/Adult
Fantomu Bureibu (Japan). Video Game
Fort Dracula (USA)
From Dusk 'til Porn (U.K.). Adult
Greasepaint and Gore: The Hammer Monsters of Phil Leakey (U.K.). Documentary
Joe Nosferatu: Homeless Vampire (USA)
Laser Fart (USA)
Lil Creepers (USA). Animation
Lust for Dracula (USA). Adult
Making Bela (USA). Documentary
McFarlane's Evil Prophecy (USA). Video Game
Mira corpora (France)
Un Petit garçon silencieux (France)
Pudelmützen Rambos (Germany)
The Revamping of Dracula (USA). Documentary
Sesame Street, episode "#35.4" (USA). Television/Animation
Sexy Adventures of Van Helsing (USA). Adult
Shaman King, episode "Vampire Ambush" (Japan). Television/Animation
The Simpsons, episode "All's Fair in Oven War" (USA). Television/Animation
Van Helsing (USA)
Van Helsing (USA). Video Game
Van Helsing: The Man and the Monsters (USA). Documentary
Vanpaia hosuto (Japan). Television
The Vulture's Eye (USA)
Walpurgis Nacht (USA)

2005

Akumajô Dorakiyura: Yami no juin (Japan). Video Game
Akumajou Dracula: Sougetsu no Juujika (Japan). Video Game
Amantul marii doamne Dracula (Romania). Television
The Batman vs Dracula: The Animated Movie (USA). Animation
Bram Stoker's Way of the Vampire (USA)
Cineastes contra magnats (Spain). Documentary
Count Spermula (USA). Adult
Danny Phantom, episode "Material Instinct" (USA). Television/Animation
Dark Angels 2: Bloodline (USA). Adult
Elmo Visits the Doctor (USA). Animation
G-String Vampire (USA). Adult
Grim & Evil, episode "Billy Idiot/Home of the Ancients" (USA). Television/Animation
Harker (USA)
Hollywood's Greatest Villains (USA). Documentary
Kibris: La ley del equilibrio (Spain)
Monster Kid Home Movies (USA)
Night People (U.K.)
The Real Life of Dracula (Romania). Documentary
Robot Chicken, episode "Nutcracker Sweet" (USA). Television/Animation
The Simpsons, episode "Treehouse of Horror XVI," segment "I've Grown a Costume on Your Face" (USA). Television/Animation
Ultimate Super Heroes, Vixens, and Villains, segment "Ultimate Super Villains" (USA). Television/Documentary

2006

Akumajou Dracula: Gallery of Labyrinth (Japan). Video Game
The Amazing Adrenalini Brothers!, episode "Fangs of Horror" (U.K./Canada). Television/Animation
Blood Son (USA)
Bloodspit (Australia/USA)
Brooke West Collection (USA). Adult
Destruction Kings (USA)
Dracula (U.K.)
Dracula Twins. Video Game
Dracula's Curse (USA)
Dracula's Curse: Behind the Scenes (USA). Documentary
Dracula's Family Visit (Netherlands)
Draculya: The Girls Are Hungry (USA). Adult
The Elder Scrolls IV: Oblivion (USA). Video Game
Ghoul Mates (USA)
Grim & Evil, episode "Fear and Loathing in Endsville" (USA). Television/Animation
Heubhyeol hyeongsa na do-yeol (Korea)
Is It Real?, episode "Vampires" (USA). Documentary
The Last Sect (Canada)
Lost Worlds, episode "The Real Dracula" (U.K.). Television/Documentary

Makai Senki Disgaea (Japan). Television/Animation
Makai Senki Disugaia Tsū (Japan). Video Game
Nosferatu's Crush (USA)
Sesame Street, episode "#37.1" (USA). Television/Animation
Shaitani Dracula (India). Adult
Vampire Secrets (USA). Television/Documentary
Wolfster, Part 1: The Curse of the Emo Vamp (USA)
Young Dracula (U.K.). Television

2007

Awake (USA)
Beloved Count (USA). Documentary
Billy & Mandy's Big Boogey Adventure (USA). Television/Animation
The Blood Is The Life: The Making of Bram Stoker's Dracula (USA). Documentary
Bloodsucking Cinema (USA). Television/Documentary
Castlevania: Order of Shadows (2007). Video Game
Cities of the Underworld, episode "Dracula's Underground" (USA). Television/Documentary
Close-Up, episode "Bela Lugosi: Dracula's Dubbelganger" (Netherlands/Germany/Belgium). Documentary
Dead to the Last Drop (USA)
Dracula: The Days of Gore (USA). Video Game
Dracula: Revamped (USA)
La Duodécima hora (Spain)
Elmo's Christmas Countdown (USA). Television/Animation
In Camera: The Naïve Visual Effects of Bram Stoker's Dracula (USA). Documentary
Method and Madness: Visualizing "Dracula" (USA). Documentary
Mysterious Journeys, episode "The Hunt for Dracula" (USA). Television/Documentary
Operation Darkness (Japan). Video Game
Sesame Street, episode "The Bookaneers" (USA). Television/Animation
Sesame Street, episode "#38.2" (USA). Television/Animation
Sesame Street, episode "Sleepy Grouchy" (USA). Television/Animation
Sphinx — Geheimnisse der Geschichte, episode "Die Vampirprinzessin" (Germany). Television/Documentary
30 Days of Night (USA)
Le Vampire déchu (France/Romania/Austria/Germany/Netherlands). Documentary
Vampires (USA). Adult

2008

The Accidental Hooker (USA). Adult
Akumajo Dorakyura: Jajimento (USA). Video Game
Akumajō Dracula: The Medal (Japan). Video Game
Akumajō Dracula: Ubawareta Kokuin (USA). Video Game
Blood Scarab (USA)
Bonnie & Clyde vs. Dracula (USA)
Canucula! (Canada)
Count Suckula (USA). Adult
Dracula: Origin (USA). Video Game
Dracula: Prince of Marketing (USA)
Dracula 3—The Path of the Dragon (Belgium/France). Video Game
Dracula's Guest (USA)
Der Goldene Nazivampir von Absam 2—Das Geheimnis von Schloß Kottlitz (Germany)
Goosebumps HorrorLand (USA). Video Game
Graf Draculas Bissige Saftfotzen (Germany). Adult
Hakaba Kitarô, episode "Yasha tai dorakyura yon sei" ("Yasha vs. Dracula IV" [USA]) (Japan). Television/Animation
Her Morbid Desires (USA)
How My Dad Killed Dracula (USA)
Kiss Attack (USA). Adult
The Lair (USA, 2007–2009). Television
Makai Senki Disugaia Surī (Japan). Video Game
Monster Kids (USA). Animation
MonsterQuest, episode "Vampires in America" (USA). Television/Documentary
New International Track & Field (Japan). Video Game
One of Those Days (U.K.)
Pachislot Akumajō Dracula (Japan). Video Game
Robot Chicken, episode "Tubba-Bubba's Now Hubba-Bubba" (USA). Television/Animation
Saturday Night Live, episode "The Mirror" (An SNL Digital Short) (USA). Television
Sesame Street, episode "Elmo & Zoe's Hat Contest" (USA). Television/Animation
Sesame Street, episode "Telly's New Shoes" (USA). Television/Animation
The Thirst: Blood Wars (USA)
A Vampyre Story: Chapter One (Germany). Video Game

2009

Akumajo Dracula: The Arcade (Japan). Video Game
Bram Stoker's Vampire Diaries: Renfield (USA)
Captain Berlin Versus Hitler (Germany)
Demons (U.K.). Television
The Dracula Files (USA). Video Game
Dracula: Forbidden Frut-a Play Benefiting the Clemente Program (USA). Documentary
Dracula's Stoker (Ireland). Documentary
40 Dana (Servia). Documentary
Scary America (USA). Documentary
Transylmania (USA)
Vampire City (Austria)

2010

The Count of Little Havana (USA).

Appendix 3. Notable Dramatizations Featuring Dracula*

Almost the Bride of Dracula; or, Why the Count Remains a Bachelor; U.S., 1980; Comedy. *Writing Credits*: Dennis Snee. The 580 year old Count is still being hassled by his mother to settle down with a nice girl.

Boys and Ghouls Together; 1965, U.S.; Comedy; Three Acts. *Writing Credits*: David Rogers. A group of young cyclists touring Europe spends the night in a castle-hotel operated by Count Dracula and his family.

Count Dracula; U.S., 1972; Mystery, Comedy; Three Acts. *Writing Credits*: Ted Tiller. This adaptation of Stoker's novel is noted by some scholars to be heavier on comic relief than other similar renditions. The story centers around Dr. Seward's Asylum for the Insane, where there is a new patient, Renfield, and a new resident in the adjacent castle, a foreigner named Count Dracula. While Dr. Seward tries desperately to tend to both his asylum and his sister, Sybil, his ward Mina takes ill following a visit from Count Dracula. Mina's fiancé, Jonathan Harker, and Professor Van Helsing, arrive in just enough time to save her.

Count Dracula; or, A Musical Mania from Transylvania; U.S., 1974; Musical, Comedy. *Writing Credits*: Lawrence O'Dwyer; *Director*: Norma Young; *Musical Lyrics*: Jac Alder; *Players/Characters*: Charles Roberts (Vlad Voivode Dracula), Bob Floyd (Van Helsing), Richard Michaels (Renfield), Gene Ross (Dr. Seward), James Burton (John Harker), Rhonda Berkman (Lucy).

The Count Will Rise Again, or Dracula in Dixie; U.S., 1980; Comedy; Two Acts. *Writing Credits*: Dennis Snee.

Countess Dracula!; Arena Theatre, Buffalo, New York, U.S., 5 January 1980; Three Acts. *Writing Credits*: Neal DuBrock; *Director*: Neal DuBrock.

Dearest Dracula; Olympia Theatre, Dublin, Ireland, 27 September 1965; Musical. *Producer*: Jay Landesman; *Writing Credits*: Margaret Hill, Charlotte Moor, Jack Murdock; *Musical Lyrics*: Fran Landesman; *Cast*: John Gower (Dracula), Mary Millar (Lucy), Robert Hornery (Jonathan Harker), David Holliday (Dr. Seward), David Morton (Sir Arthur Holmwood), Pitt Wilkinson (Dr. Van Helsing), Rita Cameron. Jonathan Harker is away at Castle Dracula where he is suffering from some illness involving great blood loss and eating flies. Seward, Holmwood, and Van Helsing, all friends of Harker's back in England, journey to the castle where they find Count Dracula and his three vampire women, who attack the gentlemen and burst into song.

Death at the Crossroads; U.S., 1975; Thriller, Suspense. *Writing Credits*: Stephen Hotchner. Dr. Van Helsing and Jonathan Harker venture, with Mina Harker, into the Transylvanian wilderness to discover Dracula's whereabouts. Mina has fallen victim to Dracula's bite, and she has but days, or perhaps hours, before turning completely into one of the undead. The three of them find themselves on a wild carriage ride with a coachman and four other passengers. Suddenly, at nearly midnight, the

---

*Many thanks are extended to David J. Skal for his helpful suggestions on earlier versions of this list. For further information on dramatizations, see also the following critical works and bibliographies: David J. Skal, "'His Hour Upon the Stage': Theatrical Adaptations of Dracula," in Dracula (New York: W.W. Norton, 1997), by Bram Stoker, ed. Nina Auerbach and David J. Skal, 371–381; Skal, Hollywood Gothic, rev. ed. (New York: Faber and Faber, 2004); Martin V. Riccardo, Vampires Unearthed (New York: Garland, 1983); and Matthew Bunson, The Vampire Encyclopedia (New York: Gramercy, 2003), 202–203.

coach breaks down at the crossroads directly beneath Dracula's castle. Wolves begin to bay nearby, and Mina begins acting strangely. A night of horrors ensues, and nearly all the passengers perish.

Dracula; U.K., Derby, Grand Theatre, 5 August 1924 (preview-premiere); U.K., London, Little Theatre, 14 February 1927 (London opening); Three Acts. *Producers*: Hamilton Deane, Harry L. Warburton; *Writing Credits*: Hamilton Deane; *General Manager*: Albert Kavanagh; *Stage Director*: Lodge Percy; *Stage Manager*: Jack Howarth; *Assistant Stage Manager*: Bernard Guest; *Players/Characters*: Edmund Blake (Count Dracula [Derby]), Raymond Huntley (Count Dracula [London]), Hamilton Deane (Abraham van Helsing), Doctor Seward (Stuart Lomath), Jonathan Harker (Bernard Guest), Quincey P. Morris (Frieda Hearn), Peter Jackson (Lord Godalming), Bernard Jukes (R.M. Renfield), Jack Howarth (The Warder), Kilda Macleod (The Parlourmaid), Betty Murgatroyd (The Housemaid), Dora Mary Patrick (Mina Harker).

Dracula; Royal Court Theatre, Warrington, U.K., September 1927. *Producer:* Harry L. Warburton; *Writing Credits*: Charles Morrell. This alternate stage adaptation was privately commissioned by Stoker's widow, Florence, but was heavily censored and only saw a brief stage life.

Dracula; Edinburgh, Scotland, U.K., 1969; London, U.K., 1972 (London opening). *Writing Credits*: Stanley Eveling, Alan Jackson, David Mowat, Robert Nye, Bill Watson, Clarisse Eriksson, John Downing.

Dracula; Macgowan Hall, University of California at Los Angeles, Los Angeles, California, U.S., May 1973; Comedy/Musical. *Writing Credits*: Larry Ferguson, David Davidson; *Director*: Larry Ferguson; *Players/Characters*: James Cady (Dracula), Cheri SU.S.n Bard (Lucy), John Peterson (Renfield), James Bohlin (Van Helsing), Joyce DeWitt (Mina), David Jorns (Seward). This is an adaptation of Stoker's novel turned rock musical.

Dracula; Royal Playhouse, New York, New York, U.S., August 1973; Two Acts. *Writing Credits*: Crane Johnson; *Director*: Crane Johnson. Lucy suffers from a bizarre illness, much to everyone's alarm, including her aunt, Mrs. Harker, and husband-to-be, Dr. Seward. Meanwhile, the good doctor must divide his time between Lucy and a mental patient named Renfield, whose strange eating habits warrant scientific inquiry. Troubled by Lucy's bizarre illness, Dr. Seward summons the renowned metaphysician Dr. Van Helsing (a female character). Just as Van Helsing begins to unravel Lucy's strange case, their

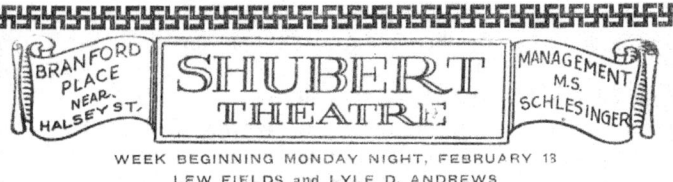

Ad from *The Magazine Theater Programme* (1927) (courtesy John Edgar Browning).

neighbor from the adjoining Carfax Hall, Count Dracula, pays Seward a visit, and Van Helsing begins to suspect the horrible truth.

Dracula; U.S., 1978; Musical. *Writing Credits*: Kingsley Day and the Chicago Premiere Society.

Dracula; U.S., 1980; Mystery; Three Acts. *Writing Credits*: John Mattera. Count Dracula has arrived to England and moved into the large estate adjacent to Dr. Seward's insane asylum. Professor Van Helsing proceeds to convince Dr. Seward that Count Dracula is actually a vampire. Renfield is in his usual role as the fly-eating lunatic who serves the Count. And the beautiful Lucy Westenra, who shares a remarkable resemblance to a girl the Count once loved in centuries past, is engaged to Jonathan Harker. New to the plot is Charles, the Westenra family butler whose poor eyesight prevents his being hypnotized.

Dracula; Royal Lyceum Theatre, Edinburgh, Scotland, 1985. *Writing Credits*: Liz Lochhead.

Dracula; U.S., 1996; Horror; Two Acts. *Writing Credits*: Steven Dietz. This adaptation follows more closely to Stoker's novel than many preceding it.

Dracula; U.K., 1998; Drama. *Writing Credits*: David Calcutt.

Dracula; Spring Street Theatre, Kingston upon Hull, Yorkshire, U.K., 25 October 1995 1998; Drama, Horror. *Writing Credits*: Janet Thornton, John Godber. With the arrival of a sudden, mysterious storm to the English coast comes, through the harbor entrance, the crash of a ship, abandoned but for a large dog and fifty boxes of grave dust. Meanwhile, a young woman sleepwalks along the edge of a cliff, unaware of the Transylvanian Count who has just arrived to England. Dracula's immortality is dependent on the blood on which he must feed.

Dracula; U.K., 2000. *Writing Credits*: Jan Needle.

Dracula: The Death of Nosferatu; U.S., 1991; Drama, Mystery, Thriller; One Act. *Writing Credits*: Christopher P. Nichols. Professor Abraham Van Helsing comes to Whitby Asylum in England to the aid of his friend and student Dr. Seward. Meanwhile, Mina Murray suffers from a strange illness that threatens to postpone her marriage to Jonathan Harker. Fortunately, Van Helsing has just come from London where he investigated a case similar to Mina's. At last, Dracula reveals himself and his plans for Mina, but Van Helsing and the others are prepared.

Dracula: The Musical?; U.S., 1982; Two Acts. *Writing Credits*: Rick Abbot; *Music by*: Rick Abbot; *Lyrics by*: Rick Abbot.

Dracula: A Musical Nightmare; U.S., 1978; Musical. *Writing Credits*: Douglas Johnson; *Lyrics by*: Douglas Johnson; *Director*: Douglas Johnson; *Music by*: John Aschenbrenner; *Music Director*: John Aschenbrenner.

Dracula: Sabbat; Loeb Playhouse, Purdue University, Indiana, West Lafayette, January 1970 (premiere); Judson Poets' Theater, New York, New York, 11 September 1970 (New York opening); Two Acts. *Writing Credits*: Leon Katz; *Director*: Word Baker (premiere), Lawrence Kornfeld; *Music*: John Herbert McDowell; *Players/Characters*: Duane Tucker (Dracula), Crystal Field (Lucy). This rendition features a Black Mass in which a bare-chested, Satanic-masked Dracula (who is wearing a dildo) is accompanied by dancing demons, witches, and vampires as he seduces Lucy and offers her to their god. Eventually, she is beheaded by Arthur, her fiancé.

Dracula: The Story You Thought You Knew; Oregon Shakespeare Festival, Oregon, U.S., 1983. *Writing Credits*: Richard Sharp.

Dracula: The Vampire Play; New Haven, U.S., Shubert Theatre, 1927 (preview-premiere); Fulton Theatre, New York, New York, U.S., 5 October 1927 (New York opening); Three Acts. *Producers*: Horace Liveright; *Writing Credits*: Hamilton Deane, John L. Balderston; *Staged by*: Ira Hands; *General Manager*: Louis Cline; *Technical Director*: Louis Cline; *Players/Characters* (in order of appearance): Nedda Harrigan (Miss Wells [maid]), Terence Neill (Jonathan Harker), Herbert Bunston (Dr. Seward), Edward Van Sloan (Abraham Van Helsing), Bernard Jukes (R. M. Renfield), Albert Frith (Butterworth), Dorothy Peterson (Lucy Seward), Béla Lugosi (Count Dracula).

Dracula, a Modern Fable; Troupe Theatre, New York, New York, U.S., 3 February 1978. *Writing Credits*: Norman Beim; *Director*: Andy Milligan.

Dracula, Baby!; Town Hall Theatre, Centerville, Ohio, U.S., 25 April 1969; Musical, Comedy; Two Acts. *Writing Credits*: Bruce Ronald; *Music by*: Claire Strauch; *Lyrics by*: John Jakes. When Count Dracula sets out for England to make Lucy his 93rd bride, Lucy's future looks pretty anemic. Little does Dracula know that he will have to contend with Arthur, Lucy's fiancé and a very, very proper gentleman, and the clumsy Professor Van Helsing. Lucy's protectors also find an unexpected ally in the nurse who works in the sanitarium, which is operated by Dr. Seward.

The Dracula Doll; US, New York, New School for Social Research, 5 December 1979; One Act. *Writing Credits*: Jeanne Youngson.

Dracula — Entre l'amour et le mort; Québec, Canada; 13 January 2006; Musical. *Writing Credits*: Bruno Pelletier, Richard Ouzounian; *Lyrics by*: Roger Tabra; *Music by*: Simon Leclerc; *Cast*: Bruno Pelletier, Martin Giroux (Count Dracula), Sylvain Cossette (Jonathan), Daniel Boucher (Renfield), Andrée Watters (Mina), Pierre Flynn (Van Helsing),

Gabrielle Destroismaisons (Lucy), Rita Tabbakh (vampiresses), Elyzabeth Diaga (vampiresses), Brigitte Marchand (vampiresses), Cassiopée (vampiresses), Louis Gagné (Grand-Lui), Claude Pineault (singer), Julie Dassylva (singer), Martin Giroux (singer). Dracula, a prince-warrior, is doomed to wander through the centuries in order to find his lost love, Elhemina. In 2050, Dracula at long last recognizes the woman who brought him immortality 500 years ago.

Dracula Is Undead and Well and Living in Purfleet; U.K., 1979; Three Acts. *Writing Credits*: Charles McKeown.

Dracula or the Un-Dead; U.K., London, Lyceum Theatre, 18 May 1897; 5 Acts. *Writing Credits*: Bram Stoker; *Stage Manager*: H. J. Loveday; *Musical Director*: Meredith Ball; *Acting Manager*: Bram Stoker; *Players/Characters*: Mr. Jones (Dracula), Herbert Passmore (Jonathan Harker), John Seward, M.D. (Mr. Rivington), Tom Reynolds (Professor Van Helsing), Quincey P. Morris (Mr. Widdicombe), Hon. Author Holmwood (Mr. Innes), M. F. Renfield (Mr. Howard), Captain Swales (Mr. Gurney), Coastguard (Mr. Simpson), Attendant at Asylum (Mr. Porter), Mrs. Westenra (Miss Gurney), Lucy Westenra (Miss Foster), Mina Murray (Miss Craig), Servant (Miss Cornfield), Vampire Woman (Mrs. Daly).

Dracula Rides Again; U.S., 2006; Western, Comedy; Two Acts. *Writing Credits*: Jeff Goode. After Doctor Frankenstein and Count Dracula fall for the same showgirl, an evening of showdowns and hoedowns ensues.

The Dracula Spectacula, U.K., 1976; Comedy/Musical. *Writing Credits*: John Gardiner; *Music by*: Andrew Parr. In this modern rendition for young audiences, Miss Nadia and her three pupils find themselves in Transylvanian where they must face the Count and his gruesome entourage.

Dracula Sucks; Horseshoe Theatre, Hollywood, California, U.S., 1969; Comedy. *Producer*: Jerry Wheeler; *Director*: Jerry Wheeler; *Writing Credits*: Jerry Wheeler; *Players/Characters*: Murray Langston (Dracula). David Manzy (Ratfield), Bob Lossier (Mr. Sewer), Chris Bailey (Jonathan Hooker), Lee Corrigan (Van Hesling). Following closely the plot of the Universal *Dracula* (1931), this dramatization features a bisexual Dracula who seeks out both male and female victims.

Dracula, "The Vampire Play"; U.S., 1978; Three Acts. *Writing Credits*: Tim Kelly.

Dracula's Treasure; U.S., 1975; Comedy, Mystery; Two Acts. *Writing Credits*: Dudley Saunders. The Boone family moves into an old house that has been unoccupied for a decade. The family soon employs a housekeeper and a carpenter, but they start disappearing behind sliding panels and vanishing walls, behind which a secret room is hidden that contains a chained coffin that knocks. Dracula emerges from the coffin during the night and hovers over Nancy while she sleeps, but then hides in the window seat when a dark figure enters through a window. Dracula soon hypnotizes the young people who happened upon his treasure, and he almost succeeds at luring them down into his underworld until his plans are foiled.

Escape from Dracula's Castle; U.S., 1975. *Writing Credits*: Stephen Hotchner. Dr. Van Helsing, the world famous scientist, warned his young friend Jonathan Harker to use caution on his trip to Transylvania where he must close a real estate deal with Count Dracula. However, the young, ambitious Jonathan discounts the warning and nearly meets his end in Transylvania.

The House of Dracula; U.K., 1992; Comedy, Horror. *Writing Credits*: Martin Downing. The Baron and Baroness Frankenstein, accompanied by their servants, Igor and Frau Lurker, stay at a Transylvania fortress where they find several of their ghoulish enemies waiting for them.

I'm Sorry, the Bridge Is Out, You'll Have to Spend the Night; Coronet Theatre, Los Angeles, California, U.S., 28 April 1970; Musical, Comedy; Two Acts. *Writing Credits*: Sheldon Allman, Bob Pickett; *Director*: Maurine Dawson; *Players/Characters*: Peter Virgo (Count Ladislav Dracula), John Ian Jacobs (Frankenstein's Monster/Count Ladislav Dracula), Tony Lane (Renfield), Glorida Dell (Natasha Dracula). This musical spoof features Dracula, along side his wife, Natasha Dracula, Dr. Frankenstein and his Monster, a hunchbacked Igor, the Mummy, and Renfield. John David Wellman and his fiancée, Mary Helen Herriman, are forced to seek shelter in Dr. Frankenstein's castle after a storm washes out the bridge. Dracula sets his sights on Mary, while the Countess begins eyeing John.

I Was a Teen-Age Dracula; US, 1958; Mystery, Comedy; Three Acts. *Writing Credits*: Gene Donovan. Marlene (who prides herself on never missing a horror play on television) considers herself an authority on werewolves, vampires, and the ghoulish. So when Steve "Dracca," a foreigner no less, comes to the home where Marlene works, Marlene takes one look at his name and assumes he is vampire.

Lady Dracula; U.S., 1980; Comedy, Drama. *Writing Credits*: Tim Kelly. Mina, a victim of Count Dracula, has searched the earth for a young man who resembles her first love, Jonathan Harker, and she finds him in Tod Wilson, a teacher who opens a school near New York City. When one student decides to investigate bats near Mina's (aka Lady Dracula's) abode, he unleashes her terror.

Mac Wellman's Dracula; SoHo Repertory, New York, New York, U.S., May 1994. *Writing Credits*:

Mac Wellman; *Director*: Julian Webber; *Set Design*: Kyle Chepulis; *Original Music*: Melissa Shiflett; *Lighting*: Brian Aldous; *Costume Design*: James Sauli; *Sound Director*: John Kilgore; *Assistant Director*: Jason Porath; *Cast*: Christopher McCann (Simmons), Julia Gibson (Lucy), Ray Xifo (Van Helsing), Thomas Jay Ryan (Dracula), Tim Blake Nelson (Jonathan Harker), Jackie Domination, Marti Domination, Patricia Dunnock, Christine Martin, Brett Rickaby, Damian Young.

Mors Draculae; Stage West, Edmonton, Alberta, Canada, 1979. *Writing Credits*: Warren Graves; *Director*: William Fisher.

Out for the Count; or, How Would You Like Your Stake?: A Vampire Yarn; U.S., 1986; Comedy. *Writing Credits*: Martin Downing. A Transylvanian Count bearing a cross-shaped birthmark is newly arrived to Dr. Sewer's asylum where he sets his sights on Bridget and Constance. The Count enlists the help of Rennet to defeat the Professor and Jonathan who stand between him and the young ladies.

The Passion of Dracula; Cherry Lane Theatre, New York City, New York, U.S., 28 September 1977; Three Acts. *Writing Credits*: Bob Hall, David Richmond; *Director*: Peter Bennett; *Stage Manager*: Andrea Naier; *Set Design*: Bob Hall, Allen Cornell; *Costume Design*: Jane Tschetter; *Lighting*: Allen Cornell; *Cast* (in order of appearance): K. Lype O'Dell (Dr. Cedric Seward), Brian Bell (Jameson), Michael Burg (Professor Van Helsing), Alice White (Dr. Helga Van Zandt), K. C. Wilson (Lord Godalming), Elliott Vileen (Mr. Renfield), Giulia Pagano (Wilhelmina Murray), Samuel Maupin (Jonathan Harker), Christopher Burnau (Count Dracula).

The Possession of Lucy Wenstrom; 1975; Drama, Mystery; One Act. *Writing Credits*: Stephen Hotchner. Dracula travels to England in search of his next victim, Mina Harker's best friend, Lucy Wenstrom, who Dr. Van Helsing must work to save.

Renfield of the Flies and Spiders; or, Tell Dracula to Bug Off; 1993, U.S.; Comedy. *Writing Credits*: Tim Kelly. Dracula's faithful servant Renfield is back, and he has been declared "sane," a ploy so that Renfield's awful brother and sister-in-law, Philip and Jessica, can lay their greedy hands on his fortune. Although Renfield could afford any place he wanted, he instead buys Curfews Castle, the old dilapidated home where Dracula once lived. Renfield knows the secret to calling Dracula back from the grave and wants revenge on all those who have treated him badly. Now Dracula is Renfield's servant.

Seven Brides for Dracula; U.S., 1980; Comedy/Musical; One Act. *Writing Credits*: Tim Kelly; *Music and Lyrics*: Larry Nestor; *Music Arrangement and Orchestration*: Paul Curnow. With vampire hunter Van Helsing in hot pursuit, Dracula takes up residence in proximity to a sanitarium, where hilarious pandemonium ensues. Adapted from Tim Kelly's *Seven Wives for Dracula* (1973), this retelling also includes a howling wolfman.

Seven Wives for Dracula; U.S., 1973; Comedy/Musical. *Writing Credits*: Tim Kelly. Mr. and Mrs. Dracula take up residence in proximity to a sanatorium. Inhabiting the sanatorium is a *mélange* of characters, including the Odd Sisters, who can never quite finish an entire sentence, Mrs. Half-Nelson, who knits with invisible yarn and needles, and Lucy, who wears garlic necklaces to ward off evil.

Unauthorized stage adaptation of *Dracula*; c.1917. Presumably North American, this adaption, according to David J. Skal, was brought to the attention of Florence Stoker by Universal Pictures during the negotiations for the 1931 film rights. Stoker was unaware of the adaptation and disavowed it. Nothing else is currently known about this production

Vampires in L.A.; U.S.; Drama, Comedy. *Writing Credits*: Norman Beim. Vlad Tepes Dracula comes to Los Angeles as a film producer with his companion Elizabeth Bathory, who becomes involved with a young poet named Leslie Hawthorne. Vlad soon glimpses an image of Leslie's sister, Laura Hawthorne, whom Vlad is soon convinced is a reincarnation of his wife who died centuries ago.

Vlad Dracula, the Impaler; Romania, 1987. *Writing Credits*: Marin Sorescu.

The World of Dracula; Troupe Theatre, New York, New York, U.S., 1978. *Writing Credits*: Norman Beim. This was an earlier version of *Vampires in L.A.*

Young Dracula; or, The Singing Bat; U.S., 1975. *Writing Credits*: Tim Kelly; *Lyrics*: Tim Kelly. A group of students on a hiking tour through Europe loses its way and ends up staying the night in Dracula's castle. However, the castle has gone bankrupt, despite the best efforts of Dracula's descendent, Bill. So, when the students offer to pay for their lodging, Bill is only too happy to accept. Dracula, on the other hand, is not as cooperative.

Bibliography

Abbot, Rick. *Dracula, the Musical?* New York: Samuel French, 1984.

Allman, Sheldon, and Bob Pickett. *I'm Sorry, the Bridge Is Out, You'll Have to Spend the Night: A Musical.* Woodstock, IL: Dramatic, 1988.

Anchorage Press Plays. http://www.applays.com.

Beim, Norman. *Infamous People: Seven Plays.* Emerson, NJ: New Concept, 2004.

The Big Cartoon Database (BCDb). http://www.bcdb.com.

The British Film Institute (BFI). http://www.bfi.org.uk.

Browning, John Edgar. "Interviews with the Vampires: The Real Story Behind New Orleans's Vampire Subculture." *Deep South Magazine* 1 (Spring 2010).

Bunson, Matthew. *The Vampire Encyclopedia.* New York: Gramercy, 2000.

The Castlevania Dungeon. http://castlevaniadungeon.net/dungeon.html.

CESPOC Library. "English-Language Vampire Comics, 1935–2000." Center for Studies on New Religions (CESNUR). http://www.cesnur.org/2008/vampire_comics.htm (accessed February 3, 2008).

Dark Shadows Journal Online. http://www.collinwood.net.

Deane, Hamilton, and John L. Balderston. *Dracula: The Vampire Play in Three Acts.* New York: Samuel French, 1933.

_____. *Dracula: The Ultimate, Illustrated Edition of the World-Famous Vampire Play.* Ed. David J. Skal. New York: St. Martin's, 1993.

Dollee. http://www.doollee.com.

Donovan, Gene. *I Was a Teen-age Dracula: A Mystery-Comedy in Three Acts.* Chicago: Dramatic, 1958.

Dramatic Publishing. http://www.dramaticpublishing.com.

Dziemianowicz, Stefan "Introduction." In *Dracula: Prince of Darkness.* Ed. Martin H. Greenebrg. New York: DAW, 1992.

GameFaqs. http://www.gamefaqs.com.

GameSpot. http://www.gamespot.com.

GameTrailers. http://www.gametrailers.com.

Glut, Donald F. *The Dracula Book.* Metuchen, NJ: Scarecrow, 1975.

Guernsey, Otis L., Jr., ed. *The Best Plays of 1977–1978.* New York : Dodd, Mead, 1978.

Hall, Bob, David Richmond, and Bram Stoker. *The Passion of Dracula: A Drama in Three Acts.* New York: Samuel French, 1979.

Halliwell, Leslie. *Halliwell's Film Guide 1996.* Eleventh Ed. Ed. John Walker. New York: HarperPerennial, 1996.

Hollinger, Veronica. "The Vampire and the Alien: Gothic Horror and Science Fiction." In *Bram Stoker's Dracula: Sucking Through the Century, 1897–1997*, ed. Carol Margaret Davison. Toronto: Dundurn, 1997.

Holte, James Craig. *Dracula in the Dark: The Dracula Film Adaptations.* Westport, CT: Greenwood, 1997.

Hotchner, Stephen. *Death at the Crossroads.* Denver: Pioneer Drama Service, 1975.

_____. *Escape from Dracula's Castle.* Denver: Pioneer Drama Service, 1975.

_____. *Possession of Lucy Wenstrom.* Denver: Pioneer Drama Service, 1975.

The Internet Movie Database. (IMDb). http://www.imdb.com.

Johnson, Crane, and Bram Stoker. *Dracula.* New York: Dramatists Play Service, 1987.

Jones, Stephen. *The Essential Monster Movie Guide.* New York: Billboard, 2000.

Kamir, Orit. *Every Breath You Take: Stalking Narratives and the Law.* Ann Arbor, MI: University of Michigan Press, 2004.

Katz, Leon. *Midnight Plays.* Venice, CA: Wavecrest, 1992.

Kelly, Tim. *Reinfield of the Flies and Spiders, or Tell Dracula to Bug Off.* Denver: Pioneer Drama Service, 1993.

_____. *Seven Brides for Dracula.* Denver: Pioneer Drama Service, 1983.

_____. *Young Dracula: or The Singing Bat.* Denver: Pioneer Drama Service, 1975.

Lentz, Harris M., III. *Science Fiction, Horror and Fantasy Film and Television Credits, Vol. 2: Filmography.* 2d ed. Jefferson, NC: McFarland, 2000.

_____. *Science Fiction, Horror and Fantasy Film and Television Credits, Vol. 3: Television Shows.* 2d ed. Jefferson, NC: McFarland, 2000.

Ludlam, Harry. *A Biography of Dracula.* London: W. Foulsham, 1962.

Lugosi, Béla. "I Like Playing Dracula." *Film Weekly* (July 1935).

Malchow, H. L. *Gothic Images of Race in Nineteenth-Century Britain.* Palo Alto, CA: Stanford University Press, 1997.

Marill, Alvin H., and William T. Leonard. *More Theatre: M–Z*. Vol. 2. Metuchen, NJ: Scarecrow, 1993.

Mattera, John, and Bram Stoker. *Dracula*. Chicago: Dramatic, 1980.

Melton, J. Gordon. "List of Vampire Movies in English (origins–2008)." Center for Studies on New Religions (CESNUR). http://www.cesnur.org/2009/vampires_movies.htm (accessed March 1, 2008).

———. "List of Vampire TV Series in English (origins–2008)." Center for Studies on New Religions (CESNUR). http://www.cesnur.org/2009/vampires_tv.htm (accessed April 15, 2008).

———. *The Vampire Book: The Encyclopedia of the Undead*. Detroit: Visible Ink, 1999.

———. *Videohound's Vampires on Video*. Detroit: Visible Ink, 1997.

Miller, Elizabeth Russell. *Bram Stoker's Dracula: A Documentary Volume* (Dictionary of Literary Biography). Vol. 304. Detroit: Thomson Gale, 2005.

MobyGames. http://www.mobygames.com.

Murphy, Michael J. *The Celluloid Vampires: A History and Filmography, 1897–1979*. Ann Arbor, MI: Pierian Press, 1979.

Nichols, Christopher P., and Bram Stoker. *Dracula: Death of Nosferatu*. Woodstock, IL: Dramatic Publishing, 1991.

Pioneer Drama Service. http://www.pioneerdrama.com.

Pirie, David. *The New Heritage of Horror*. London: I.B. Tauris, 2009.

Playdatabase.com. http://www.playdatabase.com.

Rhodes, Gary Don. "*Drakula halála* (1921): The Cinema's First Dracula." *Horror Studies* 1:1 (Spring 2010): 25–47.

Riccardo, Martin V. *Vampires Unearthed: The Complete Multimedia Vampire and Dracula Bibliography*. New York: Garland, 1983.

Riley, Philip J. *Dracula: The Original 1931 Shooting Script*. Absecon, NJ: MagicImage Filmbooks, 1990.

Rogers, David. *Boys and Ghouls Together: A Play in Three Acts*. Chicago: Dramatic Publishing, 1965.

Ronald, Bruce, and Bram Stoker. *Dracula, Baby: A Musical Comedy*. Chicago: Dramatic Publishing, 1970.

Samuel French. http://www.samuelfrench.com/store/index.php.

Skal, David J. *Hollywood Gothic*. Revised ed. New York: Faber and Faber, 2004.

Stein, Wayne, and John Edgar Browning. "The Western Eastern: Decoding Hybridity and Zyber*Zen* Goth(ic) in *Vampire Hunter D* (1985)." In *Asian Gothic: Essays on Literature, Film and Anime*. Ed. Andrew Hock Soon Ng. Jefferson, NC: McFarland, 2008. Repr. in *Draculas, Vampires, and Other Undead Forms: Essays on Gender, Race, and Culture*. Ed. John Edgar Browning and Caroline Joan (Kay) Picart. Lanham, MD: Scarecrow, 2009.

Stoker, Bram. *Dracula: Authoritative Text, Contexts, Reviews and Reactions, Dramatic and Film Variations, Criticism*. Ed. Nina Auerbach and David J. Skal. New York: W.W. Norton, 1997.

Stuart, Roxana. *Stage Blood: Vampires of the 19th-Century Stage*. Bowling Green, OH: Bowling Green State University Popular Press, 1994.

Toonarific. http://www.toonarific.com.

Vampire Erotica. http://www.vampireerotica.net.

Vampire PayPerView. http://vod.vampirepayperview.com/dispatcher/frontDoor?&.

Vampyres Online: The Vampire Movie Database. http://www.vampyres-online.com.

Willis, John. *Theatre World: 1992–1993 Season*. Vol 49. New York: Applause Theatre, 1995.

Wrong Side of the Art! http://www.wrongsideoftheart.com.

Young, R.G. *The Encyclopedia of Fantastic Film*. New York: Applause, 2000.

Youngson, Jeanne. *A Child's Garden of Vampires*. Chicago: Adams, 1980.

About the Authors and Contributors

Dodd Alley received his M.A. in film studies from Ohio University in Athens, Ohio, where he also taught cult cinema and Hollywood reflexive film. He is the author of *Gamers and Gorehounds: The Influence of Video Games on the Contemporary American Horror Film.*

John Edgar Browning, a Ph.D. candidate in English, writing and culture, teaches composition and monster theory at Louisiana State University. He is the editor, with Caroline Joan (Kay) Picart, of *Draculas, Vampires, and Other Undead Forms: Essays on Gender, Race, and Culture* and *Speaking of Monsters: A Teratological Anthology* (Palgrave, forthcoming), and author of *Movie Monsters in Print: An Illustrated History* (Schiffer, forthcoming). Recent works also include several published and forthcoming book chapters and reviews, journal and magazine articles, and encyclopedic entries on Dracula, vampires, and horror.

Robert Eighteen-Bisang, who is best-known as the owner of the world's largest private collection of vampire books, is an authority on Dracula and vampire literature. His *Bram Stoker's Notes for Dracula*, edited with Elizabeth Miller, was the recipient of the 2008 Lord Ruthven Award in Nonfiction.

Mitch Frye is a Ph.D. candidate in English at Louisiana State University. His primary area of interest is American modernism, and much of his research concerns the exclusion of genre works from the modernist canon. His essays have appeared in *The Chronicle of Higher Education*, *CRITIQUE*, and *Nabokov Studies*.

Ian Holt acquired the rights to and developed a screenplay for the best-selling nonfiction book *In Search of Dracula* (1972) by Raymond T. McNally and Radu Florescu, which Francis Ford Coppola used to research his film *Bram Stoker's Dracula* (1992). Ian's first novel is *Dracula: The Un-Dead* (2009), with Dacre Stoker.

Laura Helen Marks is a Ph.D. candidate in English and women's and gender studies at Louisiana State University. Her research focuses on representations of sexuality and gender in film and literature, with an interest in cultural and gendered perspectives on obscene and pornographic texts.

J. Gordon Melton is the director of the Institute for the Study of American Religion in Santa Barbara, California. He is also a long-time student of vampire and Dracula myth and lore, and has written, in addition to Gale's acclaimed *Encyclopedia of Occultism and Parapsychology*, 4th ed. (1996), a series of scholarly reference texts on the subject, including award-winning *The Vampire Book: The Encyclopedia of the Undead* (3rd ed., 2010); *The Vampire Gallery* (1998), and *Videohound's Vampires on Video* (1997).

Caroline Joan (Kay) Picart (M. Phil, Cambridge University; Ph.D., Pennsylvania State University) is a scholar, critic, former professor, and author or co-author of 14 published and forthcoming scholarly books on film and critical theory/philosophy. She has also authored 44 refereed and invited journal articles and book chapters, and has written for newspapers and magazines in Seoul, South Korea, and in the United States. She is a J.D. candidate at the University of Florida Levin College of Law.

David J. Skal's publications on the horror genre, and on Dracula and vampires in particular, remain some of the most highly regarded works in the field. They include *Hollywood Gothic: The Tangled Web of Dracula from Novel to Stage to Screen*; *The Monster*

Show: A Cultural History of Horror; Romancing the Vampire; and *Vampires: Encounters with the Undead.* With Nina Auerbach, he is coeditor of the Norton Critical Edition of Bram Stoker's *Dracula.*

Dacre Stoker is the great-grandnephew of Bram Stoker and lives in Aiken, South Carolina. *Dracula: The Un-Dead* (2009) is his first novel, written with Ian Holt.

Index

Abbott, Bud 41–42
The ABC Saturday Superstar Movie (TV series): "Daffy Duck and Porky Pig Meet the Groovie Goolies" 18; "The Mad, Mad, Mad Monsters" 18
ABC Weekend Specials (TV series): "Bunnicula, the Vampire Rabbit" 18
The Accidental Hooker (film) 197–198, 200
Ackerman, Forrest J 74, 75*f*, 115, 154, 178, 180, 182
Action Planet Comics 244
Addams Family 18–19, 96–97; documentaries on 28, 105
The Addams Family (TV series): "The Fastest Creepy Camper in the West" 18–19
Adjani, Isabelle 138
adult film *see* pornographic film
Adventures into Terror (comic book) 244
Adventures into the Unknown (comic book) 244
The Adventures of Elmo in Grouchland (film) 19
The Adventures of Jerry Lewis (comic book) 244
The Adventures of Olivia (comic book) 244
The Adventures of Young Indiana Jones: Masks of Evil (film) 19–20
Adventures of Young Van Helsing: The Quest for the Lost Scepter (film) 20
AFI's 100 Years ... 100 Heroes and Villains (film) 20
African Americans: and comic books 240; and pornography 197, 199*n*26, 208
El Águila Descalza (film) 20–21
AIDS 196
Akui ggot (film) 21
Akumaj Dorakyura: Yamo no Juin (manga) 261
Akumajô Dorakiyura: Yamo no juin (game) 219
Akumajô Dorakyura: Jajimento (game) 215, 219
Akumajô Dracula (game) 219–220
Akumajô Dracula: The Arcade (game) 220
Akumajô Dracula: The Medal (game) 220
Akumajô Dracula: Shikkoku taru zensôkyoku (game) 220

Akumajô Dracula: Ubawareta Kokuin (game) 220
Akumajô Dracula X: Chi no Rondo (game) 220
Akumajô Dracula X: Gekka no yasukyôoku (game) 220–221
Akumajô Dracula XX (game) 221
Akumajo Special: Boku Dracula-kun! (game) 221
Akumajou Densetsu (game) 216, 221
Akumajou Dracula: Circle of the Moon (game) 221
Akumajou Dracula: Gallery of Labyrinth (game) 221
Akumajou Dracula Mokushiroku Gaiden: The Legend of Cornell (game) 223
Akumajou Dracula: Sougetsu no Juujika (game) 221–222
Las Alegres Vampiras de Vögel (film) 21
Alf Annual (comic book) 244
Alfred Hitchcock Presents (TV series): "Night Creatures" 21
Alive! Donald Duck: Georgia Ou no Hihou (game) 232–233
All My Children (TV series) 21–22
Alley, Timothy Dodd 215–218
alternative sexuality, vampire imagery and 195–196
Alucard (film) 22
Alucarda, la hija de las tinieblas (film) 22
Amantul marii doamne Dracula (TV series) 22
The Amazing Adrenali Brothers! (TV series): "Fangs of Horror" 22
Amazing Heroes (comic book) 244
Amazing Spider Man (comic book) 240, 244
Amora (comic book) 244
And Comes the Dawn ... But Colored Red (film) 132
Animaniacs (TV series): "Draculee, Draculaa/Phranken-Runt" 22; "Randy Beaman's Pal #6" 23
Animaniacs—Spooky Stuff (film) 23
Anita Blake: Vampire Hunter (comic book) 241
Anton's Collected Drek Featuring Wendy Whitehead (comic book) 244
Anything Goes! (comic book) 244
Aqua Teen Hunger Force (TV series): "Bus of the Undead" 23; "Little Brittle" 23

Archie (comic book) 244
Archie Giant Series Magazine (comic book) 244
Archie's Double Digest Magazine (comic book) 244
Archie's Madhouse (comic book) 244
Army of Darkness (comic book) 244
Army of Darkness: Ash vs. the Classic Monsters (and More) (comic book) 244
Arozamena, Eduardo 63*f*
ARRGH! (comic book) 244
The Art of Neal Adams! (comic book) 244
Ashes of Doom (film) 23
Ashton, Roy 95
Askonas, Paul 80, 81*f*
Astin, John 96
El Ataúd del Vampiro (film) 23–25, 24*f*
Atic Atac (game) 222
Attack of the Killer Tomatoes (TV series): "Spatula, Prinze of Dorkness" 25
Aubry, Kim 104, 122
Auerbach, Nina 148
Les Avaleuses (film) 200
The Avengers (comic book) 244
Awake (film) 25
The Awesome Adventures of Victor Vector & Yondo: The Vampire's Coffin (game) 222

Il Bacio di Dracula (TV miniseries) 25–26
The Bad Flower (film) 21
Baker, Roy Ward 181
Bakula, Scott 144
Balderston, John L. 12
ballet 17, 71–72
Bandh Darwaza (film) 26
Banpaia hantâ D (film) 26–27
Banquete das Taras (film) 27
Bara no Konrei—Mayonaka ni Kawashita Yakusoku (film) 27
The Barefoot Eagle (film) 20–21
Barker, Clive 148
El Barón Brakola (film) 27
Barrymore, Drew 186
Barrymore, Lionel 119, 121
The Bash Street Kids Summer Special (comic book) 244
The Baskervilles (TV show) 27
Bassett, Angela 181

Bathory, Elizabeth 35, 46, 76; documentary on 182; *see also* Blood Countess character
Batman: censors and 241; and vampire imagery 239–240
Batman & Dracula (comic book) 244
Batman & Dracula: Red Rain (comic book) 240, 244
Batman Dracula (film) 27–28
Batman Fights Dracula (film) 28
Batman: Nosferatu (comic book) 244
Batman vs. Dracula: The Animated Movie (film) 28
Batuta ni Dracula (film) 28, 29f
BDSM 196, 198; definition of 198n5
The Beano (comic book) 244
The Beano Book (comic book) 244
Beano Comic Library 244
Beardsley, Aubrey 12, 16
The Beatles (TV series): "Misery" 28
The Beezer and Cracker (comic book) 244
The Beezer and Topper (comic book) 244
The Beezer Book (comic book) 244
The Beezer Summer Special (comic book) 245
Before the Fantastic Four: The Storms (comic book) 245
Behind the Fame: The Munsters/Addams Family (TV documentary) 28
Bela Lugosi Scrapbook (documentary) 28
Beloved Count (documentary) 28–29
Benshoff, Harry M. 195–197
Benyamin kontra Drakula (film) 29
Beowulf Dragon Slayer (comic book) 245
The Best of Buster Monthly (comic book) 245
The Best of Drag Cartoons (comic book) 245
The Best of National Lampoon (comic book) 245
The Best of Whizzer and Chips (comic book) 245
The Best of Whoopee! (comic book) 245
Big Bad Blood of Dracula (comic book) 245
Big Bang Comics 245
The Big Book of Bad (comic book) 245
The Big Comic 245
The Big Comic Holiday Special 245
Billy & Mandy's Big Boogey Adventure (film) 29–30
Billy Joe Van Helsing: Redneck Vampire Hunter (comic book) 245
Billy the Kid Versus Dracula (film) 30–31, 30f
Biography (TV series): "Bram Stoker" 31
Birth of the Vampire (film) 31
Birtwhistle, Tara 72f
A Bite of Love (film) 188
Bizarre Adventures (comic book) 245
The Bizarre Cage #3 (film) 200
Bizarre Heroes (comic book) 254
Bizarre's Dracula I (film) 196, 200–201
Bizarre's Dracula II (film) 196, 201
B.J. and the Bear (TV series): "A Coffin with a View" 31

Black Cat Mystery (comic book) 245
Black Inferno (film) 31
Blacula (film) 31, 32f
Blade (comic book) 240, 245
Blade: Trinity (film) 31–33
Blade: The Vampire Hunter (comic book) 245
Blood (film) 33
Blood Countess character: in *Ceremonia Sagrienta* 46; in *Countess Dracula* 52–53, 52f; in *Mama Dracula* 118; in *La Noche de Walpurgis* 135; in *Il Plenilunio delle vergini* 142; in *Riti, magie nere e segrete orge nel trecento* (film) 147–148; in *Vampire Blues* 179; in *Vampires* 212; *see also* Bathory, Elizabeth
Blood for Dracula (film) 33–34
Blood Hound (manga) 261
The Blood Is the Life: The Making of Bram Stoker's Dracula (documentary) 34
Blood Lines: Dracula—The Man, the Myth, the Movies (documentary) 34
Blood of Dracula (comic book) 245
Blood of Dracula (film) 34, 35f
Blood of Dracula's Castle (film) 34–35
Blood of the Innocent (comic book) 245
Blood of the Virgins (film) 150
Blood Scarab (film) 35
Blood Son (film) 35–36
Blood Suckers (film) 36
The Blood Sword (comic book) 245
Bloodhound: Vampire Gigolo (TV series) 184–185
Bloodlines: The Dracula Family Tree (documentary) 36
Bloodspit (film) 36
Bloodstone (comic book) 245
Bloodsucking Cinema (documentary) 36
Bloodsucking Doll (film) 189–190
The Bloody Vampire (film) 182
Bonnie & Clyde vs. Dracula (film) 36–37
Boo (film) 37
Boogeyman Vampire Club 4 (film) 36
Bordon, Eddie 100
Boris Karloff and Bela Lugosi (documentary) 37
Boris Karloff: Tales of Mystery (comic book) 245
BPRD (comic book) 241
Brácula Condemor II (film) 37
Bram Stoker's Dracula (comic book) 241, 245
Bram Stoker's Dracula (film) 7, 37–38, 38f; documentaries on 34, 104, 117, 122, 125
Bram Stoker's Dracula (game) 217, 224
Bram Stoker's to Die For (film) 176
Bram Stoker's Vampire Diaries: Renfield (film) 38–39
Bram Stoker's Way of the Vampire (film) 39
Breakfast with Dracula (film) 39
The Breed (film) 39
Brennan, William 195
Briant, Shane 14–16
Bridal of Rose—The Promise Exchanged at Midnight (film) 27

Bride of Heavy Metal (comic book) 245
The Bride's Initiation (film) 201
Brides of Countess Recula (film) 201
The Brides of Dracula (film) 39–41, 40f
The Brides of Dracula (game) 222
Bromfield, Louis 12
Brooke West Collection (film) 201
Brown, Jeffrey A. 240
Browning, Tod 12, 61–62, 119
Buck Rogers in the 25th Century (TV series): "Space Vampire" 41
Bud Abbott and Lou Costello Meet Frankenstein (film) 41–42
Bud Abbott and Lou Costello Meet the Monsters! (film) 42
Buenas Noches, Señor Monstruo (film) 42
Buffy the Vampire Layer (film) 201
Buffy the Vampire Slayer (film) 42–43
Buffy the Vampire Slayer (TV series): "Buffy vs. Dracula" 42–43; and comic books 241
Burger King Kids Club Adventures (comic book) 245
Buster (comic book) 245–246
Buster and Monster Fun Holiday Special (comic book) 246
Buster and Monster Fun Spring Special (comic book) 246
The Buster Book (comic book) 246
Buster Classics (comic book) 246
Buster Comic Library 246
Buster Fortnightly (comic book) 246
The Buster Holiday Special (comic book) 246
Butler, Gerard 67–68
Byron, George Gordon, Lord 3, 177

Call Him Jess (documentary) 43
Called from Darkness (comic book) 246
Campbell, Bruce 186
Canuncula! (film) 43–44
Captain America (comic book) 246
Captain Berlin Versus Hitler (film) 44
Captain N: The Game Master (TV series): "Return to Castlevania" 44
Capulina Contra los Vampiros (film) 44
Car Toons (comic book) 246
Carlson, Veronica 86
Carmilla (Le Fanu; novel) 22
Carpenter, John 36
Carradine, David 30–31, 30f, 111, 171, 186
Carradine, John 60, 101, 101f, 121, 135, 179–181
Carreras, James 194
Carreras, Michael 15
Carrey, Jim 104
Carry on Christmas (film) 44
Il Castello dei morti vivi (film) 44–45
Castle Dracula (play) 5
Castle of Horror (comic book) 246
Castlevania (film) 45
Castlevania (game) 215–217; and comic books 241; TV series based on 44
Castlevania II: Belmont's Revenge (game) 225

Castlevania II: Simon's Quest (game) 216, 225
Castlevania III: Dracula's Curse (game) 216, 221
Castlevania IV (game) 219–220
Castlevania (64) (game) 222
Castlevania: The Adventure (game) 224–225
Castlevania: Akatsuki no Minuet (game) 222
Castlevania: The Arcade (game) 220
Castlevania: Aria of Sorrow (game) 222
Castlevania: Bloodlines (game) 222–223
Castlevania: Byakuya no Concerto (game) 223
Castlevania: Circle of the Moon (game) 221
Castlevania: Concerto of Midnight Sun (game) 223
Castlevania: Curse of Darkness (game) 219
Castlevania: Curse of Darkness (manga) 261
Castlevania: Dawn of Sorrow (game) 221–222
Castlevania: Harmony of Dissonance (game) 223
Castlevania: Judgement (game) 215, 219
Castlevania: Lament of Innocence (game) 223
Castlevania: Legacy of Darkness (game) 223
Castlevania: Legends (game) 220
Castlevania: Minuet of Dawn (game) 222
Castlevania: Order of Ecclesia (game) 220
Castlevania: Order of Shadows (game) 223
Castlevania: Portrait of Ruin (game) 221
Castlevania: Rondo of Blood (game) 220
Castlevania: Symphony of the Night (game) 220–221
Castlevania: Vampire's Kiss (game) 221
Casualty (TV series): "Trials and Tribulations" 45
Cathula (film) 201
Cathula 2: Vampires of Sex (film) 201
Il Cav. Costante Nicosia demoniaco, ovvero: Dracula in Brianza (film) 45–46
Cavewoman: One-Shot Special (comic book) 246
Cemetery Girls (film) 180
censorship: and adult film 193–195; and comic books 241–243; and film 6, 13–14
Ceremonia Sagrienta (film) 46
Chair (documentary) 46
Challenge of the SuperFriends (TV series): "Attack of the Vampire" 46
Chaney, Lon, Jr. 12, 60, 74, 99, 168, 180
Chapolim x Drácula: Um Duelo Assustador (game) 223–224, 228
Chappaqua (film) 46
Les Charlots contre Dracula (film) 46–47
Cheval Noir (comic book) 246

Chi o suu bara (film) 47
Chickula: Teenage Vampire (film) 47
Children of Dracula (documentary) 47
Children of the Night (play) 16
Chiller Pocket Book (comic book) 246
Chilling Monster Tales (comic book) 246
Christopher Lee's Treasury of Terror (comic book) 246
Cinderelmo (film) 47
Cineastes contra magnats (documentary) 47–48
Cities of the Underworld (TV series): "Dracula's Underground" 48
Clarke, Harry 12
Clarke, Robert 115
Classic Horror Tales (comic book) 246
Close-Up (TV series): "Bela Lugosi: Dracula's Dubbelganger" 48
The Closed Door (film) 26
Codename: Kids Next Door (TV series): "Operation S.P.A.N.K." 49
The Collector's Dracula (comic book) 246
comic books 239–243; and video games 217
The Comic Strip (TV series): "The Mini-Monsters" 49
Comics Code Authority (CCA) 242–243
Comics to Color 246
Comix International 246
community standards, and pornography 195
The Complete Crumb Comics 246
The Complete Foo! (comic book) 246
The Complete Sally Forth (comic book) 246
Comstock law 195
Conan Saga (comic book) 246
El Conde Drácula (film) 49–50, 49f
The Conde Mácula (film) 50
Conker's Bad Fur Day (game) 224
Connery, Sean 112
Coppola, Francis Ford 34, 37–38, 117, 122
copyright issues 2, 11
Cor!! (comic book) 247
Corman, Roger 73, 141–142
Costello, Lou 41–42
The Cougar (comic book) 247
The Count (game) 224
Count Dracula (film) 50–51, 50f
Count Dracula and His Vampire Bride (film) 151, 153f
Count Dracula, the True Story (documentary) 51
Count Duckula (comic book) 247
Count Duckula (TV series) 51
Count Duckula Annual (comic book) 247
Count Duckula Winter Special (comic book) 247
Count Erotica, Vampire (film) 201
Count Frankenhausen (film) 182
The Count of Calle Ocho (film) 51
Count Spermula (film) 198, 201–202
Count Suckula (film) 198, 202
Count Yorga, Vampire (film) 51–52
Countdown Dracula (TV series) 50, 52
Countess character *see* Blood Countess character

Countess Dracula (film) 52–53, 52f
Countess Dracula's Orgy of Blood (film) 198, 202
Cracked Annuals (comic book) 247
Cracked Blockbuster (comic book) 247
Cracked Collector's Edition (comic book) 247
Cracked Digest (comic book) 247
Cracked Magazine (comic book) 247
Cracked Monster Party (comic book) 247
Cracked Summer Special (comic book) 247
Cracked's for Monsters Only (comic book) 247
Cracked's for Monsters Only Annual (comic book) 247
Cracker (comic book) 247
Craven, Wes 67–68
Crazy Comics 247
Crazy Magazine (comic book) 247
The Creeps (film) 53
Creepsville (comic book) 247
Creepy (comic book) 247–248
Creepy, The Best of (comic book) 248
Creepy: The Classic Years (comic book) 248
Crossfire (comic book) 248
Cryptic Tales (comic book) 248
Cuadecuc, vampir (documentary) 53
Cunt Dykula (film) 197, 202
Curry, Tim 149
The Curse of Dracula (comic book) 248
The Curse of Dracula (TV series) 53
Curse of the Vampires (film) 103, 104f
Curtis, Dan 57–58, 64, 100
Cushing, Peter 15; in *The Brides of Dracula* 40f, 41; in documentaries 88, 100, 181, 188; in *Dracula* 64; in *One More Time* 139; in *The Satanic Rites of Dracula* 151; in *Twins of Evil* 178
Cyberchase (TV series): "Castleblanca" 53–54

Daffy Duck (comic book) 248
Daltrey, Roger 182
Dampyr (comic book) 248
The Dandy (comic book) 248
The Dandy Book (comic book) 248
Dandy Comic Library 248
Danny Phantom (TV series): "Material Instinct" 54
Darakula (film) 54
Dark Angels 2: Bloodline (film) 198, 202
Dark Horse 239, 241
Dark Prince: The True Story of Dracula (film) 54
Dark Shadows (TV series) 54–56, 55f
Dark Shadows: Behind the Scenes (documentary) 56–57
Dark Shadows: Bloopers (documentary) 57
Dark Shadows: 1840 Flashback (film) 57
Dark Shadows: Music Videos (documentary) 57
Dark Shadows Resurrected: The Video (documentary) 57

Index

Dark Shadows' Scariest Moments (documentary) 57
Dark Shadows: 30th Anniversary Tribute (documentary) 57
Dark Shadows: 25th Anniversary Tribute (documentary) 57–58
Dark Shadows: Vampires and Ghosts (documentary) 58
Dark Shadows: Video Scrapbook (documentary) 58
Dark Wars: The Tale of Meiji Dracula (comic book) 248
The Darkness Vs. Eva: Daughter of Dracula (comic book) 248
Daughters of Dracula (film) 183
Davis, Sammy, Jr. 139
DC Comics 239–240, 242
Dead Souls (comic book) 248
Dead to the Last Drop (film) 58
Deadbeats (comic book) 248
Deadtime Stories (comic book) 248
Deafula (film) 58–59, 58*f*
Deane, Hamilton 12, 16
Death Dreams of Dracula (comic book) 248
De Carlo, Yvonne 128, 128*f,* 129
The Defenders (comic book) 248
Defenders of the Earth (TV series): "Dracula's Potion" 59
Dell, Gabriel 170–171
Demons (TV series) 59
Destruction Kings (film) 59–60
Detective Comics 239, 248
Deveraux, Tricia 199*n*22
Diary of a Vampire: Young Dracula (comic book) 248
digital media, and pornography 197–198
La Dinistía de Dracula (film) 60
Dinosaurs for Hire (comic book) 248
Disgaea: Hour of Darkness (game) 230
Disgaea 2: Cursed Memories (game) 230–231
Disgaea 3: Absence of Justice (game) 230
Disney, Walt 122
Disney Adventures (comic book) 248
Doctor Dracula (film) 60
Doctor Strange (comic book) 248
Doctor Strange: Master of the Mysic Arts (comic book) 248
Dr. Strange: Sorcerer Supreme (comic book) 248
Dr. Strange Vs. Dracula 251
Doctor Strange Vs. Dracula: The Montesi Formula (comic book) 248
Dr. Terror's Gallery of Horrors (film) 60
Doctor Who (TV series), *The Chase*: "The Executioners" 60–61; "Journey into Terror" 61
documentaries: *Behind the Fame: The Munsters/Addams Family* 28; *Bela Lugosi Scrapbook* 28; *Beloved Count* 28–29; *The Blood Is the Life: The Making of Bram Stoker's Dracula* 34; *Blood Lines: Dracula—The Man, the Myth, the Movies* 34; *Bloodlines: The Dracula Family Tree* 36; *Bloodsucking Cinema* 36; *Boris Karloff and Bela Lugosi* 37; *Call Him Jess* 43; *Chair* 46; *Children of Dracula* 47; *Cineastes contra magnats* 47–48; *Count Dracula, the True Story* 51; *Cuadecuc, vampir* 53; *Dark Shadows: Behind the Scenes* 56–57; *Dark Shadows: Bloopers* 57; *Dark Shadows: Music Videos* 57; *Dark Shadows Resurrected: The Video* 57; *Dark Shadows' Scariest Moments* 57; *Dark Shadows: 30th Anniversary Tribute* 57; *Dark Shadows: 25th Anniversary Tribute* 57–58; *Dark Shadows: Vampires and Ghosts* 58; *Dark Shadows: Video Scrapbook* 58; *Dracul cu scripca* 61; *The Dracula Business* 69; *Dracula: A Cinematic Scrapbook* 69; *Dracula: Fact or Fiction* 70; *Dracula: Forbidden Fruit* 70–71; *Dracula in the Movies* 71; *Dracula Live from Transylvania* 71; *Dracula, the Great Undead* 73; *Dracula: The True Story* 74; *Dracula's Bram Stoker* 75; *Dracula's Curse: Behind the Scenes* 76; *Dracula's Stoker* 78; *Fangs! A History of Vampires in the Movies* 86; *Flesh and Blood: The Hammer Heritage of Horror* 87–88; *40 Dana* 88; *Greasepaint and Gore* 95; *Greasepaint and Gore, Part 2* 95; *Heroes of Horror* 99; *Historical Dracula, Facts Behind the Fiction* 100; *Hollywood on Parade No. A-8* 100; *Hollywood's Greatest Villains* 100; *The Impaler: A Biographical/Historical Look...* 103–104; *In Camera: The Naïve Visual Effects of Bram Stoker's Dracula* 104; *In Search of Dracula with Jonathan Ross* 105; *In Search of History: The Real Dracula* 105; *Inside...Addams Family & The Munsters* 105; *Lugosi: Hollywood's Dracula* 115; *Lugosi: The Forgotten King* 115; *Making Bela* 117; *Making "Bram Stoker's Dracula"* 117; *Method and Madness: Visualizing "Dracula"* 122; *Mondo Lugosi* 124; *Monster by Moonlight! The Immortal Saga of "The Wolf Man"* 124; *Monster Mania* 125; *Monster Squad Forever* 126; *MonsterFest 2000: The Classics Come Alive* 126; *My Life with Count Dracula* 130; *Night Bites: Women and Their Vampires* 133; *Nightmare: The Birth of Victorian Horror* 135; *100 Years of Horror: Blood-Drinking Beings* 138; *100 Years of Horror: The Monster Makers* 138; *The Real Life of Dracula* 144; *The Revamping of Dracula* 147; *The Road to Dracula* 148; *Scary America* 153–154; *Sexy Probitissimo* 195, 210; *Universal Horror* 178–179; *La Vampire déchu* 180; *The Vampire Interviews* 181; *Vampire Secrets* 181–182; *Vampires* 182; *Van Helsing: The Man and the Monsters* 184; *Vem var Dracula* 185; *Vlad the Impaler: The True Story of Dracula* 185; *Winter with Dracula* 187
Don Dracula (TV series) 61
Don Martin Magazine (comic book) 248
Doom of Dracula (film) 61
Doomsday Album (comic book) 248
Doorway to Nightmare (comic book) 248
Doracula (film) 202
Dororon Emma-Kun (TV series) 61
D.P.7 (comic book) 248
Dracul cu scripca (documentary) 61
Dracula: absences of 7, 11–12; in comic books 239–261; markers of 4; in pornographic film 193–212; resurrections of 216–217; Russell on 16–17; Skal on 11–17; in video games 215–235
Dracula (Stoker; novel) 193; illustrated editions of 241, 248–249, 253; print editions of 265–272
Dracula (1931; film) 3, 12, 61–62, 62*f*; 1966 short version 64
Dracula (1958; film) 6, 14, 63–64, 64*f,* 194
Dracula (1966; film) 64
Dracula (1973; film) 64–66, 65*f*
Dracula (1973; TV show) 66
Dracula (1979; film) 66–67, 66*f*
Dracula (1994; adult film) 197, 203
Dracula (1999; film) 67
Drácula (1999; TV miniseries) 67
Drácula (2006; TV show) 67
Dracula (ballet) 17
Dracula (comic book) 248–249
Drácula (film; 1931 Spanish version) 12, 62–63, 63*f*
Dracula (game) 224
Dracula II: Ascension (film) 68
Dracula 2: The Last Sanctuary (game) 217, 226
Dracula II: Noroi no fūin (game) 225
Dracula III: Legacy (film) 68–69
Dracula 3—The Path of the Dragon (game) 224
Dracula 2000 (film) 67–68, 217
Dracula 3000 (film) 68
Dracula A.D. 1972 (film) 69
Dracula aema (film) 69
Dracula and the Boys (film) 195, 203
Dracula Annual (comic book) 249
Dracula: Asylum Novel (comic book) 249
Dracula Bites the Big Apple (film) 69
The Dracula Business (documentary) 69
Dracula: A Chamber Musical (TV show) 69
The Dracula Chronicles (comic book) 249
Dracula: A Cinematic Scrapbook (documentary) 69
Dracula Comics Special 249
Drácula contra Frankenstein (film) 69–70, 70*f*
Dracula: Crazy Vampire (game) 226
Dracula: The Days of Gore (game) 226
Dracula Densetsu (game) 224–225
Dracula Densetsu II (game) 225
Dracula, the Dirty Old Man (film) 195, 204
Dracula Exotica (film) 196, 203
Dracula: Fact or Fiction (documentary) 70
The Dracula Files (game) 225
Dracula: Forbidden Fruit (documentary) 70–71
Dracula/Garden of Eden (film) 71
Dracula, the Great Undead (documentary) 73

Dracula Has Risen from the Grave (film) 71
Drácula, Una História de Amor (TV series) 74
Dracula: The Illustrated Novel of Horror (comic book) 250
Dracula: The Impaler (comic book) 250
Dracula the Impaler (film) 73–74
Dracula in Hell (comic book) 249
Dracula in London (game) 225
Dracula in Pakistan (film) 190
Dracula in the Movies (documentary) 71
Dracula in Vegas (film) 71
Dracula: The Lady in the Tomb (comic book) 250
Dracula Live from Transylvania (documentary) 71
Dracula Lives (comic book) 242, 249–250
Dracula Lives Annual (comic book) 250
Dracula Lives Featuring the Legion of Monsters (comic book) 250
Dracula Lives Special (comic book) 250
Dracula: Lord of the Undead (comic book) 250
Drácula mascafierro (film) 203
Dracula Meets Jesus (comic book) 250
Dracula Meets the Outer Space Chicks (film) 203
Dracula Mon Amour (film) 71
Dracula: Origin (game) 226
Dracula: Pages from a Virgin's Diary (ballet) 71–72, 72f
Dracula père et fils (film) 72
Dracula: Prince of Darkness (film) 72–73
Dracula: Prince of Marketing (film) 73
Dracula: Reign of Terror (game) 234–235
Dracula: The Resurrection (game) 217, 226
Dracula: Return of the Impaler (comic book) 250
Dracula: Revamped (film) 73
Dracula Rising (film) 73
Dracula: The Series (TV series) 74
Dracula '79 (comic book) 250
Dracula: Sovereign of the Damned (film) 188
Dracula Sucks (comic book) 250
Dracula Sucks (film) 203–204, 204f
Dracula: The Suicide Club (comic book) 250
Dracula Summer Special (comic book) 250
Dracula: A Symphony in Moonlight and Nightmares (comic book) 249
Dracula 3-D (comic book) 250
Dracula: The True Story (documentary) 74
Dracula Twins (game) 225
Dracula-type characters: Barnabus Collins as 54–58, 55f, 100–101; in *The Breed* 39; in "Bunnicula" 18; in *Chappaqua* 46; in *Danny Phantom* 54; in *Duck Dodgers* 81–82; in *Geung see yee saang* 91; in *Ghost Fever* 92; in *Gilligan's Island* 92; in *Gravedale High* 95; in *The House That Dripped Blood* 102; in *Kulay Dugo ang Gabi* 109; in *The Lair* 110; in *Makai Senki Disgaea* 117; in *Malenka* 117–118; in *Mickey's Gala Premier* 122; in *Mystery in Dracula's Castle* 131; in "Night Creatures" 21; in *Nightmare at Elm Manor* 209; in *Onna Kyuketsuki* 140; in *Salem's Lot* 150; in *Tetsuwan Atom* 174; in *The Thirst: Blood Wars* 174; in *Twins of Evil* 178; in *Vampire Hookers* 180; in *The Vampire Hunters Club* 181; in *Vampire in Brooklyn* 181
Dracula the Undead (game) 225
Dracula: The UnDead (Stoker and Holt) 2
Dracula Unleashed (game) 217, 225–226
Dracula: El Vampiro (game) 227
Dracula Vs. Capone (comic book) 250
Dracula Vs. Frankenstein (film) 74, 75f
Dracula Versus King Arthur (comic book) 250
Dracula Vs. the Grad (comic book) 250
Dracula versus Zorro (comic book) 250–251
Dracula Versus Zorro: The Complete Saga (comic book) 250
Dracula: Vlad the Impaler (comic book) 250
Dracula Year Zero (film) 74–75
Dracula's Baby (film) 75
Dracula's Bram Stoker (documentary) 75
Dracula's Curse (*Il Bacio di Dracula*; TV miniseries) 25–26
Dracula's Curse (film) 75–76
Dracula's Curse: Behind the Scenes (documentary) 76
Dracula's Daughter (comic book) 251
Dracula's Daughter (film) 13–14, 76–77, 76f
Dracula's Dirty Daughter (film) 123
Dracula's Dog (film) 77
Dracula's Dungeon (film) 196, 204
Dracula's Family Visit (film) 77–78
Dracula's Guest (film) 78
"Dracula's Guest" (Stoker; story) 13, 77, 103, 106, 186, 268–270
Dracula's Last Rites (film) 110–111
Dracula's Revenge (comic book) 250
Dracula's Secret (game) 226–227
Dracula's Spinechillers (comic book) 251
Dracula's Stoker (documentary) 78
Dracula's Wedding Day (film) 78
Dracula's Widow (film) 78–79
Draculina (comic book) 251
Draculina Video Magazine (film) 79
Draculina's Cozy Coffin (comic book) 251
Draculito, mon Saigneur (film) 79
Draculya: The Girls Are Hungry (film) 198, 204
Drag Cartoons (comic book) 251
Dragstrip Dracula (film) 79
Dragula (film) 204–205
Dragula, Queen of Darkness (film) 196, 205
The Drak Pack (TV series) 79
Drakoulas & Sia (film) 79
O Drakoulas ton Exarheion (film) 79–80
Drakula Goes to R.P. 80, 80f
Drakula halála (film) 11–12, 80, 81f
Drakula Istanbul'da (film) 80, 81f
Drakula Mantu (film) 29
Drakulita (film) 80–81, 82f
dramatizations 284–288
Drink My Red Blood (film) 35–36
Drum bun— Jo utat! (film) 81
Duck Dodgers (TV series): "I'm Going to Get You, Fat Sucka" 81–82
Duckula (comic book) 251
Duckula Summer Special (comic book) 251
Dugo ng Vampira (film) 82
La Duodécima hora (film) 82–83
Dziemianowicz, Stefan 4

Eagle (comic book) 251
EC Comics 241–242
Echo of Future Past (comic book) 251
economic recession, and vampire imagery 7
Eerie (comic book) 251
Eighteen-Bisang, Robert 265–272
Ejacula 2 (film) 197, 205
Ejacula, la vampira (film) 197, 205
The Elder Scrolls IV: Oblivion (game) 227
The Electric Company (TV series) 83
The Electric Company Magazine (comic book) 251
Elliott, Denholm 130
Elmo Saves Christmas (film) 83
Elmo Says Boo (film) 83
Elmo Visits the Doctor (film) 83–84
Elmopalooza (film) 84
Elmo's Christmas Countdown (film) 84
Elson's Presents (comic book) 251
Elvira 125
Elvira: Mistress of the Dark (comic book) 251
Emmanuelle the Private Collection: Emmanuelle vs. Dracula (film) 205
Emotion: densetsu no gogo = itsukamita Dracula (film) 84
Ernest Le Vampire (TV show) 85
The Erotic Rites of Countess Dracula (film) 197–198, 205–206
Escala en Hi-Fi (film) 85
Essential Monster of Frankenstein (comic book) 254
Essential Tomb of Dracula (comic book) 251
Essential X-Men (comic book) 251
Eternal Knights 2 (game) 227
Eternal Romance (comic book) 251
Every Home Should Have One (film) 85
Everybody Loves Raymond (TV series): "Halloween Candy" 85–86
Evil Ernie vs The Movie Monsters (comic book) 251
Evil of Dracula (film) 47, 86
Evil Prophecy (game) 217, 231
Evolution Skateboarding (game) 227

Fade to Black (film) 86
Famous Monsters of Filmland (comic book) 251

Index

Fandom's Finest Comics 251
Fang (comic book) 251
El Fang-Dango (film) 86
Fangland (film) 86
Fangs! A History of Vampires in the Movies (documentary) 86
Fanhunter: Dracula Returns (comic book) 251
El Fantasma de la opereta (film) 86
Fantastic Fears (comic book) 251
Fantastic Four (comic book) 251
Fantomen (comic book) 251
Fantomu Bureibu (game) 227–228
Farson, Daniel 69
Fast Forward (comic book) 251
The Fearless Vampire Killers; or, Pardon Me, But Your Teeth Are in My Neck (film) 86–87
Fem dogn i august (film) 87
Femforce in the House of Horror (comic book) 251
fetish porn 196, 198
La Fiancée de Dracula (film) 87
La Fille de Dracula (film) 87
Finger, Bill 239
Flanery, Sean Patrick 19
Fleetwood, Mick 16
Flesh and Blood: The Hammer Heritage of Horror (documentary) 87–88
The Flintstones (comic book) 251
Florescu, Radu 36, 105, 185, 263, 270
Fonz and the Happy Days Gang (TV series): "The Vampire Strikes Back" 88
Foo! (comic book) 251
For Monsters Only (comic book) 251
Forbidden Mad (comic book) 251
Fort, Garrett 12, 14
Fort Dracula (film) 88
40 Dana (documentary) 88
40 gradi all'ombra del lenzuolo (film) 88–89
Fracchia Contro Dracula (film) 89
Fraiser (TV series): "Halloween" 89
Frampton, Peter 168
Franco, Jesus: and *Les Avaleuses* 200; and *El Conde Drácula* 49–50; and documentaries 28–29, 43, 53; and *Drácula contra Frankenstein* 69–70; and *La Fille de Dracula* 87; and *Killer Barbys Vs. Dracula* 108–109; and *Vampire Blues* 179; and *Vampiros Lesbos* 183
Frankenstein and Me (film) 89
The Frankenstein/Dracula War (comic book) 252
The Frankenstein Monster (comic book) 254
Frankenstein Sings (film) 125
Frankie's Frightmare (comic book) 252
Frantic (comic book) 252
Frayling, Christopher 135
Freeman, Morgan 83
Frid, Jonathan 54–55, 55*f*, 56–57, 100
Friday the 13th: The Series (TV series): "The Baron's Bride" 89–90
Fright (comic book) 252
Fright Night (comic book) 241, 252
Fright Night (film) 90
Fright Night: Part 2 (film) 90
Fright Night 3-D (comic book) 252
From Dracula with Love (film) 107
From Dusk 'til Porn (film) 206
Frye, Dwight 148
Frye, Mitch 239–243
Fujimoto, Hiroshio 107
Funny Fortnightly (comic book) 252
Funny Monthly (comic book) 252

G-String Vampire (film) 198, 207
Gable, Christopher 17
Gaiman, Neil 12, 154
Gaines, William 242
Galgali familywa Dracula (film) 90
Ganbare Goemon 2: Kiteretsu Shogun Magginesu (game) 228
Gandy Goose in G-Man Jitters (film) 91
Gandy Goose in Ghost Town (film) 90–91
Ganz, Bruno 137*f*, 138
Garfield and Friends (TV series): "Count Lasagna" 91
Gayracula (film) 196, 206, 206*f*
Gebissen wird nur nachts (film) 91
Geeksville (comic book) 252
Gegege No Kitaro : Fukkatsu! Tenma Daiou (game) 228
Gegege No Kitaro : Gyakushuu! Youkai Daichisen (game) 228
Gegege No Kitaro : Youkai Dai Makyou (game) 228
Generation X (comic book) 252
Gerard, Emily 266
Get Lost (comic book) 252
Get Smart (TV series): "The Wax Max" 91
Geung see yee saang (film) 91
Ghost Busters (TV series): "Shades of Dracula" 91–92
Ghost Fever (film) 92
Ghost House (game) 223–224, 228
Ghost in the Water (TV miniseries) 92
Ghost Rider (comic book) 252
Ghosts of Dracula (comic book) 252
Ghoul Mates (film) 92
Ghouls (comic book) 252
Giant Cracked (comic book) 252
Giant Size Action Planet Halloween Special (comic book) 252
Giant-Size Chillers (comic book) 252
Giant-Size Dracula (comic book) 252
Giant-Size Man-Thing (comic book) 252
Giant-Size Spider-Man (comic book) 252
Gilligan's Island (TV series): "Up at Bat" 92
Glut, Donald 8, 79
Go for a Take (film) 92–93
Gokujo Parodius!— Kako no Eiko o Motomete- (game) 228–229
Goldblum, Jeff 177
Der Goldene Nazivampir von Absam: 2— Das Geheimnis von Schloß Kottlitz (film) 93
gonzo porn 196; definition of 199*n*22
The Goon (comic book) 241
Goosebumps: Escape from Horrorland (game) 229
Goosebumps: Horrorland (game) 229
Gorp (film) 93
Graf Dracula beißt jetzt in Oberbayern (film) 93–94

Graf Dracula's Bissige Saftfotzen (film) 198, 206–207
Grampa's Monster Movies (film) 94
El Gran amor del conde Drácula (film) 94, 94*f*
Graphic Classics: Bram Stoker (comic book) 252
graphic novels *see* comic books
Gravedale High (TV series) 94–95
Gray Morrow's Private Commissions (comic book) 252
Greasepaint and Gore: The Hammer Monsters of Phil Leakey (documentary) 95
Greasepaint and Gore, Part 2: The Hammer Monsters of Roy Ashton (documentary) 95
The Great Bear Scare (TV series) 95
Great Books (TV series): "Dracula" 95
Grey, Nan 76*f*, 77
Grier, Pam 156
Grim & Evil (TV series): "Billy Idiot/Home of the Ancients" 95–96; "Fear and Loathing in Endsville" 96
Grimm's Ghost Stories (comic book) 252
The Groovy Ghoulies and Friends (TV series) 149–150
Die Gruft Von Dracula (comic book) 252
Guess What Happened to Count Dracula (film) 96
Gwynne, Fred 128, 128*f*, 129

Hakaba Kitarô (TV series): "Yasha vs. Dracula IV" 96
Halloween Magazine (comic book) 252
The Halloween That Almost Wasn't (TV show) 97
Halloween with the New Addams Family (TV show) 96–97
Hallow's End (film) 97
Halls of Horror Presents Dracula Comics Special 252
Hamill, Mark 122
Hamilton, George 71, 114*f*
Hamilton, Laurel K. 241
Hammer Pictures Ltd. 6, 14–15, 194, 216–217; documentaries on 87–88, 95; TV series on 187–188
Hammer's Hall of Horror (comic book) 252
Happy Hour at Casa Dracula (comic book) 252
Haram alek (film) 97
hardcore pornographic films 193, 195; definition of 198*n*2
Harker (film) 97
Hauer, Rutger 68–69
Haunt of Fear (comic book) 242
The Haunt of Horror (comic book) 252
Haunted Tales (comic book) 252
Hay que matar a Drácula (film) 97–98
Heavy Metal (comic book) 252
Heavy Metal's Dracula (comic book) 252
Hellboy (comic book) 241
Hello Dracula (film) 98
Hellsing (comic book) 252
Hellsing (TV series) 99
Helsing (comic book) 252

Helsing: Dawn of Armageddon (comic book) 252
Henaine, Gaspar 44
Henrie, Don 105
Henson, Jim 143, 156–159
Her Morbid Desire (film) 98
Herbie (comic book) 252
Hercules: The Legendary Journeys (TV series): "Darkness Visible" 98
Here Come the Munsters (film) 98–99
Heroes of Horror (documentary) 99
Herushingu (TV series) 99
Herzog, Werner 137
Heubhyeol hyeongsa na do-yeol (film) 99
The Hilarious House of Frightenstein (TV series) 99–100
Hillyer, Lambert 14
Hinds, Anthony 6
Hipara-Kun (Hipara: The Little Vampire) (manga) 261
Historical Dracula, Facts Behind the Fiction (documentary) 100
The History of Grendel: Grendel Tales (comic book) 252
Hoar, Roger Sherman 267
Hodgson, Joel 154
Hogan, David J. 193
Holden, Gloria 76f, 77
Hollinger, Veronica 3
Hollywood on Parade No. A-8 (documentary) 100
Hollywood's Greatest Villains (documentary) 100
Holstrom, Gary 58–59, 58f
Holt, Ian 2, 263–264
Home to Roost (TV series): "Open House" 100
homosexuality: and pornographic film 195–197, 199n18, 203–206, 208–209, 211; *see also* lesbianism
Hoot (comic book) 252
Hopkins, Anthony 34, 38
The Horny Vampire (film) 207
Horror Monsters (comic book) 252
Horror of Dracula see Dracula (1958; film)
Horror of Dracula and Curse of Frankenstein (comic book) 252
The Horror of Hammer (film) 100
Horror Tales (comic book) 246, 252
Hot Vampire Nights (film) 197, 207
Hotel Transylvania (film) 100
Hot'N Cold Heroes (comic book) 252
Houghton, Don 15–16
House of Dark Shadows (film) 100–101
House of Dracula (film) 101–102, 101f
House of Frankenstein (film) 102
The House of Hammer (comic book) 252
House on Bare Mountain (film) 207
The House That Dripped Blood (film) 102
How My Dad Killed Dracula (film) 102
How Sick Can You Get (comic book) 253
Howard the Duck (comic book) 253
Hrabe Drakula (film) 103
Hungarian Dracula (film) 103
Hyakumannen chikyû no tabi: Bandâ bukku (film) 103
Hysterical (film) 103

I Want to Be a Vampire (film) 36
Ibulong mo sa hangin (film) 103, 104f
IDW 239, 241
Illegal Aliens (comic book) 253
Illustrated Classex (comic book) 253
The Illustrated Dracula (comic book) 253
Impaler (comic book) 253
The Impaler: A Biographical/Historical Look at the Life of Vlad the Impaler, Widely Known as Dracula (documentary) 103–104
El Imperio de Drácula (film) 104
In Camera: The Naïve Visual Effects of Bram Stoker's Dracula (documentary) 104
In Living Color (TV series): "Bram Stoker's Wanda" 104–105
In Search of Dracula with Jonathan Ross (documentary) 105
In Search of History: The Real Dracula (documentary) 105
In the Wake of Vampire (game) 229
Informania: Vampires (comic book) 253
Inside Television's Greatest: Addams Family & The Munsters (documentary) 105
The Inspector (TV series): "Transylvania Mania" 105
Inspector Gadget (TV series): "Haunted Castle" 105
International Insanity (comic book) 253
Internet, and pornography 197–198
Invadders (comic book) 253
Irving, Henry 11, 15–16
Is It Real (TV series): "Vampries" 105
It's Science with Dr. Radium Special (comic book) 253

Jack the Ripper 268
Jackman, Hugh 184
Jackpot Comics 253
Jacula (comic book) 253
Jademan Collection (comic book) 253
The Jail Break (film) 106
Japanese manga 261
Les Jeux de la Comtesse Dolingen de Gratz (film) 106
Jikkyo Oshaberi Parodius: forever with me (game) 229
Joe Nosferatu: Homeless Vampire (film) 106
Jonathan (film) 106
Jones, Carolyn 96
Jones, Kelly 240
Jordan, Keith 20
Jourdan, Louis 50, 50f
Journey into Fear (comic book) 253
Journey into Mystery (comic book) 253
Journey into Unknown Worlds (comic book) 253
El Jovencito Drácula (film) 106–107
Jughead (comic book) 253

Kaibutsu-Kun (1968; TV series) 107
Kaibutsu-Kun (1980; TV series) 107
Kamitsukitai/Dorokiyura yori ai-O (film) 107
Kane, Bob 239
Kara boga (film) 107

Karloff, Boris 14; and comic books 245; and documentaries 37, 99, 178, 180; in *House of Frankenstein* 102; in *Mad Monster Party?* 116
Karmina (film) 107–108
Karmina 2 (film) 108
Khooni Dracula (film) 108
Kibris: La ley del equilibrio (film) 108
Kid Dracula (game) 221
Killer Barbys Vs. Dracula (film) 108–109
King, Stephen 150
King's Quest II: Romancing the Throne (game) 229
Kinski, Klaus 137f, 138
Kiss Attack (film) 207
Kiss Me Quick! (film) 195, 207–208
Kleinhans, Chuck 196, 198, 199n23
Klinger, Leslie S. 266
Knockabout (comic book) 253
Konami 217, 241
Konami Wai Wai Racing Advance (game) 229
Konami Wai Wai World (game) 229
Krazy Comic 253
Kulay Dugo ang Gabi (film) 109
Kwansukui Dracula (film) 109
Kyuketsuki Gokemidoro (film) 109
Kyûketsuki hantâ D (film) 109–110

Lady Dracula (comic book) 253
Lady Dracula (film) 110
The Lady Vampire (film) 140
Laemmle, Carl, Jr. 12–13
LaffTime Cartoon Annual (comic book) 253
The Lair (TV series) 110
Landau, Martin 117
Landis, John 124, 133
Langella, Frank 20, 66, 66f, 147
Laser Fart (film) 110
Last Rites (film) 110–111
The Last Sect (film) 111
Lathjay, Karoly 11
Laugh Comics Digest 253
Lawbreakers Always Lose (comic book) 253
Lawford, Peter 139
LCD Symphony of the Night (game) 229–230
The League of Extraordinary Gentlemen (film) 111–112
Leakey, Phil 95
Lederer, Francis 145f, 146
Lee, Bruce 113
Lee, Christopher 15; allusions to 110; and comic books 246; in documentaries 28–29, 48, 53, 75, 100, 181, 185, 187; in *Dracula* 64; in *Dracula A.D. 1972* 69; in *Dracula Has Risen from the Grave* 71; in *Dracula: Prince of Darkness* 73; in *One More Time* 139; in *The Satanic Rites of Dracula* 151, 153f; in *Scars of Dracula* 153; Skal on 216–217; in *Taste the Blood of Dracula* 173
Lee, Stan 178
Le Fanu, Sheridan 22
Legend: Horror Classics (comic book) 253
The Legend of Dracula (comic book) 253

The Legend of the 7 Golden Vampires (film) 112–113, 112f
Legion of Monsters (comic book) 242, 253
Lennon's Behold the Cartoons of Dracula (comic book) 253
lesbianism: in *Chickula: Teenage Vampire* 47; in *Mistress of Seduction* 123, 208; in *Il Plenilunio delle vergini* 142; in pornographic film 197–198, 200, 202, 204–207, 209–212; in *Vampire Blues* 179; in *Vampiros Lesbos* 183; in *Vampyres* 183
Lewis, Al 94, 128, 128f, 129
Lexx (TV series): "Walpurgis Night" 113
Li san jiao wei zhen di yu men (film) 113
Life Sucks (comic book) 253
Lil Creepers (film) 113
Little Archie (comic book) 253
Little Book of Horror: Dracula (comic book) 253
Little Dracula (comic book) 253
Little Dracula (TV series) 113–114
Little Monsters (comic book) 253
Lom, Herbert 49–50, 49f, 53
The Lonely Killer (film) 143
Look In (comic book) 253
Look In Television Annual (comic book) 253
Lorre, Peter, documentary on 99
Lost Worlds (TV series): "The Real Dracula" 114
Love at First Bite (film) 114–115, 114f
Love Bites (comic book) 253
Love Bites (film) 196–197, 208
Love Journal (comic book) 253
Lucy en Miroir (film) 115
Ludlam, Harry 15–16
Lugosi, Béla 4, 13, 13f, 14; and Batman 240; in *Bud Abbott and Lou Costello Meet Frankenstein* 41, 42f; and documentaries 28, 37, 46, 48, 73, 99, 115, 117, 124, 147, 180–181; in *Dracula* 61–62, 62f; in *Mark of the Vampire* 119; in *Mother Riley Meets the Vampire* 127; in *The Return of the Vampire* 146, 146f; and sexuality 193
Lugosi, Béla, Jr. 148, 180
Lugosi: The Forgotten King (documentary) 115
Lugosi: Hollywood's Dracula (documentary) 115
Lumley, Joanna 151
Lust for Dracula (film) 208
Lust of Blackula (film) 197, 208

Macabre Pair of Shorts (film) 115–116
Macaroni tout garni (film) 116
Mad (comic book) 253
Mad Blasts (comic book) 253
The Mad Book of Horror Stories, Yecchy Creatures, and Other Stuff (comic book) 253
Mad Brain Ticklers, Puzzlers, and Lousy Jokes (comic book) 253
Mad Duds (comic book) 253
Mad House Annual (comic book) 253
Mad House Comics 254
Mad Lobsters and Other Abominable Housebroken Creatures (comic book) 254
A Mad Look at the Future (comic book) 254
The Mad Love Life of a Hot Vampire (film) 208
Mad Monster Party (comic book) 254
Mad Monster Party? (film) 116
Mad Special/Mad Super Special (comic book) 254
Mad XL (comic book) 254
Madhouse Comics Digest 254
Mad's Al Jaffee Freaks Out (comic book) 254
The Magic Christian (film) 116–117
Magnificent Obsessions (TV series) 117
Makai Senki Disgaea (TV series) 117
Makai Senki Disugaia (game) 230
Makai Senki Disugaia Surî (game) 230
Makai Senki Disugaia Tsû (game) 230–231
Making Bela (documentary) 117
Making "Bram Stoker's Dracula" (documentary) 117
Malenka (film) 117–118
Mama Dracula (film) 118
The Man Called Nova (comic book) 254
manga 261
The Many Ghosts of Dr. Grave (comic book) 254
La Marca del Hombre-lobo (film) 119, 120f
The Mark of Dracula (film) 119
Mark of the Vampire (film) 119–120
Marks, George Harrison 208–209, 211
Marks, Laura Helen 193–199
Marshall, William 31, 156
Martin, Scott 16
Marvel Age (comic book) 254
Marvel Bumper Comic 254
Marvel Classics Comic: Dracula 254
Marvel Collection (comic book) 254
Marvel Comic 254
Marvel Comics 239–240, 242, 254
Marvel Comics Presents 254
Marvel Fanfare (comic book) 254
Marvel Madhouse (comic book) 254
Marvel Preview (comic book) 254
Marvel: Shadows and Light (comic book) 254
Marvel Team-Up (comic book) 254
Marvel Winter Special (comic book) 254
Mas vampiros en La Habana (film) 121
Matantei Loki Ragnarok (TV series): "Dorakyura Jyou no Wana" 121
Matheson, Richard 36
Matinee Theatre (TV series): "Dracula" 121
Maxwell Madd and His Wrestling Women (comic book) 254
McClanahan, Rue 115
McCloud (TV series): "McCloud Meets Dracula" 121
McCloud, Scott 239
McFarlane, Todd 217, 231
McLaughlin, John 266
McNally, Raymond 36, 263, 270
Meat Loaf 149
Megaton Man: Hardcopy (comic book) 254
Megaton Man vs. Forbidden Frankenstein (comic book) 254
Meitantei Conan (TV series): "Dracula Murder Case: Part 1" 121–122
Melton, J. Gordon 265–272
Men of Action Meet Women of Drakula (film) 122
Merrie Melodies (TV series): "Transylvania 6-5000" 122
Method and Madness: Visualizing "Dracula" (documentary) 122
Mga Manugang ni Drakula (film) 118–119, 118f
Mickey's Gala Premier (film) 122
Midnight Graffiti (comic book) 254
Might Mouse: Mighty Mouse Meets Bad Bill Bunion (film) 122
The Might World of Marvel featuring The Incredible Hulk and Dracula Lives (comic book) 254
Mignola, Mike 241
Miller, Elizabeth 265
Miller, Jonny Lee 67–68
Mina and the Count (TV series) 122
The Mini-Monsters: Adventures at Camp Mini-Mon (film) 122
Mira corpora (film) 122–123
Mr. and Mrs. Dracula (TV series) 123
Mr. T Versus Dracula (comic book) 255
Mistress of Seduction (film) 123, 197, 208
Misty (comic book) 254
Misty Annual (comic book) 254
Modern Vampires (film) 123–124
Moench, Doug 240
Mondo Lugosi (documentary) 124
The Monkees (TV series): "Monstrous Monkee Mash" 124
Monkey Business (comic book) 254
Monster by Moonlight! The Immortal Saga of "The Wolf Man" (documentary) 124
Monster Force (TV series) 124
The Monster Frankenstein (comic book) 254
Monster Fun (comic book) 254–255
Monster Fun Annual (comic book) 255
Monster Fun Summer Special (comic book) 255
Monster Howls: Humor Vision (comic book) 255
Monster Hunters (comic book) 255
Monster Kid Home Movies (film) 124
Monster Kids (film) 124–125
Monster Mania (documentary) 125
Monster Mash (film) 125
Monster Mash: The Movie (film) 125
Monster Scene (comic book) 255
The Monster Squad (film) 125–126
Monster Squad (TV series) 125
Monster Squad Forever (documentary) 126
The Monster Times (comic book) 255
Monster Wars: Magdalene Vs. Dracula (comic book) 255
Monster World (comic book) 255
MonsterFest 2000: The Classics Come Alive (documentary) 126
MonsterQuest (TV series): "Vampires in America" 126
Monsters Unleashed (comic book) 242

monstrous, and video gaming 216
Los Monstruos del terror (film) 126–127
Monty Python's Flying Circus (TV series): "You're No Fun Anymore" 127
Moon, Keith 168
Moore, Alan 111
More Fun Comics 255
Moretti, Franco 193
Mother Riley Meets the Vampire (film) 127
Ms. Marvel (comic book) 255
Munden's Bar Annual (comic book) 255
El Mundo de los vampiros (film) 127
Munsters 94, 98–99, 127–130, 128f; in comic books 255; documentaries on 28, 105
The Munsters (comic book) 255
The Munsters (TV series) 127–129, 128f
The Munsters Collected Edition (comic book) 255
The Munsters' Revenge (TV show) 129
The Munsters' Scary Little Christmas (TV show) 129–130
The Munsters Today (TV series) 130
Murnau, F.W. 2, 11, 82, 164
Murphy, Dudley 12
Murphy, Eddie 181
musicals: *Buenas Noches, Señor Monstruo* (film) 42; *Dark Shadows: Music Videos* (documentary) 57; *Dracula: A Chamber Musical* 69; *Dracula's Baby* 75; *Escala en Hi-Fi* 85; *Mad Monster Party?* 116; *Sesame Street Jam* 163–164; *Train Ride to Hollywood* 176
My Life with Count Dracula (documentary) 130
My Soul Is Slashed (film) 107
Mysterious Adventures (comic book) 255
Mysterious Journeys (TV series): "The Hunt for Dracula" 130
Mystery and Imagination (TV series): "Dracula" 130–131
Mystery Comics Digest (comic book) 255
Mystery in Dracula's Castle (film) 131

Nadja (film) 131
The Naked World of Harrison Marks (film) 208–209
National Lampoon (comic book) 255
Nattens engel (film) 131–132
Necropolis (film) 132
Negative Burns: An Anthology (comic book) 255
Nella stretta morsa del ragno (film) 132
Nelson, Jerry 19, 47, 83–84, 143, 156–164
Nem As Enfermeiras Esapam (film) 132
New England vampires, documentary on 126
New Fun: The Big Comic Magazine 255
New International Track & Field (game) 231
The New Scooby-Doo Mysteries (TV series): "Halloween Hassle at Dracula's Castle, Part 1" 132; "Halloween Hassle at Dracula's Castle, Part 2" 133

The New Shmoo (TV series): "The Return of Dracula" 133
Nicholls, John 6, 194
Night Bites: Women and Their Vampires (documentary) 133
The Night Boys (film) 197, 209
Night Court (TV series): "Death Takes a Halloween" 133
The Night Dracula Saved the World (TV show) 97
Night Gallery (TV series): "The Devil Is Not Mocked" 134; "How to Cure the Common Vampire" 134; "A Matter of Semantics" 133; "A Midnight Visit to the Neighborhood Blood Bank" 133–134
Night of the Ghouls (film) 134
Night People (film) 134–135
Night Train (film) 176
The Night Walker (comic book) 255
NightHunter (game) 231–232
Nightlinger (comic book) 255
Nightmare (comic book) 255
The Nightmare Annual (comic book) 255
Nightmare at Elm Manor (film) 209
Nightmare: The Birth of Victorian Horror (documentary) 135
Nightmare Yearbook (comic book) 255
Night's Children Vampyr! (comic book) 255
Nintendo Entertainment System 215
Niven, David 179
La Noche de Walpurgis (film) 135
Nocturna (film) 135
Nocturne in the Moonlight (game) 220–221
Nohasfrontwo (film) 135
Noroi no yakata: Chi o sû me (film) 135–136
Northern Ballet Company 17
Nosferatu (comic book) 255
Nosferatu, eine Symphonie des Grauens (1922; film) 11, 136–137, 136f
Nosferatu: Phantom der Nacht (film) 137–138, 137f
Nosferatu-Plague of Terror (comic book) 255
Nosferatu's Crush (film) 138
Not Brand Echh (comic book) 255
Nothing Generation (film) 36
Nova Girls Fun House (comic book) 255
Now Comics 241
Nutty (comic book) 255

The Occult Files of Doctor Spektor (comic book) 255
Official Handbook of the Marvel Universe (comic book) 255
Official Handbook of the Marvel Universe: Horror (comic book) 255
Oldman, Gary 4, 34, 38, 38f
Olivier, Laurence 66, 147
Olliver's Adventures (TV series): "What a Pain in the Neck" 138
100 Years of Horror: Blood-Drinking Beings (documentary) 138
100 Years of Horror: The Monster Makers (documentary) 138
One Million-Year Trip: Bandar Book (film) 103

One More Time (film) 138–139
One of Those Days (film) 139–140
Onna Kyuketsuki (film) 140
Operation Darkness (game) 232
Operazione paura (film) 140
La Orgia de los Muertos (film) 140
Otra vez Drácula (film) 140–141
Out for Blood (film) 197, 209

Pachislot Akumajô Dracula (game) 232
Palance, Jack 64, 65f, 125
Panic (comic book) 255
parodies: in pornographic film 193, 195; in video games 224, 228–229
The Passion of Dracula (film) 141
Pater Dracula (comic book) 256
Pathos (film) 141
Peck, Bob 19
Pehavý Max a strasidlá (film) 141
Penhaligon, Susan 50, 50f
Penthouse 256
Penthouse Wicked Wanda 256
Pertwee, Jon 175
Peter Porker, The Spectacular Spider-Ham (comic book) 256
Peterson, Cassandra (Elvira) 125
Un Petit Garçon silencieux (film) 141
The Phantom (comic book) 256
Phantom Brave (game) 227–228
The Phantom Eye (TV miniseries) 141–142
Phantomas 2 (game) 232
Pink Plasma (film) 142
Pirie, David 3
Plan 69 from Outer Space (film) 209
Planet of the Apes and Dracula Lives (comic book) 256
Planet of Vampires (comic book) 256
Playboy 256
Il Plenilunio delle vergini (film) 142
Plug Comic 256
Plummer, Christopher 67–68
El Pobrecito Draculín (film) 142
Poe, E. A. 12
Polanski, Roman 87
Polidori, John 3
pornographic film 193–199; in digital era 197–198; Golden Age of 195–196; listings of 200–212; term 198n2; video and 196–197
Post Halloween Left Over Monster Thanksgiving Special (comic book) 256
Previews (comic book) 256
Prez (comic book) 256
Price, Vincent 73; documentaries on 99
Der Prinz der Nacht (comic book) 248
Psycho (comic book) 256
Psycho Annual (comic book) 256
Psycho: The 1974 Fall-Special (comic book) 256
Pulse of Darkness (comic book) 256
Pumpkin Hill (film) 142–143
Purgatori Collected Edition (comic book) 256
Purgatori: The Dracula Gambit (comic book) 256
Purgatori: The Dracula Gambit Sketchbook (comic book) 256
Purgatori: Goddess Rising (comic book) 256

Index

Puss in Boots (TV series): "Nagagutsu o haita neko no boken" 143
Put Down the Duckie: A Sesame Street Special (TV series) 143
Pyasa Shaitan (film) 143

Qian li dan qi zhui xiong (film) 143
Quack! (comic book) 256
Quackshot (game) 232–233
Quantum Leap (TV series): "Blood Moon — March 10, 1975" 143–144
Quasimodo d'El Paris (film) 144
Quintero, Carlos "Che" 21

Radin, Ana 88
The Raven (film) 13
Read All About It! (TV series): "An Evil Smile" 144
The Real Life of Dracula (documentary) 144
Realm of the Undead (game) 233
Red Circle Sorcery (comic book) 256
Reed, Donald A. 130
Reed, Oliver 187–188
The Renegade (comic book) 256
Renfield: in *Bram Stoker's Vampire Diaries: Renfield* 38–39; in "Dracula's Not Gay" 151; in *Fort Dracula* 88; in *El Jovencito Drácula* 107; *see also under* Dracula
Renfield (comic book) 256
Renfield: A Tale of Madness (comic book) 256
Requiem Chevalier Vampire (comic book) 256
Requiem der Vampirritter (comic book) 256
Requiem for Dracula (comic book) 256
Requiem Vampire Knight (comic book) 256
Resident Evil (game) 217
El Retorno de Walpurgis (film) 144–145
The Return of Count Yorga (film) 145
The Return of Dracula (film) 145–146, 145f
The Return of the Vampire (film) 146, 146f
The Revamping of Dracula (documentary) 147
Revivencial (film) 147
Rice, Anne 133
Richie Rich & Casper (comic book) 256
Richie Rich Vault of Mystery (comic book) 256
Riddles of the Dead (TV series): "Dracula Unearthed" 147
Rinaldó (film) 147
Ripley's Believe It or Not! (comic book) 256
Ripley's Believe It or Not! (TV series): "The Vampire Kit" 147
Il Risveglio di Dracula (film) 147
Riti, magie nere e segrete orge nel trecento (film) 147–148
Le Rituel de la mort (comic book) 256
The Road to Dracula (documentary) 148
Robot Chicken (TV series): "Nutcracker Sweet" 148; "Tubba-Bubba's Now Hubba-Bubba" 148
Rockin' Bones (comic book) 256

Rockula (film) 148–149
The Rocky Horror Picture Show (film) 149
Romero, George 172
The Rook (comic book) 256
Rooks, Conrad 46
Roter Tango (film) 149
Roth decision 195
Runescape (game) 233
Russell, Ken 16–17
Rusty (game) 233

Saban's Mighty Morphin Power Rangers (comic book) 256
Sabrina and the Groovie Goolies (TV series) 149–150
Sabrina: The Teen-Age Witch (comic book) 256
La Saga de Los Dracula (film) 150
Saint James, Susan 114f
Salem's Lot (TV miniseries) 150
Sally Forth (comic book) 256
Sangre de vírgenes (film) 150
Santo en el Tesoro de Drácula (film) 150–151
Santo vs. Baron Brakola (film) 27
Santo y Blue Demon contra Drácula y el Hombre Lobo (film) 151, 152f
Sarandon, Susan 149
The Satanic Rites of Dracula (film) 151, 153f
Saturday Night Live (TV series): "Dracula's Not Gay" 151; "The Mirror" 151–152
Saturday the 14th (film) 152–153
Savage Action (comic book) 256
Savage Return of Dracula (comic book) 256
Savage Sword of Conan (comic book) 256–257
Scarlet in Gaslight (comic book) 257
Scarlet in Gaslight: An Adventure in Terror (comic book) 257
Scars of Dracula (film) 153, 154f
Scary America (documentary) 153–154
Scary Monsters Magazine (comic book) 257
Scary Monsters Magazine Yearbook: Monster Memories (comic book) 257
Scary Tales (comic book) 257
Schaefer, Eric 195
Schreck, Max 71, 119, 136f, 137, 164
Schusters Gespenster (TV miniseries) 154
Scooby-Doo and Scrappy-Doo (TV series): "Who's Minding the Monster" 154–155
Scooby-Doo and the Ghoul School (film) 155
Scooby-Doo and the Reluctant Werewolf (film) 155
Scooby-Doo: The Mystery Card Caper (comic book) 257
Scooby Doo Mystery Comics 257
Scooby Doo...Where Are You! (comic book) 257
Scooby-Doo! Where Are You? (TV series): "A Gaggle of Galloping Ghosts" 155–156
Scream (comic book) 257
Scream! (comic book) 257
Scream, Blacula, Scream (film) 156

Scream! Holiday Special (comic book) 257
Screen Monsters (comic book) 257
Scully (TV series) 156
The Secret of Dr. Alucard (film) 172–173
Secrets of Haunted House (comic book) 257
Sellers, Peter 116
Selznick, David O. 13
Serling, Rod 133–134
Sesame Street (TV series) 156–161; "The Bookaneers" 161; "Elmo & Zoe's Hat Contest" 161–162; "Little Furry Red Monster Parade" 162; "Miles Babysits" 162; "Sleepy Grouchy" 162–163; "Telly's New Shoes" 163
Sesame Street Jam: A Musical Celebration (TV show) 163–164
Sesame Street Stays Up Late! (TV show) 164
Sex and the Single Vampire (film) 195, 209
sexploitation films 195
Sexy Adventures of Van Helsing (film) 198, 209–210
The Sexy Dick (comic book) 257
Sexy Probitissimo (documentary) 195, 210
The Shadow of Dracula (comic book) 257
Shadow of the Vampire (film) 164
Shaitani Dracula (film) 164
Shaman King (TV series): "Vampire Ambush" 164–165; "Winged Destroyers" 165
Sherriff, R. C. 13
Shiver and Shake (comic book) 257
Shiver and Shake Annual (comic book) 257
Si Popeye, Atbp (film) 165
Sick (comic book) 257
Silver Blade (comic book) 257
Silver Scream (film) 165
Silver Surfer Vs. Dracula (comic book) 257
The Simpsons (TV series): "All's Fair in Oven War" 166; "Brawl in the Family" 166; "Sideshow Bob Roberts" 166; "Treehouse of Horror IV" 166–167; "Treehouse of Horror XVI" 167; "You Kents Alway Say What You Want" 167–168
Sin Comics 257
666: The Mark of the Beast (comic book) 257
Skal, David J. 11–17, 215–217, 267, 284, 288
Smash (comic book) 257
Snatcher (game) 233
Snipes, Wesley 33
softcore pornographic films 193, 195; definition of 198n2
Son of Dracula (1943; film) 168
Son of Dracula (1974; film) 168–169
La Sorella di Satana (film) 169
Space (TV miniseries) 169
Spermula (film) 210
Sphinx — Geheimnisse der Geschichte (TV series): "Die Vampirprinzessin" 169–170

Spider-Man and His Amazing Friends (TV series): "Transylvanian Connection" 170
Spider-Man Annual (comic book) 257
Spider-Man Comics Weekly 257
Spider-Man Team-Up (comic book) 257
Spider-Man Unlimited (comic book) 257
Spider-Woman (comic book) 257
Spider Woman (TV series): "Dracula's Revenge" 170
Spiderman Vs. Dracula (comic book) 257
Spidey Super Stories (comic book) 257
Spike Vs. Dracula (comic book) 257
SpongeBob SquarePants (TV series): "Graveyard Shift/Krusty Love" 170
Spoof (comic book) 257
Spooks'n'Monsters Howling Funny Joke Book 257
stag films 193–195, 198n8
Stagliano, John 199n22
Star Comics Magazine 257
Star Trek (comic book) 257
Star Virgin (film) 210
Starr, Ringo 116, 168
Steiger, Rod 123
The Steve Allen Show (TV series) 170–171
Stevens, Onslow 101f
Stoker, Bram 1–2; documentaries on 31, 75, 78; and performance 11; proposed biographical feature on 14–16; and video games 225; *see also under Dracula*
Stoker, Dacre 1–2
Stoker, Florence 2, 11–12, 15, 268, 288
Stoker's Dracula (comic book) 257
Stone, Jeremy 199n23
storytelling: in comic books 239; and video games 216
Strange, Glen 41, 42f
Strike the Sot! A Wizard of Id Collection (comic book) 257
Suckula (film) 210
Sundown: The Vampire in Retreat (film) 171
Super DC Giant (comic book) 257
Super Funnies (comic book) 257
Super Mario Brothers (game) 215–216
The Super Mario Bros. Super Show! (TV series): "Bats in the Basement / Mario and the Beanstalk" 171; "Count Koopula" 171
Super Spider-Man (comic book) 257
superhero genre, censorship and 242
Superman (comic book) 257
Superman: The Man of Steel (comic book) 257
Superman's Pal the New Jimmy Olsen (comic book) 257
The Supernaturals (comic book) 257
Sur les Traces de Dracula (comic book) 257
survival horror genre 217
Suspense (comic book) 258
Sutherland, Donald 95
Svengali (film) 60
Swank, Hilary 86
Sword of Dracula (comic book) 258

Taiho shichauzo (TV series): "40" 172
Tales Calculated to Drive You Bats (comic book) 258
Tales from the Darkside (TV series): "The Circus" 172; "My Ghostwriter — The Vampire" 172; "Strange Love" 172
Tales from the Tomb (comic book) 258
Tales of Horror-Dracula (comic book) 258
Tales of the Multiverse: Batman — Vampire (comic book) 258
Tales of the Wizard of Oz (TV series): "The Reunion" 172
Tales of Voodoo (comic book) 258
Tales to Tremble By (comic book) 258
Tales Too Terrible to Tell (comic book) 258
A Taste of Blood (film) 173
Taste the Blood of Dracula (film) 173
Tate, Sharon 87
Tempi dur per i vampiri (film) 173
Templesmith, Ben 241
Tendre Dracual (film) 173–174
Tentacles of Terror (comic book) 258
Terreur de Dracula (comic book) 258
Terror Tales (comic book) 258
Terrors of Dracula (comic book) 258
Terry, Ellen 16
Teta (TV series) 174
Tetsuwan Atom (TV series): "Vampire Vale" 174
The Thing (comic book) 258
The Thirst: Blood Wars (film) 174
30 Days of Night (comic book) 241
30 Days of Night (film) 174–175, 241
This Darkness: The Vampire Virus (film) 175
Thomas, Roy 240
Thor (comic book) 258
3-2-1 (TV series): "The Magic of Merlin" 175
Three's Horrible: Part 1 (film) 175
Thrills & Chills (comic book) 258
The Ticks' Big Halloween Special (comic book) 258
Tiempos duros para Drácula (film) 175
Titanic 2000 (film) 210–211
The Titans (comic book) 258
Titeuf (TV series): "Pépé Dracula" 176
To Die For (film) 176
Tomb of Dracula (comic book) 240, 242, 258
Tomb of Dracula (film) 188
Tomb of Dracula: Halloween Megazine (comic book) 258
La Tomba di Dracula (comic book) 258
Le Tombeau de Dracula (comic book) 258
Topo Gigio (TV series): "Gigio and Vampire" 176
Topo Gigio — No Castelo do Conde Drácula (TV show) 176
Topps Comics Presents 258
Toth "One for the Road" (comic book) 258
A Touch of Sweden (film) 211
Train Ride to Hollywood (film) 176
Transylmania (film) 176–177
Transylvania (game) 233
Transylvania 6-5000 (film) 177

Transylvania Twist (film) 177
Transylvania II: The Crimson Crown (game) 233
Trash (comic book) 258
Trash Comics 258
A Trip with Dracula (film) 177
La Tumba de Dracula (film) 258
TV Century 21 Annual (comic book) 258
TV Comic (comic book) 258
TV Times (comic book) 258
TV 21 (comic book) 258
TV 21 Annual (comic book) 258
The Twilight Zone (comic book) 258
Twins of Evil (film) 177–178
Twist (comic book) 258
Two on a Guillotine (comic book) 258
2000 AD (comic book) 258

U.F.O. (film) 178
Ultimate Reality (film) 196, 211
Ultimate Super Heroes, Vixens, and Villains (TV series): "Ultimate Super Villains" 178
The Uncanny X-Men (comic book) 258
The Unexpected (comic book) 258
United States v. Roth 195
Universal Horror (documentary) 178–179
Universal Monsters Cavalcade of Horror (comic book) 258
Universal Monsters: Dracula (comic book) 258–259
Universal Pictures Presents: Dracula, the Mummy, Plus Other Stories (comic book) 259
Universal Studios 12
Unknown World (comic book) 259
Urusei Yatsura (TV series): "What a Dracula!" 179

Vamperotica (comic book) 259
Vampira 154
Vampira (film) 179
Las Vampiras (film) 179
Vampire! (comic book) 259
Vampire (film) 211
Vampire (game) 232
Vampire Blues (film) 179
Vampire City (film) 180
Vampire Cop Ricky (film) 99
La Vampire déchu (documentary) 180
Die Vampire des Dr. Dracula (film) 119, 120f
Vampire Hookers (film) 180
Vampire Hunter D (*Banpaia Hantâ D*, 2000; film) 26–27
Vampire Hunter D (*Kyûketsuki hantâ D*, 1985; film) 109–110
The Vampire Hunters Club (film) 180–181
Vampire in Brooklyn (film) 181
The Vampire Interviews (documentary) 181
Vampire Jokes and Cartoons: "A Comedy of Terrors" (comic book) 259
Vampire Killer (game) 222–223
Vampire Night (game) 233–234
Vampire Secrets (documentary) 181–182
Vampire Tales (comic book) 259

Vampire Vixens (film) 211–212
Vampirella (comic book) 259
Vampirella (film) 182
Vampirella Classic (comic book) 259
Vampirella: Commemmorative Edition (comic book) 259
Vampirella/Dracula & Pantha Showcase (comic book) 259
Vampirella/Dracula: The Centennial (comic book) 259
Vampirella: The Dracula War! (comic book) 259
Vampirella: Horror Classics (comic book) 259
Vampirella of Drakulon (comic book) 259
Vampirella: Sad Wings of Destiny (comic book) 259
Vampirella: Transcending Time and Space (comic book) 259
Vampirella: 25th Anniversary Special (comic book) 259
Vampirella vs. The Cults of Chaos (comic book) 259
vampires: in comic books 239–261; literary background of 3; in pornographic film 193–212; in video games 215–235
Vampires (adult film) 212
Vampires (documentary) 182
Vampire's Empire (game) 234
Vampires of Vogel (film) 21
Vampire's Seduction (film) 212
Vampiric Jihad (comic book) 259
El Vampiro sangriento (film) 182
El Vampiro Teporocho (film) 183
¡Vampiros en La Habana! (film) 183
Vampiros Lesbos (film) 183
Vamps (film) 212
A Vampyre Story: Chapter One (game) 234
Vampyres (comic book) 259
Vampyres (film) 183
Van Dien, Casper 68, 123
Van Helsing: in *Bram Stoker's Way of the Vampire* 39; in *The Brides of Dracula* 41; in comic books 245; in *The Curse of Dracula* 53; in *Demons* 59; in *La Dinistía de Dracula* 60; in *Dracula A.D. 1972* 69; in *Dracula: Prince of Marketing* 73; in *Dracula 3000* 68; female 188, 198, 210; in *Hotel Transylvania* 100; in *El Jovencito Drácula* 107; in *The Last Sect* 111; in *The Legend of the 7 Golden Vampires* 113; in *Modern Vampires* 123–124; in *The Monster Squad* 125–126; in *The Satanic Rites of Dracula* 151; in *La Sorella di Satana* 169; in *A Taste of Blood* 173; in *This Darkness: The Vampire Virus* 175; in *Vampire City* 180; *see also under* Dracula; Hellsing
Van Helsing (film) 183–184
Van Helsing (game) 234
Van Helsing Chronicles (TV series) 184
Van Helsing: The Man and the Monsters (documentary) 184
Vanpaia (manga) 261
Vanpaia hosuto (TV series) 184–185
VCRs 196

Vegas Knights (comic book) 259
Vem var Dracula (documentary) 185
Vicious (comic book) 259
Victim of His Imagination (unfilmed script) 14–16
video, and pornography 196–197
video games 215–218; chronology of 273–283; listings of 219–235
Villarías, Carlos 63f
Vision and the Scarlet Witch (comic book) 259
Visions (comic book) 259
Vlad (film) 185
Vlad Tepes (film) 185
Vlad Tepes Dracula (game) 234–235
Vlad the Impaler (comic book) 241
Vlad the Impaler (prince of Wallachia) 264f; in comic books 250; in *Dark Prince: The True Story of Dracula* 54; documentaries on 100, 103–105, 182, 185; in *Dracula Rising* 73; in *Dracula the Impaler* 73–74; in *Dracula Year Zero* 74–75; in *Hercules: The Legendary Journeys* 98; in pornographic film 203; in *To Die For* 176
Vlad the Impaler: The True Story of Dracula (documentary) 185
von Schwarzenberg, Eleonore 170
Vorkov, Zandor 74, 75f
The Vulture's Eye (film) 185–186

Wacko (comic book) 259
Wai Wai World 2: SOS! Parsley Jo (game) 235
Wake, Rattle and Roll (TV series): "Monster Tails" 186
Wallachia *see* Vlad the Impaler
Waller, Gregory 216
Walpurgis Nacht (film) 186
Walt Disney's Goofy Adventures (comic book) 259
Walt Disney's Uncle Scrooge (comic book) 259
Warhol, Andy 27–28, 33–34, 75
Warp Graphics Annual (comic book) 259
Waxwork (comic book) 259
Waxwork (film) 186
Waxwork II: Lost in Time (film) 186–187
Waxwork 3-D (comic book) 259
Wechsberg, Peter 59
Wedding of Dracula (comic book) 259
Weird (comic book) 259
Weird Mysteries (comic book) 259
Weird Mystery Tales (comic book) 259
Weird Tales of the Macabre (comic book) 259
Weird Vampire Tales (comic book) 259
Weird War Tales (comic book) 259
Werewolf by Night (comic book) 259
Wertham, Frederic 241
Whale, James 13–14
What If...? (comic book) 259
Whedon, Joss 241
Where Creatures Roam (comic book) 259
Whitman, Walt 15
Whizzer and Chips (comic book) 259
Whizzer and Chips Holiday Special (comic book) 259

Whizzer and Chips Presents Junior Rotter Holiday Special (comic book) 259
Whoopee! (comic book) 260
Whoopee! Book of Frankie Stein (comic book) 260
Whoopee! Monthly (comic book) 260
Wilkersons, William 266
Williams, Linda 195, 198n2, 199n18
Winnipeg Free Press Canada's Leading Comic Section (comic book) 260
Winter with Dracula (documentary) 187
Witches' Tales (comic book) 260
The Witching Hour! (comic book) 260
The Wolf Man (film), documentary on 124
Wolff and Byrd, Counselors of the Macabre (comic book) 260
Wolfman, Marv 240
Wolfster, Part I: The Curse of the Emo Vamp (film) 187
Wolk, Douglas 240–241
The World of Hammer (TV series): "Christopher Lee" 187; "Costumers" 187; "Dracula and the Undead" 187–188; "Hammer" 188; "Mummies, Werewolves and the Living Dead" 188; "Peter Cushing" 188; "Vamp" 188
The World of the Vampires (film) 127
Wow! (comic book) 260
Wow! Holiday Special (comic book) 260

X-Men: Apocalypse Vs. Dracula (comic book) 260
X-Men Classic (comic book) 260
X-Men Vs. Dracula (comic book) 260

Yamadera, Kôichi 27
Yami no teio kyuketsuki Dracula (film) 188
Yi yao O.K. 188
Yikes (comic book) 260
Yin ji (film) 189
Yorugata Aijin Senmonten—Blood Hound (manga) 261
Yosemite Sam and Bugs Bunny (comic book) 260
You Wish (TV series): "Halloween" 189
Young Dracula (comic book) 260
Young Dracula (TV series) 189
Young Dracula: Prayer of the Vampire (comic book) 260
Young-guwa heubhyeolgwi dracula (film) 189
The Young Indiana Jones Chronicles (TV series): "Transylvania, January 1918" 189–190
Yûreiyashiki no kyôfu: Chi o suu ningyô (film) 190

Zane, Billy 185
Zhang Wei-Qiang 72f
Zinda Laash (*Dracula in Pakistan*; film) 190
zombie imagery 16, 202
Zora la vampiera (film) 190

www.ingramcontent.com/pod-product-compliance
Lightning Source LLC
Chambersburg PA
CBHW081540300426
44116CB00015B/2700